# MULTIPLE CRITERIA DECISION ANALYSIS IN REGIONAL PLANNING

## THEORY AND DECISION LIBRARY

General Editors: W. Leinfellner and G. Eberlein

Series A: Philosophy and Methodology of the Social Sciences
Editors: W. Leinfellner (Technical University of Vienna)
G. Eberlein (Technical University of Munich)

Series B: Mathematical and Statistical Methods
Editor: H. Skala (University of Paderborn)

Series C: Game Theory, Mathematical Programming and Operations Research
Editor: S. H. Tijs (University of Nijmegen)

Series D: System Theory, Knowledge Engineering and Problem Solving
Editor: W. Janko (University of Vienna)

---

## SERIES B: MATHEMATICAL AND STATISTICAL METHODS

Editor: H. Skala (Paderborn)



**Scope**

The series focuses on the application of methods and ideas of logic, mathematics and statistics to the social sciences. In particular, formal treatment of social phenomena, the analysis of decision making, information theory and problems of inference will be central themes of this part of the library. Besides theoretical results, empirical investigations and the testing of theoretical models of real world problems will be subjects of interest. In addition to emphasizing interdisciplinary communication, the series will seek to support the rapid dissemination of recent results.

# MULTIPLE CRITERIA DECISION ANALYSIS IN REGIONAL PLANNING

*Concepts, Methods and Applications*

FUMIKO SEO
*Kyoto Institute of Economic Research, Kyoto University, Japan*

and

MASATOSHI SAKAWA
*Department of Information Engineering, Iwate University, Japan*



D. REIDEL PUBLISHING COMPANY

A MEMBER OF THE KLUWER ACADEMIC PUBLISHERS GROUP

DORDRECHT / BOSTON / LANCASTER / TOKYO

**Library of Congress Cataloging in Publication Data**

CIP

Seo, Fumiko, 1929–
Multiple criteria decision analysis in regional planning : concepts, methods, and applications / Fumiko Seo and Masatoshi Sakawa.
p. cm.—(Theory and decision library. Series B, Mathematical and statistical methods)
Bibliography: p.
Includes index.
ISBN 90–277–2641–8
1. Regional planning—Decison making. 2. Decision-making—Mathematical models. 3. Multivariate analysis. I. Sakawa, Masatoshi, 1947– II. Title. III. Series.
HT391.S452 1987
658.4'03—dc 19 87–27337
ISBN 90–277–2641–8 CIP



Published by D. Reidel Publishing Company,
P.O. Box 17, 3300 AA Dordrecht, Holland.

Sold and distributed in the U.S.A. and Canada
by Kluwer Academic Publishers,
101 Philip Drive, Norwell, MA 02061, U.S.A.

In all other countries, sold and distributed
by Kluwer Academic Publishers Group,
P.O. Box 322, 3300 AH Dordrecht, Holland.



Printed in The Netherlands

# CONTENTS

# PREFACE

This book is devoted to presenting theoretical fundamentals for the methods of multiple criteria decision making (MCDM) in the social sciences with particular intent to their applicability to real-world decision making.

The main characteristics of the complex problems facing humans in the world today are multidimensional and have multiple objectives; they are large-scale, and have noncommensurate and conflicting objectives, such as economic, environmental, societal, technical, and aesthetic ones. The authors intend to establish basic concepts for treating these complex problems and to present methodological discussions for MCDM with some applications to administrative, or regional, planning.

MCDM is composed of two phases: analytical and judgmental. In this book, we intend to consolidate these two phases and to present integrated methodologies for manipulating them with particular interest in managerial decision making, which has not yet been properly treated in spite of its urgent necessity. Although a number of books in MCDM fields have already been published in recent years, most of them have mainly treated one aspect of MCDM. Our work specifically intends to treat the methodology in unified systems and to construct a conceptual structure with special regards to the intrinsic properties of MCDM and its "economic meanings" from the social scientific point of view.

Multiple criteria decision problems cannot be reduced to multisectoral or multivariate optimization problems. Multiple criteria decision problems have special characteristics which compare preferences on a nondominated surface. Generally, the decision maker (DM) cannot find the "best" solution among alternative plans in a feasible region. To choose the preferred policy as a compromise solution on the nondominated (or Pareto-admissible) surface is the main subject of the multiple criteria decision problems.

Thus, the question is how one find the preferred policy program. How does one derive the preferred policy with rational procedures? This is the starting point of the multiple criteria decision problem. In other words, *how* the decision is made is the crucial issue of MCDM, as distinct from classical mathematical programming in which *what* decision is made is the matter of most interest.

Multiple criteria decision analysis is an integrated approach to meet these requirements. Particularly for solving complex problems with conflicting objectives, improvement in decision making processes for present societal problems is urgently needed. Seeds for meeting the needs of the time can be found in multiobjective systems analysis, which has been rapidly developed since the 1970's. However, a conceptual structure of this approach has not yet been well established in unified systems, and thus many social scientists are still doubting the effectiveness of its contribution to a better understanding and resolution of the real-world problems. This book presents its usefulness for the social science fields and thus for administrative decision making.

There are two major approaches to MCDM. One is mathematical optimization such as multiobjective mathematical programming, which is effective for handling the analytical phase with quantitative modeling. The other is multiobjective decision analysis, which is useful for treating the judgmental phase with axiomatic and numerical representations. Multiattribute preference analyses present operational devices for multiobjective extensions of decision analysis. Fuzzy as well as stochastic extensions of both of these methods can also be discussed for handling ambiguousness and diversifications in decision making. A collective choice problem can be examined based on these extensions and game theory as the related methodologies to the above two approaches.

The third direction for treating the multiple criteria decision processes aims at combining the analytical phase with the judgmental phase of MCDM. In this book, the authors intend to combine mathematical programming for the analytical phase with decision analysis for the judgmental phase. We particularly intend to coordinate and adjust conflicting interests in societal decision problems. The main way of bridging the gap between the above two phases is to use the Kuhn-Tucker multipliers derived from mathematical programming as the basic evaluation factor, as the shadow prices or the marginal rates of substitutions, and to submit them for coordination processes via the mediation function of DM, with or without the construction of the utility or value functions. These methods are based on multilevel systems decomposition and trade-off experiments among objectives partitioned in multilevels.

In the background of MCDM research in the social sciences, there exists the situation where the market price mechanism is not any longer well-functioning and for which alternative evaluation criteria have not yet been well established. The market price mechanism combined with the efficient allocation of resources has not worked as the proper evaluation index for planning. This problem is known as "market failure." A major subject of MCDM research is thus to resolve the theoretical evaluation problem. This book concentrates on considerations of the theoretical evaluation problem for multipurpose systems, which are based on the critical succession of the inheritances of neo-classical economics. In this sense, this research presents an alternative approach to the "public goods" approach in economics for treating the nonmarket phenomena in real-world problems. Our research highly intends to take problem-solving as well as problem-finding aspects into major consideration; thus this is an "engineering", or systems economics in Stanford's sense, approach, in contrast to an "economics" approach in a conventional sense where welfare economics has been constructed in the general equilibrium framework with major intention to establish equilibrium conditions in the economic worlds.

Our background in this research is three-fold.

First is the mathematical programming approach in economic analysis (Koopmans 1951; Dorfman, Samuelson and Solow 1958; Gale 1960; and so on). This approach has provided basic concepts for the duality in resource allocation and the price determination mechanism combined with it in operational ways, and also opened the way to objectives analysis as suggested by Dantzig (1982).

Second is the early development of cost-benefit analysis and its extensions to optimal systems design problems (Eckstein 1958, Maass, Hufschmidt, Dorfman, Thomas, Marglin and Fair 1962, and so on). This research also includes the problem consciousness of multipurpose systems and has provided a stimulus to this direction of research in a combination of economic aim, engineering analysis, and administrative planning. A well-known application is the Harvard Water Program.

Third is the development of a decentralized planning theory based on the general equilibrium analysis (Koopmans 1951; Arrow and Hurwicz 1960; and so on). In this sense, our research is still conducted as a successor to the neo-classical economics. Mathematical foundations of engineering analysis with operational methods for decomposed systems have also been presented (Lasdon 1968, 1970; Wismer 1971) and applied to water resource programs (Haimes 1973; Haimes, Foley and Yu 1972; Haimes, Kaplan and Husar 1972; Haimes and Macko 1973; and so on).

In the above research works, the imputed price (or opportunity cost) is used as an evaluation factor or a regulator. This device is developed in the present research as the major theme in a more general concept, the use of the Kuhn-Tucker multiplier.

In our research, the main subject in MCDM, the imposition of the theoretical evaluation, is examined in three ways: (1) evaluation of the marginal rates of substitution among objectives (Chapters 2-4), (2) heuristic construction of the preference function of DM (Chapters 5-8), and (3) utilization of the Kuhn-Tucker multiplier as the basic evaluation factor in a transformation (Chapters 9-12). Method (1) implies assessment of the weighting parameters that are interpreted as the relative price ratios for the objectives. Thus method (1) is regarded as a surrogate for method (3), the direct evaluation of the dual variables as the shadow prices. Our research intends to bridge between the methods (2) and (3) in a consolidation.

Because of the restriction of our research intention to the above major subject, the present book does not cover all areas of MCDM research. Some discussions that are not included in the present work are shown in the bibliography for related works at the end of this book, but they still do not cover all of the research in MCDM fields.

The ultimate goal of multiple criteria decision analysis is not to satisfy just the theoretical and instrumental curiosity of researchers, but to provide effective devices to cope with the complex real-world problems with conflict-finding and conflict-solving processes. Thus the most important thing in the MCDM research is to comprehend the problems complex thoroughly and realistically and to articulate the standpoint and the contents for its structuring. Elaboration of techniques for MCDM are simply auxiliary means for that aim. Thus effectiveness in descriptive analysis for scenario writing should be highly regarded in MCDM research, and the real difficulty of the MCDM research exists in this aspect. The major concern of this book is with bridging between the theoretical fundamentals of MCDM and its empirical applications. This book particularly intends to provide intuitive interest and understanding of basic concepts and methods for MCDM, and thus proofs of theorems are not always provided. The discussions should instead be extended to behavioristic backgrounds of MCDM in this context. Our last chapter is devoted to this consideration.

This book intends to be self-contained, and thus basic concepts are explained in various ways even with some duplication. However, some preliminary knowledge of elementary matrix calculus, convex set theory, and mathematical programming are still pre-requisite for this book.

This research has primarily been performed as one part of the research projects on MCDM at the Kyoto Institute of Economic Research (KIER), Kyoto University, since 1975. Some of the material used in this book was also originally prepared during the authors' stays at the International Institute for Applied Systems Analysis (IIASA), Laxenburg, in 1979-80, and in subsequent periods occasionally, in cooperation with KIER. Through these stays, the Systems and Decision Science area chaired by Peter E. de Janosi, Andrzej Wierzbicki, and Alexander B. Kurzhanski has provided a good environment and effective support for our research activities.

The author also thanks Robert Dorfman, Professor of Political Economy at Harvard University, for his initiation and continuous stimulus to interdisciplinary research activities for public planning during and after her stay in 1973-74 as an honorary research fellow at Harvard University, and is also grateful to Howard Raiffa, Professor of Managerial Economics at Harvard School of Business Administration, for his illuminating influence on studies of the role of mediators, through the Processes of International Negotiation (PIN) Project in IIASA, 1985-87. As the developers of MCDM research, Yacov Y. Haimes, Professor of Systems Engineering at the University of Virginia, and Ralph L. Keeney, Professor of Systems Science at the University of Southern California, also provided personal encouragement to the authors through valuable discussions.

Special thanks should be extended to Yoshikazu Sawaragi, Chairman of the Japan Institute of Systems Research and Emeritus Professor of Kyoto University, and his staff for their invariant stimulus and encouragement for our research. The authors also wish to thank the following graduate students of Kobe University for their assistance through discussions and computer works: Kazuya Sawada, Kenji Arata, Takayuki Sasakura, Kohzo Tazumi, Sumio Hasegawa, Hitoshi Yano, Naohiro Mori, Kazuteru Tada, Ichiroh Nishizaki, Tohru Yumine, and Yuuji Nango.

The authors are particularly indebted to the supporting staff, Nozomi Matsuoka and Noriko Inada, who worked in the Economic Planning unit in KIER, for typing and retyping the manuscript with patience, skill, and a pleasant attitude. These works were directed by Itsuko Funayama, Executive Assistant at KIER, whose great contribution to this research during the whole period is most appreciated in every stage of it. Her work includes preparations and calculations for data for the case studies, in addition to the typing of the manuscript and the drawing of the figures.

The authors would further like to thank the Japan Ministry of Education, Science and Culture for financially supporting this work by Grant-in-Aids for Scientific Research in 1981-82, and 1985, and for also providing Grant-in-Aid for Publication of Scientific Research Result in the 1987 financial year. The Kajima Foundation is also acknowledged for a research grant in 1985-86.

Finally we would like to thank Professor Peter Nijkamp of Free University, and Dr. D. J. Larner, Publisher of the D. Reidel Publishing Company, for their assistance in the publication of this book.

Fumiko Seo
Masatoshi Sakawa
August 1987

# Chapter 1
# Introduction to Multiple Criteria Decision Making

## 1.1 Modern Society as a Problems Complex

Multiple criteria decision making (MCDM) is a major field of systems analysis, which treats the complex problems arising in modern society with the latest attainment of high technology and the rapidly changing human lives. This field has advanced during the past 30 years to cope with the consequences of the success of the modern sciences. In particular, while the sustained processes of rapid economic growth after World War II have been converted to the stable growth paths since the 1970's, new social, psychological, and environmental problems - decline of annual rates of productivity, deterioration of natural resources, increase of water and energy demands, shortage (or maldistribution) of foods, environmental pollution, urbanization, and dissolution of traditional society, etc. - have presented themselves to the people of the present world. These consequences necessitate the development of a multiple disciplinary approach for analyzing these diverse effects and initiating effective human action to cope with them. MCDM concerns methodology which can treat these wide-area problems.

This book is intended to provide an overview of the present status of MCDM along with its theoretical background, and to present integrated methods of MCDM for treating the societal systems particularly in operationally meaningful ways. Special consideration is placed on its applicability to regional planning, management, and its evaluation, which also includes technology assessment.

In the remaining sections of this chapter, characteristics of MCDM distinct from general systems research are discussed.

## 1.2 General Characteristics of Modern Systems Analysis

### 1.2.1 Historical Background

A system is defined as an entity having a purpose composed of many components which are mutually interrelated with each other. Systems research has a long history and a wide range in its field while, in its contemporary sense, there have been some new directions.

Systems science is a new field which has been rapidly developed since World War II. Cybernetics (Wiener 1948) opened a way to the general systems theory for self-organization systems based on statistical physics, communication and information theory, and biological nervous systems, etc. General Systems Theory (Ashby 1952, 1956; von Bertalanffy 1968, etc.) was intended to establish a comprehensive method for synthesizing various fields of existing sciences. The characteristics of these approaches are to describe, quantitatively and nonquantitatively, self-adaptation and control mechanisms of various kinds of systems from the point of view of homeostasis. Functions of self-adjustment, equilibrium, and stability of systems are described, leaving the inner structure of the systems as unspecified black boxes. The main interest is concentrated on the relational schemes of the adaptable control systems, with which both the physical and societal systems are structured (e.g., Lange 1962, 1965).

In another approach for societal systems, social action has been investigated in sociological research. Interpretative understanding of social action is regarded as subjective matter and a causal explanation of its course and consequences is intended (Weber 1921). Societal systems are treated as a process of interaction by plural individual actors, in which actors are motivated by their inclination toward the "optimization of gratification." The relationship of actors to their situations is culturally structured via some mediations ("symbols"). A system of expectation of the actors in response to their situations is structured relative to their own "need-dispositions" in their choice of existing alternatives. Parsons (1951) pointed out that the "need-disposition" system of the individual actors has two most primary aspects, called "gratificational" and "orientational." The latter was interpreted as the cognitive aspect. The process of a systematic integration of actions is a selective ordering among possibilities of the "cognitive orientations" relevant to the actor's interests. This process of ordered selection among alternatives is an evaluation process. Thus, social systems are recognized in the aspects of both gratification and motivation, because the orientation with evaluation motivates human action. The main characteristic of this system, however, is in the relational scheme of actions in empirical systems. There is no objectives analysis for purposeful systems, for which normative decisions should be constructed. In Parson's sense, the motivation of the social systems is interpreted as an orientation toward improvement of the gratification-deprivation balance of the actor. Because of this way of thinking, it can be asserted that the interpretation of human motivation in the social systems has been on the same line as the general systems theory or cybernetics.

### 1.2.2 Characteristics of Modern Systems Analysis

A modern systems analysis which has been rapidly developed since the 1970's has new characteristics distinct from the classical systems science, although it remains greatly influenced by preceding research.

First of all, the modern systems analysis does not attempt to construct a general systems theory and to synthesize various fields of sciences within it. The new systems analysis is intended for the objectives analysis via structuring of a problems complex. In particular, it intends to solve decision problems for effective human action in the societal as well as technological fields and to provide desirable solutions in quantitative terms. The method for treating the behavioral response of the decision maker (DM) with intent in finding solutions is called "methodology" in distinction to "theory" which is concerned purely with the logical structure of observation problems. The main concern of modern systems analysis is in the methodological development for problem-finding and problem-solving. Thus systems research is increasingly revealing its eminent properties as the science for decision support to construction of desirable programs for public policy.

Second, in articulation of the objectives included in the system, selective design of objectives composition and management of their performance levels are intended. As Dantzig (1982) has suggested for mathematical programming, the most important contribution of the modern systems analysis is in "expressing criteria for selection of good or best plans in terms of explicit goals and not in terms of ground rules which are at best only a means for carrying out the objective but not the objective itself." To set the objectives, to specify their alternative configurations, and to control and compare their performance levels are the most important tasks of the recent generation of systems analysis.

Third, for articulation of objectives in manageable terms, modeling and structuring of the decision systems become more important. No part of the whole system can be left as a "black box" unspecified. For specification of systems structure in its modeling, multidisciplinary approach in quantitative as well as qualitative terms is requested on the results of modern sciences in various fields.

Fourth, the new systems analysis is a normative approach. The objectives management cannot steer clear of normativeness in decision making. Thus modern systems analysis cannot be reduced to simulation processes. Mathematical programming and control theory, in which objective functions and constraint conditions are articulately prescribed, can provide useful tools for quantitative research in systems analysis. These methods have been greatly advanced with the development of computational algorithms during recent decades.

Fifth, the normativeness of systems research is closely combined with preference analysis. This is a new major characteristic of modern systems analysis differing from cybernetics in which preferences have been treated as external, or unconsciously given, and unspecified in "situations."

Preferences at most have been simply considered as dependent variables which respond to imbalance in the systems, such as biological wants like hunger and thirst. In Weber-Parsons' sense, preference itself has been an external phenomenon to "systems," and preference analysis has been purged from the border of science which is asserted to be value-neutral or value-free. Many economists have also succeeded along the same line which has persisted since Robbins (1932), although an exceptional assertion for the significance of value judgments as the springs of human action has been presented by von Mises (1957), a leading exponent of the Austrian School. In contrast, the modern systems analysis includes as its core the preference theory which is originally based on the von Neumann-Morgenstern expected utility hypothesis that is an offspring of the Austrian School, and has been developed as decision analysis and game theory since the late 1950's and 1960's; these approaches have been moving ahead of social systems analysis in the sense of sustaining manageability and solvability of the normative or purposeful systems.

Multiple criteria decision analysis is a method which has been developed in inheriting those fortunes from modern systems analysis. In the next section, we are concerned with describing characteristics of the multiple criteria decision analysis.

## 1.3 Characteristics of Multiple Criteria Decision Analysis

### 1.3.1 Objects to be Analyzed

**1. Multiplicity of objectives**

Multiple criteria decision analysis (MCDA) intends to analyze the objects as a problems complex which arises from modern technological society. The problems complex includes many objectives that cover economic, social, physical and chemical, psychological, administrative, engineering, ethical, and aesthetical fields. Decision making for these complex systems cannot be reduced to a single objective decision problem such as pursuit of economic efficiency. The object as a problems complex is called a multiobjective entity or an objectives complex. MCDA concerns decision complexity for the multiobjective entity.

**2. Heterogeneity of objectives**

The multiobjective entity includes heterogeneity of objectives, which cannot be reduced to multisectoral or multiregional systems. In particular, noneconomic objectives that are included in it should be explicitly specified and handled.

Due to the heterogeneity of objectives, the multiobjective entity raises specific problems.

(i) Noncommensurability, or noncomparability, among objectives. The quantities of the objectives cannot be reduced to a common unit such as a monetary (dollar, etc.) unit for evaluation. There is no measure to scale the objectives on a common standard.

(ii) Noncompatibility among objectives. The objectives are often in conflict with each other. An attainment of one objective is not necessarily compatible with that of the other objectives.

(iii) Uncertainty. Due to an augmentation of incompleteness of knowledge and information in multiobjective entity, decision making is often performed under uncertainty. Situations in which decisions are made are usually unclear for DM or the assessor.

Thus methodology for MCDM should have capabilities which can cope with these characteristics of multiobjective entities. First, the new method should be able to deal with the noncommensurability, or noncomparability, among objectives. For this purpose, a device for scalarization of vector-valued objectives should be presented. Second, for manipulating noncompatibility among objectives, value trade-offs between any pair of objectives should be articulated. Third, the method should be able to manipulate more effectively uncertainty or ambiguousness of human decision making with some rational procedures. These are the desirable criteria of MCDM.

**3. Plurality of decision makers**

The multiplicity of objectives is not the same as the

plurality of decision makers. While one decision maker can perform the multiple objectives evaluation, plural decision makers may pursue only one objective in their decision problems. The plurality of decision makers raises the diversification of evaluation for a decision problem, whereas the singularity of the decision maker ordinarily results in the unification of evaluation. Thus the multiple agents, or multiperson, decision problem possesses different properties from the single agent, or single person, decision problem, and methodologies for treating them are different from each other. Game theory usually concerns the multiple agents decision problems with a single objective, while decision analysis concerns the single agent decision problems having single or multiple objectives. This book is mainly concerned with the multiple objectives decision problems for the single decision maker who is assumed as the assessor to impersonate the disposition of other people, although the multiple agents decision problem is considered in some chapters in the context of the diversification of evaluation and is treated from the point of view of conflict-solving among plural decision makers.

### 1.3.2 General Description of Methodology

One of the methods for MCDA is known as multiobjective optimization. Multiobjective optimization is an extension of mathematical optimization, which has been primarily developed for the single objective problems, to treat the multiobjective problems. Although mathematical optimization is a well-established method and is useful for quantitative analysis of multiobjective as well as single objective systems, this approach can handle only one phase of the multiobjective entities which include a judgmental as well as an analytical phase. The multiobjective entities include, as its inherent property, not only quantitative aspects for which mathematical modeling and optimization are effectively performed, but also the qualitative - primarily nonquantitative - aspects for which modeling and evaluation depend on subjective preferences and judgment of DM. Thus MCDA has to also properly cope with the judgmental aspect of decision making.

In general, MCDM is composed of two phases - objective or analytical, and subjective or judgmental. Mathematical optimization is appropriate for the objective phase but not for the subjective phase. Decision analysis concerns the subjective phase; it deals with how to handle the subjective phase in decision processes with rational procedures. In these ways, mathematical optimization and decision analysis reveal their effectiveness for only one particular phase of MCDM. However, because the multiobjective entity includes both the analytical and judgmental phases as its inherent properties, these two approaches should be combined effectively with each other. MCDA, the method for MCDM, concerns both phases of decision making and thus is primarily composed of mathematical optimization and decision analysis. It also includes more extended and integrated devices. Naturally, the inherent characteristics of this method are different from those of conventional systems research. We will discuss them with an enumeration.

**1. Presentation of the theoretical valuation**

The objectives in the multiobjective entity are generally impossible to evaluate in a commensurate term due to their heterogeneity. The market price mechanism cannot function effectively in this situation. However, mathematical programming, which is generally used for solving optimal resource allocation problems, can simultaneously solve the valuation problems combined with the resource allocation problems. The valuation problem is known as the dual problem and is interpreted as the shadow price determination (pricing) problem. Although many economists in nonengineering fields have been exclusively involved in elucidating that finding the shadow prices is nothing more than simulating the market prices mechanism, theoretical valuation for the multiobjective entity can be derived, if it is feasible, by solving the dual problem of mathematical programming. Then the concept of shadow prices obtained via mathematical programming can be used as the indicator for theoretical valuation of any quantitative system via the system's modeling and identification.

**2. Viewpoint of systems management and control**

MCDA primarily concerns systems management and control. This method has its particular function which is not confined to simulation and prediction. Quantitative analysis with this method is performed ultimately as a part of comprehensive systems planning and management, even though it is based on information obtained via systems modeling and simulation. The shadow prices, as indicative prices, can be used as good references or measures for the systems management and control by DM.

**3. Inclusion of human preferences**

The method introduces a quantitative analysis of human preferences as its intrinsic part, which are often measured on the common scale. Although the judgmental phase of human decisions is primarily nonquantifiable, the preference structure of DM should be quantified in a comparable term if the decision processes are to be managed discretionally and evaluated comparably. The preference analysis more generally leads to articulation of the value trade-offs among objectives. The device for manipulating the quantification of the human preferences, however, cannot usually provide the optimal property with the unimodality for the selected solutions. To treat this nonunimodal characteristic in selection, which comes from existence of decision alternatives and its diversification, is an important aspect of MCDA.

**4. Pursuit of the process rationality**

As a science for planning, MCDA pursues procedural rationality in contrast to substantial rationality which has been sought by classical optimization techniques. The new method highly regards the rationality of the procedures with which decisions are made. In other words, this method regards the rationality of the process with which outcomes of decisions are obtained to be more important than the rationality of the substance of the outcome. Simon (1978, 1979) called it "process-oriented" in contrast to "outcome-oriented" in the classical optimization methods. In other words, how the decision is made is a crucial issue of MCDM, in distinction to classical approaches in which what decision is made is the matter of most interest.

**5. Interactive decision making**

One device for assuring the procedural rationality is to introduce interactive processes into decision making. Interactive decision making incorporates learning and adaptation processes in the decision making. By the enlargement of the amount and improvement of the quality of newly acquired information, decisions are modified and renewed in multistage evaluation processes, repetitively and sequentially. Computer algorithms for decision support systems (DSS) can be effectively used in these stages.

**6. Function for mediation**

The complexity of the multiobjective entity requires, for better structuring and understanding, the systems' decomposition and coordination. Objectives embedded in the systems are partitioned according to their properties, and then the objectives hierarchy, or value systems hierarchy, is constructed in multilevel. Complexity and ambiguity of decisions are also treated in multilevel. A hierarchical structure of the objectives is constructed for manipulating in order the coordination processes. The function of DM for the mediation is introduced to supremal units of the hierarchical system for coordinating the systems, for keeping consistency of the systems management and evaluation, and for compromising the value conflicts within them. This also corresponds to the judgmental phase of MCDM.

**7. Satisficing principle**

The superiority of the procedural rationality over the substantial rationality suggests use of the satisficing principle (Simon 1969, 1979; March and Simon 1958) in place of the classical optimality principle. The decisions in mathematical optimization are based on the extremal solutions obtained with marginal analysis, or differential calculus, and assert the absolute superiority of selected decisions over all of the other alternatives. It presumes omniscient rationality or perfect rationality. On the contrary, MCDA for the complex systems only requires the selected policies to be kept within some tolerable ranges or at least to correspond to some lower limits of tolerance for the sets of criteria.

**8. Decision support**

MCDA presumes existence of a policy maker and intends to support his decisions by providing information with better quality. However, it does not intend to declare any assertion or policy proposal as "absolutely best." Results of analysis with this method should be used only as a reference or as material for making decisions for finding better policy programs. This method only concerns assisting the conception of better policy programs for solving the complex problems in a scientific way, and thus presumes interaction between the analyst and the policy maker in the subsequent steps for its implementation. DM in MCDM is presumed to be the assessor, and the propriety of its results should be confined within an experimental domain.

## 1.4 Outline of the Book

In the remaining chapters of this book, the methodology of MCDA is treated in three main streams classified according to the phases of MCDM on which the methods are mainly concentrated. The first stream is concerned with the analytical phase of MCDM, for which mathematical optimization techniques can be suitably extended; it is treated in Chapters 2, 3, and 4. The second stream is concerned with the judgmental phase, for which decision analysis can be effectively used; it is treated in Chapters 5, 6, 7, and 8. The third stream intends to bridge the gap between these two phases. The main concern of this book is to explore the third direction and to present new devices which will be able to incorporate effectively both phases of MCDM - analytical and judgmental. For this purpose, the authors present an extension of the imputed price (shadow price) concept for MCDM. This device requires a combined utilization of mathematical optimization and decision analysis. The main idea is to transform the dual optimal solutions of mathematical programming to quasi-utility values, and if it is necessary, to modulate the converted "utility" values in the coordination processes of DM. This approach is discussed in Chapters 9, 10, 11, and 12. The decision processes are generally performed with human preferences in institutional and cultural conditions, which have definite effects on human nature and technological progress in a society. Descriptive analysis of the human nature embodied in DM is examined, based on recent results of behavioristic research, in the context of social implementation of the multiobjective decision analysis, and is discussed in Chapter 13.

The structure of this book is depicted in Figure 1.1.

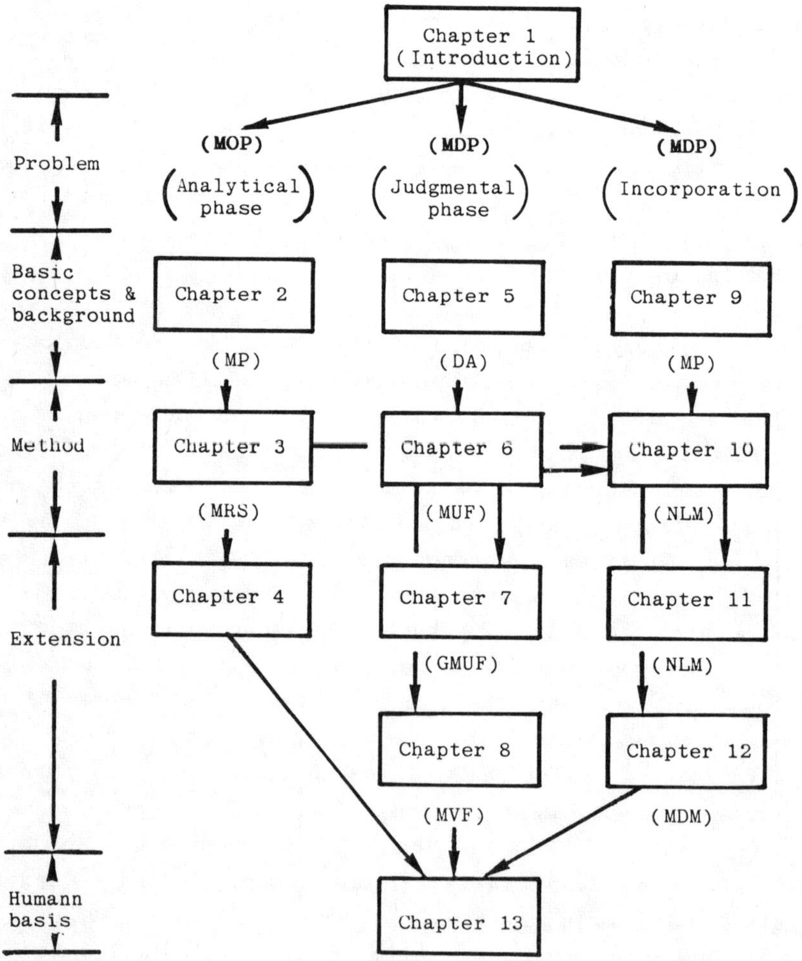


**Figure 1.1 Structure of the chapters of this book.**

# CHAPTER 2
# APPROACH TO MULTIPLE CRITERIA OPTIMIZATION

## 2.1 Pareto Optimality

### 2.1.1 Multiple Criteria Optimization

As discussed in Chapter 1, multiple criteria decision making (MCDM) has two major phases: analytical and judgmental. While the analytical phase corresponds to the deterministic and, in nature, quantifiable aspect of decision making, the judgmental phase corresponds to the indeterministic and, in nature, nonquantifiable aspect. Although mathematical modeling and optimization techniques are properly applied to the analytical or objective phase, those techniques are not necessarily appropriate for the judgmental or subjective phase where decision making depends on the preference structure of the decision maker (DM), which is not generally presumed to be known. Thus the decision process is composed of two different phases. Approaches to MCDM are concerned with filling this "phase gap" with rational procedures.

This chapter is mainly concerned with methods intended to handle the analytical phase of the multiobjective decision process, although these methods should also be able to manipulate the judgmental phase at least to some extent due to the intrinsic property of MCDM.

The method for treating the analytical phase of the multiple criteria decision process is called multiple criteria optimization or, in short, multiobjective optimization. Multiple criteria optimization has two key concepts: (i) Pareto optimality and (ii) the preferred decision (preferred solution). In general, decisions with Pareto optimality are not uniquely determined. In multiobjective optimization problems, there are many Pareto optimal solutions. Due to this plurality of optimal decisions, the most desirable decision should be selected from among the Pareto optimal solutions. The final solution selected as the most desirable, or at least the best compromised, is called the preferred solution.

Formally the procedure which solves the multiple criteria optimization problem is composed of three steps: (1) mathematical modeling of the systems structure, (2) generation of the Pareto optimal solutions, and (3) selection of the preferred solution. Steps (1) and (2) are embedded in the process of solving mathematical optimization problems. Step (3) should be inserted into the optimization process externally with subjective decisions.

In this chapter, the basic ideas about how to approach the multiple criteria optimization problems are described, and existing techniques for solving them are examined according to alternative ways for manipulating the plurality of objectives.

### 2.1.2 Concept of Pareto Optimality

In general, the multiple criteria optimization problem (MOP) is described in the following form:

MOP

$$\underset{x \in X}{\text{maximize}} \quad (f_1(x), f_2(x), \ldots, f_m(x)), \tag{2.1}$$

where $f(x) \triangleq (f_1(x), f_2(x), \ldots, f_m(x))$ is a vector-valued criterion function defined on the n-dimensional decision variables $x \triangleq (x_1, x_2, \ldots, x_n)$. $X$ is a set of feasible decisions and is defined as follows:

$$X \triangleq \{x \mid g_j(x) \leqslant 0, \quad g_j: R^n \to R^1, \quad j = 1, \ldots, J\}, \tag{2.2}$$

where $g_j(x)$ is a function representing a constraint condition. The vector-valued criterion function $f : R^n \to R^m$

is called the multiple criteria (or multiobjective) valuation function. The problem (2.1) is also called the multiobjective optimization problem or vector-valued optimization problem.

In MOP, the objective functions which are elements of the multiple criteria valuation function $f(x) \triangleq (f_1(x), f_2(x), \ldots, f_m(x))$ are usually heterogeneous and their values are noncommensurable; they cannot be measured in a common unit. In addition, they are mutually incompatible and in conflict with each other. For example, an industrial output $f_1(x)$ and a BOD effluent discharge from industrial plants $f_2(x)$ can neither be measured in a common (e.g., monetary) unit, nor can they be attained compatibly. In general, the supremal solution for (2.1) does not exist. To improve the value of one objective function often worsens the value of another objective function. All the objective functions cannot be maximized in parallel with each other.

Thus, for the solutions to MOP (2.1), noninferiority instead of superiority should be sought. These solutions are called noninferior solutions or alternatively, "optimal" solutions in the Paretian sense. The Pareto optimal or noninferior solution $x^\dagger$ of MOP (2.1) is defined as follows.

**Definition 2.1 (Noninferiority or Pareto optimal).**

The solution $x^\dagger$ of MOP (2.1) is said to be noninferior if there exist no other feasible solutions $x \in X \subseteq R^n$ such that $f(x) \geqslant f(x^\dagger)$. The $x^\dagger$ is also called Pareto optimal.

Noninferiority describes the property of "maximal" in the vector-valued maximization problem. Namely, the vector-valued maximization problem (2.1), or vector maximization, requires the maximality only in the Pareto optimal sense.

The Pareto optimality can also be defined in terms of nondominance. Let us consider a domination domain $I_+$ for a point $\hat{y}$ in an m-dimensional objective function space $R^m$, which is a positive quadrant of $R^m$ taking $\hat{y}$ as an origin in the feasible region $F$ in $R^m$ but excluding the origin $\hat{y}$.

A domination set for $\hat{y}$ is defined in $I_+$ as follows:

$$D \triangleq \{y \mid d = y - \hat{y} \geqslant 0, \quad \hat{y},\ y \in R^m\}. \tag{2.3}$$

**Definition 2.2**

$\hat{y} \in R^m$ is said to be Pareto optimal if there exists no $y$ which belongs to the domination set D (2.3) for $\hat{y}$ in the feasible region F. A cone (D) spanned by the d of (2.3) is called a domination cone.

Suppose $\mathbf{f}^\dagger$ to be a set of the Pareto optimal vector $f^\dagger(x)$ in the objective function space. Then

$$\mathbf{f}^\dagger \triangleq \{f^\dagger | f^\dagger \in F, \quad F \cap D = \phi\}, \tag{2.4}$$

where $$F \triangleq \{f(x) | x \in X, \quad f \in R^m\}. \tag{2.5}$$

The Pareto optimal is also called efficient, admissible, or maximal in the Paretian sense. A set $\mathbf{f}^\dagger$ of the Pareto optimal vector is called the Pareto efficient frontier.

The multiobjective optimization problem is a generalized form of the single objective or scalar-valued optimization problem. The scalar-valued optimization problem (SOP) is formulated as follows:

SOP

$$\underset{x \in X}{\text{Maximize}} \quad \phi(x), \tag{2.6}$$

where $\phi : R^n \to R^1$. The preference relation for values of the scalar-valued criterion function corresponding to alternative values of the decision variables $x \in R^n$ can be completely ordered according to the numerical relation represented with "larger than (>)" or "equal to (=)." Hence the supremal or the best solution $x^*$ of the SOP (2.6) can be obtained immediately from the optimization process.

In the MOP (2.1), the preference relation for values of the vector-valued function f can be only partially ordered for alternative values of x. The "maximal" solutions can be asserted only as being mutually "not inferior to." These values are usually noncomparable with each other, and thus "optimal" solutions are attained only as noninferior solutions which are indeterminate for their ordering.

Thus the concept of Pareto optimality presumes to construct a compromise among noncompatible objectives, while no standard for prescribing the content of the compromise exists. A power struggle among parties may make a forced compromise, but it may be extremely favorable for one party and extremely unfavorable for the other party. The concept of proper Pareto optimality or proper inferiority is constructed for excluding such extraordinary cases in advance.

**Definition 2.3 (Proper noninferiority) (Geoffrion 1968).**

A solution $x^{\dagger}$ to MOP (2.1) is called a proper noninferior solution, if it is noninferior and there also exists a positive scalar value $M$ such that for each $i$,

$$\frac{f_i(x) - f_i(x^{\dagger})}{f_s(x^{\dagger}) - f_s(x)} \leqslant M, \quad i,s = 1,\ldots,m, \tag{2.7}$$

where $f_s(x) < f_s(x^{\dagger})$ for some $s$, $s \neq i$, whenever $x \in X$ and $f_i(x) > f_i(x^{\dagger})$.

This concept excludes as improper the cases in which the gain of one objective can be unlimitedly increased at the loss of the other objective. It should be noted that this concept does not depend on differentiability of functions. In the subsequent discussions, it is assumed that the improper cases of the Pareto optimal have already been excluded.

MOP (2.1) can be solved with the three steps: (i) mathematical modeling of the systems structure, (ii) finding the Pareto optimal solutions, and (iii) selection of the preferred solution. In step (i), objective functions $f(x) \triangleq (f_1(x), f_2(x),\ldots, f_m(x))$ and constraint functions $g(x) \triangleq (g_1(x), g_2(x),\ldots, g_J(x))$ of MOP (2.1) are formulated and identified. In step (ii), MOP (2.1) is solved and the Pareto optimal solutions are obtained. This step is discussed in the next section 2.2. The methods to seek the preferred solution from among the Pareto optimal solutions are discussed in Section 2.3 and thereafter.

### 2.1.3 Economic Analysis and Pareto Optimality

#### 1. Pareto optimality in market exchange

The concept of Pareto optimality has appeared in relation to multiple agents decision problems in economic literature since the nineteenth century. Edgeworth (1881) analyzed, using the contract curve, the state of equilibrium in market exchange among plural parties, and defined "equilibrium" as the state in which the "utility" of one contractor becomes "relatively maximum" under the conditions that utilities of the other contractors are invariant or do not decrease.

The term Pareto optimality is combined with the name of Vilfred Pareto (1906). Pareto described the state of economic equilibrium as the situation where the members of the collectivity (community) enjoy their maximum ophelimity (ofelimita or utility). A situation is called maximum ophelimity when it is no longer possible to find a way of moving from a certain position very slightly in such a direction that the ophelimity enjoyed by each of the individuals in the collectivity increases or decreases. In other words, any small displacement in departing from the maximum ophelimity, such as increases the ophelimity for certain individual, will decrease that for others. Thus any displacement from the maximum ophelimity may be agreeable to some person but not be agreeable to others.

In Edgeworth and Pareto, the concept of Pareto optimality is used for indicating the state of maximum ophelimity which will be achieved in equilibrium in exchange in the collectivity. Thus, the concept of maximum ophelimity is defined in the context of the multiple agents decision problems. However, Pareto also suggested that the equilibrium point in production gives the maximum ophelimity for the transformation in production, and that price variables can be adjusted for obtaining the equilibrium, along the lines of Classical economics since Smith (1776) and Ricardo (1817).

#### 2. Pareto optimality in production

In activity analysis of production, Koopmans (1951) used the word efficiency in the sense of Pareto optimality. He called a point in the commodity space (a set of net products), which belongs to a technologically possible region of production, efficient when an increase in the net output of one commodity can be achieved only at the cost of a decrease in the net output of some other commodities.

**Definition 2.4 (Efficiency of production).**

Let $y$ be a point in the m-dimensional commodity space and $Y \subseteq R^m$ be a technologically possible set of $y$. Then a point $y^\dagger$ in the commodity space is called efficient if $y^\dagger \in Y$ and if there exists no other point $y \in Y$ such that

$$y - y^\dagger \geqslant 0. \tag{2.8}$$

A major accomplishment of the activity analysis is to have proved the existence of the price vector associated with efficient production which is represented by a linear (Leontief) model.

Let $a_j \in R^m$, $j = 1,\ldots,n$, be an activity of production and $A$ be a technology matrix composed of $n$ activities. In notation,

$$a \triangleq \begin{bmatrix} a_{1j} \\ a_{2j} \\ \cdot \\ \cdot \\ \cdot \\ a_{mj} \end{bmatrix}, \quad A \triangleq \begin{bmatrix} a_{11}, & a_{12}, \ldots, & a_{1n} \\ a_{21}, & a_{22}, \ldots, & a_{2n} \\ \cdot & & \cdot \\ \cdot & & \cdot \\ \cdot & & \cdot \\ a_{m1}, & a_{m2}, \ldots, & a_{mn} \end{bmatrix} \triangleq (a_1, a_2, \ldots, a_n). \tag{2.9}$$

The $m \times n$ matrix $A$ is called the Leontief activity matrix, in which an element of each row shows input of a commodity flow into an activity of production at a unit level shown by each column. Let $y$ be a point of the m-dimensional commodity space and $x \in R^n$ be an operation level of each activity. Then the $y$ is called possible in technology $A$ if there exists an activity level $x$ such that

$$y = Ax, \quad x \geqslant 0. \tag{2.10}$$

When the commodity space is partitioned into the primary

commodities $y_{pri}$ and the final commodities $y_{fin}$, then the structure of production (2.10) can be shown by

$$y \triangleq \begin{bmatrix} y_{pri} \\ y_{fin} \end{bmatrix} = \begin{bmatrix} A_{pri} & 0 \\ 0 & A_{fin} \end{bmatrix} \begin{bmatrix} x_{pri} \\ x_{fin} \end{bmatrix} = \begin{bmatrix} A_{pri} \\ A_{fin} \end{bmatrix} x. \tag{2.11}$$

Let (A) denote a cone spanned by the column vectors $a_j \in R^m$ of A, which consists of all vectors $y \in R^m$ satisfying (2.10), and $(A) \triangleq (\sum_{j=1}^{n} a_j x_j, \quad a_j \in A, \quad a_j \in R^m, \quad x_j \geqslant 0, \quad x_j \in R^1, \; j = 1,\ldots,n)$. Then a normal vector to (A) exists.

**Theorem 2.1 (Koopmans).**

A necessary and sufficient condition for a possible point $y^{\dagger} \in (A)$ in the commodity space to be efficient is that the $y^{\dagger}$ possesses a positive normal cone (p) to (A), in which the vector $p \in R^m$ satisfies that

$$pA \leqslant 0, \quad py^{\dagger} = 0, \quad p > 0. \tag{2.12}$$

This theorem implies as a necessary condition that y is a boundary point of (A). Theorem 2.1 shows that the normal vector p to (A) should be included in the negative polar $(A)^-$ for all $a_j \in (A)$; viz., the normal vector p makes an nonacute angle with all $a_j \in (A)$. In particular, the p should be included in the orthogonal complement $(A)^{\perp}$ of a cone (A), in which the p makes an orthogonal angle with all $a_j \in (A)$ on the efficient point $y^{\dagger}$.

Special interest is in the economic interpretation of the normal vector p to (A) on an efficient point $y^{\dagger}$ as the accounting price or the shadow price. From (2.10) and (2.12),

$$\begin{aligned} pa_j &= 0, \quad \text{when } x > 0, \\ pa_j &\leqslant 0, \quad \text{when } x = 0. \end{aligned} \tag{2.13}$$

(2.13) means that, while there is no activity with a negative net profit for a unit level of production, the net profit per unit of the j-th activity should be zero when its operation level is positive. This assertion provides another definition of economic efficiency.

The price concept has been extended more specifically. Consider the following production system:

$$y \triangleq \begin{bmatrix} y_{pri} \\ y_{int} \\ y_{fin} \end{bmatrix} = Ax, \quad x \geqslant 0, \quad y_{fin} \geqslant 0, \tag{2.14}$$

$$y_{int} = 0, \tag{2.15}$$

$$y_{pri} \geqslant \eta_{pri}, \quad \eta_{pri} < 0, \tag{2.16}$$

where $y_{int}$ denotes a vector of the intermediate commodities and $\eta_{pri}$ is a vector of constants of resource constraints. If there exists an activity level $x$ with which a point $y$ in the commodity space satisfies (2.14) to (2.16), then the $y$ is called attainable.

**Definition 2.5 (Efficiency of final product).**

A point $y^\dagger$ in the commodity space is called efficient if it is attainable and if there exists no other attainable point $y$ such that

$$y_{fin} - y^\dagger_{fin} \geqslant 0. \tag{2.17}$$

**Theorem 2.2 (Koopmans).**

A necessary and sufficient condition for an attainable point $y^\dagger$ in the commodity space to be efficient according to the above definition 2.5 is that there exists a normal vector $p$ to the possible cone (A) spanned by (2.9) at the point $y^\dagger$, having the following properties:

$$p_{fin} > 0, \quad p_{pri=} \geqslant 0, \quad p_{pri>} = 0, \tag{2.18}$$

where $p_{pri=}$ shows that an equality is realized in (2.16), viz., the resource constraint is binding, while $p_{pri>}$ shows that an inequality in (2.16) exists, viz., the constraint is not binding.

Koopmans called the normal vector $p$ to (A) at the efficient point $y^{\dagger}$ the price vector associated with $y^{\dagger}$ obtained by the technology A, if it satisfies the condition (2.18).

The existence of the price vectors associated with efficient production has been presented as an eminent result of economic analysis. The duality of resource allocation and price systems is the main theme throughout this book. The activity analysis has provided primal concepts for approaching the dual problem.

### 3. Pareto optimality in games

The concept of Pareto optimality is also discussed in game theory which concerns multiple agents decision problems.

In a finite n-person noncooperative game, an equilibrium point is defined as a set of mixed strategies such that each player's mixed strategy maximizes his payoff function while the strategies of the others are held fixed. Denote a set of mixed strategies $s_p$ of the player $p$, $p = 1,\ldots,n$, to be $s \triangleq (s_1, s_2, \ldots, s_n)$, and a substitution set for it to be $(s;\ r_p) \triangleq (s_1, s_2, \ldots, s_{p-1}, r_p, s_{p+1}, \ldots, s_n)$, where $s_p$ and $r_p$ show the probability vector on the set of his pure strategies and are selected as the pth player's strategic variable. It is assumed that the payoff function $z_p$ for the player $p$ be linear on the mixed strategy $s_p$ of each player. Then the equilibrium point is defined as follows.

**Definition 2.6 (Equilibrium point in a noncooporative game).**

A set $s$ of the mixed strategies is said to be an equilibrium point if and only if for every player $p$

$$z_p(s) = \max_{\text{all } r_p} [z_p(s;\ r_p)]. \tag{2.19}$$

From the linearity of $z_p(s)$ on $s_p$,

$$\max_{\text{all } r_p} [z_p(s;\, r_p)] = \max_j [z_p(s;\, \pi_{pj})], \tag{2.20}$$

where the payoff of the mixed strategy is denoted by $z_p \triangleq \sum_j s_{pj}\, \pi_{pj}$, $\pi_{pj}$ stands for a payoff of a pure strategy j of a player p, and $s_{pj} \geq 0$ and $\sum_j s_{pj} = 1$. Define $z_{pj}(s) \triangleq z_p(s;\, \pi_{pj})$ which indicates the payoff for each player p of the n-tuple mixed strategy s that is composed of a mixed strategy $s_p$ with a payoff $\pi_{pj}$ from a pure strategy j. The necessary and sufficient condition for s to be an equilibrium point is derived straightforward from Definition 2.6.

**Theorem 2.3 (Equilibrium point in game) (Nash 1951).**

An n-tuple mixed strategy s is an equilibrium point if and only if for every player p, $p = 1,\ldots,n$,

$$z_p(s) = \max_j z_p(s;\, j). \tag{2.21}$$

Then, from $z_p(s) \triangleq \sum_j s_{pj} z_{pj}(s)$, $s_{pj}$ should vanish whenever $z_{pj}(s) < \max_i z_{pi}(s)$. In other words, any pure strategy j of player p is not used in the n-tuple of mixed strategies s unless it is an optimal pure strategy for every player p. This represents the maximality condition for the equilibrium point of each player. Nash (1951) proved that every finite game has an equilibrium point. Nash's existence theorem assures that, at the equilibrium point, no player can improve his payoff by moving a mixed strategy from $r_p$ to $t_p$, which is the nondominance condition of the equilibrium point for each player.

In an n-person cooperative game, the term "imputation" is used for the payoff value $z_p$ for each player p, which has the following properties (von Neumann and Morgenstern 1944; Shaplay and Shubik 1973).

(i) Feasibility:

$$\sum_{p \in N} z_p \leqslant v(N). \qquad (2.22)$$

(ii) Individual rationality:

$$z_p \geqslant v(\{p\}) \qquad \text{for all} \quad p \in N. \qquad (2.23)$$

(iii) Collective rationality (Pareto optimality):

$$\sum_{p \in N} z_p = v(N), \qquad (2.24)$$

where $N \triangleq (1,2,,\ldots,n)$. The $v(N)$ stands for the characteristic function which maps a set (coalition) of n-players to the real number indicating the potential worth of a grand coalition among n-players.

The core, as a solution concept of a game, is defined as the set of imputations that leaves no coalition in a position to improve the payoffs of all its members. Symbolically, it satisfies the following properties.

(iv) Coalitional (group) rationality:

$$\sum_{p \subset S} z_p \geqslant v(S), \quad \text{all} \quad S \subset N, \qquad (2.25)$$

and (iii) the Pareto optimality:

$$\sum_{p \in N} z_p = v(N). \qquad (2.26)$$

The concept of core extends the Pareto optimality to assure the group rationality for every coalition $S \subset N$. The core eliminates all outcomes that any coalitions formed by a subset of the players can improve their payoff at once. Alternatively, using the domination concept, the core is also defined as the imputation which is not dominated by any other imputation in the game $\Gamma(N, v)$ except for the grand coalition.

Existence of the core has been examined by Scarf (1967), Shaplay and Shubik (1969), and others.

## 2.2 Derivation of the Pareto Optimal Frontier

### 2.2.1 Scalarization

Finding the maximum solutions to MOP (2.1) is reduced to generating a set of Pareto maximal or noninferior solutions. The procedure to find the set of noninferior solutions of MOP (2.1) is to convert it to a scalar-valued optimization problem.

MDP

$$\underset{x \in X}{\text{maximize}} \quad V(f_1(x), f_2(x), \ldots, f_m(x)), \tag{2.27}$$

where $x \in R^n$, $f_i : R^n \to R^1$, $i = 1,\ldots,m$, and $X \triangleq \{x \mid g_j \leq 0, g_J: R^n \to R^1, j = 1,\ldots,J, x \in R^n\}$.

The MDP (2.27) is called the multiple criteria decision problem (MDP), or in short, the multiobjective decision problem. The function $V(f(x))$, $V : R^m \to R^1$, is called the scalarized, vector-valued (multidimensional) valuation function, or alternatively, the scalarized (scalar-valued) multiple criteria (multiobjective) valuation function. It should be noted that finding a set of the noninferior solutions does not complete the process of solving the MDP, but only forms the first step of it. In this step, values of the valuation function $V$ can only partially be ordered. The solution process of the MDP (2.27) is completed only with the second step in which the preferred solution is found. Thus the process for solving (2.27) cannot be carried out only with the mathematical optimization process. It should also be carried out with the judgmental process by the decision maker (DM).

Transforming the vector-valued criterion function $f(x)$ in MOP (2.1) to the scalar-valued valuation function $V(f(x))$ is called scalarization. The process to find the Pareto optimal frontier of MOP (2.1) is composed of (i) scalarization of MOP, i.e., construction of the scalar-valued valuation function $V$ in MDP (2.27), and (ii) solving the MDP (2.27), i.e., derivation of the noninferior solution set of MDP (2.27) via mathematical optimization. In this section, we consider the methods for finding the noninferior or Pareto optimal solution sets of MOP (2.1).

### 2.2.2 Kuhn-Tucker Theorems

In this section, we give a brief account of the Kuhn-Tucker theorems as the theoretical fundamentals for solving the MOP (2.1).

Reformulate the vector-valued optimization problem (2.1) as follows:

MOP

$$\text{maximize} \quad f(x) \triangleq (f_1(x), f_2(x), \ldots, f_m(x)) \tag{2.28}$$

$$\text{subject to} \quad g(x) \triangleq (g_1(x), g_2(x), \ldots, g_J(x)) \leqslant 0, \tag{2.29}$$

where $f(x)$: $R^n \to R^m$ is a set of objective functions and $g(x)$: $R^n \to R^J$ is a set of constraint functions.

We define the stationarity condition for mathematical optimization with $\nabla f(x) = 0$ where $\nabla f(x) \triangleq (\nabla f_1(x), \nabla f_2(x), \ldots, \nabla f_m(x))$ is the Jacobian matrix of $f(x)$, which is written as

$$\nabla f(x) \triangleq \begin{bmatrix} \frac{\partial f_1}{\partial x_1}, & \frac{\partial f_1}{\partial x_2}, & \ldots\ldots, & \frac{\partial f_1}{\partial x_n} \\ \vdots & \vdots & \ddots & \vdots \\ \frac{\partial f_m}{\partial x_1}, & \frac{\partial f_m}{\partial x_2}, & \ldots\ldots, & \frac{\partial f_m}{\partial x_n} \end{bmatrix}.$$

The Lagrange function of MOP (2.28) (2.29) is called the vector Lagrange function, and formulated as

$$L(x, \lambda) \triangleq wf(x) - \lambda g(x) \triangleq \sum_{i=1}^{m} w_i f_i(x) - \sum_{j=1}^{J} \lambda_j g_j(x), \tag{2.30}$$

where $w \triangleq (w_1, w_2, \ldots, w_m)$ is a vector of weighting coefficients assigned to the objective functions $f(x) \triangleq (f_1(x), f_2(x), \ldots, f_m(x))$, and $\lambda \triangleq (\lambda_1, \lambda_2, \ldots, \lambda_J)$ is a vector of the Lagrange multipliers imputed to the constraint functions $g(x) \triangleq (g_1(x), g_2(x), \ldots, g_J(x))$.

When MOP (2.28) has only one objective function, i.e., $f(x)$ is a scalar, (2.30) is a Lagrange function of SOP (2.6) with the scalar $w = 1$, and is rewritten as

$$L(x, \lambda) \triangleq \phi(x) - \sum_{j=1}^{J} \lambda_j g_j(x), \tag{2.31}$$

where $\phi: R^n \to R^1$ is a scalar-valued objective function defined on a vector of decision variables $x \in R^n$. The vector Lagrange function (2.30) is a generalized form of (2.31).

The Kuhn-Tucker conditions for the vector-valued optimization problem (2.28) (2.29) are described as follows:

KTCN

$$\sum_{i=1}^{m} w_i \nabla f_i(x) - \sum_{j=1}^{J} \lambda_j \nabla g_j(x) = 0, \tag{2.32}$$

$$g_j(x) \leqslant 0, \quad \lambda_j g_j(x) = 0, \quad \lambda_j \geqslant 0, \quad j = 1,\ldots,J. \tag{2.33}$$

The formulation (2.32) states the first-order local optimality (stationarity) condition of the Lagrange function $L(x, \lambda)$ (2.30) for $x$, $\partial L/\partial x = 0$. The formulation (2.33) states the first-order local optimality (stationarity) condition of $L(x, \lambda)$ (2.30) for $\lambda$, $\partial L/\partial \lambda = 0$, along with the feasibility condition (2.29) and the sign condition for the Lagrange multiplier $\lambda_j \geqslant 0$. The second equation of (2.33) states the complementary slackness condition: Lagrange multipliers corresponding to inactive constraint conditions should be zero, where inactive means that the constraint holds the inequality. The Kuhn-Tucker conditions of the SOP (2.6) are described as follows.

SKTCN

$$\nabla \phi(x) - \sum_{j=1}^{J} \lambda_j \nabla g_j(x) = 0, \tag{2.34}$$

$$g_j(x) \leqslant 0, \quad \lambda_j g_j(x) = 0, \quad \lambda_j \geqslant 0, \quad j = 1,\ldots,J. \tag{2.35}$$

Where $\nabla \Phi(x) \triangleq (\partial \Phi/\partial x_1, \ldots, \partial \Phi/\partial x_n)$. The KTCN (2.32) (2.33) is a generalized representation of SKTCN (2.34) (2.35). The economic interpretation of KTCN is discussed in section 2.3.3.

It should be noted here that, in SOP (2.6) and MOP (2.28)

(2.29), there exists no sign condition on the decision variable $x$. If a sign condition does exist on $x$, KTCN (2.32) (2.33) should be stated in a compact vector form as follows.

$$\frac{\partial L}{\partial x} \leqslant 0, \quad x\frac{\partial L}{\partial x} = 0, \quad x \geqslant 0. \tag{2.36}$$

$$\frac{\partial L}{\partial \lambda} \geqslant 0, \quad \lambda\frac{\partial L}{\partial \lambda} = 0, \quad \lambda \geqslant 0. \tag{2.37}$$

The Kuhn-Tucker Theorem states that existence of the Lagrange multiplier $\lambda_j$, $j = 1,\ldots,J$, satisfying the Kuhn-Tucker conditions is the first-order necessary condition of mathematical optimization.

**Theorem 2.4(Necessary conditions of vector-valued optimization).**

Assume that all functions are differentiable and the Kuhn-Tucker constraint qualification (KTCQ) is satisfied in the vector-valued optimization problem (2.28) (2.29). Then the necessary condition for $x^\dagger$ to be a local noninferior solution is that there exists $w > 0$, $w \in R^m$, such that $x^\dagger \in R^n$ and some $\lambda^\dagger \in R^J$ satisfy the Kuhn-Tucker condition (KTCN) (2.32) (2.33) for the vector Lagrange function $L(x, \lambda)$ (2.30).

The Kuhn-Tucker constraint qualification (KTCQ) is stated as follows. Let the decision variable $x$ be displaced slightly from a point $x^o$ satisfying a constraint condition $g_j(x) \leqslant 0$, and denote this perturbation with $\xi$. Define a set of indices for active constraint functions $g_j(x^o)$ at $x^o$ as

$$I^o \triangleq \{j \,|\, g_j(x^o) = 0\}. \tag{2.38}$$

The perturbation $\xi$ from $x^o$ is called admissible perturbation if it satisfies the following condition:

$$g_j(x^o + \xi) \leqslant 0, \quad j \in I^o. \tag{2.39}$$

The function $g_j$ is differentiable and hence with Taylor expansion,

$$g_j(x^o) + \nabla g_j(x^o)\xi + o(\xi) \leqslant 0, \quad j \in I^o. \tag{2.40}$$

The condition for the perturbation $\xi$ to be admissible is

$$\nabla g_j(x^o)\xi \leqslant 0, \quad j \in I^o. \tag{2.41}$$

Keep in mind that $x^o$ satisfies the constraint (2.29). Let us consider an arc function $x = a(\theta)$, $a \in R^n$, emanating from a point $x^o = a(0)$, where $0 \leqslant \theta \leqslant \delta$, $\delta > 0$. It is said that the Kuhn-Tucker constraint qualification holds at $x^o$, when the admissible perturbation $\xi = da/d\theta$ at every point $\theta$ satisfying (2.41) is tangent to a differentiable arc $a(\theta)$ emanating from $x^o$ and satisfies the constraint condition (2.29). The Kuhn-Tucker constraint qualification excludes the singularity such that the outward pointing cusp exists on the boundary of the constraint set (Figure 2.1).

Theorem 2.4 provides the necessary condition for the solution $x^\dagger$ of MOP (2.28) (2.29) to be Pareto optimal, assuming the differentiability of the functions $f_i$, $i = 1,\ldots,m$, and $g_j$, $j = 1,\ldots,J$, besides ruling out the singularity of the constraint set. It should be noted that the theorem only states that if $x^\dagger$ is Pareto optimal then there exists some positive-valued weighting parameters associated with the objective

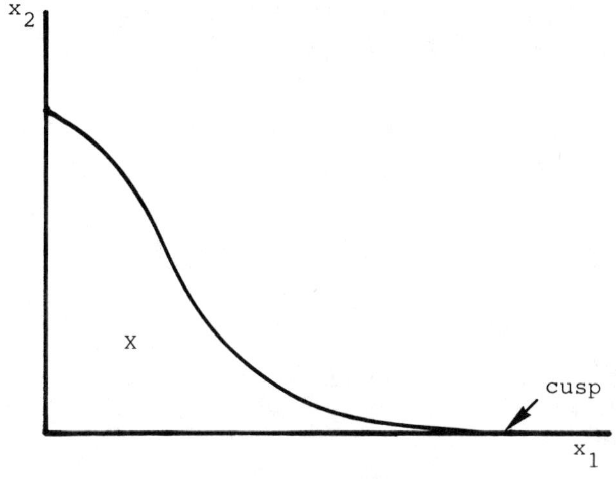


**Figure 2.1 Feasible set with cusp.**

functions; thus it does not suggest any device for finding the Pareto optimal solutions to MOP (2.28) (2.29). The theoretical basis for finding the Pareto optimal solutions is provided by the converse of the Theorem 2.4, which asserts that, if some $w > 0$ is given, then the corresponding solution $x^\dagger$ is Pareto optimal. The following theorem states the sufficiency condition for the vector-valued optimization.

**Theorem 2.5 (Sufficient condition of the vector-valued optimization).**

In order for $x^\dagger$ to be a noninferior solution of the vector-valued maximization problem (2.28) (2.29), it is sufficient that there be some $w > 0$, $w \in R^m$, such that $x^\dagger \in R^n$ and some $\lambda \in R^J$ satisfy the Kuhn-Tucker conditions (2.32) (2.33) and are the saddle point for the Lagrange function $L(x, \lambda)$ (2.30).

The saddle point $(\hat{x}, \hat{\lambda})$ of the Lagrange function $L(x, \lambda)$ is defined if it satisfies the following relation for all $x \in X$ in $R^n$ and all $\lambda \geq 0$, $\lambda \in R^J$,

$$L(x, \hat{\lambda}) \leq L(\hat{x}, \hat{\lambda}) \leq L(\hat{x}, \lambda). \tag{2.42}$$

The problem to find the saddle point is called the saddle point problem. Existence of the saddle point is assured for problems with convexity of the objective and constraint functions by Karlin's theorem (Karlin 1959).

The following theorem (Lasdon 1970) states that the conditions for a pair of $x^\dagger$ and $\lambda$ to be the saddle point are similar to the Kuhn-Tucker conditions.

**Theorem 2.6.**

Let $x^\dagger \in R^n$ and $\lambda \geq 0$, $\lambda \in R^m$. A pair of $x^\dagger$ and $\lambda^\dagger$ is a saddle point for $L(x, \lambda)$ (2.30) if and only if

(i) $x^\dagger$ maximizes $L(x, \lambda^\dagger)$,

(ii) $g_j(x^\dagger) \leq 0$, $j = 1,\ldots,J$,

(iii) $\lambda_j^\dagger g_j(x^\dagger) = 0$, $j = 1,\ldots,J$.

Theorem 2.6 states necessary and sufficient conditions for a saddle point of $L(x, \lambda)$ (2.30). This theorem shows that problems with nondifferentiable functions can be also treated for maximization. When the functions $f_i$, $i = 1,...,m$, of MOP (2.28) are concave, the functions $g_j$, $j = 1,...,J$, of (2.29) are convex, and all the functions are differentiable, KTCN is equivalent to the saddle point conditions (i)-(iii) as shown in Theorem 2.6. The Kuhn-Tucker equivalence theorem states this result.

**Theorem 2.7 (Kuhn-Tucker equivalence theorem).**

Let the functions $f_i(x)$, $i = 1,...,m$, be concave and $g_j(x)$, $j = 1,...,J$, be convex, and all the functions be differentiable for $x \geqslant 0$. Then $x^\dagger$ is a noninferior solution of the vector-valued maximization problem (MOP) (2.28) (2.29) if and only if there is some $w > 0$, $w \in R^m$, such that $x^\dagger \in R^m$ and some $\lambda^\dagger \in R^J$ give a solution of the saddle point problem for the Lagrange function $L(x, \lambda)$ (2.30).

Theorem 2.7 is used as the theoretical background for providing the algorithm to solve the vector-valued optimization problems.

In the remaining parts of this section, methods for deriving the Pareto optimal frontier (a set of noninferior solutions) are discussed.

### 2.2.3 Weighting Method

The weighting method is the well-known and established technique for solving the multiobjective optimization problem (Kuhn and Tucker 1951; Zadeh 1963). The weighting method solves the MDP (2.27) in the form of the weighting problem:

P(w)

$$\underset{x \in X}{\text{maximize}} \quad W(f) \triangleq \sum_{i=1}^{m} w_i f_i(x) \tag{2.43}$$

where $w \triangleq \{w_i | w_i \geqslant 0, \sum_{i=1}^{m} w_i = 1\}$, $w \in R^m$, is the vector of weighting coefficients assigned to the objective functions $f_i(x)$, $i = 1,\ldots,m$. The technique for solving the P(w) is called the parametric method. The parametric method generates the alternative noninferior solutions by systematically varying the weighting parameter vector w. The following theorems state the relation of the P(w) to the MOP (Geoffrion 1968).

**Theorem 2.8 (P(w) $\Rightarrow$ MOP).**

Let $w_i > 0$, $i = 1,\ldots,m$, be fixed. If $x^\dagger$ solves the P(w) (2.43), then $x^\dagger$ is the noninferior solution of the MOP (2.28) (2.29).

This theorem requests that, as the sufficient condition for $x^\dagger$ of P(w) (2.43) to solve MOP, all the weighting coefficients $w_i$, $i = 1,\ldots,m$, should take positive values.

**Theorem 2.9 (P(w) $\Leftrightarrow$ MOP).**

Let the feasible region of the constraint set X be convex and let the objective function $f_i$ be concave on X. Then $x^\dagger$ is the noninferior solution of MOP if and only if $x^\dagger$ solves P(w) with some $w > 0$.

Theorem 2.9 asserts that if the convexity conditions hold, then the existence of some positive-valued weighting coefficients $w > 0$ in P(w) is the necessary and sufficient condition for the solution $x^\dagger$ of P(w) to solve the MOP.

In intuitive descriptions, Theorem 2.8 states that if, in the feasible region of the objective function space, there exists a supporting hyperplane at the point $f(x^\dagger)$ corresponding to $x^\dagger$, then $x^\dagger$ is a noninferior solution of the MOP. Theorem 2.9 states that, when the convexity conditions hold, there exists a supporting hyperplane at the point $f(x^\dagger)$ corresponding to the noninferior solution $x^\dagger$ of MOP. Thus, if the convexity conditions hold, then the parametric method yields the entire noninferior frontier of the feasible region X by varying the vector of weighting coefficients $w > 0$

sequentially, and all of the noninferior solutions are generated. If the convexity conditions do not hold, then some noninferior solutions cannot be obtained with this method, because the supporting hyperplane does not exist at that point in the objective function space.

In short, it is noted that derivation of the Pareto optimal frontier with the weighting method does depend on the convexity of all the functions in MOP. A duality gap exists if no noninferior solutions can be found by solving the problem P(w).

### 2.2.4 Lagrangian Constraint Method

Let us formulate the Lagrange function of the problem P(w) (2.43) and extremize it under the convexity condition.

P(λ)

$$\underset{x}{\text{maximize}} \quad L(x, \lambda) \triangleq \sum_{i=1}^{m} w_i f_i(x) - \sum_{j=1}^{J} \lambda_j g_j(x) \tag{2.44}$$

where $\Lambda \triangleq \{\lambda \mid \lambda \in R^J,\ \lambda \geq 0\}$ is a set of Lagrange multipliers and $\mathbf{w} \triangleq \{w \mid w \in R^m,\ w > 0,\ \sum_{i=1}^{m} w_i = 1\}$ is a set of weighting parameters. P(λ) is called the (vector) Lagrangian problem. The Lagrangian problem (2.44) appears in the process of finding the saddle points, or equivalently, the noninferior solutions of MOP (2.28) (2.29). To solve the P(λ) is to find the solution $x^\dagger \in X$ which maximizes the function $L(x, \lambda)$ in (2.44) with $w \in \mathbf{w}$ and $\lambda^\dagger \geq 0$ satisfying $g(x) \leq 0$ and $\lambda g(x) = 0$.

The following theorems guarantee that the solution $x^\dagger$ of P(λ) is also the solution of MOP (2.28) (2.29).

**Theorem 2.10 (MOP ⇒ P(λ)) (Geoffrion 1968).**

Let all functions be differentiable and the objective function $f_i$, $i = 1,\ldots,m$, be concave on the convex set X in $R^n$. Assume that the Kuhn-Tucker constraint qualification (KTCQ) holds. If $x^\dagger$ is a noninferior solution of MOP (2.28) (2.29), then $x^\dagger$ solves the P(λ) with $w_i > 0$, $w_i \in \mathbf{w}$, $i = 1,\ldots,m$, and $\lambda_j \geq 0$, $j = 1,\ldots,J$.

Theorem 2.10 states that to solve $P(\lambda)$ with $x^\dagger$ is the necessary condition for the $x^\dagger$ to be the noninferior solution of MOP.

**Theorem 2.11 (MOP $\Leftarrow$ P($\lambda$)).**

Let all the functions be differentiable and the objective function $f$ be concave on the convex set $X$ in $R^n$. If $x^\dagger$ solves the $P(\lambda)$ with $w_i \in \mathbf{w}$, $i = 1,\ldots,m$, and $\lambda_j \geq 0$, $j = 1,\ldots,j$, then $x^\dagger$ is the noninferior solution of MOP.

Theorem 2.11 states that to solve $P(\lambda)$ with $w_i \in \mathbf{w}$ and $\lambda \in R^J$, $\lambda \geq 0$, is the sufficient condition for the $x^\dagger$ to be the noninferior solution of MOP.

The equivalence of the $P(\lambda)$ (2.44) to the original vector-valued optimization problem (2.28) (2.29) is intermediated by the Kuhn-Tucker conditions (KTCN) along with the convexity condition. The relation between MOP and KTCN is described in Theorems 2.4 and 2.5. To add the convexity conditions to KTCN guarantees that KTCN can also be a sufficient condition for solving $P(\lambda)$ as stated in Theorem 2.10. Conversely, KTCN can be the necessary condition for solving $P(\lambda)$ only along with the assumption of differentiability. However, for the solution to $P(\lambda)$ to be the solution to MOP, the convexity conditions should hold. This is implied in Theorem 2.11.

In short, for solving the $P(\lambda)$ in the process of finding the noninferior solution of MOP, the convexity of all the functions should be assured. Thus to solve globally $P(\lambda)$ (2.44) for MOP is not effective for the nonconvex problems. Some algorithms such as augmented Lagrangian methods (e.g., Pierre and Lowe 1975) have been presented to cope with this difficulty in solving nonlinear programming in practice. We will also discuss another aspect of this problem in Chapter 10.

The relationship between the vector Lagrangian problem $P(\lambda)$ and the weighting problem $P(w)$ is also established.

**Theorem 2.12 (P($\lambda$) $\Rightarrow$ P(w)).**

If $x^\dagger$ solves the problem $P(\lambda)$ (2.44) with $w \in \mathbf{w}$ and $\lambda \geq 0$, $\lambda \in R^J$, then $x^\dagger$ is the noninferior solution of $P(w)$.

**Theorem 2.13 (P(λ) ⇐ P(w)).**

Let all the objective functions $f_i$, $i = 1,\ldots,m$, be concave on the convex set $X$ in $R^n$ and let the Slater constraint qualification hold. If $x^\dagger$ solves P(w) with $w \in \mathbf{w}$, then $x^\dagger$ is the noninferior solution of P(λ).

Slater's constraint qualification (SCQ) states that there exists an inner point $x$ in the feasible region of the constraint set $X \triangleq \{x | x \in R^n,\ g_j(x) \leqslant 0,\ j = 1,\ldots,J\}$, which satisfies $g_j(x) < 0$.

Theorems 2.8-2.13 describe Geoffrion's Comprehensive Theorem, which establishes equivalence for solutions of the vector-valued optimization problem (MOP), the Kuhn-Tucker conditions (KTCN) for noninferiority, the (unconstrained) Lagrangian problem (P(λ)), and the weighting problem (P(w)). To sum up, the equivalence relations are established among the MOP (2.28) (2.29), P(w) and P(λ), if all the

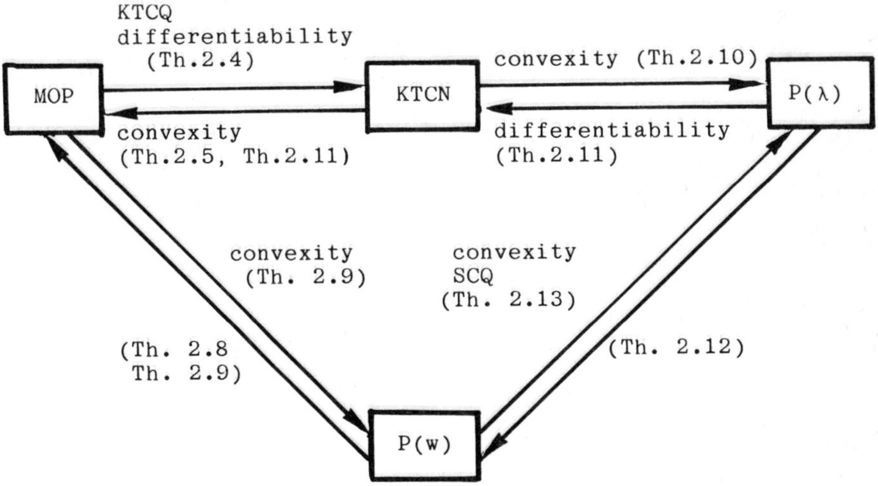


**Figure 2.2 Geoffrion's comprehensive theorem.**

assumptions such as (i) differentiability, (ii) convexity, (iii) Slater's constraint qualification (SCQ), and (iv) Kuhn-Tucker's constraint qualification (KTCQ) are satisfied (Figure 2.2). It should be noted that in Geoffrion's Comprehensive Theorem the differentiability and KTCN (2.32) (2.33) are not referred for Theorems 2.8 (MOP ⇒ P(w)) and 2.9 (P(w) ⇔ MOP), and Theorems 2.12 (P(λ) ⇒ P(w)) and 2.13 (P(λ) ⇐ P(w)), because the optimality of the solutions $x^{\dagger}$ to MOP and P(λ) implied in these theorems assumes those conditions.

The Lagrangian problem P(λ) (2.44) represents the weighting problem P(w) formulated with the Lagrange function L(x,λ). However, in the formulation (2.44), the existence of the Lagrange multiplier $\lambda \geqslant 0$ associated with the constraint function g(x) in MOP is explicitly presented. To solve the problem P(λ) is not only to obtain the noninferior solution $x^{\dagger}$ to MOP but also to get the dual optimal solution $\lambda^{\dagger} \geqslant 0$. According to Theorem 2.7, it is clear that to find $\lambda \geqslant 0$ in P(λ) is equivalent to finding the saddle point of L(x, λ) (2.30), which is generated by solving the minimax dual problem P*(λ) combined with the primal problem P(λ):

P*(λ)

$$\underset{\lambda \in D}{\text{minimize}} \quad \underset{x}{\text{maximize}} \quad L(x, \lambda) \triangleq \sum_{i=1}^{m} w_i f_i(x) - \sum_{j=1}^{J} \lambda_j g_j(x) \tag{2.45}$$

where $D \triangleq \{\lambda \mid \lambda \geqslant 0, \quad \lambda \in R^J, \quad \max L(x, \lambda) \text{ exists}\}$.

Consider the Lagrangian problem P(λ) (2.44) in a different formulation. Put one of the weighting coefficients as $w_k = 1$. Then all the other weighting coefficients $w_i$, $i = 1,\ldots,m$, $m \neq k$, can be generated in solving the Lagrangian problem, which now takes a modified form:

P(w, λ)

$$\underset{x}{\text{maximize}} \quad L = f_k(x) + \sum_{\substack{i=1 \\ i \neq k}}^{m} w_i f_i(x) - \sum_{j=1}^{J} \lambda_j g_j(x) \tag{2.46}$$

where all the other m-1 objective functions $f_i(x) \geqslant 0$,

$i = 1,\ldots,m$, except one objective function $f_k$ appear as constraint functions and the weighting coefficients $w_i$, $i = 1,\ldots,m$, $i \neq k$, are obtained as the Lagrange multipliers associated with them.

Put (2.46) in its original form (2.28) (2.29) of MOP with an artificial term $\bar{f}$. Then

$P(\bar{f})$

$$\begin{aligned} &\underset{x}{\text{maximize}} \quad f_k(x) \\ &\text{subject to} \quad f_i(x) \geq \bar{f}_i \qquad i = 1,\ldots,m, \quad i \neq k \qquad (2.47) \\ &\qquad\qquad\quad g_j(x) \leq 0 \qquad j = 1,\ldots,J. \end{aligned}$$

Everett's theorem (1963) assures that the solution $x^\dagger$ of $P(w, \lambda)$ (2.46) is also the solution of the $P(\bar{f})$ (2.47) with no restrictions such as differentiability and continuity on the functions. This theorem will be discussed in the next subsection.

The Lagrange function of (2.47) is

$$L = f_k(x) + \sum_{\substack{i=1 \\ i \neq k}}^{m} w_i(f_i(x) - \bar{f}_i) - \sum_{j=1}^{J} \lambda_i g_i(x). \qquad (2.48)$$

The constraint constant $\bar{f}_i$, $i = 1,\ldots,m$, $i \neq k$, can be obtained as the optimal value $f_i(x^*)$ of the i-th (single) objective function, which is generated by solving the following SOP.

P(i)

$$\begin{aligned} &\text{maximize} \quad f_i(x) \\ &\text{subject to} \quad g_j(x) \leq 0, \quad j = 1,\ldots,J. \qquad (2.49) \end{aligned}$$

The method which solves the MOP (2.28) (2.29) in the form of $P(w, \lambda)$ or $P(\bar{f})$ (2.47) is called the Lagrangian constraint method or, in short, the constraint method. The Lagrangian constraint method also suggests that MOP can be solved in practice by various algorithms of mathematical programming applied to SOP. However, for deriving the Pareto optimal frontier of MOP, a set of alternative solutions to $P(\bar{f})$ (2.47) should be obtained. For this purpose, perturbation to the constraint constant $\bar{f}_i$, $i = 1,\dots,m$, $m \neq k$, in (2.47) should be generated. The method for obtaining the Pareto optimal frontier in the objective function space via generating the perturbation to the constraint constant $\bar{f}_i$ is called the ε-constraint method.

### 2.2.5 ε-constraint Method

The ε-constraint method is a variation of the Lagrangian constraint method. This method is based on the perturbation function $\omega_k(\varepsilon)$ which is defined as

$$\omega_k(\varepsilon) \triangleq \text{supremum } (f_k(x) \mid f_i(x) \geqslant \varepsilon_i,\ i = 1,\dots,m,\ i \neq k), \tag{2.50}$$

where $\varepsilon \triangleq \{\varepsilon_i,\ i = 1,\dots,m,\ i \neq k\}$ is called the perturbation parameter.

The problem which obtains the perturbation function for some $\varepsilon$ is called the ε-constraint problem and is formulated as follows:

$P_k(\varepsilon)$

$$\underset{x \in X}{\text{maximize}} \quad f_k(x) \tag{2.51}$$

$$\text{subject to} \quad f_i(x) \geqslant \bar{\varepsilon}_i, \quad i = 1,\dots,m, \quad i \neq k \tag{2.52}$$

where $\bar{\varepsilon}_i^{(r)} \triangleq \bar{f}_i^{(r)} = \bar{f}_i^{(r-1)} - \varepsilon_i^{(r)}$, $\varepsilon_i^{(r)} > 0$, $X \triangleq \{x \mid x \in R^n,\ g_j(x) \leqslant 0,\ j = 1,\dots,J,\ g_j : R^n \to R^1\}$. $r$ denotes the number of times of repetitive calculation ($r = 1,\dots,T$). $\bar{f}_i^{(0)}$ is an initial value of the i-th objective function $f_i(x)$, which has been optimized for $x \in X$.

In this method, the vector-valued maximization problem (MOP) (2.1) having the m objective functions $f_i(x)$, $i = 1,\dots,m$, is reduced to the scalar-valued maximization problem

(SOP) (2.6) having only the k-th objective function $f_k(x)$, in which all the other m-1 objective functions are treated as constraint functions. The problem $P_k(\varepsilon)$ is repetitively solved for $x^{(r)} \in X$ corresponding to the value of the constraint constant $\bar{\varepsilon}_i^{(r)}$ which is parametrically varied by shifting with the perturbation parameter $\varepsilon_i^{(r)} > 0$ in each iteration. The set of the solution $x^\dagger \triangleq \{x^{\dagger(r)}, x \in R^n\}$ obtained in each iteration derives the noninferior solution set, and its locus on the decision space and its transformation on the objective function space depict the Pareto optimal frontiers.

The following theorem states that the solution of the ε-constraint problem $P_k(\varepsilon)$ (2.51) (2.52) is the noninferior solution of the MOP (2.28) (2.29) (Payne, Polak, Collins, and Meisel 1975).

**Theorem 2.14 ($P_k(\varepsilon) \Leftrightarrow$ MOP).**

A point $x^\dagger$ in the feasible region X of the constraint set is the noninferior solution of MOP (2.28) (2.29) if and only if $x^\dagger$ uniquely solves the ε-constraint problem P(ε) (2.51) (2.52) with active constraints $\bar{\varepsilon}_i > 0$, $i = 1, \ldots, m$, $i \neq k$.

Theorem 2.14 only requires that all the ε-constraints in $P_k(\varepsilon)$ should be active (binding) to assure the equivalence between $P_k(\varepsilon)$ and MOP. In particular, Theorem 2.14 does not depend on the convexity of the functions in MOP. The theorem assures that, in searching for noninferior solutions of the MOP, one can solve the $P_k(\varepsilon)$ without any regard to the convexity of all the functions. Thus this method does not suffer from the duality gap. The noninferior solutions for nonconvex problems as well as convex problems can be obtained with the ε-constraint method.

Relationship between $P_k(\varepsilon)$ and P(w) is also established. Define a set of weighting parameters $w \triangleq \{w_i \mid w_i \geq 0, \sum_{i=1}^{m} w_i = 1\}$. Then the following theorems guarantee the correspondence between $p_k(\varepsilon)$ and p(w). The proof depends on the generalized Gordan's Theorem (see Chankong 1977; Chankong and Haimes 1983).

**Theorem 2.15 ($P_k(\varepsilon) \Rightarrow P(w)$).**

Let all the functions $f_i(x)$, $i = 1,\ldots,m$, be concave on the convex set $X$ in $R^n$. If $x^\dagger$ solves the $P_k(\varepsilon)$ for any $k$, then there exists $w \in R^m$ such that $x^\dagger$ also solves the $P(w)$.

**Theorem 2.16 ($P_k(\varepsilon) \Leftarrow P(w)$).**

If there exists $w \in R^m$ for $P(w)$ and $x^\dagger$ solves $P(w)$, then $x^\dagger$ also solves the $p_k(\varepsilon)$. If $x^\dagger$ uniquely solves the $P(w)$, then $x^\dagger$ also solves the $P_k(\varepsilon)$ for all $k$.

Geoffrion's stability condition is defined on the perturbation function $\omega_k(\varepsilon)$ (2.50) (Geoffrion 1971).

GSCN

(i) The perturbation function $\omega_k(0)$ is finite, and

(ii) There exists a scalar value $M > 0$ such that for all $\varepsilon_i \neq 0$, $i = 1,\ldots,m$, $i \neq k$,

$$\frac{(\omega_k(\varepsilon_i) - \omega_k(0))}{\| \varepsilon_i \|} \leqslant M. \tag{2.53}$$

The condition GSCN means that the ratio of increase in the maximal value of the objective function in $P_k(\varepsilon)$ to the amount of perturbation $\varepsilon$ can not be made arbitrarily large. Note that, in $P_k(\varepsilon)$, the perturbation $\varepsilon_i^{(r)}$ is considered in the neighborhood of $\bar{f}_i^{(r-1)}$. ( $\| \bullet \|$ shows an arbitrarily selected norm).

Using GSCN, relationship between $P_k(\varepsilon)$ (2.51) (2.52) and $P(w, \lambda)$ (2.46) can be derived. The following theorems assert this result (Chankong 1977; Chankong and Haimes 1982, 1983a,b).

**Theorem 2.17 ($P_k(\varepsilon) \Rightarrow P(w, \lambda)$).**

Assume that $P_k(\varepsilon)$ (2.51) (2.52) satisfies Geoffrion's stability condition (GSCN) and the convexity assumption holds. If $x^\dagger$ solves the $P_k(\varepsilon)$, then there exists $w_i \geqslant 0$, $i = 1,\ldots,m$, $i \neq k$, such that $x^\dagger$ also solves $P(w, \lambda)$ (2.46).

The proof is obtained as an immediate result from Geoffrion's Strong Duality Theorem (Geoffrion 1971). The converse is provided by Everett's Theorem (1963).

**Theorem 2.18 ($P_k(\varepsilon) \Leftarrow P(w, \lambda)$) (Everett).**

If $x^\dagger \in X$ solves $P(w, \lambda)$ (2.46) for some $w_i \geqslant 0$, $i = 1,\ldots,m$, $i \neq k$, then $x^\dagger$ also solves $P_k(\varepsilon)$ (2.51)(2.52) for all $f_i(x) \geqslant \bar{\varepsilon}_i$, $i = 1,\ldots,m$, $i \neq k$.

Everett's theorem states that the optimality of $x^\dagger$ for the Lagrangian problem holds in the $\varepsilon$-constraint problem with some perturbation $\varepsilon$.

**Examples of the $\varepsilon$-constraint method**

The $\varepsilon$-constraint method has been applied, for example, to production plant and chemical plant control problems (Haimes 1973), and water resource investment problems (Cohon and Marks 1973, 1978; Miller and Byers 1973).

As seen before, derivation of the Pareto optimal frontier is only the first step for solving the multiobjective optimization problem (MOP) (2.1). The noninferior solutions generated in this step are only partially ordered because they include noncomparability or indeterminateness in their preference ordering. Thus, evaluation criteria for selecting the preferred solution among the noninferior solutions should be introduced externally to the mathematical optimization processes. In the next section, the methods for seeking the preferred solution for MOP are examined.

## 2.3 Selection of the Preferred Decisions

### 2.3.1 Search on the Pareto Optimal Frontier

Formulate the multiple criteria decision problem (MDP) (2.27) here again.

MDP

$$\underset{x \in X}{\text{maximize}} \quad V(f_1(x), f_2(x), \ldots, f_m(x)) \tag{2.54}$$

where $X \triangleq \{x \mid x \in R^n,\ g_j(x) \leq 0,\ j = 1, \ldots, J,\ g_j : R^n \to R^1\}$, and $V : R^m \to R^1$.

As seen in the preceding section, the Pareto optimal solutions are generated in the first step for solving MDP (2.54). This step corresponds to the analytical phase of MCDM. The solution process of MDP is completed in the second step, in which the preferred solution is found as the most desirable (best compromised) solution. This step corresponds to the judgmental phase of MCDM.

There are various kinds of methods for finding the preferred solution with or without deriving the Pareto optimal solutions. In this section, some devices for seeking the preferred solution based on the generated Pareto optimal frontier are discussed.

To seek the preferred solution on the Pareto optimal frontier in an m-dimensional objective function space is to find the "best" point (or the best alternative) corresponding to the preference of DM. The preference of DM is revealed by a family

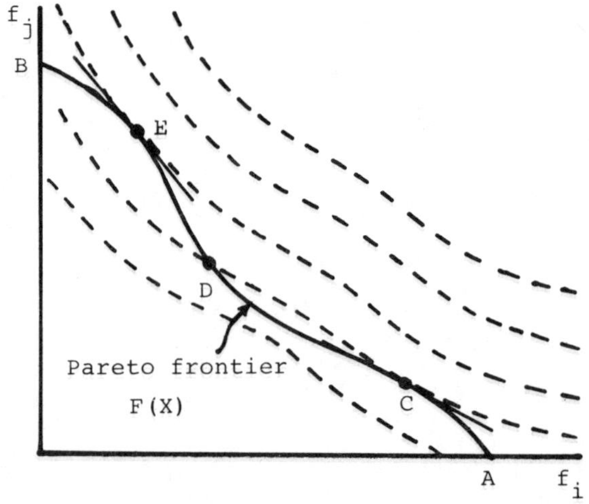


**Figure 2.3 Derivation of the preferred solution from the Pareto optimal frontier.**

of m-dimensional indifference loci which is the projection of the scalarized criterion function $V(f(x))$ as a preference function of DM on the m-dimensional objective function space. In Figure 2.3, a family of the indifference curves is depicted along with the Pareto optimal frontier A-B in the feasible region $F(X)$ in the objective function space. To obtain the preferred solution is to find the point E at which the Pareto frontier is tangent to the indifference curve; the point E represents the highest preference of DM in the feasible region.

Note that the concept of the indifference loci only requires the ordinal scale of measurement for preference, and the search for the preferred solutions on the Pareto optimal frontier is only based on assessing trade-offs among objective functions. However, the trade-offs are also calculated on derivatives of the objective functions; it requires to take the cardinal scale. The locality of the noninferior solutions is defined (Geoffrion 1968; Payne, Polak, Collins and Meisel 1975).

**Definition 2.7 (Local noninferiority).**

Consider a neighborhood $N(x^{\dagger}, \delta) \triangleq \{x \mid x \in R^n, \| x^{\dagger} - x \| < \delta\}$ of a feasible point $x^{\dagger} \in X$, which is assumed to be an open and convex set. If there exists a small number $\delta > 0$ such that $x^{\dagger}$ is noninferior in $\mathcal{N} \triangleq X \cap N(x^{\dagger}, \delta)$, then $x^{\dagger} \in \mathcal{N}$ is said to be locally noninferior. A set of the local noninferior solution $x^{\dagger}$ forms the local Pareto optimal frontier.

The trade-off rate among objective functions shows how many units of value of one objective function have to be given up in order to obtain one additional unit of value of the other objective function. The trade-off rate is said to be the local noninferior trade-off rate when it is assessed for a pair of the local noninferior solutions. To each local noninferior point in an objective function space there corresponds a trade-off rate between a pair of the objective functions. The local noninferior trade-off rate between the objective functions is defined in terms of their marginal units.

**Definition 2.8(Local noninferior marginal rate of substitution).**

Let the objective functions $f(x) \triangleq (f_1(x), \ldots, f_m(x))$ be differentiable. It is said to be a marginal rate of substitution if a trade-off rate between the objective functions is assessed in terms of a relative ratio of marginal variations for any pair $(f_i, f_j)$ of the objective functions, i.e.,

$$\Delta f_i / \Delta f_j |_{\Delta \to 0} \triangleq df_i / df_j, \quad i, j = 1, \ldots, m, \quad i \neq j. \tag{2.55}$$

It is said to be a local noninferior marginal rate of substitution if the marginal rate of substitution is assessed on the local noninferior (Pareto optimal) frontier in the objective function space. It is also said to be a partial marginal rate of substitution if a marginal rate of substitution among a pair of objective functions, $\partial f_i / \partial f_j$, is defined under the assumption that values of all the other objective functions $f_s(x)$, $s = 1, \ldots, m$, $s \neq i, j$, are not varied.

From here on, the term marginal rate of substitution is generally used for simplicity in place of the partial marginal rate of substitution.

The process to seek the preferred solution on the Pareto optimal frontier, which corresponds to the highest indifference locus of the preference of DM, is carried out by assessing the local noninferior marginal rate of substitution between the objective functions. In this process, it is decided if the marginal rate of substitution between the objective functions corresponding to the local noninferior solution $x^\dagger$ will be equivalent to the trade-off rate between the objectives of DM. If both trade-off rates coincide with one another, then the necessary condition for the preferred solution is satisfied. This is stated in the following theorem.

**Theorem 2.19 (Search for the preferred solution).**

If a point $x^*$ be a preferred solution in a feasible set $X$ in $R^n$, then the local noninferior marginal rate of substitution at the point $f(x^*)$, $f : R^n \to R^m$, corresponding to $x^*$ in the objective function space coincides with the local trade-off rate of the decision maker. When the convexity conditions for the functions are satisfied, the converse is also established.

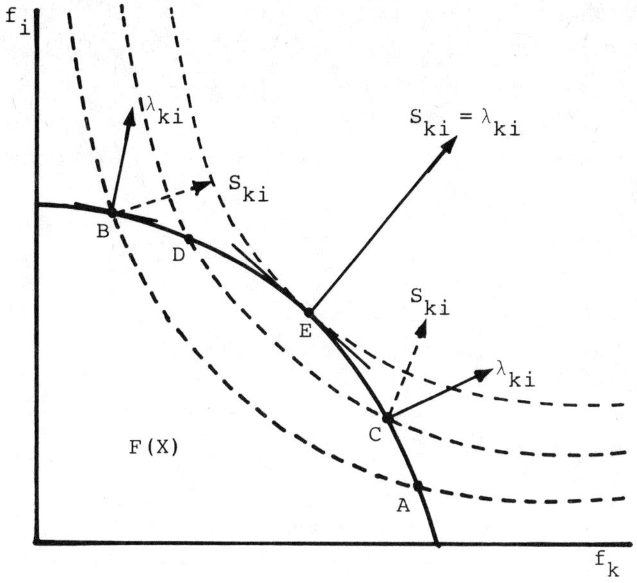


Note: $S_{ki}$ and $\lambda_{ki}$ show the gradient of the normal vector at each point.

**Figure 2.4 Evaluation of the marginal rates of substitution.**

In Figure 2.4, a local noninferior marginal rate of substitution is represented in the objective function space by a slope of a tangent line or the gradient at a point on the Pareto optimal frontier which is analytically derived, while the trade-off rate of DM is represented by a slope of a tangent line or the gradient at the point on the indifference locus of DM. Because the preference function of DM and thus the shape of his indifference loci corresponding to it are assumed to be globally unknown, the marginal rates of substitution of DM can be only locally assessed as the trade-off rates among objectives at some point.

In many cases where the convexity is not assumed, search for the preferred solution requires selecting as most desirable the marginal rates of substitution coinciding with the trade-off rates of DM from among the local noninferior marginal rates of substitution. The marginal rates of substitution at C and E in Figure 2.4 are compared with each other, and the best desirable point E is chosen. Thus finding the preferred solution on the Pareto optimal frontier is reduced to finding the preferred marginal rates of substitution.

It is noted here that the "price" concept can be combined with the marginal rate of substitution. Theorem 2.19 is restated in the following form:

**Theorem 2.20.**

If a point $x^*$ in the feasible set $X$ in $R^n$ be the preferred solution, then the feasible set $F(X)$ in $R^m$ holds a supporting hyperplane,

$$H(h) \triangleq \{f \mid p_1 f_1(k) + p_2 f_2(x) + \dots + p_m f_m(x) = \gamma\}, \qquad (2.56)$$

in common with the $\alpha$-preference set of DM at the point $f(x^*)$, $f : R^n \to R^m$, corresponding to the $x^*$ in the objective function space.

**Definition 2.9.**

Define a family of indifference loci with the parameters $C_s$, $s = 1,\dots,S$, in the m-dimensional objective function space as

$$\Psi_s(f_1, f_2, \dots, f_m) = C_s, \quad s = 1,\dots,S. \qquad (2.57)$$

Then the $\alpha$-preference set is defined as $\mathcal{F} \triangleq \{f \mid f \triangleq (f_1, f_2, \dots, f_m)\}$ such that, for any $\alpha$,

$$v[\Psi_s(f_1, f_2, \dots, f_m)] = \alpha_s \geqslant v[\Psi(f_1^\alpha, f_2^\alpha, \dots, f_m^\alpha)] = \alpha,$$
$$s = 1,\dots,S, \qquad (2.58)$$

on the m+1 dimensional preference surface.

At the point $f(x^*)$, the slope of the supporting hyperplane H on the $\alpha$-preference set coincides with the local noninferior marginal rates of substitution among objective functions according to Theorem 2.20.

Consider the function which defines the supporting

hyperplane H,

$$h(f) : p_1f_1(x) + p_2f_2(x) + \dots + p_mf_m(x) = \gamma. \tag{2.59}$$

Obtaining the total differential of the function (2.59), from the extremal condition $d\gamma = 0$, derives

$$p_1df_1 + p_2df_2 + \dots + p_mdf_m = 0. \tag{2.60}$$

Let values of all the other objective functions except any pair of $(f_i, f_k)$ be unvaried. Then, from (2.60),

$$\frac{\partial f_i}{\partial f_k}\bigg|_{f(x^*)} = -\frac{p_k}{p_i}, \qquad i,k = 1,\dots,m, \quad i \neq k. \tag{2.61}$$

The negative inverse $p_i/p_k$, which is represented by an outward normal at $f(x^*)$ is a relative ratio of weighting coefficients of the linear function $h(f)$ that is taken as a surrogate of the scalarized criterion function. The normal $p_i/p_k$ can be interpreted as the relative price ratio assigned to the objective functions. Theorem 2.20 implies that if a Pareto optimal solution $x^*$ is the preferred solution, then the relative prices assessed for the objective functions on the Pareto optimal frontier coincide with the relative marginal evaluation of DM for the objective functions. In other words, to evaluate the marginal rates of substitution among objective functions is the same as evaluating the relative prices combined with the objective functions.

The different methods for assessing the relative prices for the objective functions can be used according to the different devices for generating the Pareto optimal frontier. In the remaining parts of this section, various methods for assessing the local noninferior marginal rates of substitution and their "economic" implications are examined.

### 2.3.2 Optimal Weights and Market Prices

As shown in Section 2.2.3, the weighting or parametric

method solves MDP (2.54) in the following form:

$$P(w)\qquad \underset{x\in X}{\text{maximize}}\quad W(f) \triangleq w_1 f_1(x) + w_2 f_2(x) + \dots + w_m f_m(x) \tag{2.62}$$

where $w \triangleq (w_1, w_2, \dots, w_m)$ is the vector of weighting coefficients. This method generates alternative sets of the noninferior or Pareto optimal solutions by varying the weighting coefficient vector $w \triangleq \{w_i \mid w_i > 0, \sum_{i=1}^{m} w_i = 1\}$, $w \in R^m$.

The weighting method generates the preferred solution when an "optimal" weights vector is assigned. Thus, finding the preferred solution $x^*$ is reduced to selecting the preferred weighting coefficient $w^*$ as the optimal.

Once a set of specific weighting coefficients is chosen, then from the extremal condition

$$dW(f)\Big|_{\substack{df_r=0\\ r\neq i,j}} = w_i df_i + w_j df_j = 0, \tag{2.63}$$

$$-\frac{\partial f_j}{\partial f_i} = \frac{w_i}{w_j}, \quad i,j = 1,\dots,m, \quad i \neq j. \tag{2.64}$$

When an optimal weights vector $w^* \triangleq (w_1^*, \dots, w_m^*)$ is assigned, then the preferred marginal rates of substitution are determined corresponding to their relative ratio.

The weighting method intends to find with the preassigned optimal weights $w^*$ the preferred solution from among the noninferior solution set. However, this method has no device for selecting the optimal weight coefficients $w^*$. The preferred weights are given a priori as "optimal" without establishing any procedure for assessing them; the optimal weights are provided externally from the decision processes.

**Examples of the optimal weight.**

**1.** The market prices are often used as the optimal weights. For example, in the multisectoral optimization problem for economic activity, the market price is assigned as the optimal weight for output in each sector.

Koopmans (1951), in his activity analysis, considered the vector-valued maximization problem in the following form.

$$\underset{y_{fin} \in Y}{\text{maximize}} \quad V \triangleq p_{fin}\, y_{fin}, \tag{2.65}$$

where $Y$ denotes a possible set of production, $y_{fin}$ the vector of final output, and $p_{fin}$ the vector of prices of final output. As seen in Section 2.2.3, Theorems 2.8 and 2.9, $y^{\dagger}_{fin}$ is the efficient point in the Pareto optimal sense if and only if $p^{\dagger}_{fin} > 0$. The following theorem states this result.

**Theorem 2.21 (Koopmans).**

The point $y^{\dagger}_{fin}$ in the possible set of production $Y$ is efficient if and only if there exists a vector of positive prices $p_{fin} > 0$ with which the linear function $V$ (2.65) of the final output $y_{fin}$ is maximized in $Y$.

The price vector associated with the efficient point of production is called the efficient price. If the efficient prices are assigned, then those prices $p_{fin} = p^{*}_{fin}$ determine the preferred solution $y^{*}_{fin}$. The problem (2.65) is one of the standard weighting problem $P(w)$ (2.62) and find the preferred program of production $y^{*}_{fin}$ under technological conditions with the market prices $p^{*}_{fin}$ taken as given. Implication of the economic policy which maximizes the gross national product (GNP) is to seek the preferred solution of the multisectoral problem (2.65). A similar problem has been considered by Isard (1960), Charnes and Cooper (1961), and others.

**2.** When extending the multisectoral problem in economic analysis to the multiple criteria decision problem, it generally becomes impossible to use the market prices as the optimal weights. In this case, alternative indices should be used as the optimal weights. In a regional water quality management problem, Dorfman (1972) and Dorfman and Jacoby (1972), in setting the objective function as the weighted sum of a net benefit function for each region, treated the weighting coefficients as the "political weights." The Paretian frontier was generated by assigning alternative sets of the "political weights" for all the regions. However, for finding the preferred solution from among the Pareto optimal solutions, further selective decisions are necessary based on social philosophy that includes value judgment.

### 2.3.3 Lagrange Multiplier and Imputed Price

Now consider the weighting problem (2.62) in the form of the Lagrangian problem.

P(λ)

$$\underset{x}{\text{maximize}} \quad L = \sum_{i=1}^{m} w_i f_i(x) - \sum_{j=1}^{J} \lambda_j g_j(x). \tag{2.66}$$

The methods for assessing the weighting coefficient $w_i$ are considered in two ways: (i) to assess the parameter $w_i$, $i = 1,\ldots,m$, $w_i > 0$, $\sum_{i=1}^{m} w_i = 1$, a priori in (2.66), and (ii) to solve (2.66) in the following form:

P(w, λ)

$$\underset{x}{\text{maximize}} \quad L = f_k(x) + \sum_{\substack{i=1 \\ i \neq k}}^{m} w_i f_i(x) - \sum_{j=1}^{J} \lambda_j g_j(x), \tag{2.67}$$

where the $w_i$, $i = 1,\ldots,m$, $i \neq k$, is analytically obtained as the Lagrange multiplier along with the $\lambda_j$, $j = 1,\ldots,J$.

Implications of the $w_i$ in both cases are as follows.

In Case (i), the implication of the weighting coefficient $w_i$ assigned to the objective function $f_i$ is the same as that considered in Section 2.3.2; the weighting coefficients $w_i > 0$, $i = 1,\ldots,m$, $\sum_{i=1}^{m} w_i = 1$, are regarded as the price externally given to the decision processes, and its relative ratios correspond to the marginal rates of substitution among the objective functions. Extending this discussion to the second terms of (2.66), the Lagrange multiplier $\lambda_j$ can be interpreted with the extremal condition $dL(g) = 0$ as the price given to the constraint function $g_j(x)$. The $\lambda_j$, however, can be generated internally in the analytical processes for solving (2.62), and is regarded as the accounting price or the imputed price for the constraint.

In observing (2.66) with the price implication of weighting coefficients, $w_i$ and $\lambda_j$, the Lagrange function $L$ is regarded as the net profit function, in which the $f_i(x)$ is a gain (revenue) function and the $g_j(x)$ is a loss (cost) function representing an excess demand for a resource $j$. At the optimal, the accounting price $\lambda_j \geq 0$ for a resource j, j = 1,...,J, can be generated if the excess demand for it is nonpositive and, in particular, $\lambda_j > 0$ if the excess demand is zero. The prices $w_i$ for the gain functions are imposed externally to decision processes as are the market prices or the political weights in the weighting method.

In Case (ii), the implication of $w_i$, $i = 1,\ldots,m$, $i \neq k$, which is generated as the Lagrange multiplier, is the imputed price similar to the $\lambda_j$, $j = 1,\ldots,J$. Putting $w_k = 1$, from $dL(f) = 0$,

$$w_i = -\frac{\partial f_k}{\partial f_i}, \quad i,k = 1,\ldots,m, \quad i \neq k. \tag{2.68}$$

The relative price $w_i > 0$, of the objective function $f_i$ corresponds to the marginal rate of substitution of $f_i$ for the "standard good" $f_k$ using the $w_k = 1$ as a numéraire.

The Lagrange function $L$ in (2.67) is also regarded as the net profit function assessed with the imputed prices. The sum of the first and second term of (2.67) represents the gain function, and the third term is the loss function assessed on the excess demand function for resources. Thus the problems $P(\lambda)$ and $P(w, \lambda)$ are regarded as the net profit maximization problem in both sense.

Utilization of the Lagrange multiplier as the imputed price is the core of multiple criteria decision analysis (MCDA). With the interpretation of the Lagrange multiplier as the imputed price, economic meanings of the Kuhn-Tucker conditions are established. The KTCN (2.32) simply implies that a sum of the marginal gain is equal to a sum of the marginal loss. This is the equilibrium condition in maximizing the net profit function. The first condition of KTCN (2.33) implies that existence of the excess demand for a resource j, $g_j(x) > 0$, is not compatible with the equilibrium because, in this situation, the value of the net profit function will decrease, and thus only excess supply is admissible. The second and third conditions imply that the situation with both of $g_j(x) < 0$ and $\lambda_j > 0$ should be excluded, because in this situation the value of the net profit function would increase in contradiction to the equilibrium. It means that, when the excess supply $g_j(x) < 0$ exists, then the imputed price for this resource should be zero, i.e., $\lambda_j = 0$.

**Example of the Lagrangian constraint method**

The Lagrangian constraint method has been used by Marglin (1962) in the Harvard Water Program in which a bicriterion problem for economic efficiency in electric energy supply and for equity (minimum benefit requirement) in irrigation water supply is considered. By setting each of these two aims as the constraint condition alternately, the Lagrangian problems $P(\bar{f})$ (2.47) are solved. Both of the above methods (i) (ii) are used for assessing the weighting coefficients. In this early work, it was suggested that the Lagrange multiplier satisfying the Kuhn-Tucker conditions indicates the sensitivity of the value of an objective function to a marginal value of mitigation of a constraint condition. In other words, the Lagrange multiplier is regarded as the "shadow price," or the opportunity cost, of a constraint constant measured in terms of one marginal unit of the objective function. This concept will be examined more precisely in Chapters 9 - 12.

### 2.3.4 Surrogate Worth Trade-off Method

The constraint methods, both the Lagrangian and ε-constraint methods, have characteristics differing from the weighting method. The constraint methods generate as the weights, in the process of solving $p(w, \lambda)$ and $p_k(\varepsilon)$, the dual optimal solutions or the Lagrange multipliers $\lambda^{\dagger} > 0$ combined with the active or binding constraint conditions, while simultaneously obtaining the primal optimal solution $x^\dagger$. Thus, not all of the weighting coefficients for the vector-valued criterion function $f \triangleq \{f_i\}$ need to be preassigned. These parameters can be generated computationally with mathematical algorithms. Specifically, the ε-constant method can generate the Pareto optimal solutions without depending on the convexity of the functions. However, the constraint methods cannot derive the preferred solution by themselves. The main works of these methods concentrate on finding the Pareto optimal solutions, and the selection of the preferred solution is still left as external to these solution procedures.

The Surrogate Worth Trade-off (SWT) method (Haimes and Hall 1974; Haimes, Hall, and Freedman 1975) provides a device for deriving the preferred solution from among the Pareto optimal solutions obtained with the ε-constraint method. Outlines of this method are to obtain the noninferior solutions first and then, based on evaluation of the trade-off rate function corresponding to them, to assess the surrogate worth functions to seek the most preferable solution. The trade-off rate function $T_{ij}$ is assessed in terms of the marginal rate of substitution between the objective functions.

$$T_{ij} \triangleq T(f_i, f_j) \triangleq \frac{\partial f_i}{\partial f_j}, \quad i,j = 1,\ldots,m, \quad i \neq j. \tag{2.69}$$

The SWT method intends to find the preferred marginal rates of substitution $T_{ij}^*$ among the local noninferior marginal rates of substitution $T_{ij}^\dagger$. For this purpose, the surrogate worth functions $W_{ij}(\lambda_{ij})$ are assessed on the trade-off rate functions.

The main procedure of this method is composed of two steps. In step 1, a scalar optimization problem is sequentially solved in the form of the ε-constraint or Lagrangian problem, and noninferior solutions $x^\dagger$ are obtained. The ε-constraint problem is formulated as follows.

$P_k(\varepsilon)$

$$\underset{x \in X}{\text{maximize}} \quad f_k(x) \tag{2.70}$$

subject to $f_i(x) \geq \bar{\varepsilon}_i, \quad i = 1,\ldots,m, \quad i \neq k,$ (2.71)

where $\bar{\varepsilon}_i^{(r)} \triangleq \bar{f}_i^{(r)} = \bar{f}_i^{(r-1)} - \varepsilon_i^{(r)}$, $\varepsilon_i^{(r)} > 0$, $i = 1,\ldots,m$, $i \neq k$, and $\bar{f}_i^{(0)}$ is a maximized value of the objective function $f_i$ in the scalar optimization problem (2.49). The values of $\bar{\varepsilon}_i^{(r)}$ are revised one after another a repetitive number of times $r = 1,\ldots,T$, and the corresponding solutions $x^{\dagger(r)}$ generate the Pareto optimal frontier. The Lagrange function of the ε-constraint problem (2.70) (2.71) is

$$L = f_k(x) + \sum_{\substack{i=1 \\ i \neq k}}^{m} \lambda_{ki}(f_i(x) - \bar{\varepsilon}_i) - \sum_{j=1}^{J} \mu_j g_j(x), \qquad (2.72)$$

where $\lambda_{ki}$ and $\mu_j$ are the Lagrange multipliers. From Kuhn-Tucker's complementary slackness condition, there should exist $\lambda_{ki}(f_i(x) - \bar{\varepsilon}_i) = 0$, $\lambda_{ki} \geq 0$, $i = 1,\ldots,m$, $i \neq k$, for the second term. When the constraint conditions are active, then at optimal, $-\frac{\partial L}{\partial \bar{\varepsilon}_i} = \lambda_{ki} > 0$, and from $L = f_k(x)$ and $f_i(x) = \bar{\varepsilon}_i$, there exists the dual optimal solution:

$$\lambda_{ki}^{\dagger}(f_i(x^{\dagger})) = -\frac{\partial f_k(x^{\dagger})}{\partial f_i(x^{\dagger})} > 0, \quad i = 1,\ldots,m, \quad i \neq k, \qquad (2.73)$$

The $\lambda_{ki}^{\dagger} > 0$ in (2.73) is the Lagrange multiplier associated with the active constraint condition (2.71), and represents the local noninferior marginal rate of substitution between objective functions $f_k$ and $f_i$. Thus the trade-off rate function (2.69) is obtained from the Lagrange multiplier as the dual optimal solution to $P_k(\varepsilon)$.

Thus, in the step 1 of the SWT method, a set of the local noninferior marginal rates of substitution $\lambda_{ki}^{\dagger}(f_i(x^{\dagger})) > 0$, $i = 1,\ldots,m$, $i \neq k$, is generated analytically. For deriving the function form of $\lambda_{ki}^{\dagger}(f_i(x))$, regression analysis by the least square method (such as the fitting of a quadratic function) can be used.

In the step 2, the surrogate worth function $W_{ki}(\lambda_{ki}^{\dagger})$ is derived on the trade-off rate function $\lambda_{ki}^{\dagger}(f_i(x^{\dagger}))$ (2.73). The value of $W_{ki}$ as an ordinal number is assessed with the following criteria, setting as $\lambda_{ki} \triangleq \lambda_{ki}^{\dagger}$.

(a) $W_{ki} > 0$ is assigned for $\lambda_{ki}$ according to its relative magnitude, when DM assesses an objective function $f_i(x^{\dagger})$ relative to one marginal unit of the other objective function $f_k(x^{\dagger})$ with a value larger than the $\lambda_{ki}$. It means that DM assesses a marginal variation of $f_i(x^{\dagger})$ with a relative "price" larger than the $\lambda_{ki}$, which is represented by a smaller amount of the marginal variation of $f_i(x^{\dagger})$ to be traded-off for one additional unit of $f_k(x^{\dagger})$.

(b) $W_{ki} = 0$ is assigned for the $\lambda_{ki}$, when DM assesses an objective function $f_i(x^{\dagger})$ relative to one marginal unit of the $f_k(x^{\dagger})$ with a value equivalent to $\lambda_{ki}$. It means that DM assesses the marginal variation of $f_i(x^{\dagger})$ with the relative "price" equivalent to $\lambda_{ki}$.

(c) $W_{ki} < 0$ is assigned for the $\lambda_{ki}$ when DM assesses an objective function $f_i(x^{\dagger})$ relative to one marginal unit of $f_k(x^{\dagger})$ with a value less than the $\lambda_{ki}$. It means that DM assesses the marginal variation of $f_i(x^{\dagger})$ with a relative "price" less than the $\lambda_{ki}$, which is represented by a larger amount of the marginal variation of $f_i(x^{\dagger})$ to be traded-off for one additional unit of $f_k(x^{\dagger})$.

Figure 2.4 depicts the evaluation process of the local noninferior marginal rates of substitution for deriving the surrogate worth function. Denote the marginal rate of substitution of DM as $S_{ki} \triangleq -\left.\frac{\partial f_k}{\partial f_i}\right|_{DM} > 0$. Then the evaluation process is reduced to find the point E where $S_{ki} = \lambda_{ki}$ by the above (b). The $S_{ki}$ and $\lambda_{ki} = -\left.\frac{\partial f_k}{\partial f_i}\right|_{Pareto} > 0$ are represented by the gradients of normal vectors at the points on the supporting hyperplanes for the $\alpha$-preference set and for the feasible region in the objective function space, respectively (see Section 2.3.1). At the point E, the relative preference of DM for $f_i$ is indifferent to that which is shown with $\lambda_{ki}$; it is assessed with $W_{ki}(\lambda_{ki}) = 0$. At the point C where $S_{ki} > \lambda_{ki}$, the relative preference of DM for $f_i$ is larger than that shown with $\lambda_{ki}$, it is assessed with $W_{ki}(\lambda_{ki}) > 0$ by the above (a). At the point B where $S_{ki} < \lambda_{ki}$, the relative preference of DM for $f_i$ is less than that shown with $\lambda_{ki}$, which is assessed with $W_{ki}(\lambda_{ki}) < 0$ by the above (c).

The set of points such that $W_{ki}(\lambda_{ki}) = 0$ is called an indifference band, which can be derived with a linear combination of the evaluated points or regression analysis in the $W_{ki}-\lambda_{ki}$ space. Direct assessment of the region where $W_{ki} = 0$ is not necessarily required. If the convexity assumptions for the functions are not satisfied, then many Pareto optimal values of the objective functions $f_k^\dagger$ and $f_i^\dagger$ for $i = 1,\ldots,m$, $i \neq k$, can exist corresponding to a value of the $\lambda_{ki}$. The surrogate worth function $W_{ki}(\lambda_{ki}(f_i^\dagger))$ can also take varied values for a value of the $\lambda_{ki}$, which is represented in nonconvex function forms. When the indifference band with $W_{ki}(\lambda_{ki}^*) = 0$ is found, then the Pareto optimal solution $x^*$ corresponding to $\lambda^* \triangleq \{\lambda_{ki}^*\}$ is the preferred solution of the MDP (2.54).

Advantages of the SWT method are enumerated as follows.

First, the SWT method, differing from the other methods, has an eminent characteristic which combines the analytical phase of the decision processes with the judgmental phase as its internal procedure.

Second, the judgmental process for seeking the preferred solution is executed on the Pareto optimal frontier in the objective function space. This device makes the evaluation work in the judgmental phase more efficient than when it is executed in the decision space, although this work is still a burden.

Third, the SWT method uses as the basis of the evaluation the Lagrange multiplier (2.73) which represents the local noninferior marginal rate of substitution among objective functions. The utilization of the analytical results in the first step of the evaluations can mitigate to some extent the ambiguousness of subjective decisions in the judgmental phase.

Fourth, the assessment of the surrogate worth functions in the second step can avoid the difficulty of directly identifying the preference functions of DM.

There are still some points to be discussed.

(i) The indifference experiment in the SWT method for seeking the preferred point $f(x^*)$ corresponding to $W_{ki}(\lambda^*_{ki}) = 0$ implies a maximization process for the preference function of DM. Suppose the vector-valued criterion function $V$ in (2.54) to be the preference function of DM, and call it multiobjective utility function $U$ here. Then MDP (2.54) is represented as

$$\underset{x \in X}{\text{maximize}} \quad U(f) = U(f_1(x),\ f_2(x), \ldots,\ f_m(x)). \tag{2.74}$$

From the first order optimality condition,

$$dU = \frac{\partial U}{\partial f_1} df_1 + \frac{\partial U}{\partial f_2} df_2 + \ldots + \frac{\partial U}{\partial f_m} df_m = 0. \tag{2.75}$$

Denote a trade-off function as

$$f_k = f_k(f_1,\ f_2, \ldots,\ f_{k-1},\ f_{k+1}, \ldots,\ f_m). \tag{2.76}$$

Taking the total differential of $f_k$, from (2.73),

$$df_k = \sum_{\substack{i=1 \\ i \neq k}}^{m} \frac{\partial f_k}{\partial f_i} df_i = - \sum_{\substack{i=1 \\ i \neq k}}^{m} \lambda_{ki} df_i \tag{2.77}$$

where $df_i > 0$, $i = 1, \ldots, m$. Substitute (2.77) into (2.75),

$$dU = \sum_{\substack{i=1 \\ i \neq k}}^{m} \left( \frac{\partial U}{\partial f_i} - \frac{\partial U}{\partial f_k} \lambda_{ki} \right) df_i = 0. \tag{2.78}$$

Define

$$W_{ki}(\lambda_{ki}) \triangleq \frac{\partial U}{\partial f_i} - \frac{\partial U}{\partial f_k} \lambda_{ki} \triangleq a_i - a_k \lambda_{ki}. \tag{2.79}$$

The (2.78) is assured if and only if $W_{ki}(\lambda^{\dagger}_{ki}) = 0$, where the utility function $U(f)$ is maximized (Hall and Haimes 1976). However, the linear surrogate worth function (2.79) can be assessed meaningfully if and only if the convexity conditions are satisfied in $P_k(\varepsilon)$ (2.70) (2.71). When the convexity conditions are not satisfied, then the $x^\dagger$ corresponding to $\lambda_{ki}^\dagger$ such that $W_{ki}(\lambda_{ki}^\dagger) = 0$ is not assured to be the preferred solution. In the nonconvex problems, $W_{ki} = 0$ is a necessary condition for solving the utility maximization problem (2.74) but not a sufficient condition for it.

(ii) In the SWT method, values of the surrogate worth function $W_{ki}(\lambda_{ki})$ are supposed to be assessed only on the ordinal scale. When we want to derive a unique indifference band, however, the cardinal scale should be used. A linear combination of valuation on the ordinal scale will not necessarily produce the unique indifference band, which is still undetermined.

(iii) The SWT method includes the internal procedure for deriving the preferred solution in the decision processes. However, there is no device to improve the value of the surrogate worth function in the process of seeking the preferred point $f(x^*)$ corresponding to $W_{ki}(\lambda_{ki}^*) = 0$. This drawback of the SWT method can be eliminated by its interactive version, which is called the ISWT method. Details of the ISWT method are found in Chankong (1977) and Chankong and Haimes (1983).

**Examples of SWT method.**

Numerical examples in applications of the SWT method to water resources management programs have been presented in Haimes, Hall and Freedman (1975), Haimes (1977), Sakawa, and co-workers (1977, 1978, 1980a), Sakawa (1979), Sannomiya and Nishikawa (1978), and so on.

# Chapter 3

# Interactive Multiobjective Mathematical Programming

## 3.1 Goal Programming and Compromise Programming

### 3.1.1 Goal Programming

The term goal programming first appeared in a 1961 text by Charnes and Cooper to deal with multiobjective linear programming problems that assumed the decision maker (DM) could specify his goals or aspiration levels of the objective functions. Subsequent works on goal programming have been numerous including the texts on goal programming by Ijiri (1965), Lee (1972) and Ignizio (1976, 1982), and survey papers by Kornbluth (1973), Charnes and Cooper (1977) and Ignizio (1983).

The key idea behind goal programming is to ask DM to specify his goals or aspiration levels and to minimize the deviations from these goals or aspiration levels of DM. Goal programming therefore, in most cases, seems to yield a satisficing solution in the same spirit as March and Simon (1958) rather than an optimizing one.

In general, the multiobjective optimization problem (MOP) can be formulated as follows:

MOP

$$\underset{x \in X}{\text{maximize}} \quad f(x) \triangleq (f_1(x), f_2(x), \dots, f_m(x)) \tag{3.1}$$

where $f_1(x), \dots, f_m(x)$ are $m$ distinct objective functions of the decision vector $x$ and

$$X \triangleq \{x \in R^n \mid g_j(x) \leq 0, \quad j = 1,\ldots,J\} \tag{3.2}$$

is the feasible set.

For goal programming, however, a set of $m$ goals (or aspiration levels) is specified by DM for the $m$ objective functions $f_i(x)$ and MOP (3.1) is converted into the problem of coming "as close as possible" to the set of the specified goals which may not be simultaneously attainable.

The general formulation thus becomes:

$$\underset{x \in X}{\text{minimize}} \quad d(f(x), \hat{f}), \tag{3.3}$$

where $\hat{f} = (\hat{f}, \ldots, \hat{f}_m)$ is the goal vector specified by DM and $d(\cdot, \cdot)$ represents the distance between $f(x)$ and $\hat{f}$ according to some selected norm.

Before presenting the methodologies of goal programming, it is appropriate to review some properties of the distance measures.

Mathematically, the distance measures defined for the n-tuples $x = (x_1, \ldots, x_n)$ and $y = (y_1, \ldots, y_n)$ are known as $\ell_p$ norms and defined by:

$\ell_p$ norm:

$$d_p(x, y) = \left(\sum_{i=1}^{n} |x_i - y_i|^p\right)^{1/p} \tag{3.4}$$

where $1 \leq p \leq \infty$ .

According to the choice of $p$, the following special norms which well represent geometrical concepts of distance are derived.

Absolute value or $\ell_1$ norm:

$$d_1(x, y) = \sum_{i=1}^{n} |x_i - y_i|. \tag{3.5}$$

Euclidean or $\ell_2$ norm:

$$d_2(x,y) = \sqrt{\sum_{i=1}^{n} (x_i - y_i)^2}. \tag{3.6}$$

Tchebycheff or $\ell_\infty$ norm:

$$d_\infty(x, y) = \max_{i \leqslant i \leqslant n} |x_i - y_i|. \tag{3.7}$$

Figure 3.1 illustrates, for 2-tuples, the points satisfying $d(x, 0) \leqslant 1$ for each of the norms. Here the $\ell_1$ (absolute value) norm is represented by the diamond, the $\ell_2$ (Euclidean) norm by the circular disk and the $\ell_\infty$ (Tchebycheff) norm by the square. Concerning the $\ell_p$ norms, for $1 < p < 2$ the boundary of the "unit ball" is a symmetric convex curve lying between the

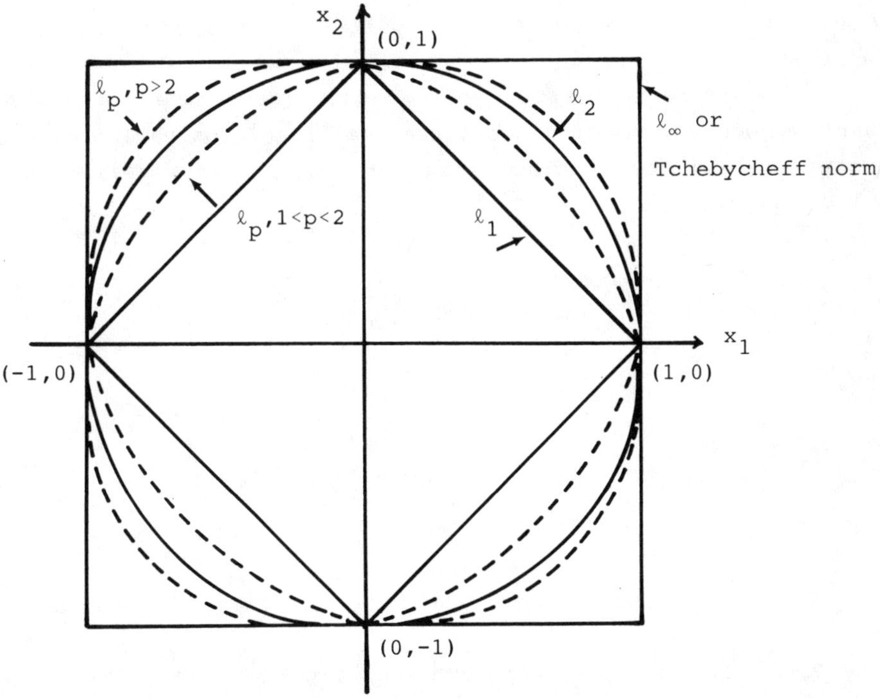


Figure 3.1 Boundary lines of unit balls for $\ell_1$, $\ell_2$, $\ell_\infty$ and $\ell_p$ norms.

diamond and the circle. For $p > 2$, the unit ball which corresponds to the $\ell_p$ norms has as its boundary a symmetric convex curve lying between the circle and the square. As the p increases, this curve comes closer and closer to the square.

Using the $\ell_p$ norm as a measure of deviation between f(x) and $\hat{f}$, the goal programming problem (3.3) becomes:

$$\underset{x \in X}{\text{minimize}} \quad d_p(f(x), \hat{f}) \triangleq \left(\sum_{i=1}^{m} |f_i(x)-\hat{f}_i|^p\right)^{1/p}, \tag{3.8}$$

or more generally, using the $\ell_p$ norm with weights (the weighted $\ell_p$ norm):

$$\underset{x \in X}{\text{minimize}} \quad d_p^w(f(x), \hat{f}) \triangleq \left(\sum_{i=1}^{m} w_i |f_i(x)-\hat{f}_i|^p\right)^{1/p}, \tag{3.9}$$

where $w_i$ is the nonnegative weight to the ith objective function.

The simplest version of (3.9), where all objective functions and constraints are linear, all decision variables are continuous and the absolute value or $\ell_1$ norm is used (i.e., p=1), becomes:

$$\underset{x \in X}{\text{minimize}} \quad d_1^w(f(x), \hat{f}) = \sum_{i=1}^{m} w_i |f_i(x) - \hat{f}_i| \tag{3.10}$$

where

$$f_i(x) = c_i x \;, \qquad i = 1,\ldots,m \tag{3.11}$$

and

$$X = \{x \in R^n \mid Ax = b, \quad x \geq 0\}. \tag{3.12}$$

This linear goal programming problem can easily be converted to an equivalent linear programming problem by introducing the auxiliary variables

$$d_i^+ = \frac{1}{2} \{|f_i(x) - \hat{f}_i| + (f_i(x) - \hat{f}_i)\} \tag{3.13}$$

and

$$d_i^- = \frac{1}{2}\{|f_i(x) - \hat{f}_i| - (f_i(x) - \hat{f}_i)\} \tag{3.14}$$

for each $i = 1,\ldots,m$. Based on (3.13) and (3.14), the equivalent linear goal programming formulation to the problem (3.10) becomes:

$$\text{minimize} \quad \sum_{i=1}^{m} w_i(d_i^+ + d_i^-) \tag{3.15}$$

$$\text{subject to} \quad f_i(x) - d_i + d_i = f_i, \quad i = 1,\ldots,m \tag{3.16}$$

$$Ax = b, \quad x \geqslant 0 \tag{3.17}$$

$$d_i^+ \cdot d_i^- = 0, \quad i = 1,\ldots,m \tag{3.18}$$

$$d_i^+ \geqslant 0, \quad d_i^- \geqslant 0, \quad i = 1,\ldots,m. \tag{3.19}$$

It is appropriate to consider here the practical significance of $d_i^+$ and $d_i^-$.

From (3.13) and (3.14) we have

$$d_i^+ = \begin{cases} f_i(x) - \hat{f}_i & (\text{if} \quad f_i(x) \geqslant \hat{f}_i) \\ 0 & (\text{if} \quad f_i(x) \leqslant \hat{f}_i) \end{cases} \tag{3.20}$$

and

$$d_i^- = \begin{cases} \hat{f}_i - f_i(x) & (\text{if} \quad \hat{f}_i \geqslant f_i(x)) \\ 0 & (\text{if} \quad \hat{f}_i \leqslant f_i(x)). \end{cases} \tag{3.21}$$

Thus $d_i^+$ and $d_i^-$ represent respectively the over-achievement and the under-achievement of the ith goal, and hence are called deviational variables. Clearly over-achievement and under-achievement can never occur simultaneously: when $d_i^+ > 0$, then $d_i^-$ must be zero, and vice versa. This fact is reflected by (3.18) which is automatically satisfied at every iteration of the simplex method of linear programming, because $d_i^+$ and $d_i^-$ never become basic variables simultaneously. Namely, nonlinear equality constraints (3.18) are always satisfied in the simplex method and consequently, it is clear that the simplex method can be applied to solve this type of linear goal programming problem.

Depending on the decision situations, sometimes DM is concerned only with either the over-achievement or the under-achievement of a specified goal. Such a situation can be incorporated into the goal programming formulation by assigning over- and under-achievement weights, $w_i^+$ and $w_i^-$, to $d_i^i$ and $d_i^-$ respectively. For example, if each $f_i(x)$ is a cost-type objective function with its goal $\hat{f}_i$, over-achievement is not desirable. For this case, we set $w_i^+ = 1$ and $w_i^- = 0$ and the problem (3.15)-(3.19) is modified as follows:

$$\underset{x \in X}{\text{minimize}} \quad \sum_{i=1}^{m} w_i^+ d_i^+ \tag{3.22}$$

$$\text{subject to} \quad f_i(x) - d_i^+ + d_i^- = \hat{f}_i, \quad i = 1,\dots,m \tag{3.23}$$

$$Ax = b, \quad x \geqslant 0 \tag{3.24}$$

$$d_i^+ \cdot d_i^- = 0, \quad i = 1,\dots,m \tag{3.25}$$

$$d_i^+ \geqslant 0, \quad d_i^- \geqslant 0, \quad i = 1,\dots,m. \tag{3.26}$$

Conversely, for benefit-type objective functions, under-achievement is not desirable. For this case, we set $w_i^- = 1$ and $w_i^+ = 0$ to replace $\sum_{i=1}^{m} w_i^+ d_i^+$ by $\sum_{i=1}^{m} w_i^- d_i^-$ as the objective function in (3.22). This particular goal programming is called one-sided goal programming.

The linear goal programming formulation can also be modified into a more general form by introducing the preemptive priorities, $P_i$, in place of or together with the numerical weights $w_i^+$, $w_i^- \geqslant 0$. When the objective functions $f_1(x),\dots,$

$f_m(x)$ are divided into $L$ ordinal ranking classes, $1 \leq L \leq m$, having the preemptive priorities $P_1, \ldots, P_L$ in decreasing order, it may be convenient to write

$$P_\ell >> P_{\ell+1}, \quad \ell = 1, \ldots, L-1 \tag{3.27}$$

to mean that no real number $t$, however large, can produce

$$t\, P_{\ell+1} >> P_\ell, \quad \ell = 1, \ldots, L-1. \tag{3.28}$$

By incorporating such preemptive priorities $P_\ell$ together with over- and under-achievement weights $w_i^+$ and $w_i^-$, the general linear goal programming (GLGP) formulation takes on the following form:

GLGP

$$\text{minimimize} \quad \sum_{\ell=1}^{L} P_\ell \Big( \sum_{i \in I_\ell} (w_i^+ d_i^+ + w_i^- d_i^-) \Big) \tag{3.29}$$

$$\text{subject to} \quad f_i(x) - d_i^+ + d_i^- = \hat{f}_i, \quad i = 1, \ldots, m \tag{3.30}$$

$$Ax = b, \quad x \geq 0 \tag{3.31}$$

$$d_i^+ \cdot d_i^- = 0, \quad i = 1, \ldots, m \tag{3.32}$$

$$d_i^+ \geq 0, \quad d_i^- \geq 0, \quad i = 1, \ldots, m, \tag{3.33}$$

where $I_\ell \neq \phi$ is the index set of objective functions in the $\ell$th priority class. Observe that when there are $m$ distinct ordinal ranking classes (i.e., $L = m$) with $f_i(x)$ belonging to the ith priority class, the objective function in (3.29) then becomes simply $\sum_{i=1}^{m} P_i (w_i^+ d_i^+ + w_i^- d_i^-)$.

To solve this type of problem, we begin by trying to achieve the goals of all objective functions in the first priority class. Having done that, we try to satisfy the goals in the second priority class, keeping the goals in the first class satisfied. The process is repeated until either a unique solution is obtained at some stage or all priority classes are considered. This is equivalent to solving, at most, $L$ linear programming problems sequentially, for which the simplex method can easily be applied with some modifications.

The extension of GLGP to nonlinear problems where objective functions $f_1(x), \ldots, f_m(x)$ and constraints $g_1(x), \ldots, g_J(x)$ may be nonlinear is straightforward. Similar to the linear case, the general nonlinear goal programming (GNLGP) formulation becomes:

GNLGP

$$\text{minimize} \quad \sum_{\ell=1}^{L} P_\ell \Big( \sum_{i \in I_\ell} (w_i^+ d_i^+ + w_i^- d_i^-) \Big) \tag{3.34}$$

$$\text{subject to} \quad f_i(x) - d_i^+ + d_i^- = \hat{f}_i, \quad i = 1, \ldots, m, \tag{3.35}$$

$$g_j(x) \leqslant 0, \quad j = 1, \ldots, J, \tag{3.36}$$

$$d_i^+ \cdot d_i^- = 0, \quad i = 1, \ldots, m, \tag{3.37}$$

$$d_i^+ \geqslant 0, \quad d_i^- \geqslant 0, \quad i = 1, \ldots, m, \tag{3.38}$$

where $I_\ell \neq \phi$ is the index set of objective functions in the $\ell$th priority class. Obviously, the solution strategy of nonlinear goal programming is the same as that of linear goal programming: namely, starting from the highest priority class, a sequence of priority class subproblems is solved successively until either a unique solution is obtained or all priority classes are considered.

It should be noted here that any existing algorithms of nonlinear programming can be used to solve a sequence of priority class nonlinear subproblems.

Another obvious approach, as suggested by Griffith and Stewart (1961), is to approximate the nonlinear functions by linear functions and to solve the resulting linear problems using the modified simplex method. Ignizio (1976), however, points out the drawbacks of this approach and suggests using a modified Hooke and Jeeves pattern search to solve the nonlinear goal programming problems directly.

Further details concerning the algorithm, extensions and applications can be found in the text of Lee (1972) and Ignizio (1976, 1982).

### 3.1.2 Compromise Programming

A well-known extension of the goal programming approach is obtained if the goal vector $\hat{f} = (\hat{f}_1, \ldots, \hat{f}_m)$ is replaced by the so-called ideal or utopia vector $f^* = (f_1^*, \ldots, f_m^*)$, where $f_i^* \triangleq \max_{x \in X} f_i(x)$, $i = 1, \ldots, m$. The resulting problem can be interpreted as an attempt to minimize deviation from the ideal or utopia vector (point). Realizing that the ideal vector is generally infeasible in most MOP with conflicting objective functions, Yu (1973) and Zeleny (1973) introduced the concept of compromise solution. Geometrically, the compromise solution defined by Yu and Zeleny is the solution which is the minimum distance from the ideal point.

To be more specific mathematically, given a weight vector $w$, $x_w^p$ is called a compromise solution of MOP (3.1) with respect to $p$ if and only if it solves

$$\underset{x \in X}{\text{minimize}} \quad d_p^w(f(x), f^*) \triangleq \left(\sum_{i=1}^{m} w_i |f_i(x) - f_i^*|^p\right)^{1/p}, \tag{3.39}$$

or equivalently, for $1 \leqslant p < \infty$,

$$\underset{x \in X}{\text{minimize}} \quad \tilde{d}_p^w(f(x), f^*) \triangleq \sum_{i=1}^{m} w_i (f_i^* - f_i(x))^p \tag{3.40}$$

and for $p = \infty$

$$\underset{x \in X}{\text{minimize}} \quad \tilde{d}_\infty^w(f(x), f^*) \triangleq \max_{1 \leqslant i \leqslant m} w_i (f_i^* - f_i(x)). \tag{3.41}$$

Observe that for $p = 1$, all deviations from $f_i^*$ are taken into account in direct proportion to their magnitudes, while for $2 \leqslant p < \infty$, the largest deviation has the greatest influence. Ultimately for $p = \infty$, the largest deviation is the only one taken into account.

It should be noted here that any solution of (3.40) for any $1 \leqslant p < \infty$ or a unique solution of (3.41) with $w_i > 0$ for all $i = 1, \ldots, m$ is a Pareto optimal solution of MOP (3.1).

The compromise set $C_w$, given the weight, is defined as the set of all compromise solutions $x_w^p$, $1 \leq p \leq \infty$. To be more explicit,

$$C_w \triangleq \{x \in X \mid x \text{ solves (3.40) or (3.41) given } w \text{ for some } 1 \leq p \leq \infty\}. \tag{3.42}$$

In the context of linear problems, Zeleny (1973) suggested that the compromise set $C_w$ can be approximated by the Pareto optimal solutions of the following two-objective problem:

$$\underset{x \in X}{\text{minimize}} \quad (\tilde{d}_1(f(x), f^*), \tilde{d}_\infty(f(x), f^*)) \tag{3.43}$$

Although it can be seen that the compromise solution set $C_w$ is a subset of the set of Pareto optimal solutions, $C_w$ may be still too large to select the final solution and hence should be reduced further.

Zeleny (1973, 1976) suggests several methods to reduce the compromise solution set $C_w$. One possible reduction method without DM's aid is to generate a compromise solution set $\bar{C}_w$ similar to $C_w$ by maximizing the distance from the so-called anti-ideal point $f_* = (f_{*1}, \ldots, f_{*m})$, where $f_{*i} \triangleq \min_{x \in X} f_i(x)$. The problem to be solved thus becomes:

$$\underset{x \in X}{\text{maximize}} \quad \left(\sum_{i=1}^{m} w_i |f_i(x) - f_{*i}|^p\right)^{1/p} \tag{3.44}$$

or equivalently, for $1 \leq p < \infty$

$$\underset{x \in X}{\text{maximize}} \quad \sum_{i=1}^{m} w_i (f_i(x) - f_{*i})^p \tag{3.45}$$

and for $p = \infty$

$$\underset{x \in X}{\text{maximize}} \quad \min_{1 \leq i \leq m} w_i (f_i(x) - f_{*i}) \tag{3.46}$$

The compromise set $\bar{C}_w$ then defined by:

$$\bar{C}_w \triangleq \{x \in X \mid x \text{ solves (3.44) or (3.41) given } w \text{ for some } 1 \leq p \leq \infty\}. \tag{3.47}$$

Naturally, the compromise set $C_w$ which is based on the ideal point is not identical with the compromise set $\bar{C}_w$ which is based on the anti-ideal point. Zeleny (1976) suggests using this fact in further reducing the compromise set by considering the intersection $C_w \cap \bar{C}_w$.

An interactive strategy for reducing the compromise solution set proposed by Zeleny (1976) is based on the concept of the so-called displaced ideal and thus called the method of the displaced ideal. In this approach the ideal point with respect to the new $C_w$ displaces the previous ideal point and the (reduced) compromise solution set eventually encloses the new ideal point, thus terminating the process.

The basic steps of the method of displaced ideal are summarized as follows:

Step 1 (Initialization).

Let $C_w^{(0)} = X$ and set the iteration index $r = 1$.

Step 2 (Ideal point).

Find the ideal point $f^{*(r)}$ by solving

$$\underset{x \in C_w^{(r-1)}}{\text{minimize}} \quad f_i(x), \qquad i = 1, \ldots, m.$$

Step 3 (Compromise solution set).

Construct the compromise solution set $C_w^{(r)}$ by finding the Pareto optimal solution set of

$$\underset{x \in C_w^{(r)}}{\text{minimize}} \quad (\tilde{d}_1(f(x), f^{*(r)}), \tilde{d}_\infty(f(x), f^{*(r)})).$$

Step 4 (Termination).

If DM can select the final solution from $C_w^{(r)}$, or if $C_w^{(r)}$ contains $f^{*(r)}$, stop. Otherwise, set $r = r + 1$ and return to step 2.

It should be noted here that the method of the displaced ideal can be viewed as the best ideal-seeking process, not the ideal itself.

Further refinements and details can be found in Zeleny

## 3.2 Interactive Frank-Wolfe Method and Its Variants

### 3.2.1 Interactive Frank-Wolfe Method

An interactive mathematical programming approach first developed by Geoffrion, Dyer and Feinberg (1972) is designed for the solution of multiobjective decision problems by assuming the existence of an underlying preference function, but never actually requires this preference function to be identified explicitly. The basic idea behind their approach is that even if the decision maker (DM) cannot specify his overall preference function explicitly, he can provide local information regarding his preference at a particular solution.

Their interactive approach is described in the context of the well-known Frank-Wolfe algorithm, a method for solving nonlinear programming problems that moves from an initial feasible solution towards the optimal solution by finding the direction of steepest ascent and the optimal step size in that direction.

It is particularly important to point out that during the solution process, explicit knowledge of the overall preference function is not essential. Instead, only local information concerning the preferences of DM is required and this, in turn, is sufficient to determine both the direction and the step size which will lead to an improvement over the current solution.

More specifically, in adopting the Frank-Wolfe algorithm, in each iteration, there are two major parts of the algorithm: the determination of the steepest ascent direction and the step size along that direction. Both subproblems require interaction with DM.

This interactive approach which combines the Frank-Wolfe algorithm for solving multiobjective decision problems with local information on DM's preference at each iteration is called the interactive Frank-Wolfe (IFW) method.

The multiobjective decision problem (MDP) considered is of the type:

MDP

$$\underset{x \in X}{\text{maximize}} \quad V(f_1(x), f_2(x), \ldots, f_m(x)), \tag{3.48}$$

where $f_1(x), \ldots, f_m(x)$ are $m$ distinct objective functions of the decision vector $x$, $V(\bullet)$ is DM's overall preference function defined on the values of the objective functions and $X$ is the constraint set defined as

$$X \triangleq \{x \in R^n \mid g_j(x) \leqslant 0, \quad j = 1, \ldots, J\}. \tag{3.49}$$

Observe that the functions $f_i(x)$ and the set $X$ are assumed to be explicitly known, but the preference function $V(\bullet)$ is assumed to be known only implicitly to DM.

In order to solve MDP (3.48) the following basic assumptions are made for the IFW method.

**Assumption 3.2.1**

$V(\bullet)$ exists and is known only implicitly to DM, which means that DM cannot specify the entire function form, but he can provide local information concerning his preference. Moreover, it is concave, strictly increasing and continuously differentiable.

**Assumption 3.2.2**

All $f_i(x)$, $i = 1, \ldots, m$ are concave and continuously differentiable in their respective domains and the constraint set $X$ is convex and compact.

Now, given a feasible solution $x^0 \in X$, a linear, or first order, approximation of the preference function $V(f(x)) \triangleq V(f_1(x), \ldots, f_m(x))$ can be made by neglecting the second and higher order terms in the Taylor series about $x^0$:

$$V(f(x)) \cong V(f(x^0)) + \nabla_x V(f(x^0))(x - x^0). \tag{3.50}$$

Using this linear approximation, the direction-finding problem to seek an increased value of $V(f(x))$ becomes as follows:

$$\underset{x \in X}{\text{maximize}} \quad \nabla_x V(f(x^0))\, x \tag{3.51}$$

Let $x^*$ be the solution to problem (3.51), then $d \triangleq (x^* - x^0)$ determines the steepest ascent direction of movement from the current point $x^0$.

Although $V(f(x))$ is not known explicitly, the concept of marginal rates of substitution of DM can be used to estimate the values of the gradient $\nabla_x V(f(x^0))$ of the preference function $V(f(x))$.

The concept of marginal rates of substitution or trade-off ratios among objective functions of DM is defined as follows:

**Definition 3.1 (Marginal rates of substitution (MRS)).**

At any point of $f = (f_1, \ldots, f_k, \ldots, f_i, \ldots, f_m)$, the amount of $f_k$ that DM is willing to acquire for sacrificing an additional unit of $f_i$ is called the MRS between $f_k$ and $f_i$. Mathematically, the MRS $m_{ki}(f)$ is represented by the negative slope of the indifference curve of a preference at f:

$$\begin{aligned} m_{ki}(f) &= [\partial V(f)/\partial f_i]/[\partial V(f)/\partial f_k] \\ &= -df_k/df_i|_{dV=0,\ df_r=0,\ r\neq k,i}, \end{aligned} \tag{3.52}$$

where each indifference curve is a locus of points in an objective function space, for which DM is indifferent.

Usually, the decision analyst assesses MRS by presenting the following prospects to DM:

$$\begin{aligned} f &= (f_1, \ldots, f_k, \ldots, f_i, \ldots, f_n), \\ f' &= (f_1, \ldots, f_k + \Delta f_k, \ldots, f_i - \Delta f_i, \ldots, f_m). \end{aligned} \tag{3.53}$$

For a small fixed $\Delta f_k$, small enough so the indifference curve is approximately linear but large enough so the increment is meaningful, the analyst varies $\Delta f_i$ until DM is indifferent between f and f'. At this level, $m_{ki}(f) \cong \Delta f_k/\Delta f_i$: in Figure 3.2, $df_k = -\Delta f_k$ and $df_i = \Delta f_i$.

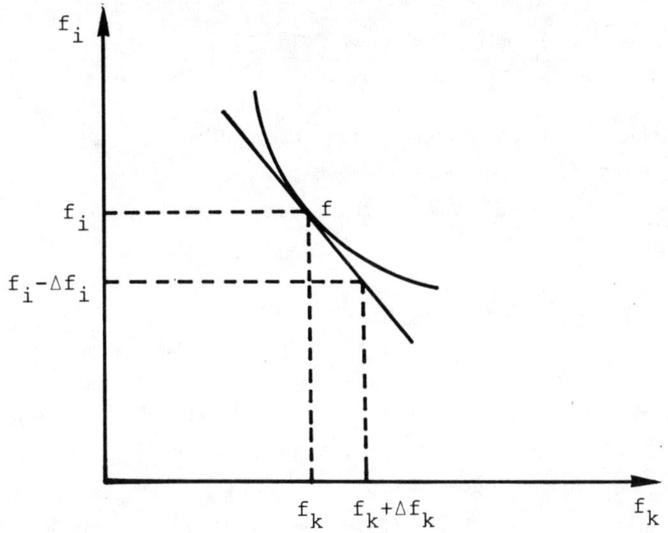


**Figure 3.2 Assessing the marginal rate of substitution.**

Now, we can formulate the gradient $\nabla_x V(f(x^0))$ of the preference function. Applying the chain rule, we have

$$\nabla_x V(f(x^0)) = \sum_{i=1}^{m} \frac{\partial V(f(x^0))}{\partial f_i} \nabla_x f_i(x^0). \tag{3.54}$$

By assuming without loss of generality that the standing objective function is the first one and using the definition of MRS $m_{1i}(f(x^0))$, the objective function in (3.51) can be expressed by:

$$\frac{\partial V(f(x^0))}{\partial f_1} \left[ \sum_{i=1}^{m} m_{1i}(f(x^0)) \nabla_x f_i(x^0)\right] x, \tag{3.55}$$

where $m_{11}(f(x^0)) = 1$. From the strict monotonicity of $V(\bullet)$ with respect to $f_1$, $\partial V(\bullet)/\partial f_1$ is always positive. Hence, by dividing the objective function by $\partial V(\bullet)/\partial f_1$ the direction-finding problem (3.51) is equivalent to:

$$\underset{x \in X}{\text{maximize}} \quad [\sum_{i=1}^{m} m_{1i}(f(x^0)) \nabla_x f_i(x^0)] x. \tag{3.56}$$

Once the steepest ascent direction $d = x^* - x^0$ is adopted, it is necessary to determine the step size $\alpha$ $(0 \leqslant \alpha \leqslant 1)$ which maximizes $V(f(x^0) + \alpha d)$ along this direction; namely, the step size problem

$$\underset{0 \leqslant \alpha \leqslant 1}{\text{maximize}} \quad V(f(x^0) + \alpha d) \tag{3.57}$$

must be solved to determine the optimal move along the direction $d$ by obtaining the best step size $\alpha$.

Since the preference function $V(\bullet)$ is not explicitly available, the step size problem must be solved through interaction with DM. One possible way to obtain the best step size $\alpha$ is to display the values of all $m$ objective functions $f_i(x + \alpha d)$ as a function of $\alpha$ over the selected values of $\alpha$ between 0 and 1 in a tabular or graphic way. DM then determines a value of $\alpha$ for the most preferred corresponding values of the objective functions according to his preference.

Based on the above discussions, we can now describe the IFW method for MDP (3.48) with an implicitly known preference function. The steps marked with an asterisk involve interaction with DM.

Step 1 (Initialization).

Select an initial point $x^{(0)} \in X$. Set the iteration index $r = 1$.

Step 2* (Assessment).

Assess the MRS $m_{1i}(f(x^{(r)}))$, $i = 2,\ldots,m$ of DM at $f(x^{(r)})$.

Step 3 (Direction vector).

Determine the direction vector

$$d^{(r)} = x^{*(r)} - x^{(r)}$$

where $x^{*(r)}$ is the optimal solution to the direction-finding problem

$$\underset{x \in X}{\text{maximize}} \quad [\sum_{i=1}^{m} m_{1i}(f(x^{*(r)})) \nabla_x f_i(x^{*(r)})] x.$$

Step 4* (Step size).

Determine the step size $\alpha^{(r)}(0 \leq \alpha \leq 1)$ which maximizes the preference function $V(f(x^{(r)} + \alpha^{(r)}d^{(r)}))$ as follows. Display the functions $f(x^{(r)} + \alpha d^{(r)})$ for the selected values of $\alpha$ $(0 \leq \alpha \leq 1)$ in a tabular or graphic way and have DM subjectively locate the best step size according to his preference.

Step 5* (Termination).

If $V(f(x^{(r)} + \alpha^{(r)}d^{(r)}) \tilde{=} V(f(x^{(r)}))$, stop. Then $x^{(r)}$ is the preferred solution of DM. Otherwise, set $x^{(r+1)} = x^{(r)} + \alpha^{(r)}d^{(r)}$, $r = r + 1$ and return to step 2.

It is important to note here that the IFW method relies mainly on DM's estimation of his MRS, which requires DM to indicate how much he would be willing to sacrifice the value of objective function $f_i(x)$ in order to acquire a specified increment in objective function $f_1(x)$ with all other objective functions held constant. In practice, however, DM usually experiences difficulty in accomplishing such a task unaided. In order to decrease this difficulty, Dyer (1972, 1973) developed an algorithmic procedure for approximating the MRS through a series of ordinal paired comparisons, where DM is required to indicate a preference for one of two possible choices, or to indicate his indifference between the two. For the fixed increment $\Delta f_1$, $\Delta f_i$ is increased if DM prefers $f$ and $\Delta f_i$ is decreased if he prefers $f'$. The process is continued until a value $\Delta f_i$ is obtained for which DM is indifferent between $f$ and $f'$.

Formally, the MRS estimate algorithm of Dyer is summarized as follows:

Step 1. Let $f = (f_1, \ldots, f_i, \ldots, f_m)$, and $i = 2$.

Step 2. Select $\Delta f_1$ small enough so the indifference curve is approximately linear but large enough so the increment is meaningful.

Step 3. Set the iteration index $s = 1$, and select a convenient value of $\Delta f_i^{(s)} > 0$.

Step 4. Let $f' = (f_1 + \Delta f_1, \ldots, f_i - \Delta f_i^{(s)}, \ldots, f_m)$. Compare $f$ and $f'$.

Step 5. If $f'$ is preferred to $f$, set $\Delta f_i^{(s+1)} = 2(\Delta f_i^{(s)})$, $s = s + 1$, and return to step 4. If $f$ is preferred to $f'$, set $\theta^{(s)} = \Delta f_i^{(s)}$, and go to step 7. If DM is indifferent between f and f', go to step 9.

Step 6. Compare f and f'. If f is preferred, go to step 7. If f' is preferred, go to step 8. If DM is indifferent between f and f', go to step 9.

Step 7. Increase the desirability of f' by letting $\Delta f_i^{(s+1)} = \Delta f_i^{(s)} - \theta^{(s)}/2$. Set $\theta^{(s+1)} = \theta^{(s)}/2$, $s = s + 1$, and return to step 6.

Step 8. Decrease the desirability of f' by letting $\Delta f_i^{(s+1)} = \Delta f_i^{(s)} + \theta^{(s)}/2$. Set $\theta^{(s+1)} = \theta^{(s)}/2$, $s = s + 1$, and return to step 6.

Step 9. Compute $m_{1i} = \Delta f_1 / \Delta f_i$. If $i \neq m$, set $i = i + 1$ and return to step 3. Otherwise, terminate.

The interactive goal programming method proposed by Dyer (1972, 1973) combines the goal programming formulation and the IFW method.

In this approach it is assumed that DM's preference for each objective function is nondecreasing, and that DM is only concerned about minimizing the under-achievement. Consequently, the goal programming formulation under consideration can be written as the following so-called one-sided goal programming problem.

$$\underset{x \in X}{\text{minimize}} \quad \sum_{i=1}^{m} w_i^- d_i^- \tag{3.58}$$

$$\text{subject to} \quad f_i(x) - d_i^+ + d_i^- = \hat{f}_i, \quad i = 1,\ldots,m \tag{3.59}$$

$$d_i^+ \cdot d_i^- = 0, \quad i = 1,\ldots,m \tag{3.60}$$

$$d_i^+ \geq 0, \quad d_i^- \geq 0, \quad i = 1,\ldots,m \tag{3.61}$$

where $w_i^-$ is the under-achievement weight for the ith objective function.

The relationship between MDP (3.48) and the one-sided goal programming problem (3.58)-(3.61) can be clarified by noting that

$$d_i^- = \hat{f}_i - f_i(x) + d_i^+, \quad i = 1,\ldots,m. \tag{3.62}$$

The objective function (3.58) in the one-sided goal programming formulation for MDP (3.48) is interpreted as the piecewise linear approximation of an implicit additive separable preference function of DM.

By considering that the one-sided goal programming formulation can be viewed as another mathematical expression of the direction-finding problem in the IFW method, Dyer (1972, 1973) proposed the interactive goal programming procedure, similar in spirit to the IFW method, with the modification that the direction-finding problem (3.8) is replaced by the one-sided goal programming problem (3.58)-(3.61).

For the interactive goal programming method of Dyer, all the assumptions postulated in the IFW method must be satisfied and each $\hat{f}_i$ should be chosen so that the marginal increase in preference associated with additional units of $f_i(x)$ beyond $\hat{f}_i$ is equal to zero; namely, $\partial V(f(x))/\partial f_i(x) = 0$ for $f_i(x) \geqslant \hat{f}_i$, $i = 1,\ldots,m$.

With these observations, the basic steps of the interactive goal programming of Dyer can be summarized as follows. The steps marked with an asterisk involve interaction with DM.

Step 0* (Goal).

Determine the goals $\hat{f}_i$, $i = 1,\ldots,m$, such that the marginal increase in preference associated with additional units of $f_i(x)$ above $\hat{f}_i$ is equal to zero (i.e. $\partial V/\partial f_i = 0$ for $f_i(x) \geqslant \hat{f}_i$). If DM finds it difficult or impossible to identify such a point for all or some objective functions $i$, the corresponding $\hat{f}_i$ should be set arbitrarily large so that $f_i(x) < \hat{f}_i$ for every $x \in X$.

Step 1 (Initialization).

Select an initial point $x^{(0)} \in X$. Set the iteration index $r = 1$.

Step 2* (Assessment).

Assess the MRS $m_{1i}(f(x^{(r)}))$, $i = 2,\ldots,m$ of DM at $f(x^{(r)})$.

Step 3 (Direction vector).

Determine the direction vector

$$d^{(r)} = x^{*(r)} - x^{(r)}$$

where $x^{*(r)}$ is the optimal solution to the one-sided goal programming problem

$$\underset{x \in X}{\text{minimize}} \quad [\sum_{i=1}^{m} m_{1i}(f(x^{*(r)}))\, d_i^-]$$

$$\text{subject to} \quad f_i(x) + d_i^- \geqslant \hat{f}_i, \quad i = 1,\ldots,m$$

$$d_i^- \geqslant 0, \quad i = 1,\ldots,m.$$

Step 4* (Step size).

Determine the step size $\alpha^{(r)}$ $(0 \leqslant \alpha \leqslant 1)$ which maximizes the preference function $V(f(x^{(r)} + \alpha^{(r)} d^{(r)}))$ as follows. Display the functions $f(x^{(r)} + \alpha d^{(r)})$ for the selected values of $\alpha$ $(0 \leqslant \alpha \leqslant 1)$ in a tabular or graphic way and have DM subjectively locate the best step size according to his preference.

Step 5* (Termination).

If $V(f(x^{(r)} + \alpha^{(r)} d^{(r)})) \tilde{=} V(f(x^{(r)}))$, stop. Then $x^{(r)}$ is the preferred solution of DM. Otherwise, set $x^{(r+1)} = x^{(r)} + \alpha^{(r)} d^{(r)}$, $r = r + 1$ and return to step 2.

It should be noted here that the interactive goal programming method can be viewed as another mathematical expression of the concept of the IFW method and therefore the computational procedures are essentially the same.

### 3.2.2 Proxy Method

With the IFW method, at each iteration, a linear approximation (3.50) to DM's overall preference function is maximized over the constraint set to determine the next feasible direction. By considering that the linear approximations of Geoffrion, Dyer and Feinberg are poor proxies for the true overall preference function of DM, Oppenheimer (1978) suggests using the sum-of-exponentials, sum-of-powers and sum-of logarithms preference functions of Barrager (1975) and Keelin (1976) as higher-order local proxies in the IFW method.

Barrager (1975) and Keelin (1976) derive the following three preference functions $V(f)$, using the deterministic additive independence condition of Keeney and Raiffa (1976) together with assumptions about marginal rates of substitution variation.

(1) sum-of-exponentials.

If $[-\partial m_{ki}(f)/\partial f_i]/m_{ki}(f) = \omega_i$, then

$$V(f) = -\sum_{i=1}^{m} a_i \exp(-\omega_i f_i). \tag{3.63}$$

This implies that if DM is indifferent between any $f^1$ and $f^2$, then he is also indifferent between $f^1 + \Delta$ and $f^2 + \Delta$ where $\Delta = (\Delta, \Delta, \ldots, \Delta)$.

(2) sum-of-powers ($\alpha_i \neq 0$).

If $[-\partial m_{ki}(f)/\partial f_i/m_{ki}(f) = (1+\alpha_i)/f_i$, then

$$V(f) = -\sum_{i=1}^{m} a_i f_i^{\alpha_i}. \tag{3.64}$$

This implies that as DM accumulates more of each attribute, he becomes less sensitive to substitutions among them.

(3) sum-of-logarithms.

If $[-\partial m_{ki}(f)/\partial f_i]/m_{ki}(f) = 1/f_i$, then

$$V(f) = \sum_{i=1}^{m} a_i \ln(f_1). \tag{3.65}$$

This preference function can be viewed as the additive form of the Cobb-Douglass function. It implies that if DM is indifferent between any $f^1$ and $f^2$, then he is also indifferent between $bf^1$ and $bf^2$ for any positive constant b.

Oppenheimer (1978) suggests using one of these preference functions only as local proxy preferences in the IFW method, because they are reasonable when assumed locally. In this procedure, at each iteration, a new MRS vector is assessed to update the proxy. Then the new proxy is maximized over the constraint set to obtain an improved feasible solution for the next iteration.

In the following, we may use the sum-of-exponentials functions

$$P(f(x)) = -\sum_{i=1}^{m} a_i \exp(-\omega_i f_i(x)) \tag{3.66}$$

as an example of a local proxy preference function. However, it should be noted here that similar discussions can be made for other types of proxy functions.

The proxy method of Oppenheimer using the sum-of-exponentials proxy is outlined below, where the steps marked with an asterisk involve interaction with DM.

Step 1 (Initialization).
Select arbitrary $x^{(0)} \in X$ and $x^{(1)} \in X$. Set the iteration index $r = 1$.

Step 2* (Assessment).
Assess the MRS $m_{1i}(f(x^{(r-1)}))$ and $m_{1i}(f(x^{(r)}))$, $i = 2,\ldots,m$ of DM at $f(x^{(r-1)})$ and $f(x^{(r)})$.

Step 3 (Local Proxy).
Fit sum-of-exponentials proxy

$$P(f(x)) = -\sum_{i=1}^{m} a_i \exp(-\omega_i f_i(x))$$

using the values of DM's MRS.

Step 4 (Maximization of Proxy).
Maximize $P(f(x))$ over $x \in X$ to obtain a new $x^{(r+1)}$.

Step 5* (Termination).
If $V(f(x^{(r+1)})) \tilde{=} V(f(x^{(r)}))$, stop. Then $x^{(r)}$ is the preferred solution of DM. If $f(x^{(r+1)})$ is preferred to $f(x^{(r)})$, assess the MRS of DM at $f(x^{(r+1)})$. Set $r = r + 1$ and return to step 3. If $f(x^{(r+1)})$ is not preferred to $f(x^{(r)})$, then find a new $f(x^{(r+1)'})$ preferred to $f(x^{(r)})$, such that $f(x^{(r+1)'}) = \alpha f(x^{(r)}) + (1 - \alpha) f(x^{(r+1)})$, $0 < \alpha < 1$. Assess the MRS of DM at $f(x^{(r+1)'})$, set $r = r + 1$ and return to Step 3.

In order to fit the sum-of-exponentials function in Step 3, the constant $a_1$ is set arbitrarily at unity and the remaining parameters, $a_2,\ldots,a_m$, $\omega_1$, $\omega_2,\ldots,\omega_m$ are determined from MRS assessment. A full set of m-1 MRS at each of two points plus a single MRS at third point are required to fit the 2m-1 parameters.

The numerical MRS actually assessed relates to the sum-of-exponential parameters $a_i$ and $\omega_i$ in the following way;

$$m_{ki}(f) = [\partial P(f)/\partial f_i]/[\partial P(f)/\partial f_k]$$

$$= [\omega_i a_i \exp(-\omega_i f_i)/(\omega_k a_k \exp(-\omega_k f_k)]$$

$$i = 1,\ldots,m, \quad i \neq k. \tag{3.67}$$

By taking the logarithm and solving a set of linear equations, the proxy parameters $a_i$ and $\omega_i$ are uniquely determined from the 2m-1 assessment of $m_{ki}(f)$. If the equations are linearly dependent, an additional assessment at the third point is required.

To ensure that the algorithm will always converge, it should be verified in step 5 that each iteration makes a sufficient improvement by asking DM after each iteration if the new point is preferred to the old one, If DM prefers the new point to the old, the next iteration may begin. If not, a movement in the $f^{\ell+1}$ direction guarantees improvement taking a small step size. There must be a point

$$f(x^{(r+1)'}) = \alpha f(x^{(r)}) + (1-\alpha)\, f(x^{(r+1)}), \quad 0 < \alpha < 1 \tag{3.68}$$

along the line determined by $f(x^{(r)})$ and $f(x^{(r+1)})$, but somewhere in between, such that $V(f(x^{(r+1)'})) > V(f(x^{(r)}))$, which can be obtained by increasing $\alpha$ from 0 until improvement is achieved.

Oppenheimer (1978) also examined techniques for checking MRS consistency and employed two types of consistency tests; the first testing MRS consistency at a single point, and the second testing the consistency at successive points.

The single point test requires a second set of assessments at each point and checks whether the MRS of DM satisfies the chain rule, i.e., $m_{ki} = m_{kj}m_{ji}$, $k, i = 1,\ldots,m$, $i \neq j$, $k \neq i$, $k \neq j$. Since only m-1 unique MRS exist among the objectives at any point, the second set can be used to measure the discrepancy e:

$$e = [(\Delta f_k/\Delta f_i) - (\Delta f_k/\Delta f_j)(\Delta f_j/\Delta f_i)]/(\Delta f_k/\Delta f_i) \quad (\%) \tag{3.69}$$

The second test checks for the decreasing marginal rates of substitution of the proxy. Oppenheimer showed that sum-of-exponentials proxy is concave and strictly increasing if and only if the parameters $a_1, \ldots, a_m$ and $\omega_1, \ldots, \omega_m$ are strictly positive.

### 3.2.3 Trade-off Cut Method

In the context of the cutting plane algorithm for nonlinear programming, Musselman and Talavage (1980) proposed a trade-off cut approach to MDP (3.48) under the same Assumptions 3.2.1 and 3.2.2 of the IFW method. This interactive approach uses the MRS obtained from DM to establish a cutting plane in the objective function space, called the trade-off cut, which removes a portion of the feasible region that has lower values of $V(f)$ than the current point $f^{(r)}$, where $r$ denotes the iteration index.

In searching for the improved values of $V(\bullet)$, one need only concentrate in the region where $V(f) \geq V(f^{(r)})$.

From the concavity assumption of $V(f)$

$$V(f) \leq V(f^{(r)}) + \nabla_f V(f^{(r)})(f - f^{(r)}). \tag{3.70}$$

Using the definition of MRS $m_{1i}(f^{(r)})$

$$\sum_{i=1}^{m} m_{1i}(f^{(r)})(f_i - f_i^{(r)}) \geq [V(f) - V(f^{(r)})]/[\partial V(f^{(r)})/\partial f_1] \tag{3.71}$$

where $\partial V(f^{(r)})/\partial f_1$ is always positive due to the strict monotonicity of $V(f)$. Thus, the region where $V(f) \geq V(f^{(r)})$ is defined by

$$\sum_{i=1}^{m} m_{1i}(f^{(r)})(f_i - f_i^{(r)}) \geq 0. \tag{3.72}$$

The left-hand side of the above inequality is called the trade-off cut.

At each iteration, when DM assesses his MRS at a particular point, one more constraint of the form (3.72) is generated in objective space in order to reduce the constraint set further. Therefore, after the rth iteration,

$$X^{(r)} \triangleq \{x \in R^n \mid g_j(x) \leq 0, \quad j = 1,\ldots,J,J+1,\ldots,J+r\} \tag{3.73}$$

represents the initial $J$ constraints

$$g_j(x) \leq 0, \quad j = 1,\ldots,J \tag{3.74}$$

plus the $r$ trade-off cuts

$$g_{J+r}(x) = -\sum_{i=1}^{m} m_{1i}(f^{(r)})(f_i(x) - f_i^{(r)}) \leq 0. \tag{3.75}$$

In order to find the next point $x^{(r+1)}$ from $x^{(r)}$, the method uses the two usual steps: finding the direction of search and the step size in that direction.

The direction of search used is not the direction of steepest ascent but rather a usable direction for improving $V(\bullet)$ that attempts to move to the center of the current feasible region in order to make the next trade-off cut as large as possible.

The usable direction $d^{(r)}$ at the rth iteration can be obtained by solving the following linear programming problem:

$$\begin{aligned} &\text{minimize} \quad z \\ &\text{subject to} \quad g_j(x^{(r)}) + \nabla_x g_j(x^{(r)})\, d \leq z, \quad j = 1,\ldots,J+r \\ &\qquad\qquad -1 \leq d_i \leq 1, \quad i = 1,\ldots,n. \end{aligned} \tag{3.76}$$

Having solved this problem to obtain the optimal solution $(z^{(r)}, d^{(r)})$, if $z^{(r)} \geq 0$, then the preferred solution is obtained, since there is no usable direction in $X^{(r)}$. On the other hand if $z^{(r)} < 0$, then the usable direction $d^{(r)}$ in $x^{(r)}$ is found.

After determining the direction of search $d^{(r)}$, a trial and error process is adopted as a means of finding the step size.

With these observations, the basic steps of the trade-off cut method of Musselman and Talavage can be summarized as follows. The steps marked with an asterisk involve interaction with DM.

Step 1 (Initialization).

Select an initial point $x^{(0)} \in X$. Set the iteration index $r = 1$.

Step 2* (Assessment).

Assess the MRS $m_{1i}(f(x^{(r)}))$, $i = 1,\ldots,m$ of DM at $f(x^{(r)})$.

Step 3 (Direction vector or Termination).

Determine the direction vector by solving the linear programming problem;

$$\text{minimize} \quad z$$

$$\text{subject to} \quad g_j(x^{(r)}) + \nabla_x g_j(x^{(r)})\, d \leqslant z, \quad j = 1,\ldots,J+r$$

$$-1 \leqslant d_i \leqslant 1, \quad i = 1,\ldots,m$$

to obtain $(z^{(r)}, d^{(r)})$.

If $z^{(r)} \geqslant 0$, stop. Then $x^{(r)}$ is the preferred solution of DM. If $z^{(r)} < 0$, then $d^{(r)}$ is the usable direction vector.

Step 4* (Step size).

Determine the step size $\alpha^{(r)}$ which maximizes the preference function $V(f(x^{(r)} + \alpha^{(r)}d^{(r)}))$ using a trial and error process. Set $x^{(r+1)} = x^{(r)} + \alpha^{(r)}d^{(r)}$, $r = r + 1$ and return to step 2.

## 3.3 Sequential Proxy Optimization Technique (SPOT)

### 3.3.1 Introduction

As was discussed in section 3.2, most of the interactive approaches for the solution of multiobjective decision problems may be viewed as extensions or modifications of the interactive Frank-Wolfe (IFW) method developed by Geoffrion, Dyer and Feinberg (1972) and assume that the decision maker (DM) is only able to give some preference information on a local level to a particular solution.

The general philosophy taken in the interactive mathematical programming approaches using the local preference information of DM is that the multiobjective decision making process should follow the 3-step procedure below.

Step 1: Generate Pareto optimal solutions.

Step 2: Obtain meaningful information to interact with DM.

Step 3: Use information obtained in step 2 to interact with DM and select the final solution based on DM's preference response.

The IFW method puts special emphasis on step 2 and 3. In step 2, DM is simply supplied with the current values of the objective functions to which DM responds by providing the marginal rates of substitution (MRS) values between two objectives. This information is then used to modify the objective function for generating a new point in step 1 of the next iteration by applying the Frank-Wolfe algorithm. Unfortunately, this method does not guarantee that the generated solution in each iteration will be Pareto optimal.

The surrogate worth trade-off (SWT) method is concerned with the relative values of additional increments of the various objectives at a given value of each objective function. In step 1, the $\varepsilon$-constraint problem is used as a means of generating areto optimal solutions. Trade-offs among objective functions, whose values can easily be obtained from the values of some strictly positive Lagrange multipliers from step 1, are used as the information carriers in step 2. And in step 3, DM responds by expressing his degree of preference over the prescribed trade-offs by assigning numerical values (on an ordinal scale of +10 to -10) to each surrogate worth function, which relates DM's preferences to the Pareto optimal solutions through the trade-offs between any two objective functions. This method guarantees the generated solution in each iteration to be Pareto optimal and DM can select his preferred solution from among Pareto optimal solutions.

However, the original version of the SWT method is noninteractive and some improvement, particularly in the way the information from DM is utilized, has been made.

Chankong and Haimes (1977, 1979) and Shimizu, Kawabe and Aiyoshi (1978) independently proposed an interactive version of the SWT method. Their methods follow all the steps of the SWT method up to the point where all the surrogate worth values corresponding to the Pareto optimal solutions are obtained from DM. An interactive scheme was constructed in such a way that the values of either the surrogate worth functions or the MRS are used to determine the direction in which values of the preference function, although unknown, increase most rapidly. In their method, however, DM must assess directly his preference at each trial solution in order to determine the step size. Such a requirement would be very difficult for DM, because he must express a preference from among the trial solutions evaluated by vector-valued objectives having no explicit knowledge of his preference function.

Oppenheimer (1978) introduced the local proxy preference functions in the IFW method. In his procedure, at each iteration, the local proxy preference function is updated by assessing a new MRS vector. Then, the proxy is maximized to find a better point. Unfortunately, this method, like the IFW method, does not guarantee the generated solution in each iteration to be Pareto optimal.

In the trade-off cut approach proposed by Musselman and Talavage (1980), the MRS assessed by DM are used to establish the cutting plane in the objective space, called the trade-off cut, which removes a portion of the feasible region having lower values of the preference function than the current point. However, having obtained the usable direction by solving the linear programming problem, their trial and error step size determination scheme requires DM to assess his MRS at each trial solution, which seems to add a considerable assessment burden.

In order to decrease the drawbacks of the above method, Sakawa (1980b, 1982a) proposed a new interactive multiobjective decision making technique, which was called sequential proxy optimization technique (SPOT), by incorporating the desirable features of the conventional multiobjective decision making methods. In his interactive on-line scheme, as will be seen below, after solving the ε-constraint problem, the values of the MRS assessed by DM are used to determine the direction in which the preference function increases most rapidly. The local proxy preference function is updated to determine the optimal step size and Pareto optimality of the generated solution is guaranteed.

### 3.3.2 Methodological Description

Consider the following multiobjective optimization problem (MOP) formulated as the vector-maximization problem:

MOP

$$\text{maximize} \quad f(x) \triangleq (f_1(x),\ f_2(x), \ldots,\ f_m(x)) \tag{3.77}$$

$$\text{subject to} \quad x \in X \triangleq \{x \in R^n \mid g_j(x) \leqslant 0,\ j = 1, \ldots, J\} \tag{3.78}$$

where $x$ is an n-dimensional vector of decision variables, $f_1(x),\ldots,f_m(x)$ are $m$ distinct objective functions of the decision vector $x$, $g_1(x),\ldots,g_J(x)$ are J inequality constraints and $X$ is the feasible set of constrained decisions.

Fundamental to MOP is the concept of a Pareto optimal solution, also known as a noninferior solution. Qualitatively, a Pareto optimal solution of MOP is one where any improvement of one objective function can be achieved only at the expense of another. Usually, the Pareto optimal solution set consists of an indefinite number of points, and some kinds of subjective judgement should be added to the quantitative analyses by DM. DM must select his preferred solution from among Pareto optimal solutions.

Then the multiobjective decision problem (MDP) we wish to solve can be stated in its most general form as follows.

MDP

$$\text{maximize} \quad V(f_1(x),\ f_2(x),\ldots,f_m(x)) \tag{3.79}$$

$$\text{subject to} \quad x \in X^P \tag{3.80}$$

where $X^P$ is the set of Pareto optimal solutions of MOP, and

$V(\bullet)$, DM's overall preference function, is assumed to exist but is known only implicitly to DM. It should be stressed here that if $V(\bullet)$ is known, then MDP reduces to a standard mathematical programming problem.

One way of obtaining Pareto optimal solutions to MOP is to solve the ε-constraint problem $P_k(\varepsilon_{\bar{k}})$ (Haimes 1977; Haimes and Chankong 1979).

$P_k(\varepsilon_{\bar{k}})$

$$\underset{x \in X}{\text{maximize}} \quad f_k(x) \tag{3.81}$$

$$\text{subject to} \quad x \in X \cap X(\varepsilon_{\bar{k}}) \tag{3.82}$$

$$\text{where} \quad \varepsilon_{\bar{k}} \triangleq (\varepsilon_1, \ldots, \varepsilon_{k-1}, \varepsilon_{k+1}, \ldots, \varepsilon_m) \tag{3.83}$$

$$X(\varepsilon_{\bar{k}}) \triangleq \{x \mid f_i(x) \geqslant \varepsilon_i,\ i = 1, \ldots, m,\ i \neq k\} \tag{3.84}$$

$$\varepsilon_{\bar{k}} \in E_{\bar{k}} \triangleq \{\varepsilon_{\bar{k}} \mid X(\varepsilon_{\bar{k}}) \neq \phi\}. \tag{3.85}$$

Note that (3.85) is a necessary condition for $P_k(\varepsilon_{\bar{k}})$ to have a feasible solution.

Let us assume that $x^*(\varepsilon_{\bar{k}})$, an optimal solution to the $P_k(\varepsilon_{\bar{k}})$, be unique for the given $\varepsilon_{\bar{k}} \in E_{\bar{k}}$. And let $AE_{\bar{k}}$ be a set of $\varepsilon_{\bar{k}}$ such that all the ε-constraints (3.84) are active, that is

$$AE_{\bar{k}} \triangleq \{\varepsilon_{\bar{k}} \mid \varepsilon_{\bar{k}} \in E_{\bar{k}},\ f_i(x^*(\varepsilon_{\bar{k}})) = \varepsilon_i,\ i = 1, \ldots, m,\ i \neq k\}. \tag{3.86}$$

Then the following theorem, which is essentially the same as in Payne and co-workers (1975), shows that the Pareto optimal solution set of MOP coincides with the solution set of $P_k(\varepsilon_{\bar{k}})$ under suitable assumptions.

**Theorem 3.1.**

$x^* \in X$ is a Pareto optimal solution of MOP if and only if $x^* \in X$ is a unique solution of $P_k(\varepsilon_{\bar{k}})$ for some $\varepsilon_{\bar{k}} \in AE_{\bar{k}}$.

If the Kuhn-Tucker condition for problem $P_k(\varepsilon_{\bar{k}})$ is satisfied, the Lagrange multiplier $\lambda_{ki}(\varepsilon_{\bar{k}})$ associated with the ith active constraint can be represented as follows:

$$\lambda_{ki} = -\{\partial f_k(\varepsilon_{\bar{k}})\}/\{\partial f_i(\varepsilon_{\bar{k}})\}, \quad i = 1,\ldots,n, \quad i \neq k. \tag{3.87}$$

By taking account of Theorem 3.1, if the unique optimal solutions of the $P_k(\varepsilon_{\bar{k}})$, denoted by $x^*(\varepsilon_{\bar{k}})$, are substituted to MDP (3.79) given desired levels of $\varepsilon_{\bar{k}} \in AE_{\bar{k}}$, MDP can be restated as the following $\varepsilon_{\bar{k}}$-parametric preference maximization problem.

$$\underset{\varepsilon_{\bar{k}} \in AE_{\bar{k}}}{\text{maximize}} \quad \bar{V}(\varepsilon_{\bar{k}}) \triangleq V(\varepsilon_1,\ldots,\varepsilon_{k-1}, f_k[x^*(\varepsilon_{\bar{k}})], \varepsilon_{k+1},\ldots,\varepsilon_m) \tag{3.88}$$

Throughout this section the following is assumed.

**Assumption 3.3.1.**

$V(\bullet)$ exists and is known only implicitly to DM, which means DM cannot specify the entire form, but he can provide local information concerning his preference. Moreover, it is concave, strictly increasing and continuously differentiable.

**Assumption 3.3.2.**

All $f_i(x)$, $i = 1,\ldots,m$ are concave and continuously differentiable in their respective domains and the constraint set $X$ is convex and compact.

**Assumption 3.3.3.**

$\varepsilon_{\bar{k}}$ is an interior point of $AE_{\bar{k}}$.

From Assumption 3.3.1 and 3.3.2 the following theorem holds (Sakawa, 1980a, 1982)

**Theorem 3.2.**

Under Assumption 3.3.1 and 3.3.2 the preference function $\bar{V}(\varepsilon_{\bar{k}})$ is concave with respect to $\varepsilon_{\bar{k}} \in AE_{\bar{k}}$.

Before formulating the gradient, $\partial\bar{V}(\varepsilon_{\bar{k}})/\partial\varepsilon_i$, of preference function $\bar{V}(\bullet)$, it would be appropriate here to review the concept of marginal rates of substitution of DM.

**Definition 3.1 (Marginal rates of substitution (MRS)).**

At any point of $f = (f_1, \ldots, f_k, \ldots, f_i, \ldots, f_m)$, the amount of $f_k$ that DM is willing to sacrifice for acquiring an additional unit of $f_i$ is called the MRS. Mathematically, the MRS $m_{ki}(f)$ is the negative slope of the indifference curve at the $f$:

$$m_{ki}(f) = [\partial V(f)/\partial f_i]/[\partial V(f)/\partial f_k]$$

$$= -df_k/df_i|_{dV=0,\ df_r=0,\ r\neq k,i} \tag{3.89}$$

Now, we can formulate the gradient $\partial\bar{V}(\varepsilon_{\bar{k}})/\partial\varepsilon_i$ $(i = 1,\ldots,m,$ $i \neq k)$ of preference function $\bar{V}(\varepsilon_{\bar{k}})$. Applying the chain rule,

$$\partial\bar{V}(\bullet)/\partial\varepsilon_i = \partial V(\bullet)/\partial\varepsilon_i + [\partial V(\bullet)/\partial f_k/\partial\varepsilon_i],$$
$$i = 1,\ldots,m, \quad i\neq k. \tag{3.90}$$

Using the relations (3.87) and (3.89), we have the following

$$\partial\bar{V}(\bullet)/\partial\varepsilon_i = [\partial V(\bullet)/\partial f_k]\ (m_{ki} - \lambda_{ki}), \quad i = 1,\ldots,n, \quad i\neq k. \tag{3.91}$$

Due to the strict monotonicity of $V(\bullet)$ with respect to $f_k$, $k = 1,\ldots,m$, $\partial V(\bullet)/\partial f_k$ is always positive. Therefore $(m_{ki} - \lambda_{ki})$ $(i = 1,\ldots,m,\ i\neq k)$ decides a direction improving the values of $\bar{V}(\bullet)$ at a current point.

Under Assumption 3.3.1-3.3.3 if the maximum is reached at an interior point of $AE_{\bar{k}}$, the optimality conditions for a maximization point $\varepsilon_{\bar{k}}$ are $\partial\bar{V}(\bullet)/\partial\varepsilon_{\bar{k}} = 0$, that is

$$m_{ki} = \lambda_{ki}, \quad i = 1,\ldots,m, \quad i\neq k. \tag{3.92}$$

This is the well known result that at the optimum the MRS of DM becomes equal to the trade-off rate.

For notational convenience, in the following, we define

$$f_k(\varepsilon_{\bar{k}}) \triangleq f_k[x^*(\varepsilon_{\bar{k}})] \tag{3.93}$$

$$(\varepsilon_{\bar{k}}, f_k) \triangleq (\varepsilon_1, \ldots, \varepsilon_{k-1}, f_k, \varepsilon_{k+1}, \ldots, \varepsilon_m) \tag{3.94}$$

$$\bar{V}(\varepsilon_{\bar{k}}, f_k(\varepsilon_{\bar{k}})) \triangleq \bar{V}(\varepsilon_1, \ldots, \varepsilon_{k-1}, f_k[x^*(\varepsilon_{\bar{k}})], \varepsilon_{k+1}, \ldots, \varepsilon_m). \tag{3.95}$$

If the optimality condition (3.92) is not satisfied at the rth iteration, the direction of search, $\Delta\varepsilon_i^{(r)}$, improving the values of $\bar{V}(\bullet)$ is

$$\Delta\varepsilon_i^{(r)} = (m_{ki}^{(r)} - \lambda_{ki}^{(r)}), \quad i = 1, \ldots, m, \quad i \neq k \tag{3.96}$$

and the corresponding direction of $\Delta f_k^{(r)}$ is given by:

$$\Delta f_k^{(r)} = [\partial f_k(\varepsilon_{\bar{k}}^{(r)})/\partial\varepsilon_{\bar{k}}^{(r)}]\Delta\varepsilon_{\bar{k}}^{(r)} = -\sum_{\substack{i=1 \\ i \neq k}}^{m} \lambda_{ki}^{(r)}\Delta\varepsilon_i^{(r)}. \tag{3.97}$$

Once the direction $\Delta f^{(r)} \triangleq (\Delta\varepsilon_{\bar{k}}^{(r)}, \Delta f_k^{(r)})$ is adopted, it is necessary to determine the step size $\alpha$ which maximizes $V(\varepsilon_{\bar{k}}^{(r)} + \alpha\Delta\varepsilon_{\bar{k}}^{(r)}, f_k^{(r)} + \alpha\Delta f_k^{(r)})$ along this direction.

To solve this linear search problem, the following two problems arise.

**Problem 3.3.1.**

Each new search point $(\varepsilon_{\bar{k}}^{(r)} + \alpha\Delta\varepsilon_{\bar{k}}^{(r)}, f_k^{(r)} + \alpha\Delta f_k^{(r)})$ $(\varepsilon_{\bar{k}}^{(r)} + \alpha\Delta\varepsilon_{\bar{k}}^{(r)} \in AE_k)$ does not always become a Pareto optimal solution.

**Problem 3.3.2.**

In order to determine the step size, DM must assess his preference at each search point $(\varepsilon_{\bar{k}}^{(r)} + \alpha\Delta\varepsilon_{\bar{k}}^{(r)}, f_k^{(r)} + \alpha\Delta f_k^{(r)})$ for several values of $\alpha$. Such a requirement would be very difficult for DM, because he must express a preference among the trial solutions evaluated by vector-valued objectives having no explicit knowledge of his preference function.

In order to overcome the problem 3.3.1 we adopt

$$(\varepsilon_{\bar{k}}^{(r)} + \alpha\Delta\varepsilon_{\bar{k}}^{(r)},\ f_k(\varepsilon_{\bar{k}}^{(r)} + \alpha\Delta\varepsilon_{\bar{k}}^{(r)}))$$

as a search point in the process of linear search instead of

$$(\varepsilon_{\bar{k}}^{(r)} + \alpha\Delta\varepsilon_{\bar{k}}^{(r)},\ f_k^{(r)} + \alpha\Delta f_k^{(r)}).$$

Our search point becomes the Pareto optimal by solving the ε-constraint problem $P_k(\varepsilon_{\bar{k}})$. Although it is necessary to solve $P_k(\varepsilon_{\bar{k}})$ for several values of $\alpha$, the generated solution in each iteration is the Pareto optimal and DM can select his preferred solution from among Pareto optimal solutions.

It is necessary to construct some kind of preference functions for the problem 3.3.2. We introduce the following local proxy preference functions like in Oppenhiemer's method (1978).

(1) sum-of-exponentials.

If $[-\partial m_{ki}(f)/\partial f_i]/m_{ki}(f) = \omega_i$, then

$$P(f) = -\sum_{i=1}^{m} a_i \exp(-\omega_i f_i). \tag{3.98}$$

(2) sum-of-powers $(\alpha_i \neq 0)$.

If $[-\partial m_{ki}(f)/\partial f_i]/m_{ki}(f) = (1+\alpha_i)/(M_i-f_i)$, then

$$P(f) = -\sum_{i=1}^{m} a_i (M_i-f_i)^{\alpha_i}. \tag{3.99}$$

where $M_i$ is a constant such that $M_i-f_i > 0$, $i = 1,\ldots, m$.

(3) sum-of-logarithms.

If $[-\partial m_{ki}(f)/\partial f_i]/m_{ki}(f) = 1/(M_i+f_i)$, then

$$P(f) = \sum_{i=1}^{m} a_i \ln(M_i+f_i). \tag{3.100}$$

where $M_i$ is a constant such that $M_i+f_i > 0$, $i = 1,\ldots,m$.

Although these preference functions are very restrictive when assumed globally, they are reasonable when assumed locally. We use one of these preference functions as a local proxy preference function to determine the best step size because it seems to be a very good model locally. To select the functional form of proxy that best represents DM's preference, estimation of the MRS variation at a number of points is recommended. However, even if none of the model fits the data, we shall still choose one of them because we will use it only as a mechanism to guide the search for the best step size.

For these three types of proxy functions, the constant $a_1$ can arbitrarily be set equal to one in P(f). The remaining parameters can be easily calculated from MRS assessment. For the sum-of-exponentials or sum-of-powers proxy, a full set of m-1 MRS at each of two points plus a single MRS at a third point are required to fit the 2m-1 parameters; whereas the sum-of-logarithms proxy requires only m-1 MRS at any point to fit the m-1 parameters. Except for the sum-of-logarithms proxy, doubling the information requirements of the other two types of proxy seems to add a considerable assessment burden. However, the extra parameters are already available since MRS are assessed at each iteration. Instead of throwing away the past information, it may be possible to use MRS at the current and previous points. Therefore, the sum-of-exponentials or powers proxy may have no additional assessment burden.

SPOT requires the MRS of DM, but it is a question of whether DM can respond with precise and consistent values of MRS through the whole searching process. Reduction of some of this erratic behaviour is usually accomplished by performing an MRS consistency test at the various iteration points. So two types of consistency tests are prepared in SPOT following Oppenheimer's method (1978); the first testing MRS consistency at a single point, and the second testing the consistency at successive points.

The single point test requires a second set of assessments at each point and checks whether the MRS of DM satisfies the chain rule, i.e., $m_{ki} = m_{kj}m_{ji}$, $j = 1,\ldots,m$, $k \neq j$, $j \neq i$, $j \neq k$. Since only m-1 unique MRS among the objectives exist at any point, the second set can be used to measure the discrepancy e:

$$e = [(\Delta f_k/\Delta f_i) - (\Delta f_k/\Delta f_j)(\Delta f_j/\Delta f_i)]/(\Delta f_k/\Delta f_i)\ (\%). \quad (3.101)$$

We set a reasonable tolerance level and if the discrepancy exceeds the tolerance, the analyst should explain the inconsistency to DM and reassess the MRS until the discrepancy is resolved.

The second test checks for decreasing marginal rates of substitution of the proxy. In Assumption 3.3.1 we assumed that the preference function $V(f)$ is strictly concave, satisfying a strictly decreasing marginal rate of substitution. So, we must check the concavity and monotonicity of the proxy $P(f)$. The necessary and sufficient condition for the three types of proxy $P(f)$ to be concave and strictly increasing can be shown using the parameter values condition.

The following theorem (Sakawa, 1980b, 1982a) can be easily proven by constructing the Hessian matrix of $P(f)$.

**Theorem 3.3.**

(1) The sum-of-exponentials proxy $P(f)$ is concave and strictly increasing if and only if

$$a_i > 0 \quad \text{and} \quad \omega_i > 0, \quad i = 1,\ldots,m. \tag{3.102}$$

(2) The sum-of-powers proxy $P(f)$ is concave and strictly increasing if and only if

$$a_i > 0 \quad \text{and} \quad \alpha_i > 1, \quad i = 1,\ldots,m. \tag{3.103}$$

(3) The sum-of-logarithms proxy $P(f)$ is concave and strictly increasing if and only if

$$a_i > 0, \quad i = 1,\ldots,m. \tag{3.104}$$

Following the above discussions, we can now describe the algorithm of the sequential proxy optimization technique (SPOT) in order to obtain the preferred solution of DM for MDP (3.79) and (3.80). The steps marked with an asterisk involve interaction with DM.

Step 1 (Initialization).

Select an initial point $\varepsilon_{\bar{k}}^{(1)} \in E_{\bar{k}}$ and set the iteration index $r = 1$.

Step 2 (Pareto optimal solution).

Solve an $\varepsilon$-constraint problem $P_k(\varepsilon_{\bar{k}}^{(r)})$ for $\varepsilon_{\bar{k}}^{(r)}$ and obtain a Pareto optimal solution $x^*(\varepsilon_{\bar{k}}^{(r)})$, a Pareto optimal value $f^{(r)} = (\varepsilon_{\bar{k}}^{(r)}, f_k^{(r)}[x^*(\varepsilon_{\bar{k}}^{(r)})])$ and corresponding Lagrange multiplier $\lambda_{ki}$ $(i = 1,\ldots,m,\ i \neq k)$. If all the $\varepsilon$- constraints are active, go to the next step. Otherwise, replace $\varepsilon_i^{(r)}$ for inactive constraints by $f_i[x^*(\varepsilon_{\bar{k}}^{(r)})]$ $(i = 1,\ldots,m,\ i \neq k)$ and solve the $\varepsilon$-constraint problem to obtain the corresponding Lagrange multipliers.

Step 3* (Assessment).

Assess the MRS of DM at $f^{(r)}$.

Step 4* (MRS consistency).

For MRS at $f^{(r)}$, evaluate discrepancy $e$. If $e < \delta_2$ go to Step 5, where the tolerance $\delta_2$ is a prescribed, sufficiently small, positive number. If $e$ exceeds the tolerance, DM reassesses the MRS until the tolerance condition is satisfied.

Step 5 (Termination or Direction vector).

If $|m_{ki}^{(r)} - \lambda_{ki}^{(r)}| < \delta_1$ for $i = 1,\ldots,m,\ i \neq k$, stop. Here the tolerance $\delta_1$ is a prescribed, sufficiently small, positive number. Then a Pareto optimal solution $(\varepsilon_{\bar{k}}(r), f_k^{(r)}[x^*(\varepsilon_{\bar{k}}^{(r)})])$ is the preferred solution of DM. Otherwise, determine the direction vector $\Delta\varepsilon_{\bar{k}}(r) = (\Delta\varepsilon_1^{(r)},\ldots,\Delta\varepsilon_{k-1}^{(r)}, \Delta\varepsilon_{k+1}^{(r)},\ldots,\Delta\varepsilon_m^{(r)})$ by $\Delta\varepsilon_i^{(r)} = (m_{ki}^{(r)} - \lambda_{ki}^{(r)})$ $(i = 1,\ldots,m,\ i \neq k)$.

Step 6* (Local proxy and MRS consistency).

Select the form of the proxy function that will be used at each iteration and calculate the parameters. If the parameter value conditions of Theorem 3.3 are passed, go to the next step. Otherwise, DM reassesses the MRS until the parameter value conditions are satisfied.

Step 7 (Step size).

Determine the step size $\alpha$ which maximizes the proxy preference function $P(\varepsilon_{\bar{k}}^{(r)} + \alpha\Delta\varepsilon_{\bar{k}}^{(r)}, f_k^{(r)}[x^*(\varepsilon_{\bar{k}}^{(r)} + \alpha\Delta\varepsilon_{\bar{k}}^{(r)}]) \triangleq P(\alpha)$ as follows. Change the step size, obtain corresponding Pareto optimal values and search for three $\alpha$ values $\alpha_A$, $\alpha_B$ and $\alpha_C$ which satisfy $\alpha_A < \alpha_B < \alpha_C$ and $P(\alpha_A) < P(\alpha_B) > P(\alpha_C)$. This step operates by either doubling or halving the step size until the maximum is bracketed. Then the local maximum of $P(\alpha)$ is in the neighborhood of $\alpha = \alpha_B$. If $f^{(r+1)}$ is preferred to $f^{(r)}$ where $f^{(r+1)} = (\varepsilon_{\bar{k}}^{(r)} + \alpha_B^{(r)} \Delta\varepsilon_{\bar{k}}^{(r)},\ f_k^{(r)}[x^*(\varepsilon_{\bar{k}}^{(r)} + \alpha_B^{(r)} \Delta\varepsilon_{\bar{k}}^{(r)})])$, set $r = r + 1$ and return to Step 2. Otherwise reduce $\alpha_B$ to be 1/2, 1/4... until improvement is achieved.

The following remarks can be made regarding the SPOT algorithm.

(1) SPOT guarantees a search along a feasible direction of improvement in the preference function, but the optimal step size is determined by maximizing the proxy numerically. To ensure that the algorithm will always converge, it is necessary to verify that each iteration makes a sufficient improvement by asking DM after each iteration if the new point is preferred to the old one. If he prefers the new point to the old, the next iteration may begin. If not, a movement in the $f^{(r+1)}$ direction guarantees improvement, taking a small step size. There must be a point $f^{(r+1)'}$ along the line determined by $f^{(r)}$ and $f^{(r+1)}$, but somewhere in between, such that $V(f^{(r+1)'}) > V(f^{(r)})$, which can be obtained by reducing $\alpha_B$ to be 1/2, 1/4,... until improvement is achieved.

(2) Under the assumption of an ideal DM, the SPOT algorithm is nothing besides a feasible direction method to solve MDP. Thus, the convergence of SPOT can be demonstrated by the convergence of the modified feasible direction method.

(3) An arbitrary change in the units of the objective functions will change the direction improving the values of $\nabla(\bullet)$ at a current point and influence the effectiveness of the algorithm of SPOT. Computational difficulty will most likely be encountered in MDP where the scales of each objective function are markedly different. One possible way to circumvent the difficulty might be to adjust the scales of each objective function by selecting suitable multipliers in advance.

The time-sharing computer program implementing the SPOT has been written in FORTRAN and is called the ISPOT (interactive sequential proxy optimization technique) program. It was designed to facilitate the interactive processes for computer-aided decision making and implemented on the ACOS-6 time-sharing system at the Kobe University, Japan (Sakawa 1981). Its application to a case study in regional planning can be found in Sakawa and Seo (1980b, 1982a).

It should be emphasized here that the difficulties of the search for a best solution along a line segment may be overcame in SPOT.

SPOT, however, requires a great number of precise MRS estimates of DM. In practice, it is a question of whether DM can respond with precise and consistent values of MRS through the whole searching process because DM's actions are often erratic, inconsistent due to the imprecise nature of human decision processes. Although by performing the MRS consistency test some of this erratic behaviour is usually reduced, it is required to cope with the imprecise nature of DM's judgements. By considering the imprecise nature of DM's judgements, techniques based on fuzzy set theory (Zadeh, 1965) which are similar to the first method of Baptistella and Ollero (1980) have been incorporated into the algorithm of SPOT. On the basis of DM's MRS presented in a fuzzy form, which can be interpreted as type L-R fuzzy numbers (Dubois and Prade, 1978), the revised version of SPOT, called the fuzzy sequential proxy optimization technique (FSPOT), has been presented (Sakawa and Seo, 1983).

Finally, it is appropriate to point out that the SPOT algorithm presented here has been extended to include the nonconvex problems by introducing the concept of local Pareto optimality (Sakawa and Mori, 1983, 1984; Sakawa and Yano, 1984b). Further extensions to the non-smooth Pareto surface are also possible by utilizing the directional derivatives.

## 3.4 Reference Point Method and Its Extensions

### 3.4.1 Reference Point Method

The reference point method (RPM), developed by Wierzbicki (1979), is a relatively practical interactive approach to multiobjective decision problems that introduces the concept of a reference point suggested by the decision maker (DM) which reflects in some sense the desired values of the objective functions. The basic idea behind the RPM is that DM can specify reference values for the objective functions and he can change his reference objective levels interactively due to learning or improved understanding during the solution process.

The RPM combines the advantages of the well-known goal programming method (Charnes and Cooper, 1963, 1977; Ignizio, 1978, 1982, 1983) and the method of the displaced ideal developed by Zeleny (1976). The RPM, therefore, seems to yield a satisficing solution in the same spirit as March and Simon (1958).

Wierzbicki introduced the penalty scalarizing functions which are able to generate all the Pareto optimal solutions regardless of the convexity assumptions. In this procedure, as will be seen below, DM specifies a reference point, and the optimization of the corresponding penalty scalarizing function provides with the Pareto optimal solution in a sense close to DM's reference point or better than that, if the reference point is attainable. Then DM either chooses the current Pareto optimal solution or modifies his reference objective levels in order to find his satisficing solution.

Now consider the following multiobjective optimization problem (MOP).

MOP

$$\underset{x \in X}{\text{maximize}} \quad f(x) \triangleq (f_1(x),\ f_2(x),\ldots,f_m(x)) \tag{3.105}$$

where $f_1(x),\ldots,f_m(x)$ are $m$ distinct objective functions and $X$ is the constraint set defined by

$$X \triangleq \{x \in R^n \mid g_j(x) \leq 0,\ j = 1,\ldots,J\}. \tag{3.106}$$

As was discussed in Chapter 2, there are several techniques for generating Pareto optimal solutions depending on the different methods for scalarizing MOP (3.105). For RPM, the utilization of the penalty scalarizing function for obtaining Pareto optimal solutions to MOP with or without convexity assumptions is suggested (Wierzbicki, 1975, 1977, 1978, 1979).

The typical penalty scalarizing function which might be convenient for nonlinear problems has the following form:

$$s_c(f(x) - \bar{f}) = \sum_{i=1}^{m} (f_i(x) - \bar{f}_i)^2 - c \sum_{i=1}^{m} (\max[0, f_i(x) - \bar{f}_i])^2. \qquad (3.107)$$

For linear problems, however, the penalty scalarizing function based on the sum of the absolute values norm

$$s_c(f(x) - \bar{f}) = \sum_{i=1}^{m} | f_i(x) - \bar{f}_i | - c \sum_{i=1}^{m} \max[0, f_i(x) - \bar{f}_i] \qquad (3.108)$$

or the Tchebycheff norm

$$s_c(f(x) - \bar{f}) = \max_{1 \leq i \leq m} | f_i(x) - \bar{f}_i | - c \max_{1 \leq i \leq m} [0, f_i(x) - \bar{f}_i] \qquad (3.109)$$

would be appropriate.

Here $c > 1$ is a scalar penalty coefficient and $\bar{f} = (\bar{f}_1, \ldots, \bar{f}_m)$ is the so-called reference point or reference objective level suggested by DM reflecting in some sense a desired level for the objective functions.

Many other forms of similar penalty scalarizing functions with analogous properties have also been proposed by Wierzbicki (1977, 1979).

It should be emphasized here that the purpose of the penalty scalarizing function is to generate a Pareto optimal point which is in some sense close to DM's reference point or better than that if the reference point is attainable.

In the RPM, the Pareto optimal solutions to MOP are obtained by solving the penalty scalarizing problem $P_c(\bar{f})$ defined by:

$P_c(f)$

$$\underset{x \in X}{\text{minimize}} \quad s\,(f(x) - \bar{f}) \qquad (3.110)$$

or equivalently, in objective function space

$$\underset{f \in F}{\text{minimize}} \quad s_c(f - \bar{f}) \qquad (3.111)$$

where

$$F = \{f(x) \mid x \in X\}. \tag{3.112}$$

The following theorems due to Wierzbicki show that the Pareto optimal solution set of MOP (3.105) coincides with the optimal solution set of $P_c(\bar{f})$ under suitable assumptions.

**Theorem 3.4.**

If $x^* \in X$ is an optimal solution of $P_c(\bar{f})$ for any $\bar{f}$, then $x^*$ is a Pareto optimal solution to MOP.

**Theorem 3.5.**

Let $x^* \in X$ be a Pareto optimal solution to MOP.

(1) If $\bar{f} = f(x^*)$, then $x^*$ is an optimal solution of $P_c(\bar{f})$ for a large enough $c$.

(2) If $\bar{f} \in \text{int } F$, then $x^*$ is an optimal solution of $P_c(\bar{f})$ for some $\bar{f}$.

(3) If $\bar{f} \notin F$, then $x^*$ is an optimal solution of $P_c(\bar{f})$ for some $\bar{f}$.

Using the penalty scalarizing problem as a means for generating Pareto optimal solutions, a relatively practical procedure can be constructed where DM interactively modifies the reference point on the basis of the knowledge gained by looking at the intermediary solutions obtained.

With these observations, the basic steps of the RPM can be sketched as follows. The steps marked with an asterisk involve interaction with DM.

Step 1* (Initialization).

Ask DM to select the initial reference point $\bar{f}^{(1)}$. If DM finds it difficult or impossible to identify such a point, the ideal point $f^* = (f_1^*, \ldots, f_m^*)$, where $f_i^* \triangleq \max_{x \in X} f_i(x)$ can be used instead of $\bar{f}^{(1)}$. Set the iteration index $r = 1$.

Step 2 (Pareto optimal solution).

Set $\bar{f} = \bar{f}^{(r)}$, solve the corresponding penalty scalarizing problem $P_c(\bar{f}^{(r)})$ to obtain a Pareto optimal solution

$x^{(r)}$ and a Pareto optimal value $f(x^{(r)})$.

Step 3* (Termination or New reference point).

If DM is satisfied with the current levels of $f_i(x^{(r)})$, $i = 1,\ldots,m$, stop. Then the current Pareto optimal solution $f(x^{(r)}) = (f_1(x^{(r)}),\ldots, f_m(x^{(r)}))$ is the satisficing solution for DM. Otherwise, ask DM to modify the current reference point $\bar{f}^{(r)}$ to a new reference point $\bar{f}^{(r+1)}$ by considering the current levels of the objective functions. Set $r = r+1$ and return to step 2.

In step 3, Wierzbicki (1979) also suggests to generate $m$ other Pareto optimal points $f(x^{(r),j})$ $j = 1,\ldots,m$ by solving the $m$ penalty scalarizing problem $P_c(\bar{f}^{(r),j})$ $j = 1,\ldots,m$, corresponding to the $m$ perturbed reference points defined by:

$$\bar{f}^{(r),j} = \bar{f}^{(r)} + e_j d^{(r)}, \qquad (3.113)$$

where

$$d^{(r)} = \| \bar{f}^{(r)} - f(x^{(r)}) \|, \quad e_j = (0,\ldots,1_j,\ldots,0). \qquad (3.114)$$

The advantages of such reference point perturbations include the following.

(1) If the reference point $\bar{f}^{(1)}$ is distant from the Pareto optimal solution set, then DM obtains a global description of the Pareto optimal solution set through the perturbed reference point $\bar{f}^{(1),j}$.

(2) If the reference point $\bar{f}^{(r)}$ is close to the Pareto optimal solution set, then the perturbed reference points $\bar{f}^{(r),j}$ provide information about the Pareto optimal solution set in the neighbourhood of the reference point $\bar{f}^{(r)}$.

This fact is illustrated for the two objective case in Figure 3.3.

Further refinements and details can be found in Wierzbicki (1979, 1981). Computer software implementing RPM has been developed. The software package called DIDASS (dynamic interactive decision analysis supporting system), written in FORTRAN 77, deals with both linear and nonlinear multiobjective

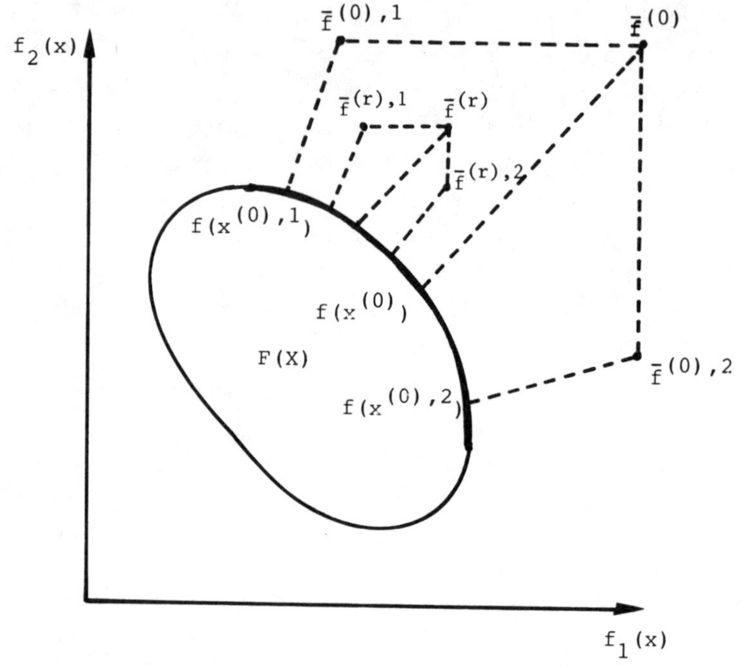


**Figure 3.3 Reference point perturbations.**

optimization problems. (Lewandowski and Grauer 1982; Grauer 1983a,b; Grauer and Kaden 1984).

### 3.4.2 Reference Point Method with Trade-off Information

Before leaving the RPM, it is important to point out a few extensions of the RPM to deal with the imprecise nature of human decision processes. Recently, Sakawa and Yano (1984a) developed an interactive fuzzy multiobjective programming method which can be viewed as the fuzzy version of the RPM. Sakawa, Yumine and Yano (1984) and Sakawa and Yano (1985b) also developed an interactive fuzzy multiobjective programming method which can be interpreted as the extended fuzzy version of the RPM in the sense that DM is supplied with the trade-off information. Although the details of these methods and extensions will be discussed in the next chapter, it would certainly be appropriate to discuss their extended nonfuzzy version of RPM.

In their nonfuzzy version, when DM specifies his reference point $\bar{f} = (\bar{f}_1, \ldots, \bar{f}_m)$, the corresponding Pareto optimal solution, which is in a sense close to his reference point or better than that if the reference point is attainable, is obtained by solving the following minimax problem instead of the penalty scalarizing problem.

$$\underset{x \in X}{\text{minimize}} \quad \max_{1 \leqslant i \leqslant m} (\bar{f}_i - f_i(x)) \tag{3.115}$$

or equivalently

$$\begin{aligned} &\underset{v,\, x \in X}{\text{minimize}} \quad v \\ &\text{subject to} \quad \bar{f}_i - f_i(x) \leqslant v, \quad i = 1, 2, \ldots, m. \end{aligned} \tag{3.116}$$

The relationships between the optimal solutions of the minimax problem and the Pareto optimal concept of MOP (3.105) can be characterized by the following theorems.

**Theorem 3.6**

If $x^*$ is a unique optimal solution to the minimax problem (3.116) for some $\bar{f} = (\bar{f}_1, \ldots, \bar{f}_m)$, then $x^*$ is a Pareto optimal solution to MOP.

**Theorem 3.7**

If $x^* \in X$ is a Pareto optimal solution to MOP, then there exists $\bar{f} = (\bar{f}_1, \ldots, \bar{f}_m)$ such that $x^*$ is an optimal solution to the minimax problem (3.116).

The proofs of these theorems follow immediately from the definitions of unique optimality and Pareto optimality by contradiction arguments.

If $x^*$, an optimal solution to (3.116), is not unique, then the Pareto optimality test for $x^*$ can be performed by solving the following problem:

$$\underset{x \in X}{\text{maximize}} \quad \sum_{i=1}^{m} \varepsilon_i \tag{3.117}$$

subject to $f_i(x) - \varepsilon_i = f_i(x^*)$, $\varepsilon_i \geqslant 0$, $i = 1,\ldots,m$

Let $\bar{x}$ be an optimal solution to (3.117). If all $\varepsilon_i = 0$, then $x^*$ is a Pareto optimal solution. If at least one $\varepsilon_i > 0$, it can be easily shown that $\bar{x}$ is a Pareto optimal solution.

Now given the Pareto optimal solution for the reference point specified by DM by solving the corresponding minimax problem, DM must either be satisfied with the current Pareto optimal solution, or modify his reference point. In order to help DM express his degree of preference, trade-off information between a standing objective function $f_1(x)$ and each of the other objective functions is very useful. Such a trade-off between $f_1(x)$ and $f_i(x)$ for each $i=2,\ldots,m$ is easily obtainable since it is closely related to the strict positive Lagrange multipliers of the minimax problem. Let the Lagrange multipliers associated with the constraints of the minimax problem be denoted by $\lambda_i$, $i=1,\ldots,m$. If all $\lambda_i > 0$ for each i, then by extending the results in Haimes and Chankong (1979), it can be proved that the following expression holds (Yano and Sakawa (1985)):

$$- \partial f_i(x)/\partial f_1(x) = \lambda_1/\lambda_i, \quad i = 2,\ldots,m. \tag{3.118}$$

Here, mathematically, it is assumed that

(1) $(v^*, x^*)$ is a regular point of the constraints of the minimax problem,

(2) the second-order sufficiency conditions are satisfied at $(v^*, x^*)$; and

(3) there are no degenerate constraints at $(v^*, x^*)$,

where $(v^*, x^*)$ is an optimal solution to the minimax problem.

It should be noted here that in order to obtain the trade-off rate information from (3.118), all the constraints of the minimax problem must be active. Therefore, if there are inactive constraints, it is necessary to replace $\bar{f}_i$ for inactive constraints by $f_i(x^*)$ and to solve the corresponding minimax problem for obtaining the Lagrange multipliers.

From the above discussions, we can now describe the interactive algorithm in order to derive the satisficing solution for DM from among the Pareto optimal solution set. The steps marked with an asterisk involve interaction with DM.

Step 0 (Individual minimum and maximum).
Calculate the individual minimum $f_{*i}$ and maximum $f_i^*$ of each objective function $f_i(x)$ under given constraints.

Step 1* (Initialization).
Ask DM to select the initial reference point $\bar{f}^{(1)}$. If DM finds it difficult or impossible to identify such a point, the ideal point $f^* = (f_1^*, \ldots, f_m^*)$ can be used instead of $\bar{f}^{(1)}$. Set the iteration index $r = 1$.

Step 2 (Pareto optimal solution).
Set $\bar{f} = \bar{f}^{(r)}$, solve the corresponding minimax problem (3.116) to obtain a Pareto optimal solution $x^{(r)}$ and a Pareto optimal value $f(x^{(r)})$ together with the trade-off rate information.

Step 3* (Termination or New reference point).
If DM is satisfied with the current levels of $f_i(x^{(r)})$, $i = 1,\ldots,m$ of the Pareto optimal solution, stop. Then the current Pareto optimal solution $f(x^{(r)}) = (f_1(x^{(r)}), \ldots, f_m(x^{(r)}))$ is the satisficing solution of DM. Otherwise, ask DM to modify the current reference point $\bar{f}^{(r)}$ to the new reference point $\bar{f}^{(r+1)}$ by considering the current levels of the objective functions together with the trade-off rates between the objective functions. Set $r = r+1$ and return to step 2. Here it should be stressed for DM that any improvement of one objective function can be achieved only at the expense of at least one of the other objective functions.

An obvious advantage of the above method over the RPM is that DM is supplied with the trade-off information as well as the levels of all objective functions in trying to express his degree of preference. It should be emphasized here that the Pareto optimality test can easily be dropped, if one replaces the minimax problem by the augmented minimax problem in a similar manner to Steuer and Choo (1983) or Choo and Atkins (1983). This fact will be discussed further in the next Chapter.

# CHAPTER 4

# INTERACTIVE FUZZY MULTIOBJECTIVE PROGRAMMING

## 4.1 Introduction

In this chapter, we continue to discuss man-machine interactive approaches for obtaining the satisficing solution of DM to the multiobjective optimization problems treated in the previous chapters. Unlike in Chapter 3, however, in this chapter our main attempt is to incorporate the inaccuracies inherent in the judgment of the decision maker (DM) in human decision making processes. To be more specific, the major purposes of this chapter are to demonstrate how imprecise or vague statements of DM can be incorporated into standard multiobjective optimization problems. The theory of fuzzy sets developed by Zadeh (1965) will be used to represent the imprecise or vague statements of DM and the advantages of applying the fuzzy set theory is that it allows the imprecise or vague aspirations of DM to be quantified and used in the multiobjective decision making processes.

### 4.1.1 Fundamentals of Fuzzy Set Theory

Before discussing some aspects of fuzzy decision making processes, it is appropriate to review the fundamentals of the fuzzy set theory which will be used in the subsequent discussions.

In general a fuzzy set is defined as follows:

**Definition 4.1 (Fuzzy Set).**

Let $X$ be a set, denumerable or not. Then a fuzzy subset $A$ of $X$ is defined by its membership function

$$\mu_A : X \to [0,1] \tag{4.1}$$

which assigns to each element $x \in X$ a real number $\mu_A(x)$ in the interval [0,1], where the value of $\mu_A(x)$ at $x$ represents the grade of membership of $x$ in $A$. Thus, the nearer the value of $\mu_A(x)$ is to unity, the higher the grade of membership of $x$ in $A$.

Observe that the membership function is an obvious extension of the idea of a characteristic function of an ordinary set because it takes on values between 0 and 1.

Several basic definitions involving fuzzy sets which are obvious extensions of the corresponding definitions for ordinary sets are as follows:

(1) Equality

The fuzzy sets $A$ and $B$ on $X$ are equal, denoted by $A = B$, if and only if their membership functions are equal everywhere on $X$:

$$A = B \Leftrightarrow \mu_A(x) = \mu_B(x) \quad \text{for all} \quad x \in X. \tag{4.2}$$

(2) Containment

A fuzzy set $A$ is contained in $B$ (or a subset of $B$), denoted by $A \subset B$, if and only if its membership function is less or equal to that of $B$ everywhere on $X$:

$$A \subset B \Leftrightarrow \mu_A(x) \leqslant \mu_B(x) \quad \text{for all} \quad x \in X. \tag{4.3}$$

(3) Complementation

The complement of a fuzzy set $A$, denoted by $\bar{A}$, is defined by:

$$\mu_{\bar{A}}(x) = 1 - \mu_A(x) \quad \text{for all} \quad x \in X. \tag{4.4}$$

(4) Intersection

The intersection of two fuzzy sets A and B on X, denoted by $A \cap B$, is defined by:

$$\mu_{A \cap B}(x) = \min(\mu_A(x), \mu_B(x)) \quad \text{for all } x \in X. \tag{4.5}$$

(5) Union

The union of two fuzzy sets A and B on X, denoted by $A \cup B$, is defined by:

$$\mu_{A \cup B}(x) = \max(\mu_A(x), \mu_B(x)) \quad \text{for all } x \in X. \tag{4.6}$$

Let us now overview the original definitions for a fuzzy decision (Bellman and Zadeh 1970).

Let X be a set of possible alternatives.

A fuzzy goal G is a fuzzy subset on X characterized by its membership function

$$\mu_G : X \to [0,1]. \tag{4.7}$$

A fuzzy constraint C is a fuzzy subset on X characterized by its membership function

$$\mu_C : X \to [0,1]. \tag{4.8}$$

The fuzzy decision D resulting from the fuzzy goal G and the fuzzy constraint C is the intersection of G and C; that is,

$$D = G \cap C, \tag{4.9}$$

and is characterized by its membership function

$$\mu_D(x) = \min(\mu_G(x), \mu_C(x)). \tag{4.10}$$

The maximizing decision is then defined as

$$\underset{x \in X}{\text{maximize}} \; \mu_D(x) = \underset{x \in X}{\text{maximize}} \min(\mu_G(x), \mu_C(x)). \tag{4.11}$$

More generally, the fuzzy decision D resulting from m fuzzy goals $G_1,\ldots,G_m$ and J fuzzy constraints $C_1,\ldots,C_J$ is defined by:

$$D = G_1 \cap \ldots \cap G_m \cap C_1 \cap \ldots \cap C_J. \tag{4.12}$$

and the maximizing decision is defined as

$$\underset{x \in X}{\text{maximize}} \quad \mu_D(x) = \underset{x \in X}{\text{maximize}} \min(\mu_{G_1}(x),\ldots, \mu_{G_m}(x), \mu_{C_1}(x),\ldots, \mu_{C_J}(x)). \tag{4.13}$$

It should be noted here that for the fuzzy decision due to Bellman and Zadeh there is no longer a difference between the fuzzy goals and the fuzzy constraints.

An application of the theory of fuzzy set to multiobjective linear programming problems was presented by Zimmermann (1978, 1983) and further studied by Leberling (1981) and Hannan (1981). Following the fuzzy decision proposed by Bellman and Zadeh (1970) together with linear, hyperbolic or piecewise linear membership functions respectively, they proved that there exists an equivalent linear programming problem.

However, suppose that the interaction with DM establishes that the first membership function should be linear, the second hyperbolic, the third piecewise linear and so forth. In such a situation, the resulting problem becomes a nonlinear programming problem and cannot be solved by a linear programming technique.

In order to overcome such difficulties, Sakawa (1983a, 1983b) has proposed a new method by combined use of bisection method and linear programming method together with five types of membership functions; linear, exponential, hyperbolic, hyperbolic inverse and piecewise linear functions. This method was further extended for solving multiobjective linear fractional (Sakawa and Yumine 1983) and nonlinear programming problems (Sakawa 1984a).

In these fuzzy approaches, however, it has been implicitly assumed that the fuzzy decision is the proper representation of DM's fuzzy preferences. Therefore, these approaches are preferable only when DM feels that the fuzzy decision is appropriate when combining the fuzzy goals and/or constraints. However such situations seem to rarely occur and consequently it becomes evident that an interaction with DM is necessary.

In this chapter, assuming that DM has a fuzzy goal for each of the objective functions in multiobjective optimization problems, we present a few interactive fuzzy multiobjective programming methods by incorporating the desirable features of both the goal programming methods and the interactive approaches discussed in Chapter 3 into the fuzzy approaches.

### 4.1.2 Problem Formulation

In general, the multiobjective optimization problem (MOP) is represented as the following vector-maximization problem:

MOP

$$\begin{aligned} &\text{maximize} \quad f(x) \triangleq (f_1(x), f_2(x), \ldots, f_m(x)) \\ &\text{subject to} \quad x \in X = \{x \in R^n \mid g_j(x) \leqslant 0,\ j = 1, \ldots, J\} \end{aligned} \tag{4.14}$$

where $x$ is an n-dimensional vector of decision variables, $f_1(x), \ldots, f_m(x)$ are $m$ distinct objective functions of the decision vector $x$, $g_1(x), \ldots, g_J(x)$ are $J$ inequality constraints, and $X$ is the feasible set of constrained decisions.

As discussed before, fundamental to MOP is the concept of a Pareto optimal solution, which is also known as a noninferior solution. In practice, however, since only local solutions are guaranteed in solving a scalar optimization problem by any standard optimization technique, unless the problem is convex, we deal with the local Pareto optimal solutions instead of global Pareto optimal solutions. The concept of local Pareto optimal solutions was first introduced by Geoffrion (1968).

**Definition 4.2 (local Pareto optimal solution).**

$x^* \in X$ is said to be a local Pareto optimal solution to MOP if and only if there exists a $\delta > 0$ such that $x^*$ is Pareto optimal in $X \cap N(x^*, \delta)$, i.e., there does not exist another $x \in X \cap N(x^*, \delta)$ such that $f_i(x) \geq f_i(x^*)$, $i = 1,\ldots,m$, with strict inequality holding for at least one i, where $N(x^*, \delta)$ denotes the set $\{x \in R^n \mid \| x - x^* \| < \delta\}$.

Usually, (local) Pareto optimal solutions consist of an infinite number of points, and therefore some kinds of subjective judgment for finding the satisficing solution should be added to the quantitative analyses by DM. In fuzzy multiobjective programming DM must select his (local) final solution from among (local) Pareto optimal solutions as the satisficing solution.

In a maximization problem, a fuzzy goal stated by DM may be to achieve "substantially greater than $a_i$". This type of statement can be quantified by eliciting a corresponding membership function. Figure 4.1 illustrates the graph of the possible shape of the membership function representing the fuzzy goal to achieve substantially greater than $a_i$.

In order to elicit a membership function $\mu_{f_i}(x)$ from DM for each of the objective functions $f_i(x)$, $i = 1,\ldots,m$, we first calculate the individual minimum $f_{i*}$ and maximum $f_i^*$ of

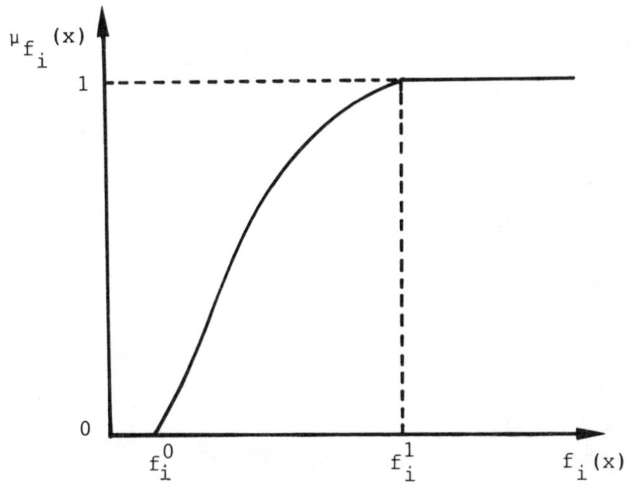


**Figure 4.1 Membership function.**

each objective function $f_i(x)$ under the given constraints. By taking account of the calculated individual minimum and maximum of each objective function together with the rate of increase of membership of satisfaction, DM must determine his subjective membership function $\mu_{f_i}(x)$, which is a strictly monotone increasing function with respect to $f_i(x)$. Here, it is assumed that $\mu_{f_i}(x) = 0$ or $\to 0$ if $f_i(x) \leqslant f_i^0$ and $\mu_{f_i}(x) = 1$ or $\to 1$ if $f_i(x) \geqslant f_i^1$, where $f_i^a$ represents the value of $f_i(x)$ such that the value of membership function $\mu_{f_i}(x)$ is a, $f_i^0$ is an unacceptable level for $f_i(x)$ and $f_i^1$ is a completely desirable level for $f_i(x)$ within $f_{i*}$ and $f_i^*$.

So far we have restricted ourselves to a maximization problem and consequently assumed that DM has a fuzzy goal such as "$f_i(x)$ should be substantially greater than $a_i$". In the fuzzy approaches, we can further treat a more general multiobjective optimization problem in which DM has two types of fuzzy goals, namely fuzzy goals expressed in words such as "$f_i(x)$ should be in the vicinity of $c_i$" (called fuzzy equal) as well as "$f_i(x)$ should be substantially greater than $a_i$ or less than $b_i$" (called fuzzy max or fuzzy min).

Such a generalized multiobjective optimization problem (GMOP) may now be expressed as:

GMOP

$$\begin{array}{lll} \text{fuzzy max} & f_i(x) & (i \in I_1) \\ \text{fuzzy min} & f_i(x) & (i \in I_2) \\ \text{fuzzy equal} & f_i(x) & (i \in I_3) \\ \text{subject to} & x \in X & \end{array} \tag{4.15}$$

where $I_1 \cup I_2 \cup I_3 = \{1,2,\ldots,m\}$.

In order to elicit a membership function from DM for a fuzzy goal like "$f_i(x)$ should be in the vicinity of $c_i$", it is obvious that we can use different functions to the left and right sides of $c_i$. As an example, Figure 4.2 illustrates the graph of the possible shape of the fuzzy equal membership

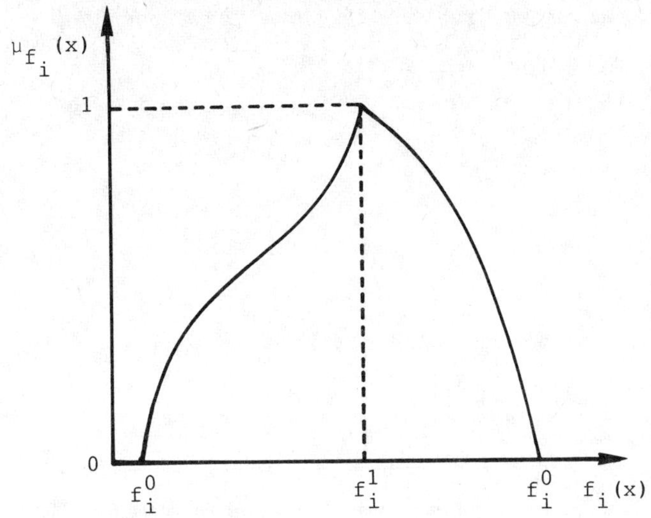


**Figure 4.2 Fuzzy equal membership function.**

functions where the left function is hyperbolic inverse and the right function is exponential.

When the fuzzy equal is included in the fuzzy goals of DM, it is desirable that $f_i(x)$ should be as close to $c_i$ as possible. Consequently, the notion of Pareto optimal solutions defined in terms of objective functions cannot be applied. For this reason, we introduce the concept of M-Pareto optimal solutions which is defined in terms of membership functions instead of objective functions, where M refers to membership.

**Definition 4.3 ((local) M-Pareto optimal solution).**

$x^* \in X$ is said to be a (local) M-Pareto optimal solution to GMOP (4.15), if and only if there does not exist another $x \in X \cap N(x^*, \delta)$ so that $\mu_{f_i}(x) \geqslant \mu_{f_i}(x^*)$, $i=1,\ldots,m$, with strict inequality holding for at least one $i$.

Observe that the set of (local) Pareto optimal solutions is a subset of the set of (local) M-Pareto optimal solutions.

Having elicited the membership functions $\mu_{f_i}(x)$, $i = 1,\ldots,m$ from DM for each of the objective functions $f_i(x)$, $i = 1,\ldots,m$, MOP (4.14) and/or GMOP (4.15) can be converted into the fuzzy multiobjective optimization problem (FMOP) defined by:

FMOP

$$\underset{x \in X}{\text{maximize}} \quad (\mu_{f_i}(x), \mu_{f_2}(x), \ldots, \mu_{f_m}(x)). \tag{4.16}$$

By introducing a general conjunctive function

$$\mu_D(\mu_f(x)) = \mu_D(\mu_{f_1}(x), \mu_{f_2}(x), \ldots, \mu_{f_m}(x)), \tag{4.17}$$

a general fuzzy multiobjective decision problem (FMDP) can be defined by:

FMDP

$$\underset{x \in X}{\text{maximize}} \quad \mu_D(\mu_f(x)). \tag{4.18}$$

Observe that the value of $\mu_D(\mu_f(x))$ can be interpreted as representing an overall degree of satisfaction with DM's multiple fuzzy goals.

The fuzzy decision or the minimum-operator of Bellman and Zadeh (1970)

$$\min_{1 \leq i \leq m} (\mu_{f_i}(x), \mu_{f_2}(x), \ldots, \mu_{f_m}(x)) \tag{4.19}$$

can be viewed only as one special example of $\mu_D(\mu_f(x))$.

In the conventional fuzzy approaches, it has been implicitly assumed that the minimum-operator is the proper representation of decision makers' fuzzy preferences, and hence FMDP (4.18) has been interpreted as follows:

$$\underset{x \in X}{\text{maximize}} \quad \min_{1 \leq i \leq m} (\mu_{f_1}(x), \mu_{f_2}(x), \ldots, \mu_{f_m}(x)) \tag{4.20}$$

or equivalently

$$\underset{v,\ x \in X}{\text{maximize}} \quad v$$
$$\text{subject to} \quad v \leq \mu_{f_i}(x), \ i = 1,\ldots,m. \tag{4.21}$$

However, it should be emphasized here that this approach is preferable only when DM feels that the minimum-operator in (4.20) is appropriate. In other words, in general decision situations, the decision makers do not always use the minimum-operator when they combine the fuzzy goals and/or constraints. Probably the most crucial problem in the FMDP is the identification of an appropriate conjunctive function which well represents the decision makers' fuzzy preferences. If $\mu_D(\bullet)$ can be explicitly identified, then the FMDP reduces to a standard mathematical programming problem. However, this rarely happens and as an alternative, an interaction with DM is necessary for finding the satisficing solution to (4.18).

Throughout this chapter we make the following assumptions.

**Assumption 4.1.**

The fuzzy goals of DM can be quantified by eliciting the corresponding membership functions through the interaction with DM.

**Assumption 4.2.**

$\mu_D(\bullet)$ exists and is known only implicitly to DM, which means DM cannot specify the entire function form of $\mu_D(\bullet)$, but he can provide local information concerning his preference. Moreover, it is increasing and continuous.

**Assumption 4.3.**

All $f_i(x)$, $i = 1,\ldots,m$ and all $g_j(x)$, $j = 1,\ldots,J$ are continuously differentiable.

Having determined the membership functions for each of the objective functions, in order to generate a candidate for the satisficing solution which is also (local) (M-) Pareto optimal, we can suggest several scalarizing methods in the membership function spaces which are based on:

(1) goal programming problems,
(2) penalty scalarizing problems,
(3) constraint problems,
(4) minimax problems and
(5) augmented minimax problems.

By adopting one of the methods, the corresponding (local) (M-) Pareto optimal solution is obtained and DM then acts on this solution until he is satisfied with the current solution. These methods are discussed in the following subsections.

## 4.2 Interactive Fuzzy Multiobjective Programming without Trade-offs

### 4.2.1 Interactive Fuzzy Goal Programming

In the interactive fuzzy goal programming method proposed by Sakawa (1984b), after determining the membership functions $\mu_{f_i}(x)$, $i = 1,\ldots,m$ for each of the objective functions $f_i(x)$, $i = 1,\ldots,m$, DM is asked to specify his aspiration levels of achievement of goals in terms of membership values, called the goal membership levels, for all the membership functions. For DM's goal membership levels $\bar{\mu}_{f_i}$, $i=1,\ldots,m$, the corresponding (local) (M-) Pareto optimal solution is obtained by solving the following goal programming problem in the membership function space.

$$
\begin{aligned}
&\underset{x \in X}{\text{minimize}} \quad \sum_{i=1}^{m} d_i^- \\
&\text{subject to} \quad \mu_{f_i}(x) + d_i^- - d_i^+ = \bar{\mu}_{f_i}, \quad i = 1,\ldots,m, \qquad (4.22) \\
&\qquad d_i^- \cdot d_i^+ = 0, \quad i = 1,\ldots,m, \\
&\qquad d_i^-,\ d_i^+ \geqslant 0, \quad i = 1,\ldots,m,
\end{aligned}
$$

where $d_i^-$ and $d_i^+$ are, respectively, the negative and positive deviation variables, which provide us with a way to measure nonachievement of goal membership levels. This particular formulation may be called one-sided fuzzy goal programming.

The relationships between the (local) optimal solutions of the fuzzy goal programming problem (4.22) and the (local) Pareto optimal concept of MOP can be characterized by the following theorems.

**Theorem 4.1.**

If $x^*$ is a (local) optimal solution to the goal programming problem (4.22) with $0 < \mu_{f_i}(x^*) < 1$ and $d_i^+ = 0$ holding for all i, then $x^*$ is a (local) Pareto optimal solution to MOP (4.14)

**Theorem 4.2.**

If $x^*$ is a (local) Pareto optimal solution to MOP (4.14) with $0 < \mu_{f_i}(x^*) < 1$ holding for all i, then $x^*$ is a (local) optimal solution to the goal programming problem (4.22) with $d_i^+ = 0$ holding for all i.

The proofs of these theorems follow directly from the definitions of (local) optimality and (local) Pareto optimality by contradiction arguments.

If $x^*$ is a (local) optimal solution to the goal programming problem (4.22), and if none of the sufficiency conditions for (local) Pareto optimality in Theorem 4.1 are satisfied (i.e., $\exists_i$, $\mu_{f_i}(x^*) = 0,1$ or $d_i^+ = 0$), then we can test the (local) Pareto optimality for $x^*$ by solving the following Pareto optimality test problem:

$$\begin{aligned} &\underset{x \in X}{\text{maximize}} \quad \sum_{i=1}^{m} \varepsilon_i \\ &\text{subject to} \quad f_i(x) - \varepsilon_i = f_i(x^*), \ \varepsilon_i \geqslant 0 \ (i=1,\ldots,m) \end{aligned} \qquad (4.23)$$

Let $\bar{x}$ be a (local) optimal solution to (4.23). If all $\varepsilon_i = 0$, then $x^*$ is a (local) Pareto optimal solution. If at least one $\varepsilon_i > 0$, it can easily be shown that $\bar{x}$ is a (local) Pareto optimal solution.

Using the concept of (local) M-Pareto optimality, the following (local) M-Pareto versions of Theorems 4.1 and 4.2 can be obtained immediately under slightly different conditions.

**Theorem 4.3.**

If $x^*$ is a (local) optimal solution to the goal programming problem (4.22) with $d_i^+ = 0$ holding for all i, then $x^*$ is a (local) M-Pareto optimal solution to GMOP (4.15).

**Theorem 4.4.**

If $x^*$ is a (local) M-Pareto optimal solution to GMOP (4.15), then $x^*$ is a (local) optimal solution to the goal programming problem (4.22) with $d_i^+ = 0$ holding for all i.

A numerical test of (local) M-Pareto optimality for $x^*$, similar to the maximization case, can be performed by solving the following M-Pareto optimality test problem:

$$\underset{x \in X}{\text{maximize}} \quad \sum_{i=1}^{m} \varepsilon_i$$

$$\text{subject to} \tag{4.24}$$

$$\mu_{f_i}(x) - \varepsilon_i = \mu_{f_i}(x^*), \quad \varepsilon_i \geqslant 0, \quad i = 1,\dots,m.$$

Let $\bar{x}$ be a (local) optimal solution to (4.24). If all $\varepsilon_i = 0$, then $x^*$ is a (local) M-Pareto optimal solution. If at least one $\varepsilon_i > 0$, $\bar{x}$ becomes a (local) M-Pareto optimal solution.

Following the above discussions, we can now present the interactive fuzzy goal programming algorithm in order to derive the (local) satisficing solution for DM from among the (local) (M-) Pareto optimal solution set. The steps marked with an asterisk involve interaction with DM.

Step 0 (Individual minimum and maximum).

Calculate the individual minimum $f_{*i}$ and maximum $f_i^*$ of each objective function $f_i(x)$ under the given constraints.

Step 1* (Membership functions).

Elicit a membership function $\mu_{f_i}(x)$ from DM for each of the objective functions.

Step 2 (Initialization).

Set the initial goal membership levels $\bar{\mu}_{f_i}^{(1)} = 1$, $i = 1,\ldots,m$

Step 3 ((M-) Pareto optimal solution).

Set $\bar{\mu}_{f_i} = \bar{\mu}_{f_i}^{(r)}$, solve the corresponding goal programming problem (4.22) to obtain the (local) (M-) Pareto optimal solution $x^{(r)}$, $f(x^{(r)})$ and the membership function value $\mu_f(x^{(r)})$.

Step 4* (Termination or New goal membership levels).

If DM is satisfied with the current levels of $\mu_{f_i}(x^{(r)})$, $i = 1,\ldots,m$ of the (local) (M-) Pareto optimal solution, stop. Then the current (local) (M-) Pareto optimal solution $f(x^{(r)}) = (f_1(x^{(r)}),\ldots, f_m(x^{(r)}))$ is the (local) satisficing solution of DM. Otherwise, ask DM to update the current goal membership levels $\bar{\mu}_{f_i}^{(r)},\ldots, \bar{\mu}_{f_m}^{(r)}$ to the new goal membership levels $\bar{\mu}_{f_1}^{(r+1)},\ldots, \bar{\mu}_{f_m}^{(r+1)}$ by considering the current values of the membership functions together with the current values of the negative deviation variables and return to Step 3. Here it should be stressed for DM that any improvement of one membership function can be achieved only at the expense of at least one of the other membership functions.

### 4.2.2 Interactive Fuzzy Penalty Scalarizing Method

An interactive fuzzy multiobjective programming method which can be interpreted as a fuzzy version of a reference point method (RPM) was proposed by Sakawa and Yano (1984a). In their method, after determining the membership functions $\mu_{f_i}(x)$, $i = 1,\ldots,m$ for each of the objective functions

$f_i(x)$, $i = 1,\ldots,m$, DM is asked to specify his reference levels of achievement of the membership values, called the reference membership levels. The concept of the reference membership levels is an extension of that of the reference point. For DM's reference membership levels $\bar{\mu}_{f_i}$, $i = 1,\ldots,m$ the corresponding (local) (M-) Pareto optimal solution, which is in a sense close to his requirement or better than that if the reference membership levels are attainable, is obtained by solving the following penalty scalarizing problem in the membership function space.

$$\underset{x \in X}{\text{minimize}} \quad \| \bar{\mu}_f - \mu_f(x) \|^2 - c \, \| [\bar{\mu}_f - \mu_f(x)]_+ \|^2 \tag{4.25}$$

where $\mu_f(x) = (\mu_{f_1}(x), \mu_{f_2}(x),\ldots,\mu_{f_m}(x))$, $\bar{\mu}_f = (\bar{\mu}_{f_1}, \bar{\mu}_{f_2},\ldots, \bar{\mu}_{f_m})$, $c > 1$ is a scalar penalty coefficient and $[\hat{\mu}_f - \mu_f(x)]_+$ denote the vector with components $\max[0, \hat{\mu}_f - \mu_f(x)]$. Note that this particular formulation is a fuzzy version of the penalty scalarizing problem discussed in section 3.4.

The relationships between the (local) optimal solutions of the penalty scalarizing problem (4.22) and the (local) Pareto optimal concept of MOP can be characterized by the following theorems.

**Theorem 4.5.**

If $x^*$ is a (local) optimal solution to the penalty scalarizing problem (4.25) for any $\bar{\mu}_f$, then $x^*$ is a (local) Pareto optimal solution to MOP (4.14).

**Theorem 4.6.**

If $x^*$ is a (local) Pareto optimal solution to MOP (4.14), then there exists a $\hat{\mu}_f$ such that $x^*$ is a (local) optimal solution to the penalty scalarizing problem (4.12).

The proofs of these theorems follow immediately from the definitions of (local) optimality and (local) Pareto optimality using contradiction arguments.

Using the concept of (local) M-Pareto optimality, the

following (local) M-Pareto versions of Theorems 4.5 and 4.6 can be established and are easy to prove.

**Theorem 4.7.**

If $x^*$ is a (local) optimal solution to the penalty scalarizing problem (4.25) for any $\bar{\mu}_f$, then $x^*$ is a (local) M-Pareto optimal solution to GMOP (4.15).

**Theorem 4.8.**

If $x^*$ is a (local) M-Pareto optimal solution to GMOP (4.15), then there exists a $\bar{\mu}_f$ such that $x^*$ is a (local) optimal solution to the penalty scalarizing problem (4.25).

From the above discussions, we can now construct the interactive algorithm in order to derive the (local) satisficing solution for DM from among the (local) (M-) Pareto optimal solution set, where the steps marked with an asterisk involve interaction with DM.

Step 0 (Individual minimum and maximum).
Calculate the individual minimum $f_{*i}$ and maximum $f_i^*$ of each objective function $f_i(x)$ under the given constraints.

Step 1* (Membership functions).
Elicit a membership function $\mu_{f_i}(x)$ from DM for each of the objective functions.

Step 2 (Initialization).
Set the initial reference membership levels $\bar{\mu}_{f_i}^{(1)} = 1$, $i = 1,\ldots,m$ and set the iteration index $r = 1$.

Step 3 ((M-) Pareto optimal solution).
Set $\bar{\mu}_{f_i} = \bar{\mu}_{f_i}^{(r)}$, solve the corresponding penalty scalarizing problem (4.25) to obtain the (local) (M-) Pareto optimal solution $x^{(r)}$, $f(x^{(r)})$ and the membership function value $\mu_f(x^{(r)})$.

Step 4* (Termination or New reference membership levels).
If DM is satisfied with the current levels of $\mu_{f_i}(x^{(r)})$, $i = 1,\ldots,m$ of the (local) (M-) Pareto optimal solution, stop. Then the current (local) (M-) Pareto optimal solution $f(x^{(r)}) = (f_1(x^{(r)}),\ldots,f_m(x^{(r)}))$ is the (local)

satisficing solution of DM. Otherwise, ask DM to update the current reference membership levels $\bar{\mu}_{f_1}^{(r)}, \ldots, \bar{\mu}_{f_m}^{(r)}$ to the new reference membership levels $\bar{\mu}_{f_1}^{(r+1)}, \ldots, \bar{\mu}_{f_m}^{(r+1)}$ by considering the current values of the membership functions. Set $r = r + 1$ and return to Step 3. Here it should be stressed for DM that any improvement of one membership function can be achieved only at the expense of at least one of the other membership functions.

## 4.3 Interactive Fuzzy Multiobjective Programming with Trade-offs

### 4.3.1 Interactive Fuzzy Constraint Method

In the interactive fuzzy satisficing method using constraint problems as a means for generating (local) (M-) Pareto optimal solutions (Sakawa and Yano 1986a), after determining the membership functions $\mu_{f_i}(x)$, $i = 1,\ldots,m$ for each of the objective functions $f_i(x)$, $i = 1,\ldots,m$, DM selects an appropriate $\mu_{f_k}(x)$ as the standing membership function and specifies his aspiration levels of achievement of the other membership values, called the constraint membership levels. For convenience in the following we assume $\mu_{f_1}(x)$ to be the standing membership function. Then for DM's constraint membership levels $\bar{\mu}_{f_i}$, $i = 2,\ldots,m$, the corresponding (local) (M-) Pareto optimal solution is obtained by solving the following constraint problem in the membership function space.

$$\begin{aligned} &\underset{x \in X}{\text{maximize}} \quad \mu_{f_1}(x) \\ &\text{subject to} \quad \mu_{f_i}(x) \geqslant \bar{\mu}_{f_i}, \quad i = 2,\ldots,m. \end{aligned} \tag{4.26}$$

The relationships between the (local) optimal solutions of the constraint problem and the (local) Pareto optimal concept of MOP can be characterized by the following theorems, whose proofs follow easily by contradiction arguments.

**Theorem 4.9.**

If $x^*$ is a unique (local) optimal solution to the constraint problem (4.26), then $x^*$ is a (local) Pareto optimal solution to MOP (4.14).

**Theorem 4.10.**

For any given (local) Pareto optimal solution $x^*$ to MOP (4.14), there always exists $(\bar{\mu}_{f_2}, \ldots, \bar{\mu}_{f_m})$ such that $x^*$ is a (local) optimal solution to the constraint problem (4.26).

If $x^*$, a (local) optimal solution to (4.26), is not unique, then we can test the (local) Pareto optimality for $x^*$ by solving the Pareto optimality test problem (4.23) as was discussed in 4.2.1.

Using the concept of (local) M-Pareto optimality, the following theorems, which are similar to Theorems 4.7 and 4.8, can easily be obtained.

**Theorem 4.11.**

If $x^*$ is a unique (local) optimal solution to the constraint problem (4.26), then $x^*$ is a (local) M-Pareto optimal solution to MOP (4.15).

**Theorem 4.12.**

For any given (local) M-Pareto optimal solution $x^*$ to MOP (4.15), there always exists $(\bar{\mu}_{f_2}, \ldots, \bar{\mu}_{f_k})$ such that $x^*$ is a (local) optimal solution to the constraint problem (4.26).

Observe that a numerical test of (local) M-Pareto optimality for $x^*$ can be performed by solving the M-Pareto optimality test problem (4.24) as was mentioned in 4.2.1.

DM must now either be satisfied with the current (local) (M-) Pareto optimal solution, or act on this solution by updating his constraint membership levels. In order to help DM express his degree of preference, trade-off information between the standing membership function $\mu_{f_i}(x)$ and each of the other membership functions is very useful. Such a trade-off between $\mu_{f_1}(x)$ and $\mu_{f_i}(x)$ for each $i = 2,\ldots,m$ is easily obtainable since it is closely related to the strict positive Lagrange multipliers of the constraint problem. Let the Lagrange multipliers associated with the ith active constraint be denoted by $\lambda_{1i}$, $i = 2,\ldots,m$. If all $\lambda_{1i} > 0$, $i = 2,\ldots,m$, then it is known that the following expression holds (Haimes and Chankong 1979).

$$- \partial\mu_{f_1}(x)/\partial\mu_{f_i}(x) = \lambda_{1i}, \quad i = 2,\ldots,m. \tag{4.27}$$

It should be noted here that in order to obtain the trade-off rate information from (4.27), all the constraints of the constraint problem must be active. Therefore, if there are inactive constraints, it is necessary to replace $\bar{\mu}_{f_i}$ for inactive constraints by $\bar{\mu}_{f_i}(x^*)$ and solve the corresponding constraint problem for obtaining the Lagrange multipliers.

Based on the above discussions, we can now construct the interactive algorithm in order to derive the (local) satisficing solution for DM from among the (local) (M-) Pareto optimal solution set. The steps marked with an asterisk involve interaction with DM.

Step 0 (Individual minimum and maximum).
Calculate the individual minimum $f_{*i}$ and maximum $f_i^*$ of each objective function $f_i(x)$ under the given constraints.

Step 1* (Membership functions).
Elicit a membership function $\mu_{f_i}(x)$ from DM for each of the objective functions.

Step 2 (Initialization).
Set the initial constraint reference membership levels $\bar{\mu}_{f_i}^{(1)} = 1$, $i = 1,\ldots,m$ and set the iteration index $r = 1$.

Step 3 ((M-) Pareto optimal solution).
Set $\bar{\mu}_{f_i} = \bar{\mu}_{f_i}^{(r)}$, solve the corresponding constraint problem (4.26) to obtain the (local) (M-) Pareto optimal solution $x^{(r)}$, $f(x^{(r)})$ and the membership function value

$\mu_f(x^{(r)})$ together with the trade-off rate information between the membership functions.

Step 4* (Termination or New Constraint membership levels).
If DM is satisfied with the current levels of $\mu_{f_i}(x^{(r)})$, $i = 1,\ldots,m$ of the (local) (M-) Pareto optimal solution, stop. Then the current (local)(M-) Pareto optimal solution $f(x^{(r)}) = (f_1(x^{(r)}),\ldots, f_m(x^{r}))$ is the (local) satisficing solution of DM. Otherwise, ask DM to update the current constraint membership levels $\bar{\mu}_{f_1}^{(r)},\ldots, \bar{\mu}_{f_m}^{(r)}$ to the new constraint membership values $\bar{\mu}_{f_1}^{(r+1)},\ldots, \bar{\mu}_{f_m}^{(r+1)}$ by considering the current values of the membership functions together with the trade-off rates between the membership functions. Set $r = r + 1$ and return to Step 3. Here it should be stressed for DM that any improvement of one membership function can be achieved only at the expense of at least one of the other membership functions.

It is significant to note here that an obvious advantage of the above method over the two methods discussed in the subsections 4.2.1 and 4.2.2 is that DM is supplied with the trade-off information between the membership functions in addition to the levels of all the membership functions in trying to express his degree of preference.

### 4.3.2 Interactive Fuzzy Minimax Method

An interactive fuzzy multiobjective programming method using minimax problems instead of the constraint problems as a means of generating (local) (M-) Pareto optimal solutions is proposed by Sakawa, Yumine and Yano (1984). The minimax problems are much more favorable than the constraint problems especially in the sense that each objective function is treated equally.

In their method, after determining the membership functions $\mu_{f_i}(x)$, $i = 1,\ldots,m$ for each of the objective functions $f_i(x)$, $i = 1,\ldots,m$, DM is asked to specify his reference membership levels for all the membership functions. For DM's reference membership levels $\bar{\mu}_{f_i}$, $i = 1,2,\ldots,m$, the corresponding (local) (M-) Pareto optimal solution which is in a sense close to his requirement or better than that if the reference membership levels are attainable, is obtained by solving the following minimax problem.

$$\underset{x \in X}{\text{minimize}} \quad \max_{i=1,\ldots,m} \{\bar{\mu}_{f_i} - \mu_{f_i}(x)\}, \tag{4.28}$$

or equivalently

$$\begin{aligned} &\underset{v,\, x \in X}{\text{minimize}} \quad v \\ &\text{subject to} \quad \bar{\mu}_{f_i} - \mu_{f_i}(x) \leq v, \quad i = 1,\ldots,m. \end{aligned} \tag{4.29}$$

The relationships between the (local) optimal solutions of the minimax problem (4.29) and the (local) Pareto optimal concept of MOP can be characterized by the following theorems.

**Theorem 4.13.**

If $x^*$ is a unique (local) optimal solution to the minimax problem (4.29) for some $\bar{\mu}_{f_i}$, $i = 1,\ldots,m$, then $x^*$ is a (local) Pareto optimal solution to MOP (4.14).

**Theorem 4.14.**

If $x^*$ is a (local) Pareto optimal solution to MOP (4.14) with $0 < \mu_{f_i}(x^*) < 1$ holding for all $i$, then there exists $\bar{\mu}_{f_i}$, $i = 1,\ldots,m$, $x^*$ is a (local) optimal solution to the minimax problem (4.29).

The proofs of these theorems follow directly from the definitions of (local) optimality and (local) Pareto optimality by making use of contradiction arguments.

If $x^*$, a (local) optimal solution to (4.29), is not unique, then we can test the (local) Pareto optimality for $x^*$ by solving the Pareto optimality test problem (4.23) as discussed in 4.2.1.

Using the concept of (local) M-Pareto optimality, the following theorem, which is similar to Theorems 4.13 and 4.14, can immediately be obtained under slightly different conditions.

**Theorem 4.15**

$x^*$ is a (local) M-Pareto optimal solution to GMOP (4.2), if and only if there exists a $\bar{\mu}_f$ such that $x^*$ is a unique (local) optimal solution to the minimax problem (4.29).

Similar to the maximization case, a numerical test of (local) M-Pareto optimality for $x^*$ can be performed by solving the M-Pareto optimality test problem (4.24) as mentioned in 4.2.1.

DM must now either be satisfied with the current (local) (M-) Pareto optimal solution, or act on this solution by updating his reference membership levels. In order to help DM express his degree of preference, as was discussed in the previous subsection, trade-off information between a standing membership function $\mu_{f_1}(x)$ and each of the other membership functions is very useful. Due to the recent results of Yano and Sakawa (1985), such a trade-off information between $\mu_{f_1}$ and $\mu_{f_i}(x)$ for each $i = 2,\ldots,m$ is easily obtainable since it is related to the strict positive Lagrange multipliers of the minimax problem (4.29). Let the Lagrange multipliers associated with the constraints of the minimax problem be denoted by $\lambda_i$, $i = 1,2,\ldots,m$. If all $\lambda_i > 0$ for each i, then by extending the results in Haimes and Chankong (1979), it can be proved that the following expression holds:

$$-\partial\mu_{f_i}(x)/\partial\mu_{f_1}(x) = \lambda_1/\lambda_i, \quad i = 2,\ldots,m. \tag{4.30}$$

In the proof of (4.30), it is assumed that

(1) $(v^*, x^*)$ is a regular point of the constraints of the minimax problem (4.29),

(2) the second-order sufficiency conditions of optimality are satisfied at $(v^*, x^*)$; and

(3) there are no degenerate constraints at $(v^*, x^*)$,

where $(v^*, x^*)$ is an optimal solution to the minimax problem (4.29).

The formal proof of this relation (4.30) can be found in Yano and Sakawa (1985). Geometrically, however, we can understand it as follows:

In the $(\mu_{f_1}, \mu_{f_2}, \ldots, \mu_{f_k}, v)$ space, the tangent hyperplane at some point on Pareto surface can be described by

$$H(\mu_{f_1}, \mu_{f_2}, \ldots, \mu_{f_k}, v) = a_1\mu_{f_1} + a_2\mu_{f_2} + \ldots + a_k\mu_{f_k} + bv = c. \tag{4.31}$$

The necessary and sufficient condition for the small displacement from this point belonging to this tangent hyperplane is

$$\Delta H = 0, \tag{4.32}$$

or, equivalently,

$$a_1\Delta\mu_{f_1} + a_2\Delta\mu_{f_2} + \ldots + a_k\Delta\mu_{f_k} + b\Delta v = 0. \tag{4.33}$$

For fixed values of $\Delta\mu_{f_j} = 0$ $(j = 2,\ldots,k,\ j \neq i)$ and $\Delta v = 0$ except $\mu_{f_1}$ and $\mu_{f_i}$, we have

$$a_1\Delta\mu_{f_1} + a_i\Delta\mu_{f_i} = 0. \tag{4.34}$$

Similarly, for fixed values of $\Delta\mu_{f_i} = 0$ $(i=1,\ldots,k, i\neq j)$ except $\mu_{f_j}$ and $v$, we have

$$a_j\Delta\mu_{f_j} + b\Delta v = 0. \tag{4.35}$$

It follows from the last two relations that

$$-\frac{\Delta\mu_{f_i}}{\Delta\mu_{f_1}} = \frac{a_1}{a_i} = \frac{(-a_1/b)}{(-a_i/b)} = \frac{(\Delta v/\Delta\mu_{f_1})}{(\Delta v/\Delta\mu_{f_i})} . \tag{4.36}$$

Consequently, it holds that

$$-\frac{\partial\mu_{f_i}}{\partial\mu_{f_1}} = \frac{(\partial v/\partial\mu_{f_1})}{(\partial v/\partial\mu_{f_i})} . \tag{4.37}$$

Now using the Lagrange multipliers $\lambda_i$, $i=1,\ldots,m$ associated with all the active constraints of the minimax problem (4.29), we observe that

$$-\frac{\partial v}{\partial\mu_i} = -\lambda_i . \tag{4.38}$$

Hence we have the result (4.30).

It should be stressed here that in order to obtain the trade-off rate information from (4.30), all the constraints of the minimax problem (4.29) must be active. Therefore, if there are inactive constraints, it is necessary to replace $\bar{\mu}_{f_i}$ for inactive constraints by $\bar{\mu}_{f_i}(x^*)$ and to solve the corresponding minimax problem for obtaining the Lagrange multipliers.

Following the above discussions, we can now construct the interactive algorithm in order to derive the (local) satisficing solution for DM from among the (local) (M-) Pareto optimal solution set where the steps marked with an asterisk involve interaction with DM. This interactive fuzzy multiobjective programming method can be also interpreted as the fuzzy version of the reference point method (RPM) with trade-off information discussed in 3.4.2.

Step 0 (Individual minimum and maximum).

Calculate the individual minimum $f_{*i}$ and maximum $f_i^*$ of each objective function $f_i(x)$ under the given constraints.

Step 1* (Membership functions).

Elicit a membership function $\mu_{f_i}(x)$ from DM for each of the objective functions.

Step 2 (Initialization).

Set the initial reference membership levels $\bar{\mu}_{f_i}^{(1)} = 1$, $i=1,\ldots,m$ and set the iteration index $r = 1$.

Step 3 ((M-) Pareto optimal solution).

Set $\bar{\mu}_{f_i} = \bar{\mu}_{f_i}^{(r)}$, solve the corresponding minimax problem (4.18) to obtain the (local) (M-) Pareto optimal solution $x^{(r)}$, $f(x^{(r)})$ and the membership function value $\mu_f(x^{(r)})$ together with the trade-off rate information between the membership functions.

Step 4* (Termination or New reference membership levels).

If DM is satisfied with the current levels of $\mu_{f_i}(x^{(r)})$, $i=1,\ldots,m$ of the (local)(M-) Pareto optimal solution, stop. Then the current (local)(M-) Pareto optimal solution $f(x^{(r)}) = (f_1(x^{(r)}),\ldots, f_m(x^{(r)}))$ is the satisficing solution of DM. Otherwise, ask DM to update the current reference membership levels $\bar{\mu}_{f_1}^{(r)},\ldots,\bar{\mu}_{f_m}^{(r)}$ to the new reference membership levels $\bar{\mu}_{f_1}^{(r+1)},\ldots,\bar{\mu}_{f_m}^{(r+1)}$ by considering the current values of the membership functions together with the trade-off rates between the membership functions. Set $r = r + 1$ and return to Step 3. Here it should be stressed for DM that any improvement of one membership function can be achieved only at the expense of at least one of the other membership functions.

### 4.3.3 Interactive Fuzzy Augmented Minimax Method

In order to circumvent the necessity to perform the (local) (M-) Pareto optimality tests in the minimax problems, an interactive fuzzy multiobjective programming method using augmented minimax problems instead of minimax problems has been proposed by Sakawa and Yano (1985b). In their method, after determining the membership functions $\mu_{f_i}(x)$, $i = 1,\ldots,m$ for each of the objective functions $f_i(x)$, $i = 1,\ldots,m$, DM is asked to specify his reference membership levels for all the membership functions. For DM's reference membership levels

$\bar{\mu}_{f_i}$, $i = 1,\ldots,m$, the corresponding (local) (M-) Pareto optimal solution, which is in a sense close to his requirement or better than that if the reference membership values are attainable, is obtained by solving the following augmented minimax problem.

$$\underset{x \in X}{\text{minimize}} \quad \left(\max_{1 \leqslant i \leqslant m} (\bar{\mu}_{f_i} - \mu_{f_i}(x)) + \rho \sum_{i=1}^{m} (\bar{\mu}_{f_i} - \mu_{f_i}(x))\right) \tag{4.39}$$

or, equivalently,

$$\begin{aligned} &\underset{v,\, x \in X}{\text{minimize}} \quad v + \rho \sum_{i=1}^{m} (\bar{\mu}_{f_i} - \mu_{f_i}(x)) \\ &\text{subject to} \quad \bar{\mu}_{f_i} - \mu_{f_i}(x) \leqslant v, \quad i = 1,\ldots,m \end{aligned} \tag{4.40}$$

or

$$\begin{aligned} &\underset{w,\, x \in X}{\text{minimize}} \quad w \\ &\text{subject to} \\ &\bar{\mu}_{f_i} - \mu_{f_i}(x) \leqslant w - \rho \sum_{i=1}^{m} (\bar{\mu}_{f_i} - \mu_{f_i}(x)), \quad i = 1,\ldots,m \end{aligned} \tag{4.41}$$

The term augmented is adopted because the term $\rho \sum_{i=1}^{m} (\bar{\mu}_{f_i} - \mu_{f_i}(x))$ is added to the standard minimax problem, where $\rho$ is a sufficiently small positive scalar. Thus the augmented minimax problem is a natural extension of the standard minimax problem, and can be regarded as a modified fuzzy version of the augmented weighted Tchebycheff norm problem of Steuer and Choo (1983) or Choo and Atkins (1983).

The relationships between the (local) optimal solutions of the augmented minimax problem and the (local) Pareto optimal concept of MOP can be characterized by the following theorems.

**Theorem 4.16.**

If $x^*$ is a (local) optimal solution to the augmented

minimax problem (4.39) for some $\bar{\mu}_f$, then $x^*$ is a (local) Pareto optimal solution to MOP (4.14).

**Proof**

Assume that $x^*$ is not a (local) Pareto optimal solution to MOP. Then there exists $x \in X(\cap N(x^*, r))$ such that $f(x) \leq f(x^*)$ or, equivalently, $\mu_f(x) \geq \mu_f(x^*)$ or $\bar{\mu}_f - \mu_f(x) \leq \bar{\mu}_f - \mu_f(x^*)$, where $\mu_f(x) = (\mu_{f_1}(x), \ldots, \mu_{f_k}(x))$. Then it holds that

$$\max_{1 \leq i \leq k} (\bar{\mu}_{f_i} - \mu_{f_i}(\bar{x})) \leq \max_{1 \leq i \leq k} (\bar{\mu}_{f_i} - \mu_{f_i}(x^*)), \tag{4.42}$$

$$\rho \sum_{i=1}^{k} (\bar{\mu}_{f_i} - \mu_{f_i}(\bar{x})) < \rho \sum_{i=1}^{k} (\bar{\mu}_{f_i} - \mu_{f_i}(x^*)). \tag{4.43}$$

This means that

$$\max_{1 \leq i \leq k} (\bar{\mu}_{f_i} - \mu_{f_i}(\bar{x})) + \rho \sum_{i=1}^{k} (\bar{\mu}_{f_i} - \mu_{f_i}(\bar{x}))$$

$$< \max_{1 \leq i \leq k} (\bar{\mu}_{f_i} - \mu_{f_i}(x^*)) + \rho \sum_{i=1}^{k} (\bar{\mu}_{f_i} - \mu_{f_i}(x^*)), \tag{4.44}$$

which contradicts the fact that $x^*$ is a (local) optimal solution to the augmented minimax problem. Hence $x^*$ is a (local) Pareto optimal solution to MOP.

**Theorem 4.17.**

If $x^*$ is a (local) Pareto optimal solution to MOP (4.14) with $0 < \mu_{f_i}(x^*) < 1$ holding for all $i$, then there exists a $\bar{\mu}_f$ such that $x^*$ is a (local) optimal solution to the augmented minimax problem (4.39).

**Proof.**

Assume that $x^*$ is not a (local) optimal solution to the augmented minimax problem for any $\bar{\mu}_f$ satisfying

$$\bar{\mu}_{f_1} - \mu_{f_1}(x^*) = \cdots = \bar{\mu}_{f_m} - \mu_{f_m}(x^*). \tag{4.45}$$

Then there exists $x \in X(N(x^*, \delta))$ such that

$$\max_{1 \leqslant i \leqslant m} (\bar{\mu}_{f_i} - \mu_{f_i}(x^*)) + \rho \sum_{i=1}^{m} (\bar{\mu}_{f_i} - \mu_{f_i}(x^*)) \tag{4.46}$$

$$> \max_{1 \leqslant i \leqslant m} (\bar{\mu}_{f_i} - \mu_{f_i}(x)) + \rho \sum_{i=1}^{m} (\bar{\mu}_{f_i}(x^*) - \mu_{f_i}(x)).$$

This implies that

$$\max_{1 \leqslant i \leqslant m} (\mu_{f_i}(x^*) - \mu_{f_i}(x)) + \rho \sum_{i=1}^{m} (\mu_{f_i}(x^*) - \mu_{f_i}(x)) < 0. \tag{4.47}$$

Now if either any $\mu_{f_i}(x^*) - \mu_{f_i}(x)$ is positive or all $\mu_{f_i}(x^*) - \mu_{f_i}(x)$, $i=1,\ldots,m$, are zero, this inequality would be violated for sufficiently small positive $\rho$. Hence

$$\mu_{f_i}(x^*) - \mu_{f_i}(x) \leqslant 0, \quad i = 1,\ldots,m \tag{4.48}$$

must hold. Since by the assumption $0 < \mu_f(x^*) < 1$, we have $f(x^*) \geqslant f(x)$, which contradicts the fact that $x^*$ is a (local) Pareto optimal solution to MOP and the theorem is proved.

Using the concept of (local) M-Pareto optimality, the following (local) M-Pareto version of Theorems 4.16 and 4.17 can also be obtained.

**Theorem 4.18.**

$x^*$ is a (local) M-Pareto optimal solution to GMOP (4.15), if and only if there exists a $\bar{\mu}_f$ such that $x^*$ is a (local) optimal solution to the augmented minimax problem.

The proof of this theorem follows in the same way as the Theorems 4.16 and 4.17.

As can be seen from the above proofs, it must be observed here that an obvious advantage of the augmented minimax problem over the standard minimax problem is that, because of the presence of the augmented terms, Pareto optimality is guaranteed without the uniqueness assumption for the solution.

Now it is significant to compare the augmented minimax problem (4.41) with the standard minimax problem, which is the special case of the augmented minimax problem (4.41) when $\rho = 0$.

Added insight can be obtained by comparing the isoquant of the augmented minimax program

$$\bar{\mu}_{f_i} - \mu_{f_i}(x) + \rho \sum_{i=1}^{m} (\bar{\mu}_{f_i} - \mu_{f_i}(x)) = \text{constant}, \quad i = 1,\ldots,m, \tag{4.49}$$

with the isoquant of the minimax problem

$$\bar{\mu}_{f_i} - \mu_{f_i}(x) = \text{constant}, \quad i = 1,\ldots,m \tag{4.50}$$

in the membership function space as depicted in Figure 4.3. Observing that, in Figure 4.3, the normal vectors of the isoquant of the augmented minimax problem and the minimax problem become $(-\rho,\ldots, -\rho, -1-\rho, -\rho,\ldots, -\rho)$ and $(0,\ldots,0, -1-\rho, 0,\ldots,0)$ respectively, it easily follows that the cosine of the angle $\theta$ between these two normal vectors is given by

$$\cos\theta = (1 + \rho) / \sqrt{1 + 2\rho + m\rho^2}. \tag{4.51}$$

Hence we have

$$\theta = \tan^{-1}(\sqrt{m-1}\ \rho/(1+\rho)). \tag{4.52}$$

This relation shows that $\theta$ is monotonically increasing with respect to $\rho$. Thus, for a sufficiently small positive scalar, the augmented minimax problems overcome the possibility to generate weak Pareto optimal solutions as was shown in Theorems 4.16, 4.17 and 4.18. Hence augmented minimax problems are

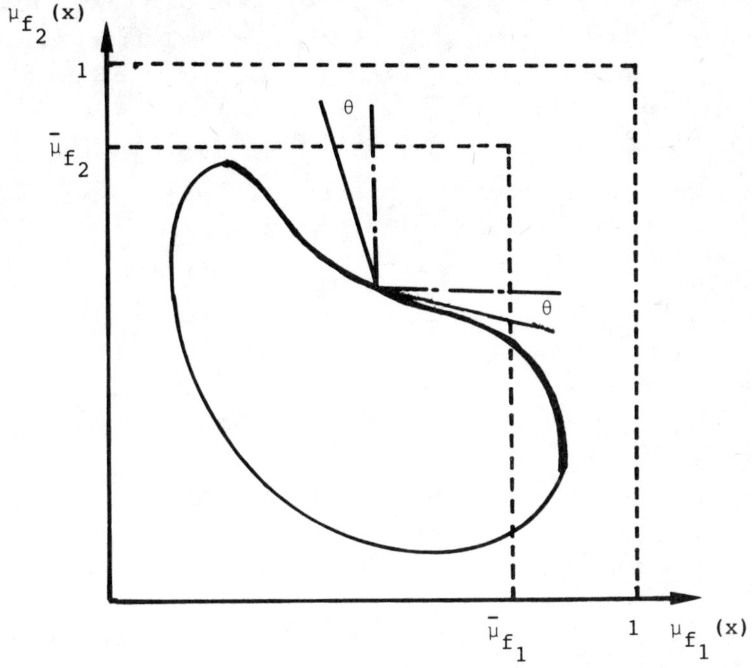


**Figure 4.3 Isoquants of the minimax problem and the augmented minimax problem.**

attractive for generating Pareto optimal solutions even if appropriate convexity assumptions are absent.

Naturally, $\rho$ should be a sufficiently small, but computationally significant, positive scalar. For practical purposes, however, a computationally significant lower bound of $\rho$ may be

$$\rho = 10^{-(a-b)}$$

where a is the number of figures indicating the degree of precision of the ,computer and b is the number of figures in each membership value for which DM can discriminate. In most cases, a computationally significant value of $\rho = 10^{-3} \sim 10^{-5}$ should suffice.

Now given the (local) (M-) Pareto optimal solution for the reference membership levels specified by DM by solving the corresponding augmented minimax problem, DM must either be satisfied with the current (local) (M-) Pareto optimal solution, or act on this solution by updating his reference membership levels. In order to help DM express his degree of preference, as discussed in the previous two subsections, trade-off information between a standing membership function $\mu_{f_1}(x)$ and each of the other membership functions is very useful. Again, due to the recent results of Yano and Sakawa (1985), such a trade-off between $\mu_{f_1}(x)$ and $\mu_{f_i}(x)$ for each $i = 2,...,m$ is easily obtainable since it is related to the strict positive Lagrange multipliers of the augmented minimax problem (4.40).

Let the Lagrange multipliers associated with the constraints of the augmented minimax problem (4.40) be denoted by $\lambda_i$, $i=1,...,m$. If all $\lambda_i > 0$ for each $i$, then similar to the minimax problems the following expression holds.

$$-\partial\mu_{f_i}(x)/\partial\mu_{f_1}(x) = (\lambda_1 + \rho)/(\lambda_i + \rho) \quad i = 2,...,m. \tag{4.54}$$

It should be pointed out here that in order to obtain the trade-off rate information from (4.54), all the constraints of the augmented minimax problem (4.40) must be active. Therefore, if there are inactive constraints, it is necessary to replace $\bar{\mu}_{f_i}$ for inactive constraints by $\mu_{f_i}(x^*)$ and solve the corresponding augmented minimax problem (4.40) for obtaining the Lagrange multipliers.

From the above discussions, we can now construct the interactive algorithm in order to derive the (local) satisficing solution for DM from among the (local) (M-) Pareto optimal solution set. The steps marked with an asterisk involve interaction with DM.

Step 0 (Individual minimum and maximum).

Calculate the individual minimum $f_{*i}$ and maximum $f_i^*$ of each objective function $f_i(x)$ under the given constraints.

Step 1* (Membership functions).

Elicit a membership function $\mu_{f_i}(x)$ from DM for each of the objective functions.

Step 2 (Initialization).

Set the initial reference membership levels $\bar{\mu}_{f_i}^{(1)} = 1$, $i = 1,\ldots,m$ and set the iteration index $r = 1$.

Step 3 ((M-) Pareto optimal solution).

Set $\bar{\mu}_{f_i} = \bar{\mu}_{f_i}^{(r)}$, solve the corresponding augmented minimax problem (4.40) to obtain the (local) (M-) Pareto optimal solution $x^{(r)}$, $f(x^{(r)})$ and the membership function value $\mu_f(x^{(r)})$ together with the trade-off rate information between the membership functions.

Step 4* (Termination or New reference membership values).

If DM is satisfied with the current levels of $\mu_{f_i}(x^{(r)})$, $i = 1,\ldots,m$ of the (local) (M-) Pareto optimal solution, stop. Then the current (local) (M-) Pareto optimal solution $f(x^{(r)}) = (f_1(x^{(r)}),\ldots, f_m(x^{(r)}))$ is the (local) satisficing solution of DM. Otherwise, ask DM to update the current reference membership levels $\bar{\mu}_{f_1}^{(r)},\ldots, \bar{\mu}_{f_m}^{(r)}$ to the new reference membership levels $\bar{r}_{f_1}^{(r+1)},\ldots, \bar{\mu}_{f_m}^{(r+1)}$ by considering the current levels of the membership functions together with the trade-off rates between the membership functions. Set $r = r + 1$ and return to Step 3. Here it should be stressed for DM that any improvement of one membership function can be achieved only at the expense of at least one of the other membership functions.

Finally, it should be noted that DM often can not specify his reference membership levels in an exact way. In such a situation, instead of trying to obtain point-valued estimates of the reference membership levels from DM, it may be more appropriate to obtain fuzzy-valued assessments of the reference membership levels such as "it should be between $\underline{\mu}_{f_i}$ and $\bar{\mu}_{f_i}$ for $f_i(x)$". Details of appropriate modifications of the above algorithm using such fuzzy-valued assessments can be found in Sakawa and Yano (1985a). Additional extensions of the above algorithm to general multiobjective optimization problems involving fuzzy parameters characterized by fuzzy numbers (Orlovski 1983a,b) which would be viewed as the more realistic version of the conventional multiobjective optimization problems can be found in Sakawa and Yan (1986b,c).

## 4.4 Interactive Computer Program

### 4.4.1 Computer Package

Interactive fuzzy decision making processes for multiobjective optimization problems include eliciting a membership function for each of the objective functions and reference membership levels from DM. Thus, mitigation and speed-up of computation works are indispensable to this approach, and interactive utilization of computer facilities is highly recommended. Based on the method described above, we have developed new interactive computer programs. Our new package includes graphical representations by which DM can visualize the shapes of his membership functions, and he can find incorrect assessments or inconsistent evaluations promptly, revise them immediately and proceed to the next stage more easily.

Our computer software package is composed of one main program and several subroutines. The main program calls in and runs the subprograms with commands indicated by the user (DM). Here we give a brief explanation of the major commands prepared in our computer software package.

(1) MINIMAX: Displays the calculated individual minimum and maximum of each of the objective functions under the given constraints.

(2) MF: Elicits a membership function from DM for each of the objective functions.

(3) GRAPH: Depicts graphically the shape of the membership function for each of the objective functions.

(4) GO: Derives the (local) satisficing solution for DM from among the (local) (M-) Pareto optimal solution set by adopting one of the interactive fuzzy multiobjective programming methods discussed in the previous section.

(5) STOP: Exists from the program.

In our computer software package, (local)(M-) Pareto optimal solutions are obtained by solving one of the scalarizing problems in the membership function spaces using the revised version of the generalized reduced gradient (GRG) program (Lasdon and co-workers, 1974, 1976) called GRG2 (Lasdon and co-workers, 1980). In GRG2 there are two optimality tests, i.e.,

(1) to satisfy the Kuhn-Tucker optimality conditions, and

(2) to satisfy the fractional change condition

$$|FM - OBJTST| < EPSTOP \times |OBJTST|$$

for NSTOP times consecutive iterations. FM is the current objective value and OBJTST is the objective value at the start of the previous one dimensional search. NSTOP has a default value of 3.

In our computer software package, DM can select his membership function in a subjective manner from by considering the rate of increase of membership satisfaction among the following five types of functions; linear, exponential, hyperbolic, hyperbolic inverse and piecewise linear functions. Then the parameter values are determined through the interaction with DM. Here, it is convenient to explain the maximization case. Then except for the hyperbolic functions, it is assumed that $\mu_{f_i}(x) = 0$ if $f_i(x) \leqslant f_i^0$ and $\mu_{f_i}(x) = 1$ if $f_i(x) \geqslant f_i^1$, where $f_i^0$ is an unacceptable level for $f_i(x)$ and $f_i^1$ is a completely desirable level for $f_i(x)$.

(1) Linear membership function

For each objective function, the corresponding linear membership function is defined as follows:

$$\mu_{f_i}(x) = [f_i(x) - f_i^0]/[f_i^1 - f_i^0]. \tag{4.55}$$

The linear membership function can be determined by asking DM to specify the two points, $f_i^0$ and $f_i^1$, within $f_i^{max}$ and $f_i^{min}$. Figure 4.4 illustrates the graph of the linear membership function.

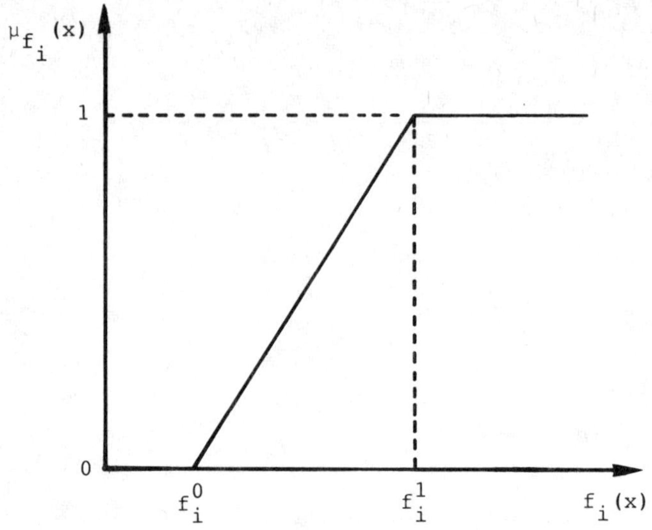


**Figure 4.4 Linear membership function.**

(2) Exponential membership function

For each objective function, the corresponding exponential membership function is defined by:

$$\mu_{f_i}(x) = a_i[1 - \exp\{- \alpha_i(f_i(x) - f_i^0)/(f_i^1 - f_i^0)\}], \quad (4.56)$$

where $a_i > 1$, $\alpha_i > 0$ or $a_i < 0$, $\alpha_i < 0$.
The exponential membership function can be determined by asking DM to specify the three points, $f_i^0$, $f_i^{0.5}$ and $f_i^1$, within $f_i^{max}$ and $f_i^{min}$, where $\alpha_i$ is a shape parameter, and $f_i^a$ represents the value of $f_i(x)$ such that the degree of the membership function $\mu_{f_i}(x)$ is a. Figure 4.5 illustrates the graph of the exponential membership function.

(3) Hyperbolic membership function

For each objective function, the corresponding hyperbolic membership function is defined by:

$$\mu_{f_i}(x) = (1/2)\tanh(\alpha_i(f_i(x) - b_i)) + (1/2), \quad (4.57)$$

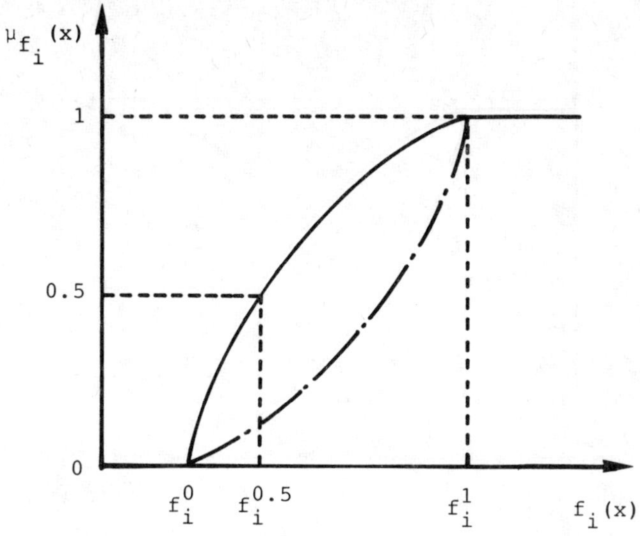


**Figure 4.5 Exponential membership function.**

where $\alpha_i > 0$ or $\alpha_i < 0$.
The hyperbolic membership function can be determined by asking DM to specify the two points, $f_i^{0.25}$ and $f_i^{0.5}$, within $f_i^{max}$ and $f_i^{min}$, where $\alpha_i$ is a shape parameter and $b_i$ is associated with the point of inflection. Figure 4.6 illustrates the graph of the hyperbolic membership function.

(4) Hyperbolic inverse membership function

For each objective function, the corresponding hyperbolic inverse membership function is defined by:

$$\mu_{f_i}(x) = a_i \tanh^{-1}(\alpha_i(f_i(x) - b_i)) + (1/2), \tag{4.58}$$

where $a_i > 0$, $\alpha_i > 0$ or $\alpha_i < 0$.
The hyperbolic inverse membership function can be determined by asking DM to specify the three points, $f_i^0$, $f_i^{0.25}$ and $f_i^{0.5}$, within $f_i^{max}$ and $f_i^{min}$, where $\alpha_i$ is a shape parameter and $b_i$ is associated with the point of inflection. Figure 4.7 illustrates the graph of the hyperbolic inverse membership function.

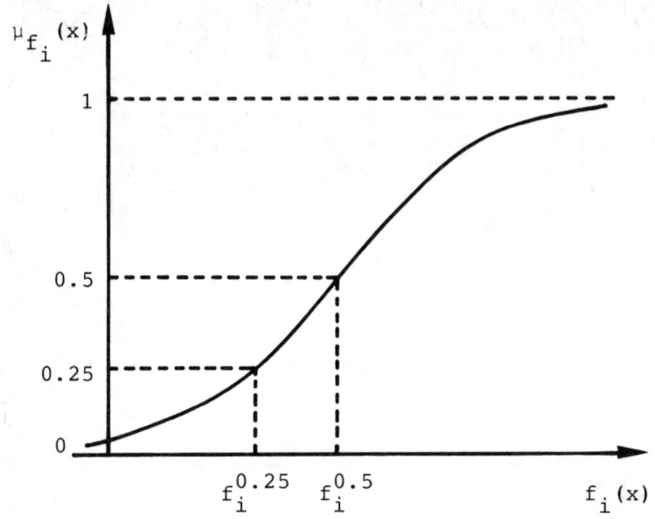


**Figure 4.6 Hyperbolic membership function.**

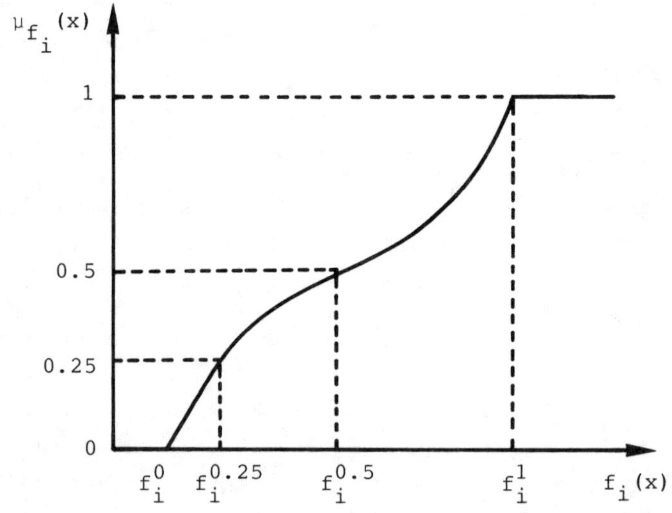


**Figure 4.7 Hyperbolic inverse membership function.**

(5) Piecewise linear membership function

For each objective function, the corresponding piecewise linear membership function is defined by:

$$\mu_{f_i}(x) = \sum_{j=1}^{N_i} \alpha_{ij} |f_i(x) - g_{ij}| + \beta_i f_i(x) + \gamma_i \tag{4.59}$$

where

$$\alpha_{ij} = (t_{i,j+1} - t_{ij})/2, \quad \beta_i = (t_{i,N_i+1} + t_{i1})/2,$$

$$\gamma_i = (s_{i,N_i+1} + s_{i1})/2. \tag{4.60}$$

That is to say, it is assumed that $\mu_{f_i}(x) = t_{ir} f_i(x) + s_{ir}$ for each segment $g_{ir-1} \leq f_i(x) \leq g_{ir}$, where $t_{ir}$ is the slope and $s_{ir}$ is the y-intercept for the section of the curve initiated at $g_{ir-1}$ and terminated at $g_{ir}$. The piecewise linear membership function can be determined by asking DM to specify the degree of membership in each of several values of objective functions within $f_i^*$ and $f_{*i}$. Figure 4.8

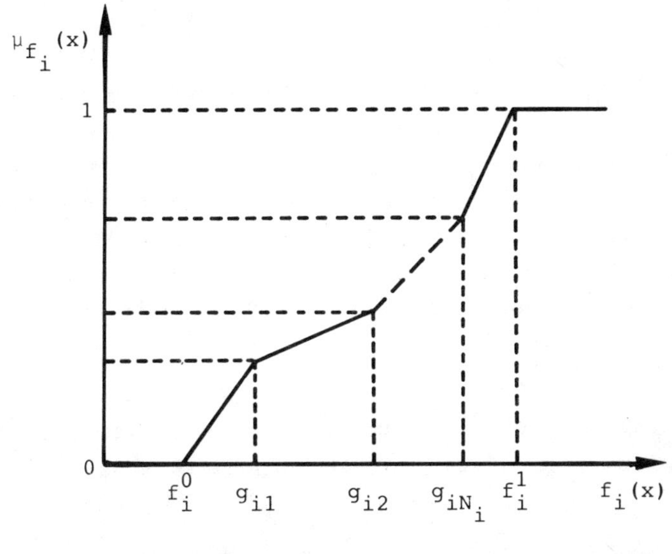


**Figure 4.8 Piecewise linear membership function.**

illustrates the graph of the piecewise linear membership function.

It should be noted here that for the fuzzy equal membership functions, DM can select his left and right functions from among the same types of membership functions previously described above (excluding the hyperbolic ones).

### 4.4.2 Illustrative Example

We now demonstrate the interaction processes using our computer program by means of an illustrative example which is designed to test the program.

Consider the following three objective decision making problem.

$$
\begin{aligned}
&\text{fuzzy max} && f_1(x) = 2x_1^2 + 4(x_2-20)^2 + 3(x_3-15)^2 \\
&\text{fuzzy min} && f_2(x) = (x_1+10)^2 + 2(x_2-25)^2 + 3(x_3+5)^2 \\
&\text{fuzzy equal} && f_3(x) = 3(x_1+15)^2 + 2(x_2+10)^2 + (x_3+20)^2 \\
&\text{subject to} && x \in X \triangleq \{(x_1, x_2, x_3) \mid \\
& && \quad (x_1+5)^2 + (x_2+8)^2 + (x_3-10)^2 \leq 200, \\
& && \quad 0 \leq x_i \leq 10,\ i=1,2,3\}
\end{aligned}
\tag{4.61}
$$

In the following illustrations, some of the interaction processes using our computer software package based on the augmented minimax problems under TSS of the ACOS-1000 digital computer in the computer center of Kobe University in Japan are explained through the aid of some of the computer outputs.

**Illustration 4.3.1.**

Using the MINIMAX command, the calculated individual minimum and maximum of each of the objective functions $f_1(x)$, $f_2(x)$ and $f_3(x)$, are displayed.

**Illustration 4.3.1.**

```
COMMAND:
=MINMAX

          INDIVIDUAL MINIMUM AND MAXIMUM

          I          MINIMUM          I          MAXIMUM
----------+-----------------------+-----------------------
  F( 1)   I          947.7585     I          2277.0000
  F( 2)   I         1239.1967     I          2202.6190
  F( 3)   I         1275.0000     I          2507.7144
```

**Illustration 4.3.2.**

```
COMMAND:
=MF
INPUT THE OBJECTIVE FUNCTION NUMBER:
=1
INPUT FUZZY GOAL:
   (1) FUZZY MAX
   (2) FUZZY MIN
   (3) FUZZY EQUAL
=1
DO YOU WANT LIST OF MEMBERSHIP FUNCTION TYPE ?
=YES
LIST OF MEMBERSHIP FUNCTION TYPE
 (1) LINEAR
 (2) EXPONENTIAL
 (3) HYPERBOLIC
 (4) HYPERBOLIC INVERSE
 (5) PIECEWISE LINEAR
INPUT MEMBERSHIP FUNCTION TYPE:
=2
INPUT THREE POINTS(F1,F2,F3) SUCH THAT
          M(F1)=0.0
          M(F2)=0.5
          M(F3)=1.0
=950 1800 2200
ANOTHER MSET ?
=YES
```

..........................................

**Illustration 4.3.2.**

The MF command is utilized to determine the membership functions for each of the objective functions $f_1(x)$, $f_2(x)$ and $f_3(x)$, sequentially. Here interaction with the hypothetical DM establishes the following membership functions and corresponding assessment values.

$f_1(x)$: exponential, $(f_1^0, f_1^{0.5}, f_1^1) = (950, 1800, 2200)$,

$f_2(x)$: hyperbolic, $(f_2^{0.25}, f_2^{0.5}) = (1900, 1750)$,

$f_3(x)$

$$\begin{cases} \text{left: exponential, } (f_3^0, f_3^{0.5}, f_3^1) \\ \qquad\qquad = (1300, 1700, 1900). \\ \text{right: linear, } (f_3^0, f_3^1) = (2500, 1900). \end{cases}$$

For each type of membership function, corresponding assessment values are input in a subjective manner by considering the calculated individual minimum and maximum of each of the objective functions.

**Illustration 4.3.3.**

The shape of the fuzzy equal membership function for $f_3(x)$ is shown graphically with the GRAPH command. Thus DM can check the properties of his membership functions visually.

**Illustration 4.3.3.**

```
COMMAND:
=GRAPH
INPUT THE MEMBERSHIP FUNCTION NUMBER:
=3
GRAPH OF THE MEMBERSHIP FUNCTION ( NO. 3)
    LEFT  TYPE --- EXPONENTIAL
    RIGHT TYPE --- LINEAR
```

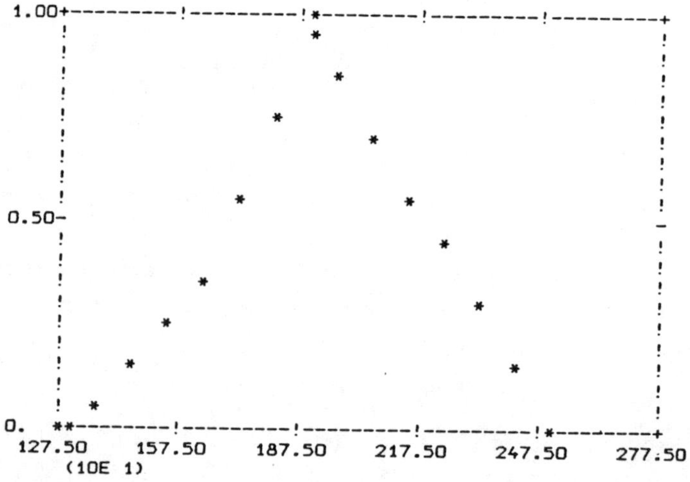

**Illustration 4.3.4.**

Using the GO command, the augmented minimax problem is solved for the initial reference membership levels and DM is supplied with the corresponding (local) (M-) Pareto optimal solution and the trade-off rates between the membership functions. Since DM is not satisfied with the current membership values, DM updates his reference membership levels.

**Illustration 4.3.4.**

```
COMMAND:
=GO

INPUT SUFFICIENTLY SMALL POSITIVE SCALAR FOR AUGMENTED TERM:
=0.001

--------------------< ITERATION 1 >--------------------

INITIATES AN INTERACTION WITH ALL THE INITIAL REFERENCE
MEMBERSHIP VALUES ARE 1

( KUHN-TUCKER CONDITIONS SATISFIED )

M-PARETO OPTIMAL SOLUTION TO THE AUGMENTED MINIMAX PROBLEM
FOR INITIAL REFERENCE MEMBERSHIP VALUES
-------------------------------------------------------
         MEMBERSHIP           I     OBJECTIVE FUNCTION
------------------------------+------------------------
   M(F1) =             0.7503 I  F(1) =       2025.2618
   M(F2) =             0.7503 I  F(2) =       1599.7956
   M(F3) =             0.7503 I  F(3) =       1812.0261
-------------------------------------------------------
   X( 1) =             3.9487    X( 2) =         0.3028
   X( 3) =             2.8597
-------------------------------------------------------

-------------------------------------------------------
TRADE-OFFS AMONG MEMBERSHIP FUNCTIONS
 -DM(F2)/DM(F1) =              0.4927
 -DM(F3)/DM(F1) =              1.2866
-------------------------------------------------------

ARE YOU SATISFIED WITH THE CURRENT MEMBERSHIP VALUES OF
THE PARETO OPTIMAL SOLUTION ?
=NO

--------------------< ITERATION 2 >--------------------

CONSIDER THE CURRENT MEMBERSHIP VALUES OF
THE PARETO OPTIMAL SOLUTION TOGETHER WITH
THE TRADE-OFFS AMONG THE MEMBERSHIP FUNCTIONS.
THEN INPUT YOUR REFERENCE MEMBERSHIP VALUES
FOR EACH OF THE MEMBERSHIP FUNCTIONS:
=0.8 0.7 0.9
```

.....................................

**Illustration 4.3.4 (continued).**

```
ARE YOU SATISFIED WITH THE CURRENT MEMBERSHIP VALUES OF
THE PARETO OPTIMAL SOLUTION ?
=YES

THE FOLLOWING VALUES ARE YOUR SATISFICING SOLUTION :

----------------------------------------------------------
          MEMBERSHIP             I      OBJECTIVE FUNCTION
---------------------------------+------------------------
   M(F1) =              0.8002   I  F(1) =        2063.4139
   M(F2) =              0.6802   I  F(2) =        1646.9619
   M(F3) =              0.8602   I  F(3) =        1853.0568
----------------------------------------------------------
   X( 1) =              4.3348     X( 2) =           0.0225
   X( 3) =              3.0358
----------------------------------------------------------

COMMAND:
=STOP


*** [ CPU-TIME =  0.244 SEC. ] ***
```

The same procedure continues in this manner, until DM is satisfied with the current values of the membership functions. In this example, at the fifth iteration, the (local) satisficing solution of DM is obtained.

An application to a case study in regional planning can be found in Sakawa and Yano (1985b).

# CHAPTER 5
# THE PREFERENCE STRUCTURE OF DECISION MAKING

## 5.1 Hypothesis of Rational Human Behavior

### 5.1.1 Introduction

This chapter concerns the preference structure of the decision maker (DM) in multiple criteria decision making (MCDM). As discussed in Chapter 1, MCDM has two phases, analytical and judgmental. This chapter treats the judgmental phase of MCDM.

As stated in Chapter 2, to solve the multiple criteria decision problem (MDP) is to find the preferred solution using a valuation function $V(f)$ that is defined on a set of objective functions $f$. For this purpose, a method for direct identification of the valuation function, or alternative devices to it, should be presented. In the preceding chapters, as the alternative devices to the direct identification of the valuation function which is usually unknown, the methods for assessing the marginal rates of substitution (trade-off rates) among the objective functions have been discussed. These methods presume that all objective functions can be analytically identified for mathematical optimization; it is not necessarily possible for the real-world problems.

In this chapter, fundamentals of the direct identification methods for the valuation function are discussed. These methods generally do not need to identify objective functions in analytical forms. In addition, the valuation function is still presumed to be unknown beforehand. Thus its construction should be carried out via heuristic identification procedures. There is a theoretical point to be discussed in constructing the heuristic identification procedures if the valuation function is treated as the preference function of DM. For identifying the preference function of DM, rationality of human behavior should be presumed. In other words, decision making should be performed in accordance with normative axioms for holding consistency among decisions. This chapter concerns theoretical backgrounds of the direct assessment methods for constructing the preference function of DM.

The multiple criteria decision problem (MDP) is described in the following form,

MDP

$$\underset{x \in X}{\text{maximize}} \quad V(f_1(x), f_2(x), \ldots, f_m(x)), \tag{5.1}$$

where $X$ is a set of the feasible decision variables in $R^n$. The function $V : R^m \to R^1$, is a scalarized valuation function defined on the $m$ objective functions $f_i(x) : R^n \to R^1$, $i = 1, \ldots, m$, for $x \in X$.

In the preceding chapters, the valuation function $V$ has been treated hypothetically as being differentiable, often concave on the convex set $X$, and nondecreasing. The valuation function $V$ in MDP (5.1) can be regarded as the preference function of DM if, in identifying the valuation function $V$ directly, the peculiarity of the valuation function as the preference function can be preserved. Only with this consideration can the valuation function $V$ be interpreted and used as the preference ("utility") function which embodies a numerical representation of the preference structure of DM. The theoretical inquiry on the preference structure is based on behavioral presumption of DM as the rational person. This section concerns the axioms that reveal rationality of human behavior.

The core of multiple criteria decision analysis (MCDA) is to recognize that it is a person that solves the decision problems. A person makes a decision according to its own preference, chooses its action, and assesses the occurrence of events as the results of the action; this process constructs repetitive cycles of actions, which form a learning process of human behavior. Assume that DM as a deliberate and wise person makes its decisions. Before an action, preference is assessed comparably for its wants or expectations, and excites its motivation, and after the action, preference is once more assessed for the results of the action. Between the wants or expectations at the outset of the behavioral cycle and the results at the end, a choice for an action and its realization are included (Figure 5.1, Table 5.1). The problem here is how DM can discretionally control the behavioral cycles according to human preferences in a consistent way; it is a management problem for the human behavior. For effective operation of the behavioral cycles, there should be a consistency of preference relations in the initialization of the cycle and in the evaluation for the results at the end. In other words, the preference structure of DM should be revealed with a consistency during every stage of the behavioral cycles. In order to

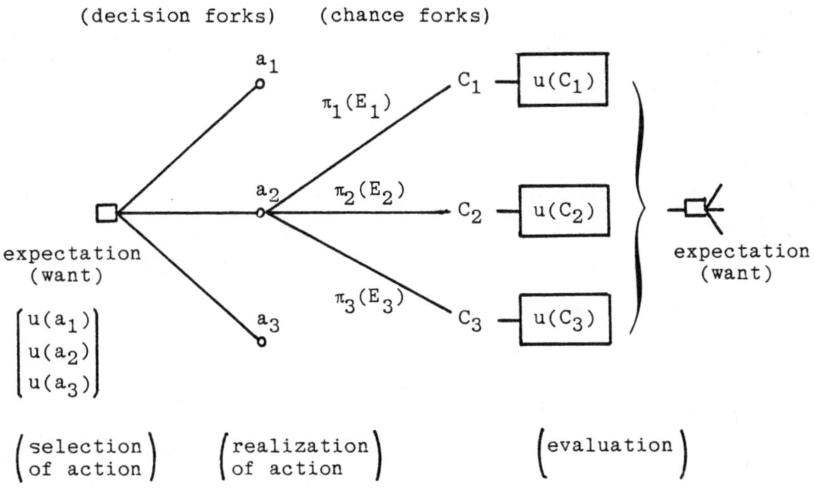


Note:

$a_1$, $a_2$, $a_3$: action $C_1$, $C_2$, $C_3$: consequence (outcome)

$E_1$, $E_2$, $E_3$: event (state) $u(\cdot)$: utility function

$\pi_1$, $\pi_2$, $\pi_3$: probability

**Figure 5.1 Administrative process of human behavior.**

**Table 5.1 Alternative action and its expected utility value (EUV)**

| Action | Event $E_1 \ldots E_j \ldots E_q$ | EUV |
|---|---|---|
| $a_1$ | $C_{11} \ldots C_{1j} \ldots C_{1q}$ | $\sum_{j=1}^{q} \pi_j u_1(C_{1j})$ |
| $a_2$ | $C_{21} \ldots C_{2j} \ldots C_{2q}$ | $\sum_{j=1}^{q} \pi_j u_2(C_{2j})$ |
| $\vdots$ | $\vdots \quad \vdots \quad \vdots$ | $\vdots$ |
| $a_m$ | $C_{m1} \ldots C_{mj} \ldots C_{mq}$ | $\sum_{j=1}^{q} \pi_j u_m(C_{mj})$ |
| Probability | | $\pi_j > 0$ |
| $\pi$ | $\pi_1 \ldots \pi_j \ldots \pi_q$ | $\sum_{j=1}^{q} \pi_j = 1$ |

accomplish this, axioms for the preference structure of DM as the "enlightened person" should be established and verified in decision processes. When human behavior is in accordance with the axioms, it is said to be rational. The axioms for rational human behavior provide general ground rules by which the preference structure of DM can be properly revealed.

The preference structure of DM is usually more complicate because it is constructed under uncertain situations. First, the choice of an action is under uncertainty due to the incompleteness and diversification of knowledge and information. Thus the choice of the best alternative is under uncertainty even though it can be made as if by reasoned judgment. Second, the events which occur as the results of the selected action are usually probabilistic phenomena in an uncertain environment. Thus, in many cases, the decisions are made under uncertainty and decision variables should be treated as uncertain quantities. The subjective probability, or alternative indices to it, should be assessed for both cases, because the probability usually cannot be found by repeated experiments like throwing regular dice.

In the following, axioms for the rational human behavior under uncertainty are examined. The occurrence of events as an outcome of the selected action is not necessarily considered to be results of the optimization, and it also embodies contingent disturbance that occurs externally to the decision processes.

### 5.1.2 Axioms for Rational Human Behavior

Let us define first the concepts of preference set and preference relation to consider the axioms for the rationality of human behavior.

The preference set is defined by a set $\chi$ whose elements are consequences of an action and objects of preference of DM. The $\chi$ is assumed to be an uncountable set, which means that it is neither finite nor denumerable; a set is said to be denumerable when its elements can be placed in one-to-one correspondence with the elements in the set of positive integers (1,2,3,...). Consider a binary relation between elements $x_i$ and $x_j$, $i = 1,...,m$, of $\chi$. The binary relation $x_i \succ x_j$ represents that $x_i$ is preferred to $x_j$, and $x_i \sim x_j$ represents that $x_i$ is indifferent to $x_j$. The binary relation among elements of the preference set $x_i \in \chi$, $i = 1,...,m$, defined with $\succ$ and/or $\sim$ is called the preference relation.

As decision analysis under uncertainty, this chapter concerns conjoint measurement of the preference relation revealed in the binary relation with probability. Extensions of the conjoint measurement to preference relation with the quaternary relation are discussed in Chapter 8.

The preference set $\chi$ is defined as the set among whose elements $x_i$, $i = 1,...,m$, the preference relations can be constructed. When preference is ordered with the preference relations ($\succ$, $\sim$), it is called preference order. In other words, the preference order is an ordered pair defined on preference relations.

The axioms for rationality of human behavior are described as follows.

(i) Coherence. There is no contradiction in the preference

ordering of DM. Coherence is generally represented in the weak ordering of the preference relations (See Section 5.2.1).

(ii) Local Nonsaturation. Increase of a quantity of an element $x_i$ of the preference set locally raises the preference order for it; i.e., when $|x_i' - x_i''| < \delta$ for a small number $\delta > 0$,

$$x_i' > x_i'' \Leftrightarrow x_i' \succ x_i'', \quad \text{for all } x_i \in \chi. \tag{5.2}$$

(iii) Inadmissibility of Dominated Actions (Pareto optimality). Let us define the domination set, for all $x_i$, $x_j \in \chi$,

$$D \triangleq \{x_i | x_i \succ x_j,\ j = 1,\ldots,m,\ i \neq j\}. \tag{5.3}$$

A decision for finding a preferred policy program $x_j^*$ is carried out in such a way that the occurrence of any other consequence $x_i$ as an element of the domination set D cannot be permitted.

(iv) Independence of Irrelevant Alternatives. The events which are not affected by the choice of an action can be excluded from the decision for the preference ordering. As a result, a consequence unaffected by the choice of an action can be substituted by another consequence having the same property.

(v) Independence Rule for Probability. The probability of an event occurring as a result of an action is imputed to only the event itself, independently of evaluation for the event.

(vi) Compactness. The preference ordering for the elements of the preference set is compact; i.e., when $x_i \succsim x_j$ for any $x_i$, $x_j \in \chi$, $i \neq j$, there exists $x_s \in \chi$, $s \neq i,j$, such that $x_i \succsim x_s$ and $x_s \succsim x_j$.

Note that the axioms for rational human behavior are normative assertion. The axioms are not required to be obtained empirically or experimentally as a result of mass observations. The axioms (i)-(vi) assert that human actions are rational, if and only if these axioms are fulfilled. Human behavior observed in the real world is at best a limitless approximation to the rationality.

In the following sections, the above axioms for rationality are assumed as the normative criteria to be fulfilled in human decision making.

## 5.2 Expected Utility Hypothesis

### 5.2.1 Preference Relation and Preference Order

Basic concepts of the preference relation and the preference order provide the fundamentals for examining the existence and properties of a number $u(x_i)$, $i = 1,\ldots,m$, combined with an element $x_i$, $i = 1,\ldots,m$, of the preference set $\chi$. (von Neumann and Morgenstern 1944; Marschak 1950; Chipman 1960; Fishburn 1970; etc.).

For the preference relations among elements $x_i$, $i = 1,\ldots,m$, of the preference set $\chi$, the following concepts are defined.

(i) Connectivity: $x_i \succsim x_j$ or $x_j \succsim x_i$ for all $x_i$, $x_j \in \chi$, which means comparability.

(ii) Weak connectivity: $x_i \succsim x_j$ or $x_j \succsim x_i$ for $x_i$, $x_j \in \chi$, $x_i \neq x_j$.

(iii) Reflexivity: $x_i \succsim x_i$ for all $x_i \in \chi$.

Clearly the connectivity includes reflexivity.

(iv) Irreflexivity: not $x_i \succsim x_i$ for all $x_i \in \chi$.

(v) Symmetry: if $x_i \succsim x_j$, then $x_j \succsim x_i$ for all $x_i$, $x_j \in \chi$.

(vi) Asymmetry: if $x_i \succsim x_j$, then not $x_j \succsim x_i$ for all $x_i$, $x_j \in \chi$.

(vii) Antisymmetry: if $x_i \succsim x_j$ and $x_j \succsim x_i$, then $x_i = x_j$ for all $x_i$, $x_j \in \chi$.

(viii) Transitivity: if $x_i \succsim x_s$ and $x_s \succsim x_j$, then $x_i \succsim x_j$ for all $x_i$, $x_s$, $x_j \in \chi$.

(ix) Negative transitivity: if not $x_i \succsim x_s$ and not $x_s \succsim x_j$, then not $x_i \succsim x_j$ for all $x_i$, $x_s$, $x_j \in \chi$. It means that if $x_i \succsim x_j$, then $x_i \succsim x_s$ or $x_s \succsim x_j$.

Note that asymmetry means irreflexivity. Conversely, if a

binary relation is irreflexive and transitive, then asymmetry holds.

Using the above concepts of the preference relation, the preference order is defined.

(i) Quasi-order (Preorder): the binary relation for elements $x_i$, $i = 1,\ldots,m$, of the preference set $\chi$ is reflexive and transitive.

(ii) Weak order: connective and transitive.

The weak order is the quasi-order with comparability and is also called total order or complete order.

(iii) Partial order: reflexive, transitive and antisymmetric.

The partial order is the quasi-order with antisymmetry. Note that the partial order does not exclude incomparability.

(iv) Linear order: connective, reflexive, transitive, and antisymmetric. It is also called simple order.

The linear order is the partial order with comparability and is also called simple order.

(v) Strict partial order: irreflexive and transitive; which is equivalent to

(vi) Strong order: transitive and asymmetry.

(vii) Semiorder (Luce 1956): the following properties hold in the binary relation for $x_i$, $x_s$, $x_r$, $x_j \in \chi$.

(a) $x_i \succ x_j$, or $x_j \succ x_i$, or $x_i \sim x_j$,

(b) $x_i \sim x_i$,

(c) If $x_i \succ x_s$, $x_s \sim x_r$, and $x_r \succ x_j$, then $x_i \succ x_j$ (semitransitive),

(d) If $x_i \succ x_s$, $x_s \succ x_r$ and $x_s \sim x_j$, then neither $x_i \sim x_j$ nor $x_r \sim x_j$ are implied.

In semiorder, transitivity for indifference relations is not implied. Thus it is semitransitive.

(viii) Equivalence: connective, transitive and symmetric.

The equivalence relation is a weak-ordered preference relation with symmetry.

The equivalence class generated by $x_s \in \chi$ is defined as

$$\mathbf{R}(x_s) \triangleq \{x_i \,|\, x_i \in \chi, \text{ and } x_i \mathbf{R}\, x_s\} \tag{5.4}$$

where **R** denotes the equivalence relation.

The binary relation with transitivity is called the order relation. All the orders (i)-(viii) define the order relation in any sense.

Consistency in preference order implies that the asymmetry holds, and coherence implies that the transitivity holds. Thus when the rationality of decision making is defined with consistency and coherence, it presumes that the strong order (or strict partial order) holds. However, asymmetry is a rigorous property of ordering, and thus is not usually fulfilled in decision processes. Instead, the weak order is adopted as a postulate for the rationality. It mitigates the requisite for rationality by only requiring the connectivity in place of the asymmetry. However, the weak order still presumes the complete transitive comparability. Relaxation of the transitivity is discussed in Chapter 8.

### 5.2.2 Existence of the Numerical Utility Function

Now we examine the existence and properties of a preference order-preserving, real-valued function $u(x_i): R^m \to R^1$, which assigns a real number corresponding to a level of an element $x_i$, $i = 1,\ldots,m$, of the preference set $\chi$. The preference order-preserving property is said, in short, to be order-preserving.

The scale of measurement is considered in two ways. One is the ordinal scale with which values of a function can be uniquely determined up to an order-preserving transformation. A real number measured on the ordinal scale is called an ordinal number. The other scale is the interval scale with which values of the function can be uniquely determined up to a positive linear transformation. In the measurement with interval scales, not only the numerical order of the values but also the numerical order of differences between the values can be preserved as well via the positive linear transformation. A real number measured on the interval scale is called a cardinal number. An origin and a unit of measurement can be chosen arbitrarily for a cardinal number, which is a numerical value

Define the set that is composed of some relations -- numerical and empirical-- as a system of relations. Consider that a system of numerical relations $\mathscr{U}$ defined on the values of the real-valued functions, $\mathbf{U} \triangleq (u_1, u_2 \ldots) \subseteq \mathscr{U}$, corresponds to a system of the empirical relations $\mathscr{R}$ that are composed of the preference relations $\mathbf{R} = (\mathbf{R}_1, R_2, \ldots) \subseteq \mathscr{R}$ defined on elements $x_i$, $i = 1, \ldots, m$, in the preference set $\chi$. If the other system of the numerical relations $\mathbf{U}'$ obtained from a transformation of $\mathbf{U}$ still corresponds to the original system of the empirical relations as $\mathbf{R}$, then the transformation is preference order-preserving and is called admissible. The numerical relations obtained from the admissible transformation are said to be formally meaningful. The numerical function $\mathbf{U}$ that is defined on the preference set and has the formally meaningful property is called the utility function.

In particular, when the utility function is measurable by the cardinal number, it is called the numerical (measurable) utility function. When the utility function is scaled with the ordinal number, it is called the ordinal utility function. For the ordinal utility function, all order-preserving transformations are admissible and the resulting ordering of preference is unvaried; the preference set that defines the utility function is treated as a countable set.

In the economic literature, the concept of the utility function has been used only in context of the theory of consumer behavior, or household under the dichotomy. In particular, since Pareto (1906) the utility function has been treated as an ordinal number. This is because the derivation of equilibrium conditions in consumer behavior only depends on identification of the ordinal utility functions.

Consider the following problem of the consumer behavior (Samuelson 1947).

$$\underset{x}{\text{maximize}} \quad u \triangleq F[\phi(x_1, x_2, \ldots, x_m] \tag{5.5}$$

$$\text{subject to} \quad \sum_{i=1}^{m} p_i x_i = Y, \tag{5.6}$$

where $x_i$, $i = 1, \ldots, m$, $x_i \in R^1$ is a quantity of a consumer good, $p_i$, $i = 1, \ldots, m$, $p_i \in R^1$ is its market price, and Y is a level of income of a consumer taken as given. $\psi$ is a "utility index" function and $u$ is an ordinal utility function transformed from $\psi$. Using the Lagrange function L, the equilibrium (stationary) condition is

$$\frac{\partial L}{\partial x_i} = \frac{\partial u}{\partial x_i} - \lambda p_i = 0, \quad i = 1, \ldots, m, \tag{5.7}$$

where $\lambda$ is a Lagrange multiplier. Taking a ratio for any $x_k$ and $x_i$, $i = 1, \ldots, m$, $i \neq k$, derives

$$\frac{\partial u}{\partial x_i} \Big/ \frac{\partial u}{\partial x_k} = \frac{\partial x_k}{\partial x_i} = \frac{p_i}{p_k}, \tag{5.8}$$

or in another expression,

$$\frac{\partial u}{\partial x_1} \Big/ p_1 = \frac{\partial u}{\partial x_2} \Big/ p_2 = \ldots = \frac{\partial u}{\partial x_m} \Big/ p_m = \lambda. \tag{5.9}$$

(5.8) and (5.9) show that, in equilibrium, the marginal rate of substitution of $x_i$ and $x_k$, or a ratio of their marginal utility, is equal to the ratio of their prices $p_i$ and $p_k$, conversely or not. In other words, the marginal utility of a commodity is in proportion to its price. It means that, in equilibrium, the marginal utility in terms of the money expended on the commodity, or the marginal utility of money, should be equal to each other. Moreover,

$$\frac{\partial u}{\partial x_i} \Big/ \frac{\partial u}{\partial x_k} = \frac{\partial F}{\partial \psi}\frac{\partial \psi}{\partial x_i} \Big/ \frac{\partial F}{\partial \psi}\frac{\partial \psi}{\partial x_k} = \frac{\partial \psi}{\partial x_i} \Big/ \frac{\partial \psi}{\partial x_k} = \frac{\partial x_k}{\partial x_i}, \quad \frac{\partial F}{\partial \psi} > 0. \tag{5.10}$$

(5.10) shows that the equilibrium condition (5.8) does not depend on selection of the "utility index" (measurable utility) function $\psi$ but only on the ordinal utility function $u$ which can be examined only on the indifference curves in the commodity space. Note that, in the equilibrium condition (5.7), only one part of the Kuhn-Tucker conditions is considered. In (5.9), the Lagrange multiplier $\lambda$ simply appears as a latent mediator and thus its particular function and implication in the optimization are not regarded.

Thus measurement of the utility function on the cardinal scale has been regarded as "unnecessary." Due to similar discussions, it has been maintained in welfare economics that the concept of the social welfare function $\mathbf{W} \triangleq F(u_1, u_2, \ldots)$, where $u_i \triangleq u(x_i)$, can be derived independently of identification of the cardinal utility functions. In other words, it has been asserted that optimality of decision making remains unvaried under the various forms of the utility functions; that is, an unlimited number of "equally good" utility index functions $u_i$ can exist for constructing the social welfare function $\mathbf{W}$, which are equally capable of deriving the optimality conditions for $\mathbf{W}$.

In MCDM where we are concerned with deriving the preferred policy programs, obtaining the equilibrium conditions cannot be the ultimate aim of DM. First, deriving the noninferior solutions is performed only as the first step, and even for this step the equilibrium condition (5.7) can provide only one part of the necessary conditions for optimality. Generation of the noninferior solutions depends on the identification of a valuation function as the cardinal number. Second, comparison among the noninferior solutions for finding the preferred solution should be performed on the interval scales for a set of complex systems. Third, assessment of the valuation functions is a decision problem under uncertainty. Thus the probability of the occurrence of an event as the result of an action should be assessed. It means that the expected values should be calculated with the cardinal numbers.

Studies on the existence of the numerical utility function have been performed by von Neumann and Morgenstern (1944) and many others (Debreu 1954, 1958; Marschack 1950, 1964; Herstein and Milnor 1953; Thrall 1954; Luce and Suppes 1965; Fishburn 1970; Coombs, Dawes and Tversky 1970; etc.).

Consider the preference set $\Omega$, whose elements $x, y, z \in \Omega$ denote imagined consequences of events to occur as the result of an action of DM and are presumed to be combined with probabilities. Consider an operation $\alpha x + (1-\alpha)y$ for the $x, y \in \Omega$ with a probability $\alpha$, $1 > \alpha > 0$, which is represented as $h(x, \alpha, y)$ showing a ternary operation. The $(x, \alpha, y)$ denotes a probability $\alpha$ - mixture which represents a lottery on the occurrences of an event $x$ with a probability $\alpha$ and another event $y$ with a probability $1-\alpha$, alternatively.

Denote the preference relation ($\succ$, $\sim$) with **R**. Then the von Neumann-Morgenstern system is defined.

**Definition 5.1 (von Neumann-Morgenstern system).**

Consider a system $\mathbf{A} \triangleq (\Omega, R, h)$. Assume that the binary relation **R** and the ternary operation $h$ for any events $x$, $y$, $z \in \Omega$ and probability $\alpha$, $\beta$, satisfy the following properties.

(i) Closure: $h(x, \alpha, y) \subseteq \Omega$.

(ii) Weak order: connective and transitive.

(iii) Reducibility: (Axiom for a Compound Lottery)

$$[\beta(\alpha x + (1-\alpha)y) + (1-\beta)y] \sim [\alpha\beta x + (1-\alpha\beta)y].$$

(iv) Replaceability: (Independence-of-Irrelevance Rule)

$$x \succsim y \Rightarrow [\alpha x + (1-\alpha)z] \succsim [\alpha y + (1-\alpha)z].$$

(v) Weak continuity: $x \succ y \Rightarrow x \succ [\alpha x + (1-\alpha)y] \succ y$.

(vi) Continuity (Axiom of Archimedes): there exists $\alpha$, $\beta$ and $\gamma$ such that

$$x \succ y \succ z \Rightarrow y \succ \alpha x + (1-\alpha)z, \quad \text{and}$$

$$x \succ y \succ z \Rightarrow \beta x + (1-\beta)z \succ y,$$

or

$$x \succ y \succ z \Rightarrow y \sim [\gamma x + (1-\gamma)z].$$

Then the system $\mathbf{A} \triangleq (\Omega, R, h)$ is called the von Neumann-Morgenstern system.

Note that the axioms (iii)-(vi) show linearity of the von Neumann-Morgenstern system. The following theorem is established for the von Neumann-Morgenstern system.

**Theorem 5.1 (von Neumann-Morgenstern).**

Assume a system $\mathbf{A} = (\Omega, R, h)$ to be the von Neumann-Morgenstern system under the axioms (i)-(vi). Then there exists the real-valued function $u$ defined on $x$, $y \in \Omega$ in **A** satisfying the following properties.

(a) $x \succsim y \Rightarrow u(x) \geqslant u(y)$ (5.11)

$$\text{(b)} \quad u[\alpha x + (1-\alpha)y] = \alpha u(x) + (1-\alpha)u(y) \tag{5.12}$$

Moreover, if u' is any other function satisfying (a) and (b), then u' can be determined up to a positive linear transformation from u.

Now we can define a von Neumann-Morgenstern type numerical utility function.

**Definition 5.2 (von Neumann-Morgenstern type utility function).**

Let **A** be the von Neumann-Morgenstern system. If there exists a correspondence between an element x of a preference set $\chi \subseteq \Omega \subseteq \mathbf{A}$ and a real number $\rho$ such that

$$u: x \to \rho, \tag{5.13}$$

and the function u satisfies the conditions (a) and (b), in Theorem 5.1, then u is called the von Neumann-Morgenstern type utility function.

Theorem 5.1(a) shows the order-preserving property of the utility function u. The (b) shows the expected utility hypothesis which asserts that the expected value of utility for a lottery (the probability $\alpha$ - mixture) on events as the result of an action is equal to the utility for an expected value of the lottery. Theorem asserts linearity of the von Neumann-Morgenstern type expected utility function, which comes from the linearity of the von Neumann-Morgenstern system.

The axiom for rational human behavior based on the von Neumann-Morgenstern Theorem 5.1 is established as the expected utility hypothesis and provides a useful criterion for decision making under uncertainty. We discuss it in the next subsection.

### 5.2.3 Expected Utility Hypothesis

The expected utility hypothesis (5.12) has a long history. Bernoulli (1738), a statistician in the eighteenth century, considered the concept of utility that was defined on monetary wealth. He asserted that, as the fundamental rule for measurement of risk, not the expected value of gain but the expected value of its utility ("emolumentum medium" or moral expectation) should be used, where the expected value of utility corresponds to the expected value of the gain with the same probability as what is used for the expected gain. No valid measurement of the value of the risk can be obtained without regard to being given to its utility. This fundamental rule for measurement of the risky prospects is described in the expected utility hypothesis (5.12) and is called Bernoulli's norm. Ramsey (1926) more generally used the concept of mathematical expectation for measuring the degree of belief for realizing a person's need for a thing being good in the psychological sense (not necessarily for "pleasure" in the Utilitarian's sense). This rule is called Ramsey's norm. Von Neumann-Morgenstern's axiom described in Theorem 5.1 (b), also asserts that the numerical utility is defined as the value for which the calculus of mathematical expectation is legitimate. The von Neumann-Morgenstern axiom presumes the existence of individuals as the utility maximizers. It should be noted here that the axiom only treats the utility of one person; it does not imply anything concerning interpersonal comparison of the utilities among different individuals.

The expected utility hypothesis is formulated as follows.

EU

$$u(x) \triangleq \sum_{i=1}^{q} \pi_i u(x_i) \tag{5.14}$$

where $\pi_i$, $\sum_{i=1}^{q} \pi_i = 1$, $1 \geqslant \pi_i \geqslant 0$, is a subjective probability for a prospect of an event i and $x_i$ is a value an event i which an action takes as its consequence. The probability is attached to the belief or the prospect about the occurrence of the event rather than to the occurrence of the event itself. Thus the probability is subjectively assessed.

Savage (1954) represented the expected utility hypothesis (5.14) in the following form.

$$u(\hat{x}) = \sum_{i=1}^{q} \pi_i u(x_i) \tag{5.15}$$

where $\hat{x}$ denotes an event having the probability one, and $x_i$, $i = 1,\ldots,q$, denotes a value (or a gain) of the consequence for an uncertain event i. $\pi_i$ is a subjective probability combined with $x_i$, and u is the von Neumann-Morgenstern numerical utility function. The right-hand side of (5.15) is regarded as the expected value of the numerical utility for a lottery having q-chance forks. Savage presented the theorem for the expected utility, which introduces the idea of numerical utility in connection with gambles.

**Theorem 5.2 (Savage).**

The real-valued function u of consequences $x_i$ and $y_j$, $i = 1,\ldots,q$, $j = 1,\ldots,r$, which each action brings about respectively, is the utility function if and only if the following equivalence relations can be established:

$$\sum_{i=1}^{q} \pi_i x_i \precsim \sum_{j=1}^{r} \pi_j y_j \Leftrightarrow \sum_{i=1}^{q} \pi_i u(x_i) \leq \sum_{j=1}^{r} \pi_j u(y_j), \tag{5.16}$$

Where $\pi_i$ and $\pi_j$ are the subjective probabilities. In particular,

$$\hat{x} \precsim \hat{y} \Leftrightarrow u(\hat{x}) \leq u(\hat{y}), \tag{5.17}$$

where $\hat{x}$ and $\hat{y}$ are the events with the probability one respectively, defined on a finite set $\Omega$ of uncertain consequences.

**Theorem 5.3.**

The utility function $u(\hat{x})$ exists.

In the proof of Theorem 5.3, the concept of a hyperutility function defined on a convex set $\Omega$ is used. The hyperutility function v is defined as a real-valued function for lotteries satisfying the following properties.

$$\text{(a)} \quad \sum_{i=1}^{q} \pi_i x_i \precsim \sum_{j=1}^{r} \pi_j y_j \Leftrightarrow v\left(\sum_{i=1}^{q} \pi_i x_i\right) \leq v\left(\sum_{j=1}^{r} \pi_j y_j\right). \tag{5.18}$$

(b) $$v(\rho \sum_{i=1}^{q} \pi_i x_i + (1-\rho) \sum_{j=1}^{r} \pi_j y_j)$$

$$= \rho v(\sum_{i=1}^{q} \pi_i x_i) + (1-\rho) v(\sum_{j=1}^{r} \pi_j y_j). \qquad (5.19)$$

If the hyperutility function $v$ exists for a set of lotteries as a straightforward extension of the von Neumann-Morgenstern theorem, then from (5.18), there exists a utility function $u(\hat{x})$ for the event $\hat{x}$ satisfying (5.17), which is extended to (5.16). It is observed that the linearity of the utility function is assumed here.

The expected utility maximization hypothesis for rational human behavior can be formulated in terms of a gamble.

$$\underset{x_i \in \Gamma}{\text{maximize}} \quad u(\hat{x}) = \sum_{i=1}^{q} \pi_i u(x_i) \qquad (5.20)$$

where $\Gamma \quad \Omega$ is a set of possible consequences of events. The utility for the event $\hat{x}$ with the probability one is actually unknown and cannot be directly assessed. However, suppose the right-hand side of (5.20) to be an expected value of utility for a lottery having q-chance forks for the event $x_i$. Then the $\hat{x}$ on the left-hand side of (5.20) is regarded as a certainty equivalent to it. The certainty equivalent is defined as a value of a certain consequence such that preference in a lottery is indifferent to the preference in the certain consequence. Thus, if a value of the right-hand side of (5.20) is known, then the $\hat{x}$ of the left-hand side can be obtained by assigning a certainty equivalent indifferent to it. This idea opens the way for measurement of the numerical utility function (Pratt, Raiffa and Schlaifer 1964; Raiffa 1968; Schlaifer 1969). This problem is examined in the next chapter.

### 5.2.4 Digressions

1. The expected utility maximization (EUMAX) hypothesis, which implies weak ordering of preferences, is based on the superiority principle (or domination rule), and is thus

different from the noninferiority criterion (Pareto optimality) which only implies partial ordering including noncomparability. The EUMAX hypothesis is appropriate for searching for the preferred solution. In particular, this hypothesis is useful for individual decision making under uncertainty based on incomplete knowledge and information. However, for multiple agents (multiperson) decision making for which interpersonal comparison of individual utility is required, the superiority principle is generally difficult to hold. Instead, the mutual regret minimization rule or the minimax principle can be used. This criterion for the multiple agents decision making has been presumed in game theory (von Neumann and Morgenstern 1944; Dantzig 1951; Luce and Raiffa 1957; Owen 1968; Harsanyi 1977; Schubik 1983, 1984; etc.).

2. The EUMAX hypothesis, however, does not necessarily have unmanageable properties compared with other hypotheses. The noninferiority still holds the transitivity which is often hard to maintain in the real world problems. The minimax principle can be regarded as an extension of the expected utility maximization hypothesis in negative terms such as the regret minimization. The regret minimization hypothesis in decision analysis discussed by Bell (1952, 1983) and others assumes the measurability of a distance between the ideal point (target) and the obtained value on a psychological scale; this also brings up a problem of intertemporal as well as interpersonal comparisons of individual utility.

3. As a descriptive model, the EUMAX hypothesis has confronted many criticism for its violations in empirical studies. One of the well-known violations is the Allais' paradox (Allais and Hagen 1979), which is discussed by Kahneman and Tversky (1979) and many others.

(1) The Allais' counterexamples show a major paradox, the certainty effect, which brings about a violation of the Independence-of-Irrelevance Rule (5.2.2.(iv)). The counter-examples demonstrate as the certainty effect that outcomes which are obtained with certainty are overweighted relative to uncertain outcomes. It is known that reducing the probability of gain from 1.0 to .25 apparently has a greater effect on decision than reducing it from .8 to .2, which leads to violate the independence rule. Ellsberg (1961, 1963) also shows that

outcomes with ambiguous probabilities are underestimated relative to outcomes with exact levels of probabilities. One approach to overcome their paradox is to replace the probability with decision weights. Recent utility theories concern a generalization of the EUMAX hypothesis with the weight function $w(\pi)$, which is defined on the probability $\pi$ (Handa 1977; Karmarkar 1978, 1979; Kahneman and Tversky 1979; Quiggin 1982; Schoemaker 1982).

(2) The reflection effect (Kahneman and Tversky) shows that, in the negative domain of prospects, the preference for the negative prospects is the mirror image of the preference for positive prospects. Thus while in the positive domain a sure gain is overweighted relative to an uncertain large gain, a probable large loss is overweighted relative to a small loss with certainty in the negative domain. The reflection effect shows that risk aversion in the positive domain is accompanied by risk seeking in the negative domain (Fishbum and Kochenberger 1979). This is another effect of the overweighting of sure gain.

(3) The reference effect shows that preferences for prospects will change due to shifts of the reference point which is usually taken to be the status quo. Thus utility assessment should be restrictive to the situation and time in which preferences are revealed. This point has been Stressed early by Bernoulli (1738) and by Schlaifer (1969). Kahneman and Tversky (1979) also suggested that the reference point can be set to be zero on the present state of wealth.

4. As a normative model, the von Neumann-Morgenstern expected utility theory still possesses an eminent property for its simple manipulatability for utility assessment in practice. Thus the theory is used as an experimental medium for constructing numerical utility function. Computer programs for assessing the expected utility functions, MANECON collection, are provided by Schlaifer (1971) and extended by ICOPSS. Detail will be discussed in Chapter 6.

5. As stated before, the expected utility theory assumes the linearity of the expected utility function. This property is used in the lottery experiment for local identification of the numerical utility functions. In other words, the utility function is assumed to be locally identifiable with a linear

function. The extension of the local identification of a utility function to its global construction presumes the satisficing principle in the value assessment for utility which concerns attainment of the utility assessment within a satisficing region. As the result, a nonlinear utility function is constructed with a smoothing procedure in a global sense.

In the next section, properties of the nonlinear utility function are discussed.

## 5.3 The Generalized Nonlinear Utility Function and Risk Attitudes

As a classical form, the Bernoulli's nonlinear utility function is represented as follows.

$$u = k \log x + c \tag{5.21}$$

where $u$ is the utility, $x$ is a gain (e.g., an increase of the wealth), $k$ and $c$ are constants, and $u, x, k, c \in R^1$. If a threshold level $A$, beyond which the degree of satisfaction with the gain changes to positive, is introduced, then

$$u = k \log (x/A), \tag{5.22}$$

(Figure 5.2).

In the Marshallian sense ( Marshall 1890), the nonlinearity shows the law of diminishing marginal utility:

$$\text{(a)} \quad \frac{du}{dx} > 0, \tag{5.23}$$

and

$$\text{(b)} \quad \frac{d^2u}{dx^2} < 0, \tag{5.24}$$

Although presentation of the law of diminishing marginal utility goes back to Gossen (1854), Jevons (1871), and Wieser (1889), who belong to the cardinal school of utility, Hicks (1939) presented in its place the principle of the diminishing marginal rate of substitution, which is revealed on the

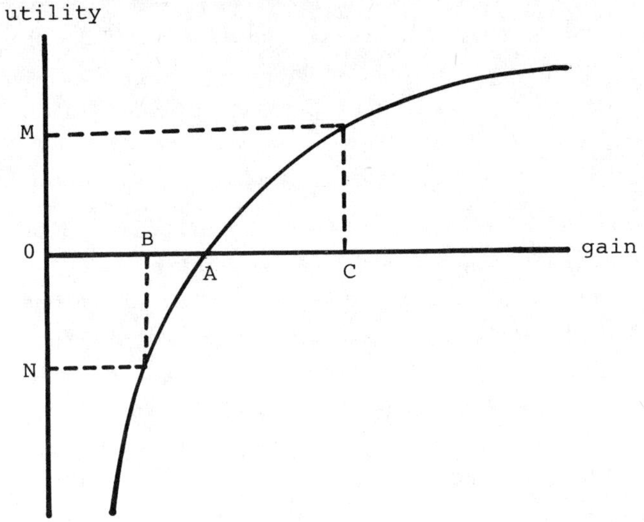


Note: The point A shows an initial holding of wealth. AC denotes an increase of the gain and AB is a decrease of it. OM and ON show increase and decrease of utility according to these changes, respectively.

**Figure 5.2 Bernoulli's utility function.**

indifference curves and does not depend on the cardinal measurement of the utility functions. Samuelson (1947) followed this approach. However, Edgeworth (1881), influenced by results of experimental psychology, defended the measurability of the cardinal utility in terms of "pleasure."

In decision analysis, the concept of utility is not confined to being used for monetary wealth or commodity bundles. Instead, $x \in \Omega$ represents the uncertain outcome of an action, and is only assumed as a prospect to be evaluated as an element of the preference set $\Omega$. $u(x)$ stands for a number corresponding to its quantum. In the context of decision analysis, the law of diminishing marginal utility does not prevail. Instead, marginal variation of a utility function can be extended to any direction and thus includes increasing marginal utility as well as constant marginal utility.

(c) $\frac{du}{dx} \gtrless 0$ (5.25)

(d) $\frac{d^2u}{dx^2} \lesseqgtr 0.$ (5.26)

The (c) shows that the nonsaturation hypothesis can be abandoned even in a local sense. We define with (c) and (d) the generalized nonlinear utility function (GNUF) hypothesis.

The GNUF hypothesis reflects the risk attitude which is described with a deviation from the linearity of a utility function. In the following, the utility function having the monotonically increasing property is discussed (Friedman and Savage 1948; Pratt 1964; Arrow 1970; Schlaifer 1971; Keeney and Raiffa 1976; etc.).

The DM's attitude of risk aversion is represented by

$$u(\sum_{i=1}^{q} \pi_i x_i) > \sum_{i=1}^{q} \pi_i u(x_i). \tag{5.27}$$

Let $\bar{x}$ denote the expected value of consequences $x_i$, $i = 1,\ldots,q$. $u(\bar{x})$ is the utility of the expected value. $\hat{x}$ denotes the certainty equivalent and $u(\hat{x})$ is its utility. Using those concepts, the risk premium $\rho$ of a lottery is defined as

$$\rho(x) = \bar{x} - \hat{x} = \sum_{i=1}^{q} \pi_i x_i - u^{-1}[\sum_{i=1}^{q} \pi_i u(x_i)] \tag{5.28}$$

where $u^{-1}$ is an inverse function of $u(\hat{x})$ and shows a value of the certainty equivalent $\hat{x}$ such that $u(\hat{x}) = \sum_{i=1}^{q} \pi_i u(x_i)$. For the risk-averse utility function,

$$\sum_{i=1}^{q} \pi_i x_i > \hat{x}, \tag{5.29}$$

which can be derived from the definition of the certainty equivalent and (5.27) with reference to the monotonically increasing property of the utility function. (5.29) means that the certainty equivalent $\hat{x}$ for a lottery is smaller than the expected value for consequences $x_i$, $i = 1,\ldots,q$, occurring as a result of the lottery. In other words, when the risk premium $\rho$ is positive, the utility function is risk-averse. The negative value of the certainty equivalent, $-\hat{x}$, is called the insurance premium for the lottery.

For the risk-prone utility function, the above properties are reversed. The DM's attitude of risk proneness is represented by

$$u\left(\sum_{i=1}^{q} \pi_i x_i\right) < \sum_{i=1}^{q} \pi_i u(x_i). \tag{5.30}$$

For the risk-prone utility function,

$$\sum_{i=1}^{q} \pi_i x_i < \hat{x}. \tag{5.31}$$

(5.31) means that the certainty equivalent $\hat{x}$ for a lottery is larger than the expected value for the consequences $x_i$. In other words, when the risk premium $\rho$ is negative, the utility function is risk-prone.

When the equality exists in (5.30), the risk attitude is risk-neutral, which is represented by the linear utility function. For the risk-neutral utility function, the expected value for a lottery is equal to the certainty equivalent. Thus the certainty equivalent can be substituted by the expected value of the lottery.

The risk function is a quantitative indicator for representing properties of the risk attitude, and is defined as follows:

$$r(x) \triangleq -\frac{u''(x)}{u'(x)} = -\frac{d}{dx}\left[\log u'(x)\right] \tag{5.32}$$

where $u'(x)$ and $u''(x)$ denote the first and second derivatives of the utility function $u(x)$ respectively for the uncertain outcome $x$. If $r > 0$ then $u''(x) < 0$, because the utility function is assumed to be monotonically increasing and hence $u'(x) > 0$. Thus the utility function $u(x)$ shows decreasing marginal utility and is risk-averse. If $r < 0$ then $u''(x) > 0$, which shows that the utility function $u(x)$ has increasing marginal utility and is risk-prone. If $r = 0$, then $u''(x) = 0$, which shows that the utility function $u(x)$ has constant marginal utility and is risk-neutral.

Variation of the value of the risk function (5.32) corresponding to a change in the value of $x$ represents the variation of the strength of the risk attitude. The variation of the risk attitude is classified as follows:

(i) Decreasing risk aversion: the utility function is risk-averse and risk premium $\rho(x)$ decreases according to the increase in $x$. The risk function $r(x)$ takes a positive and decreasing value for $x$; i.e., $r(x) > 0$, $r'(x) < 0$.

(ii) Constant risk aversion: the utility function is risk-averse and the risk premium is unvaried for any variation in $x$. The risk function $r(x)$ takes a positive constant value; i.e., $r(x) = c > 0$.

(iii) Increasing risk aversion: the utility function is risk-averse and the risk premium increases according to the increase in $x$. The risk function $r(x)$ takes a positive and increasing value for $x$; i.e., $r(x) > 0$, $r'(x) > 0$.

(iv) Decreasing risk proneness: the utility function is risk-prone and the risk premium increases according to the increase in $x$. The risk function $r(x)$ takes a negative and increasing value for $x$; i.e., $r(x) < 0$, $r'(x) > 0$.

(v) Constant risk proneness: the utility function is risk-prone and the risk premium is unvaried for any variation in $x$. The risk function $r(x)$ takes a negative constant value; i.e., $r(x) = c < 0$.

(vi) Increasing risk proneness: the utility function is risk-prone and the risk premium decreases according to the increase in $x$. The risk function $r(x)$ takes negative and decreasing values for $x$; i.e., $r(x) < 0$, $r'(x) < 0$.

Examples of these types of utility functions are as follows.

I. Risk neutral:

$$u(x) = ax + b, \tag{5.33}$$

$$r(x) = 0. \tag{5.34}$$

II. Constant risk attitude:

$$u(x) = a - be^{-cx}, \quad b > 0, \tag{5.35}$$

$$r(x) = c, \tag{5.36}$$

(a) $c > 0 \Leftrightarrow$ constant risk-averse,
(b) $c < 0 \Leftrightarrow$ constant risk-prone.

III. Decreasing risk attitude:

A. logarithmic: decreasing risk-averse.

$$\left.\begin{array}{ll} \text{(i)} & u(x) = k \log x + c \\ \text{(ii)} & u(x) = k \log(x/a) \end{array}\right\} \text{(Bernoulli type)}, \tag{5.37}$$

$$r(x) = \frac{1}{x} > 0, \quad r'(x) = -\frac{1}{x^2} < 0. \tag{5.38}$$

$$\text{(iii)} \quad u(x) = \log(x + b), \tag{5.39}$$

$$\text{(iv)} \quad u(x) = k \log(x + b) + c, \tag{5.40}$$

(iii)–(iv): $x > -b$,

$$r(x) = \frac{1}{x+b} > 0, \quad r'(x) = -\frac{1}{(x+b)^2} < 0. \tag{5.41}$$

B. exponential:

$$u(x) = ae^{-bx} + ce^{-dx} + E, \quad b > 0, \quad acd > 0, \tag{5.42}$$

$$r(x) = \frac{ab^2e^{-bx} + cd^2e^{-dx}}{abe^{-bx} + cde^{-dx}}, \tag{5.43}$$

$$r'(x) = \frac{-abcd(b-d)^2 e^{-bx} e^{-dx}}{(abe^{-bx} + cde^{-dx})^2} . \tag{5.44}$$

(a) $r(x) > 0$, and $r'(x) < 0$ ⇔ decreasing risk-averse.
(b) $r(x) < 0$, and $r'(x) > 0$ ⇔ decreasing risk-prone.

When $ac < 0$, $b \neq d$, the risk attitude (sign of r) changes beyond an inflection point $\tilde{x}$ of (5.42), where

$$\tilde{x} = \frac{1}{b-d} \log\left(- \frac{ab^2}{cd^2}\right) . \tag{5.45}$$

C. quadratic: decreasing risk-prone.

$$u(x) = ax^2 + bx + c, \quad a > 0, \quad b > 0, \tag{5.46}$$

$$r(x) = - \frac{2a}{2ax + b} < 0, \quad r'(x) = \frac{4a^2}{(2ax + b)^2} > 0, \tag{5.47}$$

$$x > - \frac{b}{2a} .$$

IV. Increasing risk attitude: increasing risk averse.

$$u(x) = -ax^2 + bx + c, \quad a > 0, \quad b > 0, \tag{5.48}$$

$$r(x) = \frac{2a}{b - 2ax} > 0, \quad r'(x) = \frac{4a^2}{(b - 2ax)^2} > 0, \tag{5.49}$$

$$x < \frac{b}{2a} .$$

V. Other utility functions

A. With changing risk attitudes and the saturation effect:

$$u(x) = abx/(1 + bx), \tag{5.50}$$

$$u(x) = a(bx)^2/(1 + (bx)^2). \tag{5.51}$$

(5.50), (5.51): $a > 0$, $b > 0$;

$$u(x) = (c - ab^x) \quad \text{(modified exponential curve)}, \qquad (5.52)$$

$$a,b,c > 0;$$

$$u(x) = a(1 - e^{-bx} - bxe^{-bx}), \quad a > 0, \quad b > 0; \qquad (5.53)$$

$$u(x) = ab^{c^x} \quad \text{(Gomperz curve)}, \quad a,b > 0, \quad 0 < c < 1; \qquad (5.54)$$

$$u(x) = a/(1 + be^{-cx}) \quad \text{(Logistic curve)}, \quad a,b,c > 0. \qquad (5.55)$$

B. With conversion from a monotonic increasing function to a decreasing function:

$$u(x) = abxe^{-bx}, \quad a > 0, \quad b > 0. \qquad (5.56)$$

**Remarks**

The GNUF characterized with its marginal properties has a twofold interpretation. First, the diminishing (or increasing) marginal utility represented in the concave (or convex) type utility function indicates that the additional satisfaction derived from an incremental quantum of a consequence of an event diminishes (or increases) with every increment of the increased quantum. This is a saturation effect and can be assessed without any regard for uncertainty. Second, changes in the risk attitude and/or in their strength are also represented in the concave (or convex) utility function, but occurs under uncertain situations like gambling. Thus, the concave type utility function does not always indicate the decrease of the DM's marginal utility, as its satisfaction with every additional increment of the consequence as the continuous quantum approaches a saturation. These two components of the nonlinear utility function can be examined separately. The decision regret theory (Bell 1982, 1983; Loomes and Sugden 1982; etc.) has been developed on the line of the risk-averse property; whereas the magnitude of the marginal value of utility includes the risk attitude as one component of the evaluation for an additional quantum, from which disutility often results.

In short, decision making is usually under uncertainty. The property of utility functions cannot be confined to the neoclassical assumptions of the law of diminishing marginal utility. Decision analysis examines the more general properties of the nonlinear utility function in a combination or a separation of the twofold interpretations of the nonlinearity.

## 5.4 Application to Technology Assessment for Substitute Energy

The EUMAX model can be applied to technology assessment under different regional conditions, which is one of major fields for making decision under uncertainty. In this section, an experimental example that uses the EUMAX model for technology assessment in fossil fuel-to-fuel conversion processes is presented (Seo and Sakawa 1979c).

Here we propose the socio-technique (SOTEC) concept as a principle for selecting the appropriate technology for the different regional conditions. This concept highly regards the social appropriateness under different resource, technology and cultural conditions in addition to the economic and energy-generating efficiency. Although the EUMAX model does not primarily intend to handle the multiobjective decision problem, we will show that the EUMAX model is still useful for selecting the appropriate technology from the point of view of multiple criteria. In this work, the expected utility concept is used as a device to make noncomparable multiple criteria commensurate.

The fossil fuel-to-fuel conversion problem is combined with a complex of resource endowment, transportation facilities, industrial, and societal conditions. Here we handle the problem in three models. In Model 1, the society has plentiful fossil fuel resources and has been highly industrialized. Thus this society has existing pipeline transportation facilities for liquefied natural gas. In Model 2, the society has limited natural resources, and largely depends on overseas transportation from fossil fuel producing countries. On the other hand, this society has highly developed heavy-chemical industries and a great deal of substitute-energy demand; thus it is well-experienced in the tanker transportation. In Model 3, the society has plentiful coal resources but they have not

**Table 5.2 (A) Comparison of alternative gasification processes**

| | Coal size | Temperature of gasfier | Pressure | Methane yield A | B | C |
|---|---|---|---|---|---|---|
| A1 | 1/8inch | 1300 1500F<br>1700 1800F<br>1800 1900F | 1000 1500psi | 0.33 | 1.69 | 0.83 |
| A2 | 12mesh | 1830F<br>1900F | 420psig | 0.098 | 0.50 | 0.29 |
| B1 | 200mesh | 1400 1700F<br>2700 2800F | 750 1500psi | 0.21 | 1.04 | 0.52 |
| B2 | 200mesh | 750F<br>1100 1470F<br>1750 1850F | 600 1000psi | 0.18 | 0.79 | 0.55 |
| C1 | 1/8inch | 1300 1500F | 1000 1500psi | | no data | |
| C2 | 1/8inch | 1300 1500F | 1000 1500psi | 0.25 | 1.27 | 0.64 |
| C3 | 50×100mesh | 1650F | 1000psi | 0.50 | 2.90 | 0.95 |
| D | 1/4 to 1/8 inch (lignite) | 1500F | 140psig<br>300psig | 0.16 | 0.90 | 0.46 |

Source: Hottel and Howard, New Energy Technology.

Note: All based on feed of Illinois No. 6 coal, except CSG(Renner Cove Lignite), Molton Carbonate (Pittsburgh seam coal) and Bureau of Mines Hydrogasification (Pittsburgh seam coal).
A = (Methane leaving gasifier)/(Carbon in solids feeds stream to gasifier);
B = (Methane leaving gasifier)/(Methane-equivalent of hydrogen in coal);
C = (Methane leaving gasifier)/(Methane in final pipeline gas).

been highly developed yet. However, if it does not desire to return to the previous colonial situation, industrialization must be the main object of economic policies. A typical society of Model 1 (M1) is the U.S.A.. Model 2 (M2) is Japan, and Model 3 (M3) is a society like South Africa or Australia which still has large unknown capabilities for development.

Data have been obtained mainly from research at MIT (Hottel and Howard, 1971) and partially from research in the Chemistry Division of the National Industrial Research Institute, Japan, 1977.

The procedure for assessing the desirability of the alternative technological processes for gasification and liquefaction of coal is as follows.

First, most of the basic data for assessing each

**Table 5.2 (B) List of alternative processes for substitute-energy technologies from coal**

| Gasification | Process | Characteristics (energy supply, etc.) |
|---|---|---|
| A1 | Hygas-electrothermal (IGT) | electrothermal & hydrogasifier |
| A2 | Molten Carbonate (Kellogg) | molten carbonate gasifier |
| B1 | Bigas (BCR) | oxygen and steam |
| B2 | Synthane (Bureau of mines) | oxygen and steam |
| C1 | Hygas-oxygen (IGT) | oxgen and steam hydrogasifier |
| C2 | Steam-Irom (IGT) | air and steam hydrogasifier use of iron oxide |
| C3 | Hydrogasification (Bureau of mines) | air hydrogasifier |
| D | $CO_2$ Acceptor (CSG) | hot air use of dolomite |
| Liquefaction | | |
| A | Solvent refining of coal (SRC) (CSC) | hydrogen |
| B | Consol process (HRI) | hydrogen use of zinc chloride catalyst |
| C | H-coal (HRI) | hydrogen use of cobalt molybdate catalyst |
| D | COED | oxygen and steam hydrogen |
| E | Solvolysis (KKS) | use of asphalt as slovent |

technological process is provided in nonquantitative terms. Thus the subjective scale for the nonquantified data must be constructed instead of utilization of the objective scale for quantified data. The data for the performance of each process are formed as a composite of multiple attributes and thus treated as a single attribute for assessment $x \in R^1$ for each process. Some examples of the original data are shown in Table 5.2. Measures for the consideration are scaled with subjective judgment in the range of 0 to 10. The composite data is supposed to be random variables.

Second, a utility function $u(x)$ of coal gasification and liquefaction for each model is assessed. The utility functions with decreasing risk aversion are assessed with an assistance by

**Table 5.3 Parameters of the utility function and values of the risk functions**

| Parameter of utility function $(u_i(x_i) = -e^{-Ax_i} - Ce^{-Bx_i} + E)$ | | | | Value of risk function | | | |
|---|---|---|---|---|---|---|---|
| | A | B | C | r(2.5) | r(5.0) | r(7.5) | r(9.5) |
| Gasification processes | | | | | | | |
| M1 | 0.7272 | 0.0102 | 127.9 | 0.071 | 0.021 | 0.021 | 0.011 |
| M2 | 0.4064 | -0.0218 | -6.294 | 0.194 | 0.089 | 0.024 | -0.001 |
| M3 | 0.3438 | -0.2737 | -0.0149 | 0.311 | 0.217 | 0.005 | -0.154 |
| Liquefaction Processes | | | | | | | |
| M1 | 0.5145 | 0.0940 | 13.89 | 0.145 | 0.113 | 0.101 | 0.097 |
| M2 | 0.5744 | 0.0333 | 23.73 | 0.119 | 0.058 | 0.040 | 0.036 |
| M3 | 0.5762 | -0.0180 | -7.512 | 0.274 | 0.089 | 0.010 | -0.009 |

Note: Parameter $E = C + 1$. $x_i$: $0 < x_i < 10$.

the MANECON computer program SUMEXFIT. Input data for depicting utility curves are derived by assessing certainty equivalents with 50-50 chance lottery techniques.

Parameters of the utility functions are shown in Table 5.3. The MANECON program PREFEVAL can evaluate and print out the values of the attributes and the corresponding utility values. Using these results, the utility functions for the oil-from-coal as well as gas-from-coal conversion processes in each model can be graphically depicted. The numerical values of the risk function for the decreasing risk-aversion functions are also shown in Table 5.3. The magnitudes of numerical values of the risk-aversion function $R(x)$ are, in a descending order, M3 > M2 > M1 for the gasification process. In Model 3, it is supposed that DM is most risk-averse in the first half of the whole range of the attributes and becomes rather risk-prone in the end. For the liquefaction process, the situation in Model 3 is same. However, unlike in the gasification case, in Model 2 is less risk-averse than in Model 1. This is because the liquefaction process in Japan is in the relatively advanced stage of R & D.

**Table 5.4 Expected utility of alternative processes**

| M1 | Preference | M2 | Preference | M3 | Preference |
|---|---|---|---|---|---|
| GAS A1 | 0.7517 | GAS A1 | 0.7303 | GAS A1 | 0.7476 |
| A2 | 0.4933 | A2 | 0.5239 | A2 | 0.5621 |
| B1 | 0.6518 | B1 | 0.5994 | B1 | 0.5872 |
| B2 | 0.5971 | B2 | 0.6468 | B2 | 0.6616 |
| C1 | 0.7559 | C1 | 0.7107 | C1 | 0.7656 |
| C2 | 0.6902 | C2 | 0.6963 | C2 | 0.7686 |
| C3 | 0.7822 | C3 | 0.7847 | C3 | 0.8042 |
| D | 0.6842 | D | 0.7063 | D | 0.7880 |
| OIL A | 0.8237 | OIL A | 0.7233 | OIL A | 0.7678 |
| B | 0.7648 | B | 0.6566 | B | 0.6820 |
| C | 0.7095 | C | 0.6396 | C | 0.6991 |
| D | 0.7037 | D | 0.6161 | D | 0.6346 |
| E | 0.7913 | E | 0.7707 | E | 0.7642 |

Third, the probability distribution function of the attribute of each process is assessed with subjective judgment. The different characteristic of each technological process is treated as being reflected not in the form of the utility function, but in the characteristic of probability distribution. In fact, the value x of the cumulative distribution function $P(x \leqslant \tilde{x})$ is assessed for several fractiles of the distribution. Using the MANECON program CDISPRI, continuous piecewise quadratic distributions are assessed and graphically printed in the form of the mass functions as well as cumulative functions. Characteristics of the distribution such as mean, standard derivation, and variance are also calculated.

Finally, expected value of utility for each process is calculated with the MANECON program PREFEVAL. The numerical values of the expected utility of the alternative processes are shown in Table 5.4.

# CHAPTER 6
# MULTIATTRIBUTE UTILITY ANALYSIS

## 6.1 Representation Theorem of Multiattribute Utility Functions

Multiattribute utility analysis is concerned with the judgmental phase of MCDM. This method provides a heuristic device for constructing the scalar-valued valuation function defined on multiple objectives. This device for scalarization of vector-valued objectives intends to directly cope with the noncommensurability of the multiple objectives and to assess the value trade-offs among these criteria. The theoretical background of this method is founded on the von Neumann-Morgenstern expected utility hypothesis. This chapter provides a methodological description of multiattribute utility analysis. In this section, the main concepts of multiattribute utility analysis are examined and the representation theorems are discussed.

Formulate the multiple criteria decision problem (MDP) as

MDP

$$\underset{x \in X}{\text{maximize}} \quad V(f_1(x), f_2(x), \ldots, f_m(x)) \tag{6.1}$$

where $x \in R^n$ is a vector of decision variables, $X$ in $R^n$ is a feasible set of the decision variables, $f_i : R^n \to R^1$, $i = 1, \ldots, m$, is an objective function, and $V : R^m \to R^1$ is a scalar-valued valuation function defined on the vector-valued criterion (objective) function $f(x) \triangleq (f_1, f_2, \ldots, f_m)$.

As stated in the previous chapter, the valuation function

V is generally unknown to DM. However, the von Neumann-Morgenstern Theorem 5.1 opens a way to construct the valuation function V. With the concept of the probability mixture or lottery, the method for measuring the numerical utility function for a single attribute treated as an uncertain quantity has been developed (Pratt, Raiffa and Schlaifer 1964; Raiffa 1968; Schlaifer 1969). This method has been absorbed into multiattribute utility analysis. The valuation function V in MDP (6.1) is identified as the multiattribute utility function. In this section, the representation theorem for MUF is discussed.

The core of multiattribute utility analysis is to reduce MDP (6.1) to an evaluation problem of MUF in the following form:

MUP

$$\sup_{\mathbf{x}_i \in S_i \subset \Gamma} U(\mathbf{x}_1, \mathbf{x}_2, \ldots, \mathbf{x}_m) \tag{6.2}$$

where $\mathbf{x}_i \in R^1$, $i = 1,\ldots,m$, is an uncertain quantity as an element of an uncertain preference set $\Omega$ and denotes a measure of effectiveness of a consequence, which indicates a level of an objective to be achieved. The objective $\mathbf{X}_i$ is called an attribute, and its value $\mathbf{x}_i$ shows its performance level without any concern for the mathematical optimization processes. Thus an objective function $f_i(x)$ in MDP (6.1) is replaced by $\mathbf{x}_i$ in (6.2). $\mathbf{S}_i$ is a feasible set of the attributes, and $\Gamma \subset \Omega$ is a feasible set of all attributes in the system. The function $U : R^m \to R^1$ is called the multiattribute utility function (MUF). The multiattribute utility analysis is concerned with finding the preferred policy program as a set of $\mathbf{x}_i^*$ in terms of MUP (6.2).

The main step of the MUF method is to evaluate (6.2) in terms of single attribute utility functions, based on a partition of the whole system, and then to coordinate their functions into a MUF with assessment of value trade-offs. Thus MUP (6.2) is assessed in the following form.

MUP

$$\sup_{\mathbf{x}_i \in S_i \subset \Gamma} U(u_1(\mathbf{x}_1), u_2(\mathbf{x}_2), \ldots, u_m(\mathbf{x}_m)), \tag{6.3}$$

where $u_i(\mathbf{x}_i)$ is a single attribute utility function (SUF), and U is a MUF defined on the SUF. In the following discussion, representation theorems for MUF are treated on the same line as Keeney (1974) and Keeney and Raiffa (1976).

For the MUF U in (6.3) to be assessed on the SUF, every attribute $\mathbf{x}_i$, $i = 1,\ldots,m$, should be presumed to be evaluated independently of the others. For this purpose, the independence assumptions are introduced.

**Definition 6.1 (Utility independence).**

An attribute $\mathbf{x}_i$ is said to be utility independent of its complement $\mathbf{x}_{\bar{i}}$ if the conditional preference order for lotteries with probabilities for variations in the level of an attribute $\mathbf{x}_i$ does not depend on the levels of other attributes $\mathbf{x}_{\bar{i}}$ which are held fixed.

**Definition 6.2 (Preferential independence).**

A set of attributes $(\mathbf{x}_i, \mathbf{x}_j)$ is said to be preferentially independent of its complement $\mathbf{x}_{\bar{i}\bar{j}}$ if the conditional preference order for the consequences with variations in levels of the attributes $(\mathbf{x}_i, \mathbf{x}_j)$ does not depend on the levels of other attributes $\mathbf{x}_{\bar{i}\bar{j}}$ which are held fixed.

The utility independence is concerned with preferences for uncertain consequences or lotteries which have chance-forks with probabilities of occurrence of events. The preferential independence is concerned with preferences for certain consequences, and implies that trade-off ratios among varied values of attributes can be assessed independently of all the other attribute levels. If a certain state is considered as an event occurring with a probability one, then the preferential independence is regarded as the utility independence for a degenerated lottery to such a limit state. Thus if the utility independence is satisfied, then the preferential independence can also be implied in it. In particular, when mutual utility independence among attributes is assumed, then both independence properties are generally fulfilled.

**Definition 6.3 (Mutual utility independence).**

Attributes $\mathbf{x}_1, \ldots, \mathbf{x}_m$ are said to be mutually utility independent, if every subset of the attribute set $(\mathbf{x}_1, \ldots, \mathbf{x}_m)$ is utility independent of its complement.

Then, using the definition of mutual utility independence, the representation theorems for MUF are presented.

**Theorem 6.1 (Keeney and Raiffa).**

If attributes $\mathbf{x}_1, \mathbf{x}_2, \ldots, \mathbf{x}_m$ are mutually utility independent, then a general representation form of MUF can be derived:

$$U(\mathbf{x}) = \sum_{i=1}^{m} k_i u_i(\mathbf{x}_i) + K \sum_{\substack{i=1 \\ j>i}}^{m} k_i k_j u_i(\mathbf{x}_i) u_j(\mathbf{x}_j) + K^2 \sum_{\substack{i=1 \\ j>i \\ s>j}}^{m} k_i k_j k_s u_i(\mathbf{x}_i) u_j(\mathbf{x}_j) u_s(\mathbf{x}_s) + \ldots\ldots\ldots + K^{m-1} k_1 k_2 k_3 \ldots k_m u_1(\mathbf{x}_1) u_2(\mathbf{x}_2) u_3(\mathbf{x}_3) \ldots u_m(\mathbf{x}_m). \tag{6.4}$$

(i) $U : R^m \to R^1$ is normalized between $U(\mathbf{x}_{10}, \mathbf{x}_{20}, \ldots, \mathbf{x}_{m0}) = 0$ and $U(\mathbf{x}_{11}, \mathbf{x}_{21}, \ldots, \mathbf{x}_{m1}) = 1$, where $\mathbf{x}_{i0}$ denotes the worst level of the attribute $\mathbf{x}_i$ and $\mathbf{x}_{i1}$ denotes its best level. (ii) $u_i(\mathbf{x}_i)$ is a conditional utility function on $\mathbf{x}_i$ normalized between $u_i(\mathbf{x}_{i0}) = 0$ and $u_i(\mathbf{x}_{i1}) = 1$ with all the other attributes $\mathbf{x}_{\bar{i}}$ held fixed. (iii) $k_i$ is a scaling constant, $0 < k_i < 1$, and $k_i = u(\mathbf{x}_{i1}, \mathbf{x}_{\bar{i}0})$. (iv) $K$ is a scaling constant that is a solution to

$$1 + K = \prod_{i=1}^{m} (1 + Kk_i), \tag{6.5}$$

and $K > -1$.

It has been proved that $K > -1$ can be obtained uniquely in any high-order equation (6.5). If $\sum_{i=1}^{m} k_i < 1$, then $K > 0$; and if $\sum_{i=1}^{m} k_i > 1$, then $-1 < K < 0$ (Keeney and Raiffa 1976, Appendix 6B).

**Corollary 6.1 (Additive form).**

When $\sum_{i=1}^{m} k_i = 1$ in (6.4), then $K = 0$, and (6.4) is reduced to the additive form of MUF:

$$U(\mathbf{x}) = \sum_{i=1}^{m} k_i u_i(\mathbf{x}_i). \tag{6.6}$$

**Corollary 6.2 (Multiplicative form).**

When $\sum_{i=1}^{m} k_i \neq 1$, then $K \neq 0$, and for $K > -1$, (6.4) can be reduced to the multiplicative form of MUF:

$$KU(\mathbf{x}) + 1 = \prod_{i=1}^{m} (Kk_i u_i(\mathbf{x}_i) + 1), \tag{6.7}$$

or

$$U(\mathbf{x}) = \frac{1}{K} \left[ \prod_{i=1}^{m} (Kk_i u_i(\mathbf{x}_i) + 1) - 1 \right]. \tag{6.8}$$

Before proof of Theorem 6.1 and Corollaries 6.1 and 6.2, some remarks should be added.

If an attribute $\mathbf{x}_i$ and its complement $\mathbf{x}_{\bar{i}}$ are mutually utility independent, then the preference order of a lottery for $\mathbf{x}_i$ is independent of $\mathbf{x}_{\bar{i}}$. Thus certainty equivalents (CE) $\hat{\mathbf{x}}$ and $\hat{\mathbf{x}}'$ for the following two lotteries $\ell_1$ and $\ell_2$ are equal without any dependence on variation of the value of $\mathbf{x}_{\bar{i}}$.

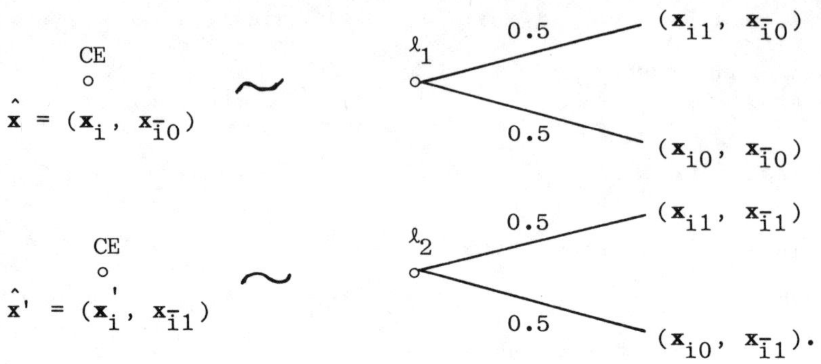


In general, conditional utility functions $u(\mathbf{x}_i, \mathbf{x}_{\bar{i}})$ and $u'(\mathbf{x}_i', \mathbf{x}_{\bar{i}})$ are said to be strategically equivalent when the preference orders for any two lotteries corresponding to their attribute values are equivalent to each other. The lotteries $\ell_1$ and $\ell_2$ for which the conditional utility functions are strategically equivalent can be substituted for each other. This represents the independence-of-irrelevance rule in terms of the substitutability of lotteries.

**Theorem 6.2.**

When two utility functions $u_i^1(\mathbf{x}_i)$ and $u_i^2(\mathbf{x}_i)$ for an attribute $\mathbf{x}_i$ are strategically equivalent, there exists constants c and h satisfying

$$u^1(\mathbf{x}_i, \mathbf{x}_{\bar{i}1}) = h(\mathbf{x}_{\bar{i}1}) + c(\mathbf{x}_{\bar{i}1})u^2(\mathbf{x}_i, \mathbf{x}_{\bar{i}0}), \tag{6.9}$$

$$i = 1,\ldots,m$$

where $h > 0$, $c > 0$.

**Proof.** Consider a $\pi$-probability mixture (lottery) for values $\mathbf{x}_{i1}$, $\mathbf{x}_{i0}$ of an attribute $\mathbf{x}_i$. Let $\mathbf{x}_i$ be a certainty equivalent to that. Then

$$u^j(\mathbf{x}_i, \mathbf{x}_{\bar{i}1}) = \pi u^j(\mathbf{x}_{i1}, \mathbf{x}_{\bar{i}1}) + (1-\pi)u^j(\mathbf{x}_{i0}, \mathbf{x}_{\bar{i}1}). \tag{6.10}$$

From (6.10), for some $j = 2$,

$$\pi = \frac{u^2(\mathbf{x}_i, \mathbf{x}_{\bar{i}1}) - u^2(\mathbf{x}_{i0}, \mathbf{x}_{\bar{i}1})}{u^2(\mathbf{x}_{i1}, \mathbf{x}_{\bar{i}1}) - u^2(\mathbf{x}_{i0}, \mathbf{x}_{\bar{i}1})} . \tag{6.11}$$

Substituting (6.11) into (6.10) for the other strategically equivalent utility function, j = 1, we can get (6.9).

(6.9) shows that the utility functions $u^1$ and $u^2$ can represent each other with a positive linear transformation. Evaluating (6.9) with $\mathbf{x}_i = \mathbf{x}_{i0}$ yields

$$u^1(\mathbf{x}_{i0}, \mathbf{x}_{\bar{i}1}) = h(\mathbf{x}_{\bar{i}1}) + c(\mathbf{x}_{\bar{i}1})u^2(\mathbf{x}_{i0}, \mathbf{x}_{\bar{i}0}). \tag{6.12}$$

From $u^2(\mathbf{x}_{i0}, \mathbf{x}_{\bar{i}0}) = 0$,

$$u^1(\mathbf{x}_{i0}, \mathbf{x}_{\bar{i}1}) = h(\mathbf{x}_{\bar{i}1}). \tag{6.13}$$

Substituting (6.13) into (6.9) yields

$$u^1(\mathbf{x}_i, \mathbf{x}_{\bar{i}1}) = u^1(\mathbf{x}_{i0}, \mathbf{x}_{\bar{i}1}) + c(\mathbf{x}_{\bar{i}1})u^2(\mathbf{x}_i, \mathbf{x}_{\bar{i}0}). \tag{6.14}$$

Considering that $\mathbf{x}_i$ and $\mathbf{x}_{\bar{i}}$ are mutually utility independent, and from $u_i(\mathbf{x}_{i0}) = 0$ and $u_{\bar{i}}(\mathbf{x}_{\bar{i}0}) = 0$, (6.14) can be represented by

$$u(\mathbf{x}) = u(\mathbf{x}_{\bar{i}}) + c(\mathbf{x}_{\bar{i}})u(\mathbf{x}_i) \tag{6.15}$$

or, substituting $\mathbf{x}_i$ and $\mathbf{x}_{\bar{i}}$ for each other, by

$$u(\mathbf{x}) = u(\mathbf{x}_i) + c(\mathbf{x}_i)u(\mathbf{x}_{\bar{i}}), \quad i = 1,\dots,m. \tag{6.16}$$

**The proof of Theorem 6.1.**

If $\mathbf{x}_i$ and $\mathbf{x}_{\bar{i}}$ are mutually utility independent, then from (6.16),

$$u(\mathbf{x}) = u(\mathbf{x}_i) + c_i(\mathbf{x}_i)u(\mathbf{x}_{\bar{i}}), \quad i = 1,2,\dots, m-1. \tag{6.17}$$

Let all the $\mathbf{x}_i$ except $\mathbf{x}_1$ and $\mathbf{x}_j$, j = 2,3,..., m-1, be $\mathbf{x}_i = \mathbf{x}_{i0}$. Then, from $u(\mathbf{x}_{i0}) = 0$,

$$u(\mathbf{x}_1, \mathbf{x}_j) = u(\mathbf{x}_1) + c_1(\mathbf{x}_1)u(\mathbf{x}_j) \tag{6.18}$$
$$= u(\mathbf{x}_j) + c_j(\mathbf{x}_j)u(\mathbf{x}_1).$$

Dividing both sides by $u(\mathbf{x}_1)u(\mathbf{x}_j)$ yields

$$\frac{c_j(\mathbf{x}_j) - 1}{u(\mathbf{x}_j)} = \frac{c_1(\mathbf{x}_1) - 1}{u(\mathbf{x}_1)} = K, \tag{6.19}$$

where $u(\mathbf{x}_j) \neq 0$ and $K$ is a constant. When $u(\mathbf{x}_j) = 0$, $c_j(\mathbf{x}_j) = 1$. It follows that

$$c_i(\mathbf{x}_i) = Ku(\mathbf{x}_i) + 1, \quad i = 1,2,\ldots, m-1. \tag{6.20}$$

By using (6.17) repeatedly,

$$\begin{aligned} u(\mathbf{x}) &= u(\mathbf{x}_1) + c_1(\mathbf{x}_1)u(\mathbf{x}_2, \mathbf{x}_3,\ldots, \mathbf{x}_m) \\ &= u(\mathbf{x}_1) + c_1(\mathbf{x}_1)[u(\mathbf{x}_2) + c_2(\mathbf{x}_2)\, u(\mathbf{x}_3, \mathbf{x}_4,\ldots, \mathbf{x}_m)] \\ &= u(\mathbf{x}_1) + c_1(\mathbf{x}_1)u(\mathbf{x}_2) + c_1(\mathbf{x}_1)c_2(\mathbf{x}_2)[u(\mathbf{x}_3) \\ &\qquad + c_3(\mathbf{x}_3)u(\mathbf{x}_4, \mathbf{x}_5,\ldots, \mathbf{x}_m)] \\ &\vdots \\ &= u(\mathbf{x}_1) + c_1(\mathbf{x}_1)u(\mathbf{x}_2) + c_1(\mathbf{x}_1)c_2(\mathbf{x}_2)u(\mathbf{x}_3) + \cdots \\ &\qquad + c_1(\mathbf{x}_1)c_2(\mathbf{x}_2) \cdots c_{m-1}(\mathbf{x}_{m-1})u(\mathbf{x}_m). \end{aligned} \tag{6.21}$$

Substituting (6.20) into (6.21),

$$\begin{aligned} u(\mathbf{x}) &= u(\mathbf{x}_1) \\ &+ (Ku(\mathbf{x}_1) + 1)u(\mathbf{x}_2) \\ &+ (Ku(\mathbf{x}_1) + 1)(Ku(\mathbf{x}_2) + 1)u(\mathbf{x}_3) \\ &\vdots \\ &+ (Ku(\mathbf{x}_1) + 1)(Ku(\mathbf{x}_2) + 1) \ldots (Ku(\mathbf{x}_{m-1}) + 1)u(\mathbf{x}_m) \end{aligned} \tag{6.22}$$

$$= u(\mathbf{x}_1) + \sum_{j=2}^{m} \prod_{i=1}^{j-1} (Ku(\mathbf{x}_i) + 1)u(\mathbf{x}_j).$$

When $K = 0$, (6.22) is reduced to

$$u(\mathbf{x}) = \sum_{i=1}^{m} u(\mathbf{x}_i). \tag{6.23}$$

When $K \neq 0$, multiplying both sides of (6.22) by $K$ and adding one to each side yields

$$Ku(\mathbf{x}) + 1 = \prod_{i=1}^{m} (Ku(\mathbf{x}_i) + 1). \tag{6.24}$$

Because $\mathbf{x}_i$ is utility independent,

$$u(\mathbf{x}_i) = u(\tilde{\mathbf{x}}_1, \ldots, \tilde{\mathbf{x}}_{i-1}, \mathbf{x}_i, \tilde{\mathbf{x}}_{i+1}, \ldots, \tilde{\mathbf{x}}_m), \tag{6.25}$$

where $\tilde{\mathbf{x}}_j$, $j \neq i$, $j = 1,\ldots,m$, is a fixed value of $\mathbf{x}_j$. Then, putting $\tilde{\mathbf{x}}_j = \tilde{\mathbf{x}}_{j0}$, we can define it with a linear conversion of scaling as

$$u(\mathbf{x}_i) = k_i u_i(\mathbf{x}_i). \tag{6.26}$$

Substituting (6.26) into (6.23) yields Corollary 6.1 (6.6) and substituting (6.26) into (6.24) yields Corollary 6.2 (6.7) or (6.8).

The MUF has another general representation form.

**Theorem 6.3 (Multilinear utility function) (Keeney and Raiffa).**

Given a set of attributes $\mathbf{x} \triangleq (\mathbf{x}_1, \mathbf{x}_2, \ldots, \mathbf{x}_m)$ for $m \geq 2$. If $\mathbf{x}_i$ is mutually utility independent of $\mathbf{x}_{\bar{i}}$, then we can obtain the multilinear utility function:

$$U(\mathbf{x}) = \sum_{i=1}^{m} k_i u_i(\mathbf{x}_i) + \sum_{i=1}^{m} \sum_{j>i}^{m} k_{ij} u_i(\mathbf{x}_i) u_j(\mathbf{x}_j)$$

$$+ \sum_{i=1}^{m} \sum_{j>i}^{m} \sum_{s>j}^{m} k_{ijs} u_i(\mathbf{x}_i) u_j(\mathbf{x}_j) u_s(\mathbf{x}_s) \qquad (6.27)$$

$$+ \ldots + k_{123,\ldots,m} u_1(x_1) u_2(x_2), \ldots, u_m(x_m)$$

where U and $u_i$ are normalized between 0 and 1. The scaling constants can be assessed by

$$k_i = u(\mathbf{x}_{i1}, \mathbf{x}_{\bar{i}0})$$

$$k_{ij} = u(\mathbf{x}_{i1}, \mathbf{x}_{j1}, \mathbf{x}_{\bar{i}\bar{j}0}) - k_i - k_j$$

$$= u(\mathbf{x}_{i1}, \mathbf{x}_{j1}, \mathbf{x}_{\bar{i}\bar{j}0}) - u(\mathbf{x}_{i1}, \mathbf{x}_{\bar{i}0}) - u(\mathbf{x}_{j1}, \mathbf{x}_{\bar{j}0})$$

$$k_{ijs} = u(\mathbf{x}_{i1}, \mathbf{x}_{j1}, \mathbf{x}_{s1}, \mathbf{x}_{\bar{i}\bar{j}\bar{s}0})$$

$$- k_{ij} - k_{is} - k_{js} - k_i - k_j - k_s$$

$$= u(\mathbf{x}_{i1}, \mathbf{x}_{j1}, \mathbf{x}_{s1}, \mathbf{x}_{\bar{i}\bar{j}\bar{s}0}) - u(\mathbf{x}_{i1}, \mathbf{x}_{j1}, \mathbf{x}_{\bar{j}\bar{i}0})$$

$$- u(\mathbf{x}_{i1}, \mathbf{x}_{s1}, \mathbf{x}_{\bar{i}\bar{s}0}) - u(\mathbf{x}_{j1}, \mathbf{x}_{s1}, \mathbf{x}_{\bar{j}\bar{s}0})$$

$$+ u(\mathbf{x}_{i1}, \mathbf{x}_{\bar{i}0}) + u(\mathbf{x}_{j1}, \mathbf{x}_{\bar{j}0}) + u(\mathbf{x}_{s1}, \mathbf{x}_{\bar{s}0})$$

$$\vdots$$

$$k_{1,2,3\ldots m} = u(\mathbf{x}^*) - \sum_{i}^{m} k_{i\ldots(i-1)(i+1)\ldots m} - \ldots$$

$$- \sum_{i,j>i}^{m} k_{ij} - \sum_{i=1}^{m} k_i = 1 - \sum_{i=1}^{m} u(\mathbf{x}_{i0}, \mathbf{x}_{\bar{i}1}) + \ldots \qquad (6.28)$$

$$+ (-1)^{m-2} \sum_{i,j>i} u(\mathbf{x}_{i1}, \mathbf{x}_{j1}, \mathbf{x}_{\bar{i}\bar{j}0}) + (-1)^{m-1} \sum_{i=1}^{m} u(\mathbf{x}_{i1}, \mathbf{x}_{\bar{i}0}).$$

**Proof.** From the assumption of mutually utility independence, (6.15) can be used. Assuming $u(\mathbf{x}_i) = k_i u_i(\mathbf{x}_i)$ for any $k_i > 0$, and substituting it into (6.15),

$$u(\mathbf{x}) = u(\mathbf{x}_{\bar{i}}) + d_i(\mathbf{x}_{\bar{i}}) u_i(\mathbf{x}_i), \quad i = 1,\ldots,m \qquad (6.29)$$

where $d_i > 0$, and $d_i(\mathbf{x}_{\bar{i}}) \triangleq k_i c(\mathbf{x}_{\bar{i}})$. Evaluating (6.29) with $\mathbf{x}_i = x_{i1}$,

$$u(\mathbf{x}_{i1}, \mathbf{x}_{\bar{i}}) = u(\mathbf{x}_{i0}, \mathbf{x}_{\bar{i}}) + d_i(\mathbf{x}_{\bar{i}})u_i(\mathbf{x}_{i1}). \tag{6.30}$$

From $u_i(\mathbf{x}_{i1}) = 1$,

$$d_i(\mathbf{x}_{\bar{i}}) = u(\mathbf{x}_{i1}, \mathbf{x}_{\bar{i}}) - u(\mathbf{x}_{i0}, \mathbf{x}_{\bar{i}}), \quad i = 1,\ldots,m. \tag{6.31}$$

Substituting (6.31) into (6.29), and from $u(\mathbf{x}_{\bar{i}}) = u(\mathbf{x}_{i0}, \mathbf{x}_{\bar{i}})$

$$u(\mathbf{x}) = u_i(\mathbf{x}_i)u(\mathbf{x}_{i1}, \mathbf{x}_{\bar{i}}) + [1 - u_i(\mathbf{x}_i)]u(\mathbf{x}_{i0}, \mathbf{x}_{\bar{i}}). \tag{6.32}$$

Now assessing (6.32) with $i = 1$ derives

$$u(\mathbf{x}) = u_1(\mathbf{x}_1)u(\mathbf{x}_{11}, \mathbf{x}_{\bar{1}}) + [1 - u_1(\mathbf{x}_1)]u(\mathbf{x}_{10}, \mathbf{x}_{\bar{1}}). \tag{6.33}$$

Then, by assessing (6.32) with $i = 2$ and by substituting it into (6.33) with

$$\begin{aligned} u(\mathbf{x}_{11}, \mathbf{x}_{\bar{1}}) &= u_2(\mathbf{x}_2)u(\mathbf{x}_{11}, \mathbf{x}_{21}, \mathbf{x}_{\bar{1}\bar{2}}) \\ &\quad + [1 - u_2(\mathbf{x}_2)]u(\mathbf{x}_{11}, \mathbf{x}_{20}, \mathbf{x}_{\bar{1}\bar{2}}), \\ u(\mathbf{x}_{10}, \mathbf{x}_{\bar{1}}) &= u_2(\mathbf{x}_2)u(\mathbf{x}_{10}, \mathbf{x}_{21}, \mathbf{x}_{\bar{1}\bar{2}}) \\ &\quad + [1 - u_2(\mathbf{x}_2)]u(\mathbf{x}_{10}, \mathbf{x}_{20}, \mathbf{x}_{\bar{1}\bar{2}}), \end{aligned} \tag{6.34}$$

(6.33) becomes

$$\begin{aligned} u(\mathbf{x}) = u_1(\mathbf{x}_1)[&u_2(\mathbf{x}_2)u(\mathbf{x}_{11}, \mathbf{x}_{21}, \mathbf{x}_{\bar{1}\bar{2}}) \\ &+ (1 - u_2(\mathbf{x}_2))u(\mathbf{x}_{11}, \mathbf{x}_{20}, \mathbf{x}_{\bar{1}\bar{2}})] \\ &+ [1 - u_1(\mathbf{x}_1)][u_2(\mathbf{x}_2)u(\mathbf{x}_{10}, \mathbf{x}_{21}, \mathbf{x}_{\bar{1}\bar{2}}) \\ &+ (1 - u_2(\mathbf{x}_2))u(\mathbf{x}_{10}, \mathbf{x}_{20}, \mathbf{x}_{\bar{1}\bar{2}})]. \end{aligned} \tag{6.35}$$

By repeating this procedure, (6.27) and (6.28) are obtained.

**Corollary 6.3.**

For the two attributes utility function, if the attributes $\mathbf{x}_1$ and $\mathbf{x}_2$ are mutually utility independent, then the representation form

$$k_1u_1(\mathbf{x}_1) + k_2u_2(\mathbf{x}_2) + (1 - k_1 - k_2)u_1(\mathbf{x}_1)u_2(\mathbf{x}_2) \qquad (6.36)$$

is obtained.

The identification process of MUF, based on the above representation theorems and corollaries, is composed of three steps: (i) assessment of the single attribute utility functions (SUF) $u_i(\mathbf{x}_i)$, $i = 1,\dots,m$, as components of the MUF; (ii) assessment of the scaling constants $k_i$, $i = 1,\dots,m$, for SUF; and (iii) structural identification of the representation form of the MUF, additive or multiplicative, with the scaling constant K obtained from (6.5). Finally, the MUF-value is calculated for alternative set of observed or predicted data for the attributes. The result is used for selecting a preferred policy program.

In the next section, the identification method for SUF is described. In Section 6.3, the identification method for MUF is discussed. The effectiveness of the MUF method is founded on the decomposition of objectives to be evaluated. The decomposition device and its structuring is discussed in Section 6.4.

## 6.2 Identification of the Single Attribute Utility Function

The identification method of the single attribute utility function (SUF) is based on the von Neumann-Morgenstern expected utility hypothesis, which opens a way for assessing the utility function $u_i(\mathbf{x}_i): R^1 \to R^1$ in the following form:

$$u_i(\hat{\mathbf{x}}_i) = \sum_{j=1}^{q} \pi_{ij}u_{ij}(\mathbf{x}_{ij}), \qquad (6.37)$$

where $u_{ij}$, $0 < u_{ij} < 1$, is a utility index that measures the degree of preference in the von Neumann-Morgenstern sense and is assessed for a level of an occurrence $\mathbf{x}_{ij}$, $j = 1,\ldots,q$, of an attribute $\mathbf{X}_i$, $i = 1,\ldots,m$; $\pi_{ij}$ is a judgment or the degree of belief for the occurrence of an attribute level $\mathbf{x}_{ij}$, $j = 1, \ldots,q$, and scaled on $0 \leq \pi_{ij} \leq 1$, $\sum_{j=1}^{q} \pi_{ij} = 1$. The $u_{ij}$ shows a utility of the decision maker (DM) for the consequence $\mathbf{x}_{ij}$, and the $\pi_{ij}$ is its assessment of the probability for $\mathbf{x}_{ij}$. The right-hand side of (6.37) defines a real-valued expected

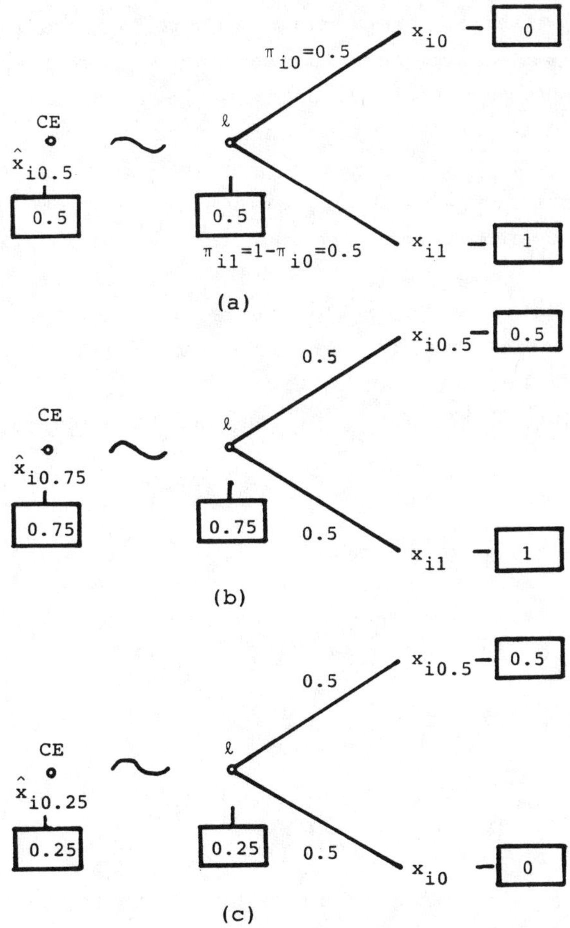


**Figure 6.1 Indifferent experiment for identification of a single attribute utility function.**

utility. $\hat{\mathbf{x}}_i$ shows a certainty equivalent (CE).

(6.37) can be interpreted such that the right-hand side shows an expected utility of a lottery having a q-chances fork and the left-hand side shows a utility value equivalent to the lottery. Thus, if the expected utility value of the lottery can be assessed, then by assessing the corresponding CE $\hat{\mathbf{x}}_i$ we can find each pair of $\hat{\mathbf{x}}_i$ and $u_i(\hat{\mathbf{x}}_i)$. This device derives a utility function $u_i(\mathbf{x}_i)$ in a two-dimensional space. Since to evaluate $\sum_{j=1}^{q} \pi_{ij}u_{ij}(\mathbf{x}_{ij})$ in an arbitrary form is difficult, canonical lotteries are constructed to calculate the expected utility values in sequence to find the utility function $u(\hat{\mathbf{x}})$.

The canonical lottery technique is a device for identifying the SUF with a heuristic procedure. The canonical lottery has a two-chance fork taking the worst value $\mathbf{x}_{i0}$ or the best value $\mathbf{x}_{i1}$ alternatively with a probability of fifty percent each. Indifference experiments between the canonical lottery $\ell$ on the right-hand side of (6.37) and CE $\hat{\mathbf{x}}$ on the left-hand side proceed for other alternative values of $\mathbf{x}_i$. Then the numerical utility function can be derived (Pratt, Raiffa and Schlaifer 1964; Raiffa 1968) (Figure 6.1).

Consider (6.37) first in the following canonical form for j = 0,1,

$$\begin{aligned} u_i(\hat{\mathbf{x}}_i) &= \sum_{j=0,}^{1} \pi_{ij}u_{ij}(\mathbf{x}_{ij}) \\ &= 0.5 \times u_{i0}(\mathbf{x}_{i0}) + 0.5 \times u_{i1}(\mathbf{x}_{i1}) \qquad (6.38) \\ &= 0.5 \end{aligned}$$

where $u_{i0}(\mathbf{x}_{i0}) = 0$ and $u_{i1}(\mathbf{x}_{i1}) = 1$. By assessing $\hat{\mathbf{x}}$, we can obtain a pair of $\hat{\mathbf{x}}_i = \mathbf{x}_{i0.5}$ and $u_i(\hat{\mathbf{x}}_i) = u_{i0.5}(\mathbf{x}_{i0.5}) = 0.5$.

Second, with this value, by assessing (6.37) in the following form for $j = 0.5, 1$,

$$u_i(\hat{\mathbf{x}}_i) = \sum_{j=0.5,}^{1} \pi_{ij} u_{ij}(\mathbf{x}_{ij})$$

$$= 0.5 \times u_{i0.5}(\mathbf{x}_{i0.5}) + 0.5 \times u_{i1}(\mathbf{x}_{i1})$$

$$= 0.5 \times 0.5 + 0.5 \times 1 \tag{6.39}$$

$$= 0.75,$$

we can obtain a pair of $\hat{\mathbf{x}}_i = \mathbf{x}_{i0.75}$ and $u_i(\hat{\mathbf{x}}_i) = u_{i0.75}$ $(\mathbf{x}_{i0.75}) = 0.75$. Calculation is continued in the same way. With those pairs of values, the utility function $u_i(\mathbf{x}_i)$ is obtained on the $\hat{\mathbf{x}}_i - u_i(\hat{\mathbf{x}}_i)$ plane (Figure 6.2). Assuming appropriate forms of SUF such as

(i) $\quad u_i(\mathbf{x}_i) = a - be^{-c\mathbf{x}_i}, \quad b > 0 \tag{6.40}$

(ii) $\quad u_i(\mathbf{x}_i) = -e^{-b\mathbf{x}_i} - ce^{-d\mathbf{x}_i}, \quad b, c, d > 0, \tag{6.41}$

parameters can be calculated.



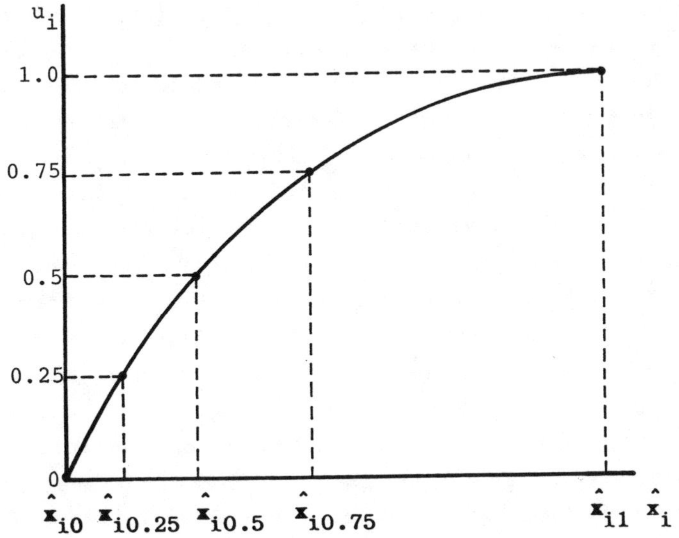

**Figure 6.2  Derivation of the single attribute utility function.**

**Remarks.**

1. The independence assumptions imply that DM's preference for one attribute is assessed independently of the other attributes without any interest in these attributes even though they are functionally interrelated with each other. Thus, although the independence assumptions presume that a system to be evaluated can be partitioned into subsystems which are all independent of each other from the point of view of value assessment, it does not imply any structural independency among the numerical values of the attributes.

2. The identification of the numerical utility function is decision making under uncertainty. Numerical values for attributes $\mathbf{x}_i$, $i = 1,\ldots,m$, are only assumed to take a probable range from the worst value $\mathbf{x}_{i0}$ to the best value $\mathbf{x}_{i1}$ and the numerical structure of SUF depends to a considerable extent on the probable range of attributes taken as the data.

3. Properties of the attributes are classified into three cases. (i) The case in which some intermediate values of the attributes can be measured with certainty. (ii) The case in which some intermediate values of the attributes are measured with a specified probability within a specified range. These numerical values can be represented by a "tabular" form. (iii) The case in which some intermediate values of the attributes are measured as continuous quantities with a probability density function. In the cases (ii) and (iii), the utility function is evaluated, via assessing their probabilities, in terms of the expected utility function. These probabilities are assessed subjectively, because the mass observation for finding them usually cannot be performed.

4. For assessing the probability density function subjectively, a cumulative distribution function $F_i(\mathbf{x}_i) = P(\mathbf{x}_i \leqslant \tilde{\mathbf{x}}_i)$ is derived. The values of cumulative distributions, $F_i^r(\mathbf{x}_i \leqslant \tilde{\mathbf{x}}_i^r)$, $r = 1,\ldots,s$, are assessed on s-fractiles for an attribute $\mathbf{x}_i$. Then, it is transformed to the probability density function $f_i(\mathbf{x}_i) = p(\mathbf{x}_i = \tilde{\mathbf{x}}_i)$ (Schlaifer 1969). The expected utility function for the uncertain quantity $\mathbf{x}_i$ is assessed as

$$E[u_i(\mathbf{x}_i)] = \sum_{r=1}^{s} f_i^r(\mathbf{x}_i^r)u_i^r(\mathbf{x}_i^r). \tag{6.42}$$

5. Identification of parameters of the nonlinear utility functions requires a repetitive calculation process by approximation. For calculating the expected value of a utility function (6.42) via the assessment of the probability density function, Schlaifer (1971) provides the computer program MANECON collection. This program supplies a function for revising the evaluation of the utility by DM interactively, along with an algorithm for calculating parameters of the risk-averse utility functions. In addition, the program has facilities for calculating the statistics for the probability distributions such as mean, standard deviation, and variance, and for printing out the distribution functions as well as density functions graphically. The value of a probability distribution at every fractile point designated by DM can be also calculated. The MANECON collection has been largely revised, and is combined with the computer program MUFCAP for calculation and assessment of MUF. This new program is called ICOPSS (Interactive Computer Program for Subjective Systems) which will be presented in Section 6.5.

## 6.3 Identification of the Multiattribute Utility Function

### 6.3.1 Independence Check

The representation theorems for MUF presume the utility and preferential independence assumptions. Thus, before numerical identification of MUF, the independence assumptions should be checked.

For checking the preferential independence of the attributes, an indifference experiment is performed. Assume all the attributes $\mathbf{x}_{\overline{ij}} \in \Gamma$ except $\mathbf{x}_i$ and $\mathbf{x}_j$ take their worst values and denote them $\mathbf{x}_{\overline{ij}0}$, where $\Gamma$ is a possible set of attributes in the system. First find an indifference pair $(\mathbf{x}_i^1, \mathbf{x}_j^1) \sim (\mathbf{x}_i^2, \mathbf{x}_j^2)$, for the two attributes $\mathbf{x}_i$ and $\mathbf{x}_j$. Then change the values of all the other attributes $\mathbf{x}_{\overline{ij}}$ to their best values $\mathbf{x}_{\bar{i}\bar{j}1}$ and check if the indifference relation will still hold for that pair. If the answer is "yes," then take another indifferent pair $(\mathbf{x}_i^3, \mathbf{x}_j^3) \sim (\mathbf{x}_i^4, \mathbf{x}_j^4)$ for $\mathbf{x}_i$ and $\mathbf{x}_j$ and check if the indifference relation will still hold when the other attributes $\mathbf{x}_{\bar{i}\bar{j}}$ change their values. If all those experiments can be performed with the answer "yes," then the attributes $\mathbf{x}_i$ and $\mathbf{x}_j$ are confirmed to be preferentially independent of the other attributes $\mathbf{x}_{\bar{i}\bar{j}}$ .

For checking the utility independence, another indifference experiment is performed. Assume all the attributes $\mathbf{x}_{\bar{i}} \in \Gamma$ except $\mathbf{x}_i$ be at a fixed level. Consider a lottery for an attribute $\mathbf{x}_i$ which takes an alternative value $x_i^1$ or $\mathbf{x}_i^2$ with a probability of fifty percent each. Assess CE $\hat{\mathbf{x}}_i^1$ indifferent to the lottery. Change the values of all the other attributes $\mathbf{x}_{\bar{i}}$, and check if the CE $\hat{\mathbf{x}}_i^1$ to the lottery will still be unvaried. If the answer is "yes," then change the values which the lottery takes to $\mathbf{x}_i^3$ and $\mathbf{x}_i^4$ and assess CE $\hat{\mathbf{x}}_i^2$ to the new lottery. Change again the values of the other attributes $\mathbf{x}_{\bar{i}}$ and check if the CE $\hat{\mathbf{x}}_i^2$ to the new lottery will still be unvaried. The same procedure is applied to the other lotteries with changed values of the attributes. If the CE $\hat{\mathbf{x}}_i^1$ , $\hat{\mathbf{x}}_i^2$ ,..., to those lotteries are all unvaried, then the attribute $\mathbf{x}_i$ is confirmed to be utility independent of all the other attributes $\mathbf{x}_{\bar{i}}$.

### 6.3.2 Assessment of Scaling Constants

According to Corollaries 6.1, 6.2 and 6.3, if the independence assumptions are satisfied, then identification of MUF can be performed. In this subsection, the assessment method of the scaling constants $k_i$ and $K$ for MUF is discussed.

#### 1. Ranking of $k_i$

The scaling constants for MUF are regarded as weights placed on the component utility functions which are primarily assessed as SUF, and thus their assessment represent a coordination process by DM. In the process of assessing the scaling constants, value trade-offs among attributes should be revealed. Before numerical calculation of the scaling constants, numerical order of $k_i$, $i = 1,\dots,m$, should be determined corresponding to the preference order of attributes $X_i$, $i = 1,\dots,m$, which shows the degree of their relative importance in the system. For example,

$$X_s \succ X_k \succ X_r \dots \succ X_t \Leftrightarrow k_s > k_k > k_r \dots > k_t. \tag{6.43}$$

## 2. Determination of relative ratio of $k_i$

Based on the preference order of $X_i$, $i = 1,\dots,m$, in a system, relative ratios of the scaling constants $k_i$ are determined. Taking the most preferable attribute $X_s$ as the base, value trade-offs between the $X_s$ and the other attributes $X_i$, $i = 1,\dots,m$, $i \neq s$, are assessed. An indifference experiment determines how many units of the most preferable attribute $X_s$ can be given up to gain an additional one unit of the other attribute $X_i$. In practice, we assess how much of the attribute $\mathbf{x}_s$ should be given up for changing the value of the other attribute $\mathbf{x}_i$, $i = 1,\dots,m$, $i \neq s$, traded-off for the $\mathbf{x}_s$ from the worst value $\mathbf{x}_{i0}$ to the best value $\mathbf{x}_{i1}$. The indifference experiment is depicted in Figure 6.3.

From the representation theorems or corollaries, it is known that to find, by the indifference experiment, the point $\mathbf{x}_{sx}$ such that

$$u(\mathbf{x}_{i1}, \mathbf{x}_{s0}) = u(\mathbf{x}_{i0}, \mathbf{x}_{sx}) \tag{6.44}$$

is reduced to finding the point $\mathbf{x}_{sx}$ such that

$$k_i u_{i1}(\mathbf{x}_{i1}) = k_s u_{sx}(\mathbf{x}_{sx}). \tag{6.45}$$

From $u_{i1}(\mathbf{x}_{i1}) = 1$,

$$k_i = k_s u_{sx}(\mathbf{x}_{sx}), \quad i = 1,\dots,m, \quad i \neq s \tag{6.46}$$

or

$$\frac{k_i}{k_s} = u_{sx}(\mathbf{x}_{sx}). \tag{6.47}$$

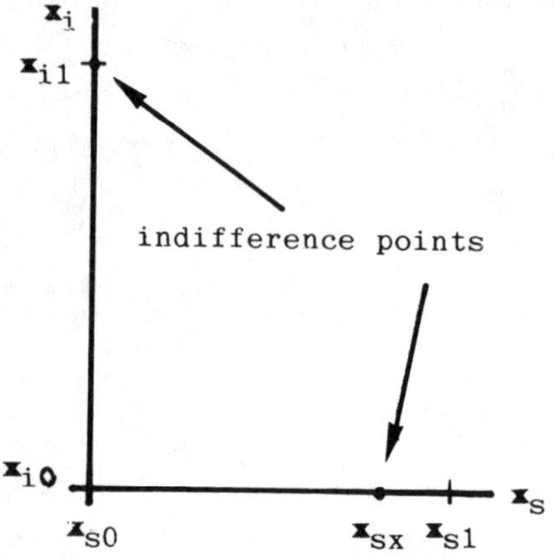


**Figure 6.3 Indifference experiment for assessing scaling constants.**

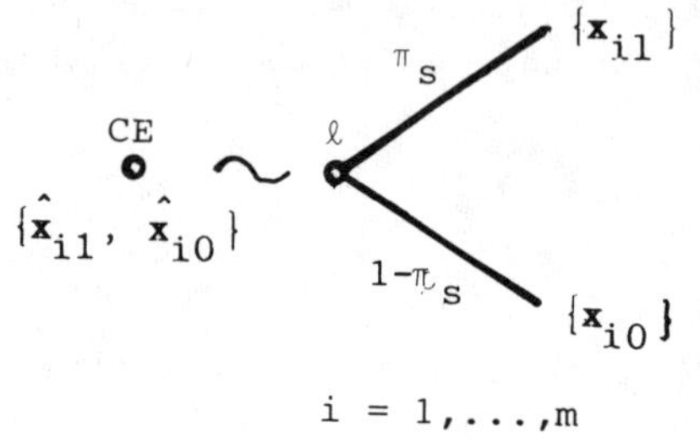


**Figure 6.4 $x_s$-probability experiment.**

By assigning $x_{sx}$, $u_{sx}(x_{sx})$ can be known. Thus, if the $x_{sx}$-value is obtained for every $x_{i1}$ in (6.44), $i = 1,\ldots,m$, $i \neq s$, then the relative ratios of the scaling constants $k_i/k_s$, $i = 1,\ldots,m$, $i \neq s$, can be determined from (6.47).

### 3. Determination of the basic value $k_s$

For obtaining the numerical values $k_i$, $i = 1,\ldots,m$, $i \neq s$, the value of the scaling constant $k_s$ taken as the base should be determined. The $k_s$-value can be determined by the $\pi_s$-probability experiment which is depicted in Figure 6.4. Consider, on the one hand, a certain event in which the most preferable attribute $X_s$ takes its best value and all the other attributes $X_{\bar{s}}$ take their worst values and, on the other hand, a lottery in which all the attributes take their best values with a probability $\pi_s$ or their worst values with a probability $1-\pi_s$, alternatively. Assess the value of the probability $\pi_s$ with which the certain event and the lottery come to be indifferent to each other. From the representation theorems or corollaries for MUF, this indifference experiment is reduced to finding the $\pi_s$-value such that

$$k_s u_{s1}(x_{s1}) = \pi_s, \tag{6.48}$$

or $k_s = \pi_s$.

The value of the basic scaling constant $k_s$ can be determined with the probability $\pi_s$. Then all the numerical values of the scaling constants $k_i$, $i = 1,\ldots,m$, can be determined from (6.46).

**4. Calculation of K**

From Corollary 6.2., when $\sum_{i=1}^{m} k_i \neq 1$, the MUF U takes the multiplicative form. The scaling constant K is a solution to

$$1 + K = \prod_{i=1}^{m} (1 + Kk_i). \tag{6.49}$$

As has already been suggested, any high-order equation (6.49) has a unique solution $K > -1$. When $\sum_{i=1}^{m} k_i > 1$, $-1 < K < 0$. When $\sum_{i=1}^{m} k_i < 1$, $\infty > K > 0$.

**Remark.**

The assessment of the scaling constant $k_i$, $i = 1,\ldots,m$, corresponds to the coordination process of DM. While evaluation of SUF for an attribute $\mathbf{X}_i$ is performed independently of all the other attributes $\mathbf{X}_j$, $j = 1,\ldots,m$, $j \neq i$, in a partitioned subsystem i, the coordination process for the evaluation in each subsystem is introduced in assessing the scaling constants as adjustment parameters for reconciling value conflicts among the subsystems. The value trade-off experiment is performed for this purpose.

Thus MUF can be constructed corresponding to an objectives configuration of a whole system. This problem is discussed in the next section.

### 6.3.3 Checks for the Representation Forms and for Coherence of the Preference Order

**1. Check for the representation forms**

The representation forms, additive or multiplicative, of MUF are determined by whether the sum of the scaling constants $\sum_{i=1}^{m} k_i$ is 1 or not. The result of this evaluation should be checked to confirm the validity of the obtained representation forms. For this purpose, an indifference experiment between two lotteries is performed. The one lottery $\ell_1$ takes the best values or the worst values for all the attributes $\mathbf{x}_{i1}$, $i = 1,\ldots,m$, alternately, with an equal probability of 50 %. The other lottery $\ell_2$ takes the best values for a set of attributes $\{\mathbf{x}_i\}$ and the worst values for its complement $\{\mathbf{x}_{\bar{i}}\}$, or takes reverse values for these attributes alternately, with the equal probability of 50 %. If the two lotteries $\ell_1$ and $\ell_2$ are indifferent to each other, then the MUF is additive. If not, the MUF is multiplicative (Figure 6.5). This can be proved with the representation theorems or corollaries for MUF.

**2. Check for coherence of preference order**

Numerical ordering of the scaling constants $k_i$ in deriving MUF should correspond to the preference ordering for the attributes $X_i$, $i = 1,\ldots,m$. However, the indifference

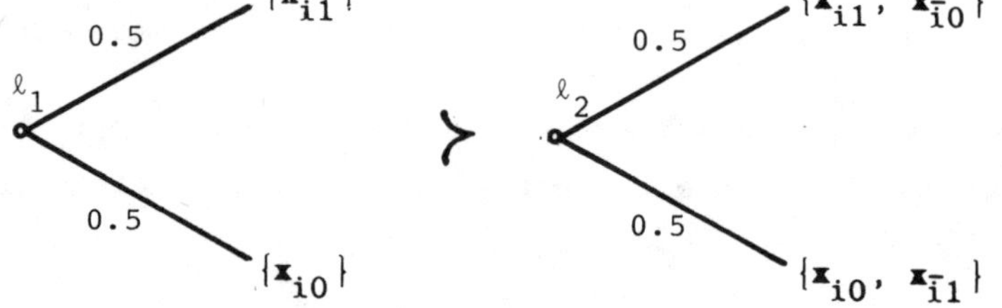


**Figure 6.5 Check of the representation forms of the multiattribute utility function.**

experiments for assessing relative ratios of the scaling constants are performed for every pair of attributes. Thus when MUF is defined on many attributes, assuring the consistency in assessment of the scaling constant for SUF will be difficult. The coherence check is used for this purpose. For checking the coherence, the trade-off experiment (6.44) is performed between the $\mathbf{X}_j$, $j \neq s$, selected as the new base and the other attributes $\mathbf{X}_i$, $i = 1,\dots,m$, $i \neq s,j$. Then similarly to (6.46) or (6.47),

$$k_i = k_j u_{jx}(\mathbf{x}_{jx}), \quad i = 1,\dots,m, \quad i \neq s,j, \tag{6.50}$$

or

$$\frac{k_i}{k_j} = u_{jx}(\mathbf{x}_{jx}) \tag{6.51}$$

is obtained. If the preference order for the attributes is not coherent, then the $k_i$-value in (6.50) will not be the same as in (6.46). Correction of evaluation for the scaling constants can be performed in three ways.

(i) To modify the indifference point $\mathbf{x}_{sx}$ between $X_i$ and $\mathbf{X}_s$. With this device, the value of $u_{sx}(\mathbf{x}_{sx})$ in (6.46) is revised and the $k_i$-value is corrected with $k_s$ unvaried.

(ii) To modify the indifference point $\mathbf{x}_{sx}$ between $X_j$ and $\mathbf{X}_s$. With this device, the value of $u_{sx}(\mathbf{x}_{sx})$ in (6.46) is revised and the $k_j$-value is corrected with $k_s$ unvaried.

(iii) To modify the indifference point $\mathbf{x}_{jx}$ between $X_i$ and $\mathbf{X}_j$. With this device, the value of $u_{jx}(\mathbf{x}_{jx})$ in (6.51) is revised and the $k_i$-value is corrected with $\mathbf{k}_j$ unvaried .

By using any one or more of these, the evaluation of scaling constants is corrected to keep coincidence between (6.46) and (6.50).

**Remark.**

In practice, the coherence check cannot be performed effectively for many attributes. The systems decomposition, in which one subsystem includes only the small number of attributes, will provide a proper device for avoiding such incoherence in the assessment.

## 6.4 Hierarchical Structuring of Preferences: Nesting

### 6.4.1 Decision Hierarchy

The effectiveness of multiattribute utility analysis largely depends on construction of an objectives hierarchy in multilevel. The reasons are the following.

First, the representation theorems of MUF are based on the mutual utility independence assumption, which is difficult to satisfy when a large number of attributes must be considered. Second, for assuring the coherence in preference ordering of attributes, the number of attributes should be confined within a manageable range. If not, incoherence will often occur. Third, the properties of the attributes to be assessed have great variety they are physical, ecological, economical, social, psychological, aesthetic, managerial, administrative, and so forth. Not all of the preferences for those attributes are properly comparable with each other even by the trade-off assessment, and consequently they cannot be assessed in only one level all at once. Fourth, even the attributes having similar properties often must be evaluated from different points of view, such as different interests, different times, different regions, different functions, different cultural point of view, etc. Thus, the attributes of the whole system should be classified and structured according to their properties from different points of view. For coping with these characteristics, systems decompositions such as (a) regional, (b) functional, (c) interest (such as industrial and residential), and (d) time decompositions are used, and these decomposed subsystems are consolidated into a multilevel system for keeping consistency and comparability.

The hierarchical structure of multilevel systems has been considered by Mesarović, Macko and Takahara (1970), Haimes, Lasdon, and Wismer (1971), Haimes and Macko (1973), and others. The main concepts for the multilevel decomposition are classified in the following terms.

(i) Stratum: decomposition based on levels of abstraction in description of systems.

For example, physical processes facilitate physical

modeling, operation, and control, and are laid at the lowest level in a decision hierarchy. Mathematical processes are appropriate to mathematical modeling and optimization, and are at a higher level. Economic and social processes need an abstract description, and thus are at the highest level. This decomposition corresponds to the levels of abstraction in the systems description.

(ii) Layer: decomposition based on levels of complexity of decision making.

Incompleteness of information, the great number of decision alternatives, contingencies for making decisions, and the value conflicts which DM faces increase the complexity in decision. More complex strategic judgments are made at higher levels, which are also concerned with wider-range and longer-term decision problems. Thus, the higher levels in a hierarchical system include more uncertainties and more ambiguousness in decision making, which prevent definite judgment of DM. The decisions should be made more deliberately and more constructively to maintain mutual coherence and consistency at the higher levels. This decomposition corresponds to the levels of decision complexity.

(iii) Echelon: decomposition based on levels of organizational hierarchy.

Decisions in higher levels exercise their authority on decisions in lower levels via intervention. The higher-level decision units send prescribed policies down to the lower-level units, and make them execute these policies. The lower-level decision units send their responses to the indicated policies back up to the higher levels. Within these information and performance feedback channels, learning and adaptation processes are embedded. This decomposition corresponds to levels of an indicative decision hierarchy.

The above three categories for systems decomposition are related with each other. The stratum and layer are usually included into the echelon. The partition of the whole system into subsystems represents specialization and decentralization of the different functions of the system. Thus, the whole system can be treated as an interactive information and management system, which is operated by the partitioned decision units functioning with their own specialized authorization and responsibility in multilevels. Simulation, prediction, and optimization processes can be included with a proper order in some decision units at some levels. Thus a methodological systems configuration constructs another aspect of the decision hierarchy.

### 6.4.2 Nesting of Preferences

An objectives hierarchy is constructed corresponding to the hierarchical configuration of the multilevel systems. For example, a set of attributes in a system can be partitioned according to their properties as follows:

$$\mathbf{x} \triangleq ([(\mathbf{x}_1, \mathbf{x}_2, \mathbf{x}_3)_1, (\mathbf{x}_4, \mathbf{x}_5, \mathbf{x}_6)_2, (\mathbf{x}_7, \mathbf{x}_8, \mathbf{x}_9)_3]^1, [\mathbf{x}_{10}, (\mathbf{x}_{11}, \mathbf{x}_{12})_4]^2). \tag{6.52}$$

In terms of the utility functions,

$$U(\mathbf{x}) \triangleq U[U^1(U_1(u_1(\mathbf{x}_1), u_2(\mathbf{x}_2), u_3(\mathbf{x}_3)), U_2(u_4(\mathbf{x}_4), u_5(\mathbf{x}_5), u_6(\mathbf{x}_6)), U_3(u_7(\mathbf{x}_7), u_8(\mathbf{x}_8), u_9(\mathbf{x}_9))), U^2(u_{10}(\mathbf{x}_{10}), U_4(u_{11}(\mathbf{x}_{11}), u_{12}(\mathbf{x}_{12})))], \tag{6.53}$$

where $\mathbf{x} \in R^{12}$.

In (6.53), the MUF $U$ for the whole system is represented with two MUFs in a lower level, $U^1$ and $U^2$, where the $U^1$ itself has three MUFs $U_1$, $U_2$ and $U_3$, and the $U^2$ has one SUF, $u_{10}$, and one MUF $U_4$. (6.53) shows that the twelve attributes in the whole system are consolidated into five subsystems, which are consolidated again into two subsystems. Finally, this system is evaluated with an overall MUF $U(\mathbf{x})$. (6.53) represents a hierarchical configuration based on the four-level decomposition.

Representing a MUF in terms of many MUFs which are incorporated in it is called nesting. By using a general form of nesting, the decision problem (6.3) with MUF U is formulated.

$$\sup_{\mathbf{x}^j \in S^j \subset \Gamma} U[U^1(\mathbf{x}^1), U^2(\mathbf{x}^2), \ldots, U^q(\mathbf{x}^q)], \tag{6.54}$$

or

$$\sup_{\mathbf{x}_i \in S_i \subset \Gamma} U[U^1(u_1(\mathbf{x}_1), u_2(\mathbf{x}_2), \ldots, u_t(\mathbf{x}_t)),$$

$$U^2(u_{t+1}(\mathbf{x}_{t+1}), \ldots, u_r(\mathbf{x}_r)), \ldots,$$

$$U^q(u_{s+1}(\mathbf{x}_{s+1}), \ldots, u_m(\mathbf{x}_m))]. \tag{6.55}$$

(6.55) shows the structuring which consolidates the $m$ attributes in the system into $q$ subsystems. The formulation (6.55) can be represented in more complex forms by regarding some or all of $u_i(\mathbf{x}_i)$, $i = 1, \ldots, m$, as MUF.

The representation theorems 6.1 and 6.3 and corollaries 6.1-6.3 can be extended to (6.55). When $u_i(\mathbf{x}_i)$, $i = 1, \ldots, m$, is also a MUF, the scaling constant $k_i$, $i = 1, \ldots, m$, can be assessed by the trade-off experiments for each pair of attributes which are selected as the most preferable in each subsystem $i = 1, \ldots, m$.

The systems decomposition and coordination in a hierarchical, multilevel system is a useful device for a better understanding of the properties of a system and for its effective management and control. While multiattribute utility analysis is not concerned with the mathematical optimization in any level at all, MDP (6.1) probably includes some objectives for which mathematical optimization can be effectively performed. Thus, although the multiattribute utility analysis exclusively concerns the subjective identification of the preference structure of DM, this identification process is better executed at a higher level of the decision hierarchy. This problem is discussed in later chapters.

## 6.5 Interactive Computer Program for Subjective Systems

### 6.5.1 Discussion on Multiattribute Utility Analysis

Multiattribute utility analysis provides a heuristic method for directly assessing the preference of DM in a commensurable term: MUF. The MUF is measured with interval scales which make it possible not only to determine a preference order of DM but also to get its numerical assessment, which corresponds to the preference structure for the entire system. Because the assessment of MUF does not depend on the mathematical optimization and thus a mathematical modeling of the attributes is not required, the multiattribute utility analysis is particularly effective when applied to objects having descriptive properties which are difficult to identify in mathematical function forms.

One of the main characteristics of multiattribute utility analysis is its use of interactive processes for making decisions, or selecting the numerical order of preferences. Evaluation processes of MUF proceed sequentially and iteratively. The major part of assessment and calculation of MUF is composed of repetitive computation procedures. The processes include assessment of the single or component utility functions and various types of probability distributions, evaluation of expected utility functions, calculation of MUF with alternative scaling constants, and also sensitivity analysis. Indifference experiments for deriving MUF are performed. Assessors must know promptly about alternative results of evaluation that have been calculated with alternative parameters, and then must proceed to the next stage sequentially. Constructing alternative policy proposals based on the sensitivity analysis and comparing final results of the numerical evaluation for alternative policy programs are included as an important aspect in the interactive processes. Thus, facilities for speed-up of computation works will be expected. For this purpose, effective utilization of an interactive computer program is highly recommended as a decision support system (DSS) in MCDM.

The following discussion provides some examples of DSS for MCDM.

### 6.5.2 Assistance by Computer Programs

As described in Section 6.2, computer programs for assessing and calculating the SUF as well as the probability distribution functions have been developed by Schlaifer (1971), which have been written in FORTRAN and are called the MANECON collection. The MANECON collection has many eminent characteristics for assessing the various types of SUF and probability distribution functions, and for calculating the expected utility values. In particular, the MANECON collection has interactive characteristics which assist DM in checking and revising the consistency of his assessments. Sicherman (1975) developed a new computer program for assessing and calculating MUF based on the representation theorems of Keeney (1974) and Keeney and Raiffa (1976). His program is written in PL/1 and is called MUFCAP (Multiattribute Utility Function Calculation and Assessment Package). MUFCAP is designed to facilitate the assessment and calculation of the DM's utility functions. These utility functions are assessed in order through a preference structure that is configured in a hierarchical, multilevel system and represented in a tree diagram. MUFCAP also has excellent facilities for changing the systems attributes and their levels and for revising the construction of the nested preference structures. Despite this progress, MUFCAP still has some room to be improved for treating decision problems under uncertainty because it lacks some techniques for calculating probability distribution functions and the expected utility values which are included in MANECON collection.

Thus, the MANECON programs can be combined with the MUFCAP program for assisting the evaluation of MUF more effectively through the large-scale and complex preference structure. This revised computer package is called ICOPSS (Interactive Computer Program for Subjective Systems) (Sakawa and Seo 1980a, 1982b), which is written in FORTRAN. A medium-size computer facility is sufficient for loading the program packages written in FORTRAN. This new package has the capability for graphical representations by which assessors can figure the shapes of their utility functions, probability distributions, and indifference curves. Thus assessors can find incorrect assessments or unnatural evaluations promptly, revise them immediately, and proceed to the next stage more reasonably. An overall preference structure can also be represented in a tree diagram visually. The facilities for assessing the scaling constants are also revised and enlarged.

ICOPSS, along with MANECON collection and MUFCAP, is a computer program which offers a new direction for computer-assisted decision making. This type of computer utilization, which intends to interactively assess human preferences, includes human factors explicitly in computer-aided systems analysis. While computer-assisted decision analysis is still an experimental field to be developed, the combination of computer utilization with preference analysis is increasingly becoming more crucial in DSS fields for coping with complex systems in the present world where human preferences are diversified and independent of each other, and tends to have unmanageable properties.

### 6.5.3 Assessment of the Scaling Constants for MUF

In this subsection, facilities of ICOPSS for assessment of the scaling constraints are discussed.

Three types for assessment of the scaling constant $k_i$ in MUF are considered in ICOPSS. Alternative methods for assessing $k_i$ in the representation forms (6.6)-(6.8) are: (1) to input $k_i$ directly with subjective assessment, or (2) to select one pair of indifference points between the attributes and a probability for a prescribed lottery, or (3) to select the two pairs of indifference points between any two attributes.

The method (2) proceeds responding to the following questions.

**Question 1.** What are the level $\mathbf{x}_{ix}$ of an attribute $\mathbf{X}_i$ and the level $\mathbf{x}_{sx}$ of another attribute $\mathbf{X}_s$ taken as a base, such that, for fixed levels of all the other attributes $\mathbf{x}_{\overline{is}}$, you are indifferent between

(i) a consequence yielding $\mathbf{x}_{ix}$ and $\mathbf{x}_{s0}$ together, and

(ii) a consequence yielding $\mathbf{x}_{sx}$ and $\mathbf{x}_{i0}$ together ?

Responses to Question 1 provide relative values of $k_i/k_s$,

$i = 1,\ldots,m$, from the representation theorems.

**Question 2.** Consider a lottery such that all the attributes $\mathbf{X}_i$, $i = 1,\ldots,m$ take alternately their best levels $\mathbf{x}_{i1}$, $i = 1,\ldots,m$, with a probability $p$, or worst levels $\mathbf{x}_{i0}$, $i = 1,\ldots,m$, with a probability $1 - p$. Then, for which value of the probability $p$ are you indifferent between the lottery and a certain consequence that takes the best value for $\mathbf{x}_s$ and the worst value for $\mathbf{x}_{\bar{s}}$ ? In other words, what value can be assigned to the probability $p$ such that

(i) the lottery that has a chance $p$ of $\{\mathbf{x}_{i1}\}$ and a chance $1 - p$ of $\{\mathbf{x}_{i0}\}$, and

(ii) the certain consequence $(\mathbf{x}_{s1}, \mathbf{x}_{\bar{s}0})$ are indifferent ?

A response to Question 2 provides the $k_s$-values for the most preferable attribute $\mathbf{x}_s$ taken as the base of evaluation. The method (3) proceeds responding to the following question:

**Question 3.** What are the levels A, B, C, D in two indifferent pairs for attributes $\mathbf{X}_i$ and $\mathbf{X}_s$, $i = 1,\ldots,m$, $i \neq s$, such that

$$A[\mathbf{x}_{ix}, \mathbf{x}_{sx}] \sim B[\mathbf{x}_{ix}, \mathbf{x}_{sx}],$$

$$C[\mathbf{x}_{ix}, \mathbf{x}_{sx}] \sim D[\mathbf{x}_{ix}, \mathbf{x}_{sx}],$$

taking $\mathbf{X}_s$ as a base.

In method (2), taking the most preferable (or highly regarded) attribute $\mathbf{X}_s$ as the base, one indifference point between each pair of the attributes $\mathbf{X}_i$ and $\mathbf{X}_s$ is sought with all levels of the other attributes $\mathbf{X}_{\overline{is}}$ held fixed. The indifference point represents the trade-off which measures how much DM is willing to give up of an attribute $\mathbf{X}_s$ in order to gain an amount of the other attribute $\mathbf{X}_i$.

Using Question 1, one indifferent pair of attributes $\mathbf{X}_i$ and $\mathbf{X}_s$ is sought as follows:

$$\begin{pmatrix} \mathbf{x}_{ix} & : ? \\ \mathbf{x}_{s0} & : \text{worst} \end{pmatrix} \sim \begin{pmatrix} \mathbf{x}_{i0} & : \text{worst} \\ \mathbf{x}_{sx} & : ? \end{pmatrix}, \quad \begin{matrix} i = 1,\ldots,m, \\ i \neq s. \end{matrix} \tag{6.56}$$

Utilities for (6.56) are equated, and yield

$$k_i u_i(\mathbf{x}_{ix}) = k_s u_s(\mathbf{x}_{sx}), \quad i = 1,\ldots,m, \quad i \neq s, \tag{6.57}$$

$$k_i = k_s u_s(\mathbf{x}_{sx})/u_i(\mathbf{x}_{ix}). \tag{6.58}$$

In this way, the relative values of all the scaling constants $k_1,\ldots,k_m$ are expressed in terms of $k_s$. It can be seen that, when $\mathbf{x}_{ix}$ takes its best value $\mathbf{x}_{i1}$, the indifference experiment (6.56) will be performed more easily.

Using Question 2, if the p-value is determined to be $\hat{p}$, the expected utility of the lottery is $\hat{p}$ and the utility value of the certain consequence is $k_s$. Thus we find, from the indifference relation,

$$k_s = \hat{p}. \tag{6.59}$$

In method (3), taking the attribute $\mathbf{X}_s$ as the base, two pairs of the indifference points are assessed. In the additive case, it is necessary to assess only one pair of the different values. In the multiplicative case, two pairs of indifference points (A,B) and (C,D) should be shown to calculate $k_i$ and K. For convenience, we use new notations $([\mathbf{x}_i^A, \mathbf{x}_s^A], [\mathbf{x}_i^B, \mathbf{x}_s^B])$, and $([\mathbf{x}_i^C, \mathbf{x}_s^C], [\mathbf{x}_i^D, \mathbf{x}_s^D])$ instead of $(A[\mathbf{x}_{ix}, \mathbf{x}_{sx}], B[\mathbf{x}_{ix}, \mathbf{x}_{sx}])$, and $(C[\mathbf{x}_{ix}, \mathbf{x}_{sx}], D[\mathbf{x}_{ix}, \mathbf{x}_{sx}])$ for showing different points. Using the definition of the multiplicative utility function (6.8), utilities in indifference points (A,B) and (C,D) are equated to each other with other attributes fixed at their worst levels. Then taking the difference,

$$k_i(u_i(\mathbf{x}_i^A) - u_i(\mathbf{x}_i^B)) + k_s(u_s(\mathbf{x}_s^A) - u_s(\mathbf{x}_s^B))$$
$$+ k_i k_s K(u_i(\mathbf{x}_i^A)u_s(\mathbf{x}_s^A) - u_i(\mathbf{x}_i^B)u_s(\mathbf{x}_s^B)) = 0, \tag{6.60}$$
$$i = 1,\ldots,m, \quad i \neq s,$$

$$k_i(u_i(\mathbf{x}_i^C) - u_i(\mathbf{x}_i^D)) + k_s(u_s(\mathbf{x}_s^C) - u_s(\mathbf{x}_s^D))$$

$$+ k_i k_s K(u_i(\mathbf{x}_i^C)u_s(\mathbf{x}_s^C) - u_i(\mathbf{x}_i^D)u_s(\mathbf{x}_s^D)) = 0, \qquad (6.61)$$

$$i = 1,\ldots,m, \quad i \neq s,$$

where $K$ is the non-zero scaling constant satisfying the equation

$$1 + K = \prod_{i=1}^{m} (1 + Kk_i). \qquad (6.62)$$

From equations (6.59), (6.60), and (6.61), the $k_i$ and $K$ can be determined. Putting

$$P \triangleq u_i(\mathbf{x}_i^A)u_s(\mathbf{x}_s^A) - u_i(\mathbf{x}_i^B)u_s(\mathbf{x}_s^B) \neq 0, \qquad (6.63)$$

and

$$Q \triangleq u_i(\mathbf{x}_i^C)u_s(\mathbf{x}_s^C) - u_i(\mathbf{x}_i^D)u_s(\mathbf{x}_s^D) \neq 0, \qquad (6.64)$$

and solving equations (6.60) and (6.61) yields

$$k_i/k_s = -\frac{R}{S}, \qquad (6.65)$$

$$k_s K = \frac{F}{R}, \qquad (6.66)$$

where

$$F \triangleq (u_i(\mathbf{x}_i^C) - u_i(\mathbf{x}_i^D))(u_s(\mathbf{x}_s^A) - u_s(\mathbf{x}_s^B))$$

$$- (u_s(\mathbf{x}_s^C) - u_s(\mathbf{x}_s^D))(u_i(\mathbf{x}_i^A) - u_i(\mathbf{x}_i^B)),$$

$$R \triangleq (u_i(\mathbf{x}_i^A) - u_i(\mathbf{x}_i^B))Q - (u_i(\mathbf{x}_i^C) - u_i(\mathbf{x}_i^D))P \neq 0, \qquad (6.67)$$

and

$$S \triangleq (u_s(\mathbf{x}_s^A) - u_s(\mathbf{x}_s^B))Q + (u_s(\mathbf{x}_s^C) - u_s(\mathbf{x}_s^D))P \neq 0. \qquad (6.68)$$

Equation (6.62) is rewritten as

$$1 + K = \prod_{i=1}^{m} (1 + (k_i/k_s)k_sK). \qquad (6.69)$$

Substituting (6.65) and (6.66) into (6.69), the value of $K$ can be determined. Substituting the value of $K$ into (6.66), $k_s$ is determined. Then $k_i$, $i = 1,\ldots,m$, $i \neq s$, can be determined from (6.65).

### 6.5.4 The Computer Package: ICOPSS

ICOPSS is composed of one main program and many subroutines. The main program calls in and runs the subroutines with commands indicated by the user.

INPUT command initiates a dialogue by indicating a name of an overall MUF for a preference structure, and requests in order the numbers and names of attributes that are included in MUF through the hierarchical preference structure. A prompt "ANOTHER INPUT?" asks whether the input process should continue or not. The input processes can be interrupted and the input data can be saved at any level of the MUF structure. This device helps to mitigate the burden of the work for putting in a large-scale data set in order all at once.

SAVE command saves all the information, which has been put in and calculated, in a file.

READ command restores the information which has been saved in the file.

STRUCT command displays the MUF structure with the names of all the attributes or the single attribute utility functions UNIF, and the names of all MUF, in a tree diagram, which is called out with an overall MUF name.

UNISET command constructs a data set for UNIF by indicating the UNIF-names. The UNISET command provides a list of UNIF-types such as

(1) LINEAR,
(2) PIECEWISE LINEAR,

(3) CONSTANT RISK,
(4) DECREASING RISK AVERSE, and
(5) INCREASING RISK PRONE,

for an option.

In constructing the data set for each UNIF-type, information for each attribute is required. For (1), the range (worst or best) of the attribute; for (2), the range of the attribute and numerical values for the specified points in abscissa and ordinate in the $\mathbf{x}_i-u_i(\mathbf{x}_i)$ plane; for (3), the range of attributes and specified values of CE for the 50-50 chance lottery. The type (3) is available both for constant risk averse and constant risk prone.

Types (4) and (5) have two options for data input: (a) to input the five levels of the attribute for which the UNIF-values are 0, 0.25, 0.5, 0.75, and 1. respectively, or (b) to input a range for the attribute and each CE for three 50-50 chance lotteries which can be arbitrarily chosen. If assessments for the decreasing risk averse or increasing risk prone type of UNIF are unsuccessful with the input data, a warning message prompts for putting in revised data. For the UNIF types (4) and (5), users can express and revise their preference more accurately via these interactive processes.

KSET command makes a data set for all scaling constants for each MUF by indicating the MUF names. Three types of options for calculating scaling constants are available:

(1) BY INPUT OF K'S VALUES DIRECTLY,
(2) BY INDIFFERENCE PAIRS AND LOTTERY, and
(3) BY INDIFFERENCE PAIRS.

For type (1), by inputting $k_i$-values directly, a corresponding value of the scaling constant K for each MUF is calculated.

Type (2) is based on Questions 1 and 2. Taking an attribute $\mathbf{x}_S$ as the base, an indifference pair of $\mathbf{x}_i$ and $\mathbf{x}_S$ is input. With the selected $\hat{p}$-value, all the scaling constants $k_i$, $i = 1,\ldots,m$, for each UNIF, and K are calculated.

Type (3) requires to input any two pairs of indifference points. In the case of nested MUF, the indifference experiments are executed in terms of the utility values of the most preferable attributes. Computer utilization is more effective in this respect. The KSET, INDIF1, and INDEF2 commands in the MUFCAP are unified in (3), which also includes a function for consistency check.

DEBUG command lists at once all information of UNIF and MUF in the MUF Structure. For the MUF, the name and its scaling constant K are listed. For the UNIF, the name, a range of the attribute, its scaling constant $k_i$, and the UNIF type are listed.

ADDALT command constructs alternative data sets called by assigned names. These data sets are composed of alternative levels of all the attributes included in the overall MUF structure. Four types of attributes are available, which can be used in combination in a data set:

(1) CERTAINTY,
(2) PROBABILITY: DISCRETE DISTRIBUTION,
(3) PROBABILITY: CONTINUOUS DISTRIBUTION (PIECEWISE LINEAR),
(4) PROBABILITY: CONTINUOUS DISTRIBUTION (PIECEWISE QUADRATIC).

DROPALT command deletes the specified alternative data sets from the data file.

EVAL command calculates numerical values of UNIF and MUF in the alternative data set.

GRAD command calculates the gradients for the specified UNIF and MUF in terms of attributes and component utility functions:

$$\left(\frac{\partial u_1}{\partial \mathbf{x}_1}, \frac{\partial u_2}{\partial \mathbf{x}_2}, \ldots, \frac{\partial u_m}{\partial \mathbf{x}_m}\right), \quad \text{and} \quad \left(\frac{\partial U}{\partial u_1}, \frac{\partial U}{\partial u_2}, \ldots, \frac{\partial U}{\partial u_m}\right). \tag{6.70}$$

DISPLAY command displays information of each UNIF or MUF separately by calling out with its name. For UNIF, a range of the attribute, parameters, and a UNIF-type are listed. For MUF, its partial system's structure is depicted with the component UNIF-names or MUF-names in a tree diagram, and values of their scaling constants $k_i$ and K are also listed.

IMAP command generates indifference points in a specified attributes (uname1-uname2) plane. A point through which the indifference curve will pass is requested. A value of one attribute (uname1) is input and then a value of another attribute (uname2) is requested to maintain an indifference of preference.

GRAPHU command depicts graphically the shape of a UNIF.

GRAPHI command depicts graphically the shape of an indifference curve in a uname1-uname2 plane. A specified pair of indifference points through which the curve will pass is requested.

LISTU and LISTK commands display UNIF-and MUF-values and $k_i$-and K-values with their names respectively in a multilevel construction.

STOP command terminates the assessment and calculation process. A word of gratitude to the operator is listed out and the job ends.

### 6.5.5 Application to Prior Assessment for the Bullet Train Network

**1. The object area**

Multiattribute utility analysis with computer assistance by ICOPSS has been applied to prior assessment of the Hokuriku Shinkansen Project (the Bullet Train network construction project) in the north-western coastal area in Japan. Opening of the super-express railway system will be accompanied by various kinds of impacts on economic, environmental, social, cultural and administrative aspects in the region. This case study has been particularly concerned with the multiobjective impact analysis for Ishikawa prefecture which is located in the middle of the new railway (Hokuriku Shinkansen) system.

Ishikawa Prefecture faces the Sea of Japan and, having less sunshine time and more precipitation during all seasons than the average in Japan, suffers from severe meteorological conditions. However, Ishikawa has a long history and has been developed with the historical and cultural traditions of the "Kaga-millionaire" during the sixteenth to nineteenth centuries.

Those traditions still remain in their own local character and make Ishikawa an independent cultural area different from neighboring prefectures. As a result, Ishikawa holds the second to fifth positions in ranking in Japan for living space in houses, for the number of libraries and community centers, and for the number of doctors and beds for patients per capita of the resident in 1982. The number of criminal cases is also quite small compared with the average in Japan. Economic activities, which are shown by ratios of the employed labor force to population and the annual amounts of commodity sales per employed labor force, are in the ninth position in the ranking. Farm income per farm families and prefectural income per capita are in the twelfth and fourth positions, respectively, which are at the upper level in the 47 prefectures of Japan. Ishikawa is still one of the representative rice-producing areas in Japan and is also a major forestry and fishery area where these primary industries are still actively operating. Ishikawa has special local products with historical reputation, such as Kutani pottery, Wajima, Yamanaka, and Kanazawa lacquer wares, Kaga yuzen (Japanese silk cloth), and Kanazawa and Nanao home Buddhist altars, etc. Modern industries such as electric machinery have also been developed. Electric power plants are located in Ishikawa and supply energy resources. Construction of atomic power plants is also scheduled. Thus this region forms a complex problématique, and the Hokuriku Shinkansen Project will have particularly wide-ranging impacts on Ishikawa Prefecture as a historical as well as a well-administrated region.

## 2. Method

The impact assessment on this region has been performed in a combination of macroeconometrics and multiattribute utility analysis. The case study intends to combine those two approaches in multiobjective systems analysis. On the one hand, the impact assessment should properly be based on a prediction, and the econometric method can be effectively used for providing macroeconomic forecasting based on a quantitative structuring of economic aspects under given parameters obtained via statistical estimation and testing. On the other hand, multiattribute

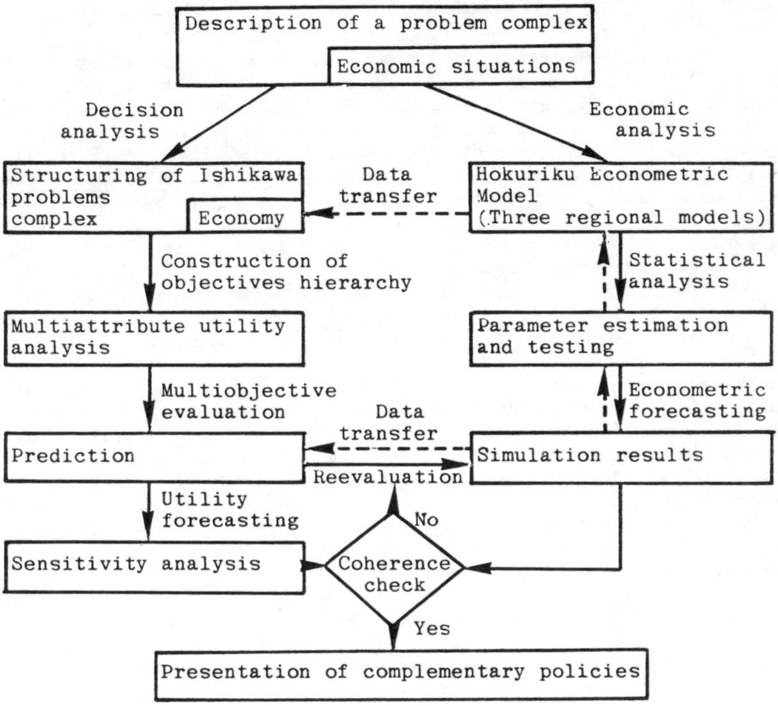


**Figure 6.6 Large-Scale systems analysis for Hokuriku Shinkansen construction.**

utility analysis concerns a comprehensive evaluation of multiple objectives systems, even though it depends on subjective evaluation for future prediction. In this case study, multiattribute utility analysis is combined with the results of simulation using the macroeconometric model in the first step (Figure 6.6). Both methods are used for future prediction in an interactive combination, and sensitivity analysis for UNIFs and MUFs is performed to present complementary policies based on the efficiency criterion in utility analysis.

The whole system is decomposed in regional, industrial, and functional subsystems in a nine-level hierarchical configuration, in which 166 subsystems are included and 5 regions, 15 industries, and 18 noneconomic factors are examined.

## 3. Structuring of a problems complex

The multiobjective impact assessment of the Hokuriku Shinkansen construction is performed based on structuring of the complex problems which the local communities face. The whole system is decomposed in regional, industrial and functional subsystems; which are structured in nine levels of a hierarchical system. The first level concerns a comprehensive evaluation of the Ishikawa prefecture. The second level is partitioned into "region" which can be separately evaluated for each subregion and "prefectural administration" which can not be separately evaluated. In the third level, the "region" is partitioned into "Kanazawa", "Hakusan", "Kaga" and "Noto" districts and evaluated according to each peculiarity for each district. "Kanazawa" is an urban area which include the capital city of Ishikawa prefecture, Kanazawa city, where the administrative functions of the prefecture are agglomerated and traditional small industries such as the Kutani potteries, Lacquer ware, and Japanese cloth and cakes are located. "Hakusan" is a natural environment conservation area which is mainly composed of the Hakusan National Park, but also partially includes industrial areas such as Mikawa, Tsurugi and Nonoich towns where some modern industries are located. "Kaga" is a famous sightseeing and health resort area which is composed of the Kaga Hotsprings country (Yamanaka, Yamashiro, Katayamazu, and Awazu Hotsprings, etc.) and the Kaga Beach, but also includes major industrial areas such as Komatsu city, where the Komatsu Manufacturing Company and the Komatsu airport are located, and Yamanaka town which is famous for the Yamanaka Lacquer ware. "Noto" is well known for the Noto Peninsula National Park and includes the Wajima city, which is famous for Wajima Lacquer ware, and electric and atomic power plants sites in Nanao city and in the Hagui district. Noto is also important forestry and fishery areas.

Those areas are evaluated in three subsystems such as "industry" "environment" and "public service". The industrial decomposition is performed in six levels from the fourth to the ninth. For "manufactures", eight industries are examined which are largely partitioned to "local" and "newly developed". For "commerce", eleven groups are considered, which are largely divided into "retail trades" and "sightseeing". The functional decompositions are performed for each industry. Each manufacturing industry is evaluated for its "activity" and "stability". "Retail trade" is evaluated for "activity" (amount of sales), and "sightseeing" is for "activity" and "earnings". For manufactures, the "activity" is examined from different points of view of interest. Measurements are the value of shipment per capita from the social point of view, the earnings (value added) per employed person from the point of view of entrepreneurs, and the wage income per employed person from that of laborers. The "stability" is also considered from different points of view of interest. Measurements are the change in share of the value of shipment from the social point of view, the change in the number of business establishments from the point of view of entrepreneurs and the availability of production factors in terms of opportunity of employment from that of laborers.

"Environment" for each subregion is partitioned into "pollution" and "natural environment" in the fifth level. "Pollution" is evaluated for "stench", "noise and vibration", "air pollution" and "water pollution" in the sixth level. "Public service" is partitioned into "sanitation" and "medical care" in the fifth level, and "sanitation is evaluated for "garbage treatment", "sanitary service" and "pervasion of flush-toilet" in the sixth level.

"Prefectural administration" is decomposed in six levels. It is partitioned into "economy", "resources" "environment" and "administration" in the third level. In the fourth level, "economy" is partitioned into "construction", "finance" and "exports". "Resource" is partitioned into "water" and "electric power" supply, and "environment" is partitioned into "cultural", "social" and "natural" environments. In the fifth level, "cultural environment" is evaluated for "preservation of traditional culture" and "university and college education". "Social environment" is evaluated for "stability" which is assessed with the number of criminal cases per capita. "Natural environment" is evaluated for "nature preservation" and "pollution control". "Pollution control" is partitioned into "solid waste treatment" and "water pollution" in the sixth level, and the "water pollution" is evaluated for "rivers", "lakes and marshes" and "estuaries", with the number of cases of unfitness to each environmental standard, respectively, in the seventh level. "Administration" is evaluated for "equity" using an index which shows economic equality compared with the average of national income per capita.

The attribute or UNIF (singleattribute utility function) names and MUF names are formed by combinations of code names corresponding to the hierarchical systems structure. For example, INMNEMCO is an attribute name which represents the value of shipment per capita for measuring "activity" of "electric machinery" in the "newly developed industry" of "manufactures". ENPOW is a MUF name which represents the "water pollution" in "environment". In performing multiattribute utility analysis, 269 attributes in total are selected for assessment. The number of UNIF-values to be assessed also amounts to the same. This numerous attributes is not easy to be evaluated individually. However the system's decomposition into a hierarchical structure shown in the above configuration makes the evaluation work much easier than at first sight.

## 4. Result

The evaluation process is effectively assisted by the computer program ICOPSS.

The STRUCT command in ICOPSS depicts visually a bird's eye picture of all 269 attributes in a tree diagram which represents the whole systems structure (Figure 6.7).

The data set for UNIF is constructed with the UNISET command (Figure 6.8). UNIF is assessed for (1) LINEAR and (2) CONSTANT RISK attitudes. When DM chooses (1) LINEAR form, evaluation is performed in the form of U(X) = A + BX and, when (2) CONSTANT RISK, U(X) = A + B * EXP(-C * X). (3) DECREASING RISK attitude is also available in the form of U(X) = A * EXP(-B * X) + C * EXP(-D * X) + E. The DISPLAY command demonstrates the function form of UNIF and the results of the parameter calculation. The scaling constants in the representation forms of MUF are assessed with the KSET command (Figure 6.9). In total, 269 UNIFs for all the attributes and 167 MUFs for all the systems are assessed in a nested preference structure.

For documentation, the LISTU and LISTK commands demonstrate all the data of UNIF and MUF in a tabular form according to all the levels. This device will make it easy to compare the scale-value assessment for each subsystem.

```
STRUCTURE FOR KANAZAWA
level 4     level 5     level 6     level 7      level 8      level 9
----IN      ----INM     ----INML    ----INMLFO   ----INMLFOC  ----INMLFOCO
  !           !           !           !            !            !
  !           !           !           !            !            !--INMLFOCP
  !           !           !           !            !            !
  !           !           !           !            !            !--INMLFOCW
  !           !           !           !            !
  !           !           !           !            !--INMLFOS  ----INMLFOSN
  !           !           !           !                         !
  !           !           !           !                         !--INMLFOSL
  !           !           !           !                         !
  !           !           !           !                         !--INMLFOSS
  !           !           !           !
  !           !           !           !--INMLTE  ----INMLTEC  ----INMLTECO
  !           !           !           !            !            !
  !           !           !           !            !            !--INMLTECP
*
  !           !           !           !            !            !
  !           !           !           !            !            !--INMLTECW
  !           !           !           !            !
  !           !           !           !            !--INMLTES  ----INMLTESN
  !           !           !           !                         !
  !           !           !           !                         !--INMLTESL
  !           !           !           !                         !
  !           !           !           !                         !--INMLTESS
  !           !           !           !
  !           !           !           !--INMLFR  ----INMLFRC  ----INMLFRCO
  !           !           !           !            !            !
  !           !           !           !            !            !--INMLFRCP
  !           !           !           !            !            !
  !           !           !           !            !            !--INMLFRCW
  !           !           !           !            !
  !           !           !           !            !--INMLFRS  ----INMLFRSN
  !           !           !           !                         !
  !           !           !           !                         !--INMLFRSL
  !           !           !           !                         !
  !           !           !           !                         !--INMLFRSS
  !           !           !           !
  !           !           !           !--INMLWO  ----INMLWOC  ----INMLWOCO
  !           !           !           !            !            !
*
  !           !           !           !            !            !--INMLWOCP
  !           !           !           !            !            !
  !           !           !           !            !            !--INMLWOCW
  !           !           !           !            !
  !           !           !           !            !--INMLWOS  ----INMLWOSN
  !           !           !           !                         !
  !           !           !           !                         !--INMLWOSL
  !           !           !           !                         !
  !           !           !           !                         !--INMLWOSS
  !           !           !           !
  !           !           !           !--INMLCL  ----INMLCLC  ----INMLCLCO
  !           !           !                        !            !
  !           !           !                        !            !--INMLCLCP
  !           !           !                        !            !
  !           !           !                        !            !--INMLCLCW
  !           !           !                        !
  !           !           !                        !--INMLCLS  ----INMLCLSN
  !           !           !                                     !
  !           !           !                                     !--INMLCLSL
  !           !           !                                     !
                                                                !--INMLCLSS
```

**Figure 6.7** Problem structure for Kanazawa district: part (Illustration with STRUCT command).

```
COMMAND:
=READ
INPUT FILE NAME:
=HAKUSAN
DATA IS READ.

COMMAND:
=UNISET
INPUT UNIF NAME:
=INMLFOCO
WANT LIST OF UNIF TYPE?
=YES
LIST OF UNIF TYPE


 (1) LINEAR
 (2) PIECEWISE LINEAR
 (3) CONSTANT RISK
 (4) DECREASING RISK
INPUT UNIF TYPE:
=3
INPUT RANGE(WORST & BEST) OF THIS UNIF:
=0.0 50.0
INPUT 50-50 LOTTERY(WORSE PAYOFF,BETTER PAYOFF & C.E.):
=0.0 50.0 21.0
ANOTHER UNISET?
=YES
INPUT UNIF NAME:
=INMLFOCP
WANT LIST OF UNIF TYPE?
=NO
INPUT UNIF TYPE:
=3
INPUT RANGE(WORST & BEST) OF THIS UNIF:
=0.0 1500.0
INPUT 50-50 LOTTERY(WORSE PAYOFF,BETTER PAYOFF & C.E.):
=0.0 1500.0 625.0
ANOTHER UNISET?
```

**Figure 6.8 Illustration of UNISET command.**

Utility prediction is performed on the predicted levels of attributes to change under the assumption that the type and parameters of each utility function are unvaried in future prediction (Table 6.1).

One merit of the MUF method is to provide alternative policy programs based on efficiency criteria in terms of the utility values. For this purpose, sensitivity analysis is performed on the data set composed of current values of the attributes, UNIFs and MUFs (Table 6.2). Using numerical results of the sensitivity analysis (Table 6.3-6.4), the attributes which will bring the most efficient improvement of

```
COMMAND:
=KSET
INPUT MNAME:
=INMLFOC
WANT LIST OF THE METHOD FOR KSET?
=YES
LIST OF THE METHOD FOR KSET
  (1) INPUT K'S VALUES DIRECTLY
  (2) INPUT ONE INDIFFERENCE PAIR AND LOTTERY
  (3) INPUT TWO INDIFFERENCE PAIRS
WHICH METHOD DO YOU USE?
=2
INPUT REFERENCE UNAME:
=INMLFOCO

INPUT THE FOLLOWING ANS1 AND ANS2:
( INMLFOCO , INMLFOCP ) = ( ANS1          ,      0.      )
        IS INDIFFERENT TO (      0.       , ANS2         )
(INPUT ATTRIBUTE VALUES)
=35.0 1500.0
( INMLFOCO , INMLFOCW ) = ( ANS1          ,      0.      )
        IS INDIFFERENT TO (      0.       , ANS2         )
(INPUT ATTRIBUTE VALUES)
=32.5 800.0
INPUT P SUCH THAT
     LOTTERY --- ALL ARE BEST WITH PROBABILITY P
              !- ALL ARE WORST WITH PROBABILITY 1-P
AND
     CERTAINTY CONSEQUENCE --- INMLFOCO IS BEST
                            !- THE OTHERS ARE WORST
ARE INDIFFERENT:
=0.75
K( INMLFOCO ) =    0.7500
K( INMLFOCP ) =    0.7064
K( INMLFOCW ) =    0.6936
* CAPITAL K =   -0.97266
ANOTHER KSET?
=YES
```

**Figure 6.9 Illustration of KSET command.**

the utility values are selected and their values are changed discretionally from different administrative points of view. Alternative data sets are constructed with the changed levels of the selected attributes, which show alternative policy programs.

Details of this research are published in Seo, Sakawa, Yamane and Fukuchi (1986a,b).

## 5. Remarks

(i) Large-scale systems analysis is usually confronted with incompatible requirements: preciseness in problem structuring and ocmprehensiveness in problem setting. On the one hand,

**Table 6.1 Evaluation of UNIF and MUF values: part (KANAZAWA)**

| | current value<br>EVALUTION OF ALT1<br>NAME | UTIL VALUE | predicted value<br>EVALUTION OF ALT2<br>NAME | UTIL VALUE |
|---|---|---|---|---|
| | KANAZAWA | 0.9560 | KANAZAWA | 0.9621 |
| level 1 | IN | 0.9330 | IN | 0.9569 |
| | EN | 0.5332 | EN | 0.5058 |
| | PB | 0.8971 | PB | 0.9120 |
| level 2 | INM | 0.9216 | INM | 0.9517 |
| | INC | 0.9373 | INC | 0.9527 |
| | ENPO | 0.7617 | ENPO | 0.7225 |
| | PBSN | 0.8552 | PBSN | 0.8836 |
| | PBMD | 0.9117 | PBMD | 0.9117 |
| level 3 | INML | 0.9473 | INML | 0.9693 |
| | INMN | 0.8857 | INMN | 0.9277 |
| | INCR | 0.9419 | INCR | 0.9294 |
| | INCH | 0.8338 | INCH | 0.9301 |
| | ENPOS | 0.7452 | ENPOS | 0.7452 |
| | ENPOZ | 0.5000 | ENPOZ | 0.4483 |
| | ENPOA | 0.5000 | ENPOA | 0.4102 |
| | ENPOW | 0.5613 | ENPOW | 0.5613 |
| | PBSNG | 0.7522 | PBSNG | 0.6496 |
| | PBSNU | 0.8755 | PBSNU | 0.9237 |
| | PBSNT | 0.5000 | PBSNT | 0.7500 |
| level 4 | INMLFO | 0.8074 | INMLFO | 0.8903 |
| | INMLTE | 0.8045 | INMLTE | 0.8787 |
| | INMLFR | 0.6855 | INMLFR | 0.7670 |
| | INMLWO | 0.7161 | INMLWO | 0.7400 |
| | INMLCL | 0.8000 | INMLCL | 0.8031 |
| | INMNMC | 0.8838 | INMNMC | 0.9176 |
| | INMNEM | 0.8165 | INMNEM | 0.9070 |
| | INCRX | 0.8818 | INCRX | 0.8451 |
| | INCRY | 0.9455 | INCRY | 0.9436 |
| | INCRZ | 0.8899 | INCRZ | 0.8662 |
| | INCRWFL | 0.7875 | INCRWFL | 0.7875 |
| | INCHN | 0.8750 | INCHN | 0.9961 |
| | INCHE | 0.6852 | INCHE | 0.8064 |
| level 5 | INMLFOC | 0.8314 | INMLFOC | 0.9155 |
| | INMLFOS | 0.6090 | INMLFOS | 0.7279 |
| | INMLTEC | 0.8034 | INMLTEC | 0.9004 |
| | INMLTES | 0.6131 | INMLTES | 0.5885 |
| | INMLFRC | 0.7014 | INMLFRC | 0.7920 |
| | INMLFRS | 0.5274 | INMLFRS | 0.5929 |
| | INMLWOC | 0.7120 | INMLWOC | 0.7577 |
| | INMLWOS | 0.6875 | INMLWOS | 0.6535 |
| | INMLCLC | 0.8058 | INMLCLC | 0.8302 |
| | INMLCLS | 0.5927 | INMLCLS | 0.5466 |
| | INMNMCC | 0.9232 | INMNMCC | 0.9574 |
| | INMNMCS | 0.6270 | INMNMCS | 0.6718 |
| | INMNEMC | 0.7850 | INMNEMC | 0.8920 |
| | INMNEMS | 0.7786 | INMNEMS | 0.8416 |

**Table 6.2 Sensitivity analysis: part (KANAZAWA)**

GRADIENT FOR KANAZAWA

| NAME | : UTILITY GRAD | (ATTRIBUTE GRAD) |
|---|---|---|
| level 1 | | |
| IN | 0.26081 | |
| EN | 0.06037 | |
| PB | 0.10078 | |
| level 2 | | |
| INM | 0.15263 | |
| INC | 0.10575 | |
| ENPO | 0.04226 | |
| PBSN | 0.05306 | |
| PBMD | 0.03298 | ( 0.00484 ) |
| level 3 | | |
| INML | 0.04859 | |
| INMN | 0.08454 | |
| INCR | 0.05282 | |
| INCH | 0.02331 | |
| ENPOS | 0.00339 | ( -0.00706 ) |
| ENPOZ | 0.01485 | ( -0.03148 ) |
| ENPOA | 0.00927 | ( -0.48268 ) |
| ENPOW | 0.00758 | ( -0.05062 ) |
| PBSNG | 0.01674 | ( 0.01964 ) |
| PBSNU | 0.00830 | ( 0.00696 ) |
| PBSNT | 0.00993 | ( 0.01259 ) |
| level 4 | | |
| INMLFO | 0.00380 | |
| INMLTE | 0.00873 | |
| INMLFR | 0.00230 | |
| INMLWO | 0.00176 | |
| INMLCL | 0.00108 | |
| INMNMC | 0.05660 | |
| INMNEM | 0.01850 | |
| INCRX | 0.01241 | |
| INCRY | 0.00652 | |
| INCRZ | 0.00782 | |
| INCRWFL | 0.00331 | ( 0.00009 ) |
| INCHN | 0.01036 | ( 0.00028 ) |
| INCHE | 0.00902 | ( 0.00063 ) |
| level 5 | | |
| INMLFOC | 0.00258 | |
| INMLFOS | 0.00089 | |
| INMLTEC | 0.00694 | |
| INMLTES | 0.00116 | |
| INMLFRC | 0.00170 | |
| INMLFRS | 0.00054 | |
| INMLWOC | 0.00126 | |
| INMLWOS | 0.00047 | |
| INMLCLC | 0.00066 | |
| INMLCLS | 0.00028 | |
| INMNMCC | 0.04439 | |
| INMNMCS | 0.00895 | |
| INMNEMC | 0.01488 | |
| INMNEMS | 0.00168 | |

**Table 6.3 Selected attributes by sensitivity analysis ($\partial u_i / \partial x_i$)**

| District | Item |
|---|---|
| Kanazawa | Pollution: noise, air, water<br>Public Service: garbage disposal, pervasion of flash-toilet |
| Hakusan | Pollution: air, water<br>Public service: garbage disposal, medical care |
| Kaga | Pollution: stench, noise, water<br>Natural environment<br>Public service: medical care |
| Noto | Industry: nonelectrical machinery (stability: share of shipment)<br>Pollution: noise, air, water<br>Natural environment<br>Public service: medical care |
| Prefectural administration | Equity (in national economy):<br>Social environment: stability<br>Electric power supply |

**Table 6.4 Selected utility functions by sensibirity analysis ($\partial U_j / \partial u_s$) (level 4 and level 5 in industry)**

| Item / District | Manufactures | Commerce |
|---|---|---|
| Kanazawa | Nonelectrical machinery: activity<br>Electric and electronic equipment: activity | Sightseeing: number of visitors,<br>Apparel |
| Hakusan | Textiles: activity<br>Nonelectrical machinery: activity<br>Electric and electronic equipment: activity | Sightseeing: number of visitors, gross sales<br>Apparel |
| Kaga | Nonelectrical machinery: activity, stability<br>Electric and electronic equipment: activity | Sightseeing: number of visitors, gross sales |
| Noto | Nonelectrical machinery: activity<br>Electric and electronic equipment: activity | Sightseeing: number of visitors, gross sales<br>Apparel |

problems included in a system should be structured in more precise forms quantitatively. For meeting this request, the problem setting for the large-scale systems analysis should be confined to a rather narrow particular range. On the other hand, the systems analysis demands as its intrinsic property more wide-ranging recognition of problems. Thus systems analysis should provide a combined utilization of different methods which possess their own characteristics for treating the complex systems. Our research intends to meet the gap between the precise problem structuring and the wide-ranging problem setting. As an example, our approach is composed of the macroeconometric modeling and the multiattribute utility analysis.

(ii) It has been found that the magnitude of MUF-values has a tendency to be gradually distorted (heightened) in the upper levels of the hierarchical preference structure because of cumulative effects of scaling constants in the multiplicative MUF forms. The MUF-values include upward biases in the process of nesting MUFs, and thus comparison of MUF-values should be performed mainly among those in the same levels of the preference structure.

(iii) In practice, the interaction via brainstorming processes between practitioners and MCDM researchers has confronted no difficulty in each stage for assessing the MUF. The assessment could be done with a prompt understanding of the method. A compromise among the assessors has been easily attained through a common recognition of the problems in the light of their experiences and knowledge. Thus, the assessment has been done as if it was performed by the single decision maker. Even so, however, manipulation of diversity and ambiguity of assessment can explicitly be taken into consideration. This device introduces a multiple agents decision problem to some extent. Biases of assessment due to the singularity of each DM can be considered on examining the multiple agents (multiple actors) decision problem. This problem will be discussed in the next chapter.

# CHAPTER 7

# VALUE CONFLICTS IN MULTIPLE AGENTS DECISION MAKING

## 7.1 Extension of Multiattribute Utility Analysis

Multiattribute Utility analysis concerns a heuristic method for directly assessing the multitudinous preferences of the decision maker (DM) in a commensurate term that is called multiattribute utility function (MUF). The main characteristics of this method are as follows.

First, multiattribute utility analysis intends to manipulate the judgmental phase in MCDM, and does not depend on mathematical derivation of the Pareto optimal frontier (the noninferior solution set) as its pretreatment. The obtained preferred set of attributes (preferred policy programs), however, is supposed to implicitly satisfy the Pareto optimality. If not, the other attribute set having higher utility values than those for the preferred set will exist in the feasible region of the attributes. This contradicts the aim of multiattribute utility analysis, which intends to select the policy program having the highest values of MUF. The main idea of multiattribute utility analysis, as depicted in Figure 7.1., is to select the point (attribute set) E tangent to the highest indifference surface of preference of DM from among alternative sets of attributes (A, B, C, D, E, F, G, H, etc.) in the feasible region.

Second, in the process for deriving MUF, value trade-offs among conflicting objectives are articulated. This device corresponds to the procedure for finding the preferred solution for the multiobjective optimization problems (MOP). When

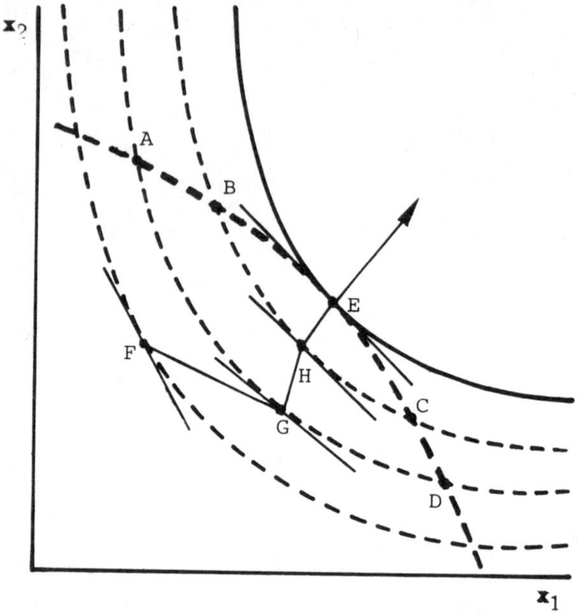


**Figure 7.1 Illustration of multiattribute utility analysis.**

alternative sets of attributes are only composed of solutions to MOP as discussed in Chapter 2-4, the set of alternative policy programs can be constructed as a Pareto optimal set (A, B, C, D, E) in the objective function space. The preferred solution is chosen from among the Pareto optimal solutions by assessing the marginal rates of substitution (MRS) among the objective functions without identification of the scalarized valuation function or the preference function of DM. In the multiattribute utility analysis, identification of the preference function is intended without any regard for mathematical optimization process, and thus MRS is not calculated analytically. Instead, value trade-offs among attributes or the component utility functions are assessed, and preferred trade-offs are found. The search process proceeds, for example, like F → G → H → E without any concern about components other than E in the Pareto optimal set (A, B, C, D, E). Thus, multiattribute utility analysis does not assure the Pareto optimality for all alternatives (F, G, H, E) of the policy program examined during the assessment process. Only in the final selection of E, is the Pareto optimality implied.

Third, about identification of SUF (UNIF), the assessment is executed only with local information for the function form in the neighborhood of the current values of system's attributes which are taken as the reference point. Thus, criticism may be raised here for deriving a utility function having de facto a global property by using the local information. However, the defense for the dispute is that, because the assessment does not depend on strict extremalization but rather on the satisficing principle, as long as monotonic and smooth utility function forms are assumed, local information on the surrounding region of the current values of attributes can be used with some bounded rationality. Specific distant values far from the current values are rarely used for evaluation without some aid by other complementary information.

Fourth, derivation of the MUF depends on the subjective judgment of the assessor who is presumed to be a single decision maker. The method ultimately has some individual assert a set of its preferences as "socially" desirable. Collective choice or group decision problems are not taken into account. For maintaining the appropriateness of this approach, the assessor or DM is assumed to be a "knowledgeable person" having mature experience and wisdom. Variation and ambiguousness of preference evaluation due to multiple agent (multiactor) decision making are not explicitly considered. These multiplicity and ambiguity of the evaluation are interrelated with one another to some extent.

In the following sections, some extensions of the multiattribute utility analysis for treating the collective choice or multiple agents (multiperson) decision making are discussed. The multiple agent decision making (MADM) requests some additional considerations for preference evaluation. First, for social acceptance and its sustainment of decisions had been made, a fairness or an equity should be satisfied as the result of a compromise among multiple decision makers (MDM). Second, for this purpose, value trade-offs among assessors should be articulated in the process of finding the fair point. Thus the extensions of multiattribute utility analysis to collective choice should embody these new criteria and, in this sense, be useful for MADM. The following discussions are particularly concerned with this aspect.

## 7.2 Approaches to Collective Choice

### 7.2.1 Construction of Group Utility Functions

The difficulty of collective choice is well known. Arrow (1950b, 1951) established the possibility theorem in deriving the social utility (welfare) function which is compatible with the following assumptions: (i) weak ordering of individual preferences; (ii) Pareto principle that means positive, or at least nonnegative, response of social preference ordering to changes of individual values; (iii) independence of irrelevant alternatives; it means that an individual's choice in an alternative set S is independent of the preferences of other individuals for alternatives not in the set S; (iv) nonimposition requirement that social choice is not imposed; and (v) nondictatorship that there exists no special individual to represent social preference. His theorem is derived on the order-preserved utility functions scaled with the ordinal number.

**Theorem 7.1 (Arrow's possibility theorem I).**

The social preference function satisfying the above assumptions (i)-(iii) must be either imposed or dictatorial.

It should be noted here that the main intention of this theorem is on an affirmative assertion for construction of the social preference function, even though it must be imposed or dictatorial. Naturally, more interest will be in the case of its imposition. The imposition is regarded as adequate not only in the Platonic case where its construction is best apprehended via philosophic inquiry among people, but also in the concession case where the recognition of common interest in society leads to a compromise.

This assertion results from excluding the possibility of interpersonal comparison of individual preferences, which needs to measure the strength of preferences. Under this presumption, the theorem opens a way for constructing the social preference function with some procedural rationality, with which cooperation in a society satisfying the assumptions (i) to (ii) will be obtained and its results can be accepted as to be imposed. The following theorem asserts this result.

**Theorem 7.2 (Arrow's possibility theorem II) (Arrow 1963 p.59).**

If we exclude the possibility of interpersonal comparison of preferences, then the only method for passing from individual tastes to social preferences, which will be satisfactory (with the assumptions (i) and (ii)) and defined for a wide range of sets of individual ordering, is either imposed or dictatorial.

Approaches to multiple agent decision making (MADM) based on construction of the social preference function primarily depend on Arrow's theorems. However, if we are interested in constructing the social preference function not only for sure outcomes but also for uncertain prospects, the cardinal social preference function or the von Neumann-Morgenstern type group utility function should be introduced.

Construction rules of the social preference function for multiple decision makers (MDM) were examined originally in an additive form in terms of the measurable (cardinal) utility functions under uncertainty (Fleming 1952; Harsanyi 1955) and developed in more general forms (Keeney and Kirkwood 1975; Keeney 1976). Harsanyi, following some ethical postulates by Fleming similar to Arrow's assumptions, which make social choice dependent solely on the individual interests directly affected, pointed out that the postulates does not exclude "the widespread habit of judging the fairness or unfairness" of the income distribution among the members of a society. He stressed that, in the presence of "external economy and diseconomy of consumption," the utility of a given income for any person depends not only on the absolute size of its own income but also on the relation to other people's incomes, and thus the value judgment on the income distribution between individuals should be influenced by the income distribution in the rest of the society. This assertion is crucial to the imposition of the social preference function upon the members based on the independence-of-irrelevant rule, and to the acceptance in the society. We should assert that an individual's preference is composed of both of its "ethical" (impersonal and impartial) preference and its personal preference. In the following discussions, we assume that the individual preference includes the "ethical" preference for the other persons in the society. The social preference functions will be discussed with the terminology of the group utility function, which treats the measurable social preference function for uncertain consequences and is composed of individual measurable utility functions representing individual preferences for the uncertain consequences. The term "group" utility is used because the word "social" preference presents a somewhat metaphysical evaluation problem with an unlimited number of anonymous decision makers. We are concerned with psychologically revealed individual preferences here, and intend to restrict the evaluation problem to that for a limited number of unanonymous members of a society. Thus, we use the word "group" utility as to represent specified preferences revealed by its members. The following discussions are mainly based on Keeney and Kirkwood.

The group utility function (GUF) U with a cardinal measure are represented in terms of the individual utility functions (IUF) of the group members as follows:

$$U(\mathbf{x}_j) \triangleq U(u_1(\mathbf{x}_j), u_2(\mathbf{x}_j), \ldots, u_S(\mathbf{x}_j)), \tag{7.1}$$

where $\mathbf{x} \triangleq \{\mathbf{x}_j\}$, $\mathbf{x} \in R^n$, is a set of possible consequences or prospects with an n-chance fork for the uncertain outcomes of an alternative action, and $u_p$, $p = 1,\ldots,S$, is IUF of the p-th group member. The expected utility hypothesis requests to find $\max_k U^k(\mathbf{x})$ such that

$$U^k(\mathbf{x}) \triangleq \sum_{j=1}^{n} U(\mathbf{x}_j)\, P^k(\mathbf{x}_j), \tag{7.2}$$

where $P^k$ is the group subjective probability function for the uncertain consequences $\mathbf{x} \in R^n$ of an alternative action $a^k$, $k = 1,\ldots,K$.

$$p^k(\mathbf{x}_j) \triangleq P[p_1^k(\mathbf{x}_j), p_2^k(\mathbf{x}_j), \ldots, p_S^k(\mathbf{x}_j)]. \tag{7.3}$$

where $U(\mathbf{x}_j)$ and $p^k(\mathbf{x})$, $\mathbf{x} \in R^n$, are supposed to be unknown functions beforehand.

The representation form of the expected utility function (7.2) can be used for heuristic construction of GUF via dialogues by MDM. It can be shown, the same as for assessment of IUF, that the right-hand side of the expected utility function (7.2) can be regarded as representing the utility for a lottery over the consequences $\mathbf{x}$, and that the $\mathbf{x}$ on the left-hand side is treated as the certainty equivalent (CE). Thus, based on the chance lottery techniques for deriving SUF, which has been discussed in Chapter 5, GUF can be constructed.

For GUF (7.1) to be derived from the IUF, some positive correspondence between an individual's preference and the group preference should be established. The positive correspondence should also obey the independence-of-irrelevant rule.

**Condition 7.1.**

For an individual $p$, $p = 1,\ldots,S$, as a member of a group, if all the other $S - 1$ members are indifferent among all possible consequences, then the preferences of the group for any lotteries over these consequences will correspond to the preferences of the individual $p$ over these lotteries.

**Condition 7.2.**

For any two individuals $p$ and $h$, $p \neq h$, as members of a group, if all the other $S - 2$ members are indifferent among all possible consequences, then preferences of the group for trade-offs among these consequences will correspond to the preferences of the individuals $p$ and $h$ for the trade-offs.

These conditions represent Arrow's positive association rule (ii) and the irrelevance rule (iii) for social choice, and also have similar implications to the utility and preference independence conditions in the multiattribute utility analysis. In fact, these conditions presume that all members of the group will mutually not care what happens concerning the preferences of the other members. Those conditions (7.1) and

(7.2) are called the group correspondence conditions.

**Theorem 7.4 (Representation theorem of the group utility function) (Keeney and Kirkwood).**

Under the group correspondence conditions, a representation form for the group utility function (GUF) is derived:

$$U(\mathbf{x}_j) = \sum_{p=1}^{S} \lambda_p u_p(\mathbf{x}_j) + \lambda \sum_{\substack{p=1 \\ t>p}}^{S} \lambda_p \lambda_t u_p(\mathbf{x}_j) u_t(\mathbf{x}_j) + \cdots$$

$$+ \lambda^{S-1} \lambda_1 \lambda_2 \cdots \lambda_S u_1(\mathbf{x}_j) u_2(\mathbf{x}_j) \cdots u_S(\mathbf{x}_j), \tag{7.4}$$

where $U$ and $u_p$ are scaled from zero to one. The $\lambda$ and $\lambda_p$ are the scaling constants, $0 < \lambda_p < 1$ for all $p$, and $\lambda > -1$. When $\lambda = 0$, the $U(\mathbf{x}_j)$ takes the additive form:

$$U(\mathbf{x}_j) = \sum_{p=1}^{S} u_p(\mathbf{x}_j). \tag{7.5}$$

When $\lambda \neq 0$, by multiplying both sides of (7.4) by $\lambda$ and adding one, the multiplicative form is obtained:

$$\lambda U(\mathbf{x}_j) + 1 = \prod_{p=1}^{S} [\lambda \lambda_p u_p(\mathbf{x}_j) + 1]. \tag{7.6}$$

Proof for the representation forms (7.4) to (7.6) of the GUF can be derived on the same line as those of MUF.

The IUF $U_p(\mathbf{x}_j)$ as a component in (7.5)(7.6) can be a MUF of an individual $p$. Thus the representation forms of the GUF can be discussed in terms of group multiattribute utility functions (GMUF). The nesting procedure discussed in Chapter 6 is applied with some conceptual modifications for group decision making.

The scaling constants $\lambda_p$, $p = 1,\ldots,S$, show value trade-offs among MDM, which should represent a "fair" compromise among preferences of all individuals as the members of a society. Thus, externality as the ethical consideration for fairness can be introduced into the trade-off evaluation in the process of construction of the GUF.

There are two ways to specify the GUF. One is to presume the "benevolent dictator" who specifies scaling constants of the GUF (7.4)-(7.6) impartially, wishing to incorporate the preference of all group members into its decision processes. Another is to treat the "collective response" to a decision problem by the entire group as participatory group decision making. If complete information is available for preferences of all members, then the construction of GUF from IUF is trivial in the former case and is, in result, under the assumption of revealed individual preferences, only nominally different from multiattribute utility analysis for the single decision maker (SDM). In the latter case, however, the "collective response" should be specified in the process of assessing the scaling constants.

It should be remarked here that the collective response of individual preferences revealed by the IUF in constructing the GUF can be represented as an "aggregation" of individual responses. For simplicity, according to Margolis's suggestion (1982), it can be supposed that the IUF is composed of two components; the utility from the point of view of purely individualistic self-interest and the utility from the point of view of altruistic group-interest. We will also presume that the collective response of each person can be revealed by a value of an individual group utility function which is founded on the group-interest utility that every person has but reflects both of the components of IUF that are represented in their relative ratios. Define an individual group utility function (IGUF) $U_p(u_p)$ for a person $p$ on its IUF $u_p$. Then the various types of individual responses are represented by the diversified function forms of $U_p$, $p = 1,\ldots,S$, which reveal the degree of the ethical attitude or an altruistic attitude of an individual $p$, such as egoistic, nice, or philanthropic. Taking a value of IUF at a fixed level as $\hat{u}_1 = \hat{u}_2 = \ldots = \hat{u}_S$, the relative individual responses in constructing the GUF are represented by the slopes of IGUF, which are shown as $\frac{a}{\alpha}$, $\frac{b}{\alpha}$, $\frac{c}{\alpha}$, etc., in Figure 7.2(a). For example, $U_1$ shows a more egoistic attitude toward the group utility, $U_2$ is nice, and $U_3$ shows a more philanthropic attitude.

The property of IGUF for the collective response is

generally classified as follows.

(i) When $\frac{dU_p}{du_p} > 0$, IGUF is increasing altruistic.

(ii) When $\frac{dU_p}{du_p} < 0$, decreasing altruistic.

(iii) When $\frac{d^2U_p}{du_p^2} > 0$, relatively increasing altruistic.

(iv) When $\frac{d^2U_p}{du_p^2} < 0$, relatively decreasing altruistic.

(v) When $\frac{d^2U_p}{du_p^2} = 0$, an invariant social attitude.

Define the social response function as

$$S(x) \triangleq -\frac{d^2U_p}{du_p^2} \bigg/ \frac{dU_p}{du_p} \,. \tag{7.7}$$

S(x) indicates quantitatively a relative strength of the social attitude in terms of the changing altruistic property.

The ratios between the group utility levels, $\frac{c}{\alpha} / \frac{a}{\alpha} = \frac{c}{a}$, $\frac{b}{\alpha} / \frac{a}{\alpha} = \frac{b}{\alpha}$, etc., at the given individual utility level represent interpersonal value trade-offs in deriving GUF. These value trade-offs can be used for assessing indifferent points between individual group utility values at a given level of individual utilities for the two persons. Namely, in Figure 7.2 (b), indifferent points for constructing the GUF are assessed as $\frac{C}{A} = \frac{c}{a}$ and $\frac{B}{A} = \frac{b}{a}$. With this device, a heuristic construction of GUF is performed straight forward as a weighted "aggregation" from every IGUF.

This "aggregation" process of the individual responses includes interpersonal comparisons of individual preferences. Even though different individuals will have different scales and origins for measuring their utility values, the value trade-off

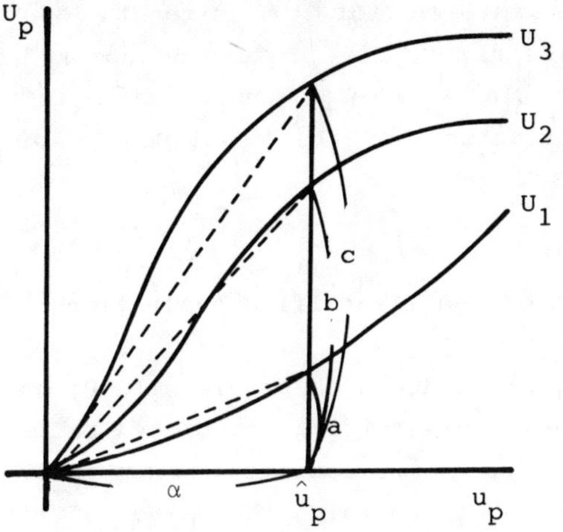


**(a) Individual group utility functions in a common scale.**

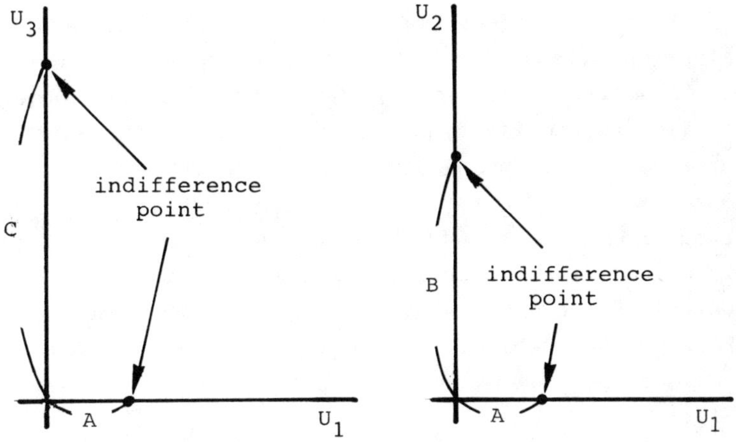


**(b) Interpersonal value trade-offs.**

**Figure 7.2 The "aggregation" process of individual responses to the group utility function.**

assessment among multiple persons make it possible to compare their incremental value assessment in relative ratios. This device is similar to that in the construction process of MUF. However, the interpersonal comparison of preferences includes the interpersonal comparison of preference differences, which requires the measurement of the strength of the individual preference. This aspect for preference comparison is not easy to manipulate. In the remaining sections of this chapter, alternative approaches for the construction of group utility function are discussed.

### 7.2.2 Treatment of the Diversified Evaluation

In general, group decision problems (GDP) have two aspects; one is to consider a diversification of evaluation and the other is to reconcile the value conflicts among MDM. Although the major problem of GDP is to solve the value conflicts in multiple agents decision making, the value conflicts usually are embeded in the diversification of evaluation. Thus, measuring the degree of disagreement for an evaluation result will provide a measure for finding a range of the value conflicts among MDM.

There are three ways to treat the diversification of evaluation without any regard to construction of GUF. First is the probabilistic approach, which treats the objects to be evaluated as uncertain quantities and assesses their probability distributions to represent the diversification of evaluation among MDM. As a modification of the probabilistic approach, an entropy model can be used for assessing the probabilities. In this method, the probability is regarded as an index showing the diversification of evaluations by anonymous multiple decision makers or the "public." The entropy approach is primarily based on the prior assessment of events to occur and is calculated analytically.

Second is the fuzzy approach, which is nonprobabilistic and treats the linguistic ambiguity of some assertions with semantic unpreciseness. It is based on a posterior assessment via subjective decisions. Compared with a fuzzy statement, a probabilistic description is crisp. Neither of these approaches are concerned with any identification of GUF.

Third is the stochastic dominance approach, which is concerned with partial identification of GUF. Although this method is also another version of the probabilistic approach, it requires to assess the risk attitudes of the presumed group utility functions. Thus it is worthwhile to discuss it separately from the other probabilistic approaches.

In the following sections, the above three approaches are discussed in the context of extending multiattribute utility analysis to GDP. Concerning the probabilistic and fuzzy approaches, devices for measuring the "risk of disagreement" in implementing selected policy programs are discussed. In Section 7.3, the entropy approach is presented for maximizing the variety of evaluation by anonymous MDM and is used to detect the magnitudes of risk of failure in implementation of the selected policy programs. In Section 7.4, the fuzzy approach is examined for use in treating the ambiguousness of the utility assessment that results from the diversified evaluation by MDM. In Section 7.5, the stochastic dominance rules are discussed to present the criteria for the final choice from alternative policy programs based on a partial identification of GUF.

## 7.3 Probability Assessment and Entropy Model

### 7.3.1 Probability Assessment and Collective Choice

MADM is primarily concerned with the mutual "compensation" or weighting problems for diversified preference assessments by MDM. The diversity of evaluation by MDM is revealed in a distribution of the preference assessments. Thus, in an elementary form, the diversity of evaluation by MDM can be scaled with a score or a rating such as the number of votes for an assessment, and the result can be treated as a probability distribution, via normalization procedures. In this sense, the probability assessment can be used for manipulating MADM.

Consider the expected utility function in collective choice:

$$u(\mathbf{x}) \triangleq \sum_{p=1}^{S} p_p u_p(\mathbf{x}) \tag{7.8}$$

where $u_p(\mathbf{x})$ shows an IUF or IMUF revealing a different assessment by a person $p$, and $p_p$, $1 > p_p > 0$, $\sum_{p=1}^{S} p_p = 1$, denotes a probability that the $u_p$-value takes, which represents a weight or, for example, the number of votes for the evaluation. n is the number of the different assessment (scores). Thus, the probability assessment is reduced, with normalization, to scoring the IUF- or IMUF-values based on unanonymous evaluation of IUF. Using smoothing procedures, the probability density function can be derived.

The probabilistic approach is also extended in more sophisticated terms. The next subsection is concerned with discussing the entropy model used in information theory.

### 7.3.2 Entropy Model and Default Index: The Entropy Evaluation Method (EEM)

As discussed in Chapter 6, multiattribute utility analysis is used for constructing alternative policy programs via sensitivity analysis for current values of attributes and for component utility functions. With the sensitivity analysis, some attributes can be chosen as "most effective" for improving the current or predicted utility values, and then the values of the selected attributes are changed within their feasible ranges. Alternative policy programs are composed of these changed values according to alternative policy aims. However, such evaluation results include some biases. First, the evaluation is based on the "efficiency" criterion in terms of the improvement of utility values; it is implied by the sensitivity analysis. Alternative criteria such as "equity" are disregarded. Second, although the whole assessment is executed as if by SDM, some constituents may not agree with the evaluated results. These people may complain about the results due to large discrepancies among individual preferences for the selected policy programs. This hazardous possibility makes the selected policy programs "risky" in the sense that these programs may default in their implementation. The entropy evaluation method is concerned with supplying compensations for those shortcomings which the multiattribute utility analysis usually faces.

The entropy evaluation method (EEM) proceeds in the following steps: (1) to solve an entropy problem, and (2) to construct the default index for the risk assessment.

(1) First, an entropy problem is formed and solved under the assumption of the existence of anonymous MDM.

Assume that the sensitivity analysis for utility functions derived with the MUF method has been performed and alternative policy programs have been constructed on its results. Assume that the inclusion of a selected attribute $\mathbf{x}_i$ into the alternative policy program be a random event having a probability $p_i$, which is regarded as reflecting a result of choice by anonymous individual decision makers. We are concerned with reexamining the set of selected attributes for the alternative policy program from the point of view of ambiguity in the occurrence or the inclusion of the attribute. It is assumed that only one attribute will be chosen independently in each selection by one of the anonymous MDM. The current values $\mathbf{x}_1, \mathbf{x}_2, \ldots, \mathbf{x}_r$ of the selected attributes $\mathbf{X}_1, X_2, \ldots, X_r$ are presumed to occur independently with the probability $p_1, p_2, \ldots, p_r$ in an alternative policy program, and are evaluated with the u-values, $u_1, u_2, \ldots, u_r$, that are treated as the values of one characteristic factor, the utility, for the entropy model. The attributes set for an alternative program h, $\mathbf{X}^h \triangleq (\mathbf{X}_1, X_2, \ldots, X_r)$ which has been selected with sensitivity analysis is reexamined from the point of view of two additional criteria: equity and diversification of evaluation.

This bicriterion problem can be solved in the form of an entropy model which solves an entropy maximization problem under a minimization of the average characteristic value, the $\bar{u}$-value. In the entropy model, diversification of evaluation is treated as entropy maximization. The equity criterion is treated as a bottom-up policy which is represented as the minimization of the average u-values of selected attributes for the alternative policy programs.

The entropy model is formulated as follows.

(i) Bottom-up policy: The average characteristic value $\bar{u}$ is minimized.

$$\text{minimize} \quad \bar{u} \triangleq p_1u_1 + p_2u_2 + \ldots + p_ru_r. \tag{7.9}$$

This means that the average u-value in the selected attributes set $\mathbf{X}^h$ should be minimized.

(ii) Maximization of diversification: The entropy $H \triangleq H(p_1, \ldots, p_r)$, $\sum_{i=1}^{r} p_i = 1$, is maximized.

$$\text{maximize} \quad H \triangleq -p_1 \log p_1 - \cdots - p_r \log p_r, \tag{7.10}$$

where the entropy represents the ambiguity in the selection of the characteristic value $u_1, \ldots, u_r$ by the anonymous MDM.

The entropy problem is to solve the bicriterion problem, (i) and (ii), and to find the probability distribution, $p_1, p_2, \ldots, p_r$, $\sum_{i=1}^{r} p_i = 1$, $0 \leq p_i \leq 1$, $i = 1, \ldots, r$.

The probability $p_i$, $i = 1, \ldots, r$, shows a frequency in the occurrence or the inclusion of the attribute $\mathbf{x}_i$ in the alternative h. By solving the entropy problem (i) and (ii), variety in selecting the attributes is allowed to be as large as possible under the "bottom-up" constraint, or the equity consideration in this sense.

An algorithm to solve the entropy problem (i) and (ii) has been presented by Kunisawa (1975). After rearranging the u-values, $u_1, u_2, \ldots, u_r$, as an integer ratio whose elements are mutually prime numbers $\hat{u}_1, \hat{u}_2, \ldots, \hat{u}_r$, the following equation is solved, and a positive root $\mathbf{W}^*$ is obtained.

$$\mathbf{W}^{-\hat{u}_1} + \mathbf{W}^{-\hat{u}_2} + \cdots + \mathbf{W}^{-\hat{u}_r} = 1. \tag{7.11}$$

Then the solution $p_i$, $i = 1, \ldots, r$, of the entropy problem (i) and (ii) is obtained in the following form:

$$p_i = \mathbf{W}^{*-\hat{u}_i}, \quad i = 1, \ldots, r. \tag{7.12}$$

The probability $p_i$ is a rate in the random selection, or the frequency in the occurrence of $\mathbf{x}_i$, measured with the characteristic value $u_i$, and it represents a magnitude of the frequency in selecting the attribute $\mathbf{x}_i$ as to be included in the alternative policy program. Then, we shall proceed to evaluate the risk of default in implementing those alternative programs in an uncertain environment due to MADM.

(2) Second, using the solution $p_i$, $i = 1, \ldots, r$, an index

which measures the "risk" of failure in implementing the alternative programs is constructed.

For this risk assessment, representatives are elected beforehand from among constituents of the group and entrusted with examining the alternatives. An admissible lower limit $u_{is}(\mathbf{x}_i^*)$ of the u-value for a selected attribute $\mathbf{x}_i$, $i = 1,\ldots,r$, is evaluated by the representatives, $s = 1,\ldots,q$. Each representative $s$ is assumed to have its own opinion on the minimum admissible level $\mathbf{x}_{is}^*$ for the value of a selected attribute $\mathbf{x}_i$, and assesses its own u-value $u_{is}^*(\mathbf{x}_i)$ for the admissible level $\mathbf{x}_{is}^*$, where $u_{is}^*(\mathbf{x}_{is}) \triangleq u_{is}(x_{is}^*)$.

Then the risk assessment for the alternative program $h$ by the representative $s$ is performed quantitatively with the sum of the probability $p_i^h$, which is combined with the u-value $u_i^h(\mathbf{x}_i)$ for the selected attribute $\mathbf{x}_i$ in the alternative $h$, and for which the estimated u-value is below the minimum admissible level $u_{is}^{h*}(\mathbf{x}_i)$. Naturally including attributes with smaller u-values in the alternative programs is more desirable from the point of view of the bottom-up policy that is taken as a surrogate for equity here. The risk index assessed by the representative $s$ is formulated in the following form.

$$d_s^h = \left( \sum_{\substack{i=1 \\ u_i^h(\mathbf{x}_i) < u_{is}^{h*}(\mathbf{x}_i)}}^{r} p_i^h [u_i^h(\mathbf{x}_i)] \right)^{-1} . \tag{7.13}$$

(7.13) means that when the sum of the probability $\sum_{i=1}^{r} p_i^h$ is large under the condition $u_i^h < u_{is}^{h*}$, the occurrence or the inclusion of the selected attributes $\mathbf{x}_i$ in the alternative $h$ is more acceptable. In other words, the alternative $h$, which is composed of the set of the selected attribute $\mathbf{x}_i$, is more acceptable because it satisfies the minimum utility requirement for the representative $s$ under the condition that the largest discrepancy of assessment is allowed. Thus the risk index is constructed with the inverse of the summation.

The default index $D^h$ of the alternative $h$ for all the representatives is calculated as the sum of the $d_s^h$ in (7.3) as follows:

$$D^h = \sum_{s=1}^{q} d_s^h = \sum_{s=1}^{q} \left( \sum_{\substack{i=1 \\ u_i^h(\mathbf{x}_i) < u_{is}^{h*}}}^{r} p_i^h[u_i^h(\mathbf{x}_i)] \right)^{-1}. \qquad (7.14)$$

The default index $D^h$ is used as a measure of risk for implementation of the alternative $h$ to fail.

The $d_s^h$ and $D^h$ can be modified by weighting the probability $p_i^h$ with the deviation:

$$v_{is}^h = \alpha(u_{is}^{h*}(\mathbf{x}_i) - u_i^h(\mathbf{x}_i)). \qquad (7.15)$$

Thus the weighted risk index

$$\hat{d}_s^h = \left( \sum_{\substack{i=1 \\ u_i^h(\mathbf{x}_i) < u_{is}^{h*}(\mathbf{x}_i)}}^{r} v_{is}^h p_i^h(u_i\{\mathbf{x}_i)) \right)^{-1}, \qquad (7.16)$$

and the weighted default index

$$\hat{D}_s^h = \sum_{s=1}^{q} \hat{d}_s^h = \sum_{s=1}^{q} \left( \sum_{\substack{i=1 \\ u_i^h(\mathbf{x}_i) < u_{is}^{h*}(\mathbf{x}_i)}}^{r} v_{is}^h p_i^h[u_i(\mathbf{x}_i)] \right)^{-1} \qquad (7.17)$$

are obtained. With those measures, the degree or magnitude of the value conflict implied in the alternative policy programs is numerically assessed. The difficulty for forming a consensus on each alternative can be compared quantitatively with each other.

### 7.3.3 Application to Regional Planning

The entropy evaluation method (EEM) is applied to a regional planning problem to assess current satisfaction levels in Osaka Prefecture in Japan and to construct and evaluate alternative regional policy programs (Seo and Sakawa 1984a).

**1. Object area**

The object area is composed of three cities: Kishiwada (KI) Kaizuka (KA), and Izumi (IZ), which are located in the northern-Senshu area in Osaka Prefecture. The regional planning problem includes many objectives that are noncommensurate and often in conflict with each other. The hierarchical configuration is composed of eight layers, corresponding to regional, industrial, and functional decompositions. The 130 attributes in total are chosen at the lowest level.

**2. Utility assessment**

The utility assessment is performed with the MUF method. In the utility assessment, different types of SUF (UNIF)(u-types) are assigned for all attributes depending on the risk attitude of DM. The u-type for each attribute for primary industries is assumed to be the same in each city. For secondary industries, each industry is classified from Category 1 to Category 5 according to the average size of business establishments within the industry. The u-types are assigned differently in those categories (Table 7.1). The UNIF-values and the MUF-values for the current situation are calculated with the assistance of the computer program ICOPSS.

Based on the utility assessments, sensitivity analysis for the current attribute values is executed and alternative regional policy programs for improving the current regional situations are constructed. The alternative policy programs are composed of revised values for the selected attributes according to alternative policy aims: (A) agricultural development-oriented, or (B) fishery and forestry preservation-oriented, or (C) local industry-oriented. These attributes are selected such that they would improve the current u-values most effectively. The revised MUF-values of all the alternatives are calculated with the same scaling constants as those for the current MUF-values and compared with each other.

**Table 7.1 Details of categories for utility assessment:(secondary industries)**

| Category | Manufacturing shipment (million yen) | Item | Labor productivity:L | Wage Revenue:W | Entrepreneur's gross revenue:F |
|---|---|---|---|---|---|
| I | over | Best value of attribute: | 30. | 6. | 700. |
| | 500 | u-type: | DR | DR | DR |
| II | 250 | Best value of attribute: | 30. | 6. | 300. |
| | ~ 499 | u-type: | CR | CR | CR |
| III | 150 | Best value of attribute: | 20. | 6. | 200. |
| | ~ 249 | u-type: | LI | LI | CR |
| IV | 50 | Best value of attribute: | 20. | 6. | 100. |
| | ~ 149 | u-type: | LI | CP | LI |
| V | under | Best value of attribute: | 20. | 6. | 20. |
| | 50 | u-type: | CP | DP | CP |

Note.

DR: decreasing risk aversion (u-type 4)

CR: constant risk aversion (u-type 3)

LI: linear (u-type 1)

CP: constant risk prone (u-type 3)

DP: decreasing risk prone (u-type 5)

## 3. Assessment of probability and the default index

After constructing and solving the entropy problem (7.1) and (7.2), the default index is calculated (Table 7.2).

Each representative, R1, R2, or R3 has its own peculiarity for the utility function. R1 represents citizens who are diversity-of-consumption oriented and have a strong inclination to favor nature preservation; its u-type is risk averse. R2 represents employees of firms who are wage-income oriented and have a mild preference for nature preservation; its u-type is also risk averse. R3 represents industrial entrepreneurs who have a profit-seeking property and have no inclination to favor nature preservation; its u-type is rather risk prone. For simplicity, the admissible lower limits for the u-values of each representative are assumed to be the same among the industries and cities. It can be found that, for Alternatives A and B, there is a discrepancy of interests between the representatives

**Table 7.2 Assessment of the default index**

(A) equal weight case

| | $d_s^h$ for | | | $D^h$ |
|---|---|---|---|---|
| | R1 | R2 | R3 | |
| Alternative A | 2.070 | 2.070 | 10.0 | 14.140 |
| Alternative B | 2.049 | 2.227 | 10.0 | 14.276 |
| Alternative C | 1.028 | 1.006 | 1.188 | 3.222 |

(B) weighted with $v_{is}^h$ case

| | $\hat{d}_s^h$ for | | | $\hat{D}^h$ |
|---|---|---|---|---|
| | R1 | R2 | R3 | |
| Alternative A | 0.899 | 1.588 | 10.0 | 12.487 |
| Alternative B | 2.008 | 5.299 | 10.0 | 17.307 |
| Alternative C | 0.471 | 0.251 | 1.991 | 2.713 |

Note: R1, R2, R3 are the representatives.

R1 and R2 and the representative R3. Although the Alternatives A and B are acceptable for the citizen and the employee, they will be rejected by the entrepreneur. It will be easier to form a consensus for Alternative C among those representatives. Inspecting those results along with the MUF-values for the alternatives, it is confirmed that, although Alternative B has the highest and Alternative A has the second highest MUF-values, there is a basic discrepancy of interests between the group of the citizen (R1) and the employee (R2), and the entrepreneur (R3). Thus, the risk of default is considerably large for the Alternatives A and B. In contrast, Alternative C is almost equally acceptable to all the representatives, although it has lower MUF-values. When the risk and default indices are weighted with the deviation $v_{is}^{h}$ (7.14), the discrepancies in interest among the representatives are enlarged. It is evident that there is a conflict even between the citizen and the employee to some extent. In general, there is a tendency that the risk for implementation to default be large for nature preservation-oriented policies (Alternative A and B) and much less for the industrial wage-oriented policy (Alternative C).

## 7.4 Fuzzy Multiattribute Utility Analysis

### 7.4.1 Fuzzy Extension of Multiattribute Utility Analysis

Another approach for MADM is the fuzzy approach. Fuzzy multiattribute utility analysis is based on a fuzzy extension of multiattribute utility analysis. The fuzzy multiattribute utility analysis concerns the conceptual imprecision, or the linguistic ambiguity, which accrues from a multiplicity of evaluation. The fuzzy multiattribute utility function (FMUF) is constructed as a natural extension of the multiattribute utility function (MUF) to the fuzzy preference evaluation, which is based on fuzzy preference relations and fuzzy number operations. Although this approach does not intend to construct the group utility function (GUF) and to treat the value trade-offs among MDM directly, it articulates quantitatively the levels or ranges of value-conflicts among MDM.

Concepts of fuzzy preference relations are based on fuzzy

set theory developed by Zadeh (1965, 1971). Fuzzy number operations and comparisons have been developed by Dubois and Prade (1978, 1980a,b). The collective choice problem based on the fuzzy set theory has been considered by Blin (1974), and Blin and Whinston (1974), although they have not attempted to construct fuzzy utility functions. In this section, we are concerned with presenting the fuzzy evaluation of MUF for the collective choice, and providing devices for measuring agreement levels or ranges in the collective choice in terms of FMUF.

Recall the representation forms of MUF.

Additive:

$$U(\mathbf{x}_1, \ldots, \mathbf{x}_m) = \sum_{i=1}^{m} k_i u_i(\mathbf{x}_i), \text{ when } \sum_{i=1}^{m} k = 1. \tag{7.18}$$

Multiplicative:

$$1 + KU(\mathbf{x}_1, \ldots, \mathbf{x}_m) = \prod_{i=1}^{m} (1 + Kk_i u_i(\mathbf{x}_i)), \text{ when } \sum_{i=1}^{m} k_i \neq 1. \tag{7.19}$$

where $U$ and $u_i$ are utility functions scaled 0 to 1. $K$ and $k_i$ are scaling constants, and $0 < k_i < 1$, $K > -1$. When $\sum_{i=1}^{m} k_i \neq 1$, $K$ is a non-zero solution to $1 + K = \prod_{i=1}^{m} (1 + Kk_i)$. The unique solution $K$ takes the range of $0 < K < \infty$ when $\sum_{i=1}^{m} k_i < 1$, and $-1 < K < 0$ when $\sum_{i=1}^{m} k_i > 1$.

The procedure of assessing MUF is composed of three steps: (i) evaluation of the single attribute utility functions (UNIF) $u_i$, $i = 1,\ldots,m$, (ii) assessment of the scaling constants $k_i$ and $K$ on them, and (iii) determination of the representation form (7.18) or (7.19) of MUF. Step (i) corresponds to the decomposition of the system. Step (iii) is simply a calculation process. Thus the fuzzification device is introduced in the value assessment in Step (ii), which is the coordination process by DM and where diversified evaluations by MDM can be included.

In Step (ii), fuzzification can be performed twofold: before and after the value trade-off experiment among the attributes, which is executed for deriving relative values of the scaling constants $k_i$. In the first phase of the fuzzification, before the trade-off experiment, attributes $\mathbf{X}_i$, $i = 1,\ldots,m$, as objects for evaluation are compared with each other, and a fuzzy preference ordering among the attributes is constructed as a result of the diversified evaluation in collective choice. Then with a defuzzification device, a nonfuzzy collective preference ordering is derived. A numerical ordering of the scaling constants $k_i$ is determined corresponding to the non-fuzzy preference ordering among $\mathbf{X}_i$, $i = 1,\ldots,m$. The relative values $k_i/k_s$, $i \neq s$, of the scaling constants are found deterministically with the trade-off experiment based on their numerical ordering. In the second phase of the fuzzification, after the value trade-off experiment, a numerical value of the fuzzy scaling constant $\tilde{k}_s$ on UNIF $u_s(\mathbf{x}_s)$ for the most preferable attribute $\mathbf{X}_s$ is assessed as a fuzzy number. Thus, all values of the fuzzy scaling constants $\tilde{k}_i$, $i = 1,\ldots,m$, can be numerically determined.

Finally, in Step (iii), FMUF is calculated as the fuzzy number. Then fuzzy comparison among alternative policy programs is performed in terms of FMUF.

In the following subsections, main aspects of the fuzzification processes are discussed.

### 7.4.2 Fuzzy Preference Ordering

The first phase of the fuzzification process in Step (ii) concerns constructing the nonfuzzy collective preference ordering among attributes from fuzzy individual preference orderings.

The concepts of fuzzy preference relation are defined with the membership function $\mu_R(\mathbf{X}_i, X_j)$ for all pairs of attributes $\mathbf{X}_i \in \tilde{X}_i$ and $\mathbf{X}_j \in \tilde{\mathbf{X}}_j$, $i, j = 1,\ldots,m$, where $\tilde{X}_i$ and $\tilde{X}_j$ are fuzzy sets of the attributes. The membership function $\mu_R(\mathbf{X}_i, \mathbf{X}_j)$ associates with each pair $(\mathbf{X}_i, \mathbf{X}_j) \subseteq \tilde{X}_i \times \tilde{X}_j$ its "grade of membership" $\mu_R$, where R is a fuzzy binary relation ($\succ$, $\sim$) for preferences defined on the ordered pairs of the attributes.

The value of the membership function $\mu_R(\mathbf{X}_i, X_j)$, which takes a range of interval [0, 1], represents the strength of the preference relation R between $\mathbf{X}_i$ and $\mathbf{X}_j$.

Some basic concepts of a fuzzy binary relation are defined. The symbols $\vee$ and $\wedge$ denote max and min, respectively.

**Definition 7.1 (Fuzzy relation).**

(i) The domain of a fuzzy relation R is denoted by dom R and is a fuzzy set defined by

$$\mu_{\text{dom } R}(\mathbf{X}) \triangleq \bigvee_{\mathbf{X}_j} \mu_R(\mathbf{X}_i, X_j), \quad \text{for} \quad \mathbf{X}_i \in \tilde{X}_i, \quad \mathbf{X}_j \in \tilde{X}_j. \tag{7.20}$$

The range of R is denoted by ran R, and

$$\mu_{\text{ran } R}(\mathbf{X}) \triangleq \bigvee_{\mathbf{X}_i} \mu_R(\mathbf{X}_i, X_j) \tag{7.21}$$

(ii) The height of R is denoted by h(R) and is defined by

$$h(R) \triangleq \bigvee_{\mathbf{X}_i} \bigvee_{\mathbf{X}_j} \mu_R(\mathbf{X}_i, X_j). \tag{7.22}$$

A fuzzy relation is said to be subnormal when $h(R) < 1$ and normal when $h(R) = 1$.

(iii) The containment of a fuzzy relation R in a fuzzy relation S is denoted by $R \subset S$, and is defined by

$$\mu_R(\mathbf{X}_i, X_j) \leqslant \mu_S(\mathbf{X}_i, X_j) \quad \text{for all} \quad (\mathbf{X}_i, X_j) \subseteq \tilde{\mathbf{X}}_i \times \tilde{\mathbf{X}}_j. \tag{7.23}$$

(iv) The union of fuzzy relations R and S is denoted by R + S (or $R \cup S$), and is defined by

$$\begin{aligned} \mu_{R+S} &\triangleq \mu_R \vee \mu_S \\ &\triangleq \max(\mu_R(\mathbf{X}_i, X_j), \mu_S(\mathbf{X}_i, X_j)). \end{aligned} \tag{7.24}$$

(v) The intersection of R and S is denoted by $R \cap S$, and is defined by

$$\mu_{R \cap S} \triangleq \mu_R \wedge \mu_S \tag{7.25}$$

$$\triangleq \min\,(\mu_R(\mathbf{X}_i, X_j),\ \mu_S(\mathbf{X}_i, X_j)).$$

(vi) The complement of R is denoted by $\bar{R}$, and is defined by

$$\mu_{\bar{R}} = 1 - \mu_R. \tag{7.26}$$

(vii) When $R \subset \mathbf{X}_i \times \mathbf{X}_j$ and $S \subset \mathbf{X}_j \times X_k$, the (max-min) composition of R and S is denoted by $R \bullet S$, and is defined by

$$\mu_{R \circ S}(\mathbf{X}_i, X_j) = \bigvee_{\mathbf{X}_j} (\mu_R(\mathbf{X}_i, X_j) \wedge \mu_s(\mathbf{X}_i, X_k)),$$

$$\text{for} \quad \mathbf{X}_i \in \tilde{\mathbf{X}}_i, \quad \mathbf{X}_k \in \tilde{\mathbf{X}}_k. \tag{7.27}$$

Properties of the fuzzy preference relation are defined with the membership function $\mu_R(\mathbf{X}_i, X_j)$.

**Definition 7.2 (Fuzzy preference relation).**

(i) Connectivity:

$$\mathbf{X}_i \neq \mathbf{X}_j \Rightarrow \mu_R(\mathbf{X}_i, X_j) > 0 \quad \text{or} \quad \mu_R(\mathbf{X}_j, X_i) > 0. \tag{7.28}$$

(ii) Reflexivity:

$$\mu_R(\mathbf{X}_i, X_i) = 1, \quad \text{for all } \mathbf{X}_i \text{ in dom R}. \tag{7.29}$$

(iii) Transitivity:

$$\mu_R(\mathbf{X}_i, X_k) \geqslant \bigvee_{x_j} (\mu_R(\mathbf{X}_i, X_j) \wedge \mu_R(\mathbf{X}_j, X_k)). \tag{7.30}$$

(iv) Symmetry:

$$\mu_R(\mathbf{X}_i, X_j) = \mu_R(\mathbf{X}_j, X_i). \tag{7.31}$$

(v) Asymmetry:

$$\mu_R(\mathbf{X}_i, X_j) > 0 \Rightarrow \mu_R(\mathbf{X}_j, X_i) \not> 0. \tag{7.32}$$

(vi) Antisymmetry:

$$\mu_R(\mathbf{X}_i, X_j) > 0 \quad \text{and} \quad \mu_R(\mathbf{X}_j, X_i) > 0 \Rightarrow \mathbf{X}_i = X_j. \tag{7.33}$$

(vii) Similarity relation: reflexive, symmetric, and transitive.

**Definition 7.3 (Fuzzy preference ordering).**

(i) fuzzy weak ordering: connective and transitive.

(ii) fuzzy strong ordering: transitive and asymmetric.

(iii) fuzzy partial ordering: reflexive, transitive, and antisymmetric.

(iv) fuzzy quasi-ordering: reflexive and transitive.

(v) fuzzy linear ordering: connective, transitive, and antisymmetric.

In general, rationality of human behavior is expressed in terms of consistency and coherence of preference ordering. Consistency presumes asymmetry, and coherence presumes transitivity. Thus the rationality in fuzzy preference ordering holds in a fuzzy strong ordering (viz. asymmetry and transitivity). However, it is not easy to fulfill both properties in actual decision processes. Thus we use a fuzzy weak (complete) ordering with connectivity as a relaxed surrogate of asymmetry along with the transitivity in place of the strong ordering.

### 7.4.3 Derivation of a Nonfuzzy Collective Preference Ordering

#### 1. Hierarchical structure of the fuzzy preference ordering

A hierarchical structure of the fuzzy preference ordering is constructed in the resolution of the fuzzy binary relation $R$ into a union of several nonfuzzy sets. For a number $\alpha$ in $[0, 1]$, an $\alpha$-level set $R_\alpha$ of a fuzzy relation $R$ is defined by

$$R_{\alpha} \triangleq \{(\mathbf{X}_i, \mathbf{X}_j) \mid \mu_R(\mathbf{X}_i, \mathbf{X}_j) \geq \alpha\}. \tag{7.34}$$

The $R_{\alpha}$ is a non-fuzzy set of $\hat{\mathbf{X}}_i \times \hat{\mathbf{X}}_j$ and those $\alpha$-level sets form a nested sequence of non-fuzzy relations with $\alpha_i \geq \alpha_j \Rightarrow R_{\alpha_i} \subset R_{\alpha_j}$. The $\alpha$ is interpreted as an agreement level of the collective choice.

According to Zadeh's proposition (1971), any fuzzy relation $R$ defined on $\mathbf{X} \subseteq (\tilde{\mathbf{X}}_1 \times \ldots \times \tilde{\mathbf{X}}_m)$ admits of the resolution

$$R = \sum_{\alpha} \alpha R_{\alpha}, \quad 0 < \alpha \leq 1, \tag{7.35}$$

where $\sum_{\alpha}$ stands for the union $\cup_{\alpha}$ and $\alpha R_{\alpha}$ denotes a non-fuzzy set defined by

$$\mu_{\alpha R_{\alpha}}(\mathbf{X}_i, X_j) = \alpha \mu_{R_{\alpha}}(\mathbf{X}_i, X_j), \tag{7.36}$$

or equivalently,

$$\mu_{\alpha R_{\alpha}}(\mathbf{X}_i, X_j) = \begin{cases} \alpha & \text{for } (\mathbf{X}_i, X_j) \in R_{\alpha} \\ 0 & \text{otherwise.} \end{cases} \tag{7.37}$$

For the resolution of a fuzzy preference relation $R$ into the nonfuzzy subsets $R_{\alpha}$, the relation matrix $[\mu_R]$ whose elements are composed of $\mu_R$ is constructed. The collective preference ordering can be generated by a permutation mapping $\psi : \mathbf{X} \to \mathbf{X}$ where $\mathbf{X}$ denotes a preference set defining a preference ordering. This permutation operation can be executed for constructing a nonfuzzy collective ordering from the fuzzy set of the individual preference orderings.

The hierarchical structure of the fuzzy preference ordering is constructed for deriving a compromised preference ordering from a diversified evaluation in the multiple agents decision making.

## 2. Construction of relation matrices

Derivation of the nonfuzzy collective preference ordering

from a fuzzy set composed of individual preference orderings of MDM depends on selection rules for the collective choice.

(1) Simple majority rule:

$$\mu_R(\mathbf{X}_i, X_j) \triangleq \frac{1}{n} N(O_{ij}), \tag{7.38}$$

where $n$ is a number of assessors and $N(O_{ij})$ denotes a total score (e.g., the number of votes) for the pair-wise preference ordering $O_{ij}$ between the attributes $\mathbf{X}_i$ and $\mathbf{X}_j$. Suppose that $n = 20$, $\mathbf{X} \triangleq (\mathbf{X}_1, \mathbf{X}_2, \mathbf{X}_3, \mathbf{X}_4)$, and a score sheet for diversified quaternary assessments has been obtained as follows:

$$\begin{aligned}
O^1 &= (\mathbf{X}_1, X_2, X_3, X_4), & N(O^1) &= 4 \\
O^2 &= (\mathbf{X}_1, X_2, X_4, X_3), & N(O^2) &= 2 \\
O^3 &= (\mathbf{X}_2, X_1, X_3, X_4), & N(O^3) &= 2 \\
O^4 &= (\mathbf{X}_2, X_1, X_4, X_3), & N(O^4) &= 1 \\
O^5 &= (\mathbf{X}_3, X_1, X_2, X_4), & N(O^5) &= 2 \\
O^6 &= (\mathbf{X}_3, X_1, X_4, X_2), & N(O^6) &= 1 \\
O^7 &= (\mathbf{X}_1, X_3, X_2, X_4), & N(O^7) &= 3 \\
O^8 &= (\mathbf{X}_4, X_1, X_2, X_3), & N(O^8) &= 2 \\
O^9 &= (\mathbf{X}_4, X_1, X_3, X_2), & N(O^9) &= 1 \\
O^{10} &= (\mathbf{X}_2, X_4, X_3, X_1), & N(O^{10}) &= 2 \,.
\end{aligned} \tag{7.39}$$

The preference ordering $O \triangleq \{O_{ij}\}$, which appeared on the score sheet (7.39), is a fuzzy set. The score sheet (7.39) for the collective choice derives a $4 \times 4$ relation matrix $[\mu_R]$(7.40), whose elements are values of the membership function $\mu_R(\mathbf{X}_i, X_j)$ for the fuzzy preference relation $R$ on $(\mathbf{X}_i, \mathbf{X}_j) \subseteq \tilde{X}_i \times \tilde{X}_j$, $i,j = 1,\ldots,4$, $i \neq j$.

$$[\mu_R] = \begin{bmatrix} 0. & 0.75 & 0.75 & 0.7 \\ 0.25 & 0. & 0.65 & 0.8 \\ 0.25 & 0.35 & 0. & 0.6 \\ 0.25 & 0.2 & 0.4 & 0. \end{bmatrix} \tag{7.40}$$

(2) Strength-of-preference rule:

$$\mu_R(\mathbf{x}_i, \mathbf{x}_j) = \frac{1}{m} \sum_k w^k N^k(O_{ij}) = S(O_{ij})/m, \tag{7.41}$$

where $N^k(O_{ij})$ denotes a total score (e.g., the number of votes) for a preference ordering $O_{ij}$ for an ordered pair $(\mathbf{X}_i, \mathbf{X}_j)$. The weighting coefficient $w^k$ represents the strength of individual preferences for each ordered pair $(\mathbf{X}_i, \mathbf{X}_j)$ of attributes. m is the number of voters multiplied by a maximum value of $w^k$, viz. $m \triangleq \max(w^k n)$. For instance, suppose that $w \triangleq (w^1, w^2, w^3) = (3, 2, 1)$. Then $m = 60$, and the following scores (7.42) for the binary relations $O_{ij}$ can be obtained from the original score sheet (7.39).

$$\begin{array}{lll}
O_{12} = (\mathbf{X}_1, \mathbf{X}_2), & N(O_{12}) = 15, & S(O_{12}) = 38 \\
O_{13} = (\mathbf{X}_1, \mathbf{X}_3), & N(O_{13}) = 15, & S(O_{13}) = 37 \\
O_{14} = (\mathbf{X}_1, \mathbf{X}_4), & N(O_{14}) = 14, & S(O_{14}) = 35 \\
O_{21} = (\mathbf{X}_2, \mathbf{X}_1), & N(O_{21}) = 5, & S(O_{21}) = 13 \\
O_{23} = (\mathbf{X}_2, \mathbf{X}_3), & N(O_{23}) = 13, & S(O_{23}) = 32 \\
O_{24} = (\mathbf{X}_2, \mathbf{X}_4), & N(O_{24}) = 16, & S(O_{24}) = 42 \\
O_{31} = (\mathbf{X}_3, \mathbf{X}_1), & N(O_{31}) = 5, & S(O_{31}) = 12 \\
O_{32} = (\mathbf{X}_3, \mathbf{X}_2), & N(O_{32}) = 7, & S(O_{32}) = 16 \\
O_{34} = (\mathbf{X}_3, \mathbf{X}_4), & N(O_{34}) = 12, & S(O_{34}) = 28 \\
O_{41} = (\mathbf{X}_4, \mathbf{X}_1), & N(O_{41}) = 5, & S(O_{41}) = 10 \\
O_{42} = (\mathbf{X}_4, \mathbf{X}_2), & N(O_{42}) = 4, & S(O_{42}) = 8 \\
O_{43} = (\mathbf{X}_4, \mathbf{X}_3), & N(O_{43}) = 8, & S(O_{43}) = 21 ,
\end{array} \tag{7.42}$$

where, for example, $S(O_{12}) = 9 \times 3 + 5 \times 2 + 1 \times 1 = 38$.

Using the score sheet (7.42), the relation matrix (7.43) can be derived.

$$[\mu_R] = \begin{bmatrix} 0. & 0.63 & 0.62 & 0.58 \\ 0.22 & 0. & 0.53 & 0.7 \\ 0.2 & 0.26 & 0. & 0.47 \\ 0.17 & 0.13 & 0.53 & 0. \end{bmatrix} \tag{7.43}$$

**3. Transitivity checks**

Now the problem is to find the nonfuzzy collective preference ordering from the fuzzy set (7.39) or (7.42). The relation matrix can usually represent connectivity, but intransitivity often occurs in some triples $(\mathbf{X}_i, \mathbf{X}_j, \mathbf{X}_k) \subseteq \tilde{\mathbf{X}}_i \times \tilde{\mathbf{X}}_j \times \tilde{\mathbf{X}}_k$.

For example, in the relation matrix (7.40) under the simple

majority rule, the intransitivity occurs in triples ($\mathbf{X}_1$, $\mathbf{X}_2$, $\mathbf{X}_4$), ($\mathbf{X}_4$, $\mathbf{X}_1$, $\mathbf{X}_2$), and ($\mathbf{X}_4$, $\mathbf{X}_3$, $\mathbf{X}_2$). The relation matrix (7.43) under the strength-of-preference rule also includes the intransitivity in triples ($\mathbf{X}_1$, $\mathbf{X}_2$, $\mathbf{X}_4$), ($\mathbf{X}_3$, $\mathbf{X}_2$, $\mathbf{X}_1$), ($\mathbf{X}_4$, $\mathbf{X}_1$, $\mathbf{X}_2$), and ($\mathbf{X}_4$, $\mathbf{X}_3$, $\mathbf{X}_2$).

Thus, the problem is to ensure the transitivity for every binary preference relation. According to the definition of fuzzy transitivity (7.30), there are three ways to revise the original relation matrix: (i) to augment the value of $\mu_R(\mathbf{X}_i, \mathbf{X}_k)$, (ii) to lessen the value of $\mu_R(\mathbf{X}_i, \mathbf{X}_j) \wedge \mu_R(\mathbf{X}_j, \mathbf{X}_k)$, and (iii) to lessen the value of $\mu_R(\mathbf{X}_i, \mathbf{X}_j)$ or the value of $\mu_R(\mathbf{X}_j, \mathbf{X}_k)$ discretionally. With those alternative devices, different revised relation matrices with transitivity can be obtained. Transitivity checks can be performed sequentially in the revising processes. An effective computer program, ICOPSS/FR, is available for the transitivity checks to obtain the weak-ordered preference relations. This computer program can generate the matrix with transitivity internally. For example, the way (i) can derive the following revised matrix (7.44) with transitivity from the original intransitive relation matrix (7.40) under the simple majority rule.

$$[\mu_R'] = \begin{bmatrix} 0. & 0.75 & 0.75 & 0.75 \\ 0.25 & 0. & 0.65 & 0.8 \\ 0.25 & 0.35 & 0. & 0.6 \\ 0.25 & 0.35 & 0.4 & 0. \end{bmatrix} \tag{7.44}$$

Illustration 7.1 shows the sequential procedure for revising the original matrix (7.40) with transitivity checks to obtain the revised matrix (7.44).

The way (ii) can derive another revised matrix (7.45) with transitivity from the original intransitive relation matrix (7.40) under the simple majority rule.

$$[\mu_R''] = \begin{bmatrix} 0. & 0.7 & 0.75 & 0.7 \\ 0.25 & 0. & 0.65 & 0.8 \\ 0.20 & 0.2 & 0. & 0.6 \\ 0.2 & 0.2 & 0.4 & 0. \end{bmatrix} \tag{7.45}$$

The original relation matrix (7.43) under the strength-of-

## Illustration 7.1 Transitivity check with the way (i) (ICOPSS/FR)

RELATION MATRIX

| | 1 | 2 | 3 | 4 |
|---|---|---|---|---|
| 1 | 0. | 0.750 | 0.750 | 0.700 |
| 2 | 0.250 | 0. | 0.650 | 0.800 |
| 3 | 0.250 | 0.350 | 0. | 0.600 |
| 4 | 0.250 | 0.200 | 0.400 | 0. |

TRANSITIVITY CHECK 1

| ( I J K ) | (I J)AND(J K) | | (I K) |
|---|---|---|---|
| ( 1 2 3 ) | 0.650 | < | 0.750 |
| ( 1 2 4 ) | 0.750 | > | 0.700 |
| ( 1 3 2 ) | 0.350 | < | 0.750 |
| ( 1 3 4 ) | 0.600 | < | 0.700 |
| ( 1 4 2 ) | 0.200 | < | 0.750 |
| ( 1 4 3 ) | 0.400 | < | 0.750 |
| ( 2 1 3 ) | 0.250 | < | 0.650 |
| ( 2 1 4 ) | 0.250 | < | 0.800 |
| ( 2 3 1 ) | 0.250 | = | 0.250 |
| ( 2 3 4 ) | 0.600 | < | 0.800 |
| ( 2 4 1 ) | 0.250 | = | 0.250 |
| ( 2 4 3 ) | 0.400 | < | 0.650 |
| ( 3 1 2 ) | 0.250 | < | 0.350 |
| ( 3 1 4 ) | 0.250 | < | 0.600 |
| ( 3 2 1 ) | 0.250 | = | 0.250 |
| ( 3 2 4 ) | 0.350 | < | 0.600 |
| ( 3 4 1 ) | 0.250 | = | 0.250 |
| ( 3 4 2 ) | 0.200 | < | 0.350 |
| ( 4 1 2 ) | 0.250 | > | 0.200 |
| ( 4 1 3 ) | 0.250 | < | 0.400 |
| ( 4 2 1 ) | 0.200 | < | 0.250 |
| ( 4 2 3 ) | 0.200 | < | 0.400 |
| ( 4 3 1 ) | 0.250 | = | 0.250 |
| ( 4 3 2 ) | 0.350 | > | 0.200 |

FOR ENSURING THE TRANSITIVITY,
THE FOLLOWINGS MUST BE REEXAMINED

| | | | |
|---|---|---|---|
| ( 1 2 4 ) | 0.750 | > | 0.700 |
| ( 4 1 2 ) | 0.250 | > | 0.200 |
| ( 4 3 2 ) | 0.350 | > | 0.200 |

REVISED VALUES

| | | | |
|---|---|---|---|
| ( 1 2 4 ) | 0.750 | = | 0.750 |
| ( 4 1 2 ) | 0.250 | < | 0.350 |
| ( 4 3 2 ) | 0.350 | = | 0.350 |

REVISED RELATION MATRIX 1

| | 1 | 2 | 3 | 4 |
|---|---|---|---|---|
| 1 | 0. | 0.750 | 0.750 | 0.750 |
| 2 | 0.250 | 0. | 0.650 | 0.800 |
| 3 | 0.250 | 0.350 | 0. | 0.600 |
| 4 | 0.250 | 0.350 | 0.400 | 0. |

TRANSITIVITY CHECK 2

| ( I J K ) | (I J)AND(J K) | | (I K) |
|---|---|---|---|
| ( 1 2 3 ) | 0.650 | < | 0.750 |
| ( 1 2 4 ) | 0.750 | = | 0.750 |
| ( 1 3 2 ) | 0.350 | < | 0.750 |
| ( 1 3 4 ) | 0.600 | < | 0.750 |
| ( 1 4 2 ) | 0.350 | < | 0.750 |
| ( 1 4 3 ) | 0.400 | < | 0.750 |
| ( 2 1 3 ) | 0.250 | < | 0.650 |
| ( 2 1 4 ) | 0.250 | < | 0.800 |
| ( 2 3 1 ) | 0.250 | = | 0.250 |
| ( 2 3 4 ) | 0.600 | < | 0.800 |
| ( 2 4 1 ) | 0.250 | = | 0.250 |
| ( 2 4 3 ) | 0.400 | < | 0.650 |
| ( 3 1 2 ) | 0.250 | < | 0.350 |
| ( 3 1 4 ) | 0.250 | < | 0.600 |
| ( 3 2 1 ) | 0.250 | = | 0.250 |
| ( 3 2 4 ) | 0.350 | < | 0.600 |
| ( 3 4 1 ) | 0.250 | = | 0.250 |
| ( 3 4 2 ) | 0.350 | = | 0.350 |
| ( 4 1 2 ) | 0.250 | < | 0.350 |
| ( 4 1 3 ) | 0.250 | < | 0.400 |
| ( 4 2 1 ) | 0.250 | = | 0.250 |
| ( 4 2 3 ) | 0.350 | < | 0.400 |
| ( 4 3 1 ) | 0.250 | = | 0.250 |
| ( 4 3 2 ) | 0.350 | = | 0.350 |

preference rule can derive a revised matrix (7.46) assuring the transitivity with the way (i).

$$[\mu_R'] = \begin{bmatrix} 0. & 0.63 & 0.62 & 0.63 \\ 0.22 & 0. & 0.53 & 0.7 \\ 0.22 & 0.26 & 0. & 0.47 \\ 0.22 & 0.26 & 0.35 & 0. \end{bmatrix} \tag{7.46}$$

The way (ii) derives another revised matrix (7.47) from the original matrix (7.43).

$$[\mu_R''] = \begin{bmatrix} 0. & 0.58 & 0.62 & 0.58 \\ 0.2 & 0. & 0.53 & 0.7 \\ 0.13 & 0.13 & 0. & 0.47 \\ 0.13 & 0.13 & 0.35 & 0. \end{bmatrix} \tag{7.47}$$

Finally, the revised matrices which embody the transitivity are presented to the assessors as candidates for acceptance. The values of the membership function $\mu_R$ appearing in the alternative relation matrices are regarded as alternatives of average weights for preferences revealed in the pair-wise comparisons under a selection rule. Thus, in practice, it is asked if the changed values of the weights in an alternative would be more acceptable for the assessors than those in the others. If the revised values in one of the transitive matrices are most acceptable to the assessors, a nonfuzzy weak-ordered preference set has been obtained.

## 4. Construction of a nonfuzzy preference ordering with confirmation of its acceptance level

The algorithm for deriving a nonfuzzy preference ordering among the attributes is based on the $\alpha$-level decomposition of fuzzy binary relations. The procedure is to decompose the fuzzy set of preference orderings like (7.39) into a union of the $\alpha$-level sets based on the finally obtained relation matrix with transitivity ensured. For instance, assume that the revised matrix (7.46) is finally accepted. Then the $\alpha$-level decomposition can be obtained as follows.

$$R_{\alpha=.7} = (\mathbf{X}_2, X_4)$$

$$R_{\alpha=.6} = R_{\alpha=.7} \cup ((\mathbf{X}_1, X_2), (\mathbf{X}_1, X_3), (\mathbf{X}_1, X_4))$$

$$R_{\alpha=.5} = R_{\alpha=.6} \cup (\mathbf{X}_2, X_3) \tag{7.48}$$

$$R_{\alpha=.4} = R_{\alpha=.5} \cup (\mathbf{X}_3, X_4)$$

$$R_{\alpha=.3} = R_{\alpha=.4} \cup (\mathbf{X}_4, X_3)$$

$$R_{\alpha=.2} = R_{\alpha=.3} \cup ((\mathbf{X}_2, X_1), (\mathbf{X}_3, X_1), (\mathbf{X}_3, X_2), (\mathbf{X}_4, X_1), (\mathbf{X}_4, X_2))$$

The classes of the nonfuzzy weak-ordered set are defined corresponding to the $\alpha$-level decomposition (7.48). The class $C^i$ is defined as a set of all orderings for the quaternary relation compatible with $C^i$, and is shown as follows.

$$\begin{array}{lll} C^1 : (\mathbf{X}_2, X_4) & \ldots \text{ level } 0.7 & \\ C^2 : ((\mathbf{X}_1, X_2), (\mathbf{X}_1, X_3), (\mathbf{X}_1, X_4)) & \ldots \text{ level } 0.6 & (7.49) \\ C^3 : (\mathbf{X}_2, X_3), & \ldots \text{ level } 0.5 & \\ C^4 : (\mathbf{X}_3, X_4) & \ldots \text{ level } 0.4 \;. & \end{array}$$

Taking the intersection, we can find the nonfuzzy collective ordering

$$C^1 \cap C^2 \cap C^3 \cap C^4 = (\mathbf{X}_1, X_2, X_3, X_4), \tag{7.50}$$

or in another expression,

$$\mathbf{X}_1 \succ X_2 \succ X_3 \succ X_4. \tag{7.51}$$

Taking the minimum $\alpha$-level in (7.49) from the definition of fuzzy intersection (7.25), we can call (7.51) the nonfuzzy weak-rodered preference relation in the level 0.4 for our decision problem. Or preferably, using the membership function $\mu_{C^1 \cap C^2 \cap C^3 \cap C^4}(\mathbf{X}_i, X_j) = 0.47$ in (7.46), we can say about the collective preference ordering (7.51) that "the degree of agreement is 0.47."

With this device, the range or the degree of disagreement for the collective preference ordering (7.51) can also be ascertained. For instance, each counterordering class can be obtained from the $\alpha$-level set (7.48) as a set of all orderings for the quaternary relation compatible with:

$$C^{1'} : (\mathbf{X}_4, X_3) \qquad \ldots \text{ level } .3$$
$$C^{2'} : ((\mathbf{X}_2, X_1), (\mathbf{X}_3, X_1), (\mathbf{X}_3, X_2), (\mathbf{X}_4, X_1), (\mathbf{X}_4, X_2)) \qquad \ldots \text{ level } .2 \quad (7.52)$$

Taking the intersection, we can find a counterordering of (7.51)

$$C^{1'} \cap C^{2'} = (\mathbf{X}_4, X_3, X_2, X_1). \quad (7.53)$$

Taking the maximum $\alpha$-level, we can say about (7.51) that "it is disagreeable in level 0.3." Or preferably, using the membership function $\mu_{C^{1'}+C^{2'}}(\mathbf{X}_i, \mathbf{X}_j) = 0.35$, we can say "the degree of disagreement for (7.51) is 0.35." A transitivity closure representing the finally obtained relation matrix can be depicted with a modified Hasse diagram (Figure 7.3).

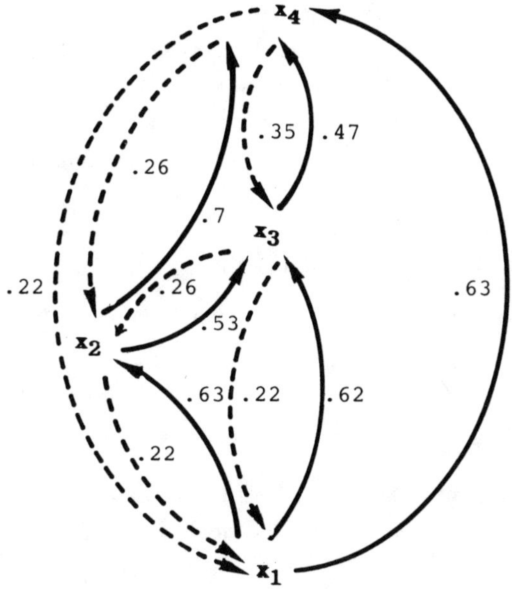


**Figure 7.3 A transitivity closure for a collective choice.**

Clearly, in the case of the strength-of-preference rule, the agreement level of the nonfuzzy weak-ordered relation (7.51) will usually be lower in comparison to the simple majority case: like from 0.6 to 0.4. In other words, the strength-of-preference rule usually admits a higher degree of fuzziness in the agreement level for the collective choice.

### 7.4.4 Construction of the Fuzzy Multiattribute Utility Function

The second phase of the fuzzification process in Step (ii) concerns assessing the values of the scaling constants $k_i$, $i = 1,\ldots,m$, for constructing FMUF. The numerical ordering of the scaling constants has been already determined corresponding to the nonfuzzy collective preference ordering for the attributes $\mathbf{X}_i$, $i = 1,\ldots,m$, obtained with the articulation of its agreement level. Thus even though the indifference experiments among the attributes $\mathbf{X}_i$ for assessing the relative values of scaling constants have been executed as if they were a single person's decision processes, the derivation of the collective preference ordering in the prior stage will have mitigated to some extent the arbitrariness due to MADM, which must be included in relative magnitude of the scaling constants.

Now after the indifference experiments, the FMUF is derived with numerical values of the fuzzy scaling constants $\tilde{k}_i$, $i = 1,\ldots,m$, which are treated as the fuzzy number such as the L-R type. The L-R type fuzzy number is defined by Dubois and Prade (1978).

**Definition 8.4 (L-R type fuzzy number).**

An L-R type fuzzy number $\tilde{n}$ is expressed in the following form:

$$\tilde{n} \triangleq (\bar{n}, \ \alpha, \ \beta), \tag{7.54}$$

where $\bar{n}$ is a "mean" value and $\alpha$ and $\beta$ show left-and right-hand side dispersion. A membership function of the fuzzy number $\tilde{n}$ (7.54) is

$$\mu_{\tilde{n}} = \begin{cases} L((\bar{n} - z)/\alpha), & z \leqslant \bar{n}, \quad \alpha > 0 \\ R((z - \bar{n})/\beta), & \bar{n} \leqslant z, \quad \beta > 0, \end{cases} \tag{7.55}$$

where $L(0) = R(0) = 1$.

After obtaining the relative values $k_i/k_s$ of the scaling constants in (7.18) and (7.19) with the indifference experiments, the numerical value of $k_s$ on $u_s(\mathbf{x}_s)$ for the most preferable (highly regarded) attribute $\mathbf{x}_s$ must be determined. For this purpose, the lottery experiment on m attributes is executed to answer the following question:

**Question.** On the one hand, let us consider the lottery which will take alternatively with a probability $p_s$ the best values $\mathbf{x}_{i1}$ for all attributes $\mathbf{X}_i$, $i = 1,\ldots,m$, or with a probability $1 - p_s$ the worst values $\mathbf{x}_{i0}$ for all the attributes. On the other hand, let us consider the certain consequence in which the most preferable attribute takes its best value $\mathbf{x}_{s1}$ and all the other attributes take their worst values $\{\mathbf{x}_{\bar{s}0}\}$, $\bar{s} \triangleq 1,\ldots, s-1, s+1,\ldots,m$. Then what is the numerical value of the probability $p_s$ with which the lottery and the certain consequence will become indifferent ?

The fuzzification device takes the probability $p_s$ as a fuzzy number $\tilde{p}_s \triangleq (\bar{p}_s, \beta, \gamma)$, where $\bar{p}_s$ denotes a "mean" value of $\tilde{p}_s$, and $\beta$ and $\gamma$ denote respectively the left-and right side spreads from $\bar{p}_s$. The parameters $\beta$, $\gamma$, and $\bar{p}_s$ can be obtained as minimum, maximum, and medium valuations of the probability $p_s$ in the collective choice. Then the scaling constant $k_s$ can be assessed by

$$\tilde{p}_s = \tilde{k}_s \triangleq (\bar{k}_s, \beta, \gamma) \tag{7.56}$$

from the representation theorem (7.18)(7.19).

We can use the L-R type fuzzy number (7.55) for $\tilde{k}_s$, and perform the fuzzy algebraic operations on it. The corresponding UNIF-value $u_s$ in (7.18) and (7.19) can also be reexamined as a fuzzy number $\tilde{u}_s \triangleq (\bar{u}_s, \delta, \eta)$, where the parameters $\delta$, $\eta$ and $\bar{u}_s$ can also be obtained respectively as minimum, maximum, and medium values in collective choice. With these fuzzy numbers $\tilde{k}_s$ and $\tilde{u}_s$, all the fuzzy scaling constants $\tilde{k}_i$, $i = 1,\ldots,m$, $i \neq s$, can be obtained (See Chapter 6).

The fuzzification of the scaling constants will have some effects on choosing a representation form, multiplicative or additive, of MUF. For this reason, the fuzzy representation check should be performed.

$$\begin{aligned} &\text{(a)} \quad \text{If} \quad \sum_{i=1}^{m} \tilde{k}_i > 1, \quad \text{then} \quad -1 < K < 0 \text{ (multiplicative).} \\ &\text{(b)} \quad \text{If} \quad \sum_{i=1}^{m} \tilde{k}_i < 1, \quad \text{then} \quad K > 0 \text{ (multiplicative).} \\ &\text{(c)} \quad \text{If} \quad \sum_{i=1}^{m} \tilde{k}_i = 1, \quad \text{then} \quad K = 0 \text{ (additive).} \end{aligned} \tag{7.57}$$

Because the scaling constant $\tilde{k}_i$, $i = 1,\ldots,m$, is a fuzzy number, the assertion ( > and < ) for that in (7.57) is still fuzzy. Thus it should be asked what the truth value of the assertion " $\sum_{i=1}^{m} \tilde{k}_i$ is greater (or smaller) than 1" is. The separation theorem for two fuzzy sets (Zadeh 1965) can be applied to the comparison of the fuzzy numbers $\sum_{i}^{m} \tilde{k}_i$ and $\tilde{1} \triangleq (\bar{1}, 0, 0)$. The separation theorem asserts that when $M$ is the maximum grade of the intersection of two bounded convex fuzzy sets, the degree of separation $D$ of these sets is obtained by $D = 1 - M$. To answer the question, we can choose a threshold level $\theta$, $1 > \theta > 0$. If $M > \theta$, then it can be assured that $\sum_{i=1}^{m} \tilde{k}_i = \tilde{1}$ in the level $\theta$ (Figure 7.4).

In the result, FMUF can be derived as a fuzzy number in the additive form,

$$\tilde{U}(\mathbf{x}_1,\ldots,\mathbf{x}_m) = \sum_{i=1}^{m} \tilde{k}_i \tilde{u}_i(\mathbf{x}_i), \tag{7.58}$$

or in the multiplicative form,

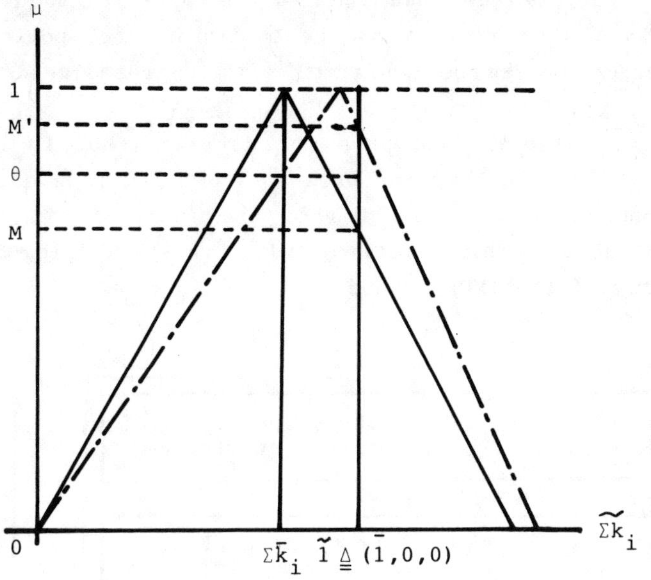


Note: M' > θ : additive
M < θ : multiplicative

**Figure 7.4 The fuzzy representation check with the separation theorem.**

$$1 + K\tilde{U}(\mathbf{x}_1, \ldots, \mathbf{x}_m) = \prod_{i=1}^{m} (Kk_i\tilde{u}_i(\mathbf{x}_i) + 1). \qquad (7.59)$$

The values of FMUF are calculated for alternative policy programs in which different numerical values of the attributes $\mathbf{x}_i$, $i = 1,\ldots,m$, are assigned. The values of SUF (UNIF) $u_i(\mathbf{x}_i)$, $i = 1,\ldots,m$, $i \neq s$, can also be assessed as the fuzzy number $\tilde{u}_i = (\bar{u}_i, \xi, \nu)$, where $\bar{u}_i$, $\xi$, and $\nu$ can be determined from the evaluation by MDM.

Finally, based on the assessment of FMUF for the alternative policy programs A, B, C,..., a preference ordering among these alternatives can be found. For instance,

$$\tilde{U}(C) > \tilde{U}(B) > \tilde{U}(A) > \ldots \Leftrightarrow C \succ B \succ A \succ \ldots \qquad (7.60)$$

Because the comparison (7.60) on the fuzzy number $\tilde{U}$ is still fuzzy, the previous procedure for ascertaining if the value of

$\tilde{U}(C)$ is truly larger than that of $\tilde{U}(B)$, etc., should be used here again. The priority of the best preferred policy program C, for example, can be confirmed with a preassigned threshold level $\theta$.

The operational procedure for deriving FMUF is summarized in Figure 7.5. The computer program ICOPSS/FR is also available for evaluation and calculation of the fuzzy scaling constants and the FMUF. This facility will raise applicability and feasibility of the FMUF method.

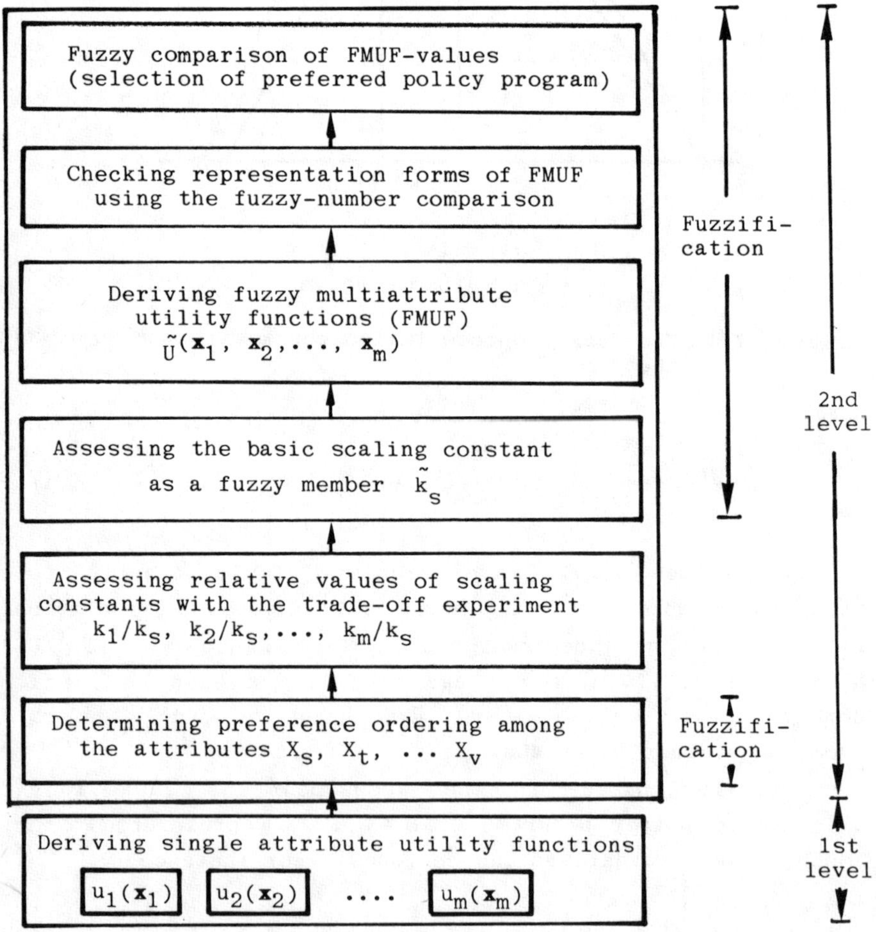


**Figure 7.5 The algorithm of FMUF method**

## 7.5 Stochastic Dominance Rules for Collective Choice

In this section, stochastic dominance rules for collective choice are discussed as a surrogate for deriving GUF. Constructing GUF requires an "aggregation" of individual preferences, and measuring it on the cardinal scale requires perfect knowledge about the strength of preference of each individual. However, since perfect information on individual preferences scaled on a common unit is generally unavailable, selection rules based on partial identification of GUF can be better established. Although this method has no concern about constructing the GUF and thus cannot provide any final selection rule for the preferred policy programs, it will contribute to narrow down the admissible set for the final selection among alternative programs.

The stochastic dominance rules (SDR) are used for finding an efficient set with the partial identification of GUF. The SDR has been developed by Quirk and Saposnik (1962), Fishburn (1964), Hanock and Levy (1969), Levy and Sarnat (1970), Hadar and Russell (1969, 1971), Whitmore (1970), Bawa (1975), Fishburn and Vickson (1978), and others. The SDR has been developed as an alternative to the mean-variance selection rule (MVR) for ordering uncertain prospects, or risky policy programs (e.g., in the portfolio selection). The MVR, which has been developed since Markowitz's famous work (1959), can generate an admissible or efficient set by excluding the prospects with a lower mean and a higher variance of utility values. It means that policy programs having a lower likely return and a higher uncertainty of return are eliminated as "inefficient." However, it has been pointed out that the MVR is valid only under the assumptions of the quadratic (increasing risk averse) utility function and the normal distributions of probability (Hicks 1962, Arrow 1971). Thus the MVR will have a very limited generality in practice. The SDR is based on the expected utility hypotheses, as is the MVR, but intends to establish more general selection rules for uncertain prospects.

The expected utility maximization (EUMAX) hypothesis is expressed in a compact and continuous form as follows:

$$\underset{x}{\text{maximize}} \quad Eu \triangleq \int_a^b u(x)p(x)dx, \tag{7.61}$$

where $x$ is an uncertain prospect, $p(x)$ is a probability density function and $u(x)$ is a utility function. Supposing the function form of $u(x)$ be unknown, an order of priority of $E_u$ (7.61) can be determined based on the stochastic dominance rule (SDR) for $p(x)$. In this approach, only partial identification of $u(x)$ in terms of risk properties is required. Risk properties of the von Neumann-Morgenstern type utility function have been discussed in Chapter 5. A classification of the risk properties of the utility functions is defined as follows:

**Definition 7.4.**

(1) A class $\mathscr{U}^1$ of the utility function represents the set of all bounded and strictly increasing utility functions:

$$\mathscr{U}^1 \triangleq \{u(x) \mid u \in C^1, \quad u'(x) > 0, \quad x \in \Xi\}, \tag{7.62}$$

where $\Xi$ is a closed value-interval of the uncertain quantity x, and denotes $\Xi \triangleq [a, b]$.

(2) $\mathscr{U}^2$ represents the set of all bounded, strictly increasing, risk averse (decreasing marginal) utility functions:

$$\mathscr{U}^2 \triangleq \{u(x) \mid u \in C^2, \quad u \in \mathscr{U}^1, \quad u''(x) < 0, \ \forall x \in \Xi\}. \tag{7.63}$$

(3) $\mathscr{U}^3$ represents the set of all bounded, strictly increasing, risk averse utility functions with positive third derivatives.

$$\mathscr{U}^3 \triangleq \{u(x) \mid u \in C^3, \quad u \in \mathscr{U}^2, \quad u'''(x) > 0, \ \forall x \in \Xi\}. \tag{7.64}$$

(4) $\mathscr{U}^4$ represents the set of all bounded, strictly increasing and decreasing, risk averse utility functions:

$$\mathscr{U}^4 \triangleq \{u(x) \mid u \in C^3, \quad u \in \mathscr{U}^2, \quad r'(x) < 0, \quad \forall x \in \Xi\}, \tag{7.65}$$

where $r(x)$ is the risk function, $r(x) \triangleq -u''(x)/u'(x)$, and

$\gamma'(x) = \frac{\partial}{\partial x}(-u''(x)/u'(x)) = (-u'''(x)u'(x) + u''(x)^2)/u'(x)^2$.
The $u'$, $u''$, and $u'''$ show the first, second, and third derivatives of the utility function $u(x)$, respectively. $C^i$ denotes a set of i-times continuously differentiable functions, or a set of functions of class $C^i$.

It should be noted that $\mathscr{U}^3$ can include both of $r' > 0$ and $r' \leqslant 0$ (increasing and nonincreasing risk aversion).

Let the $p(x)$ and $q(x)$ be nondecreasing, continuous probability functions. According to the expected utility maximization hypothesis, p is preferred to q if

$$\Delta Eu \triangleq \int_a^b u(x)p(x)dx - \int_a^b u(x)q(x)dx > 0 \tag{7.66}$$

In terms of Stieltjes-Lebesques integrals,

$$\Delta Eu \triangleq \int [F(x) - G(x)]\, du(x) > 0, \tag{7.67}$$

where $F(x)$ and $G(x)$ are cumulative distribution functions for $p(x)$ and $q(x)$, respectively.

**Definition 7.5 (Stochastic dominance).**

The i-th degree stochastic dominance $F >^i G$ for all utility functions in Class $\mathscr{U}^i$ is defined whenever $\Delta Eu \geqslant 0$ for all $u \in \mathscr{U}^i$ and $\Delta Eu > 0$ for some $u \in \mathscr{U}^i$ in (7.67).

A theorem about the stochastic dominance rules is established.

**Theorem 7.5.**

(1) $F >^1 G \Leftrightarrow F(x) \leqslant G(x), \quad \forall x \in \Xi,$ (7.68)
and $F(x) < G(x)$ for some $x \in \Xi$.

(2) $F >^2 G \Leftrightarrow \int_a^x F(t)dt \leqslant \int_a^x G(t)dt, \quad \forall x \in \Xi,$ (7.69)

and $\int_a^x F(t)dt < \int_a^x G(t)dt$ for some $x \in \Xi$.

(3) $F >^3 G \;\Rightarrow\; m_F \geq m_G$,

$$\text{and} \quad \int_a^x \int_a^y F(t)dtdy \leq \int_a^x \int_a^y G(t)dtdy, \quad \forall x \in \Xi, \tag{7.70}$$

$$\text{and} \quad \int_a^x \int_a^y F(t)dtdy < \int_a^x \int_a^y G(t)dtdy,$$

for some $x \in \Xi$.

(4) $F >^4 G \;\Leftrightarrow\;$ (7.70), when $m_F = m_G$,
where $m_F$ denotes the mean of the distribution function F, etc.

Theorem 7.5 presents the criteria with which an efficient set of the uncertain prospects, or policy programs, is chosen. The theorem shows that the cumulative distribution functions are used for finding the nondominated set, depending only on the risk properties of the utility functions for the prospects without any regard for identification of their function forms.

Distribution properties of the stochastic dominance are also examined, which will enhance its usefulness for empirical studies.

**Corollary 7.1.**

(1) (Hanock and Levy 1969)

$$F >^1 G \;\Leftrightarrow\; m_F > m_G, \text{ when } F \leq G \text{ for } a < x < x^\circ, \tag{7.71}$$

$F < G$ for some $x < x^\circ$, and $F \geq G$
for $b > x \geq x^\circ$, $x^\circ \in \Xi$.

(2) (Hadar and Russell 1971)

(a) $$F >^2 G \;\Leftrightarrow\; m_F \geq m_G, \tag{7.72}$$

(b) When $m_F = m_G$, then $$F >^2 G \;\Rightarrow\; \nu_F < \nu_G, \tag{7.73}$$
where $\nu_F$ denotes a variance of the distribution function F.

(3) (Bawa 1975)

(a) $F >^4 G \;\Leftarrow\; m_F \geq m_G$, and

$$\int_a^x \int_a^y (F(t) - G(t))dtdy \leqslant 0, \quad \forall x \in \Xi,$$

$$\text{and} \quad \int_a^x \int_a^y (F(t) - G(t))dtdy < 0 \quad \text{for some} \quad x \in \Xi. \tag{7.74}$$

(b) $F >^4 G \Rightarrow m_F \geq m_G$, and for some $x^\circ \in \Xi$,

$$\int_a^x \int_a^y (F(t) - G(t))dtdy \leqslant 0 \quad \text{for some} \quad a \leqslant x \leqslant x^\circ,$$

$$\text{and} \quad \int_a^x \int_a^y (F(t) - G(t))dtdy < 0 \quad \text{for some} \quad a < x < x^\circ. \tag{7.75}$$

As Bawa pointed out, there is no known selection rule which is both necessary and sufficient for the fourth degree stochastic dominance in the general case with unequal means for two distribution functions. Thus the third degree stochastic dominance rule (TSDR) can be used as a reasonable approximation to the optimal selection rule for the entire class of the distribution functions.

The SDR has been extended to multiattribute decision problems (Levy 1973, Levy and Proush 1974, Huang, Vertinsky, and Ziemba 1978). The following theorem for multiattribute utility analysis is provided (Huang, Kira and Vertinsky 1978).

**Theorem 7.6.**

Let us define

$$\mathscr{U}^{i*} \triangleq \{U(\mathbf{x}_1, \mathbf{x}_2, \ldots, \mathbf{x}_m) = u(v(\mathbf{x}_1, \mathbf{x}_2, \ldots, \mathbf{x}_m) | u \in \mathscr{U}^i$$

$$\text{and} \quad v \in \mathscr{U}^i\}, \quad \text{for} \quad i = 1, \ldots, 4, \tag{7.76}$$

where $\mathbf{x}_i$ shows a value of an attribute, $v$ is a multivariate function, and $u$ is SUF. Then $\mathscr{U}^{i*} = \mathscr{U}^i$.

**Proof.**

Since $u(v) \in \mathscr{U}^i$ from $u \in \mathscr{U}^i$ and $v \in \mathscr{U}^i$ for all

$i = 1,\ldots 4, \mathscr{U}^{i*} \subset \mathscr{U}^{i}$. Moreover, for $u(v) = v$ where $u \in \mathscr{U}^{i}$, $\{U(\mathbf{x}_1, \mathbf{x}_2, \ldots, \mathbf{x}_m) = v(\mathbf{x}_1, \mathbf{x}_2, \ldots, \mathbf{x}_m) | v \in \mathscr{U}^{i}\} \subset \mathscr{U}^{i*}$. Thus from $\mathscr{U}^{i*} \subset \mathscr{U}^{i*}$, $\mathscr{U}^{i} = \mathscr{U}^{i*}$.

A research bibliography for SDR has been provided by Bawa (1982), which includes many application studies with efficient algorithms.

Now an alternative method to incorporate the diversity of evaluation under the SDR can be discussed.

Let the utility function u be GUF. Under the SDR, the GUF should be assessed only for its risk property. However, SDR requires an entire evaluation for the probability functions, and for this purpose, the distribution of the diversified evaluation by MDM must be assessed entirely with or without some weighting device.

Let us consider a two-layer system for systems evaluation (Figure 7.6).

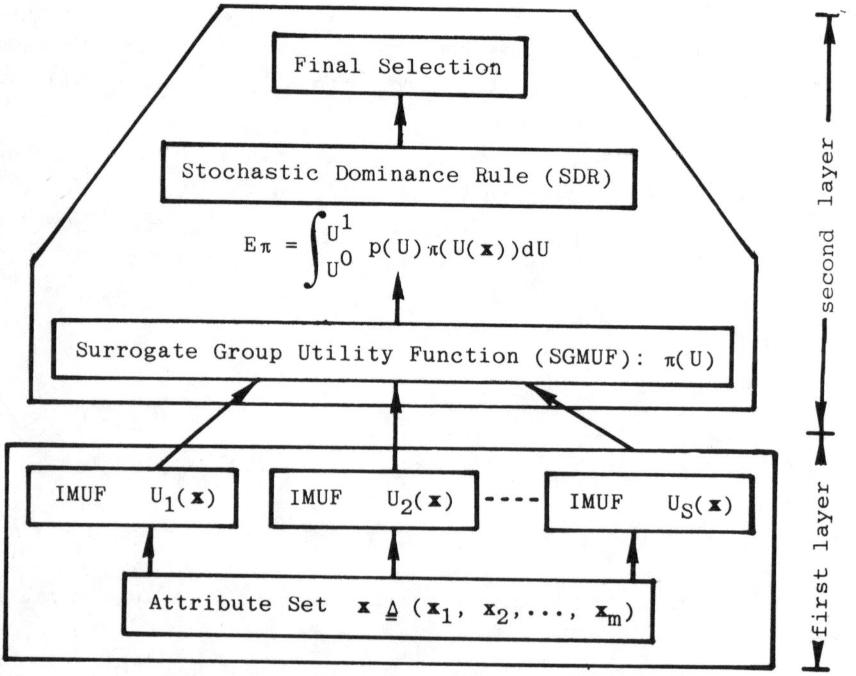


**Figure 7.6 Multiattribute utility analysis with the stochastic dominance rule.**

In the first layer, for alternative sets $\mathbf{x}^k \triangleq (\mathbf{x}_1, \mathbf{x}_2, \ldots, \mathbf{x}_m)^k$, $k = 1,\ldots,K$, of attributes, $\mathbf{x}_i$, $i = 1,\ldots,m$, an IMUF $U_p^k(\mathbf{x}^k)$ for each individual decision maker (IDM), $p = 1,\ldots,S$, is assessed with the usual procedure.

In the second layer, the collective choice problem is introduced. Assume the surrogate function (SGMUF) $\pi(U^k(\mathbf{x}^k))$ for the group multiattribute utility function (GMUF) $U^k(\mathbf{x}^k)$ be partially known, i.e., $\pi(U^k) \in (\mathscr{U}^1 \cup \mathscr{U}^2 \cup \mathscr{U}^3 \cup \mathscr{U}^4)$, and assume the $U^k$ be an uncertain quantity taking its values, $U_1^k$, $U_2^k, \ldots, U_S^k$, at random, where $U_p^k$, $p = 1,\ldots,S$, is an IMUF value. The expected group utility function is defined with a smoothing procedure as follows ($k$ is omitted):

$$E\pi \triangleq \int_{U^0}^{U^1} p(U)\pi(U)dU, \tag{7.77}$$

where $U^0$ and $U^1$ show the lower and upper limits of the range of the IMUF-values $U_p$, $p = 1,\ldots,S$. The probability density function $p(U)$ is constructed from a diversified evaluation of the IMUF-values with or without some weights which represent the strength-of-preference. Once the distribution function $F(U_k)$ is derived from the specified values of the probability function $p(U_k)$ assessed for alternative policy programs $k = 1,\ldots,K$, the SDR can be applied as efficiency criteria for the selection of the "optimal" or nondominated values. The order of priority among the alternative policy programs is derived and a final selection among the efficient policy programs can be performed.

**Remarks.**

1. For treating the judgmental phase in MCDM, multiattribute utility analysis has been well-developed for direct assessment of human preferences. However, methodological development for treating collective choice decision problems still remains behind the public needs. Although many theoretical researches on the multiattribute utility analysis has focused upon the decomposition of MUF particularly with its nonlinearity, and they will greatly contribute to constructing GUF or GMUF, their feasibility in practice still lags behind

their theoretical progress. To cope with this situation, alternative ways which are not based on identifying the GUF or GMUF are considered; they are probabilistic and linguistic. In this section, we discussed an intermediate approach between these two ways, which is based on partial identification of the surrogate group multiattribute utility functions (SGMUF). Although this approach does not treat the value trade-offs or the agreement levels among MDM directly, they restrict the range of the admissible set from which the final choice can be made.

2. This method treats the IMUF-values $U_p$, $p = 1,\ldots,S$, as uncertain prospects, and regards them as the values that a collective utility function U takes. SGMUF $\pi(U^k(\mathbf{x}))$ for a policy program k is defined as a surrogate for an intrinsic group utility function (7.1) composed of the derived IMUFs, on the collective utility function U which is treated as a random variable. The SGMUF is only assessed for its risk attitude, and thus it is not necessary to identify the entire function form. The SDR can be used to compare the distributions of IMUFs for alternative policy programs without resorting to precise identification of the function forms of the GMUF.

3. As has already been discussed, the construction of the intrinsic group utility function (GUF) representing the collective response requires an interpersonal comparison of individual preferences that includes the measurement of strength of preference in a common unit. The strength of preference should be measured in terms of preference differences, and the value function is defined in distinction from the utility function as embodying the preference differences. In the next chapter, the preference structure which includes the strength of preference is discussed in terms of the value function.

# CHAPTER 8

# RECONSIDERATION OF PREFERENCE STRUCTURE

## 8.1 Strength of Preference and Measurable Value Functions

### 8.1.1 Beyond the Concept of the Utility Function under Uncertainty

Multiattribute utility analysis, discussed in the preceding chapters, treats the preference structure based on the von Neumann-Morgenstern expected utility hypothesis. The von Neumann-Morgenstern expected utility hypothesis presents the fundamentals for measurable utility functions under uncertainty, and has the following characteristics, which presume the von Neumann-Morgenstern System in Definition 5.1:

(1) order-preserving

$$\mathbf{x}_i \succsim \mathbf{x}_s \quad \Leftrightarrow \quad u(\mathbf{x}_i) \geqslant u(\mathbf{x}_s), \qquad i,s = 1,\dots,m, \tag{8.1}$$

(2) expected utility hypothesis

$$u(\mathbf{x}_i) = \sum_{j=1}^{n} p_{ij}\, u(\mathbf{x}_{ij}), \tag{8.2}$$

where $\mathbf{x}_i \in X$ is an uncertain quantity in the preference set such that an outcome $\mathbf{x}_{ij}$ occurs with a probability $p_{ij}$ and $\mathbf{x}_i$ can be represented as $\mathbf{x}_i \triangleq \sum_{j=1}^{n} p_{ij}\mathbf{x}_{ij}$ under the assumption of linearity since Bernoulli (1738).

The 50-50 chance lottery technique is used for constructing the measurable utility function $u(\mathbf{x}_i)$, based on the expected utility hypothesis, via treating the $x_i$ as equal in preference to the certainty equivalent $\hat{x}_i$. This device does not depend on measuring the strength of preference of DM. However it has already been pointed out that, in linear or nonlinear aggregation processes of the individual utility functions, which can be individual single attribute utility functions (ISUF) or individual MUF (IMUF), for deriving the group utility function (GUF), interpersonal comparisons of preferences are required. This notion presumes that the differences in preferences are measurable and comparable with each other and thus the strength of preference is also measurable and commensurable.

In this section, the preference analysis for incorporating comparisons of preference differences is examined. Although comparisons of preference differences can be conducted in terms of interpersonal comparisons of the strength of preferences, as long as any individual preference function is measured as a cardinal number, the strength of preferences cannot really be compared among people in a commensurate term, because the origin and scale of their measurement cannot be determined with a common unit, with which the preference differences among multiple decision makers (MDM) can be compared. Thus, we are concerned here simply with examining the comparison of preference differences in terms of some particular property of a preference attitude of a single decision maker (SDM). The interpersonal comparisons of preference differences are postponed until the end of the present discussions.

The comparison of the preference differences is primarily a matter of a crisp and nonrandom evaluation. Thus the concept of value function under certainty is discussed apart from the uncertain situations under which the utility functions are examined.

### 8.1.2 Concepts of the Value Function under Certainty

Ellsberg (1954), and Luce and Raiffa (1957) suggested that the utility concept under uncertainty should not be confused with the value concept which compares the preference differences under certainty. The preference function based on a comparison of the preference differences is defined as a value function. As a theoretical background, axioms and representation theorems for measurement of the difference structures have been provided by Krantz, Luce, Suppes and Tversky (1971). In particular, the following theorem for an algebraic-difference structure is presented.

**Definition 8.1 (Algebraic-difference structure).**

An algebraic difference structure is defined for the pair $(\mathbf{X} \times \mathbf{X}, \succsim^*)$ of a nonempty set $\mathbf{X}$ and a quaternary relation $\succsim^*$ on $\mathbf{X}$, if and only if the following axioms are satisfied for all $\mathbf{w}$, $\mathbf{x}$, $\mathbf{y}$, $\mathbf{z}$, $\mathbf{w}'$, $\mathbf{x}'$, $\mathbf{y}'$, $\mathbf{y}'' \in \mathbf{X}$ and for all sequences $\mathbf{w}_1, \mathbf{w}_2, \ldots \in \mathbf{X}$:

(i) $(\mathbf{X} \times \mathbf{X}, \succsim^*)$ is a weak order.

(ii) $\mathbf{w} - \mathbf{x} \succsim^* \mathbf{y} - \mathbf{z} \Rightarrow \mathbf{z} - \mathbf{y} \succsim^* \mathbf{x} - \mathbf{w}$.

(iii) $\mathbf{w} - \mathbf{x} \succsim^* \mathbf{w}' - \mathbf{x}'$ and $\mathbf{x} - \mathbf{y} \succsim^* \mathbf{x}' - \mathbf{y}'$
$\Rightarrow \mathbf{w} - \mathbf{y} \succsim^* \mathbf{w}' - \mathbf{y}'$.

(iv) $\mathbf{w} - \mathbf{x} \succsim^* \mathbf{y} - \mathbf{z} \succsim^* \mathbf{w} - \mathbf{w}$
$\Rightarrow \mathbf{z}', \mathbf{z}'' \in \mathbf{X}$ exist such that $\mathbf{w} - \mathbf{z}' \sim^* \mathbf{y} - \mathbf{z} \sim^* \mathbf{z}'' - \mathbf{x}$.

(v) $\mathbf{w}_1, \mathbf{w}_2, \ldots, \mathbf{w}_i, \ldots$ is a strictly bounded standard sequence.
$\Rightarrow$ It is finite.

The strictly bounded standard sequence is defined as that, for every $\mathbf{w}_i, \mathbf{w}_{i+1} \in \mathrm{X}$ in a sequence $\mathbf{w}_1, \mathbf{w}_2, \ldots, \mathbf{w}_i, \ldots, \mathbf{w}_{i+1} - \mathbf{w}_i \sim^* \mathbf{w}_2 - \mathbf{w}_1$, not $\mathbf{w}_2 - \mathbf{w}_1 \sim^* \mathbf{w}_1 - \mathbf{w}_1$, and there exist $\mathbf{z}', \mathbf{z}'' \in \mathbf{X}$ such that $\mathbf{z}' - \mathbf{z}'' \succ^* \mathbf{w}_i - \mathbf{w}_1 \succ^* \mathbf{z}'' - \mathbf{z}'$ for all $\mathbf{w}_i$ in the sequence.

**Theorem 8.1 (Measurable value function).**

Suppose $\mathbf{X}$ be a nonempty preference set and $\succsim^*$ be a quaternary preference relation on $\mathrm{X}$, i.e., a binary relation on $\mathrm{X} \times \mathrm{X}$. If a pair $(\mathrm{X} \times \mathrm{X}, \succsim)$ is a (weak-ordered) algebraic-difference structure, then there exists a real-valued function $\phi$ on $\mathbf{X}$ such that, for all $\mathbf{w}$, $\mathbf{x}$, $\mathbf{y}$, $\mathbf{z} \subset \mathbf{X}$,

$$\mathbf{w} - \mathbf{x} \succsim^* \mathbf{y} - \mathbf{z} \Leftrightarrow \phi(\mathbf{w}) - \phi(\mathbf{x}) \geqslant \phi(\mathbf{y}) - \phi(\mathbf{z}). \tag{8.3}$$

Moreover, $\phi$ is unique up to a positive linear transformation, i.e., if $\phi'$ has the same property as $\phi$, then there are real-valued constants $\alpha$, $\beta$, such that $\phi' = \alpha\phi + \beta$ where $\alpha > 0$.

If $\mathbf{x}$ and $\mathbf{z}$ are fixed as $\mathbf{x} = \mathbf{z}$, then the formulation (8.3) is reduced to the representation axiom for the von Neumann-Morgenstern type measurable utility function (8.1). The function $\phi(\bullet)$ is interpreted as the measurable value function $v(\mathbf{x})$. Consider the following representation for the measurable value function:

$$\mathbf{w} - \mathbf{x}_o \succsim^* \mathbf{y} - \mathbf{x}_o \Leftrightarrow v(\mathbf{w}) - v(\mathbf{x}_o) \geq v(\mathbf{y}) - v(\mathbf{x}_o). \quad (8.4)$$

Then $v(\mathbf{w})$ and $v(\mathbf{y})$ are defined as the measurable value functions incorporating the preference differences or the strength of preference. Note that the expressions (8.3) and (8.4) do not include any uncertainty.

The multiattribute value functions (MVF) under certainty are derived in terms of a (weak-ordered) positive difference structure which does not allow negative differences.

Let $X_i$ denote an attribute and $x_i$ denote its value. A representation theorem of MVF in the multiplicative as well as additive form is presented under the assumptions of mutual preference independence and weak difference independence (Dyer and Sarin 1979a).

**Definition 8.2 (Mutual preference independence).**

The attributes $X_1, \ldots, X_m$ are mutually preferentially independent if, for every subset $\tilde{I} \subset I \triangleq (1, \ldots, m)$, the set $X_{\tilde{I}}$ of these attributes is preferentially independent of its complement $\bar{X}_{\tilde{I}}$. Namely, if $(\mathbf{w}_{\tilde{I}}, \bar{\mathbf{w}}_{\tilde{I}}) \succsim (\mathbf{x}_{\tilde{I}}, \bar{\mathbf{w}}_{\tilde{I}})$ for any $\mathbf{w}_{\tilde{I}}, \mathbf{x}_{\tilde{I}} \in X_{\tilde{I}}$ and $\bar{\mathbf{w}}_{\tilde{I}} \in \bar{X}_{\tilde{I}}$, then $(\mathbf{w}_{\tilde{I}}, \bar{\mathbf{x}}_{\tilde{I}}) \succsim (\mathbf{x}_{\tilde{I}}, \bar{\mathbf{x}}_{\tilde{I}})$ for all $\bar{\mathbf{x}}_{\tilde{I}} \in \bar{X}_{\tilde{I}}$.

**Definition 8.3 (Weak difference independence).**

$X_{\tilde{I}}$ is weak difference independent of $\bar{X}_{\tilde{I}}$ if, given any $\mathbf{w}_{\tilde{I}}, \mathbf{x}_{\tilde{I}}, \mathbf{y}_{\tilde{I}}, \mathbf{z}_{\tilde{I}} \in X_{\tilde{I}}$ and some $\bar{\mathbf{w}}_{\tilde{I}} \in \bar{X}_{\tilde{I}}$ such that $(\mathbf{w}_{\tilde{I}}, \bar{\mathbf{w}}_{\tilde{I}}) - (\mathbf{x}_{\tilde{I}}, \bar{\mathbf{w}}_{\tilde{I}}) \succ^* (\mathbf{y}_{\tilde{I}}, \bar{\mathbf{w}}_{\tilde{I}}) - (\mathbf{z}_{\tilde{I}}, \bar{\mathbf{w}}_{\tilde{I}})$, then $(\mathbf{w}_{\tilde{I}}, \bar{\mathbf{x}}_{\tilde{I}}) - (\mathbf{x}_{\tilde{I}}, \bar{\mathbf{x}}_{\tilde{I}}) \succ^*$

$(\mathbf{y}_{\tilde{I}}, \bar{\mathbf{x}}_{\tilde{I}}) - (\mathbf{z}_{\tilde{I}}, \bar{\mathbf{x}}_{\tilde{I}})$ for any $\bar{\mathbf{x}}_{\tilde{I}} \in \bar{\mathbf{X}}_{\tilde{I}}$.

That is, if the ordering of preference differences depends only on the values of the attributes in $\mathbf{X}_{\tilde{I}}$ and not on the fixed values of their complements in $\bar{\mathbf{X}}_{\tilde{I}}$, then the attribute set $\mathbf{X}_{\tilde{I}}$ is weak difference independent of $\bar{\mathbf{X}}_{\tilde{I}}$.

**Theorem 8.2 (Dyer and Sarin).**

Define $\mathbf{x}$ as a vector of values which an attribute set $X \triangleq (X_1, \ldots, X_m)$ takes. If there exists a measurable value function $v(\mathbf{x})$ on $\mathbf{x} \in R^m$, if $X_1, \ldots, X_m$ are mutually preferentially independent, and if $\mathbf{X}_{\tilde{I}}$ is weak difference independent of $\bar{\mathbf{X}}_{\tilde{I}}$, then for $i \in \tilde{I}$ the multiattribute value function (MVF) is represented as either

$$1 + \lambda v(\mathbf{x}) = \prod_{i=1}^{m} [1 + \lambda\lambda_i v_i(\mathbf{x}_i)], \quad \sum_{i=1}^{m} \lambda_i \neq 1, \tag{8.5}$$

or

$$v(\mathbf{x}) = \sum_{i=1}^{m} \lambda_i v_i(\mathbf{x}_i), \quad \sum_{i=1}^{m} \lambda_i = 1, \tag{8.6}$$

where $v(\mathbf{x})$ is the MVF which takes $v(\mathbf{x}^*) = 1$ and $v(\mathbf{x}^o) = 0$, and $v_i(\mathbf{x}_i)$ is the single attribute value function (SVF) that takes $v_i(\mathbf{x}_{i1}) = 1$ and $v_i(\mathbf{x}_{i0}) = 0$. $\lambda_i = v(\mathbf{x}_{i1}, \bar{\mathbf{x}}_{i0})$ and $\lambda$ are scaling constants such that $\lambda > -1$, $\lambda \neq 0$, and $\lambda$ solves $1 + \lambda = \prod_{i=1}^{m} (1+\lambda\lambda_i)$. $\mathbf{x}^* \triangleq \{\mathbf{x}_{i1}\}$ and $\mathbf{x}^o \triangleq \{\mathbf{x}_{i0}\}$ are sets of the best and worst values of the attributes respectively.

The proof of Theorem 9.2 can be carried out along the same line as the one for the multiattribute utility functions under the assumption of mutual utility independence.

The device to verify the weak difference independence is analogous to that for the preferential independence in the MUF method; it is asked if the order of preference differences between attributes is invariant to changes in all the other attribute values. If a trade of $(\mathbf{x}_{\tilde{I}}, \bar{\mathbf{w}}_{\tilde{I}})$ to $(\mathbf{w}_{\tilde{I}}, \bar{\mathbf{w}}_{\tilde{I}})$ is preferred to another trade of $(\mathbf{z}_{\tilde{I}}, \bar{\mathbf{w}}_{\tilde{I}})$ to $(\mathbf{y}_{\tilde{I}}, \bar{\mathbf{w}}_{\tilde{I}})$, or in another expression, if $(\mathbf{w}_I^{\sim}, \bar{\mathbf{w}}_I^{\sim}) - (\mathbf{x}_I^{\sim}, \bar{\mathbf{w}}_I^{\sim}) \succ^* (\mathbf{y}_I^{\sim}, \bar{\mathbf{w}}_I^{\sim}) - (\mathbf{z}_I^{\sim}, \bar{\mathbf{w}}_I^{\sim})$, and if this preference order is held for several different values of $\mathbf{w}_I^{\sim}, \mathbf{x}_I^{\sim}, \mathbf{y}_I^{\sim}, \mathbf{z}_I^{\sim} \in \mathbf{X}_I^{\sim}$ and $\bar{\mathbf{w}}_I^{\sim}, \bar{\mathbf{x}}_I^{\sim}, \bar{\mathbf{y}}_I^{\sim}, \bar{\mathbf{z}}_I^{\sim} \in \bar{\mathbf{X}}_I^{\sim}$, then $\mathbf{X}_I^{\sim}$ is weak difference independent of $\bar{\mathbf{X}}_I^{\sim}$.

Several kinds of experimental methods, nonprobabilistic and probabilistic, for constructing the value functions have been discussed (e.g., Fishburn 1967a).

For SVF, the direct (i.e., nonprobabilistic) midpoint (equisection or bisection) method is recommended. In the direct midpoint method, setting the worst and best values as $v_i(\mathbf{x}_{i0}) = 0$ and $v_i(\mathbf{x}_{i1}) = 1$ for an attribute $\mathbf{x}_i$, the attribute level $\mathbf{x}_{ix}$ corresponding to a midpoint of the value function $v_i(\mathbf{x}_{ix}) = 0.5$ is assessed. Then the attribute levels corresponding to midpoints among the assessed values are further assessed in the same way until enough points to derive a value function can be obtained on the value-attribute plane. This method resembles a direct assessment method for the single attribute utility function (SUF) except that it is based on a direct estimation of value intervals.

It is noted here that although the value function which can compare the preference differences is derived under certain conditions, heuristic procedures for constructing the value functions often use lottery techniques in which the value functions are treated as if they are defined on uncertain quantities and are combined with some probabilities. As experimental methods to construct the value functions, the lottery techniques are used in canonical forms.

The probabilistic midpoint method can be used for assessing the midpoints with the 50-50 chance lottery. Using the representation of the expected value function, the attribute level $\mathbf{x}_{ix}$ corresponding to the midpoint of the value function $v_i(\mathbf{x}_{ix}) = 0.5\ v_i(\mathbf{x}_{i0}) + 0.5\ v_i(\mathbf{x}_{i1})$ is assessed, and so forth.

Alternatively, four different levels of an attribute $\mathbf{x}_i$ are used in two 50-50 chance lotteries, one of which is a canonical lottery and derives the above midpoint value. For the other lottery, taking an attribute level $\mathbf{x}_i$ as fixed and setting another attribute level $\mathbf{x}_{ix}$ as unknown, we are concerned with assessing the $\mathbf{x}_{ix}$ such that both lotteries are indifferent. With this device, an equal value interval can be estimated. For example, consider the following two lotteries.

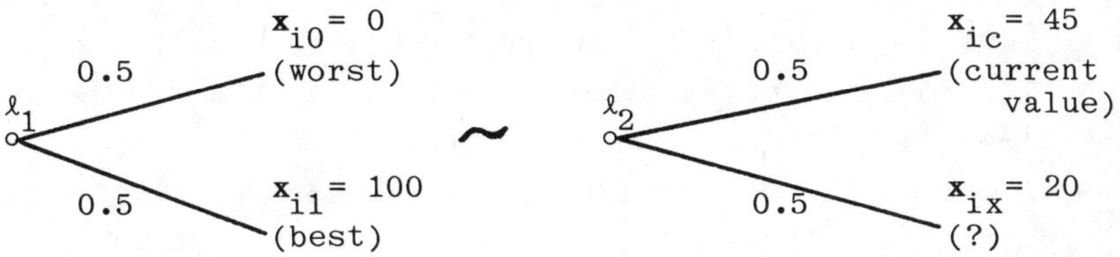


Then, from $v_i(100) - v_i(45) = v_i(20) - v_i(0)$, Figure 8.1 can be depicted.

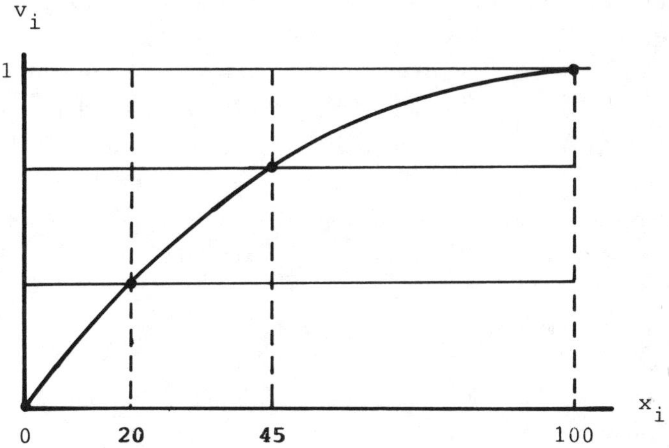


**Figure 8.1 Probabilistic midpoint method.**

Another estimation method, called the direct ordered metric method, ranks in ascending (or descending) order the differences of preferences between adjacent and nonadjacent preferences.

As an alternative to the direct ordered metric method, the probabilistic ordered metric method also uses the 50-50 chance lotteries for comparing preference differences between ordered preference values. Consider the following two lotteries.

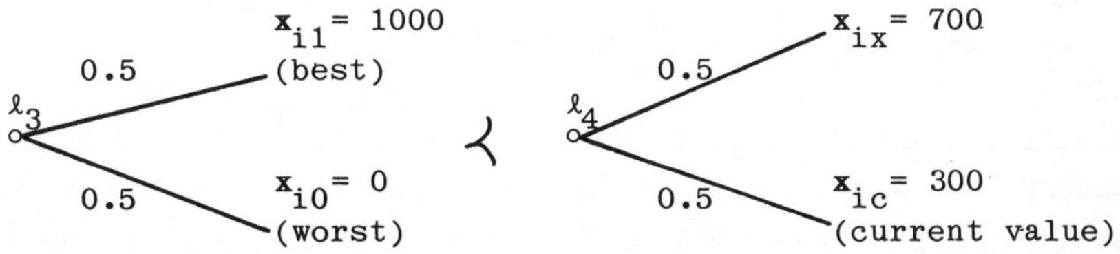

Then $[v_i(1000) - v_i(700)] < [v_i(300) - v_i(0)]$. The lottery $\ell_4$ can also be treated as degenerated and as a quantity of the attribute, say 500. Then $[v_i(1000) - v_i(500)] < [v_i(500) - v_i(0)]$. The numbers are assigned for ranking of the ordered metric value intervals in a descendent order. For example, assuming that $0 < [v_i(1000) - v_i(700)] < v_i(700) - v_i(300)] < [v_i(1000) - v_i(300)] \leqslant [v_i(300) - v_i(0)] < [v_i(700) - v_i(0)] < [v_i(1000) - v_i(0)]$, we get $v_i(0) = 0$, $v_i(300) = 3$, $v_i(700) = 5$, $v_i(1000) = 6$; these values can be normalized 0 to 1 for deriving the SVF.

The trade-off methods for assessing the scaling constants of MVF are based on indifference experiments between attributes as well as direct equality judgments. (Fishburn 1967a, Keeney and Raiffa 1976, Chapter 3). A similar method to the direct rating approach assigns relatively-scaled "weights" to conditional value differences (Dyer and Sarin 1979a).

For assessing the scaling constants of the MVF, the indifference experiment, being similar to the MUF method, can be used for deriving $\lambda_i/\lambda_s$ in the form of

$$\lambda_i = \lambda_s v_s(\mathbf{x}_s), \quad i = 1,\ldots,m, \quad i \neq s, \tag{8.7}$$

where $\lambda_s \geqslant \lambda_i$. $\lambda_s$ can be assessed directly by scaling the preference difference between $\mathbf{x} \triangleq \{\mathbf{x}_{s1}, \mathbf{x}_{\bar{s}0}\}$ and $\mathbf{x}^o \triangleq \{x_{i0}\}$ relatively to the preference difference between $\mathbf{x}^* \triangleq \{x_{i1}\}$ and $\mathbf{x}^o$, or by the indifference experiment with the lottery similar to that in the MUF method.

With those devices, the MVF based on the strength of preference or preference differences is constructed. In practice, probabilistic experimental methods are recommended because sequential procedures for assessment using the lottery experiments will more efficiently assure the commensuration and compensation, or weighting, of preference evaluations for many attributes, compared with an ad hoc evaluation process under certainty. In addition, indifference experiments among preference differences may make it possible to ensure interpersonal comparisons; as a result, it will lead to construction of a multivariate value function by approximately taking the similar origin and scale in multiperson evaluations and keeping consistency among them. Thus this device can be extended for multiple agent decision making.

### 8.1.3 Aggregation Rule of the Measurable Value Function

Extensions of the measurable value function to the collective choice are not straightforward. The existence of the group value functions (GVF) under assumptions analogous to those for Arrow's possibility theorem has suggested by Keeney (1976), and concepts of the measurable group value functions and their aggregation rule have been developed by Dyer and Sarin (1978, 1979b). Assuming the axiom for the measurable value function in Theorem 8.1 (8.3) be satisfied for all individuals and the group, representation forms of the GVF are derived just the same as in (8.4) and (8.5) for the MVF.

**Condition 8.1 (Ordinal preference independence).**

If any subset $\tilde{I}$ of individuals $p \in I \triangleq (1,2,...,S)$ as the member of a group is indifferent between two consequences $\mathbf{x}_i$ and $\mathbf{x}_k$, then the group preference is determined only by the preferences of the individuals in the complement of subset $\tilde{I}$.

**Condition 8.2 (Weak substitution independence).**

If all individuals except an individual $p$ are indifferent between two substitutions for the attributes, then the group will prefer the same substitution for the attributes as the individual $p$.

These conditions assert the independence conditions which are similar to those for MUF and were discussed as the group correspondence conditions for GUF in Chapter 7.

The preference aggregation rule for the measurable value function is established on Conditions 8.1 and 8.2.

**Theorem 8.3 (Representation of the group value function).**

For $S \geqslant 3$, if the axiom (8.3) for the measurable value function (Theorem 8.1) holds for the group preference as well as for the individual preference of all the group members, if Conditions 8.1 and 8.2 hold, and if all attributes are bounded from the worst to the best, then either

$$1 + \lambda V(\mathbf{x}) = \prod_{p=1}^{S} [1 + \lambda\lambda_p v_p(\mathbf{x})] \quad \text{if} \quad \sum_{p=1}^{S} \lambda_p \neq 1, \tag{8.8}$$

or

$$V(x) = \sum_{p=1}^{S} \lambda_p v_p(\mathbf{x}) \quad \text{if} \quad \sum_{p=1}^{S} \lambda_p = 1, \tag{8.9}$$

where $S$ is the number of individuals in a group, $\mathbf{x}$ is the attribute taken as a scalar or a vector, and $V$ and $v_p$ are scaled from 0 to 1. The $\lambda_p$ is a scaling constant, $0 < \lambda_p < 1$, $p = 1,\dots,S$, and $\lambda > -1$.

The proof of Theorem 8.3 can be provided on a similar line to the representation theorem for MUF.

The representation forms (8.8) (8.9) of GVF are similar to those for MVF and also can be constructed as the group multiattribute value function (GMVF), if the attribute $\mathbf{x}$ denotes a vector value $\mathbf{x} \in R^m$ and thus $v_p(\mathbf{x})$ shows an individual multiattribute value function (IMVF). The individual value function (IVF) or IMVF $v_p(\mathbf{x})$ is a revealed preference of an individual $p$ defined in terms of preference differences (8.3). The scaling constants represent value trade-offs among individuals and can be assessed by DM as the mediator, or if not, collective response of individuals to the GVF or GMVF should be examined (see Chapter 7).

**Remarks**

1. It should be noted that conditions for Theorem 8.3 primarily correspond to those in Arrow's theorem, except that Theorem 8.3 is constructed in terms of cardinal numbers instead of ordinal numbers as in Arrow's theorem. Conditions 8.1 and 8.2 assert the positive association of social and individual preference, which also implies Pareto optimality, the citizen's sovereignty, and the independence of irrelevant rule. The weak order property is implied in the axiom for the measurable value function.
2. As mentioned in the preceding subsection 8.1.1, the

interpersonal comparison of strength of preference is required when the aggregation of the measurable value functions is intended, which is not always feasible because every individual as a group member has a particular function form and parameters for the value function and reveals his preference on different personal scales depending on his disposition, sensitive or carefree, etc. In this sense, commensuration of plural IVFs is difficult and the construction of GVF as an aggregate still remains an unresolved matter. However, as we suggested before, the indifference experiments among the plural IVFs provide some reconciliation for value trade-offs; it may properly lead to derivation of an aggregation with a common scale of measure for constructing GVF.

## 8.2 The Measurable Value Function for Risky Choice

### 8.2.1 Measurable Value Function under Uncertainty

In classical works on the measurable value function, such as those by Suppes and Winet (1955 p.259), Davidson and Marshak (1959), and Debreu (1960), stochastic acts of choice have been taken into account. In subsequent works, however, it has been discussed that the axiomatic development for the notion of preference difference or strength of preference does not include any quantitative implication for the risk element in the representation of the value function. Thus, the measurable value function cannot be derived simply from an affine transformation of the von Neumann-Morgenstern utility function defined on some set of consequences of acts. Even so, it will still be practically useful as well as conceptually interesting to examine the conditions under which the measurable value function can be equivalent to the utility function under uncertainty. In fact, in the discussion on the assessment methods for the measurable value functions, the probabilistic approach has seemed to be more recommendable. In the same sense that the even chance lottery techniques have contributed to enhance the practical usefulness of the measurable utility functions under uncertainty, extensions of the measurable value function under certainty to risky choice situations will also contribute to widen its applicability.

This section is concerned with examining the conceptual and practical development of the measurable value function under uncertainty. All discussions at present concern single agent (person) decision making. Preference differences or strength of preferences are supposed to be assessed on a particular preference function of an individual decision maker.

### 8.2.2 Gambles Embodied Preference Differences

Comparison between preferences represented by the 50-50 chance lottery and its axiomatic development for representation of the utility function have been well-developed (Savage 1954, Debreu 1959a Theorem). This development is based on the definition of the von Neumann-Morgenstern expected utility function in terms of gambles, which is described as follows:

**Proposition 8.1 (Expected utility hypothesis for gambles).**

A gamble $\tilde{\mathbf{x}}'$ is preferred to $\tilde{\mathbf{x}}''$ if and only if $\tilde{\mathbf{x}}'$ has a higher expected utility value than $\tilde{\mathbf{x}}''$ does, or symbolically

$$\tilde{\mathbf{x}}' \succsim \tilde{\mathbf{x}}'' \Leftrightarrow Eu(\tilde{\mathbf{x}}') \geqslant Eu(\tilde{\mathbf{x}}''), \tag{8.10}$$

where $Eu(\tilde{\mathbf{x}}')$ and $Eu(\tilde{\mathbf{x}}'')$ are expected utility functions for the gambles $\tilde{\mathbf{x}}'$ and $\tilde{\mathbf{x}}''$, respectively, and are defined as

$$Eu(\tilde{\mathbf{x}}) \triangleq \sum_{j=1}^{n} p_j u(\mathbf{x}_j), \tag{8.11}$$

where $\mathbf{x}_j \in \mathbf{X}$, $\mathbf{X} \subset R^n$ is a consequence of a gamble $\tilde{\mathbf{x}}$ with n chance-forks, with which a probability or a degree of belief $p_j$ is combined. The function $u(\bullet)$ is the von Neumann-Morgenstern type utility function, which is uniquely determined up to positive linear transformations.

Following Bell and Raiffa (1982), the primal idea of the risky measurable value function can be provided by using a gamble to compare the preference differences. Consider a 50-50 chance lottery between consequences $\mathbf{x}_i \in \mathbf{X}$ and $\mathbf{x}_j \in \mathbf{X}$, $\mathbf{X} \subset R^n$, and denote this as $\langle \mathbf{x}_i, \mathbf{x}_j \rangle$. Clearly if, adding an increment $\Delta > 0$,

$$\langle \mathbf{x}_i + \Delta, \mathbf{x}_j \rangle \succsim \langle \mathbf{x}_i, \mathbf{x}_j + \Delta \rangle, \tag{8.12}$$

then

$$[\mathbf{x}_i \rightarrow \mathbf{x}_i + \Delta] \succsim [\mathbf{x}_j \rightarrow \mathbf{x}_j + \Delta]. \tag{8.13}$$

Thus we can construct the following axiom with changed notations, $\mathbf{x}_r \triangleq \mathbf{x}_i + \Delta$ and $\mathbf{x}_s \triangleq \mathbf{x}_j + \Delta$:

$$\langle \mathbf{x}_r, \mathbf{x}_j \rangle \succsim \langle \mathbf{x}_i, \mathbf{x}_s \rangle \Leftrightarrow (\mathbf{x}_r - \mathbf{x}_i) \succsim^* (\mathbf{x}_s - \mathbf{x}_j). \tag{8.14}$$

Suppose that $\hat{\mathbf{x}}$ is the certainty equivalent (CE) of $\langle \mathbf{x}_i, \mathbf{x}_j \rangle$. Then from (8.14),

$$\hat{\mathbf{x}} \sim \langle \mathbf{x}_i, \mathbf{x}_j \rangle \Leftrightarrow (\hat{\mathbf{x}} - \mathbf{x}_i) \sim^* (\mathbf{x}_j - \hat{\mathbf{x}}). \tag{8.15}$$

This device makes the preference differences or the strength of a preference tangible in terms of the gamble questions. If the gamble $\langle \mathbf{x}_i, \mathbf{x}_j \rangle$ is constructed with the even chance, then (8.15) holds. When the values of preference $v(\mathbf{x}_i)$ and $v(\mathbf{x}_j)$ for the consequences of the 50-50 chance lottery $\langle \mathbf{x}_i, \mathbf{x}_j \rangle$ are assessed, assessment of CE $\hat{\mathbf{x}}$ provides a midpoint $v(\hat{\mathbf{x}})$ of the preference difference $v(\mathbf{x}_j) - v(\mathbf{x}_i)$. Thus the measurable value function can be constructed as depicted in Figure 8.2. The axioms (8.14) and (8.15) represent the equivalence between the value functions embodied difference structures and gamble representations in terms of expectation with the even chance. Based on this equivalence, using the 50-50 chance lottery technique, derivation of the value functions embodying preference differences among consequences can be performed straightforwardly.

In the next subsection, some theoretical fundamentals to prove the equivalence of representations of the measurable value and utility functions in terms of the expectation are discussed.

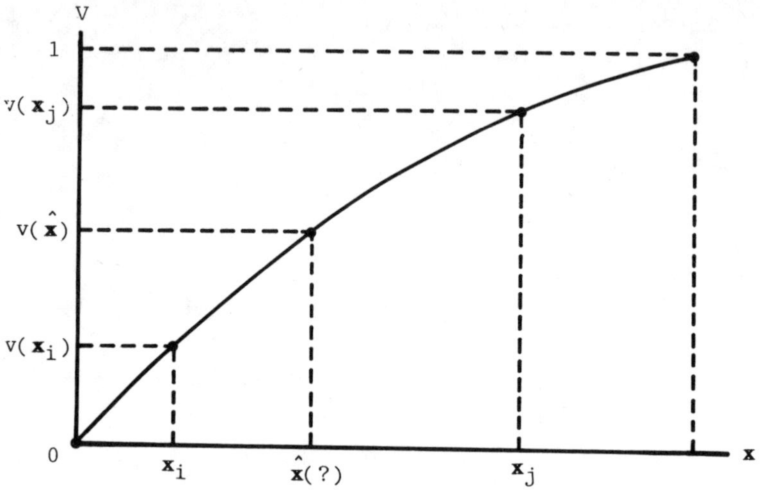


**Figure 8.2 Construction of the value function**

### 8.2.3 Foundations of the Expected Value Function

An axiomatic development of the expected value function concerns providing numerical representations for comparing preference differences among gambles. This development has been carried out in analogous ways to represent the expected utility function.

Savage (1954), Debreu (1960), Fishburn (1970) and Marshak and Radner (1972) have considered primitive conditions which lead to the existence theorem of a numerical utility function with an additive conjoint measurement. The conjoint measurement concerns simultaneous measurement of a composite object and its components, where the object preserves their observed order with respect to their attribute (preference) and the scale value of each object is a function of the scale values of its components. The expected utility hypothesis is constructed on the additive conjoint measurement. Basic axiomatizations for comparison of the expected utility functions having subjective probability have been established with the even-chance lottery concept (Davidson and Suppes 1956; Fishburn 1967b).

Krantz, Luce, Suppes, and Tversky (1971) have established the general representation theorem for a numerical function in an additive conjoint structure with quaternary preference relations.

**Definition 8.4 (Additive conjoint structure).**

Let $\mathbf{A}$ denote a nonempty set. Let $(\mathbf{A}_I, A_{II})$ be a partition of the set $\mathbf{A}$. The triple $(\mathbf{A}_I, A_{II}, \succsim^*)$ is an additive conjoint structure if and only if the following axioms are satisfied.

(i) Weak ordering.

Let $\succsim^*$ be a quaternary relation on $\mathbf{A}$, i.e., a binary relation on $\mathbf{A} \times \mathbf{A}$. $\succsim^*$ on $\mathbf{A}$ is a weak order.

(ii) Independence condition (monotonicity).

A relation $\succsim^*$ on $\mathbf{A}_I \times \mathbf{A}_{II}$ is independent. Namely for $a, b \in \mathbf{A}_I$, $(a, g) \succsim^* (b, g)$ for some $g \in \mathbf{A}_{II}$ implies that $(a, h) \succsim^* (b, h)$ for every $h \in \mathbf{A}_{II}$; and for $g, h \in \mathbf{A}_{II}$, $(a, g) \succsim^* (a, h)$ for some $a \in \mathbf{A}_I$ implies that $(b, g) \succsim^* (b, h)$ for every $b \in A_I$.

(iii) Thomsen condition.

A relation $\succsim^*$ on $\mathbf{A}_I \times \mathbf{A}_{II}$ satisfies the following condition: for every $a, b, c \in \mathbf{A}_I$ and $g, h, k \in \mathbf{A}_{II}$, if $(a, k) \sim^* (c, h)$ and $(c, g) \sim^* (b, k)$, then $(a, g) \sim^* (b, h)$. (The weaker condition of the double cancellation where $\sim^*$ is replaced by $\succsim^*$).

The indifference curves of preference depict the Thomsen condition.

(iv) Restricted solvability.

Whenever there exist $a, \bar{b}, \underline{b} \in \mathbf{A}_I$ and $g, h \in \mathbf{A}_{II}$ for which $(\bar{b}, h) \succsim^* (a, g) \succsim^* (\underline{b}, h)$, then there exists $b \in \mathbf{A}_I$ such that $(b, h) \sim^* (a, g)$. A similar condition holds for the component of $\mathbf{A}_{II}$.

(v) Essentialness.

There exist $a, b \in \mathbf{A}_I$ and $g \in \mathbf{A}_{II}$ such that not $(a, g) \sim^* (b, g)$. A similar condition holds for $\mathbf{A}_{II}$.

(vi) Archimedean property.

Every strictly bounded standard sequence (i.e., a set of elements on one component that are equally spaced, weak-ordered) is finite.

**Theorem 8.4 (Krantz, Luce, Suppes, and Tversky).**

Suppose $(\mathbf{A}_I, \mathbf{A}_{II}, \succsim^*)$ is an additive conjoint structure. Then

(i) there exist functions $\phi_i$ from $\mathbf{A}_i \subset \mathbf{A}$, i = I, II, into the real numbers such that, for all a, b $\in \mathbf{A}_I$, and g, h $\in \mathbf{A}_{II}$,

$$(a, g) \succsim^* (b, h) \Leftrightarrow \phi_I(a) + \phi_{II}(g) \geqslant \phi_I(b) + \phi_{II}(h). \quad (8.16)$$

(ii) If $\phi_I'$ and $\phi_{II}'$ are two other functions with the same property, then there exist constants $\alpha > 0$, $\beta_I$, and $\beta_{II}$ such that

$$\phi_I' = \alpha\phi_I + \beta_I \quad \text{and} \quad \phi_{II}' = \alpha\phi_{II} + \beta_{II}. \quad (8.17)$$

Sarin (1982) provided the representation theorem of the expected value function which orders the preference differences among consequences of events in terms of alternative acts (Table 8.1). He added a few conditions restating some of the above axioms, where **A** denotes a set of alternative acts and a, b,..., show its elements.

**Condition 8.1 (Natural ordering) (Krantz and others).**

$(a, c) \succsim^* (b, c) \Leftrightarrow a \succsim^* b$ for all a, b $\in \mathbf{A}_I$ and for some c $\in \mathbf{A}_{II}$.

**Table 8.1 Example of notations**

| Act \ Events | | $X_I$ | | $X_{II}$ | |
|---|---|---|---|---|---|
| | | $S_1$ | $S_2$ | $S_3$ | $S_4$ |
| $A_I$ | a | $x_1$ | $x_2$ | $x_3$ | $x_4$ |
| | b | $x_1'$ | $x_2'$ | $x_3$ | $x_4$ |
| $A_{II}$ | c | $x_1$ | $x_2$ | $x_3'$ | $x_4'$ |
| | d | $x_1'$ | $x_2'$ | $x_3'$ | $x_4'$ |

**Condition 8.2 (Substitution of equal exchange).**

Let $(\mathbf{X}_I, X_{II})$ be a partition of a set of events $\mathbf{X}$. Let a consequence $\mathbf{x}_{aj}$ of an act $a \in A_I$ be represented by an outcome function

$$\rho(s_j, a) = \mathbf{x}_{aj}, \quad j = 1,\ldots,n, \tag{8.18}$$

where $s_j$ is an uncertain event in $\mathbf{X}$. Let $a, b \in \mathbf{A}_I$ and $c, d \in \mathbf{A}_{II}$ satisfy

$$\left.\begin{array}{l}\rho(s_j, a) = \rho(s_j, c)\\ \rho(s_j, b) = \rho(s_j, d)\end{array}\right\} \quad \text{for} \quad s_j \in \mathbf{X}_I, \qquad \left.\begin{array}{l}\rho(s_j, a) = \rho(s_j, b)\\ \rho(s_j, c) = \rho(s_j, d)\end{array}\right\} \quad \text{for} \quad s_j \in \mathbf{X}_{II}, \tag{8.19}$$

then $(a, b) \sim^* (c, d)$.

This condition is a strengthened statement of Savage's postulates P2 and P3 which lead to the sure-thing principle (Savage's Theorem 2 and 3 1954 Chapter 2; Marschak and Radner 1972). The sure-thing principle asserts that if a preference relation is established among acts in every state, then the preference relation among the acts is generally established.

**Condition 8.3 (Independence of tastes for states) (Marshak and Radner).**

(i) If $(\mathbf{x}_i, x_{\bar{i}}) \succsim (\mathbf{x}_i', x_{\bar{i}})$, then $(\mathbf{x}_j, x_{\bar{j}}) \succsim (\mathbf{x}_j', x_{\bar{j}})$ for all $\mathbf{x}_i = x_j$, $\mathbf{x}_i' = x_j'$, $i, j = 1,\ldots,n$, $j \neq i$.

(ii) If $((\mathbf{x}_i, x_{\bar{i}}), (\mathbf{x}_i', x_{\bar{i}})) \sim^* ((\mathbf{x}_i', x_{\bar{i}}), (\mathbf{x}_i'', x_{\bar{i}}))$, then $((\mathbf{x}_j, \mathbf{x}_{\bar{j}}), (\mathbf{x}_j', \mathbf{x}_{\bar{j}})) \sim^* ((\mathbf{x}_j', x_{\bar{j}}), (\mathbf{x}_j'', x_{\bar{j}}))$, for $\mathbf{x}_i = x_j$, $\mathbf{x}_i' = \mathbf{x}_j'$ and $\mathbf{x}_i'' = \mathbf{x}_j''$ for any $i \neq j$.

(i) states that DM takes the same conditional ordering of consequences irrespective of the states under which the consequences occur, and (ii) states that his preference differences among the consequences are also conditionally ordered irrespective of the states.

The representation theorem for preference differences among acts is derived, with those conditions and axioms for the additive conjoint structure, in terms of expected value functions.

**Theorem 8.5 (Existence of Expected Value Function) (Sarin).**

Let $\Gamma$ be the set of all possible consequences $\mathbf{x}_j$, $j = 1,\dots,n$. If $\succsim$ and $\succsim^*$ are weak-ordered, the restricted solvability and essentialness are held, and Conditions 8.1 to 8.3 are satisfied; then there exists a function $v : \Gamma \to R^1$ and positive numbers $\pi_1, \pi_2, \dots, \pi_n$ such that, for all $a, b \in \mathbf{A}_I$, and $c, d \in \mathbf{A}_{II}$,

(i) $$(a, b) \succsim^* (c, d) \Leftrightarrow \sum_{j=1}^{n} \pi_j v(\rho(s_j, a)) - \sum_{j=1}^{n} \pi_j v(\rho(s_j, b)) \geqslant$$

$$\sum_{j=1}^{n} \pi_j v(\rho(s_j, c)) - \sum_{j=1}^{n} \pi_j v(\rho(s_j, d)), \tag{8.20}$$

(ii) $$a \succsim b \Leftrightarrow \sum_{j=1}^{n} \pi_j v(\rho(s_j, a)) \geqslant \sum_{j=1}^{n} \pi_j v(\rho(s_j, b)). \tag{8.21}$$

(iii) $v$ is measured with an interval scale and $\pi_j$, $j = 1,\dots,n$, is unique up to its multiplication by a positive constant.

Using the main result (8.20), comparison of preference differences among acts is reduced to the comparison of preference differences among lotteries for consequences. Note that (ii) is a similar representation to the expected utility hypothesis for $u(\rho(s_j, a))$ with a probability $p(s_j)$. From Theorem 8.4 (ii), we can scale the $v$ in Theorem 8.5 to be the same as $u$ in this representation such that $v(\mathbf{x}^o) = u(\mathbf{x}^o) = 0$ and $v(\mathbf{x}^*) = u(\mathbf{x}^*) = 1$, and with further scaling, we can also obtain $\pi_j = p(s_j)$ such that $\pi_j > 0$ and $\sum_{j=1}^{n} \pi_j = 1$.

### 8.2.4. Relative Risk Attitude

An increment of the measurable value function embodied risky choice can be decomposed into two components: a marginal change of the strength of preference and a marginal change of the intrinsic risk attitude for an uncertain consequence (Bell and Raiffa 1982). The distinction between those two components is shown by a simple example. Suppose DM to declare that both $1000 for certain and a canonical even chance lottery with an alternative gain, $0 for the worst or $3000 for the best, be indifferent. This assertion will imply twofold responses under the assumption of the monotonically increasing value function: (i) a monetary difference going from $0 to $1500 is assessed with greater worth than that going from $1500 to $3000, and (ii) DM has an aversion about the risk in the gamble. Bell (1982, 1983) discussed this situation with the "decision regret" concept as a component of decision making under uncertainty. By explicitly incorporating the regret for wrong decision into a utility function, Bell intends to support the EUMAX hypothesis as a better guide for human behavior.

There will still be different discussions for the incremental value. In a nonlinear value function, an incremental value of the preference difference or the strength of preference is also assumed gradually to change. What is the cause of this change? Doesn't a fear of failure, or decision regret, make this value psychologically decrease? Doesn't a risk seeking attitude, or the decision venture, make it increase? Thus the regret attitude can be regarded as a cause of the change of strength of preference. Therefore, alternative interpretation of the partitioned components for the risky choice can be presented. They are the marginal degree of relative saturation and the regret attitude, where the former component is revealed as the decreasing (or increasing) marginal value of preference. In this case, another question will also be raised: what is the psychological result of the access to saturation? Isn't it a change in the strength of preference? Thus a causal relation will make a tie between the access to saturation and the strength of preference as well as between the regret attitude and the strength of preferences. In other words, the change in the strength of preference seems to represent both of the psychological results for a change in the regret attitude and for a change in the marginal degree of relative saturation. In this subsection, two components of the nonlinear value function are distinguished. The changing marginal value of preference is assessed in terms of the degree of relative saturation and the regret attitude, both of which are revealed in a change of the preference differences. Based on this recognition, the measure of risk attitudes defined relative to the strength of preference presented by Dyer and Sarin (1982) is reconsidered.

Let $\mathbf{X}$ denote a set of all possible consequences. The local value satiation function $m(\mathbf{x})$ (8.22) is defined in the analogous terms to Pratt's risk function $r(x)$ (8.23):

$$m(\mathbf{x}) \triangleq \frac{-v''(\mathbf{x})}{v'(\mathbf{x})}, \quad v'(\mathbf{x}) > 0, \tag{8.22}$$

$$r(\mathbf{x}) \triangleq \frac{-u''(\mathbf{x})}{u'(\mathbf{x})}, \quad u'(\mathbf{x}) > 0, \tag{8.23}$$

where $\mathbf{x} \in X$, $X \subset R^n$, and $v'(\mathbf{x})$ and $v''(\mathbf{x})$ are the first and second derivatives of the measurable value function $v(\mathbf{x})$, respectively. We can interpret that $m(\mathbf{x})$ scales a marginal change of the degree of relative saturation of an individual, which is revealed in a change of the magnitude of preference differences or the strength of preferences. $m(\mathbf{x}) > 0$ indicates a decreasing marginal value of $v(\mathbf{x})$, or a decreasing marginal degree of relative saturation, at $\mathbf{x}$. $m(\mathbf{x}) < 0$ indicates an increasing marginal value, or an increasing marginal degree of relative saturation, at $\mathbf{x}$. $m(\mathbf{x}) = 0$ indicates a constant marginal value, or a constant marginal degree of relative saturation, at $x$. The relative risk attitudes to the degree of relative saturation (Satisfaction) are defined as follows:

**Definition 8.5**

At $\mathbf{x} \in \mathbf{X}$, $X \subset R^n$, an individual is relatively risk averse to his decreasing marginal degree of satisfaction if $0 < m(\mathbf{x}) < r(\mathbf{x})$, relatively risk prone to his increasing marginal degree of satisfaction if $0 > m(\mathbf{x}) > r(\mathbf{x})$, and relatively risk neutral for a constant marginal value if $m(\mathbf{x}) = r(\mathbf{x}) = 0$.

Now let us define the risky value function $v^* : u \to R^1$ that embodies the risk attitude, where $u : \mathbf{x} \to u$ is the measurable utility function. The rationale for constructing the risky value function $v^*(u(\mathbf{x}))$ is based on the above-mentioned twofold implication of the strength of preference, and the function $v^*$ is defined on the risk attitude revealed in $u(\mathbf{x})$. As the inverse function $v^{-1*}(u(\mathbf{x}))$ of the risky value function, the new utility function $u^*(v(\mathbf{x})) \triangleq u(v^*(\mathbf{x}))$ is defined, i.e., $u^* : v \to R^1$, which is defined on the measurable value function. The relative risk attitudes can be derived from the risk function according to the following theorem:

**Theorem 8.7 (Dyer and Sarlin).**

Let us define the new risk function $r^*(v)$ for the risky value function in terms of the new utility function.

$$r^*(v) \triangleq -u^{*''}(v(\mathbf{x}))/u^{*'}(v(\mathbf{x})). \tag{8.24}$$

At $\mathbf{x} \in \mathbf{X}$, $X \subset R^n$, an individual is relatively risk averse if and only if $r^*(v) > 0$, relatively risk prone if and only if $r^*(v) < 0$, and relatively risk neutral if and only if $r^*(v) = 0$.

For proof, define

$$u^*(v(\mathbf{x})) \triangleq u(\mathbf{x}). \tag{8.25}$$

Then, considering that $u'(\mathbf{x}) = u^{*'}(v(\mathbf{x}))v'(\mathbf{x})$ and $u''(\mathbf{x}) = u^{*'}(v(\mathbf{x}))v''(\mathbf{x}) + u^{*''}(v(\mathbf{x}))(v'(\mathbf{x}))^2$, from the definitions (8.22) (8.23) (8.24),

$$r(\mathbf{x}) - m(\mathbf{x}) = v'(\mathbf{x})r^*(\mathbf{v}). \tag{8.26}$$

From (8.26) and $v'(\mathbf{x}) > 0$, Theorem 8.7 is straightforward.

**Corollary 8.1 (Dyer and Sarin).**

(i) when $r(\mathbf{x}) = 0$, then $r^*(v) = -m(\mathbf{x})/v'(\mathbf{x})$.

(ii) when $r(\mathbf{x}) = \alpha$, then $r^*(v) = (\alpha - m(\mathbf{x}))/v'(\mathbf{x})$.

(iii) when $m'(\mathbf{x}) < 0$ and $r^{*'}(v) < 0$, then $r'(\mathbf{x}) < 0$. If $m'(\mathbf{x}) < 0$ and $r^*(v) = t > 0$, then $r(\mathbf{x}) = tv'(\mathbf{x}) + m(\mathbf{x})$ is decreasing.

**Remarks**

1. Although the notion of the measurable value functions have been developed primarily for scaling the preference differences in nonrisky situations, DM often faces some difficulty in their assessment processes. The extension for treating risky situations, which is based on the representation theorem of the expected value function, will greatly enhance their practical usefulness by making it possible to use the lottery techniques for their identification.

2. It has been discussed that, for the risky value function $v^*(u(x))$, two components of the "risk" property which are represented by the nonlinearity of function forms should be discerned. One represents a change in the marginal degree of satisfaction and the other represents a change in the regret attitude which is psychologically an intrinsic risk attitude. The concept of the relative risk attitudes will contribute to discriminate the intrinsic risk property from the changing marginal degree of relative saturation.

3. Construction of the new utility function defined on the measurable value function makes it possible for DM to decompose the assessment process of the risky value function in two levels. As Dyer and Sarin have suggested, this device will make it relatively easy to aggregate the risky value functions into a new multiattribute utility function, because the risk attitude of DM can separately be taken into account only in the last part of the assessment (see Chapter 7, 7.5).

4. It should be noted for collective choice here that interpersonal comparisons of both of the marginal degree of relative saturation and the intrinsic risk attitudes still need to measure with the same interval scales among individuals. This requirement duplicates the difficulty of the group decision making due to different personal dispositions of individuals concerning both the components. However some theoretical points which may mitigate the above difficulty to some extent still remain. In the next subsection, some topics are examined.

### 8.2.5 Extensions to Collective Choice

**1. Multivariate risk attitude**

In general, extension of the concept of the measurable risky value function $v^*(u(\mathbf{x}))$ to a multivariate function $v^*: u \rightarrow R^1$, $u \in R^m$, is not straightforward. The main reason is that the multivariate function should include multivariate risk attitudes. The risk parameters should not only be extracted independently of the degree of relative saturation, as discussed in the preceding subsection 8.2.4., but also should reflect the multivariate risk attitude. Although numerous works concerning multivariate risk attitudes have been presented, basic concepts of multivariate risk analysis for MUF was presented by Richard (1975). On the same line of this discussion, the risky group multiattribute value function (GMVF) is shown as to embody the similar properties of multivariate risk attitudes for MUF. In the following, $v(\mathbf{x})$ is used for $v^*(u(\mathbf{x}))$.

**Definition 8.6.**

Consider the following two lotteries $\ell_1$ and $\ell_2$ for any $\mathbf{x}_0$, $\mathbf{x}_1$, $\mathbf{y}_0$, $\mathbf{y}_1 \in X$, where $\mathbf{x}_0 < \mathbf{x}_1$ and $\mathbf{y}_0 < \mathbf{y}_1$.

(i) $\ell_1$ takes alternative values $(\mathbf{x}_0, \mathbf{y}_0)$ or $(\mathbf{x}_1, \mathbf{y}_1)$ with an even chance.

(ii) $\ell_2$ takes alternative values $(\mathbf{x}_0, \mathbf{y}_1)$ or $(\mathbf{x}_1, \mathbf{y}_0)$ with an even chance.

If $\ell_2 \succsim \ell_1$ for all $\mathbf{x}_0$, $\mathbf{x}_1$, $\mathbf{y}_0$, and $\mathbf{y}_1$, then the risk attitude of DM is multivariate risk averse (MRA). If $\ell_1 \sim \ell_2$ for all $\mathbf{x}_0$, $\mathbf{x}_1$, $\mathbf{y}_0$, and $\mathbf{y}_1$, then DM is multivariate risk neutral (MRN). If $\ell_1 \succsim \ell_2$ for all $\mathbf{x}_0$, $\mathbf{x}_1$, $\mathbf{y}_0$, and $\mathbf{y}_1$, then DM is multivariate risk prone (MRP).

**Theorem 8.8.**

Let $\mathbf{x}, \mathbf{y} \in \mathbf{X}$. GMVF is MRA if and only if $v_{\mathbf{xy}}(\mathbf{x}, \mathbf{y}) \leqslant 0$, MRP if and only if $v_{\mathbf{xy}}(\mathbf{x}, \mathbf{y}) \geqslant 0$, and MRN if and only if $v_{\mathbf{xy}}(\mathbf{x}, \mathbf{y}) = 0$; where $v_{\mathbf{xy}}$ denotes $\partial v(\mathbf{x}, \mathbf{y}) / \partial \mathbf{x} \partial \mathbf{y}$.

The proof is based on the following representation for the difference in the expected utility values of the two lotteries, $\ell_1$ and $\ell_2$, and is obtained from the definitions of MRA, MRP, and MRN in terms of the lotteries and Proposition 8.1.

$$\frac{1}{2}\left(v(\mathbf{x}_o, \mathbf{y}_1) + v(\mathbf{x}_1, \mathbf{y}_o) - v(\mathbf{x}_o, \mathbf{y}_o) - v(\mathbf{x}_1, \mathbf{y}_1)\right)$$

$$= -\frac{1}{2}\int_{\mathbf{x}_o}^{\mathbf{x}_1}\int_{\mathbf{y}_o}^{\mathbf{y}_1} v_{\mathbf{xy}}(\mathbf{x}, \mathbf{y})d_{\mathbf{y}}d_{\mathbf{x}}. \tag{8.27}$$

Define the following representation forms (8.28) (8.29) (8.30) of GMVF under the assumptions of mutual preferential independence and weak difference independence,

$$V(\mathbf{x}) = a \pm b \sum_{p=1}^{S} v_p(\mathbf{x}_p) \qquad \text{(additive)}, \tag{8.28}$$

$$V(\mathbf{x}) = a + b \prod_{p=1}^{S} v_p(\mathbf{x}_p) \qquad \text{(multiplicative)}, \tag{8.29}$$

$$V(\mathbf{x}) = a - b \prod_{p=1}^{S} (v_p(\mathbf{x}_p)) \quad \text{(negative multiplicative)}, \tag{8.30}$$

where $b > 0$, and $v_p(x_p) > 0$.

Those functions are derived with equal weights from the general representation forms (8.5) and (8.6) for MVF of a person p, via linear transformations. Then a theorem which describes the properties of GMVF is derived.

**Theorem 8.9.**

Assume that the mutual preferential and weak difference independence conditions hold. Then, for GMVF, the additive form (8.28) has the multivariate risk neutral (MRN) property, the positive multiplicative form (8.29) has the strictly multivariate risk prone (SMRP) property, and the negative multiplicative form (8.30) has the strictly multivariate risk averse (SMRA) property for all attributes.

The proof is provided from twice differentiating the representation forms (8.28)-(8.30) considering Theorem 8.8.

Thus the multivariate risk attitude can be extended for collective choice, and represents the multiperson risk attitude of the group members. Although the interpersonal comparison of preference differences is difficult in real situations, the recognition of properties for the risk attitude in the GMVF will provide some information for manipulating the collective choice problems, as discussed in Chapter 8.

## 2. Equality

Equality consideration is another problem to be discussed in collective choice. It has been discussed that the additive representation of group preference function is the only form that guarantees a Pareto optimality in multiple agents decision making (Kirkwood 1978, 1979). The additive form also presumes the postulate that if two consequences are indifferent from the point of view of every individual, then they are also indifferent from a social (group) point of view (Harsanyi 1955). Those discussions conclude that the group preference function can be obtained, if at all, only as a weighted sum of individual preference functions if the Pareto optimality should hold. However, it is asserted that the additive form implies the multivariate risk neutral, which brings a limitation in applications to the real world. Moreover, the equality (or distributional equity) concern is not taken into account in the additive forms. In other words, there does not exist a group preference function embodying both the Pareto optimality and equality criterion (Diamond 1967, Kirkwood 1978, 1979).

For proof of the above assertions, assume the additive form of the group value function (GVF) $V(\mathbf{x}) = \sum_{p=1}^{S} \lambda_p v_p(\mathbf{x})$, where p denotes an individual as the group member. The following representation of the expected group value functions for an alternative i, where $\lambda_p$ is the scaling constant,

$$E^i(V(\mathbf{x})) = E^i(\sum_{p=1}^{S} \lambda_p v_p(\mathbf{x})) = \sum_{p=1}^{S} \lambda_p E^i(v_p(\mathbf{x})), \qquad (8.31)$$

assures that, when two alternatives, i = a and i = b, are indifferent from every individual's point of view, then these alternatives are also indifferent from the social point of view in terms of GVF. Now consider the following two 50-50 chance lotteries: (1) $\ell_1$ that has alternative consequences taking the same value of all best (better) or all worst (worse) for every individual and (2) $\ell_2$ that has alternative consequences with a mixture of these events in even chance and for every individual. Although these two lotteries are indifferent from every individual point of view, $\ell_1$ will be preferred to $\ell_2$, if the decision is made with the equality concern among individuals, and $\ell_2$ will be indifferent or preferred to $\ell_1$, if an inequality among the group members is accepted. The additive group value function excludes the former case by (8.31).

A more important comment can be made about the generality of the additive group value functions. Extended discussions about preference structures incorporating equitable distributions of public risk have also been presented in terms of a multiplicative utility function and its modified form, which are defined on the risk profile ($p_1$, $p_2$,..., $p_S$) and the fatality profile taken as the attributes, where the fatality is defined as losing human life or an annihilation (Keeney 1980a, b). Some propositions are presented, which assert that the risk equality holds if and only if the utility function defined on the number of fatalities is risk prone and that catastrophe avoidance holds if and only if the utility function is risk averse.

It should be noted here that these equality considerations are regarded as the complete egalitarian principle under risky situations, or unpredictable fates, for the group members. This concept is rather stiff and seems to presume extreme cases in the real world.

The equality consideration is introduced into the preference structure without resort to the risk equity concern which has a hazardous implication for human fate. The equality attitude is examined in terms of GVF under certainty and is defined separately from the multivariate risk attitude under uncertainty (Bodily 1981). Assume GVF $v(\mathbf{x})$ be revealed with the representation forms similar to the multiattribute value function (8.5) and (8.6). Then the local inequality function is defined.

**Definition 8.7 (Bodily).**

Let $\mathbf{x}_p$ and $\mathbf{x}_r$ denote an endowment, or a distribution, to individuals p and r. Let $v(\mathbf{x})$ be a strictly concave group value function. The local inequality function for $\mathbf{x}_p$ and $\mathbf{x}_r$ in $X = \overset{S}{\underset{p=1}{\times}} X_p$ is defined with

$$f_{pr}(\mathbf{x}) \triangleq \begin{cases} \dfrac{-v_{pp}(\mathbf{x}) + 2v_{pr}(\mathbf{x}) - v_{rr}(\mathbf{x})}{\left| \dfrac{\partial v}{\partial x_p} - \dfrac{\partial v}{\partial x_r} \right|} & \text{when } \dfrac{\partial v}{\partial \mathbf{x}_p} \neq \dfrac{\partial v}{\partial \mathbf{x}_r} \\ 0 & \text{otherwise,} \end{cases} \tag{8.32}$$

where $v_{pr} \triangleq \dfrac{\partial^2 v(\mathbf{x})}{\partial \mathbf{x}_p \partial \mathbf{x}_r}$ .

The local inequality function (8.32) represents the situation that, when marginal values evaluated by any two members in a group are different from each other, the inequality attitude is indicated according to whether a sum of the change in a marginal value assessed by each individual exceeds the sum of a cross-personal evaluation of the change of the marginal values. The sum of the cross-personal evaluation is interpreted as showing an "average" of the marginal value evaluations and thus as representing an equality consideration. When a numerator of (8.32) is positive, it is strict inequality averse. When the numerator is negative, it is strict inequality prone. When the numerator is zero, it is inequality neutral. If the marginal value evaluations are all equal between two individuals, then they are mutually indifferent to their evaluations and the inequality neutrality is supposed to hold. Thus the following theorem is established:

**Theorem 8.10 (Bodily).**

If the local inequality function $f_{pr}(\mathbf{x}) > 0$, then the value function $v(\mathbf{x})$ exhibits strict inequality aversion in $\mathbf{x}_p$ and $\mathbf{x}_r$ at $\mathbf{x} \in R^S$. If $f_{pr}(\mathbf{x}) = 0$, then $v(\mathbf{x})$ exhibits inequality neutrality. If $f_{pr}(\mathbf{x}) < 0$, then it exhibits strict inequality proneness. Let $v^1$ and $v^2$ be measurable value functions with inequality aversion functions $f^1_{pr}$ and $f^2_{pr}$, respectively. If $f^1_{pr}(\mathbf{x}) > f^2_{pr}(\mathbf{x})$, then $v^1$ exhibits greater inequality aversion in $\mathbf{x}_p$ and $\mathbf{x}_r$ at $\mathbf{x}$ than $v^2$ does. If this property holds for all $\mathbf{x}$, then $v^1$ is globally more inequality averse for $\mathbf{x}_p$ and $\mathbf{x}_r$ than $v^2$ is.

It is easy to demonstrate that both $v(\mathbf{x})$ and $a + bv(\mathbf{x})$, $b > 0$, have the same local inequality property.

Note that the inequality attitudes represent local preferences for attributes at certain levels, while the multivariate risk attitudes represent local preferences for attributes with probability distributions.

## 8.3 Partial Comparable Axioms without Transitivity

### 8.3.1 Value Function with Indifference Intransitiveness

As discussed in the preceding chapters, quantitative analyses of preference structures are generally founded on weak-ordered binary or quaternary relations which imply connectivity (i.e., comparability) and transitivity. Those axioms are not necessarily fulfilled in practical situations. Decision processes often confront a "hesitation" in discernment of indifference or strict preference. Armstrong (1939, 1948) early suggested that indifference can be recognized when a utility-difference is sufficiently small and preference can be recognized when it is sufficiently large, and thus that utility theory should deny the transitiveness of indifference because recognition of strict preference or indifference below a certain threshold of a cognizance is difficult. Luce (1956) discussed, using his famous "a cup of coffee with sugar" example, that small changes of utility are not perfectly discernible and thus transitivity of indifference relations is contrary to human experiences. For treating this situation, recognition of the indifference threshold, or the "just noticeable difference" in preference relations, should be established. The semiorder concept (5.2.1) by Luce allows for the intransitive indifference relations. A revised definition of the utility function embodying the semiordering is also provided. In this subsection, we discuss this concept in terms of the value function measuring preference differences.

First, the just noticeable difference function (Luce) is defined to characterize a discernible band for the change from indifference to preference in utility.

Let $\mathbf{X}$ be a preference set and I be an indifference relation defined on $\mathbf{X}$. Define the upper just noticeable difference function for $\mathbf{x}, \mathbf{y} \in \mathbf{X}$ as

$$\overline{\delta}(\mathbf{x}) = \sup_{\substack{\mathbf{y} \\ \mathbf{x}I\mathbf{y}}} [v(\mathbf{y}) - v(\mathbf{x})], \tag{8.33}$$

and the lower just noticeable difference function as

$$\underline{\delta}(\mathbf{x}) = \inf_{\substack{\mathbf{x} \\ \mathbf{x}I\mathbf{y}}} [v(\mathbf{y}) - v(\mathbf{x})], \tag{8.34}$$

where $\overline{\delta}(\mathbf{x}) > 0$, $\underline{\delta}(\mathbf{x}) > 0$ and $v(\bullet)$ is an order-preserved measurable value function.

The new definition of the value function which admits the intransitive indifference relations is described as follows:

**Definition 8.8 (Quasi-weak order without transitivity).**

Let $(\succ, \sim)$ be a set of binary relations defined on a preference set $\mathbf{X}$. Then $(\succ, \sim)$ is a set of quasi-weak order on $\mathbf{X}$ if

(i) for every $\mathbf{x}, \mathbf{y} \in X$, one of $\mathbf{x} \succ \mathbf{y}$, $\mathbf{y} \succ \mathbf{x}$ or $\mathbf{x} \sim \mathbf{y}$ is obtained,

(ii) $\sim$ is an equivalence relation,

(iii) $\succ$ is transitive.

**Definition 8.9.**

Let $\mathscr{R} \triangleq (\succ, \sim)$ be semiorder on $\mathbf{X}$ and v be a real-valued function defined on $\mathbf{X}$. Then v is called a value function of $(\mathbf{X}, \mathscr{R})$, if (i) v is an order-preserved function defined on $(\mathbf{X}, \mathscr{R}')$, where $\mathscr{R}'$ is quasi-weak order on $\mathbf{X}$ induced by $\mathscr{R}$, and (ii) for any $\mathbf{x} \in \mathbf{X}$, there exist $\mathbf{y}, \mathbf{z} \in \mathbf{X}$

such that $v(\mathbf{y}) = v(\mathbf{x}) + \overline{\delta}(\mathbf{x})$, $\mathbf{x}I\mathbf{y}$, and $v(\mathbf{z}) = v(\mathbf{x}) - \underline{\delta}(\mathbf{x})$, $\mathbf{x}I\mathbf{z}$.

Properties of the value function are described in the following theorem.

**Theorem 8.11 (Luce).**

Let $\mathscr{R} \triangleq (\succ, \sim)$ be semiorder on $\mathbf{X}$. Suppose that there is a value function $v$ of $(\mathbf{X}, \mathscr{R})$. Then

(i) $\mathbf{x} \sim \mathbf{y}$ if and only if $v(\mathbf{y}) - \underline{\delta}(\mathbf{y}) \leqslant v(\mathbf{x}) \leqslant v(\mathbf{y}) + \overline{\delta}(\mathbf{y})$, and $\mathbf{x} \succ \mathbf{y}$ if and only $v(\mathbf{x}) > v(\mathbf{y}) + \overline{\delta}(\mathbf{y})$.

(ii) $v(\mathbf{x}) \leqslant v(\mathbf{y}) + \overline{\delta}(\mathbf{y})$ if and only if $v(\mathbf{x}) \leqslant v(\mathbf{y}) + \underline{\delta}(\mathbf{x})$.

(iii) if $v(\mathbf{x}) < v(\mathbf{y})$, then either $v(\mathbf{x}) + \overline{\delta}(\mathbf{x}) < v(\mathbf{y}) + \overline{\delta}(\mathbf{y})$, or $v(\mathbf{x}) + \underline{\delta}(\mathbf{y}) < v(\mathbf{y}) + \underline{\delta}(\mathbf{x})$.

Remark that the relation $\mathscr{R}' \triangleq (\succ, \sim)'$ induced on $\mathbf{X}$ by a given relation $\mathscr{R}$ on $\mathbf{X}$ is defined: if, for $\mathscr{R} \triangleq (\succ, \sim)$, either

(i) $\mathbf{x} \succ \mathbf{y}$,

(ii) $\mathbf{x} \sim \mathbf{y}$, and there exists $\mathbf{z} \in \mathbf{X}$ such that $\mathbf{x} \sim \mathbf{z}$ and $\mathbf{z} \succ \mathbf{y}$, or

(iii) $\mathbf{x} \sim \mathbf{y}$, and there exists $\mathbf{w} \in \mathbf{X}$ such that $\mathbf{x} \succ \mathbf{w}$ and $\mathbf{w} \sim \mathbf{y}$,

then $\mathbf{x} \succ' \mathbf{y}$. If neither $\mathbf{x} \succ' \mathbf{y}$ nor $\mathbf{y} \succ' \mathbf{x}$, then $\mathbf{x} \sim' \mathbf{y}$.

Thus although the preference relation $\mathscr{R}'$ does not generally include the indifference transitivity, if $\mathscr{R}$ is weak order, then naturally the induced relation $\mathscr{R}'$ is weak order because of the transitivity of the indifference relation. Furthermore, Luce has proved a theorem that $\mathscr{R}$ is semiorder if and only if $\succ$ in $\mathscr{R}$ is transitive and $\mathscr{R}'$ is weak order.

The value function with indifference intransitiveness presumes the satisficing principle in preference theory, which admits for some assertion on preference order to be held in a cognitive range and treats them as a rational recognition. Relaxation of transitivity can also be extended to strict preference. With this device, the preference theory based on the satisficing principle can be established and thus becomes more testable in psychological experiments. Concepts based on the intransitive preference relations are discussed in the next subsection.

**Remark.**

A measurable utility function which does not depend on the independence axiom as well as the transitivity has been presented as a skew-symmetric bilinear (SSB) function that represents preference by a real-valued function $\phi$ defined on a set of probability measures $P \times P$, for which $\phi(p, q) > 0$ if and only if $p$ is preferred to $q$ (Fishburn 1982). This SSB theory uses continuity, dominance, and symmetry axioms, and shows that the preferences are uniquely determined up to a similarity transformation with the ratio scale measurement. This theory is in another stream of preference theory which does not consider the imprecise capability of discrimination in preference ordering. The SSB theory can be extended to treat the distortion of probability evaluation that is the source of nonlinearity of preference assessment based on the probability measure.

## 8.3.2. Large Preference and Indistinctive Outranking

An alternative axiom on partial comparability has been presented by Roy (1977a,b). The partial comparability axiom treats the imprecise discrimination for preference relations, which are defined without transitivity. We will discuss it in a more compact form.

The cognitive preference relations without transitivity are defined as follows.

(i) Indifference (I): reflexive and symmetric.

(ii) Strict preference (P): irreflexive and asymmetric.

(iii) Large preference (L): irreflexive and antisymmetric.

(iv) Presumed preference (M): $I \cup L$.

(v) Incomparability (N): irreflexive and symmetric.

Note that the transitivity is not included in these concepts. In particular, it is necessary to establish a threshold of human discernment capability for discriminating the indifference and the large preference. The indifference threshold is denoted as $\delta(s)$, and the presumed preference threshold is shown as $\omega(s)$, where $s$ is a preference level assigned to a numerical value of an attribute $\mathbf{x} \in \mathbf{X}$. The above concepts are redefined with those concepts as follows:

(i)' Indifference (I): $s(\mathbf{x}) - \underline{\delta}(\mathbf{x}) \leqslant s(\mathbf{y}) \leqslant s(\mathbf{x}) + \bar{\delta}(\mathbf{x})$.

(iii)' Large preference (L): $s(\mathbf{x}) + \bar{\delta}(\mathbf{x}) < s(\mathbf{y}) \leqslant s(\mathbf{x}) + \bar{\omega}(\mathbf{x})$

$$s(\mathbf{x}) - \underline{\delta}(\mathbf{x}) > s(\mathbf{y}) \geqslant s(\mathbf{x}) - \underline{\omega}(\mathbf{x}),$$

where $\bar{\delta}(\mathbf{x}) > 0$ and $\underline{\delta}(\mathbf{x}) > 0$ are the same as the values of the just noticeable difference function previously defined, and show deviations from the "strict" recognition of a preference. For simplicity, $\delta(\mathbf{x}) \triangleq \delta(s(\mathbf{x}))$ and $\omega(\mathbf{x}) \triangleq \omega(s(\mathbf{x}))$. Figure 8.3 shows a large preference relationship between $\mathbf{x}$ and $\mathbf{y}$.

With these concepts, numerical outranking relations with an indiscriminative preference band $\omega$ are constructed. A cognitive outranking relation $R_\delta^\omega$, with an indiscriminative preference band $\omega$ and an indifference threshold $\delta$, is based on the partial comparability axiom and is defined on a discernible difference between numerical values of the value functions. A set of actions "a" for a decision problem is evaluated in comparison with another set "a'" in terms of the cognitive outranking relation.

The cognitive outranking relation $R_\delta^\omega$ is defined as follows:

(i) $R_\delta^\omega$ is distinctive outranking with strict preferences,
if $\underline{\omega}(a) > v(a') - v(a)$, $v(a') - v(a) > \bar{\omega}(a)$,

(ii) $R_\delta^\omega$ is indistinctive outranking with presumed preference,
if $\underline{\omega}(a) \leqslant v(a') - v(a) \leqslant \bar{\omega}(a)$,

(iii) $R_\delta^\omega$ is indistinctive outranking with indifference,
if $\underline{\delta}(a) \leqslant v(a') - v(a) \leqslant \bar{\delta}(a)$,

(iv) $R_\delta^\omega$ is distinctive nonoutranking with incomparability otherwise,

where $v$ is a value function.

The outranking function is defined on the outranking relation as $\gamma(a', a) \triangleq \psi(v(a') - v(a))$, where $\psi$ is a transfer function of the numerical difference between value functions for alternative actions to a value of the outranking

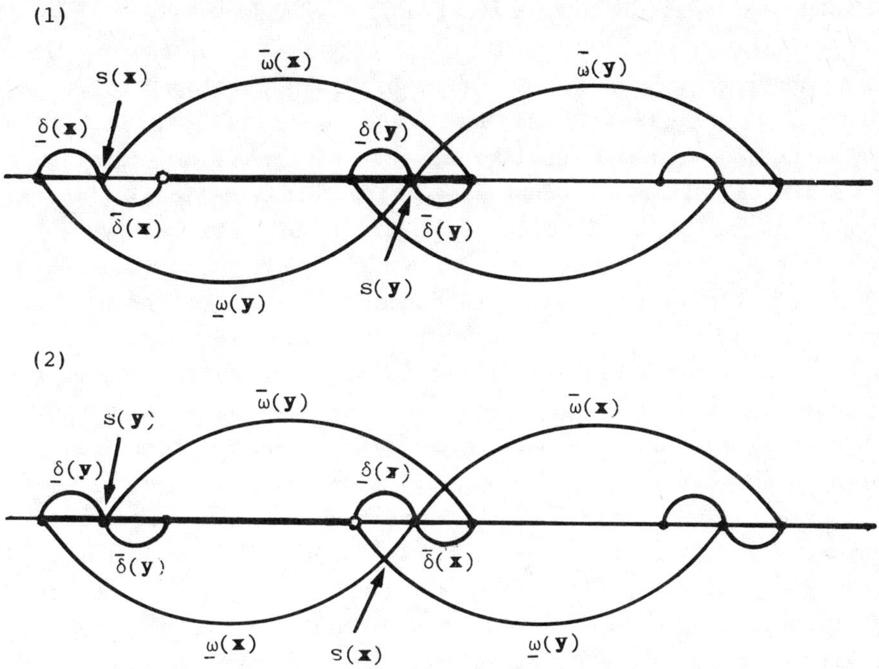


**Figure 8.3 Large preference relationship.**

function. The outranking function represents the numerical degrees of the cognitive outranking relations and takes integer values according to the cognitive outranking relations. For example, when (i), $\gamma(a', a) = 3$, when (ii), $\gamma(a', a) = 2$, when (iii), $\gamma(a', a) = 1$, when (iv), $\gamma(a', a) = 0$.

Indistinctive outranking relations can be used appropriately for preference evaluations of societal events. These events usually cannot be evaluated with the recognition of strict preference or indifference relations. In particular, socio-psychological and organization-psychological phenomena in a community are not assessed with strict preferences; they are sensitive to suggestions, persuasion, and prevalence, and obey capricious changes of preference to some extent. Thus the concepts of cognitive outranking relations with some discernible bands will provide an effective measure for recognizing the degree of satisfaction of the human constituents.

In the next subsection, an application is presented.

### 8.3.3. Application to Organizational Decision Making

Modern organization theory, which was developed by Barnard (1938), Simon (1945), and March and Simon (1958), defines an organization as a cooperative system and treats its function as a decision making process involving organizational (mutual) conflicts as well as cognitive limits of rationality. This analysis is also appropriate to an association in a community. In this subsection, we are concerned with extending their contributions to multiple criteria decision analysis in axiomatic forms. In particular, using the cognitive outranking relation, we intend to embed conflict-finding processes into organizational decision making. Here we use the term "utility" without any concern about its exact definition.

Assume an organizational structure be composed of three components: goal (G), act (a), and agent or actor (A). In operating an organization, inducement (I) to the goal, contribution (C) to the act, and return (R) to the agent are regarded as objects of major concern, or attributes, for the above basic components. For the organization (community) to be operated effectively, some propositions are presented.

**Proposition 1 (On-going condition of the organization).**

The three concerns (I, C, R) for the components of an organization must be in equilibrium if the organization is to operate continuously.

We regard the function of an organization as utility exchange processes among the components, G, a, and A. The utility exchange processes are executed via the mutual expectation-realization processes in terms of utility about the attribute levels from both sides of the components (Figure 8.4). In order that the organization may be in equilibrium, it is necessary and sufficient to keep utility balances in the expectation-realization processes for their attributes.

**Proposition 2 (The equilibrium condition of the organization).**

For assuring that an organization is in equilibrium, a utility balance for the concerned attribute must be realized in

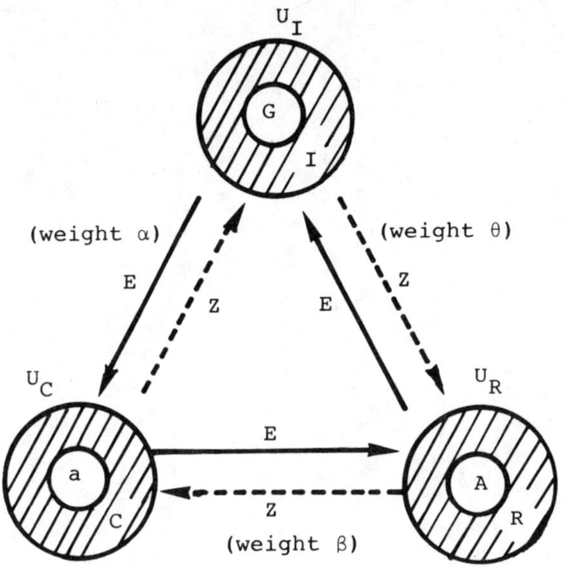


**Figure 8.4 Utility exchange process among organization constituents.**

its expectation-realization process. In other words, utility for inducement, utility for contribution, and utility for return should be balanced respectively for its expectation and realization.

**Proposition 3 (Well-functioning or stability condition of the organization).**

If the organization is well behaved, conflict-finding as well as conflict-solving functions must be embedded in the utility exchanges processes.

The utility assessment from the point of view of the expectation for one component is regarded to provide an evaluation for a scenario "a" of a decision problem. Another utility assessment from the point of view of the realization for the component reflects an evaluation for an alternative scenario "a'", which represents the expectation by the counterpart component. Conflicts among the components can be revealed by the discrepancy among the utility values that are evaluated for the alternative scenarios by both parties. Since, in the utility exchange processes, the realization for one party means the expectation for the other party as the counterpart, the discrepancy between both parties reflects the existence of a conflict in the utility exchange processes. This discrepancy between the parties can be measured numerically with the cognitive outranking relations. In addition, the magnitude of the indistinctiveness reflects the strength of the conflicts which exist within the organization.

**Example**

Let us consider a simple city model which concerns "amenity" as its goal, "activities" as its act, and "entrepreneur" as its agent or actor. Then main attributes for the concerns are "degree of attractiveness" as inducement for the amenity, "producing" as contribution for the activity, and "profit" as return for the entrepreneur. Assume the assessor or DM calculate the U-values as MUF-values defined on $\mathbf{x}$ taken as a set of attributes via multiattribute utility analysis, and assess the $\gamma$-values of the cognitive outranking relation for $U_i(\mathbf{x})$ of each concern i with or without a weight according to the degree of importance from the organizational point of view. Let us suppose the weights are like $\alpha = 100$, $\beta = 1000$, $\theta = 10000$, and assess alternative U-values for the expectation $(a = a_E)$ and the realization $(a' = a_Z)$. Calculated values are shown as:

(i) $\alpha\gamma(\mathbf{x}_Z, \mathbf{x}_E) = \alpha\Psi(U_I(\mathbf{x}_Z) - U_I(\mathbf{x}_E))$,

(ii) $\beta\gamma(\mathbf{x}_Z, \mathbf{x}_E) = \beta\Psi(U_C(\mathbf{x}_Z) - U_C(\mathbf{x}_E))$,

(iii) $\theta\gamma(\mathbf{x}_Z, \mathbf{x}_E) = \theta\Psi(U_R(\mathbf{x}_Z) - U_R(\mathbf{x}_E))$.

The assessor can interpret those results as the alarm index for finding the conflicts which may be expressed with some counteraction. For example,

value (i) ..... enervation
value (ii) ..... stagnation
value (iii) ..... escape or remodeling.

# Chapter 9

# Resource Allocation and Duality

## 9.1 Introduction

The ultimate aim of multiple criteria decision analysis (MCDA) is to provide a device for combining the analytical phase and the judgmental phase of multiple criteria decision making (MCDM). As we have discussed in preceding chapters, MCDM has two phases: analytical and judgmental. Mathematical optimization can effectively be executed in the analytical phase and decision analysis can be properly used in the judgmental phase. However, there exists a decision gap between these two phases, which should be bridged with some devices; this is the intrinsic property of MCDM. In the multiobjective mathematical programming techniques discussed in Chapters 2 to 4, the judgmental phase is reduced to assess the marginal rates of substitution among objectives, and is inserted externally into the solution algorithm without any concern about construction of the preference functions of DM. In the decision analysis discussed in Chapters 5 to 8, the judgmental phase is exclusively treated in construction of the preference functions of DM without any concern about mathematical optimization processes. In both of these approaches, the subjective evaluation processes in MCDM are definitely separated from the mathematical optimization processes for obtaining Pareto optimal solutions. We are concerned with constructing a proper device which can more effectively combine both phases of MCDM. This device can primarily be based on duality of mathematical programming.

This chapter presents some backgrounds for using the theoretical imputed prices as the basis of evaluation in the judgmental phase of MCDM. The fundamentals can be found in modern economic analysis and its extensions to inherently unmarketable goods.

## 9.2 Economic Analysis and Equilibrium Prices

The imputed price concept has primarily appeared in economic analysis for multicommodity and multiagent resource allocation in a general equilibrium system. In this section, the price concept embedded in the general equilibrium system is examined to provide the basis of the price concept for MCDM, although market prices cannot by nature be used for MCDA except as given parameters.

In economic literature, the equilibrium price systems are combined with resource allocations for production and consumption. The property of the general equilibrium system in the competitive market can be represented in a duality. Denote an abstract economic system as

$$E \triangleq (A_1(a_1), \ldots, A_S(a_S) \mid \Omega_1, \ldots, \Omega_S;\ f_1, \ldots, f_S). \tag{9.1}$$

The economic system is composed of a set of acts of individual decision makers. Every individual $p$, $p = 1, \ldots, S$, selects his "best" alternative program $A_p^*$ for acts $a_p$ with his criterion function $f_p$ under the constraints for a feasible set of his actions $\Omega_p \in \Omega$. The characteristics of this economic system are as follows:

(i) An economic structure is described as a set of Leibnizian monadic (separate and independent) agents with homogeneity which are devoted to economic activities. There are no intrinsic differences among the agents, who are occasionally divided in their functions between consumers and producers.

(ii) Decision making of an individual is mutually independent of each other and exclusively depends on his own preference function. This is a Benthamian world of individualistic utilitarianism.

(iii) The feasible set $\Omega$ of selection is a subset of the comprehensive commodity (and service) space, in which no other objects for preference are included.

The properties of the general equilibrium system which is defined on (9.1) have been analyzed mathematically and precisely in the neoclassical school of economics, such those by Arrow (1950a), Arrow and Debreu (1954), Debreu (1954, 1959b), Arrow and Hurwicz (1960), and Koopmans (1957). The main results are summarized in a few theorems. There are some assumptions for the consumers and the producers.

**Assumption 9.1 (Consumption program).**

A set of the possible consumption program $x_i \in X_i$, $X_i \subseteq R^{\ell}$, of every consumer (consumption unit) i, $i = 1,\ldots,m$, $I \triangleq \{i\}$, $I \in R^S$, has the following properties:

(i) The possible consumption set $X_i$ is closed, convex, and bounded from below. Namely, for all $x_i \in X_i$, $X_i \subseteq R^{\ell}$, there exists a vector value $\xi_i \in R^{\ell}$ such that $\xi_i \leqslant x_i$.

(ii) The utility function of the consumer is a continuous quasi-concave function on the possible consumption set $x_i$. Namely, when $u_i(x_i^2) > u_i(x_i^1)$, then $u_i(\alpha x_i^2 + (1-\alpha)x_i^1) > u_i(x_i^1)$, which means that an indifference surface of the consumer is convex to the origin.

(iii) There exists no saturation point for an attainable consumption program $x_i$ under the current technological and resource constraints.

(iv) There exist initial holdings $H_i \in R^{\ell}$ of available commodities for every consumer i, and $0 \leqslant x_i < H_i$. (In the case of labor service, $0 \geqslant x_i > H_i$). It means that a consumption program $x_i$ of the consumer is less than his initial holdings $H_i$ for commodities and still holds some available quantities for market transactions.

(v) Every consumer i has a contractual claim to the share $\beta_{ij}$ of the profit of the producer j, where $\beta_{ij} \geqslant 0$, $\sum_{i=1}^{m} \beta_{ij} = 1$, $j = 1,\ldots,n$, $J \triangleq \{j\}$, $J \in R^S$.

**Assumption 9.2 (Production program).**

A set of the possible production program $y_j \in Y_j$, $Y_j \subseteq R^\ell$, for every producer (production unit) $j$, $j = 1,\ldots,n$, $J \triangleq \{j\}$, $J \in R^S$, has the following properties:

(i) Nonincreasing returns to scale. Namely, $0 \in Y_j$ and $Y_j$ is a closed and convex set.

(ii) Nonexistence of the Land of Cockaigne; there exists no possible production set with a positive component (i.e., output) unless at least one component is negative (i.e., input). Namely, $Y \cap I_+ = 0$, where $Y \triangleq \bigcup_{j=1}^{j=n} Y_j$, and $I_+ \triangleq \{y_j | y_j \in R^\ell,$ $y_j \geqslant 0\}$. $y_j < 0$ denotes input, $y_j > 0$ is output.

(iii) Irreversibility of production processes. Namely, $Y \cap -Y = 0$.

**Definition 9.1 (Competitive equilibrium).**

A set of commodity vectors composed of the possible consumption program $x_i^*$ and possible production program $y_j^*$, and a price vector $p^* \triangleq \{p_r,\ r = 1,\ldots,\ell\}$, having the following properties, is said to be a competitive equilibrium.

(i) The production program in the equilibrium $y_j^* \in Y_j$ of every producer $j$, $j = 1,\ldots,n$, maximizes his profit function $py_j^*$ on the possible set of production $Y_j$.

(ii) The consumption program in the equilibrium $x_i^* \in X_i$ of every consumer $i$, $i = 1,\ldots,m$, maximizes his utility function $u_i(x_i)$ on the possible set of consumption $X_i \triangleq \{x_i \mid px_i^* \leqslant pH_i + \sum_{j=1}^{n} \beta_{ij} py_j\}$, where $px_i^*$ shows a net amount of expenditure in excess of his wage income.

(iii) The price vector in the equilibrium $p^*$ is nonnegative and normalized as relative prices such that

$$p^* \in P \triangleq \{p \mid p \in R^\ell,\ p \geqslant 0,\ \sum_{r=1}^{\ell} p_r = 1\}. \tag{9.2}$$

(iv) Existence of a positive excess demand is incompatible with the equilibrium and, when an excess supply exists, the prices in equilibrium should be necessarily zero. Namely, for the excess demand $z \triangleq x - (y - H)$,

$$z^* \leqslant 0 \quad \text{and} \quad p^*z^* = 0, \tag{9.3}$$

where $x \triangleq \sum_{i=1}^{m} x_i$, $y \triangleq \sum_{j=1}^{n} y_i$ and $H \triangleq \sum_{i=1}^{m} H_i$.

Commodities whose prices are zero in the equilibrium are called the free goods.

The existence theorems for the competitive equilibrium (Arrow and Debreu 1954) are derived under the above assumptions.

**Theorem 9.1 (Existence of the competitive equilibrium I).**

There exists a competitive equilibrium in the economic system satisfying Assumptions 9.1 and 9.2.

In Theorem 9.1, Assumption 9.1 (iv) requests that, in the equilibrium, it should be possible for a consumer to supply with at least one positive price some quantities of commodities including labor services. This assumption is too rigorous in the real world. A weaker assumption is substitute for (iv).

**Assumption 9.3.**

(i) Quantities of consumption by the consumer i cannot exceed his initial holdings. Namely, $x_i \leqslant H_i$ for $x_i \in X_i$ and $x_{hi} < H_{hi}$ for at least one $h \in \rho$, where $\rho$, is an index set showing productive labor.

(ii) An excess supply of all commodities can be achieved. Namely, there exists a consumption program $x \in X$, and a production program $y \in Y$ such that $\sum_{j=1}^{n} y_i + \sum_{i=1}^{m} H_i > \sum_{i=1}^{m} x_i$, where $x \triangleq \sum_{i=1}^{m} x_i$ and $y \triangleq \sum_{j=1}^{n} y_j$, $X \triangleq \bigcup_{i=1}^{m} X_i$, and $Y \triangleq \bigcup_{j=1}^{n} Y_j$.

(iii) The set of desired commodities in the possible consumption set of every consumer is not empty. Namely the set of the commodities $x_i$ such that the utility function $u_i(x_i)$ of every consumer is always an increasing function of the consumed quantity $x_i$ is not empty.

(iv) The set of productive labors used for the possible production is not empty. Namely marginal productivity of at least one type of labor should be positive in terms of one desired commodity.

Now the modified existence theorem of competitive equilibrium is presented.

**Theorem 9.2 (Existence of competitive equilibrium II)**

There exists a competitive equilibrium in an economic system satisfying Assumptions 9.1, 9.2(i)-(iii), (v), and 9.3.

The theorems assert, under the appropriate assumptions which are not very singular, existence of the equilibrium price system $p^*$ defining the competitive equilibrium. The equilibrium prices are regarded as the market prices on their "ideal" averages, which have been discussed in classical school of economics. Adam Smith (1776) presented the "Providence of Invisible Hands" in the context of the "natural" prices, whereby the quantity of every commodity brought to the market naturally suits itself to the effectual demand (Bk. I, p. 57). Ricardo (1817 Chap. 4) presented an excellent classical description of the functions of the market price mechanism with which demand and supply in markets coincide with each other. The coincidence of the total amounts of "social labor" expended in "social commodities" with the total amounts of "social wants" with solvency is also discussed in Marxian market value theory (Marx 1894 Bd. III, pp. 203-219), which provides a theoretical basis for balanced economy in a planned society.

The new contribution of modern economic analysis is to presents the Pareto optimality of the competitive equilibrium. The Pareto optimality is defined for a distribution such that any redistribution of commodities cannot improve the present situation of any individual without worsening that of at least one other individual.

**Definition 9.2 (Pareto optimality).**

Let $X^{\dagger} \triangleq \{X_{rp}, r = 1,\ldots,\ell, p = 1,\ldots,S\}$ be a vector showing an allocation of a commodity r to an individual p.

$X_p^\dagger \triangleq \{X_{1p},\ldots, X_{\ell p}\}$ denotes a commodity vector given to an individual p. $X^\dagger$ is said to be a Pareto optimal allocation if no other allocation X, such that $u_p(X_p) \geqslant u_p(X_p^\dagger)$ for every individual p and $u_t(X_t) > u_t(X_t^\dagger)$ for at least one individual t, exists on a condition $\sum_{p=1}^{S} X_p^\dagger \leqslant \sum_{j=1}^{n} y_j$ in the possible production set Y.

The following theorem is mainly from Arrow (1950a).

**Assumption 9.4.**

(i) All quantities of consumption are nonnegative. Let $x \triangleq \{x_r\}$ be a commodity bundle. Then $x \geqslant 0$.

(ii) Local nonsaturation. The preference order of an individual is continuous and weak ordered, and his utility function is represented by a strictly concave function.

(iii) Desirability of an allocation X for every individual is represented only by the desirability of the commodity bundle $X_p$ allocated for the individual p, which is independent of the desirability of any other person.

(iv) The possible production set Y has a nonincreasing return-to-scale property which is a convex and compact (i.e., bounded and closed) set that includes the origin.

The competitive equilibrium is redefined with an equilibrium price vector but without the sign conditions.

**Definition 9.3 (Competitive equilibrium II).**

An allocation X* and a price vector p* satisfying the following conditions (i) and (ii) are said to be a competitive equilibrium.

(i) An allocation $X_p^*$ for every individual p maximizes his utility function $u_p(x)$, $x \triangleq \{x_1,\ldots,x_\ell\}$, under the constraint $\sum_{r=1}^{\ell} p_r x_r \leqslant \sum_{r=1}^{\ell} p_r X_{rp}^*$ which implies the budget constraint.

(ii) The profit function $\sum_{r=1}^{\ell} p_r y_r$ for $y^* \in Y$ is maximized. Namely, there exists a production $y_r^* \geqslant \sum_{p=1}^{S} X_{rp}^*$ for all commodities $r$ and $y^* \in Y$, under the constraint $\sum_{r=1}^{\ell} p_r y_r \leqslant \sum_{r=1}^{\ell} p_r y_r^*$ which implies the technological condition.

The price vector $p^*$ satisfying the competitive equilibrium (i) and (ii) is said to equalize demand and supply at the resource allocation $X^*$ and thus is the equilibrium price vector.

**Theorem 9.3 (Pareto optimality of competitive equilibrium I).**

The resource allocation $X^*$ satisfying the competitive equilibrium (i) and (ii) under Assumption 9.4 (i)-(iii) is Pareto optimal. Conversely, a Pareto optimal allocation $X^*$ under Assumption 9.4 (i)-(iv) is the competitive equilibrium, and there exists a price vector whose components are not all zero.

It should be noted here that the convexity of the possible production set is assumed only for the sufficiency of the Pareto optimality of the competitive equilibrium. The existence of a price system with all nonzero components implied in the competitive equilibrium is assured only in the sufficiency which presumes the convexity condition (Assumption 9.4(iv)). The sufficiency, however, does not assure nonnegativity of all components of the price system. As Arrow pointed out with scrupulous and foresighted deliberation, the appearance of "unwanted or nuisance goods" ("bads") in consumption that comes from the use of some material for producing some commodities is not excluded here. The possibility of including negative price components within the equilibrium price system is the core of this theorem.

For assuring the existence of a price vector having all nonnegative components in the competitive equilibrium system with Pareto optimality, the following assumption should be added.

**Assumption 9.5 (Free disposal).**

If an amount $y_r^1$ of $y_r$ is in a possible production set $Y$, then another amount $y_r^2$ of $y_r$ such as $0 \leqslant y_r^2 \leqslant y_r^1$, $r = 1,\dots,\ell$, is also possible.

Assumption 9.5 describes the possibility of producing an amount $y_r^2$ by producing $y_r^1$ and discarding $(y_r^1 - y_r^2)$ for a commodity r. It means that a producer can dispose of an amount of a superfluous product r without any charge for it. This assumption is called free disposal; it plays a crucial role in assuring the nonnegativity of the equilibrium price systems.

**Theorem 9.4.**

Under Assumptions 9.4 and 9.5, if an allocation $X^\dagger$ is Pareto optimal, then there exists a price vector p* where at least one component is positive and the other components are all nonnegative.

The Pareto optimality of the competitive equilibrium system is one of the most essential conclusions in modern economic analysis. It asserts not only the Pareto optimality of the equilibrium system for resource allocation but also the existence of the price systems, as its dual, combined with the equilibrium resource allocation. Although this assertion provides a primal concept of the equilibrium, limitations of the modern economic analysis should also be discussed.

First, classical and modern (or neoclassical) economic analyses are founded on the paradigm of Benthamian (individualistic) utilitarianism. Adam Smith (1759), one of the most eminent founders of the Classical Economic School, continued his reflections on human nature in the basis of modern societies parallel with the construction of his economic theory up to the last period of his life. Smith regarded the feelings of "compassion" or "sympathy", which citizens in modern societies hold in their minds for other people, as having a function for guarding and protecting societies. He thought that usefulness of things is seldom the first grounds of a people's approbation and that the sentiment of approbation always involves in it a sense of propriety which is distinct from the perception of "utility" with which people approve of a convenient and well-contrived building (Bk.IV, Chap. 2, p. 326). The sentiment of approbation is founded upon a "perception of coincidence" or "correspondent affection" in ourselves (Bk.I, Chap. 3, p. 18, p. 21). "Moral faculties" or "our sensitivity to the feeling of others" is one basis of humanity (Bk.III, Chap. 3, p. 257). By nature, an original desire to please and an original aversion to offend his brethren are endowed (Chap. 2, p. 200). In Smith's paradigm, existence of the impartial spectator is assumed. The impartial spectator, or the impartial bystander, is supposed to be "some other being who is the natural judge of the person that feels [the sentiments]" (Bk.IV. Chap. 2, p. 334), who is an impersonation of the citizen's community implicitly based on modern Christianity and idealized. In contrast with the classical founder's reflection, in the neoclassical economic analysis, an individual considered as an economic unit is isolated from the citizen's community and detached from the fellow-feeling. An individual decision maker is only interested in his own utility or profit maximization. The assumption of individualism in this sense, however, seems rather unrealistic in the actual world.

Second, the equilibrium price systems, whose components are all nonnegative, are formed only under the assumption of free disposal (Theorem 9.4). However, in actual production processes where harmful goods (bads) appear, the free disposal (Assumption 9.5) cannot be realized; the disposal of wastes should be charged a cost. In this situation, which is more universal in modern industrial societies, existence of the competitive equilibrium for resource allocation with Pareto optimality cannot be assured without proper assessment of the negative prices to be imposed as the disposal costs on waste or nuisance goods.

Third, suppose that the Pareto optimal resource allocation may represent a realistic situation. Even so, as discussed in previous chapters, Pareto optimality cannot prescribe the preferred solution. For deriving the preferred solution from among the Pareto optimal solution set, either at least local identification of the social preference function or numerical determination of an equilibrium price system should be performed. The first discussion requires the possibility of the construction of the social utility function, and the second statement requires that the market price systems should assure the general equilibrium property of the market with the Pareto optimality. The paradigm of modern economic analysis contradicts these requests. Thus the preferred solution to the optimal resource allocation problems must be undetermined.

These criticisms toward modern economic analysis do not imply any forfeiture of the effectiveness in dual analysis. The duality, which describes the correspondence of quantities and prices in the optimal resource allocation, i.e. the existence of the equilibrium price systems combined with that, can still be effective and extended to further approaches. In the next section, some discussions about the duality are presented.

## 9.3 Shadow Market and Imputed Prices

### 9.3.1 Negative Utility and Shadow Prices

Theoretical backgrounds of the extended discussions about the duality are as follows.

First of all, in the general equilibrium system of production and consumption without free disposal, the evaluation for nuisance goods (bads) with negative utility should be included.

Second, the negative utility goods are treated as "products" formed by individual producers and consumers, which are not primarily "external" but rather "internal" to the market in spite of the appearance that social accounting for them is not actually imputed to the source of their occurrence. As Arrow (1950a) and Koopmans (1957) have properly pointed out, the nuisance goods can be included in the same plane as the utility goods even within the equilibrium analysis.

Third, as for the possibility of the social utility function, persistence of individuals for their own personal preference orders should be reconsidered. A person as DM can be supposed to be the person who possesses, as Smith has stressed, the pleasure of mutual sympathy, or "correspondent affection" towards other people, and the sense of "propriety." He is assumed to have a great regard for the virtues of prudence and self-discipline, which will lead a society to a graceful and agreeable mind. We can call such concerns "externality" following Ellsberg's term (1954). The "externality" consideration is a crucial factor of competency for DM. However, this aspect will be discussed in the last chapter of this book.

In the following, concepts of imputed prices are examined in relation to the first and second points of the above arguments.

Consider the activity of production from the social point of view and define it as a social production activity which is composed of activity of production and activity of negative production (waste discharge, or harmful item production, processes). The negative production processes can be combined with the (positive) production processes in the elementary terminology of activity analysis.

An activity (or a process) for producing an item $j$ is denoted by a vector $a_j$, $j = 1,\ldots,n$, whose components are $a_{ij}$, $i = 1,\ldots,m$. The $a_{ij}$ is a technological coefficient which shows an amount of an item $i$ (as a commodity, service, etc.) necessary to operate the activity $j$ in a unit level. Input $i$ in the activity $j$ is usually denoted by $-a_{ij} \leqslant 0$, $1 > a_{ij} \geqslant 0$. Output is denoted by $a_{i+1j} \triangleq 1$.

An activity matrix $A$ is a set of $n$ activities $a_j$, $j = 1,\ldots,n$, and shown as

$$a_j \triangleq \begin{bmatrix} a_{1j} \\ a_{2j} \\ \vdots \\ a_{mj} \end{bmatrix}, \quad A \triangleq (a_1,\ldots,a_j,\ldots,a_n) \triangleq \begin{bmatrix} a_{11},\ldots,a_{1j},\ldots,a_{1n} \\ a_{21},\ldots,a_{2j},\ldots,a_{2n} \\ \vdots \qquad \vdots \qquad \vdots \\ a_{m1},\ldots,a_{mj},\ldots,a_{mn} \end{bmatrix}, \tag{9.4}$$

which is also called an input coefficient matrix.

A set of the output levels for all activity, $y \triangleq (y_1,\ldots, y_j,\ldots, y_n)$, $y_j \in R'$, represents a production program. An input of each item $i$ to each activity $j$ is denoted by $x_{ij}$.

$$\begin{bmatrix} x_{11},\ldots, x_{1j},\ldots, x_{1n} \\ x_{21},\ldots, x_{2j},\ldots, x_{2n} \\ \vdots \qquad \vdots \qquad \vdots \\ x_{m1},\ldots, x_{mj},\ldots, x_{mn} \end{bmatrix} \tag{9.5}$$

**Assumption 9.6 (Linearity).**

(i) $x_{ij}$ is nonnegative.

(ii) The proportionality condition is satisfied, which means that each activity can be proportionally expanded or reduced. Namely, $x_{ij} = a_{ij}y_j$, $a_{ij} \geqslant 0$, where $y_j$ shows the total amount of production of an item $j$. The input coefficient $a_{ij}$ is defined as $a_{ij} \triangleq x_{ij}/y_j$.

(iii) Each activity is additively separable. Namely, we can obtain a net output $Y_i$ of an item $i$ as $Y_i = \sum_{j=1}^{n} a_{ij}y_j$.

From the linearity assumption 9.6, the negative production processes can be treated as independent activities distinct from the production activities. The input coefficient matrix (9.4) also includes the negative production activities. The activity matrix for social production is denoted as:

$$\tilde{A} \triangleq \begin{bmatrix} \tilde{a}_{11}, & \tilde{a}_{12}, & \cdots & \tilde{a}_{1n} \\ \vdots & \vdots & \ddots & \vdots \\ \tilde{a}_{m1}, & \tilde{a}_{m2} & \cdots & \tilde{a}_{mn} \end{bmatrix} \tag{9.6}$$

$$\triangleq \begin{bmatrix} (a_{11}, \bar{a}_{11}), & (a_{12}, \bar{a}_{12}), & \cdots, & (a_{1n}, \bar{a}_{1n}) \\ \vdots & \vdots & \ddots & \vdots \\ (a_{m1}, \bar{a}_{m1}), & (a_{m2}, \bar{a}_{m2}), & \cdots, & (a_{mn}, \bar{a}_{mn}) \end{bmatrix}, \tag{9.7}$$

where $\bar{a}_{ij}$, $i = 1,\ldots m$, $j = 1,\ldots,n$, shows an activity of the negative production.

Consider a simple example. Suppose that an activity of production $a_1$ produces an output $y_1$ (e.g., paper) with an input $x_{11}$ (e.g., wood pulp). The activity $a_1$ simultaneously produces a waste $\bar{y}_1$ (e.g., sludge) from the social point of view. The waste discharging process can be conceptually considered as an activity $\bar{a}_1$ additively separated from the production activity $a_1$. The social production activity $a_s$ is composed of both activities under the linearity assumption and

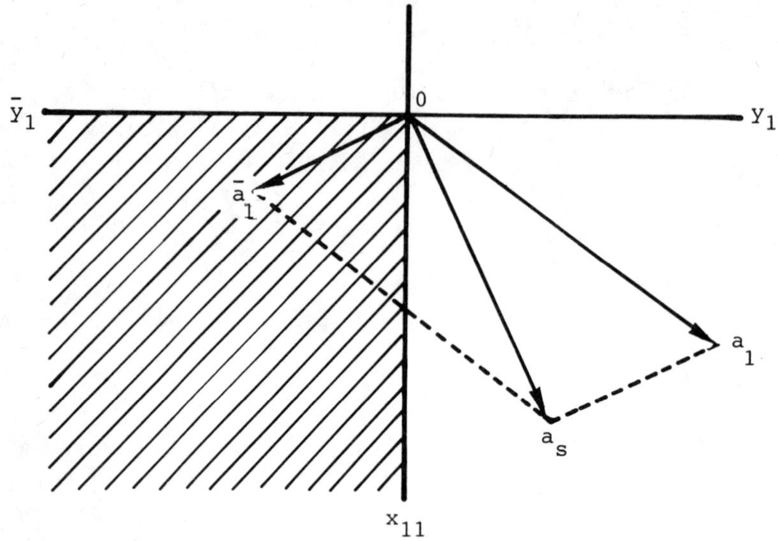


**Figure 9.1 Social production activity: linear case.**

depicted in Figure 9.1. In the economic market, only the production activity $a_1$ is recognized and the activity of negative production $\bar{a}_1$ forms an unrecognized "shadow" market. The evaluation price system for the product $\bar{y}_1$ of the activity $\bar{a}_1$ is not established in the market. Thus, efficiency of the social production measured with an average productivity $y_s/x_s$ is clearly different from efficiency of the private production $y_p/x_p$ and is lower than the latter.

The social production function $F(x, y, \bar{y})$ is represented under the assumption of additive separability in a general form:

$$F(x, y, \bar{y}) = F(x, y) + \bar{F}(x, \bar{y}) = 0, \tag{9.8}$$

where $F(x, y)$ shows a production function and $\bar{F}(x, \bar{y})$ denotes the negative production function from the social point of view. In terms of an additive utility function, a social utility function for the social products can be represented in simple terms (the subscript s is omitted):

$$U(y, \bar{y}) = U(y) - \bar{U}(\bar{y}), \tag{9.9}$$

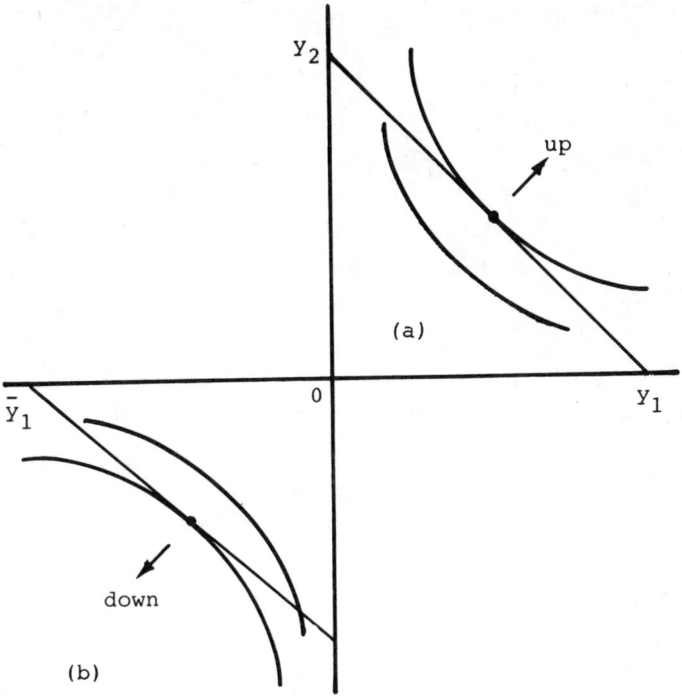


**Figure 9.2 Indifference curves for utility and negative utility goods.**

where $\bar{U}(\bar{y})$ is a negative utility function for the negative product $\bar{y}$.

An indifference curve for negative utility goods is depicted in two dimensional space in Figure 9.2 (b) in contrast to (a) for (positive) utility goods. While a movement toward the northeastern direction shows climbing on the utility surface in Figure 9.2 (a), the movement toward the southwestern direction shows moving down on the negative utility surface in (b).

### 9.3.2 Derivation of the Negative Demand Function

A negative demand (or aversion) function for the negative utility goods $\bar{y}$ can be derived in a manner analogous to the demand function.

Consider the following problem:

$$\underset{\bar{y}}{\text{minimize}} \quad \bar{U}(\bar{y}) \tag{9.10}$$

$$\text{subject to} \quad \bar{p}\bar{y} \leqslant \Gamma, \tag{9.11}$$

where $\bar{y} \in R^n$ is a vector whose components $\bar{y} \triangleq (\bar{y}_1, \ldots, \bar{y}_n)$ denote negative utility goods. $\bar{p} \in R^n$ is a "Price" vector whose components $\bar{p} \triangleq (\bar{p}_1, \ldots, \bar{p}_n)$ denote negative evaluation ("negative price") for the negative utility goods. $\Gamma$ shows an admissible level of total evaluation of the negative products at a given point of time. The problem (9.10) (9.11) is to find the level of the negative products which minimizes the negative utility function under the constraint that the total evaluation of the negative utility goods does not exceed the preassigned admissible level.

From the Lagrange function

$$z = \bar{U}(\bar{y}_1, \ldots, \bar{y}_n) + \mu\left(\sum_{i=1}^{n} \bar{p}_i \bar{y}_i - \Gamma\right), \tag{9.12}$$

the optimality conditions for (9.10) (9.11) are derived:

$$\frac{\partial z}{\partial \bar{y}_i} = \bar{U}_i + \mu \bar{p}_i = 0, \quad i = 1, \ldots, n \tag{9.13}$$

$$\frac{\partial z}{\partial \mu} = \sum_{i=1}^{n} \bar{p}_i \bar{y}_i - \Gamma = 0, \tag{9.14}$$

where $\bar{U}_i$ denotes $\partial \bar{U}/\partial \bar{y}_i$ and $\mu$ is a Lagrange multiplier.

From the $n+1$ optimality conditions (9.13) (9.14), we obtain the following $n+1$ values with "price" $\bar{p}_i$, $i = 1, \ldots, n$, taken as given and with the preassigned admissible level $\Gamma$.

$$\bar{y}_i = \phi_i(\bar{p}_1, \ldots, \bar{p}_n, \Gamma), \quad i = 1, \ldots, n \tag{9.15}$$

$$\mu = \phi_\mu(\bar{p}_1, \ldots, \bar{p}_n, \Gamma). \tag{9.16}$$

(9.15) is the negative demand function for $\bar{y}_i$ defined on the "price" of all negative utility goods. Properties of the negative utility function are as follows.

(i) From (9.13),

$$\mu = -\frac{\partial \bar{U}}{\partial \bar{y}_i} / \bar{p}_i, \quad i = 1,\ldots,n. \tag{9.17}$$

It means that the marginal negative utility (disutility) for each negative product $\bar{y}_i$ in terms of its price $\bar{p}_i$, $i = 1,\ldots,n$, is equal to each of the others. This corresponds to the well-known Law of Equal Marginal Utility in textbooks of economics.

(ii) From (9.17),

$$\frac{\partial \bar{y}_j}{\partial \bar{y}_i} = \frac{\bar{p}_i}{\bar{p}_j}, \quad i, j = 1,\ldots,n, \quad i \neq j, \tag{9.18}$$

which means that the ratios of prices for the negative utility goods are inversely equal to the marginal rates of substitution between their goods.

(iii) From the Kuhn-Tucker conditions, when $\mu > 0$,

$$-\frac{\partial z}{\partial \Gamma} = \mu = -\frac{\partial \bar{U}}{\partial \Gamma} \tag{9.19}$$

which means that the marginal disutility in terms of its price (9.17) can also be represented in terms of the marginal decrease of disutility for the increase of the admissible level.

When the social demand functions are considered, the market demand function for transactions of the utility goods, $y_i = \phi_i(p_1,\ldots,p_n, \Sigma)$ where $\Sigma$ denotes an income level, should be combined with the negative demand function (9.15) with which presumable transactions of the negative utility goods in the shadow market are explicitly recognized.

Consider the simple example. In Figure 9.3, the demand curve in the first quadrant $D(y_i)$ represents the demand function $\phi_i$ for the utility good $y_i$ defined on its price $p_i$. The negative demand curve $\bar{D}(\bar{y}_i)$ in the third quadrant

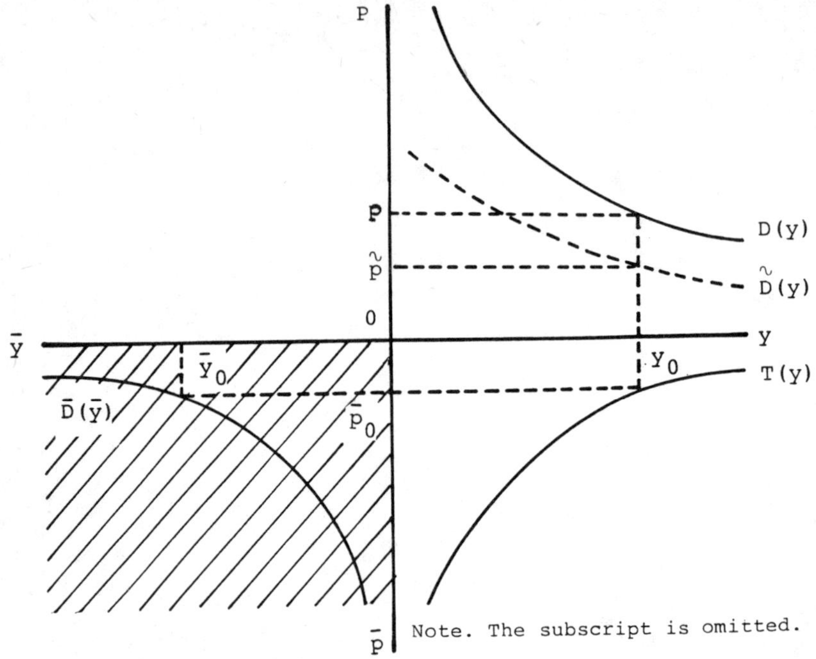


**Figure 9.3 Derivation of the social demand function.**

represents the negative demand function $\psi_i$ for the disutility good $\bar{y}_i$ defined on its negative price $\bar{p}_i$. The shape of $\bar{D}(\bar{y}_i)$ shows that, when the negative evaluation $\bar{p}_i$ per unit for the disutility good $\bar{y}_i$ is larger (in an absolute value) in equilibrium, the amount of the negative demand $\bar{y}_i$ is smaller. In other words, when the degree of aversion for the $\bar{y}_i$ is higher, one unit of the $\bar{y}_i$ is assessed with a larger negative evaluation $\bar{p}_i$. The transfer curve $T(y_i)$ which combines $\bar{p}_i$ with $y_i$ can be derived via a product-residual function which represents the technological interrelation between $y_i$ and $\bar{y}_i$. Using $T(y_i)$, a negative evaluation $\bar{p}_{i0}$ for an amount of the negative utility good $\bar{y}_{i0}$ is plotted for the corresponding amount of the product $y_{i0}$. The transfer curve $T(y_i)$ is mapped in the fourth quadrant with the $y_{i0}$. Then the social demand curve $\tilde{D}(y_i)$ can be derived. The social demand function $\tilde{y}_i = \tilde{\phi}_i(\tilde{p}_i)$ is defined on a new valuation price $\tilde{p}_i$ in which the negative evaluation $\bar{p}_i$ is deducted from the market price $p_i$ for the utility good $y_i$. The "shadow market" is a conceptual field in which an evaluation system for the disutility goods is established via the negative demand functions.

In the above analysis, it should be noted that the evaluation systems of $p_i$, $i = 1,\ldots,n$, and $\bar{p}_i$, $i = 1,\ldots,n$, are presumed to be given in commensurable units. Thus the problem is to establish a method for evaluating the negative utility goods in the shadow market which can never be recognized in market activity. The calculation of shadow prices is a purely theoretical problem. In addition, the evaluation of the shadow prices is not only concerned with the simulation of the status quo, but also with the management and control of the present situations. Therefore, the evaluation problem for the shadow prices must be combined with managerial decision making.

In the next subsection, some examples for approaching evaluation of the negative utility goods are discussed.

### 9.3.3 Evaluation of the Negative Utility Goods

The negative evaluation for the negative utility goods is imputed to the degree of their harmfulness for humans. Thus treatment of the harmful goods will bring about a decrease of the negative evaluation through the elimination of the harmfulness; it generates positive evaluation in the treatment processes. This subsection concerns two major approaches; input-output analysis and mathematical programming.

#### 1. Input-output analysis

Interindustry analysis (an input-output model) including pollution preventing activities has presented since Leontief (1970).

From the interindustry (input-output) table with the pollution preventing activities, the $n \times n$ input coefficient matrix is obtained, which is partitioned as follows:

$$A \triangleq [A_1 : A_2] \triangleq \begin{bmatrix} A_{11} \triangleq \{a_{ij}\} & \vdots & A_{12} \triangleq \{a_{ik}\} \\ \cdots\cdots\cdots & \vdots & \cdots\cdots\cdots \\ A_{21} \triangleq \{\bar{a}_{gj}\} & \vdots & A_{22} \triangleq \{\bar{a}_{gk}\} \end{bmatrix}, \tag{9.20}$$

where $A_1$ is the input coefficient matrix for production activities, and $A_2$ is the input coefficient matrix for pollution preventing activities, and $i, j = 1,\ldots,m$, $k, g = m+1,\ldots,n$. Each input coefficient is defined as:

$$\begin{aligned} a_{ij} &= x_{ij}/y_j, & i, j &= 1,\ldots,m \\ a_{ik} &= x_{ik}/\bar{y}_k, & i &= 1,\ldots,m, \quad k = m+1,\ldots,n \\ \bar{a}_{gj} &= \bar{x}_{gj}/y_j, & g &= m+1,\ldots,n, \quad j = 1,\ldots,m \\ \bar{a}_{gk} &= \bar{x}_{gk}/\bar{y}_k, & g, k &= m+1,\ldots,n, \end{aligned} \tag{9.21}$$

where $\bar{x}_{gj}$ is an amount of a pollutant $g$ generated in an production activity $j$, and $\bar{x}_{gk}$ is an amount of a pollutant $g$ generated in a pollution preventing activity $k$. $y_j$ is the total output of a commodity $j$, and $\bar{y}_k$ the total amount of pollutant $k$ eliminated. $a_{ij}$ is input of a commodity $i$ per unit of output of a commodity $j$ (i.e., the input coefficient of the commodity producing sector), $a_{ik}$ is input of a commodity $i$ per unit of elimination of a pollutant $k$ (i.e., the input coefficient to the pollution preventing sector), $\bar{a}_{gj}$ is generation of a pollutant $g$ per unit of output of a commodity $j$ (i.e., the pollution generating coefficient of the commodity producing sector), and $\bar{a}_{gk}$ is generation of a pollutant $g$ per unit of elimination of a pollutant $k$ (i.e., the pollution generating coefficient of the pollution preventing sector). Let $z_i$ be an amount of commodity $i$ supplied to the final demand sector and $\bar{z}_k$ be the final discharge of a pollutant $k$. Then for $i = 1,\ldots,m$, $k = m+1,\ldots,n$,

$$\begin{bmatrix} Y_1 \\ \cdots \\ Y_2 \end{bmatrix} \triangleq \begin{bmatrix} y_1 \\ \vdots \\ y_m \\ \cdots \\ \bar{y}_{m+1} \\ \vdots \\ \bar{y}_n \end{bmatrix}, \quad \begin{bmatrix} Z_1 \\ \cdots \\ Z_2 \end{bmatrix} \triangleq \begin{bmatrix} z_1 \\ \vdots \\ z_m \\ \cdots \\ \bar{z}_{m+1} \\ \vdots \\ \bar{z}_n \end{bmatrix}, \quad I \triangleq \begin{array}{c c} & \begin{array}{cc} m & n-m \end{array} \\ \begin{array}{c} m \\ n-m \end{array} & \left[\begin{array}{c:c} I_1 & 0 \\ \hdashline 0 & I_2 \end{array}\right] \end{array} \tag{9.22}$$

where $I_1$ and $I_2$ are the unit matrix.

Using (9.20) and (9.22), the input-output relationship in the equilibrium is formulated as follows:

$$\begin{aligned} &[I_1 - A_{11}]Y_1 - A_{12}Y_2 = Z_1 \\ &\qquad A_{21}Y_1 - [I_2 - A_{22}]Y_2 = Z_2, \end{aligned} \tag{9.23}$$

or

$$\left[\begin{array}{c:c} I_1 - A_{11} & -A_{12} \\ \hdashline A_{21} & -I_2 + A_{22} \end{array}\right] \begin{bmatrix} Y_1 \\ \cdots \\ Y_2 \end{bmatrix} = \begin{bmatrix} Z_1 \\ \cdots \\ Z_2 \end{bmatrix}. \tag{9.24}$$

The first equation of (9.23) describes the total supply-demand equality relation that includes the pollution preventing activities. The second equation describes the quantitative balance for pollutants generated in all sectors; it shows that the total quantity of a pollutant generated in all sectors is equal to the amount eliminated in the pollution preventing sector plus the final discharge.

From (9.24), the solution is obtained with the predetermined coefficients and the final deliveries.

$$\begin{bmatrix} Y_1 \\ \cdots \\ Y_2 \end{bmatrix} = \left[\begin{array}{c:c} I_1 - A_{11} & -A_{12} \\ \hdashline A_{21} & -I_2 + A_{22} \end{array}\right]^{-1} \begin{bmatrix} Z_1 \\ \cdots \\ Z_2 \end{bmatrix}, \tag{9.25}$$

where

$$\left[\begin{array}{c:c} I_1 - A_{11} & -A_{12} \\ \hdashline A_{21} & -I + A_{22} \end{array}\right]^{-1} \triangleq C \tag{9.26}$$

is the Leontief type inverse matrix. Let a component of the inverse matrix C (9.26) be $r_{ij}$, i, j = 1,...,n. Then the solution $\hat{y}_i$ to (9.24) is represented with its component:

$$y_i = \tilde{r}_{i1}z_1 + \tilde{r}_{i2}z_2 + \dots + \tilde{r}_{im}z_m + \tilde{r}_{i,m+1}\bar{z}_{m+1} + \dots$$
$$\dots + \tilde{r}_{in}\bar{z}_n, \qquad i = 1,\dots,n. \tag{9.27}$$

specifically for the eliminated pollutant g,

$$\bar{y}_g = \tilde{r}_{g1}z_1 + \tilde{r}_{g2}z_2 + \dots + \tilde{r}_{gm}z_m + \tilde{r}_{g,m+1}\bar{z}_{m+1} + \dots$$
$$+ \dots + \tilde{r}_{gn}\bar{z}_n, \qquad g = m+1,\dots,n. \tag{9.28}$$

The equation (9.28) shows that the elimination level of a pollutant g is proportionally determined in terms of the final deliveries per unit of all items (commodities and pollutants); it is similar to the commodity production level represented in the equation (9.27).

The input-output structure describes the resource allocation in balance, and within it a price determination mechanism is implied. Note that a price is equal to a total unit cost for primal and intermediate input under the zero-surplus assumption for the competitive market. The price system is derived as the dual to the production program $\hat{y}_i$, as given the input coefficient matrix. In the extended form for (9.24),

$$\begin{aligned} [I_1 - A_{11}]^T P_1 \qquad &= A_1^o \\ - A_{12}^T P_1 + P_2 &= A_2^o, \end{aligned} \tag{9.29}$$

where $P_1 \triangleq (p_1,\dots,p_m)$ is a price vector whose component $p_j$ denotes a price of a commodity j, j = 1,...,m. $P_2 \triangleq (\bar{p}_{m+1},\dots, \bar{p}_n)$ is a price vector whose component $\bar{p}_k$ denotes a "price" of a pollutant k, k = m+1,...,n. $A_1^o \triangleq (a_1^o,\dots, a_m^o)$ is a vector whose component $a_i^o$ shows the value added per unit of output of a commodity i, i = 1,...,m, and $A_2^o \triangleq (a_{m+1}^o,\dots, a_n^o)$ is a vector whose component $a_k^o$ shows the value added per unit of the elimination of a pollutant k, k = m+1,...,n. The first equation of (9.29) shows that the commodity price $P_1$ is equal to the total unit cost of the intermediate input $A_{11}^T P_1$ and the primary input $A_1^o$ whose price is normalized as $P_1^o \triangleq 1$. The second equation shows that the "price" $P_2$ of the pollutant is equal to the total cost for the intermediate input per unit of the elimination of pollutants $A_{12}^T P_1$ and the cost for the primal input (value added) per unit of the elimination of pollutants $A_2^o$, where $p_2^o \triangleq 1$. Thus it is seen that the price of pollutants is equal to their disposal cost.

Rewriting (10.29) in the following form

$$\begin{bmatrix} I_1 - A_{11}^T & \vdots & 0 \\ \cdots & \cdots & \cdots \\ - A_{12}^T & \vdots & I_2 \end{bmatrix} \begin{bmatrix} P_1 \\ \cdots \\ P_2 \end{bmatrix} = \begin{bmatrix} A_1^o \\ \cdots \\ A_2^o \end{bmatrix} \tag{9.30}$$

yields the solution

$$\begin{bmatrix} P_1 \\ \cdots \\ P_2 \end{bmatrix} = \begin{bmatrix} I_1 - A_{11}^T & \vdots & 0 \\ \cdots & \cdots & \cdots \\ - A_{12}^T & \vdots & I_2 \end{bmatrix}^{-1} \begin{bmatrix} A_1^o \\ \cdots \\ A_2^o \end{bmatrix} . \tag{9.31}$$

Let $\tilde{r}_{ij}$ be a component of the inverse matrix $\tilde{C}$ in (9.31)

$$\tilde{C} \triangleq \begin{bmatrix} 1 - A_{11}^T & \vdots & 0 \\ \cdots & \cdots & \cdots \\ - A_{12}^T & \vdots & I_2 \end{bmatrix}^{-1} . \tag{9.32}$$

Then

$$p_j = a_1^o \tilde{r}_{1j} + a_2^o \tilde{r}_{2j} + \dots + a_n^o \tilde{r}_{nj}, \quad j = 1, \dots, n. \tag{9.33}$$

Specifically for a pollutant $k$,

$$p_k = a_1^o \tilde{r}_{1k} + a_2^o \tilde{r}_{2k} + \dots + a_n^o \tilde{r}_{nk}, \quad k = m+1, \dots, n. \tag{9.34}$$

When internal treatment processes of pollutants is introduced within industries, a modification is required. Let a proportion $\theta_{gj}$ of a pollutant $g$ generated by commodity producing activity $j$ be eliminated at the expense of that activity (i.e., industry) and denote its amount $q_{gj}$, i.e., $q_{gj} \triangleq \theta_{gj}\bar{a}_{gj}$. Then (9.30) becomes

$$\begin{bmatrix} I_1 - A_{11}^T & \vdots & -Q_{21}^T \\ \cdots\cdots & \vdots & \cdots\cdots \\ -A_{21}^T & \vdots & I_2 - Q_{22}^T \end{bmatrix} \begin{bmatrix} P_1 \\ \cdots \\ P_2 \end{bmatrix} = \begin{bmatrix} A_1^o \\ \cdots \\ A_2^o \end{bmatrix}, \tag{9.35}$$

where $Q_{21} \triangleq \{q_{gj}\}$, $g = m+1,\ldots,n$, $j = 1,\ldots,m$, and $Q_{22} \triangleq \{q_{gk}\}$, $g, k = m+1,\ldots,n$. Thus

$$\begin{bmatrix} P_1 \\ \cdots \\ P_2 \end{bmatrix} = \begin{bmatrix} I - A_{11}^T & \vdots & -Q_{21}^T \\ \cdots\cdots & \vdots & \cdots\cdots \\ -A_{12} & \vdots & I_2 - Q_{22}^T \end{bmatrix}^{-1} \begin{bmatrix} A_1^o \\ \cdots \\ A_2^o \end{bmatrix}. \tag{9.36}$$

Let $\tilde{\tilde{r}}_{ij}$ be a component of the inverse matrix $\tilde{\tilde{C}}$ in (9.36),

$$\tilde{\tilde{C}} \triangleq \begin{bmatrix} I - A_{11}^T & \vdots & -Q_{21}^T \\ \cdots\cdots & \vdots & \cdots\cdots \\ -A_{12}^T & \vdots & I_2 - Q_{22}^T \end{bmatrix}^{-1}. \tag{9.37}$$

Then

$$P_j = a_1^o\tilde{\tilde{r}}_{1j} + a_2^o\tilde{\tilde{r}}_{2j} + \ldots + a_n^o\tilde{\tilde{r}}_{nj}, \quad j = 1,\ldots,n. \tag{9.38}$$

Particularly for a pollutant $k$,

$$P_k = a_1^o\tilde{\tilde{r}}_{1k} + a_2^o\tilde{\tilde{r}}_{2k} + \ldots + a_n^o\tilde{\tilde{r}}_{nk}, \quad k = m+1,\ldots,n. \tag{9.39}$$

The equations (9.34) and (9.39) show that the price of a pollutant $k$ is proportionally determined in terms of the values added (or primary input) per unit for all the activities, similarly to the commodity price.

**Remark.**

The input-output analysis has the intrinsic properties of "supply-side" economics. The evaluation problem for the negative utility goods is solved only from one-side, that is, from the point of view of activity analysis of production. Thus when the imputed prices for pollutants are added to commodity prices, the supply curve for a commodity is raised upward. The input-output analysis shows this situation. On the contrary, demand analysis discussed in the preceding subsection shows that generation of negative evaluation for a pollutant will pull down the social demand curve for a commodity. Thus pollution generating processes combined with commodity producing processes bring down the social demand function and, at the same time, raise the supply function. As a result, a contracted equilibrium will occur in the economic market. This means that, in the shifted equilibrium, the output level will decrease with the unvaried price level. In that case, when the market price level is determined with the market demand curve, there will be still over-production due to over-assessment for the commodity. The price mechanism in actual markets cannot be adjusted autonomously to the non free-disposal situation. This is another explanation of the market failure by the signal, discussed by Bator (1958).

## 2. Mathematical programming

The pollution control program is also constructed in the form of mathematical programming. As a simple example, a regional water pollution treatment program is considered.

The polluted water is regarded as a pollutant complex, such as sludge, whose components consist of pollutants, such as cadmium, cyanide, mercury, COD, and other noxious chemical or biochemical substances. Each pollutant is assumed to be discharged from each activity of an industrial plant.

Each pollutant is denoted by $i = 1,\ldots,m$, each industry by $s = 1,\ldots,q$, each plant by $k = 1,\ldots,h$, and each region by $j = 1,\ldots,n$. The data for pollutants generated in region $j$ is shown by a matrix $U_j \triangleq \{{}_{sk}u^i_j\}$, whose component ${}_{sk}u^i_j$ denotes the quantity of a pollutant $i$ (e.g., cadmium, cyanide, mercury) discharged by a plant $k$ of an industry $s$ in a region $j$ during a given period of time. Consequently, each column of the matrix $U_j$ is a vector whose elements are pollutants (cadmium, cyanide, etc.) included in polluted waste (sludge, etc.) discharged by plant $k$ belonging to the industry s, and each row is a vector whose elements show the generating sources of the pollutants.

With the above data, a disposal coefficients matrix is obtained.

$$D_j \triangleq \{ {}_{sk}\delta^i_j \} \qquad \begin{array}{ll} i = 1,\ldots,m, & s = 1,\ldots,q \\ j = 1,\ldots,n, & k = 1,\ldots,h, \end{array} \tag{9.40}$$

where ${}_{sk}\delta^i_j \triangleq \dfrac{{}_{sk}u^i_j}{{}_{sk}U_j}$. ${}_{sk}U_j$ denotes an amount of waste discharge.

The waste treatment program is formulated as a cost minimization problem:

$$\underset{{}_{sk}x_j}{\text{minimize}} \quad \sum_{s=1}^{q} \sum_{k=1}^{h} {}_{sk}c_j \; {}_{sk}x_j \tag{9.41}$$

$$\text{subject to} \quad \sum_{s=1}^{q} \sum_{k=1}^{h} {}_{sk}\delta^i_j \; {}_{sk}x_j \geqslant \tau^i_j, \quad i = 1,\ldots,m \tag{9.42}$$

$${}_{sk}x_j \leqslant {}_{sk}U_j, \quad s = 1,\ldots,q \tag{9.43}$$

$${}_{sk}x_j \geqslant 0, \quad k = 1,\ldots,h, \tag{9.44}$$

where ${}_{sk}c_j$ is the treatment cost per unit of discharged waste from a plant k belonging to an industry s located in a region j, and $\tau^i_j$ is a target level for treating pollutant i in the region j. ${}_{sk}x_j$ is a policy variable representing a quantity of waste treatment discharged by the plant k belonging to the industry s in the region j, which takes a range $0 \leqslant {}_{sk}x_j \leqslant {}_{sk}U_j$.

A set of quantities of the waste treatment in each process is termed "project" and a set of the quantities of each pollutant to be treated in a project is termed "design." A project should be constructed with a specific design.

The problem is to select a project level which minimizes the total cost of the waste treatment under the constraints that the treated quantity of each pollutant should at least satisfy the target level.

The waste treatment program (9.41)-(9.44) as a primal problem is combined with a evaluation program as its dual problem:

$$\underset{\mu_j^i,\ {}_{sk}\omega_j}{\text{maximize}} \quad \Phi_j = \sum_{i=1}^{m} \mu_j^i \tau_j^i - \sum_{s=1}^{q} \sum_{k=1}^{h} {}_{sk}\omega_j \, {}_{sk}U_j \tag{9.45}$$

$$\text{subject to} \quad \sum_{i=1}^{m} \mu_j^i \, {}_{sk}\delta_j^i - {}_{sk}\omega_j \leqslant {}_{sk}c_j, \tag{9.46}$$

$$s = 1,\ldots,q, \quad k = 1,\ldots,h,$$

$${}_{sk}\omega_j \geqslant 0 \tag{9.47}$$

$$\mu_j^i \geqslant 0, \quad i = 1,\ldots,m, \tag{9.48}$$

where ${}_{sk}\delta_j^i$ is a component of the disposal coefficients matrix and ${}_{sk}c_j$ is the disposal cost per unit of the discharged waste from plant $k$ of the industry $s$ in the region $j$.

The $\mu_j^i$ and ${}_{sk}\omega_j$ are generated as the dual variables. $\mu_j^i$ is an estimated value per unit of disposal of the pollutant $i$ in the region $j$ and is interpreted as the imputed price. The fictitious price accrues in the transformation process of the biochemical composition of a pollutant, or the elimination of its disutility. The ${}_{sk}\omega_j$ is an opportunity cost per unit of the waste discharge by plant $k$ of the industry $s$ in the region $j$. The constraint (9.46) shows that the net estimated value for all the pollutant disposal per unit of waste discharge by plant $k$ belonging to the industry $s$ in the region $j$ should not exceed the cost per unit of the waste treatment; this is the condition that permits no positive surplus gain in each project. The objective function (9.45) shows the net estimated value for this waste treatment program, which is defined as the sum of estimated values for all the pollutant disposal indicated by the target levels minus the sum of opportunity costs for all the waste discharge in this region.

The problem is to select the nonnegative imputed price vector that maximizes the net estimated value obtained from attainment of the target levels for all pollutant disposal in the region $j$ under the above constraints (9.46) and the nonnegativity conditions of the dual variables (9.47) and (9.48).

The solution $\mu_j^{i*}$ to the evaluation problem combined with the waste treatment program provides the accounting price or the estimated value per unit of each pollutant, which is a positive value given for the disappearance or decrease of disutility for each pollutant, accruing from the elimination of each pollutant. From (9.46), the total of the estimated value per unit of pollutant disposal in each process is, in the optimal, equal to a sum of the treatment cost per unit of the project level (i.e., direct cost) and the opportunity costs (i.e., indirect cost) for the waste discharge. Such estimated values are different according to different industrial characteristics in each region.

There is an alternative formulation of the waste treatment program as a net benefit maximization problem.

Let ${}_{sk}x_j$ be the project level for the waste treatment in the plant $k$ belonging to the industry $s$ in the region $j$, and ${}_{sk}\beta_j$ be the net benefit obtained from the waste treatment per unit of each project level in the region $j$. Then, the net benefit maximization problem is formulated as:

$$\underset{{}_{sk}x_j}{\text{maximize}} \quad \sum_{s=1}^{q} \sum_{k=1}^{h} {}_{sk}\beta_j \; {}_{sk}x_j \tag{9.49}$$

$$\text{subject to} \quad \sum_{s=1}^{q} \sum_{k=1}^{h} {}_{sk}r_j^i \; {}_{sk}x_j \leqslant Q_j^i, \quad i = 1,\ldots,m, \tag{9.50}$$

$${}_{sk}x_j \leqslant {}_{sk}U_j, \tag{9.51}$$

$$s = 1,\ldots,q, \quad k = 1,\ldots,h,$$

$${}_{sk}x_j \geqslant 0, \tag{9.52}$$

where ${}_{sk}r_j^i$ is an element of a matrix of public resources (e.g., funds) $\Gamma_j \triangleq \{{}_{sk}r_j^i\}$ to be distributed to each project for the elimination of a pollutant $i$ per unit of the waste treatment. $Q_j^i$ is the sum of available public resources for elimination of the pollutant $i$ in the region $j$.

The problem is to select the optimal project levels (a set of program variables) so as to maximize the total net benefit obtained from the waste treatment under the constraint that the sum of public resources to be allocated for each pollutant elimination should not exceed the total amount of available public resources in each region.

The net benefit obtained from the waste treatment program can be calculated from the net benefit function which can be defined in terms of the negative consumer surplus. Let ${}_{sk}\bar{D}_j({}_{sk}\bar{y}_j)$ denote the negative demand function derived for all the "nuisance goods" (waste) ${}_{sk}\bar{y}_j$ which are socially supplied by plant $k$ of the industry $s$ in the region $j$. Let ${}_{sk}x_j$ be a policy variable and denote a treated quantity. Let ${}_{sk}w_j > 0$, $\sum_{k=1}^{h} {}_{sk}w_j = 1$, be a weight allotted to plant $k$ in the industry $s$ in the region $j$. The gross benefit $\tilde{B}_j({}_{sk}x_j)$ is measured in terms of the negative demand function for a nuisance good (waste) discharged by the plant $k$. Define the net benefit as gross benefit minus gross cost. Let ${}_{sk}\gamma_j({}_{sk}x_j)$ be the gross cost as a function of waste treatment ${}_{sk}x_j$ in each plant. The net benefit function ${}_{sk}B_j({}_{sk}x_j)$ of the waste treatment in the region $j$ is defined as

$$ {}_{sk}B_j({}_{sk}x_j) \triangleq {}_{sk}w_j \int_0^{{}_{sk}x_j^0} {}_{sk}\bar{D}_j({}_{sk}\eta_j)\, d_{sk}\eta_j - {}_{sk}\gamma_j({}_{sk}x_j). \tag{9.53} $$

The net benefit for the waste treatment is nothing but a positive evaluation accrued from the elimination of the negative consumer's surplus included in the negative demand functions when the cost ${}_{sk}\gamma_j$ is evaluated with the "negative price" multiplied by the amounts of the waste treatment.

The waste treatment program (9.49)-(9.52) as a primal problem is combined with an evaluation program as its dual problem. The evaluation problem is formulated as:

$$ \underset{\hat{\mu}_j^i,\ {}_{sk}\hat{\omega}_j}{\text{minimize}} \quad g_j = \sum_{i=1}^{m} \hat{\mu}_j^i Q_j^i + \sum_{s=1}^{q} \sum_{k=1}^{h} {}_{sk}\hat{\omega}_j\, {}_{sk}U_j \tag{9.54} $$

subject to

$$\sum_{i=1}^{m} \hat{\mu}_j^i \, {}_{sk}r_j^i + {}_{sk}\hat{\omega}_j \geq {}_{sk}\beta_j, \qquad s = 1,\ldots,q, \quad k = 1,\ldots,h, \tag{9.55}$$

$$\hat{\mu}_j^i \geq 0, \qquad i = 1,\ldots,m, \tag{9.56}$$

$${}_{sk}\hat{\omega}_j \geq 0, \qquad s = 1,\ldots,q, \quad k = 1,\ldots,h, \tag{9.57}$$

where $\hat{\mu}_j^i$ and ${}_{sk}\hat{\omega}_j$ are the dual variables. $\hat{\mu}_j^i$ is the imputed price, or the buying-out price for the other processes, per unit of public resources allocated for disposal of a pollutant i in the region j, and the ${}_{sk}\hat{\omega}_j$ is the opportunity cost per unit of waste treatment of the plant k belonging to the industry s. The constraint (9.55) shows that the sum of the total estimated prices (buying-out prices) of public resources per unit of the pollutant disposal and the opportunity cost per unit of the waste treatment should not be smaller than the net benefit per unit of the waste treatment for the plant k. It means that no surplus gain in each project is permitted.

The problem is to select the imputed price $\hat{\mu}_j^i$ and the opportunity cost ${}_{sk}\hat{\omega}_j$ to minimize the sum of the total estimated values (i.e., direct costs) for the available public resources and the total opportunity cost (i.e., indirect cost) for the waste treatment under the constraint (9.55) and the nonnegativity conditions (9.56) and (9.57).

Note that solving the evaluation problem (9.54)-(9.57), combined with the waste treatment program (9.49)-(9.52), results in deriving the social cost of the waste treatment. The social opportunity cost ${}_{sk}\hat{\omega}_j$ per unit of the waste treatment is, in optimal, equal to the net social benefit per unit of waste treatment minus the opportunity cost for the allocation of the public resources. It should be noted here that the social cost is also characterized by different industrial properties in each region.

### 3. Decomposition algorithm in two-level planning

The regional waste treatment program can be consolidated into a comprehensive treatment program in the two-level planning. One example is to use the decomposition algorithm by Dantzig and Wolfe (1960, 1961), whose economic implications have been discussed by Dantzig (1963) and Baumol and Fabian (1964). The way to consolidate a regional waste treatment program into a central treatment program is straightforward.

A two-level waste treatment program based on the problem (9.41)-(9.44) is formulated as follows:

$$\underset{x_j}{\text{minimize}} \quad f_0 = \sum_{j=0}^{n} c_j x_j \tag{9.58}$$

$$\text{subject to} \quad \sum_{j=0}^{n} A_j x_j \geqslant \tau_0 \tag{9.59}$$

$$B_j x_j \geqslant \tau_j, \quad j = 1,\ldots,n \tag{9.60}$$

$$x_j \leqslant U_j, \quad j = 0,\ldots,n \tag{9.61}$$

$$x_j \geqslant 0, \quad j = 0,\ldots,n, \tag{9.62}$$

where $j = 0$ denotes the central agency and $j = 1,\ldots,n$, shows each region. The number of constraints (10.60) and (10.61) is $\sum_{j=0}^{n} m_j$ in total and the number of variables is $\sum_{j=0}^{n} p_j$. $c_j$ is a row vector having $p_j$ components, $j = 0,\ldots,n$, $\tau_j$ is a column vector having $m_j$ components, $j = 0,\ldots,n$. $x_j$ is a column vector having $p_j$ components, $j = 0,\ldots,n$. $A_j$ is an $m_0 \times p_j$ matrix, $j = 0,\ldots,n$, and $B_j$ is an $m_j \times p_j$ matrix, $j = 1,\ldots,n$. The $m_0$ denotes the number of pollutants which are recognized through interregional or external pollution information available only at the central waste treatment agency. The $m_j$ denotes the number of pollutants in the region $j$. The $p_j$, $j = 1,\ldots,n$, is the number of industries in each region and $p_0$ is the number of processes for the central treatment agency. The $c_j$ is the disposal cost per unit of waste treatment. $A_j$ is a matrix of regional disposal coefficients for the activities of the joint treatment center. $B_j$ is a matrix of inner-regional disposal coefficients. $U_j$ is a column vector having $p_j$ components which denote the quantity of waste discharge. $\tau_j$ is the target level of each pollutant disposal, and $x_j$ is the program variable and the quantity of

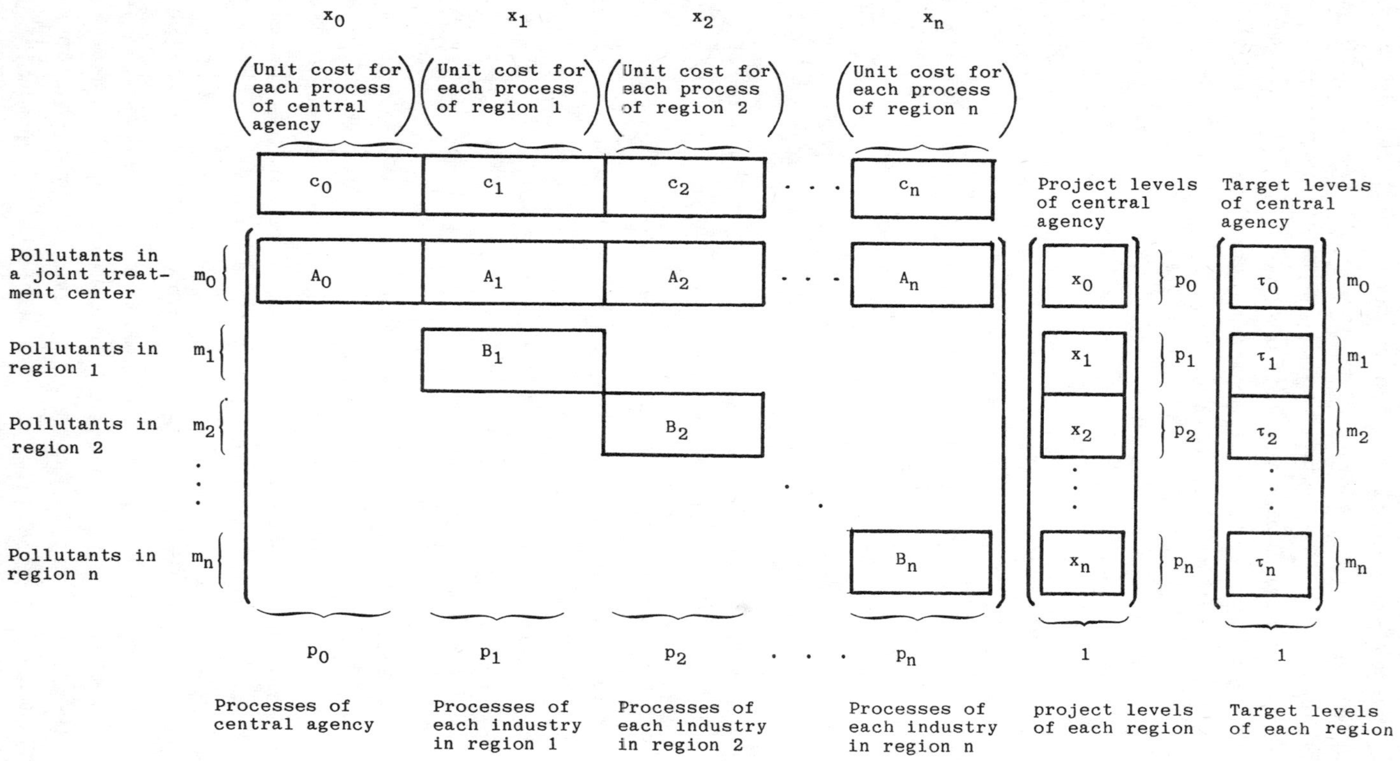


**Figure 9.4** Consolidation into the central treatment program: decomposition algorithm.

treated waste in each process (Figure 9.4).

The problem is to find the waste treatment level that minimizes the total treatment costs as defined in (9.58). The optimal solution is found as a linear convex combination of all extreme-point solutions so as to satisfy the constraints (9.60)-(9.62) for each region and also to satisfy the constraints (9.59) and (9.61) (9.62) for the central agency. The operation which minimizes (9.58) under the constraints (9.59) (9.61) and (9.62) forms a unique field of the central treatment program.

The regional program as a subproblem of the comprehensive waste treatment program is formed as follows; for a region $j$, $j = 1,\dots,n$,

$$\underset{x_j}{\text{minimize}} \quad (c_j - \pi_1 A_j)x_j \tag{9.63}$$

$$\text{subject to} \quad B_j x_j \geqslant \tau_j \tag{9.64}$$

$$x_j \leqslant U_j \tag{9.65}$$

$$x_j \geqslant 0, \tag{9.66}$$

where $\pi_1$ is a part of a vector of the simplex multiplier $\Pi \triangleq (\pi, \bar{\pi})$, $\pi \triangleq (\pi_1, \pi_2)$. The vector $\pi_1$ has $m_0$ components corresponding to the constraint (9.68) in the row vector $\pi$ which is combined with the transfer row of the following master problem. The $\pi_2$ is a vector having $p_0$ components corresponding to the constraint (9.69). The $\bar{\pi}$ is a vector having $n$ components corresponding to the convex constraint condition (9.70). The components of $\pi_1$ are interpreted as the "transfer" price for pollutant disposal per unit. The $\pi_1 A_j x_j$, $j = 1,\dots,n$, is a scalar.

Let $x_{dj}$ be the d-th extreme-point solution vector of the subproblem $j$. Then the central waste treatment program is formed as the extremal problem:

$$\underset{x_0,\ \lambda_{dj}}{\text{minimize}} \quad c_0 x_0 + \sum_{j=1}^{n} \sum_{d=1}^{N_j} c_j x_{dj} \lambda_{dj} \tag{9.67}$$

$$\text{subject to} \quad A_0x_0 + \sum_{j=1}^{n} \sum_{d=1}^{N_j} A_jx_{dj}\lambda_{dj} \geq \tau_0 \tag{9.68}$$

$$x_0 \leq U_0 \tag{9.69}$$

$$\sum_{d=1}^{N_j} \lambda_{dj} = 1, \qquad j = 1,\ldots,n, \tag{9.70}$$

$$x_0 \geq 0 \tag{9.71}$$

$$\lambda_{dj} \geq 0, \qquad d = 1,\ldots,N_j, \quad j = 1,\ldots,n. \tag{9.72}$$

The optimal solution vector $x_0^*$ and the scalar $\lambda_{dj}^*$, $j = 1,\ldots,n$, $d = 1,\ldots,N_j$, in the form of $x_j = \sum_{d=1}^{N_j} \lambda_{dj}x_{dj}$, provide the optimal solution vectors $x_0^*$, $x_j^*$ to the original problem (9.58)-(9.62), where the suffix $N_j$ denotes the number of the extreme-point solution vectors to the subproblem $j$, $j = 1,\ldots,n$.

The simplex criterion is given with

$$\sigma_{dj} = (c_j - \pi_1A_j)x_{dj} - \bar{\pi}_j, \qquad d = 1,\ldots,N_j, \quad j = 1,\ldots,n, \tag{9.73}$$

$$\sigma_{do} = c_{do} - \pi_1A_{do} - \pi_2, \qquad d = 1,\ldots,N_0, \tag{9.74}$$

as

$$\sigma_d = \min \left[ \min_j \sigma_{dj}, \ \min_d \sigma_{d0} \right]. \tag{9.75}$$

When $\sigma_d \geq 0$, the current basic feasible solution to the extremal problem provides the optimal solution to the comprehensive treatment program (9.58)-(9.62). When $\sigma_d < 0$, the processes which compose the basic solution to the extremal problem are replaced and the simplex multipliers are revised.

The economic meaning of the simplex criterion $\sigma_{dj}$ and $\sigma_{do}$ has been considered as a "reduced cost," while $c_j$ and

$c_{do}$ are direct disposal costs per unit of each process (project level). It can be shown that $\pi_1 A_j x_{dj} + \bar{\pi}_j$ and $\pi_1 A_{do} + \pi_2$ represent the costs for linear combinations of each process, respectively. Consequently the simplex criterion shows that, in the case where the direct cost occurring from the introduction of a new treatment process into the basis is lower than the cost occurring from the linear combination of the existing processes, the new treatment process is introduced into the treatment program for improving the objective function. Otherwise, it is implied that the existing treatment program attains the optimal solution to the two-level mathematical programming problem.

When the decomposed algorithm is set up as the net benefit maximization problem , the simplex criterion is defined from

$$\hat{\sigma}_{dj} = (\beta_j - \pi_1 A_j)\, x_{dj} - \bar{\pi}_j, \qquad d = 1,\ldots,N_j, \quad j = 1,\ldots,n, \tag{9.76}$$

$$\hat{\sigma}_{do} = \beta_{do} - \pi_1 A_{do} - \pi_2, \qquad d = 1,\ldots,N_o, \tag{9.77}$$

as

$$\hat{\sigma}_d = \max\,[\max_j \hat{\sigma}_{dj},\ \max_d \hat{\sigma}_{do}]. \tag{9.78}$$

When $\hat{\sigma}_d \leqslant 0$, then the existing basic feasible solution to the extremal problem provides the optimal solution. When $\hat{\sigma}_d > 0$, the replacement of the existing processes is performed for improvement of the objective function. It means that, in the case where the net benefits $\beta_j$ and $\beta_{do}$ per unit of the project level are greater than the benefits $\pi_1 A_j x_{dj} + \bar{\pi}_j$ and $\pi_1 A_{do} + \pi_2$, respectively, which are obtained by linear combinations of the existing processes, the objective function can be improved by introducing the new processes into the program. Otherwise, the net benefit of the existing processes can no longer be improved by any replacement of processes. Then the treatment program composed of the existing processes is accepted as the optimal.

In the decomposition algorithm, the extremal problem as a master program (9.67)-(9.72) carries out iterative improvements of the waste treatment program using the simplex criterion

(9.73)-(9.75), while in regional subproblems (9.63)-(9.66) the simplex multiplier $\pi_1$ is iteratively changed and is imposed within the regional objective functions (9.63). The simplex multiplier $\pi_1$ is interpreted as the "indicative price" which shows a transfer price vector indicating a transferable component (adjustable price component) among the simplex multiplier vector $\Pi$.

The iterative processes for the comprehensive waste treatment program (9.58)-(9.62) are carried on in the following way. First, the vector of provisional optimal solutions, a set of selected project levels obtained from the subproblem (9.63)-(9.66) in each region, is presented to the central treatment agency, based on the matrices of disposal coefficients obtained in each region and on the information of provisional "transfer cost" sent down from the central treatment agency. Second, the central treatment agency examines the possibilities for improving the collective objective function (9.67) by using the simplex criterion based on the proposed regional programs. The selected processes in the master program (extremal problem) are replaced and a new simplex multiplier vector is calculated, if necessary. The central treatment agency sends down the transfer price components as the revised price information of each pollutant to each region. Each region forms a new subproblem based on the newly indicated transfer price vector $\pi_1$ and sends the revised regional treatment program to the central agency. In this manner, the procedure is repeated until the revised regional program can meet the simplex criterion generated from the central treatment program.

The economic meaning of these repetitive processes is as follows. The transfer price $\pi_1$ implies a premium which is added to the regional objective function. Consider the cost minimization problem. When a regional treatment program can provide a new solution with a lower cost without any consideration about the other regional treatment programs, the central treatment agency provides a premium $\pi_1 > 0$ to the regional objective function, or otherwise adds a penalty $\pi_1 < 0$. Thus the central treatment agency as a coordinator, via adjusting all the treatment programs to be feasible, guides them to obtain an optimal project level via the execution of the master program. The $\pi_1 > 0$ indicates the opportunity benefit (external economy) and $\pi_1 < 0$ the opportunity cost (external diseconomy) for the other regions. In the case of the net benefit maximization problem, $\pi_1 > 0$ indicates the penalty and $\pi_1 < 0$ indicates the premium, which imply the opportunity cost and the opportunity benefit, respectively, for other regions.

While, in the regional waste treatment program, the dual price vector derived from the pollutant disposal possesses regional characteristics, the consolidation of each regional treatment program into a comprehensive treatment program can provide an unified evaluation for the pollutant disposal. It is known that the simplex multiplier is the shadow price as the dual variable; the simplex multiplier $\pi$ represents a marginal change of a value of the objective function in the original primal problem gained by a small change in the constraint constant. The proof is simply derived from the definition of the simplex multiplier and the formal structure of the linear programming (Lasdon 1970). The transfer price $\pi_1$ is nothing but an evaluation of the opportunity cost for the target constraints in terms of the objective function in the central waste treatment problem (master program). Thus, the comprehensive waste treatment program in the two-level planning can also provide as its by-products a comprehensive evaluation system for the pollutant disposal.

# CHAPTER 10

# IMPUTATION OF DUAL PRICES

## 10.1 Introduction

This chapter presents a device for using the dual optimal solutions, or the Kuhn-Tucker (Lagrange) multipliers generated from mathematical programming as the theoretical valuation prices for MCDM, with which multiple criteria can be made commensurate in a comparable term and based on which the judgmental phase of MCDM can be meaningfully combined with the analytical phase.

Although the theoretical valuation prices play a role corresponding to the function of the market prices in the economic systems, the intrinsic characteristic of MCDA is to introduce the coordination function of DM as the mediator for reconciling conflicting objectives in the judgmental phase. Thus the methods for assessing the theoretical valuation prices should include a device for assessing public weights to the primal evaluation accrued from the analytical processes, judgmentally and discretionally, and for providing it with some modifications from the managerial point of view.

In the preceding chapter, the preliminary dual concepts were discussed with some examples. After a general discussion on the treatment of the judgmental phase (9.1), functions of the market prices for achieving the optimal resource allocation were examined in the context of general equilibrium analysis (9.2). Then the theoretical imputed prices or opportunity costs obtained as the dual solutions are used as valuation prices for the negative utility goods (9.3). In this chapter, a generalization of the evaluation problem for MCDM is discussed, and the imputation of the dual prices to multiple criteria decision problems is examined with some extended discussions.

## 10.2 Nonlinear Programming and Dual Prices

### 10.2.1 Duality of Convex Programming and Its Implication

Duality of mathematical programming in a convex form has been examined since Wolfe (1961), and its economic interpretations were discussed in detail by Balinski and Baumol (1968). We will consider the duality of the convex programming problem including multiple objectives.

CP

$$\underset{x}{\text{maximize}} \quad f(x) \tag{10.1}$$

$$\text{subject to} \quad g_j(x) \leqslant b_j, \quad j = 1,\ldots,J \tag{10.2}$$

where $f(x)\colon R^n \to R^m$ is a set of objective functions, $x \in R^n$ is a vector of decision variables and $g_j(x)\colon R^n \to R^1$ is a constraint function. f is a concave function, $g_i$ is a convex function and both are assumed to be continuous and differentiable. The dual problem to the primal problem CP is formulated as

CP*

$$\underset{\omega}{\text{minimize}} \quad L(x,\omega) = \sum_{i=1}^{m} w_i f_i(x) - \sum_{j=1}^{J} \omega_j (g_j(x) - b_j) \tag{10.3}$$

$$\text{subject to} \quad \sum_{i=1}^{m} w_i \nabla f_i(x) - \sum_{j=1}^{J} \omega_j \nabla g_j(x) = 0 \tag{10.4}$$

$$\omega_j \geqslant 0, \quad j = 1,\ldots,j \tag{10.5}$$

where $w_i \geqslant 0$. $\nabla f_i(x) \triangleq (\partial f_i/\partial x_1,\ldots, \partial f_i/\partial x_n)$ and $\nabla g_j(x) \triangleq (\partial g_j/\partial x_1,\ldots, \partial g_j/\partial x_n)$ are the gradients of the functions $f_i$ and $g_j$, and $\omega \triangleq (\omega_1,\ldots, \omega_J)$ is the Lagrange multiplier.

The dual problem CP* is to minimize the Lagrange function $L(x, \omega)$ (10.3) formed for the primal problem CP (10.1) (10.2) under the constraint (10.4), which indicates that the primal problem CP is optimized, and the nonnegativity constraint (10.5) for the Lagrange multiplier $\omega_j$, $j = 1,\dots,J$. The duality theorem for the convex programming problem CP is established.

**Theorem 10.1.**

Assume $f_i$ be a concave function and $g_j$ be a convex function in (10.1) (10.2). If the primal problem CP possesses the solution $x^* \triangleq (x_1^*,\dots, x_n^*)$, then there exists the solution $\omega^* \triangleq (\omega_1,\dots, \omega_J) \geqslant 0$, which solves the dual problem CP*, and $wf(x^*) = L(x^*, \omega^*)$ for $w \triangleq (w_1,\dots, w_m) > 0$.

Suppose the problem CP be a resource allocation problem. Then the solution $x^*$, to the primal problem CP indicates the performance levels corresponding to the optimal resource allocation. Assume $f_i(x)$ be a concave net benefit function, $g_j(x)$ be a convex function for resource input and $b_j$ be a preassigned resource constraint. Then the problem CP is to find the performance levels $x^* \triangleq (x_1^*,\dots, x_n^*)$ as to maximize the net benefit under the resource constraints (10.2). The solution $\omega_j^*$, $j = 1,\dots,J$ to the dual problem CP* is interpreted to be an imputed price to an input resource j. Then (10.4) shows that the weighted sum of marginal benefit is equal to the total marginal cost. This equality should hold in a competitive equilibrium. (10.3) shows that a surplus of the weighted sum of the net benefit plus the initial holding (supply) of resources over the total cost for the resource requirement should be minimized. (10.5) is the sign condition.

The duality theorem 10.1 assures the possibility to simultaneously solve the evaluation problem for the input resources combined with the optimal resource allocation problem. Theorem 10.1 presumes the convexity and differentiability of the functions, and this seems to bring about a lack of generality in treating realistic decision problems. Even so, when solution procedures start from appropriate initial values, the optimal solutions can be found with local search. DM often is satisfied with finding local optimal solutions when they are in some acceptable ranges. Thus it is not necessary to insist that the duality should be globally established as indicated rigorously in the duality theorem 10.1. We will proceed to treat more generally nonconvex programming, based only on local satisfaction of the duality theorem.

### 10.2.2 Generalized Multiobjective Nonlinear Programming and the Dual Prices

In this subsection, the generalized multiobjective optimization problem and its duality are discussed. Multiobjective mathematical programming is formulated in a general form:

MOP

$$\underset{x \in S}{\text{maximize}} \quad f(x) \tag{10.6}$$

$$\text{subject to} \quad g_j(x) \leq b_j, \quad j = 1, \ldots, J, \tag{10.7}$$

where $x \in R^n$ is the decision variable, $f: R^n \to R^m$ is the vector-valued criterion function, $g_j: R^n \to R^1$ is the constraint function, $b_j \in R^1$ is the constraint constant, and $S$ is an arbitrary nonempty set, $S \subset R^n$. Using the Lagrange function of MOP,

$$L(x, \omega) \triangleq \sum_{i=1}^{m} w_i f_i(x) - \sum_{j=1}^{J} \omega_j (g_j(x) - b_j), \tag{10.8}$$

the Lagrangian problem is formed:

$\tilde{L}$

$$\underset{x \in S}{\text{maximize}} \quad L(x, \omega) \triangleq \sum_{i=1}^{m} w_i f_i(x) - \sum_{j=1}^{J} \omega_j (g_j(x) - b_j) \tag{10.9}$$

where $w^i$ is the weighting coefficient and $\omega_j \geq 0$ is the

Lagrange multiplier. The Lagrangian problem finally concerns finding $\omega^* \geqslant 0$, $\omega^* \in R^J$, such that for some $x = x^*$ (10.9) is solved. Thus the unknown variables in the Lagrangian problem are the pair $(x^*, \omega^*)$, for which (10.9) satisfies to the Kuhn-Tucker conditions:

KTCN

$$\frac{\partial L}{\partial x} = \sum_{i=1}^{m} w_i \nabla f_i(x) - \sum_{j=1}^{J} \omega_j \nabla g_j(x) = 0 \tag{10.10}$$

$$\frac{\partial L}{\partial \omega_j} = g_j(x) - b_j = 0 \tag{10.11}$$

$$\omega_j(g_j(x) - b_j) = 0, \quad \omega_j \geqslant 0 \quad j = 1,\ldots,J. \tag{10.12}$$

(10.10) and (10.11) are the first-order local optimality conditions for the unknown variables $x$ and $\omega_j$. (10.12) shows the complementary slackness condition.

If $(x^*, \omega^*)$ solves the Lagrangian problem, then $x^*$ solves the primal problem of MOP (10.6) (10.7) and $\omega^*$ solves the dual problem. $(x^*, \omega^*)$ are a local saddle point for the Lagrange function (10.8). The dual problem to MOP (10.6) (10.7) is formed as the minimax dual problem:

MOP*

$$\underset{\omega \in D}{\text{minimize}} \ \underset{x \in S}{\text{maximize}} \ L(x, \omega), \tag{10.13}$$

where $D \triangleq \{\omega | \omega \geqslant 0, \ \omega \in R^J, \ \max_{x \in S} \tilde{L}(x, \omega) \text{ exist}\}$. It is not necessary for the set $D$ to be convex. Putting the solution to the Lagrangian problem $\tilde{L}$ (10.9) as $x^*(\omega)$, (10.13) is rewritten as

MOP*

$$\underset{\omega \in D}{\text{minimize}} \ h(x^*(\omega), \omega) = h(\omega), \tag{10.14}$$

where $h(\omega) = \max_{x \in S} L(x, \omega)$. $h(\omega)$ is called the dual function.

(10.13) or (10.14) is a generalization of Wolfe's dual problem CP* (10.3)-(10.5).

**Theorem 10.2 (Minimax duality).**

If $x^*$ is a feasible solution to the primal problem MOP and $\omega^*$ is a feasible solution to the dual problem MOP* such that $f(x^*) = h(\omega^*)$, then $x^*$ is optimal to MOP and $\omega^*$ is optimal to MOP*.

In Theorem 10.2, the necessary and sufficient condition for $x^*$ to be the optimal solution to MOP is equivalent to $x^*$ and $\omega^*$ being the saddle points of $L(x, \omega)$. For $x^*$ and $\omega^*$ to be the saddle points, the convexity assumption that the function f is concave on the convex set $x \in S$, $S \subset R^n$, and the function $g_j$ is convex on the x should be satisfied, as Karlin's theorem (1959) points out. Thus only in the convex programming problem, global existence of the saddle points, $x^*$ and $\omega^*$, to MOP or MOP* and the duality of the solutions are assured. However, as suggested in the previous subsection, the possibility of finding the saddle point solution $(x^*, \omega^*)$ holds locally even in nonconvex programming problems, if the search with heuristic algorithms can start from appropriate initial values. Thus Theorem 10.2 does not lose its generality and usefulness for the local optimization. The general theorem for the minimax dual problems is presented under some assumptions, along with the related algorithm (Lasdon 1968, 1970; Wismer 1971).

**Assumption 10.1.**

(i) $S \subset R^n$ is a closed and bounded set.
(ii) $f(x)$ and all $g_j(x)$, $j = 1,\ldots,j$, are continuous functions on $x \in S$.

**Theorem 10.3 (Lasdon).**

Let assumptions (i) and (ii) hold. Let $\omega^*$ solve the dual problem MOP* and let the dual function $h(\omega)$ be differentiable at $\omega^*$. Then the solution $x^*$ to the Lagrangian problem $\tilde{L}$ (10.9) solves the primal problem of MOP (10.6)-(10.7).

Note that for function forms of MOP no assumptions such as convexity are presumed, except for the differentiability of the dual function $h(\omega)$ and Assumption 10.1. As a result, by solving the dual problem $MOP^*$ according to Theorem 10.3, the primal problem MOP is solved in more general cases. Thus the algorithm to solve nonlinear programming based on the duality theorem 10.3 establishes the evaluation system combined with the optimal allocation system.

The primal problem of MOP (10.6) (10.7) is regarded in any sense as the plural output maximization problem under the input of constraints, and the primal solution $x^*$ indicates an optimal allocation program for the decision variable $x$. The output shows performance levels of the allocation program as the goals from the point of view of multiple criteria. The input of constraints shows the means for achieving the performance levels, and the dual solutions $\omega^*$ indicate the valuation prices or the opportunity costs imputed to the plural input. The imputed prices $\omega^*$ can be used as the evaluation factor for the input of constraints in controlling and managing the multiobjective systems.

Consider the algorithm which solves MOP and MOP* as a two-level decision system. The outline of the algorithm is as follows. First, solve the Lagrangian problem $\tilde{L}$ (10.9) with the dual variable $\omega^o$ held fixed at the first level. Then solve the dual problem MOP* (10.14) to find the Lagrange multiplier $\omega^1$, using the dual function $h(\omega)$ which is evaluated with the obtained solution $x^o$, at the second level. The obtained $\omega^1$ is sent to the first level and the new solution $x^1$ is obtained there. This process is reiterated sequentially until the optimal solutions $(x^*, \omega^*)$ are obtained. When the Lagrange function $L(x, \omega)$ (10.8) is separable, individual Lagrangian problems composed for independent subsystems are solved at the first level, and dual prices are calculated as the adjusting parameter at the second level.

Consider a nonlinear system composed of $q$ subsystems separable from each other. The primal problem is

DMOP

$$\underset{x_s \in S}{\text{maximize}} \quad \sum_{s=1}^{q} f_s(x_s) \tag{10.15}$$

$$\text{subject to} \quad \sum_{s=1}^{q} g_{js}(s_x) \leqslant b_j, \quad j = 1,\ldots,J, \tag{10.16}$$

where $x_s \in R^n$, $f_s$: $R^n \to R^m$, $g_{js}$: $R^n \to R^1$, $b_j \in R^1$, $s = 1,\ldots q$.

Let the objective functions $f_s(x_s)$ be the net benefit functions obtained on performance levels $x_s$ in a region $s$, and the constraint function $g_{js}(x_s)$ be an input function of resource $j$ for some activities in the region $s$. The problem DMOP is to find the performance levels $x_s$, $s = 1,\ldots,q$ in each region so as to maximize the regional net benefit function under the constraint that total demand of a resource $j$ does not exceed total supply, $b_j$, $j = 1,\ldots,J$. Let each region perform its activity independently.

The Lagrange function of DMOP is, with $w_i > 0$,

$$L_D = \sum_{i=1}^{m} w_i \sum_{s=1}^{q} f_{is}(x_s) - \sum_{j=1}^{J} \omega_j \left( \sum_{s=1}^{q} g_{js}(x_s) - b_j \right). \tag{10.17}$$

Each subproblem is constructed using the partitioned part of the Lagrange function $L_D$.

$\tilde{L}_D^p$

$$\underset{x_s \in S}{\text{maximize}} \quad L_D^p(x_s, \omega) = \sum_{i=1}^{m} w_i f_{is}(x_s) - \sum_{j=1}^{J} \omega_j g_{js}(x_s),$$

$$s = 1,\ldots,q, \tag{10.18}$$

where $\omega_j$ is an imputed price to a resource $j$. $L_D^p(x_s, \omega)$ is interpreted as a surplus gain or a rent in each region, which is the difference between the total net benefit and the total accounting cost of the resource input. The dual function is constructed using a sum of optimized values for the partitioned problem $\tilde{L}_D^p$.

$$h(\omega) = \sum_{s=1}^{q} L_s^{p*} \, (x_s^*(\omega), \; \omega) + \sum_{j=1}^{J} \omega_j b_j \tag{10.19}$$

$$= \sum_{i=1}^{m} w_i \sum_{s=1}^{q} f_{is}^*(x_s^*) - \sum_{j=1}^{J} \omega_j \Big( \sum_{s=1}^{q} g_{js}(x_s^*) - b_j \Big). \tag{10.20}$$

The dual problem is

DMOP*

$$\underset{\omega \geqslant 0}{\text{minimize}} \quad h(\omega), \tag{10.21}$$

where $\omega \in R^J$ is dual variables. DMOP* is a problem to find a system of the nonnegative evaluation prices $\omega^* \triangleq (\omega_1^*, \omega_2^*, \ldots, \omega_J^*)$ for resource $j$, $j = 1,\ldots,J$, so as to minimize a sum of the total surplus gain (rent) for each region and the total of the imputed values to the resource endowment. DMOP* forms the evaluation problem combined with the optimal allocation problem DMOP. Economic interpretation of the algorithm to solve the dual problem DMOP* is shown using the steepest gradient method (Lasdon 1968, 1970; Wismer 1971). Applications of this algorithm are found in Haimes, Foley and Yu (1972), and Haimes, Kaplan and Husar (1972).

Step 1. Select an initial value $\omega^o \geqslant 0$, $\omega \in R^J$ with $r = 0$, where $r$ denotes the number of times of calculation.

Step 2. Solve the Lagrangian problem $\tilde{L}_D^p$ (10.18) with $\omega = \omega^r$ for each subproblem $s$, and obtain the solution $x_s(\omega^r)$, where $s = 1,\ldots,q$.

Step 3. Form the dual function $h(\omega^r)$ (10.19) and calculate its gradient $\nabla h(\omega^r) \triangleq \left(\frac{\partial h}{\partial \omega_1}, \ldots, \frac{\partial h}{\partial \omega_J}\right)\Big|_{\omega^r}$. The components of the gradient are shown as

$$-\frac{\partial h}{\partial \omega_j}\Big|_{\omega^r} = \Big( \sum_{s=1}^{q} g_{js}(x_s(\omega^r)) - b_j \Big) = e_j(\omega^r), \quad j = 1,\ldots,J, \tag{10.22}$$

which represents an excess demand $e_j(\omega^r)$ for a resource $j$.

Step 4. Define a direction of search $d_j^r$ using the gradient $\nabla h(\omega^r)$ as follows:

$$d_j^r \triangleq \begin{cases} \left.\dfrac{\partial h}{\partial \omega_j}\right|_{\omega^r} & \text{when } \omega_j^r > 0 \\ \min\left(0, \left.\dfrac{\partial h}{\partial \omega_j}\right|_{\omega^r}\right) & \text{when } \omega_j^r = 0 \end{cases} \qquad i = 1,\ldots,J. \tag{10.23}$$

A revised $\omega^{r+1}$ is determined with a step size $\alpha_j > 0$.

$$\omega_j^{r+1} = \omega_j^r - \alpha_j d_j^r, \quad j = 1,\ldots,J. \tag{10.24}$$

For selecting the step size $\alpha_j$ such that

$$h(\omega^{r+1}) < h(\omega^r), \tag{10.25}$$

a one-dimensional search problem is solved:

$$\underset{\alpha \geq 0}{\text{minimize}} \quad h(\omega^r - \alpha d^r) \tag{10.26}$$

$$\text{subject to} \quad \omega^{r+1} = \omega^r - \alpha d^r \geq 0. \tag{10.27}$$

The meaning of the gradient method is clear from (10.22)-(10.27). When the excess demand $e_j(\omega^r) > 0$ for a resource exists, the "price" $\omega_j$ is increased by (10.23) (10.24). When the excess supply $e_j(\omega^r) < 0$ exists, the "price" $\omega_j$ is decreased or unvaried. When $e_j(\omega^r) = 0$, the imputed price $\omega_j$ does not change and the equilibrium is achieved where the objective function is not improved any more by (10.25) and the optimal prices $\omega^*$ are obtained.

Step 5. When (10.25) is satisfied, return to Step 2 with $r = r+1$.

In the algorithm using the gradient method for solving the dual problem, the movement of $\omega^r$ resembles the way to vary the market prices. The calculation process to obtain the accounting or imputed price system indicates the evaluation corresponding to the "tâtonnements" processes in the market to obtain the equilibrium price system; it is regarded as a simulation of the market mechanism. Note, however, that the imputed price system should hold the nonnegativity condition, differing from the market price system in the equilibrium where the free disposal assumption is not necessarily satisfied.

Considering the general property of MOP, the dual prices $\omega^*$ can be generated for wide-ranging evaluation problems in general for multiple criteria decision analysis (MCDA). In the next section, a more precise interpretation of the Lagrange multiplier $\omega^*$ as the imputed price for MOP is scrutinized.

## 10.3 The Kuhn-Tucker Multiplier as General Evaluation Factor

The Kuhn-Tucker multiplier is defined as the Lagrange multiplier that satisfies KTCN (10.10)-(10.12) and indicates the attainment of dual optimality in mathematical programming according to Theorem 10.3. In Chapter 2, it has been discussed that the relative "price" ratio assessed in the multiple criteria decision problem shows a trade-off ratio between objectives and thus is used as an index for relative weights among the multiple objectives. The trade-off ratio between objectives is interpreted to represent the opportunity cost of one objective expressed in terms of the other objective. To give the trade-off ratio the meaning of the relative opportunity costs has merit to concretely ascertain the substance of the trade-offs. Therefore this device is useful for providing information to achieve the best-compromised decisions for the preferred policy program. Furthermore, as discussed in the same chapter, although the interpretation of the Lagrange multiplier as the shadow price has been suggested in economic literature since Hicks (1939) and Samuelson (1947), the intention to attain the preferred solution with it has not appeared in their discussions. This section concerns the interpretation of the Kuhn-Tucker multiplier as the shadow price to represent the relative evaluation among objectives in MCDM with the clarification of its contents. The intervention, or mediation, for their coordination in managerial decision making is discussed in the subsequent section.

Consider the multiobjective programming problem in a vector form.

MOP

$$\underset{x}{\text{maximize}} \quad f(x) \tag{10.28}$$

$$\text{subject to} \quad g(x) \leqslant b, \tag{10.29}$$

where $x \in R^n$, $f: R^n \to R^m$, $g: R^n \to R^J$, $b \in R^J$.

The Lagrange function of (10.28) (10.29) is in a vector form

$$\tilde{L} \triangleq wf(x) - \lambda(g(x) - b), \tag{10.30}$$

where $w \in R^m$ is the weighting coefficient and $\lambda \in R^J$ is a vector of the Lagrange multiplier. Let $x = x(b)$ and $\lambda = \lambda(b)$. Then by vector differentiation

$$\frac{\partial \tilde{L}}{\partial b} = (w\frac{\partial f}{\partial x} - \lambda\frac{\partial g}{\partial x}) \frac{\partial x}{\partial b} - \frac{\partial \lambda}{\partial b} (g(x) - b) + \lambda. \tag{10.31}$$

At the optimal, from the Kuhn-Tucker conditions, $w\frac{\partial f}{\partial x} - \lambda\frac{\partial g}{\partial x} = 0$, $g(x) \leqslant b$, $\lambda(g(x) - b) = 0$, $\lambda \geqslant 0$, when $\lambda > 0$,

$$\frac{\partial \tilde{L}}{\partial b} = w\frac{\partial f}{\partial b} = \lambda. \tag{10.32}$$

(10.32) represents that the Kuhn-Tucker multiplier $\lambda$ indicates a sensitivity, or a relative ratio, of a marginal variation of the weighted objective function $wf(x)$ to a marginal variation of the constraint constant $b$. In other words, the $\lambda$-value shows a trade-off ratio indicating how many units of the constraint constant $b$ should be given up in order to increase one marginal unit of the weighted objective function $wf$. It indicates the trade-off rates with the weights $w$ between the objectives and the constraints, where the constraint constants $b$ also represent the other objectives. Thus the $\lambda$ is interpreted as the theoretical price that represents the weighted trade-off rate between the objectives, which is the opportunity cost of the constraint constant b measured in terms of the weighted objective function. Thus the Lagrange multiplier satisfying the Kuhn-Tucker conditions is interpreted as the imputed price to which specific substance is bestowed. In other words, the dual price, the Kuhn-Tucker multiplier, obtained in the analytical phase of MCDM can be treated as an evaluation factor with substantial contents, and used as the basis of a further manipulation in its judgmental phase.

The problem is to verify that the differentiation (10.31) with $x = x(b)$ and $\lambda = \lambda(b)$ exists for the Lagrange function (10.30). This problem has been treated in the sensitivity theorem for mathematical programming (Phipps 1952; Luenberger 1973; Robinson 1974; Fiacco 1976, 1983; Armacost and Fiacco 1976; etc.). For the discussion, the second-order optimality conditions should be considered.

The Hessian matrix for $x$ of the Lagrange function $\tilde{L}$ (10.30) is denoted as

$$\nabla_x^2 \tilde{L}(x) \triangleq \begin{bmatrix} \frac{\partial^2 \tilde{L}}{\partial x_1 \partial x_1}, & \frac{\partial^2 \tilde{L}}{\partial x_1 \partial x_2}, & \ldots, & \frac{\partial^2 \tilde{L}}{\partial x_1 \partial x_n} \\ \frac{\partial^2 \tilde{L}}{\partial x_2 \partial x_1}, & \frac{\partial^2 \tilde{L}}{\partial x_2 \partial x_2}, & \ldots, & \frac{\partial^2 \tilde{L}}{\partial x_2 \partial x_n} \\ \vdots & \vdots & & \vdots \\ \frac{\partial^2 \tilde{L}}{\partial x_n \partial x_1}, & \frac{\partial^2 \tilde{L}}{\partial x_n \partial x_2}, & \ldots, & \frac{\partial^2 \tilde{L}}{\partial x_n \partial x_n} \end{bmatrix}, \tag{10.33}$$

where $\dfrac{\partial^2 \tilde{L}}{\partial x_s \partial x_t} = \sum_{i=1}^{m} w_i \dfrac{\partial^2 f_i}{\partial x_s \partial x_t} - \sum_{j=1}^{J} \lambda_j \dfrac{\partial^2 g_j}{\partial x_s \partial x_t}$.

The regularity condition for the constraint (10.29) is defined.

**Definition 10.1.**

Let $x^*$ satisfy the constraint (10.29) and $I$ be a set of indices $j$, $j = 1,\ldots,J$, such that $g_j(x^*) = b_j$, i.e., the constraint is active. Then $g_j$, $j \in I$, is said to satisfy the regularity condition at $x^*$ and $x^*$ is said to be a regular point of the constraint (10.29), if the gradient vectors $\nabla g_j(x^*)$, $j \in I$, are linearly independent.

The second-order necessary conditions are shown with those concepts.

**Theorem 10.4.**

Suppose the functions $f_i$, $g_j \in C^2$, and $x^*$ be a regular point of the constraints (10.29). If $x^*$ is a local optimal point of MOP (10.28) (10.29), then there exists the Lagrange multiplier $\lambda \in R^J$, $\lambda \geqslant 0$, such that the Kuhn-Tucker conditions hold and the Hessian matrix (10.33) of the Lagrange function (10.30) is negative semidefinite on the tangent subspace of the active constraints at $x^*$.

A subset $M \subset R^n$ is said to be a subspace of $R^n$, if $x + y \in M$ and $\alpha x \in M$ for a vector $x, y \in M$ and a scalar $\alpha \in R^1$. The vectors $y^1, \ldots, y^k \in R^n$ are said to span the subspace $M$, if $M$ is represented as a set of all linear combinations of the vectors $y^1, \ldots, y^k$ such as

$$M \triangleq \{y \in R^n \mid y = \alpha_1 y^1 + \alpha_2 y^2 + \ldots + \alpha_k y^k, \quad \alpha_1, \ldots, \alpha_k \in R^1\}. \tag{10.34}$$

The tangent subspace of the active constraints is defined as a subspace $M$ composed of all tangent vectors $y \in R^n$ such that $\nabla g_j(x)^T y = 0$ for all $j \in I^*$, $I^* \subset I$, where $I^* \triangleq \{j \mid g_j(x) = b_j,\ \lambda_j > 0,\ j = 1, \ldots, J\}$. The Hessian matrix $\nabla_x^2 \tilde{L}(x, \lambda)$ is said to be negative semidefinite if $y^T \nabla_x^2 \tilde{L}(x, \lambda) y \leqslant 0$ for all non-zero vectors $y$. If $y^T \nabla_x^2 \tilde{L}(x, \lambda) y < 0$, then the Hessian matrix is said to be negative definite. The superscript $T$ denotes a transposition of the vector.

The second-order necessary condition in Theorem 10.4 can be stated differently. The necessary condition for $x^*$ to be the local optimal solution of MOP (10.28) (10.29) is that there be a Lagrange multiplier $\lambda \geqslant 0$ holding the Kuhn-Tucker conditions and that, for all tangent vectors $y \neq 0$, $y \in M$, such that

$$\nabla g_j(x^*)^T y = 0, \quad j \in I^*, \tag{10.35}$$

there holds

$$y^T \nabla^2 \tilde{L}(x^*, \lambda) y \leqslant 0. \tag{10.36}$$

When there is a degenerated inequality constraint, namely when there is a Lagrange multiplier $\lambda_j = 0$ combined with an active constraint $g_j(x) = b_j$, (10.35) should be replaced by

$$\begin{aligned} &\nabla g_j(x^*)^T y \leqslant 0, \quad j \in I - I^* \\ &\nabla g_j(x^*)^T y = 0, \quad j \in I^*. \end{aligned} \tag{10.37}$$

Putting it differently, (10.36) should hold for all $y \in M$, $y \neq 0$, satisfying (10.37).

The second-order sufficiency condition of optimality is presented.

**Theorem 10.5.**

Suppose the functions $f_i$, $g_j \in C^2$. The sufficient conditions for $x^*$ to be the locally optimal (maximum) solution of MOP (10.28) (10.29) are that there exists the Lagrange multiplier $\lambda \in R^J$, $\lambda \geqslant 0$, satisfying the Kuhn-Tucker conditions and that the Hessian matrix (10.33) is negative definite on the tangent subspace of the active constraint at $x^*$.

Theorem 10.5 indicates that, for $x^*$ to be a local optimal solution of (10.28) (10.29), the Lagrange multiplier $\lambda \geqslant 0$ satisfying the Kuhn-Tucker conditions should exist, and also

$$y^T \nabla_x^2 \tilde{L}(x^*, \lambda) y < 0 \tag{10.38}$$

should hold for all $y \neq 0$ in the subspace $M$ to satisfy (10.37).

The second-order sufficient conditions only assure the local, not global, optimality of $x^*$ because the convexity of the functions is not assumed. However, as stated before, the local optimality searched from proper initial values can reveal enough usefulness of the algorithms for nonconvex cases.

The second-order sufficient conditions of optimality are used to describe the sensitivity theorem.

Rewrite MOP (10.28) (10.29) with a perturbation $\varepsilon$ in the constraint condition.

MOP($\varepsilon$)

$$\underset{x}{\text{maximize}} \quad f(x) \tag{10.39}$$

$$\text{subject to} \quad g_j(x) \leqslant \bar{\varepsilon}_j \qquad j = 1,\ldots,J \tag{10.40}$$

where $f : R^n \to R^m$, $x \in R^n$, and $\bar{\varepsilon}_j \triangleq b_j + \varepsilon_j$. Note that, taken $b_j$ as an origin, the perturbation is generated in the neighborhood of $b_j$. The problem is to perturb the constraint constant $b_j$ and to show the property of the sensitivity of the objective function with respect to the perturbation. The Lagrange function of MOP($\varepsilon$) is

$$\tilde{L}(x, \lambda, \varepsilon) = \sum_{i=1}^{m} w_i f_i(x) - \sum_{i=1}^{J} \lambda_j (g_j(x) - \bar{\varepsilon}_j) \tag{10.41}$$

where $\lambda_j$ is the Lagrange multiplier.

The existence theorem of sensitivity defined by the Kuhn-Tucker multiplier (Armacost and Fiacco 1975, 1976; Fiacco 1983) is extended for MOP($\varepsilon$) as follows.

**Theorem 10.6 (Sensitivity theorem).**

If (i) the functions $f \in R^m$, $g_j$, $j = 1,\ldots,J$, in (10.39) (10.40) are twice continuously differentiable for $(x, \bar{\varepsilon})$, $\bar{\varepsilon} \in R^J$, in the neighborhood of $(x^*, b)$, (ii) the second-order sufficient conditions for local optimality of MOP(0) hold at $x^* \in R^n$ with the associated Lagrange multiplier $\lambda^* \in R^J$, (iii) the gradient vectors $\nabla_x \hat{g}_j(x^*, b) \triangleq \partial \hat{g}_j(x^*, b)/\partial x$ for all active constraints $\hat{g}_j(x^*, b) = 0$ are linearly independent, and (iv) $\lambda_j > 0$ when $\hat{g}_j(x^*, b) = 0$, $j = 1,\ldots,J$, (i.e., strict complementarity holds), then

(a) $x^*$ is a local optimal solution to MOP(0) and the associated Lagrange multiplier $\lambda^* \in R^J$ is uniquely determined.

(b) Put the local optimal solution to MOP(0) as $\xi(0) \triangleq (x^*, \lambda^*)$. There exists a unique, once continuously differentiable vector-valued function $\xi^*(\bar{\varepsilon}) \triangleq (x^*(\bar{\varepsilon}), \lambda^*(\bar{\varepsilon}))$, $\bar{\varepsilon} \triangleq \{\bar{\varepsilon}_j\}$, $j = 1,\ldots,J$, satisfying the second-order sufficient conditions as a local optimal solution to MOP($\varepsilon$) for $\bar{\varepsilon}$ in a neighborhood of b. Hence the $x^*(\bar{\varepsilon})$ with the associated Lagrange multiplier $\lambda^*(\bar{\varepsilon})$ is a locally unique optimal solution.

(c) For $\bar{\varepsilon}$ in a neighborhood of b,

$$wf^*(\bar{\varepsilon}) = \tilde{L}^*(\bar{\varepsilon}). \tag{10.42}$$

(d) Strict complementarity for the active constraint and linear independence of the gradient vector $\nabla g_j(x(\bar{\varepsilon}))$, $j \in I$, hold at $x(\bar{\varepsilon})$ for $\bar{\varepsilon}$ in a neighborhood of b.

(e) For $\bar{\varepsilon}$ in a neighborhood of b,

$$w\nabla_{\bar{\varepsilon}} f^*(\bar{\varepsilon}) \triangleq w\,\frac{\partial f^*(x(\bar{\varepsilon}))}{\partial \bar{\varepsilon}} = \lambda^*(\bar{\varepsilon}). \tag{10.43}$$

(f) For $\bar{\varepsilon}$ in a neighborhood of b,

$$w\nabla^2_{\bar{\varepsilon}}\, f^*(\varepsilon) \triangleq w\,\frac{\partial^2 f^*(\bar{\varepsilon})}{\partial \bar{\varepsilon}^2} = \frac{\partial \lambda^*(\bar{\varepsilon})}{\partial \bar{\varepsilon}}. \tag{10.44}$$

The (e) and (f) provide the sensitivity result for the Kuhn-Tucker multiplier $\lambda$. Particularly (10.43) represents that a weighted sum of variations (sensitivity) of the optimal values $f^*(x(\bar{\varepsilon}))$ of the objective functions (10.39) relative to a variation of a perturbation $\varepsilon$ on the constraint constant b in (10.40) is shown as a value of the Kuhn-Tucker multiplier $\lambda^*(\bar{\varepsilon})$.

Comparing MOP($\varepsilon$) with the perturbation $\varepsilon$ (10.39) (10.40) with the problem MOP (10.28) (10.29), Theorem 10.6 (b) (e) assures that when $\varepsilon \to 0$

$$w \frac{\partial f^*(x(\bar{\varepsilon}))}{\partial \bar{\varepsilon}} = \lambda^*(\bar{\varepsilon}) \Rightarrow w \frac{\partial f^*(x(b))}{\partial b} = \lambda^*(b). \tag{10.45}$$

In short, the component of the gradient vector of the weighted objective functions indicates a weighted marginal variation in the optimal value of the objective function for a marginal variation in the constraint constant, and is represented by the Kuhn-Tucker multiplier $\lambda^*(\bar{\varepsilon})|_{\varepsilon\to 0} \approx \lambda^*(b)$. The Kuhn-Tucker multiplier is interpreted as the imputed price, or the opportunity cost, of the constraint constant measured in terms of a marginal unit of the weighted objective function. This value can be interpreted as representing a trade-off value between various policy aims assigned in different levels.

Theorem 10.6 (b) assures that there exist vectors $x^*(\bar{\varepsilon})$ and $\lambda^*(\bar{\varepsilon})$ to make the differentiation (10.43) possible for the local optimal values of MOP($\varepsilon$).

**Proof of Theorem 10.6.** Consider the equations showing the Kuhn-Tucker conditions for MOP($\varepsilon$) (10.39) (10.40):

$$\nabla_x L(x, \lambda, \bar{\varepsilon}) = 0 \tag{10.46}$$

$$\lambda \hat{g}(x, \bar{\varepsilon}) = 0. \tag{10.47}$$

The Jacobian matrix of (10.46) and (10.47) is shown, at $(x^*, \lambda^*, \varepsilon) \in R^n \times R^J \times R^J$, by

$$J^o \triangleq \begin{bmatrix} \nabla_x^2 L(x^*, \lambda^*, \bar{\varepsilon}), \ldots, & -\nabla_x g_j(x^*, \bar{\varepsilon}), \ldots \\ \vdots & \ddots \\ \lambda_j^* \nabla_x \hat{g}_j(x, \bar{\varepsilon})^T, & g_j(x^*, \bar{\varepsilon}), \\ \vdots & \ddots \end{bmatrix}. \tag{10.48}$$

The $(n + J) \times (n + J)$ Jacobian matrix (10.48) is known to be nonsingular ($\det J^o \neq 0$), or to have an inverse matrix ${J^o}^{-1}$, under the assumptions (i)-(iv) of Theorem 10.6. Hence the implicit function theorem can be applied to (10.46) and (10.49): there exist continuously differentiable functions $x(\bar{\varepsilon})$ and $\lambda(\bar{\varepsilon})$ such that

$$x^* = x(\bar{\varepsilon}), \qquad \lambda^* = \lambda(\bar{\varepsilon}) \tag{10.49}$$

and satisfying

$$\nabla_x L(x(\bar{\varepsilon}), \lambda(\bar{\varepsilon}), \bar{\varepsilon}) = 0 \tag{10.50}$$

$$\lambda(\bar{\varepsilon})\hat{g}(x(\bar{\varepsilon}), \bar{\varepsilon}) = 0, \tag{10.51}$$

in a proper neighborhood $\mathcal{N}$ of b. Note that the nonsingular matrix has linearly independent columns. Taking the neighborhood $\mathcal{N}$ as sufficiently small, x(b) and λ(b) is assured.

Using $x(\bar{\varepsilon})$ and $\lambda(\bar{\varepsilon})$, the complementary slackness condition $\lambda(\bar{\varepsilon})(g(x(\bar{\varepsilon})) - \bar{\varepsilon}) = 0$ yields from (10.41)

$$\tilde{L}^*(x(\bar{\varepsilon}), \lambda(\bar{\varepsilon}), \bar{\varepsilon}) = wf^*(x(\bar{\varepsilon}), \bar{\varepsilon}), \tag{10.52}$$

which is Theorem 10.6 (c).

Differentiating (10.41) as

$$\nabla_{\bar{\varepsilon}} L(x(\bar{\varepsilon}), \lambda(\bar{\varepsilon}), \bar{\varepsilon}) = [w\nabla_x f(x(\bar{\varepsilon})) - \lambda(\bar{\varepsilon})\nabla_x g(x(\bar{\varepsilon}))]\nabla_{\bar{\varepsilon}} x(\bar{\varepsilon})$$

$$- \nabla_{\bar{\varepsilon}}\lambda(\bar{\varepsilon})(g(x(\bar{\varepsilon})) - \bar{\varepsilon})) + \lambda(\bar{\varepsilon}) \tag{10.53}$$

yields, for $\lambda^* > 0$ from the Kuhn-Tucker conditions,

$$\nabla_{\bar{\varepsilon}} L^*(x(\bar{\varepsilon}), \lambda(\bar{\varepsilon}), \bar{\varepsilon}) = w\nabla_{\bar{\varepsilon}} f^*(x(\bar{\varepsilon}), \bar{\varepsilon}) = \lambda^*(\bar{\varepsilon}), \tag{10.54}$$

which is Theorem 10.6 (e).

Theorem 10.6 (e) implies that the Kuhn-Tucker multiplier $\lambda^*$, combined with the local optimal solution $x^*$ in the neighborhood of x(b) and λ(b), indicates the sensitivity of the objective function to the marginal variation of the constraint constant b. In other words, the $\lambda^*(b)$-value in (10.45) indicates a marginal evaluation (the opportunity cost) of the constraint constant b measured in terms of the marginal variation of the weighted objective function; it represents quantitatively how many units of the constraint constant should be relaxed for varying one marginal unit of the weighted objective function.

Thus the Kuhn-Tucker multiplier in multiobjective mathematical programming can be used effectively as a measure for performing logical experiments for multiobjective evaluation by articulating value trade-offs among objectives which can be structured in multiple levels. As discussed in Chapter 2, the weighting parameter w in MOP is also assessed as representing the value trade-offs between objective functions. However, the assessment for w as the optimal weight must be performed entirely with subjective decisions even though DM can use complete information for it. In general, the optimal solutions to MOP (10.28) (10.29) only provide the Pareto optimal solutions depending on alternative w-values taken by decision makers. Thus multiobjective mathematical programming still includes some arbitrariness in its original form. Furthermore, the preferred solution to MOP should be obtained with some additional devices for manipulating the judgmental phase. In the next section, a method for modifying the analytical results with some coordination processes is presented. This method is used for numerical evaluation to determine preferred policy programs in MCDM.

## 10.4 Nested Lagrangian Multiplier (NLM) Method

### 10.4.1 Introduction

In this section, we are concerned with an extended utilization of the Kuhn-Tucker multiplier as a basic evaluation factor in MCDM. The Kuhn-Tucker multiplier, represented in the form of (10.45), is interpreted as the imputed price, or the opportunity cost, for the systems objective, which is imputed to a marginal unit of the constraint constant revealed in terms of the marginal change of the objective function and analytically articulates the value trade-offs among policy aims represented in these values. This implication as the systems evaluator can be primarily held in the single objective optimization problem (SOP). This form is simpler to manipulate because it does not include any subjective decision process in the optimization.

Specifically, the weighting coefficients for the multiple objective functions can be simply put as 1 for SOP. Although the ε-constraint method is an alternative device with the same idea that reduce MOP to SOP, the ε-constraint method primarily concerns generating the Pareto optimal solutions. Thus the assessor (DM) must resort to a tremendous amount of work to complete it. In this section, the utilization of the Kuhn-Tucker multiplier in SOP is extended to the multiobjective decision problem (MDP). With this device, the MDP can once be reduced to a set of plural SOP, and then reintegrated in MDP. In this process, the coordination process of DM for the systems valuation is also included. For this purpose, the valuation price system generated as the Kuhn-Tucker multipliers is converted to more commensurate terms of the quasi-utility function and then integrated into multiattribute utility function (MUF) which takes as their components (arguments) the quasi-utility functions. This method once distinctly separates the analytical phase of MCDM from the judgmental phase and then integrate the analytical results in the judgmental phase with deliberate procedures for determining the preferred policy program. Considerations for integrating both phases are the core of MCDM.

The main idea of this method is based on the following considerations.

(i) Multiobjective interpretation of mathematical programming, which is based on a hierarchical structuring of the problem complex. The systems' objectives that are noncommensurable and conflicting with each other are configured in a multilevel according to their properties.

(ii) Generation of the Kuhn-Tucker multipliers and their utilization as the basic evaluation factor. This process is performed at an infimal level of the hierarchical configuration.

(iii) Introducing the multiattribute preference analysis. Multiattribute utility analysis is used at a supremal level, in integration with the analytical results of mathematical programming.

Using this device, MOP is reduced to a set of SOP in the first step of MCDM, and then is coordinated into an overall MDP in the second step. This procedure is primarily based on the duality of mathematical programming and the multiattribute preference analysis, which have been discussed through the preceding chapters.

This method is named the nested Lagrangian multiplier (NLM) method (Seo 1977, 1978a,b, 1980; Seo and Sakawa 1979a,b). In the following sections, the above aspects of the NLM method will be discussed in some detail.

### 10.4.2 Multiobjective Interpretation of Mathematical Programming

The multiobjective interpretation of mathematical programming is based on a hierarchical configuration of multiple objectives. A multiple criteria decision problem is regarded as an objectives complex, or an objectives system, composed of many noncommensurate and conflicting objectives. Those objectives are decomposed into subsystems in multilevel according to their peculiarities and consolidated into a hierarchical configuration. The objectives configuration is considered in two major groups. One objectives group G1 has more clear-cut properties to be mathematically defined and is appropriate for quantitative modeling and optimization. The other objectives group G2 has more comprehensive and ambiguous properties and is appropriate for discretionary and coordinating functions of DM. Those two groups can be treated in two layers which correspond to the analytical and judgmental phases of MCDM and are structured in a hierarchical modeling. Mathematical programming treats the objectives in G1 in the infimal level of the hierarchical configuration, and decomposes them into further subsystems.

Consider the multiple criteria decision problem (MDP).

MDP

$$\sup_{\mathbf{x}_j \in \Gamma} V(\mathbf{x}_1, \mathbf{x}_2, \ldots, \mathbf{x}_m, \mathbf{x}_{m+1}, \ldots, \mathbf{x}_r) \tag{10.55}$$

where $\mathbf{x}_j \in R^1$ is a systems attribute which denotes a performance level of a systems objective and takes a value in a feasible set $\Gamma$. $V: R^r \to R^1$ is a vector-valued criterion function of DM. Using the mathematical programming formulation, MDP (10.55) is rewritten as

MDP

$$\underset{x_i \in X}{\text{Maximize}} \quad V(f_1(x_1), f_2(x_2), \ldots, f_q(x_q)) \tag{10.56}$$

where $x_i \in R^n$ is a vector of decision variables for subsystem $i$, $f_i: R^n \to R^1$, is an objective function defined on the n-dimensional decision vector $x_i$, and $X \subset R^n$ is a feasible set for the overall system:

$$x_i \in X \triangleq \{x_i \,|\, x_i \in R^n, \; g_j(x) \leqslant b, \quad j = 1, \ldots, J\}. \tag{10.57}$$

The criterion function $V: R^q \to R^1$ is interpreted as a preference function of DM for the overall decision problem defined on the multiple objective functions $f_i(x_i)$, $i = 1, \ldots, q$.

Note that, in MDP (10.56), the $m$ objectives in the original system of MDP are structured into $q$ subsystems and that for each subsystem a mathematical programming problem can be constructed, in which multiple objectives are also structured in the hierarchical configuration.

Each subsystem is described independently as follows.

DMDP

$$\underset{x_i \in X_i}{\text{maximize}} \quad f_i(x_i), \quad i = 1, \ldots, q, \tag{10.58}$$

where $X_i \subset R^n$ is a feasible set for the subsystem $i$.

MDP (10.56) corresponds to the supremal level of the hierarchical configuration and DMDP (10.58) corresponds to the infimal level. The hierarchical configuration is depicted in Figure 10.1. In the infimal level, or the first layer, mathematical optimization for the partitioned subsystem is executed independently without any regard to other subsystems. In the supremal level, or the second layer, the coordination process of DM is introduced to the results of the mathematical optimization for each subsystem and a search for the preferred

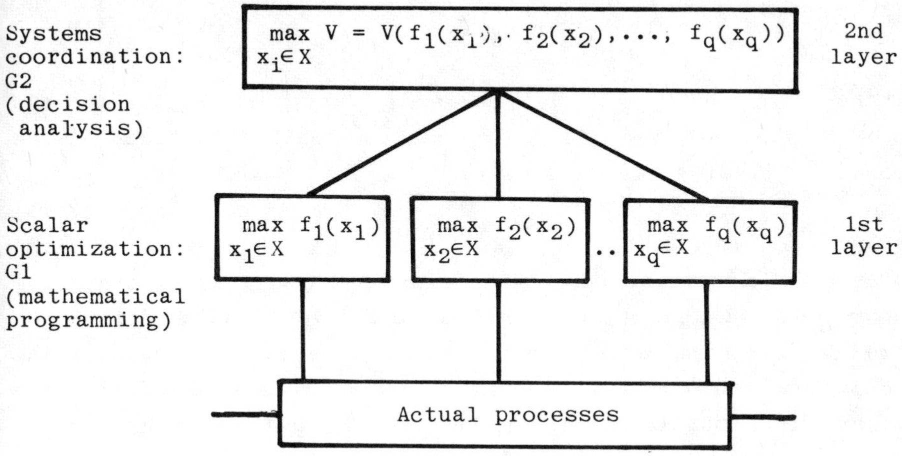


**Figure 10.1 Systems decomposition and coordination in a hierarchical system (two-layer configuration).**

policy program is performed. In the infimal level, mathematical programming is applied. In the supremal level, multiattribute decision analysis is applied, where $\mathbf{x}_{m+1},\ldots,\mathbf{x}_r$ are taken into account in the process to evaluate V (10.56).

In the two-layer system, the first layer problem is represented as the primal problem of mathematical programming, and the second layer treats the evaluation based on the dual prices generated from the dual problem combined with the primal problem. In this way, in the hierarchical interpretation of mathematical programming (Ijiri 1965), we will introduce the dual price implication of the mathematical programming.

Consider the mathematical programming problem for a subsystem i, i = 1,...,q, in a standard form.

DMDP

$$\underset{x_i}{\text{maximize}} \quad f_i(x_i) \tag{10.59}$$

$$\text{subject to} \quad g_{si}(x\ ) \leqslant d_{si}, \quad s = 1,\ldots,p_i \tag{10.60}$$

$$h_{ki}(x_i) \leqslant b_{ki}, \quad k = p_i+1,\ldots,J_i \tag{10.61}$$

$$a_i \leqslant x_i \leqslant c_i, \tag{10.62}$$

where $x_i \in R^n$ is the decision variable, $a_i \in R^n$ and $c_i \in R^n$ are lower-and upper-bounds constraint constants on the policy variable $x_i$, respectively, $g_{si}: R^n \to R^1$ is a policy (soft) constraint function, $d_{si} \in R^1$ is a policy (soft) constraint constant, $h_{ki}: R^n \to R^1$ is a technical (hard) constraint function, $b_{ki} \in R^1$ is a technical (hard) constraint constant, and $f_i: R^n \to R^1$ is an objective function defined on the decision variables in a subsystem $i$. The constraint condition (10.60) is determined by a policy aim, and the constraint constant $d_{si}$ on the right-hand side can be mitigated to some extent. The constraint condition (10.61) is determined technically, and the constraint constants $b_{ki}$ on the right-hand side cannot discretionally be relaxed. The constraint (10.62) has special properties, and is separately treated in the computer algorithms.

Thus, in the decision process formulated with DMDP (10.59)-(10.62), only value trade-offs between (10.59) and (10.60) are left under investigations. A set $(f_i, d_{si}, x_i)$ represents an objectives configuration determined by policy aims. The $f_i$, an objective function of a subsystem $i$, is a lower-level objective in the repartitioned objectives hierarchy in the first layer, and the policy constraint constant $d_{si}$, $s = 1,\ldots,p_i$, indicates an upper-level objective. The policy variable $x_i$ is the lowest level objective or a policy means. Thus the problem DMDP (10.59)-(10.62) represents a multiobjective representation in a hierarchical configuration in the first layer.

In the first layer, the solution to DMDP is generated independently of each of the others. On the one hand, the primal optimal solution $x_i^*$ is presented to the actual processes to indicate a policy program for an optimal resource allocation in each subsystem. On the other hand, the dual optimal solution $\lambda_{si}^*$ (Kuhn-Tucker multiplier) is reported to the second layer to indicate the valuation price system for each subsystem. This two layer system in mathematical programming is depicted in Figure 10.2.

**Example.** In the case of regional planning, the $\lambda_{si}^*$ is used as the basic evaluation factor for the policy constraint constant

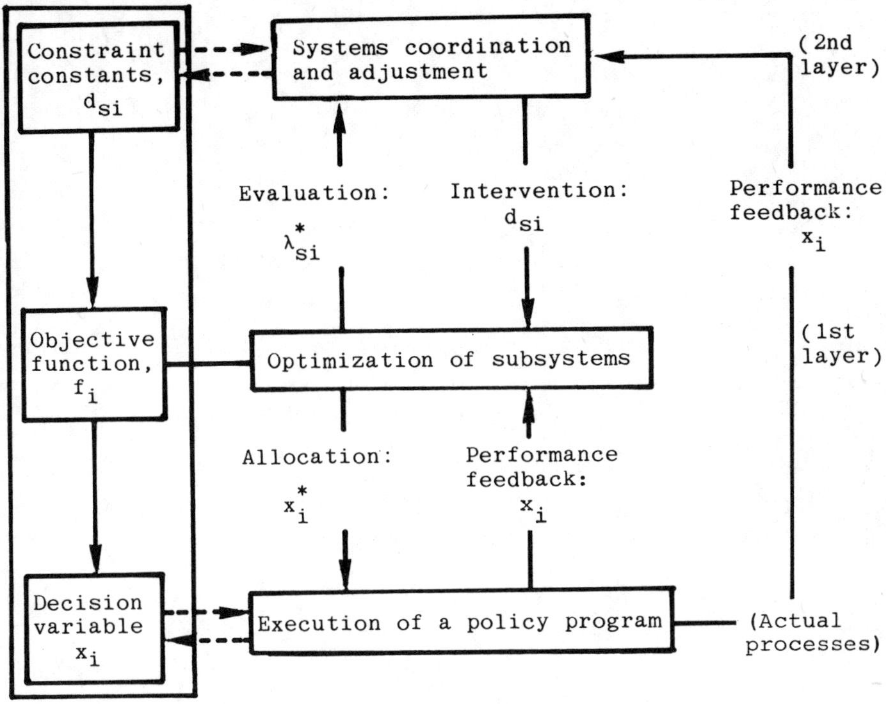


**Figure 10.2 Mathematical programming as a multilevel objectives composition.**

$d_{si}$, such as the environmental standard imposed by the regional authority as an upper-level decision unit, which is examined from the point of view of maximizing a local objective function such as industrial output in a subregion $i$ as a lower-level decision unit. $g_{si}$ is a constraint function for the subregion $i$ such as a local pollution discharge function, and $x_i$ is the local decision variable such as capital formation and land-use in each subregion.

### 10.4.3 The Kuhn-Tucker Multiplier as the Basic Evaluation Factor

Interpretation of the Kuhn-Tucker multiplier as the valuation price is reconsidered for the above systems structure. A Lagrange function of DMDP for (10.59)-(10.61) is formulated as, for $x_i \in S \triangleq \{x_i \mid a_i \leq x_i \leq c_i\}$,

$\bar{L}$

$$\bar{L}_i(x_i, \lambda_i) \triangleq f_i(x_i) - \sum_{s=1}^{p_i} \lambda_{si}(g_{si}(x_i) - d_{si})$$

$$- \sum_{k=p_i+1}^{J_i} \lambda_{ki}(h_{ki}(x_i) - b_{ki}) \qquad (10.63)$$

where $\lambda_{si} \in R^1$, and $\lambda_{ki} \in R^1$, are the Lagrange multipliers. Suppose the DMDP has the optimal solution $x_i^*$. Then the Kuhn-Tucker theorem guarantees, under the conditions $f_i \in C^1$, $g_{si}$, $h_{ki} \in C^1$ and holding the constraint qualification, the existence of the Lagrange multiplier $\lambda_i^* \geq 0$, $\lambda_i^* \in R^{J_i}$, satisfying the Kuhn-Tucker conditions for $x_i \in S$.

$$\nabla f_i(x_i) - \sum_{s=1}^{p_i} \lambda_{si} \nabla g_{si}(x_i) - \sum_{k=p_i+1}^{j_i} \lambda_{ki} \nabla h_{ki}(x_i) = 0, \qquad (10.64)$$

$$\lambda_{si} \geq 0, \quad \lambda_{si}(g_{si}(x_i) - d_{si}) = 0, \quad s = 1,\ldots,p_i, \qquad (10.65)$$

$$\lambda_{ki} \geq 0, \quad \lambda_{ki}(h_{ki}(x_i) - b_{ki}) = 0, \quad k = p_i+1,\ldots,J_i, \qquad (10.66)$$

Recall here that the Kuhn-Tucker theorem shows the existence of the Kuhn-Tucker multiplier as the first-order necessary condition for the $x_i^*$ to be locally optimal in DMDP assuming only differentiability and KTCQ. Thus existence of the Kuhn-Tucker vector $\lambda_i^*$ corresponding to the $x_i^*$ is guaranteed as the necessary condition of optimality in a nonconvex as well as a convex problem.

From the discussions following Theorem 10.6, under the appropriate conditions, we can perform meaningful differentiation of $\bar{L}$ (10.63) for $x_i(d_i, b_i)$, $\lambda_i(d_i, b_i)$ with the perturbation $\varepsilon \to 0$ for DMDP (10.59)-(10.61). In particular,

$$\frac{\partial \bar{L}}{\partial d_i} = \left[\frac{\partial f_i}{\partial x_i} - \lambda_i^1 \frac{\partial g_i}{\partial x_i} - \lambda_i^2 \frac{\partial h_i}{\partial x_i}\right] \frac{\partial x_i}{\partial d_i} \tag{10.67}$$

$$- \left[g_i(x_i) - d_i\right] \frac{\partial \lambda_i^1}{\partial d_i} - \left[h_i(x_i) - b_i\right] \frac{\partial \lambda_i^2}{\partial d_i} + \lambda_i^1,$$

where $x_i \in R^n$, $\lambda_i^1 \in R^{p_i}$, $\lambda_i^2 \in R^{J_i - p_i}$, $g_i$, $d_i \in R^{p_i}$ and, $h_i$, $b_i \in R^{J_i - p_i}$.

At the optimal,

$$\frac{\partial \bar{L}}{\partial d_i} = \frac{\partial f_i(x_i^*(d_i, b_i))}{\partial d_i} = \lambda_i^{1*}(d_i, b_i), \quad \text{for} \quad \lambda_i^{1*} > 0. \tag{10.68}$$

In short, the component of the gradient vector for $d^i$ of the objective function (10.59) indicates a marginal variation of the optimal value of the objective function $f_i(x_i)$ in terms of a marginal variation of the constraint constant $d_i$, and is represented by the Kuhn-Tucker multiplier $\lambda_i^1(d_i) \triangleq \{\lambda_{si}(d_i)\}$.

The component $\lambda_{si}^* > 0$ is used as the systems evaluator. The $\lambda_{si}^* = \partial f_i^* / \partial d_{si}$ shows a ratio of a marginal variation of the objective function $f_i$ (system output) to a marginal variation of the policy constraint constant $d_{si}$ (system input). In other words, the $\lambda_{si}^*$ inversely indicates the imputed prices, or the shadow prices, of the system's constraints measured in terms of a marginal value of the objective function. In the hierarchical system, the $\lambda_{si}^*$ inversely shows a marginal variation of the upper-level objective evaluated in terms of a marginal variation of the lower-level objective, which represents a value trade-off among these objectives. The larger the $\lambda_{si}^*$ is, the larger a marginal variation of the $f_i$ to be traded off to a marginal variation of the $d_{si}$ is. This means that one additional unit of $f_i$ is assessed with a relatively smaller worth (opportunity cost) compared to the incremental value in $d_{si}$ and thus that the degree of satisfaction with the presentation of the marginal change of the $d_{si}$ in the subsystem $i$ is relatively high in terms of a marginal unit of the $f_i$. Thus the $\lambda_{si}^*$ represents proportionally the degree of marginal satisfaction with the upper-level objective in term of the lower-level objective. We can use the $\lambda_{si}^{*}$ as an indicator representing the degree of satisfaction with the $d_{si}$ for the subsystem i. Note that the market prices vary in inverse proportion to a degree of satisfaction (sufficiency) with a commodity: a higher price indicates a lower degree of satisfaction (sufficiency) with a commodity. Similarly the inverse of the trade-off rate $1/\lambda_{si}^{*}$ is the opportunity cost or the imputed price of the $d_{si}$ for the subsystem i. This interpretation of the shadow price looks the same as that of Luenberger (1973) and Intriligator (1971), but it is a new version based on the hierarchical structuring of multiple objectives in mathematical programming. Write (10.68) with * omitted as

$$\lambda_{si}(d_{si}) = \frac{\partial f_i}{\partial d_{si}}, \quad s = 1,\ldots,p_i \tag{10.69}$$

Then,

$$\begin{aligned}\lambda_{si} &= \frac{\text{marginal change of system's output}}{\text{marginal change of system's input}} \\ &= \text{sensitivity of the system's output to the systems input} \\ &= \text{marginal productivity of system's input.}\end{aligned} \tag{10.70}$$

Thus as the imputed price or the opportunity cost of the $d_{si}$, $1/\lambda_{si}$ is in inverse proportion to the marginal productivity of the system's input, similarly to the market price.

**Example 1.**

Let the objective function (10.59) of DMDP be a net benefit function in a region i and the constraint (10.60) be resource constraints such as coal, steel, and electricity, etc. A constraint constant $d_{si}$ shows a resource availability in the region. When a numerical value of the Kuhn-Tucker multiplier combined with one resource constraint (e.g., coal) is larger than that for the other resource (e.g., steel), it means that the marginal productivity of the coal availability is larger than that for steel availability. Under the assumption that selection of the units of measurement for all the resources is empirically reasonable and practically meaningful, it means that for this region, the marginal importance, or the opportunity cost, of the coal availability to the regional net benefit is relatively small compared with that of steel, etc. It represents that the degree of satisfaction with the coal availability relative to the regional net benefit is higher than that for steel. The comparison of the imputed prices can also be done for any one resource (e.g., coal) among the regions.

**Example 2**

Let the objective function (10.59) of DMDP be a regional industrial production function in a region $i$ and the constraint condition (10.60) be an environmental restriction such as COD, $SO_2$, etc. A constraint constant $d_{si}$ shows a regulation standard for environmental management. The inverse of the Lagrange multiplier $1/\lambda_{si}$ is the opportunity cost of the environmental restriction in terms of the regional industrial production, and indicates quantitatively how many units of the environmental constraint $d_{si}$ sent down from the upper-level decision unit should be relaxed for increasing one marginal unit of the industrial production in the region $i$. The larger the $\lambda_{si}$ is, the smaller the amount of $d_{si}$ to be relaxed, or increased, for one marginal unit of increase of the $f_i$-value is. It means that the opportunity cost of the system's constraint $d_{si}$ (upper-level objective) for the region $i$ is relatively low, or that the degree of satisfaction with the $d_{si}$ for the region $i$ is relatively high.

### 10.4.4 Transformation of the Kuhn-Tucker Multiplier to a Quasi-Utility Function and Its Nesting

The derivation of a quasi-utility function $u_i(\lambda_i^*(d_i))$, where $\lambda_i^* \triangleq \lambda_i^{1*}$, is based on the Kuhn-Tucker multiplier generated from the mathematical optimization. The problem is how to convert the Kuhn-Tucker multiplier $\lambda_i^*$ with a positive sign into a utility index function with a cardinal measure. From now on the asterisk * in $\lambda_i^*$ is omitted.

Define a mapping $\phi$ such that $\phi : \Lambda \to T$, $\Lambda \subseteq R^{p_i}$, $T \subseteq R^{p_i}$.

Let $\lambda_i \in \Lambda$, $u_i \in T$. $u_i$ is an image of $\lambda_i$ by $\psi$. A power set $\mathscr{P}(T)$ is a set composed of the total of the subsets of the set $T$. Let a subset of the set $T$ be $\mathcal{U}$. For $\mathcal{U} \subset \mathscr{P}(T)$,

$$\psi^{-1}(\mathcal{U}) = \{\lambda_i \mid \lambda_i \in \Lambda,\ \psi(\lambda_i) \in \mathcal{U}\} \tag{10.71}$$

is an inverse image of $\mathcal{U}$. Define $\Lambda \triangleq \{\lambda_i \mid \lambda_i > 0\}$ and $\psi(\Lambda) \triangleq \{\psi(\lambda_i) \geqslant 0,\ \lambda_i \in \Lambda\}$. Then, in construction of the linear function, the Kuhn-Tucker multiplier $\lambda_i$ is used as an inverse image of $u_i$ which is interpreted as a surrogate of a preference function of DM and called a quasi-utility function.

By the property of the cardinal number, a positive linear transformation of $\lambda_i$ to $u_i$ is admissible. Define a system of relations $A \triangleq \langle \Omega, \mathbf{R} \rangle$. Here $\Omega$ is a nonempty preference set and $\mathbf{R}$ is a binary relation defined on components of $\Omega$. The von Neumann-Morgenstern theorem for the numerical representation of a utility function is restated.

**Theorem 10.7.**

Under the preference relation $\mathbf{R}$ defined on the preference set $\Omega$ satisfying the von Neumann-Morgenstern system, there exists a real-valued function $S$ such that, for every $\boldsymbol{x}$ and $\boldsymbol{y}$ in $\Omega$ and a parameter $\alpha$ in [0, 1],

(i) $\boldsymbol{x}\ \mathbf{R}\ \boldsymbol{y}$ if and only if $S(\boldsymbol{x}) \geqslant S(\boldsymbol{y})$,

(ii) $S\{\alpha \boldsymbol{x} + (1 - \alpha)\boldsymbol{y}\} = \alpha S(\boldsymbol{x}) + (1-\alpha)S(\boldsymbol{y})$.

Moreover, if $S'$ is any other function satisfying (i) and (ii), then $S'$ is admissible and related to $S$ by a positive linear transformation.

The problem is to prove that, according to the interpretation of the Kuhn-Tucker multiplier as the imputed price or opportunity cost, the Kuhn-Tucker multiplier $\lambda_i^*$ can be replaced for the $S$ in Theorem 10.7.

Consider the real-valued functions $\lambda_i(\boldsymbol{x})$ and $S(\boldsymbol{x})$ defined on the decision set $D \triangleq \{\boldsymbol{x}, \boldsymbol{y}\}$, $D \subset \mathcal{X}$, $\mathcal{X} \subseteq \Omega$, when $\mathcal{X}$ is a possible set of preference.

The following proposition can be presented about the

equivalence of the Kuhn-Tucker multiplier $\lambda_i$ interpreted as the imputed price to the real-valued function S defined on the preference set $\Omega$ as described in Theorem 10.7.

**Proposition 10.1.**

Two real-valued functions $\lambda_i(\boldsymbol{x})$ and $S(\boldsymbol{x})$ defined on the decision set D are in an equivalence class. Namely,

(i) A binary relation **R** for numerical magnitudes of $\lambda_i$ defined on the set D is reflexive, or $\lambda_i \mathbf{R} \lambda_i$, for every $\lambda_i(\boldsymbol{x})$, $\boldsymbol{x} \in D$.

(ii) The binary relation **R** for the $\lambda_i$ and S is symmetric, or if $\lambda_i \mathbf{R} S$ then $S\mathbf{R}\lambda_i$ for every $S(\boldsymbol{x})$, $\lambda_i(\boldsymbol{x})$, $\boldsymbol{x} \in D$.

(iii) The binary relation **R** for $\lambda_i$ and S is transitive; i.e., if $\lambda_i \mathbf{R} S$, $S\mathbf{R}\lambda_i'$, then $\lambda_i \mathbf{R} \lambda_i'$; or if $S\mathbf{R}\lambda_i$, $\lambda_i \mathbf{R} S'$, then $S\mathbf{R}S'$.

Thus, in the definition

$$\mathbf{R}(S) \triangleq \{\lambda_i \mid \lambda_i \in \Lambda \text{ and } \lambda_i \mathbf{R} S\},$$

**R** is an equivalence relation and $\mathbf{R}(S)$ is the equivalence class generated by S, and $\mathbf{R}(S) = \mathbf{R}(\lambda_i)$ if and only if $S\mathbf{R}\lambda_i$. Thus S in Theorem 10.7 is replaced with the $\lambda_i$.

**Theorem 10.8.**

Under the preference relation **R**, for every $\boldsymbol{x}$ and $\boldsymbol{y}$ in the decision set D, the following properties are preserved for the function $\lambda_i(\boldsymbol{x})$.

$$\text{(i)} \quad \boldsymbol{x}\ \mathbf{R}\ \boldsymbol{y} \text{ if and only if } \lambda_i(\boldsymbol{x}) \geqslant \lambda_i(\boldsymbol{y}),$$

$$\text{(ii)} \quad \lambda_i\{\alpha \boldsymbol{x} + (1-\alpha)\boldsymbol{y}\} = \alpha\lambda_i(\boldsymbol{x}) + (1-\alpha)\lambda_i(\boldsymbol{y}). \tag{10.72}$$

Proof of Theorem 10.8 can be derived immediately by regarding the components $\boldsymbol{x}$ and $\boldsymbol{y}$ of the preference set as values of some implicit evaluation functions for the system's constraints $d_{ri}$ and $d_{si}$, respectively, in mathematical programming. From the preceding discussions in 10.4.3, we can write $\lambda_i(\boldsymbol{x})$ as $\lambda_i(\psi(d_{ri})) = \lambda_{ri}$, and $\lambda_i(\boldsymbol{y})$ as $\lambda_i(\psi(d_{si}))$

$= \lambda_{si}$, where $s, r \in I \triangleq [1, \ldots, p_i]$. According to the discussion about (10.45), the Kuhn-Tucker multiplier $\lambda_i$ for DMDP has the representation

$$\lambda_i \triangleq (\ldots, \lambda_{ri}, \ldots, \lambda_{si}, \ldots)$$

$$= \frac{\partial f_i}{\partial d_i} \triangleq (\ldots, \frac{\partial f_i}{\partial d_{ri}}, \ldots, \frac{\partial f_i}{\partial d_{si}}, \ldots), \quad \lambda_i > 0. \tag{10.73}$$

Remind that the $\lambda_i$ indicates inversely the opportunity cost or the imputed price of the system's constraint constant $d_i \triangleq (\ldots, d_{ri}, \ldots, d_{si}, \ldots)$, $1 \leqslant r, s \leqslant p_i$. Thus the $\lambda_i$ is supposed to be determined corresponding to the numerical function $\psi$ which measures the satisfaction of a subsystem i with the policy constraint constant $d_i$. Then $\mathscr{x}$ and $\mathscr{y}$ in Theorem 10.8 can be replaced by $\psi(d_{ri})$ and $\psi(d_{si})$.

**Theorem 10.9.**

A quasi-von Neumann-Morgenstern system is defined for a preference set $(\ldots, \psi(d_{ri}), \ldots, \psi(d_{si}), \ldots) \subset D$ and a binary relation $\mathbf{R} \triangleq (\succ, \sim)$ on D, which are defined on the system's constraints $d_i \triangleq (\ldots, d_{ri}, \ldots, d_{si}, \ldots)$, $r, s = 1, \ldots, p_i$, $r \neq s$, presented in the mathematical programming problem DMDP (10.59)-(10.62). Then the Kuhn-Tucker multiplier $\lambda_i \triangleq (\ldots, \lambda_{ri}, \ldots, \lambda_{si} \ldots)$ combined with the policy constraints $d_i \triangleq (\ldots, d_{ri}, \ldots, d_{si} \ldots)$ holds the following properties:

$$\text{(i)} \quad \psi(d_{ri}) \mathbf{R} \psi(d_{si}) \Leftrightarrow \lambda_i(\psi(d_{ri})) \geqslant \lambda_i(\psi(d_{si})) \tag{10.74}$$

$$\text{(ii)} \quad \lambda_i(\gamma\psi(d_{ri}) + (1-\gamma)\psi(d_{si}))$$

$$= \gamma\lambda_i(\psi(d_{ri})) + (1-\gamma)\lambda_i(\psi(d_{si})), \tag{10.75}$$

where $\psi(d_{\cdot i})$ is a component of the preference set for $d_i$.

The function $\lambda_i$ can be linearly transformed to the function $u_i$ which satisfies (i) and (ii).

**Theorem 10.10.**

The Kuhn-Tucker multiplier function $\lambda_i(\psi(d_i))$ having the properties (10.74) and (10.75) is admissible up to positive linear transformations which generate the quasi-utility function $u_i(\lambda_i(\phi(d_i)))$ defined on 0 to 1.

The word, "quasi"-utility function, is used because the numerical values are derived by the positive linear transformation of the Kuhn-Tucker multiplier (10.73), which is generated with the mathematical optimization and does not depend on the direct assessment of preference of DM.

The quasi-utility function can be represented in the following forms:

$$u_i = u_i(\lambda_i(d_i)) \tag{10.76}$$

$$= \alpha_i + \beta_i \lambda_i(d_i). \tag{10.77}$$

Note that only discrete values appear originally in the domain and the range of the quasi-utility function. In order to apply the concept of the von Neumann-Morgenstern system to the present case where the quasi-utility function corresponds to the Kuhn-Tucker multiplier, a smoothing procedure must be introduced. The basic idea for deriving the quasi-utility function is shown in Figure 10.3. The conversion of the $\lambda_i$ into the $u_i$ is shown in Figure 10.4. In practice, we choose the lower and upper bounds, $\underline{\lambda}_i$ and $\bar{\lambda}_i$, of the $\lambda_i$ such as

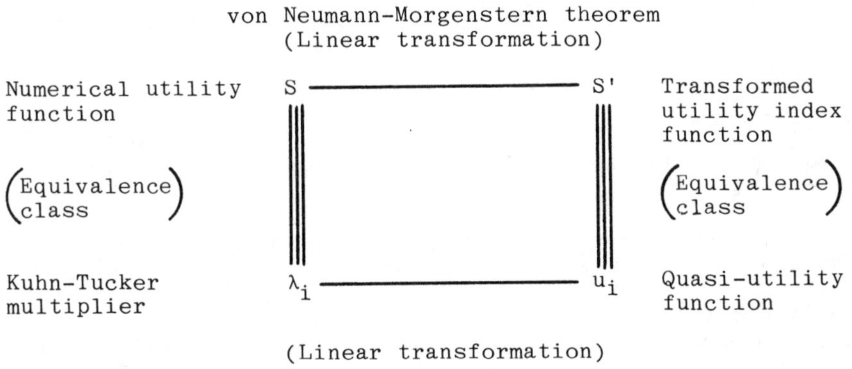


**Figure 10.3 Derivation of quasi-utility functions.**

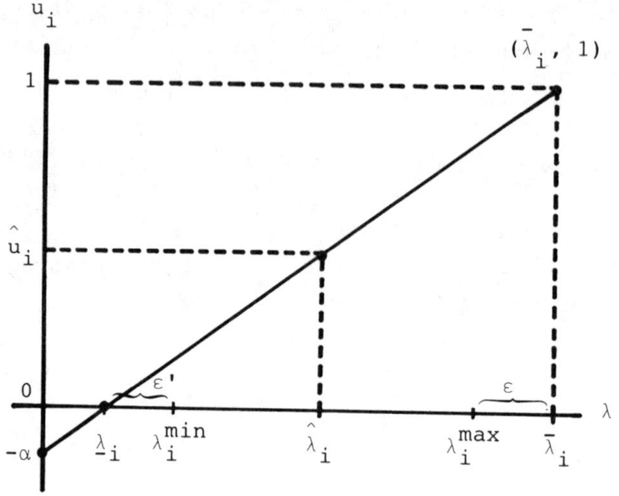


**Figure 10.4 Scaling of the quasi-utility function.**

$0 < \underline{\lambda}_i < \lambda_i^{min}$ and $\bar{\lambda}_i > \lambda_i^{max} > 0$, where $\lambda_i^{max}$ and $\lambda_i^{min}$ are actually obtained as maximum and minimum values of $\lambda_i$. The quasi-utility function $u_i$ is scaled between $u_i(\underline{\lambda}_i) = 0$ and $u_i(\bar{\lambda}_i) = 1$.

**Example.**

For a regional planning problem in Example 2 in 10.4.3, values of the quasi-utility function $u_i(\lambda_i(d_i))$ are used as the utility index of the environmental restriction for the region i, which indicates inversely the opportunity cost of the environmental restrictions for the economic aim of the region i.

The quasi-utility function $u_i$ (10.76) is derived as an analytical result based on the Kuhn-Tucker multiplier, which is generated independently in each subsystem i without any concern about external considerations. Thus, for solving the original MDP (10.55) or (10.58) and finding the preferred policy program, the coordination process of DM for the whole system should be introduced. This process is executed as the judgmental phase of MCDM in which weighting coefficients on the analytical results should be assessed. Multiattribute utility analysis provides a proper device to assess the weighting coefficients as the scaling constants and is used on the quasi-utility functions. From the quasi-utility function $u_i(\lambda_i(d_i), i = 1,\ldots,q, 0 \leqslant u_i \leqslant 1,$ the multiattribute utility functions (MUF) are constructed and nested with the coordination function of DM. The procedure for deriving MUF is similar to the technique of multiattribute utility analysis by Keeney and Raiffa, except that here the assessment of trade-offs between attributes is executed on the values of the quasi-utility functions which are already normalized from zero to one. Thus the trade-off experiments can be performed more easily.

Consider a two-level coordination process. In the first level, a component multiattribute utility function (CMUF) is assessed for the policy constraint $s$, $s = 1,\ldots, p_i$, of each subsystem $i$ in the form of the additive,

$$U_i(u_{1i}, u_{2i},\ldots, u_{p_i i}) = \sum_{s=1}^{p_i} k_{si}u_i(\lambda_{si}), \tag{10.78}$$

$$\sum_{s=1}^{p_i} k_{si} = 1,$$

or the multiplicative,

$$U_i(u_{1i}, u_{2i},\ldots, u_{p_i i}) = \frac{1}{K_i}\left(\prod_{s=1}^{p_i} (1 + K_i k_{si} u_i(\lambda_{si})) - 1\right),$$

$$\sum_{s=1}^{p_i} k_{si} \neq 1, \quad K_i > -1, \tag{10.79}$$

where $0 \leqslant u_{si}, U_i \leqslant 1$.

In this process, the trade-off experiments are executed among policy constraints to assess the scaling constants $k_{si}$, $s = 1,\ldots,p_i$.

In the second level, nesting of CMUF for each subsystem $i$, $i = 1,\ldots,q$, into an overall multiattribute utility function (OMUF) is executed in the form of the additive,

$$U = (U_1, U_2, \ldots, U_q) = \sum_{i=1}^{q} k_i U_i(u_{1i}, \ldots, u_{p_i i}),$$

$$\sum_{i=1}^{q} k_i = 1, \tag{10.80}$$

or the multiplicative,

$$U = (U_1, U_2, \ldots, U_q) = \frac{1}{K}\left(\prod_{i=1}^{q} (1 + Kk_i U_i(u_{1i}, \ldots, u_{p_i i}))-1\right),$$

$$\sum_{i=1}^{q} k_i \neq 1, \quad K_i > -1, \tag{10.81}$$

where $0 \leqslant U_i, U \leqslant 1$.

In this process, the trade-off experiments are executed for each subsystem $i$, $i = 1,\ldots,q$, to assess the scaling constant $k_i$. Finally, a valuation index for an overall decision system (10.55) is derived in the representation form of OMUF.

$$U[U_1(u_{11}(\lambda_{11}(d_{11}), u_{21}(\lambda_{21}(d_{21})),\ldots,u_{p_1 1}(\lambda_{p_1 1}(d_{p_1 1}))),\ldots,$$
$$U_q(u_{1q}(\lambda_{1q}(d_{1q})), u_{2q}(\lambda_{2q}(d_{2q})),\ldots,u_{p_q q}(d_{p_q q})))]. \tag{10.82}$$

The coordination process can be further decomposed into multilevels, and the nesting can be executed sequentially to construct a more intricate structure of OMUF, which corresponds to a more complex objectives hierarchy.

Thus the analytical results of the mathematical optimization for each subsystem are coordinated, via the normalized valuation using the quasi-utility function, to make a comprehensive adjustment. In this process, some other systems objectives in G2 $(\mathbf{x}_{m+1},\ldots,\mathbf{x}_r)$, which are not included in mathematical modeling, are taken into account. This is the judgmental phase of MCDM.

In short, for incorporating the judgmental phase into the analytical phase of MCDM, the two-layer decision system is

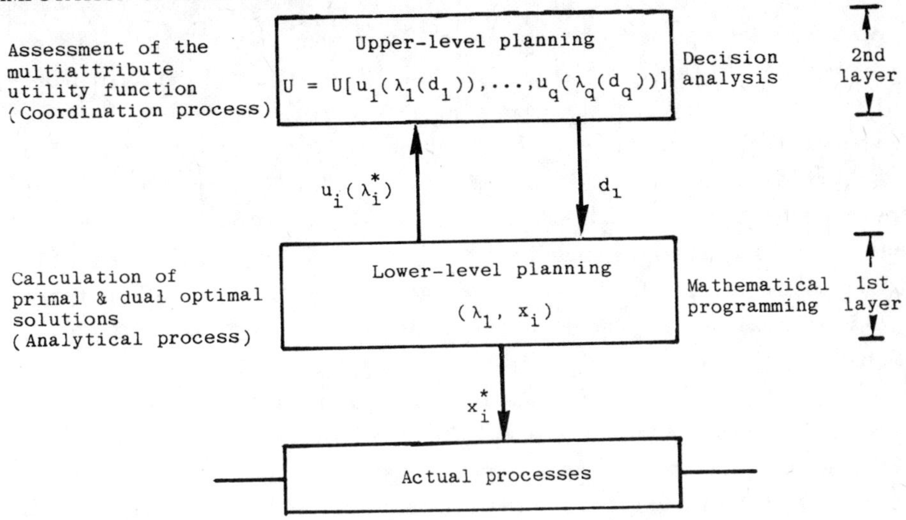


**Figure 10.5 Structure of a two-layer decision system.**

constructed as depicted in Figure 10.5, which is composed as the dual to the primal system depicted in Figure 10.1. In the first layer, mathematical programming is solved independently in each subsystem and the dual optimal solutions $\lambda_i^*$ are converted to the quasi-utility functions $u_i(\lambda_i^*)$. Then, in the second layer, a coordination process based on the analytical information is executed. Using the quasi-utility functions, MUFs are constructed in various levels and used for an overall system's evaluation.

### 10.4.5 Summary and Remarks

As discussed in Chapter 1, the ultimate purpose of MCDM is to find the preferred policy program among the alternatives having many noncommensurate and conflicting objectives. There are three major directions to systems evaluation. Direction I is to seek the preferred solutions interactively in repetitive processes of the analytical phase in MCDM according to a mathematical algorithm without any concern about identification of the preference function of DM. Direction II intends to identify the preference function of DM in order to determine the preferred policy program with the highest (expected) preference value. In the direction I, the preference of DM is inserted externally and a priori in a step of the mathematical algorithms. In contrast, in the direction II, derivation of the preference function of DM using the rational procedures is intended, exclusively depending on the judgmental phase of DM without resorting to the analytical optimization processes. Those two methods intend to seek the preferred policy program utilizing only one of the two intrinsic phases of MCDM.

The third direction concerns intrinsically treating both of the analytical and judgmental phases in MCDM and intends to bridge between these two phases. This method is based on the mathematical optimization in its use of analytical results on the one hand and also on the construction of the preference function of DM on the other hand.

The nested Lagrangian multiplier (NLM) method is intended for the third direction and is summarized as follows.

This method is primarily composed of two steps which correspond to a two-layer hierarchical decision system. In Step 1, which is performed in the first layer, a mathematical programming problem is solved separately and independently for each subsystem $i$, $i = 1,\ldots,q$, where policy constraint constants $d_i$, $i = 1,\ldots, p_i$ and policy parameters are imposed from DM in the second layer of the decision hierarchy. The optimal solution $x_i^*$ is presented as a reference index to the actual processes, and the dual optimal solution $\lambda_i^*$ is sent to the second layer as information of valuation prices for the policy constraint $d_i$ imposed by the upper-level DM. In Step 2, which is performed in the second layer, the analytical results obtained from Step 1 as the quasi-utility function $u_i(\lambda_i(d_i))$ $i = 1,\ldots,q$, are coordinated with some modification via discretional functions of DM as the mediator. The systems' coordination can be executed in multilevel. As the final valuation, MUF is assessed for determining a preference order of alternative policy programs and is utilized for selecting the preferred policy program. This method can be applied to posterior as well as prior evaluation of multiobjective decision problems.

The main characteristics of the NLM method are as follows.

(1) multiobjective systems as *un complex problématique* are hierarchically structured according to properties of objectives for better understanding and management of multipurpose systems.

(2) Duality of mathematical programming is utilized. With this device, a valuation problem combined with a resource allocation problem can be simultaneously solved.

(3) In analytical processes, it is not necessary for the analyst to be bothered with generating the Pareto optimal solutions prior to solving the multiobjective decision problem. Thus computational works for solving mathematical programming can be greatly reduced. The preferred policy program obtained as the result holds the Pareto optimality. If it does not, a better policy program would exist in the feasible region, which contradicts the definition of the preferred policy program.

(4) Use of the Kuhn-Tucker multiplier as the basic evaluation factor can remove ambiguousness in decision making at least in the first step of the assessment.

(5) Functions of DM as a coordinator are articulately introduced via the value trade-off experiments to assess MUF. To compromise the value conflicts, which are an intrinsic characteristic of MCDM, is properly performed in this process.

(6) The function of the systems coordination is executed not all at once but interactively in multiple levels corresponding to the complex systems structure. In this process, procedural rationality is highly regarded.

(7) A comparable evaluation for alternative systems designs is quantitatively performed with a common unit of measurement in terms of the quasi-utility function and MUF. By identification of these criterion functions, noncommensurate systems objectives can be compared with each other in the common units for alternative policy programs and their components.

(8) Use of the Kuhn-Tucker multiplier can reflect the differences in relative scales of the systems attributes included in different systems. This property can be used effectively for comparing and examining volumetric characteristics of different systems with different scales of magnitude, as long as the selection of measurement units are relatively reasonable and practically meaningful.

(9) Because the NLM method uses mathematical programming in the first step, the efficiency of this method depends on the development of effective computer algorithms for performing mathematical optimization, which is particularly important because the method requires that all the policy constraints be activated for obtaining the Kuhn-Tucker multiplier. There are many restrictions such as computational costs and technical difficulty. Those difficulties can be reduced to a considerable extent by the systems decomposition as a prior treatment. Solving small-sized scalar optimization problems in the first step will greatly increase effectiveness of this method. The decomposition device will also support the construction of appropriate mathematical models particular to each subsystem, avoiding any redundant effort toward unnatural modeling.

(10) The device to decompose an overall system into many small independent subsystems is also recommendable for assuring the independence conditions for deriving MUFs in the second layer. The independence assumptions among the systems attributes can be ensured more easily in the derivation of MUFs based on the Kuhn-Tucker multiplier generated for each subsystem, because the quasi-utility function is derived without any direct concern with preferences of DM.

(11) The NLM method can be used along with any other simulation techniques which can be included in treatment of some decomposed subsystems and whose results are transferred to the other subsystems via input-output channels of information.

# CHAPTER 11

# APPLICATIONS OF THE NESTED LAGRANGIAN MULTIPLIER (NLM) METHOD

## 11.1 The Nested Lagrangian Multiplier (NLM) Method in Application

In this chapter, applications of the nested Lagrangian multiplier (NLM) method to regional planning are discussed.

The NLM method proceeds in the following steps (Figure 11.1).

**Step 1.** Constructing of an objectives hierarchy.

The first step is to obtain an overview of the whole system with multiple objectives. The whole system as an objectives complex is decomposed into independent subsystems and structured in a hierarchical configuration in two layers which correspond to the analytical and judgmental phases of MCDM. At the first (or lower) layer, decision in each subsystem is concerned with restricted ranges of problems. Each subsystem is structured quantitatively and more precisely, and decision can be made straightforward, using mathematical optimization and simulation techniques. At the second (or upper) layer, decisions are concerned with a broader scope of problems. Descriptions of problems are relatively ambiguous and indeterministic, and decision making is more complex, depending on subjective judgment of DM. The second layer is particularly concerned with modifying and coordinating the decision obtained independently for each subsystem at the first layer.

**Step 2.** Solving mathematical programming problems.

At the first layer, mathematical programming problems are

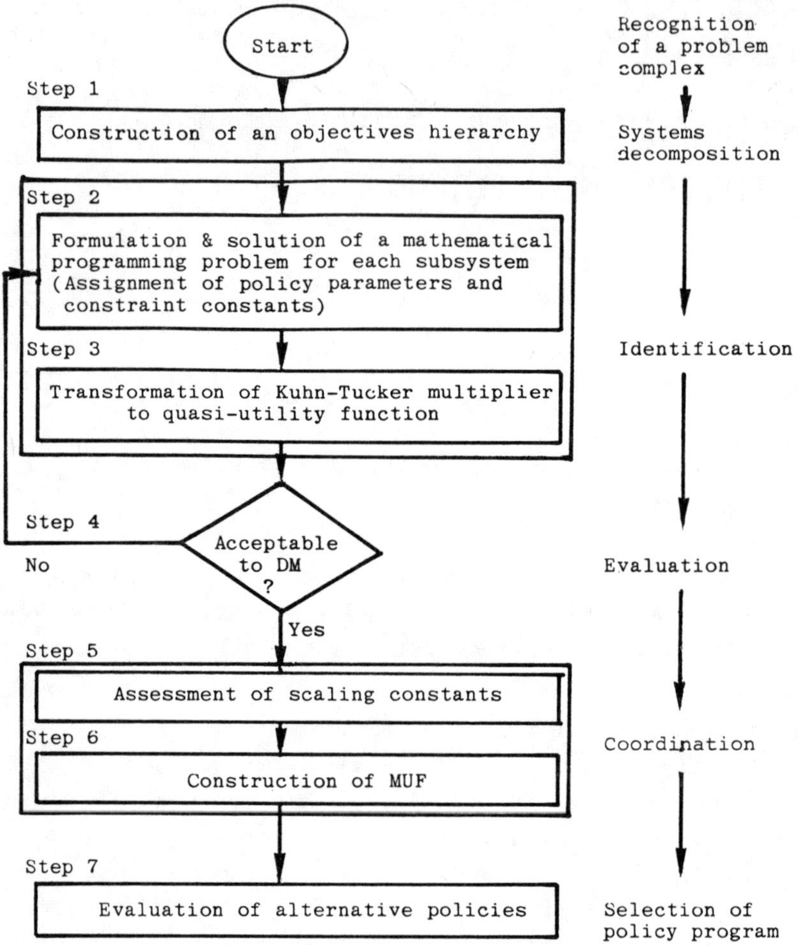


**Figure 11.1 Algorithm of the NLM method**

formulated and solved independently for each subsystem with specific parameters and constraint constants, some of which are imposed as indicative modulators from the second layer.

**Step 3.** Transforming of the Kuhn-Tucker multiplier to the quasi-utility function.

The Kuhn-Tucker multipliers obtained from mathematical optimization are used as the basic evaluators for the components in each subsystem and are converted to the quasi-utility function. Due to the correspondence of the numerical ordering of the Kuhn-Tucker multipliers interpreted as the imputed prices or opportunity costs to the preference ordering of DM, the Kuhn-Tucker multiplier is used as an inverse image of the quasi-utility function for a constraint. The numerical utility function is derived from a positive linear transformation of the Kuhn-Tucker multiplier.

**Step 4.** Checking acceptability of the quasi-utility value.

DM in the lower level examines the quasi-utility values for each subsystem and checks their acceptability. If they are acceptable, then DM proceeds to the next step. If not, the response is fed back to the upper layer and a request is made for modification of the modulators (policy parameters and constraint constants) imposed to the subsystems. Based on the response, new indicator are sent to the lower layer.

**Step 5 and Step 6.** Assessing the scaling constants and deriving the multiattribute utility functions (MUF).

By the coordination function of DM at the upper layer, scaling constants for the quasi-utility functions are assessed. The results from assessment of the scaling constants may also be sent down to the lower layer for confirming the response of the subsystems. If necessary, scaling constants are reassessed by DM at the upper layer. Then MUFs are derived using the scaling constants finally obtained. Similar procedures are executed in the process of nesting of the MUFs in various levels. Finally an overall MUF can be derived with the sequential nesting procedures corresponding to the objectives hierarchy.

**Step 7.** Determining preference priority of alternative policy programs.

Using the numerical value of an overall MUF, alternative policy programs are compared with each other and preference priority among them is determined. The evaluation results are presented to the administrative agency and used for supporting decisions of the administrators.

In the following sections, some case studies are presented.

**Remark.**

In multiple criteria evaluation of regional planning using the NLM method, problems are constructed with empirical data compiled and calculated for the regions. Various kinds of complementary devices for decision support can be combined in the execution process of the NLM method for making its use more effective. Some devices for mixed data manipulation and evaluation, which are not discussed in this book, are presented by Nijkamp (1977, 1979, 1980), Voogd (1983), Nijkamp and Spronk (1981), Hinloopen and others (1983), Rietveld (1980), and so on. These researches are more policy analysis-oriented, and some of them can be used for data-base construction and examination in regional planning from the multiobjective point of view in appropriate stages of the analysis. Independent utilizations of their devices are also recommended in comparison with our method.

## 11.2 Multiobjective Evaluation of Regional Planning in the Greater Osaka Area: A Static Case

### 1. The objective area

The central area of Osaka Prefecture is one of the highly industrialized districts in Japan. It faces Osaka Bay and is located between the Yodo River and the Yamato River basins. The Yodo River has many branches, the largest one being the Kanzaki River, which defines the boundary between Osaka Prefecture and Hyogo Prefecture. Osaka City, which is the second largest industrial and commercial area in Japan, is located between the Kanzaki and the Yamato Rivers and contains many small rivers which are branches of the Yodo River. The Neya River passes through newly industrialized areas in the East Osaka district, and also has many small branches which flow into branches of the Yodo. Acting as a network of waterways for carrying industrial and other wastes, these rivers and their branches finally flow into Osaka Bay which is a part of the Inland Sea, which has been the most important fishing area in Japan (Figure 11.2). The Yodo River is also an important source of drinking water for residents in Osaka, but water pollution in the Yodo River basin

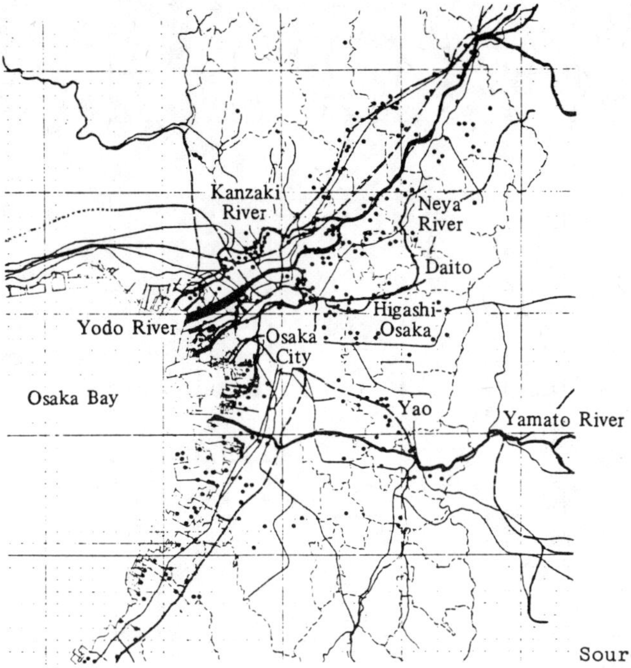


Source: Osaka Big Plan (Osaka Prefecture, 1973)

**Figure 11.2 Major sources of water pollution in Osaka Prefecture**

has become an increasingly serious issue as a result of rapid industrial development that has occurred since 1960. Air pollution is also at a critical level in and around Osaka City. In addition, the water-supply capacity is limited in these areas. The limitations of land use in and near Osaka are also becoming a serious problem since it is one of the most densely populated areas in Japan. In addition, the enlargement of newly developed industries has created a problem of wage differentials among industries.

## 2. Problem formulations and evaluation

The hierarchical system of the industrialized Yodo River basin area is constructed as in figure 11.3.

The regional system is decomposed according to functions of interest groups as well as administrative districts. The region is divided into Osaka City and the East Osaka district which consists of three cities: Yao, Daito, and Higashi-Osaka.

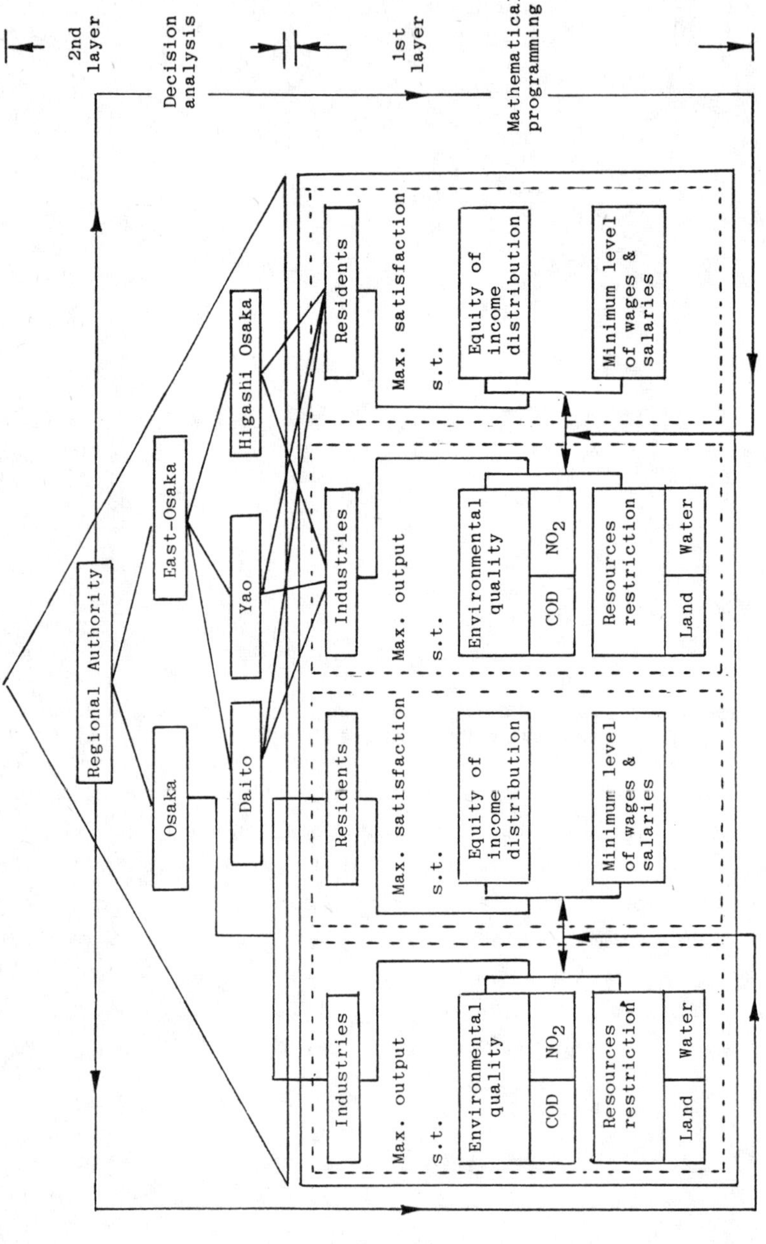


Figure 11.3 A hierarchical environmental system in the industrialized Yodo River basin.

Interest groups in each city are divided into an industrial group and a residential group. For each group in each city, an independent subproblem is constructed. The industrial group is interested in maximizing the output of each industry in each city, whereas the residential group, which is defined here as the daytime population and thus consists of wage and salary earners, is interested in maximizing the satisfaction from their earnings. Since DM must place some restrictions on activities of both groups from the social point of view, environmental quality standards and resource restrictions as well as equity considerations and minimum-wage requirements are introduced.

The sources for the data are mainly from statistical publications of the Statistical Office of Osaka Prefecture (1974), the Ministry of International Trade and Industry (1973), and the Osaka Bureau of Trade and Industry (1973).

The regional problem for the residents is as follows:

$$\underset{w_j}{\text{maximize}} \quad f(w) = \sum_{j=1}^{n} (C - AB^{w_j}) \tag{11.1}$$

subject to

$$w_j \geqslant \tilde{w}_j, \quad j = 1, \ldots, n, \tag{11.2}$$

$$\sum_{j=1}^{n} |w_j - \bar{w}| \leqslant \nu, \tag{11.3}$$

where

$j$ denotes an industry in the region,

$n$ the number of industries in each region,

$w_j$ the wages and salaries per employee in industry $j$ (decision variable),

$w$ the vector whose components are $(w_1, \ldots, w_n)$,

$\tilde{w}_j$ the actual amount of wages and salaries in industry $j$,

$\bar{w}$ the mean value of compensation per employee in all industries,

$\nu$ the sum of the deviation in each industry from the mean value of wages and salaries in all industries, and

$A$, $B$, $C$ are parameters.

Constraints (11.2) represent the minimum requirement for wages and salaries in each industry, and constraint (11.3) is an equity requirement for the wages and salaries among all industries. The objective function is estimated in the form of a modified exponential function.

$$f(w) = \sum_{j=1}^{n} (1.0102 - 0.9926 \times 0.76808^{w_j}). \tag{11.4}$$

After both primal and dual optimal solutions are obtained, the Kuhn-Tucker multipliers are converted into the quasi-utility functions. The numerical results are shown in Table 11.1 and 11.3. It has been found that more than half of all the industries in each region do not meet the minimum wage requirement. Increase of the wage levels for employees in these industries is recommended. This situation is assessed with negative values of the converted utility function for the present situation. In other industries, the actual levels of the compensation fulfill the minimum requirement. This situation is assessed with positive values of the converted utility function. The numerical values of the utility show the varying degrees of satisfaction in the present situation of the industries. In Osaka, the iron and steel industry which is mainly composed of large corporations has the highest level of satisfaction, but the nonelectrical machinery industry which is largely composed of small businesses has the lowest level. In Yao, the nonferrous metal industry has the highest level of satisfaction, the iron and steel industry is second, and the pulp and paper product industry has the lowest. By contrast, in Daito, the machinery industry has the highest level of satisfaction, and the lumber and related-products industry has the lowest level. In Higashi-Osaka, the iron and steel industry still has the highest level of satisfaction, and the machinery industry has the lowest.

For the equity requirement for wages among all the industries, the satisfaction level is the highest in Higashi-Osaka and the lowest in Osaka City. In other words, Osaka City is the richest, but the worst city in the region from the point of view of economic equity.

Table 11.1 Assessment of utilities for minimum level of wages: $u_m$

| Industry code | $b_j$ (million yen /yr.) | $w_j^*$ (million yen/yr.) | $w_j^*/b_j-1=\beta$ [1] | $\lambda_j^*$ (10−n means $10^{-n}$) | $u_j$ |
|---|---|---|---|---|---|
| Osaka | | | | | |
| 18.19 | 1.356 | 1.818 | .3407 | 0.0 | −0.20 |
| 20 | 1.361 | 1.818 | .3358 | 0.0 | −0.20 |
| 21 | .986 | 1.818 | .8438 | 0.0 | −0.20 |
| 22 | 1.687 | 1.818 | .0780 | 0.0 | −0.20 |
| 23 | 1.562 | 1.818 | .1638 | 0.0 | −0.20 |
| 24 | 1.595 | 1.818 | .1398 | 0.0 | −0.20 |
| 25 | 2.064 | 2.064 | .0 | 1.0172 × 10−4 | 0.1439 |
| 26 | 2.226 | 2.226 | .0 | 1.6530 × 10−4 | 0.3630 |
| 27 | 2.310 | 2.310 | .0 | 1.9720 × 10−4 | 0.4731 |
| 28 | 1.583 | 1.818 | .1485 | 0.0 | −0.20 |
| 29 | 1.121 | 1.818 | .6218 | 0.0 | −0.20 |
| 30 | 1.786 | 1.818 | .0179 | 0.0 | −0.20 |
| 31 | 2.640 | 2.640 | .0 | 3.1594 × 10−4 | 0.8825 |
| 32 | 2.134 | 2.134 | .0 | 1.2953 × 10−4 | 0.2397 |
| 33 | 1.690 | 1.818 | .0757 | 0.0 | −0.20 |
| 34 | 1.977 | 1.977 | .0 | 6.6442 × 10−5 | 0.2221 × 10−1 |
| 35 | 1.663 | 1.818 | .0932 | 0.0 | −0.20 |
| 36 | 2.031 | 2.031 | .0 | 8.8435 × 10−5 | 0.9805 × 10−1 |
| 37 | 1.457 | 1.818 | .2478 | 0.0 | −0.20 |
| 39 | 1.437 | 1.818 | .2651 | 0.0 | −0.20 |
| Yao | | | | | |
| 18.19 | 1.590 | 1.715 | .0780 | 0.0 | −0.08 |
| 20 | 1.516 | 1.715 | .1306 | 0.0 | −0.08 |
| 21 | 1.007 | 1.715 | .7021 | 0.0 | −0.08 |
| 22 | 1.367 | 1.715 | .2538 | 0.0 | −0.08 |
| 23 | 1.450 | 1.715 | .1821 | 0.0 | −0.08 |
| 24 | 1.771 | 1.771 | .0 | 2.4553 × 10−5 | 0.1821 × 10−1 |
| 25 | 1.461 | 1.715 | .1732 | 0.0 | −0.08 |
| 26 | 1.985 | 1.985 | .0 | 1.1467 × 10−4 | 0.3787 |
| 29 | 1.055 | 1.715 | .6246 | 0.0 | −0.08 |
| 30 | 1.642 | 1.715 | .0438 | 0.0 | −0.08 |
| 31 | 2.068 | 2.068 | .0 | 1.4827 × 10−4 | 0.5131 |
| 32 | 2.352 | 2.352 | .0 | 2.5784 × 10−4 | 0.9514 |
| 33 | 1.590 | 1.715 | .0790 | 0.0 | −0.08 |
| 34 | 1.776 | 1.776 | .0 | 2.6717 × 10−5 | 0.1069 |
| 35 | 1.448 | 1.714 | .1837 | 0.0 | −0.08 |
| 36 | 1.784 | 1.784 | .0 | 3.0174 × 10−5 | 0.4070 × 10−1 |
| 37 | 2.038 | 2.038 | .0 | 1.3621 × 10−4 | 0.4648 |
| 39 | 1.373 | 1.714 | .2484 | 0.0 | −0.08 |
| Daito | | | | | |
| 18.19 | 1.408 | 1.762 | .2514 | 0.0 | −0.04 |
| 20 | 1.569 | 1.762 | .1230 | 0.0 | −0.04 |
| 21 | .882 | 1.762 | .9977 | 0.0 | −0.04 |
| 22 | 1.780 | 1.780 | .0 | 7.7563 × 10−6 | 0.4133 × 10−2 |
| 23 | 1.748 | 1.762 | .0080 | 0.0 | −0.04 |
| 24 | 1.593 | 1.762 | .1061 | 0.0 | −0.04 |
| 25 | 1.732 | 1.762 | .0173 | 0.0 | −0.04 |
| 26 | 2.128 | 2.128 | .0 | 1.5142 × 10−4 | 0.7892 |
| 28 | 1.902 | 1.902 | .0 | 5.9629 × 10−5 | 0.2876 |
| 29 | .718 | 1.762 | .4540 | 0.0 | −0.04 |
| 30 | 1.919 | 1.919 | .0 | 6.6726 × 10−5 | 0.3264 |
| 31 | 2.101 | 2.101 | .0 | 1.4074 × 10−4 | 0.7308 |
| 32 | 1.626 | 1.762 | .0836 | 0.0 | −0.04 |
| 33 | 1.467 | 1.762 | .2011 | 0.0 | −0.04 |
| 34 | 2.207 | 2.207 | .0 | 1.8224 × 10−4 | 0.9576 |
| 35 | 1.626 | 1.762 | .0836 | 0.0 | −0.04 |
| 36 | 1.872 | 1.872 | .0 | 4.7028 × 10−5 | 0.2187 |
| 39 | 1.550 | 1.762 | .1368 | 0.0 | −0.04 |

1) β shows the required rate of increase of wages in this model.

Table 11.1 (continued)

| Industry code | $b_j$ (million yen/yr.) | $w_j^*$ (million yen/yr.) | $w_j^*/b_j - 1 = g^{1)}$ | $\lambda_j$ (10-n meas $10^{-n}$) | $u_j$ |
|---|---|---|---|---|---|
| Higashi-Osaka | | | | | |
| 18.19 | 1.251 | 1.663 | .3297 | 0.0 | -0.01 |
| 20 | 1.295 | 1.663 | .2845 | 0.0 | -0.01 |
| 21 | 1.070 | 1.663 | .5546 | 0.0 | -0.01 |
| 22 | 1.411 | 1.663 | .1789 | 0.0 | -0.01 |
| 23 | 1.591 | 1.663 | .0455 | 0.0 | -0.01 |
| 24 | 1.526 | 1.663 | .0900 | 0.0 | -0.01 |
| 25 | 1.562 | 1.663 | .0649 | 0.0 | -0.01 |
| 26 | 2.048 | 2.048 | .0 | 1.6295 × 10-4 | 0.4578 |
| 28 | 1.350 | 1.663 | .2321 | 0.0 | -0.01 |
| 29 | 1.218 | 1.663 | .3657 | 0.0 | -0.01 |
| 31 | 2.477 | 2.477 | .0 | 3.2624 × 10-4 | 0.9311 |
| 32 | 1.916 | 1.961 | .0 | 1.0887 × 10-4 | 0.3011 |
| 33 | 1.532 | 1.663 | .0858 | 0.0 | -0.01 |
| 34 | 1.676 | 1.676 | .0 | 5.5974 × 10-6 | 0.1732 × 10-2 |
| 35 | 1.581 | 1.663 | .0521 | 0.0 | -0.01 |
| 36 | 1.951 | 1.951 | .0 | 1.2340 × 10-4 | 0.3432 |
| 37 | 1.706 | 1.706 | .0 | 1.8868 × 10-5 | 0.4020 × 10-1 |
| 39 | 1.449 | 1.663 | .1480 | 0.0 | -0.01 |

Table 11.2 Classification of industries

| Code | Industry | Code | Industry |
|---|---|---|---|
| 18,19 | Food | 30 | Clay and stone products |
| 20 | Textile-mill products | 31 | Iron and steel |
| 21 | Apparel products | 32 | Nonferrous metals |
| 22 | Lumber and related products | 33 | Fabricated metal products |
| 23 | Furniture | 34 | Machinery |
| 24 | Pulp and paper products | 35 | Electrical machinery |
| 25 | Printing and publishing | 36 | Transportation equipment |
| 26 | Chemicals and related products | 37 | Precision machinery |
| 27 | Coal and petroleum products | 38 | Ordnance |
| 28 | Rubber products | 39 | Miscellaneous |
| 29 | Leather products | | |

**Remarks.**

This example shows a case in which the negative values of the quasi-utility function can be meaningfully used as an index indicating particular spots that require improvement of the present situation.

Table 11.3 shows that the quasi-utility values reveal a positive relationship to the statistical standard deviation

**Table 11.3 Assessment of utility for equity rquirement in each region: $u_e$ (10-n means $10^{-n}$)**

| | Osaka | Yao | Daito | Higashi-Osaka |
|---|---|---|---|---|
| $\lambda_o^i$ | 1.6209 ×10-3 | 1.6659 ×10-3 | 1.6452 ×10-3 | 1.6886 ×10-3 |
| $u_e^i$ | 0.2099 | 0.6593 | 0.4524 | 0.8864 |
| $\sigma^i$ | 41.53 | 34.60 | 38.60 | 34.15 |

Note: $\sigma^i$ denotes the standard deviation among industries for wages and salaries in each city.

which is another conventional index indicating the equity of compensations among the industries.

Now, by using the quasi-utility functions for residential attributes, the nesting procedure is carried out. First, via the trade-off experiments between the quasi-utility values for the minimum-wage requirement and the equity requirement, a MUF is derived in each region. Then, using these MUFs for each region, a MUF is constructed for residents in the East-Osaka area. Finally, by nesting these MUFs for Osaka and East-Osaka, a regional MUF for residents is derived. Numerical values of the residential MUFs are assessed with the following forms.

Osaka City:

$$U_O^R = \frac{1}{0.61}\left[(1+0.43u_O^m)(1+0.13u_O^e) - 1\right]; \tag{11.5}$$

East Osaka:

Yao:

$$U_Y^R = \frac{1}{1.36}\left[(1+1.22u_Y^m)(1+0.06u_Y^e) - 1\right], \tag{11.6}$$

Daito:

$$U_D^R = \frac{1}{0.31}\left[(1+0.25u_D^m)(1+0.05u_D^e) - 1\right], \tag{11.7}$$

Higashi-Osaka:

$$U_H^R = \frac{1}{0.12}\,[(1+0.11u_H^m)(1+0.01u_H^e) - 1], \tag{11.8}$$

East-Osaka:

$$U_{EO}^R = 1/-0.82[(1-0.65u_{ya})(1-0.39u_{da})(1-0.13u_{hg})-1]; \tag{11.9}$$

Region:

$$U_R = 1/1.63[(1+1.14u_{eo})(1+0.23u_{os})-1], \tag{11.10}$$

where $u^m$ and $u^e$ are the quasi-utility functions for the minimum-wage requirement and the equity requirement respectively, and the subscripts O, Y, D, and H denote Osaka City and Yao, Daito, and Higashi-Osaka cities respectively.

The environmental management problem for industries is formulated with particular parameters and constraint constants for each subregion as follows:

$$\underset{K_j,\ L_j}{\text{maximize}} \quad \sum_j^{n_i} f_j(K_j,\ L_j) = \sum_j^{n_i} c_j K_j^{a_j} L_j^{b_j} \tag{11.11}$$

subject to

$$\sum_{j=1}^{n_i} \frac{\omega_{sj}}{\kappa_j} K_j \leqslant \tau_s, \quad s = 1,\ldots,4, \tag{11.12}$$

$$\sum_{j=1}^{n_i} K_j / \sum_j^{n_i} L_j \leqslant \gamma, \tag{11.13}$$

$$\alpha\tilde{K}_j \leqslant K_j \leqslant \beta\tilde{K}_j, \quad j = 1,\ldots,n_i, \tag{11.14}$$

$$\alpha'\tilde{L}_j \leqslant L_j \leqslant \beta'\tilde{L}_j, \quad j = 1,\ldots,n_i, \tag{11.15}$$

where

$n_i$ is the number of industries in each region $i$

$s$ an environmental factor [s=1: chemical oxygen demand (COD), s=2: sulphur dioxide ($SO_2$), s=3: land, and s=4: water]

$K_j$ the capital value (the book value of tangible fixed assets) in industry j (decision variable),

$\tilde{K}_j$ the actual capital value in industry j,

$L_j$ the number of employees in industry j (decision variable),

$\tilde{L}_j$ the actual number of employees in industry j,

$\omega_{sj}$ the requirement or discharge of environmental or resource factor s per unit of industrial shipments in industry j,

$\kappa_j$ the capital coefficient, namely capital value per unit of industrial shipments, in industry j,

$\tau_i$ the policy constraint constant or target level for the ith environmental factor,

$\gamma$ the overall capital intensity (ratio of the total capital value to the total number of employees),

$a_j$, $b_j$, $c_j$ parameters of the production function for each industry j, and

$\alpha$, $\beta$, $\alpha'$, $\beta'$ are parameters which represent friction (resistance) to the transfer of capital and labor ($0 \leqslant \alpha, \alpha' \leqslant 1$; $1 \leqslant \beta, \beta'$).

The objective function is a Cobb-Douglas type of production function which is homogeneous of degree one (i.e., $a_j + b_j = 1$), and thus if each production factor is paid its marginal product, total output is distributed between labor and capital in proportions $a_j$ and $b_j$, respectively. The constraints (11.12) are the target constraints showing that the amount of an environmental factor required or discharged by each industry should not exceed a constraint imposed by DM. Constraint (11.13) is the technical constraint showing capital intensity as a whole, which is used to indicate the direction of changes of technological composition of capital and labor to occur as a result of the reformation of the industrial structure in each region. Constraints (11.14) and (11.15) are frictional constraints. The frictional coefficients are imposed as the upper and lower bounds for each decision variable because drastic changes in the current industrial structure are supposed to be undesirable.

The problem is to find the optimal allocation of production factors (capital and labor) to each industry under the constraints (11.12) to (11.15). The computer program for the augmented Lagrangian method presented by Pierre and Lowe (1975) was used effectively in solving the nonlinear optimization problem (11.11)-(11.15).

The data for environmental restrictions are shown in Table 11.4.

The quasi-utility functions $u(\lambda)$ derived from the $\lambda$ are presented in Table 11.5. The diagnosis based on the numerical results is given in Table 11.6.

The primal optimal solutions, $K_j^*$ and $L_j^*$, for the decision variables show the optimal allocation of capital and labor to each industry (Table 11.7). The code numbers of the industrial classification are shown in Table 11.2. Some of the main results are that capital formation in the iron and steel industry and in the chemicals and related-products industry should be reduced in all subregions, and that the nonferrous metals industry and the fabricated metal products industry should decrease their capital investment in Osaka City. On the other hand, in consumer industries such as the apparel, lumber, and furniture, as well as in machine industries such as electrical machinery, capital investment can be promoted. In the East Osaka district, capital investment in other machine industries such as general machinery and precision machinery is also recommended.

As a result, the capital values in industry as a whole will be greatly reduced in Osaka City. Although capital-saving technological changes will occur, industrial shipments in Osaka City will also decrease drastically by 24.1-28.5%. On the other hand, capital values in the East Osaka district will increase and, as a result, labor will be transferred from Osaka City to the East Osaka district. The increase of industrial shipments in the East Osaka district can compensate for only about 7.8-9.2% of the decrease in Osaka City. However, from the prefectural point of view, development of the other areas in Osaka Prefecture (which contains thirty-one cities, eleven towns, and two villages) will make it possible to compensate for almost all of the decrease in industrial shipments in Osaka City within the prefecture. It should be noted that the industrial reallocation program can be obtained simultaneously with the evaluation of the environmental management program. Although our main concern is with evaluating the numerical quasi-utility values imputed to the environmental management program, the industrial reallocation program combined with the evaluation can

**Table 11.4 Environmental restrictions and reduction rates**

| | COD | | $SO_2$ | | Land | | Water | |
|---|---|---|---|---|---|---|---|---|
| | $\tau_1$ (tons per year[a]) | $\rho$[b] (%) | $\tau_2$ (tons per year[a]) | $\rho$[b] (%) | $\tau_3$ ($100m^2$) | $\rho$[c] (%) | $\tau_4$ ($100m^3$) | $\rho$[c] (%) |
| Osaka City | | | | | | | | |
| Case 1 | 84095 | -47.50[d] | 62250 | -46 | 156065 | -9 | 150923 | 0 |
| Case 2 | 95227 | -40.00 | 70060 | -40 | 171253 | 0 | 173561 | +15 |
| Yao | 9864 | -32.75 | 6358 | -20 | 25544 | -5 | 14600 | +15 |
| Daito | 2194 | -25.00 | 1917 | -20 | 13904 | -5 | 7980 | +15 |
| Higashi-Osaka | 11824 | -32.75 | 10417 | -27 | 58162 | -5 | 33382 | +15 |

[a] 1 year = 290 days.

[b] Rate of reduction estimated from the input-output table for 1973 (Osaka Bureau of Trade amd Industry, 1973).

[c] Rate of reduction estimated from the 1974 Industrial Statistics Survey (Statistical Office of Osaka Prefecture, 1974).

[d] Rate of reduction from predicted value in 1981.

**Table 11.5 Assessment of utility for environmental control**

| Area | COD | | $SO_2$ | | Land | | Water | |
|---|---|---|---|---|---|---|---|---|
| | $\lambda_s$ | $u_s$ | $\lambda_s$ | $u_s$ | $\lambda_s$ | $u_s$ | $\lambda_s$ | $u_s$ |
| Osaka City | | | | | | | | |
| case 1 | 2.1642 | 0.0323 | 0.9474 | 0.0012 | 0.0000 | -0.0230 | 37.5866 | 0.9383 |
| case 2 | 0.2275 | 0.0008 | 14.4730 | 0.4101 | 4.7484 | 0.1307 | 30.3245 | 0.8656 |
| Yao | 0.0000 | 0.0000 | 11.5712 | 0.7714 | 8.1213 | 0.5414 | 6.1050 | 0.4070 |
| Daito | 10.9544 | 0.7121 | 0.9618 | 0.0008 | 7.2767 | 0.4503 | 0.0000 | -0.0676 |
| Higashi-Osaka | 15.5528 | 0.7760 | 0.1605 | 0.0005 | 7.0646 | 0.3483 | 9.1199 | 0.4519 |

**Table 11.6 Diagnosis**

| Area | Satisfaction level | | Slackness | Technological change (capital-saving) |
|---|---|---|---|---|
| | minimum | maximum | | |
| Osaka | | | | |
| Case 1 | $SO_2$ | water | land[a] | drastic |
| Case 2 | COD | water | none | drastic |
| Yao | COD | $SO_2$ | none | medium |
| Daito | $SO_2$ | COD | water[b] | medium |
| Higashi-Osaka | $SO_2$ | COD | none | medium |

Note: [a]32.54($100m^2$). [b]1025.56($1000m^3 year^{-1}$).

## Table 11.7 Capital reallocation plan

| Industry code | 1974 capital: million yen | % | Proposed capital: Case I: million yen | % | Proposed capital: Case 2: million yen | % | 1974 capital: million yen | % | Proposed capital: million yen | % |
|---|---|---|---|---|---|---|---|---|---|---|
| | Osaka city | | | | | | Yao | | | |
| 18,19 | 29409 | 4.43 | 14704 | 3.69 | 17645 | 4.09 | 5033 | 7.78 | 3830 | 5.63 |
| 20 | 21375 | 3.22 | 10687 | 2.68 | 12825 | 2.97 | 1619 | 2.50 | 971 | 1.43 |
| 21 | 8423 | 1.27 | 12634 | 3.17 | 6273 | 1.45 | 223 | 0.34 | 312 | 0.46 |
| 22 | 13873 | 2.09 | 20808 | 5.23 | 18456 | 4.28 | 310 | 0.48 | 434 | 0.64 |
| 23 | 8474 | 1.28 | 12711 | 3.19 | 11864 | 2.75 | 697 | 1.08 | 976 | 1.43 |
| 24 | 36375 | 5.49 | 18187 | 4.57 | 21825 | 5.06 | 4655 | 7.19 | 2793 | 4.10 |
| 25 | 66016 | 9.96 | 37401 | 9.39 | 39610 | 9.18 | 998 | 1.54 | 599 | 0.88 |
| 26 | 80134 | 12.08 | 40066 | 10.06 | 48080 | 11.14 | 2800 | 4.33 | 1680 | 2.47 |
| 27 | 1327 | 0.20 | 663 | 0.17 | 796 | 0.18 | - | - | - | - |
| 28 | 4414 | 0.67 | 2207 | 0.55 | 2649 | 0.61 | - | - | - | - |
| 29 | 3709 | 0.56 | 1854 | 0.47 | 2225 | 0.52 | 193 | 0.30 | 116 | 0.17 |
| 30 | 14496 | 2.19 | 7247 | 1.82 | 8697 | 2.01 | 1229 | 1.90 | 737 | 1.08 |
| 31 | 102399 | 15.44 | 51199 | 12.86 | 61439 | 14.23 | 2398 | 3.71 | 1439 | 2.11 |
| 32 | 28008 | 4.22 | 14003 | 3.52 | 16805 | 3.89 | 3498 | 5.40 | 4683 | 6.88 |
| 33 | 69314 | 10.45 | 34657 | 8.70 | 41589 | 9.63 | 10267 | 15 86 | 9919 | 14.57 |
| 34 | 90014 | 13.57 | 56049 | 14.08 | 54008 | 12.51 | 9223 | 14.25 | 11369 | 16.70 |
| 35 | 29360 | 4.43 | 35113 | 8.82 | 33286 | 7.71 | 9612 | 14.85 | 13457 | 19.76 |
| 36 | 27687 | 4.18 | 13843 | 3.48 | 16612 | 3.85 | 2465 | 3.81 | 1479 | 2.17 |
| 37 | 4009 | 0.60 | 2004 | 0.50 | 2405 | 0.56 | 2961 | 4.58 | 4145 | 6.09 |
| 38 | - | - | - | - | - | - | - | - | - | - |
| 39 | 24323 | 3.67 | 12161 | 3.05 | 14594 | 3.38 | 6538 | 10.10 | 9154 | 13.44 |
| Total | 663139 | 100.00 | 398198 | 100.00 | 431683 | 100.00 | 64719 | 100.00 | 69093 | 100.00 |
| Industrial shipment (million yen) | (a) 4,688,885 | | (b) 3,351,800 | | (c) 3,556,930 | | (a) 414,812 | | (b) 454,474 | |
| Share in Osaka Prefecture (%) | 35.67 | | 25.5 | | 27.06 | | 3.16 | | 3.46 | |
| | | | 100(b/a-1): -28.5(%) | | 100(c/a-1): -24.1(%) | | | | 100(b/a-1): 9.6% | |

**Table 11.7 Capital reallocation plan (continued)**

| Industry | 1974 capital | | Proposed capital | | 1974 capital | | Proposed capital | |
|---|---|---|---|---|---|---|---|---|
| code | million yen | % | million yen | % | million yen | % | million yen | % |
| | Daito | | | | Higashi-Osaka | | | |
| 18,19 | - | - | - | - | 3106 | 2.53 | 1864 | 1.50 |
| 20 | 1099 | 4.04 | 659 | 2.44 | 2036 | 1.66 | 1222 | 0.99 |
| 21 | - | - | - | - | 894 | 0.73 | 609 | 0.49 |
| 22 | 91 | 0.33 | 128 | 0.47 | 508 | 0.41 | 711 | 0.57 |
| 23 | 473 | 1.74 | 662 | 2.45 | 3281 | 2.67 | 4594 | 3.71 |
| 24 | 938 | 3.45 | 563 | 2.08 | 4967 | 4.04 | 2980 | 2.41 |
| 25 | 627 | 2.30 | 376 | 1.39 | 4683 | 3.81 | 2810 | 2.27 |
| 26 | 850 | 3.12 | 510 | 1.88 | 3571 | 2.91 | 2143 | 1.73 |
| 27 | - | - | - | - | - | - | - | - |
| 28 | 523 | 1.92 | 705 | 2.61 | 322 | 0.26 | 193 | 0.16 |
| 29 | - | - | - | - | 259 | 0.21 | 155 | 0.13 |
| 30 | 977 | 3.59 | 586 | 2.17 | - | - | - | - |
| 31 | 3601 | 13.23 | 2617 | 9.67 | 15844 | 12.90 | 9910 | 8.00 |
| 32 | 817 | 3.00 | 1143 | 4.22 | 8100 | 6.60 | 5430 | 4.38 |
| 33 | 2584 | 9.49 | 2905 | 10.73 | 23735 | 19.33 | 27872 | 22.50 |
| 34 | 6423 | 23.59 | 5016 | 18.54 | 20100 | 16.37 | 26130 | 21.09 |
| 35 | 5002 | 18.37 | 7003 | 25.88 | 6903 | 5.62 | 9664 | 7.80 |
| 36 | 398 | 1.46 | 239 | 0.88 | 8872 | 7.22 | 5730 | 4.63 |
| 37 | - | - | - | - | 1204 | 0.98 | 1685 | 1.36 |
| 38 | - | - | - | - | - | - | - | - |
| 39 | 2821 | 10.36 | 3949 | 14.59 | 14414 | 11.74 | 20179 | 16.29 |
| Total | 27224 | 100.00 | 27061 | 100.00 | 122799 | 100.00 | 123881 | 100.00 |
| Industrial shipment (million yen) | (a) 225,834 | | (b) 257,625 | | (a) 944,655 | | (b) 977,408 | |
| Share in Osaka Prefecture (%) | 1.72 | | 1.96 | | 7.19 | | 7.44 | |
| | | | 100(b/a-1): 14.1% | | | | 100(b/a-1): 3.5% | |

also be acquired by the NLM method.

**Remark.**

In the environmental management problem, negative values of the quasi-utility function are used as a checking point for finding the occurrence of slacks in natural resources, which is a different utilization from the residential problem.

The MUFs for the environmental management problem for the industrial pollution control (denoted by $U^{IPC}$) are assessed through the nesting procedure as follows:

Osaka City:

$$U_O^{IPC} = \frac{1}{-0.8268} [(1-0.6614u_O^{COD})(1-0.2646u_O^{SO_2}) \times (1-0.1984u_O^{land})(1-0.1323u_O^{water}) - 1]; \tag{11.16}$$

East Osaka:

Yao:

$$U_Y^{IPC} = \frac{1}{-0.8871} [(1-0.2395u_Y^{COD})(1-0.07984u_Y^{SO_2}) \times (1-0.7984u_Y^{land})(1-0.1996u_Y^{water}) - 1], \tag{11.17}$$

Daito:

$$U_D^{IPC} = \frac{1}{-0.6704} [(1-0.5363u_D^{COD})(1-0.1073u_D^{SO_2}) \times (1-0.1341u_D^{land})(1-0.0804u_D^{water}) - 1], \tag{11.18}$$

Higashi-Osaka:

$$U_H^{IPC} = \frac{1}{-0.5855} [(1-0.1317u_H^{COD})(1-0.4391u_H^{SO_2}) \times (1-0.1098u_H^{land})(1-0.0439u_H^{water}) - 1]. \tag{11.19}$$

The nesting of these MUFs for the environmental management problem along with the MUFs for the residential problem gives the composite MUF for both problems. The composite MUF for each subregion is assessed as follows:

Osaka City:

$$U_O = \frac{1}{0.1020} [(1+0.02856U_O^R)(1+0.714U_O^{IPC}) -1]; \qquad (11.20)$$

East Osaka:

Yao:

$$U_Y = \frac{1}{0.3125} [(1+0.05U_Y^R)(1+0.25U_Y^{IPC}) - 1], \qquad (11.21)$$

Daito:

$$U_D = \frac{1}{0.2076} [(1+0.0265U_D^R)(1+0.1765U_D^{IPC}) - 1], \qquad (11.22)$$

Higashi-Osaka:

$$U_H = \frac{1}{0.1481} [(1+0.0333U_H^R)(1+0.1111U_H^{IPC}) - 1]. \qquad (11.23)$$

Now an overall regional MUF $U$ is derived. First the nesting of equations (11.21)-(11.23) forms a composite MUF for the East Osaka district:

$$U_E = \frac{1}{0.6406} [(1+0.5125U_Y)(1+0.05765U_D)(1+0.0256U_H) - 1]. \qquad (11.24)$$

Then the nesting of equations (11.20) and (11.24) derives an overall regional MUF.

$$U = U(U_E, U_O) = \frac{1}{0.3125} [(1+0.25U_O)(1+0.05U_E) - 1]. \qquad (11.25)$$

Numerical values of the scaling constants as the results of the trade-off experiments are shown in Table 11.8.

The numerical results of the utility assessment are shown in Figure 11.4, which reveals the following results.

(i) In general, utility values for the residential problems are lower than those for the environmental management problems, and the worst for the minimum-wage requirement in each region.

(ii) The satisfaction levels in Osaka City are generally lower than in the East Osaka district. Higashi-Osaka, which

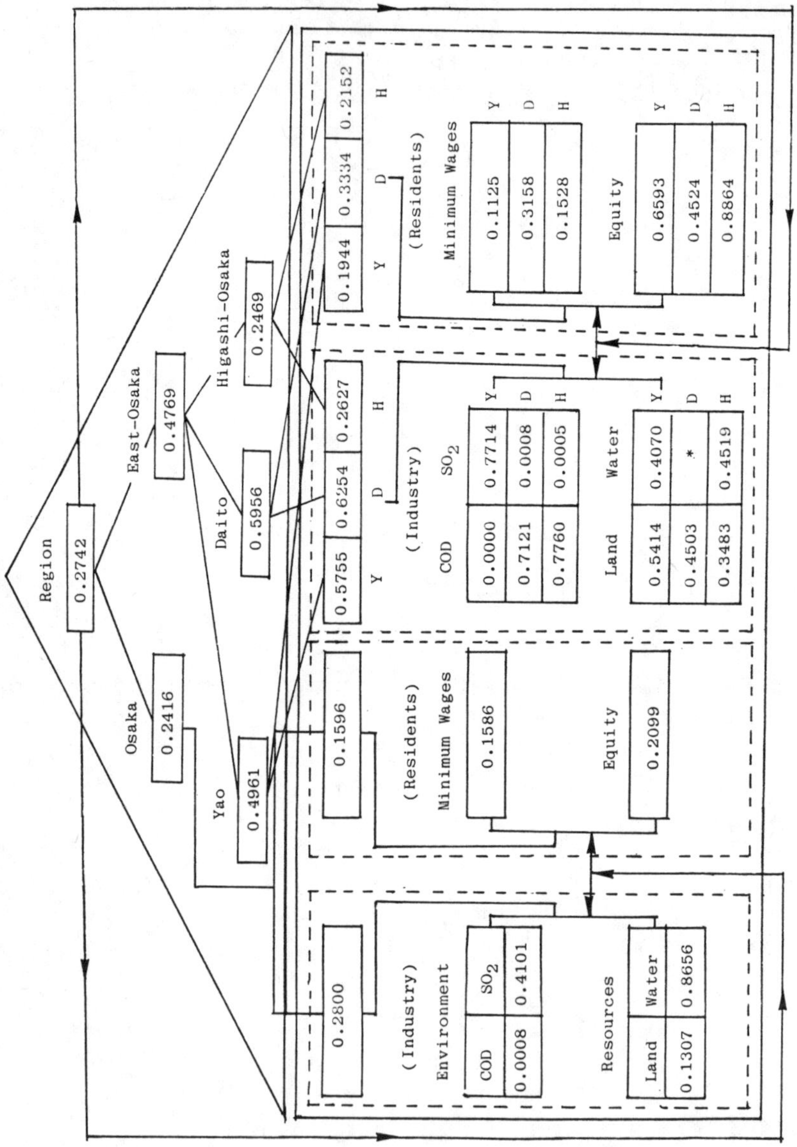


**Figure 11.4 Regional utility assessment for the industrialized Yodo River basin area.**

**Table 11.8 Numerical values of scaling constants**

I. Local MUF for the industrial problem in each subregion

Osaka($U_{OSIN}$):

| | |
|---|---|
| $k_{SO_2}=0.4k_{COD}$ | $k_{COD}=0.8$ |
| $k_{land}=0.3k_{COD}$ | $K_{IN}=-0.8268$ |
| $k_{water}=0.2k_{COD}$ | |

$k_{COD}=0.8 > k_{SO2}=0.32 > k_{land}=0.24 > k_{water}=0.16$

Yao($U_{YAIN}$):

| | |
|---|---|
| $k_{COD}=0.3k_{land}$ | $k_{land}=0.9$ |
| $k_{water}=0.25k_{land}$ | $K_{IN}=-0.8871$ |
| $k_{SO_2}=0.1k_{land}$ | |

$k_{land}=0.9 > k_{COD}=0.27 > k_{water}=0.225 > k_{SO2}=0.09$

Daito($U_{DAIN}$):

| | |
|---|---|
| $k_{land}=0.25k_{COD}$ | $k_{COD}=0.8$ |
| $k_{SO_2}=0.2k_{COD}$ | $K_{IN}=-0.6704$ |
| $k_{water}=0.15k_{COD}$ | |

$k_{COD}=0.8 > k_{land}=0.2 > k_{SO2}=0.16 > k_{water}=0.12$

Higashi-Osaka($U_{HGIN}$):

| | |
|---|---|
| $k_{COD}=0.3k_{SO2}$ | $k_{SO2}=0.75$ |
| $k_{land}=0.25k_{SO2}$ | |
| $k_{water}=0.1k_{SO2}$ | $K_{IN}=-0.5855$ |

$k_{SO_2}=0.75 > k_{COD}=0.225 > k_{land}=0.1875 > k_{water}=0.075$

II. Composite MUF for each subsystem

| | | |
|---|---|---|
| Osaka($U_{OS}$): | | |
| $k_{OSR}=0.4k_{OSIN}$ | $k_{OSIN}=0.7$ | $K_{OS}=0.1020$ |
| Yao($U_{YA}$): | | |
| $k_{YAR}=0.2k_{YAIN}$ | $k_{YAIN}=0.8$ | $K_{YA}=0.3125$ |
| Daito($U_{DA}$): | | |
| $k_{DAR}=0.15k_{DAIN}$ | $k_{DAIN}=0.85$ | $K_{DA}=0.2076$ |
| Higashi-Osaka($U_{HG}$): | | |
| $k_{HGR}=0.3k_{HGIN}$ | $k_{HGIN}=0.75$ | $K_{HG}=0.1481$ |
| Higashi-Osaka district($U_{EO}$): | | |
| $k_{DA}=0.11k_{YA}$ | $k_{YA}=0.8$ | $K_{EO}=0.6406$ |
| $k_{HG}=0.05k_{YA}$ | | |

III. An overall regional MUF(U):

| | | |
|---|---|---|
| $k_{EO}=0.2k_{OS}$ | $k_{OS}=0.8$ | $K=0.3125$ |

comes to resemble Osaka City, has the lowest level of overall satisfaction. The lowest level of satisfaction for a residential problem, which is found in Yao, results from the low level of satisfaction with the minimum-wage requirement in the city.

(iii) The poor satisfaction level for the residential problem in Osaka City is caused by the low level of satisfaction with the equity requirement in the city, whereas the residential problem in the East Osaka district has the highest satisfaction level from this point of view. Daito, however, which has had the most rapid economic development recently, has the lowest level of satisfaction with the equity requirement in the three cities in the East Osaka district.

(iv) With regard to restrictions on resources, the utility level for land limitation in Osaka City is the worst among all resources in all subregions.

These results coincide with a common understanding of the present situation in the greater Osaka area. The numerical results of the utility assessment indicate, in more sophisticated forms, the places where the difficulties exist to be resolved in the present systems.

For further results, see Seo (1978a), and Seo and Sakawa (1979a).

## 11.3 Multiobjective Evaluation of Regional Planning in the Greater Osaka Area: A Dynamic Case

The regional industrial management problem is extended to a dynamic model over multiple periods (Seo and Sakawa 1979b).

For the overall industrial management problem, temporal decompositions (short term: $t = 1,2$; intermediate term: $t = 3,4$; and long term: $t = 5$) and the regional decompositions (Osaka City and East Osaka district: Yao, Daito, and Higashi-Osaka cities) are introduced. Each period is composed of two years. This system is constructed in two layers: local level planning and regional level planning. In the local level planning, a functional decomposition is constructed in the form of mathematical programming. In the regional level planning, functions for modulations and interventions by DM are introduced. Based on this coordination process, an overall systems evaluation is performed.

First, at the first layer, an industrial management problem is formulated as a mathematical programming problem and solved independently in each subregion $i$. The different values of constraint constants and parameters are assigned for each subregion according to its characteristics. The problem formulation is as follows:

$$\underset{K_j,\, L_j}{\text{maximize}} \quad F(K, L) = \sum_{t=1}^{5} \sum_{j=1}^{n_i} A_j e^{\mu_j t} K_j(t)^{1-b_j} L_j(t)^{b_j} \tag{11.26}$$

$$\text{subject to} \quad \sum_{j=1}^{n_i} (\omega_{sjt_0} e^{-\rho_s t} / \kappa_j) K_j(t) \leqslant \tau_s(t), \tag{11.27}$$

$$t = 1, \ldots, 5, \quad s = 1,2$$

$$\sum_{j=1}^{n_i} (\gamma_{sj}(t)/\kappa_j)\, K_j(t) \leqslant \Gamma_s(t), \tag{11.28}$$

$$t = 1, \ldots, 5, \quad s = 3,4$$

$$\sum_{j=1}^{n_i} K_j(t) / \sum_{j=1}^{n_i} L_j(t) \leqslant q_t, \quad t = 1, \ldots, 5 \tag{11.29}$$

$$K_{jt_0} e^{-\pi t} \leqslant K_j(t) \leqslant K_{jt_0} e^{\pi' t}, \tag{11.30}$$

$$j = 1, \ldots, n_i, \quad t = 1, \ldots, 5,$$

$$L_{jt_0} e^{-\pi t} \leqslant L_j(t) \leqslant L_{jt_0} e^{\pi' t}, \tag{11.31}$$

where $n_i$ is the number of industries in the subregion $i$.

The objective function (11.26) is the sum of the dynamic production functions of the Cobb-Douglas type for each industry $j$, $j = 1, \ldots, n_i$. Constraints (11.27) and (11. 28) are target constraints and show environmental and resource constraints respectively.

The $\omega_{sj}(t) \triangleq \omega_{sjt_0} e^{-\rho_s t}$ and $\gamma_{sj}(t)$ indicate unit loads of environment and resource factors $s$, $s \triangleq (1,2,3,4) = $ (COD, $SO_2$; land, water), per industrial shipment in industry $j$. These parameters are changed for each planning period $t$. $\kappa_j$ is a capital coefficient in industry $j$. Constraint constants $\tau_s(t)$ and $\Gamma_s(t)$ on the right-hand side are assigned by the upper-level decision unit and are also changed for each period. Constraint (11.29) is a technical constraint which shows that the capital intensity (capital-labor ratio) cannot exceed its present level. This constraint (11.29) is shown in fact to be generally inactive. Constraints (11.30) and (11.31) are frictional constraints for capital and labor transfer among industries. The number of industries $n_i$ varies from 15 to 20 in each subregion $i$. Each problem includes 150 to 200 decision variables and 25 constraints besides the upper-and lower-bound constraints (11.30) and (11.31).

The mathematical programming problem constructed as the local level planning is to find the optimal allocation of capital and labor among industries that will maximize the industrial output (11.26) under the environmental and resource constraints (11.27) (11.28) considering the technical and frictional restrictions (11.29)-(11.31). The following assumptions are used.

(1) The production function is of the Cobb-Douglas type with the Hicks-neutral technological progress (i.e., not embodied to capital and labor). Parameter $\mu_j$ representing a rate of technological progress is based on 1970-1975 data and extended to the period 1975-1985.

(2) The predicted rates of the change $\rho_s$ of the unit load of the environmental as well as the resource factor $s$ are assumed to be the same for each industry. The rates of COD and $SO_2$ are based on the trends of actual data in the Pollution White Paper for Osaka Prefecture (1977). For water, an increase of 20 percent during 10 years is assumed.

(3) Capital coefficients $\kappa_j$ and rates of distribution $b_j$ are average values calculated from time-series data and are taken as constants over the planning period.

(4) For frictional constraints, $\pi = 0.102$, $\pi' = 0.067$ in Osaka and $\pi = 0.071$, $\pi' = 0.139$ in other subregions are assigned. (For ten years, they show (-)40 percent, 40 percent, and (-)30 percent, 100 percent, respectively)

**Table 11.9 Assessment of utility for environmental management program in the regions**

| | t=1 | | t=2 | | t=3 | | t=4 | | t=5 | |
|---|---|---|---|---|---|---|---|---|---|---|
| | λ | u | λ | u | λ | u | λ | u | λ | u |
| **Osaka** | | | | | | | | | | |
| COD | 43.34 | 0.85 | 15.82 | 0.16 | 83.15 | 0.21 | 50.81 | 0.70 | 56.30 | 0.68 |
| $SO_2$ | 47.17 | 0.94 | 0.08 | 0.00 | 343.96 | 0.86 | 67.19 | 0.96 | 74.88 | 0.93 |
| Land | 7.21 | 0.05 | 96.69 | 0.97 | 6.96 | 0.02 | 23.76 | 0.29 | 24.76 | 0.24 |
| Water | 12.51 | 0.17 | 72.37 | 0.72 | 25.34 | 0.06 | 7.31 | 0.04 | 8.44 | 0.02 |
| **Yao** | | | | | | | | | | |
| COD | 1.42 | 0.09 | 1.05 | 0.07 | 1.57 | 0.09 | 0.00 | - | 5.56 | 0.08 |
| $SO_2$ | 0.24 | 0.02 | 1.98 | 0.13 | 0.04 | 0.00 | 2.42 | 0.05 | 23.79 | 0.39 |
| Land | 10.85 | 0.72 | 8.09 | 0.54 | 8.31 | 0.46 | 8.60 | 0.26 | 5.53 | 0.08 |
| Water | 3.27 | 0.22 | 12.65 | 0.84 | 14.80 | 0.82 | 26.05 | 0.86 | 57.54 | 0.96 |
| **Daito** | | | | | | | | | | |
| COD | 1.43 | 0.06 | 106.64 | 0.12 | 265.58 | 0.52 | 282.34 | 0.56 | 285.91 | 0.56 |
| $SO_2$ | 2.00 | 0.10 | 370.18 | 0.71 | 409.20 | 0.81 | 453.02 | 0.90 | 460.23 | 0.92 |
| Land | 0.00 | - | 72.40 | 0.05 | 24.98 | 0.03 | 25.43 | 0.03 | 25.99 | 0.03 |
| Water | 13.42 | 0.89 | 111.71 | 0.14 | 133.73 | 0.25 | 138.26 | 0.26 | 133.44 | 0.25 |
| **Higashi-Osaka** | | | | | | | | | | |
| COD | 82.76 | 0.31 | 7.98 | 0.79 | 0.00 | - | 9.98 | 0.09 | 28.95 | 0.80 |
| $SO_2$ | 0.00 | - | 0.60 | 0.03 | 60.06 | 0.85 | 50.69 | 0.83 | 11.52 | 0.22 |
| Land | 43.61 | 0.08 | 8.32 | 0.83 | 8.56 | 0.05 | 7.81 | 0.05 | 6.43 | 0.05 |
| Water | 174.05 | 0.85 | 0.00 | - | 13.08 | 0.12 | 10.69 | 0.10 | 22.14 | 0.57 |

As a result, it is known that, in the dynamic case, both economic growth and environmental management are compatible with one another. In particular, promotion of electric machinery, apparel, and nonferrous metal industries is recommended, which is consistent with the results of the static model in the previous analysis.

The Lagrange multipliers combined with the primal solutions are converted via positive linear transformation to the quasi-utility values. Numerical results are shown in Table 11.9. It is known that, in Osaka, land and water constraints are the worst in terms of the local production functions. In Yao, COD and $SO_2$ are the worst; however, these difficulties are decreasing during the planning period. On the contrary, difficulty for land is increasing. In Daito and Higashi-Osaka, satisfaction with the availability of land is the worst. Thus it can be seen that, in the dynamic model, difficulties caused by the land constraint form the major problem for this region.

Finally, the component utility functions are nested into MUF. The numerical representation of MUF $U^j$ is generally presented in multiplicative form:

$$1 + K^j U^j = \prod_{i=1}^{m} (1 + K^j k_i u_i) \tag{11.32}$$

or

$$U^j = 1/a_0 \left[ \prod_{i=1}^{m} (1 + a_i u_i) - 1 \right], \tag{11.33}$$

where $a_0 \triangleq K^j$ and $a_i \triangleq K^j k_i$. $k_i$, $K^j$ are scaling constants, and $\sum_{i=1}^{m} k_i \neq 1$, $0 < k_i < 1$ and $K^j > -1$. Parameters for the scaling constants are shown in Table 11.10.

The numerical values of these utility functions obtained from present situations are calculated and shown in Table 11.11.

## 11.4. Industrial Land-use Program Combined with Water Quality Control: A Dynamic Case

In an application of the nested Lagrangian multiplier (NLM) method to a regional land-use program combined with water quality control, the hierarchical two-layer modeling of the multiobjective decision system is used. However, in the first (lower) layer, we incorporate a physical simulation model into water quality control processes. In the second (upper) layer, probability assessment is used to determine the expected value of the quasi-utility functions for mitigating the appearance of some extreme values.

The object area in this study is the Otsu River Basin in the northern Senshu area of Osaka Prefecture in Japan.

The hierarchical structure and its decomposition of the Otsu River Basin system is shown in Figure 11.5. The first layer is composed of one main program unit and two subsidiary simulation units. The main program unit is decomposed into two levels which correspond to regional (Izumi-Otsu City, Tadaoka-Cho, and Izumi City) and time ($t = 1,\ldots,5$) decompositions where each period is composed of two years. For each subsystem, a mathematical programming problem is independently formulated and solved with its specific parameters and constraint constants.

Table 11.10 Parameters of multiattribute utility functions

| | Short term: t = 1,2 | | | | | Intermediate term; t = 3,4 | | | | | Long term: t = 5 | | | | |
|---|---|---|---|---|---|---|---|---|---|---|---|---|---|---|---|
| | $a_0$ | $a_1$ | $u_1$ | $a_2$ | $u_2$ | $a_0$ | $a_1$ | $u_1$ | $a_2$ | $u_2$ | $a_0$ | $a_1$ | $u_1$ | $a_2$ | $u_2$ |
| **Osaka:** | | | | | | | | | | | | | | | |
| $U_{OS}$ | -0.2083 | -0.1666 | $u_{env}$ | -0.0500 | $u_{res}$ | 0.3207 | 0.2245 | $u_{env}$ | 0.0786 | $u_{res}$ | 1.1111 | 0.6667 | $u_{env}$ | 0.2667 | $u_{res}$ |
| $U_{env}$ | -0.2083 | -0.0500 | $u_{COD}$ | -0.1666 | $u_{SO_2}$ | -0.2222 | -0.0667 | $u_{COD}$ | -0.1667 | $u_{SO_2}$ | -0.4082 | -0.1714 | $u_{COD}$ | -0.2857 | $u_{SO_2}$ |
| $U_{res}$ | -0.6633 | -0.3714 | $u_{land}$ | -0.4643 | $u_{water}$ | -0.6983 | -0.3666 | $u_{land}$ | -0.5237 | $u_{water}$ | -0.7292 | -0.3500 | $u_{land}$ | -0.5834 | $u_{water}$ |
| **Yao:** | | | | | | | | | | | | | | | |
| $U_{YA}$ | 0.3125 | 0.2500 | $u_{env}$ | 0.0500 | $u_{res}$ | 0.4445 | 0.3334 | $u_{env}$ | 0.0833 | $u_{res}$ | 0.6122 | 0.4285 | $u_{env}$ | 0.1236 | $u_{res}$ |
| $U_{env}$ | -0.4082 | -0.1714 | $u_{COD}$ | -0.2857 | $u_{SO_2}$ | -0.6984 | -0.3667 | $u_{COD}$ | -0.5238 | $u_{SO_2}$ | -0.8035 | -0.4500 | $u_{COD}$ | -0.6428 | $u_{SO_2}$ |
| $U_{res}$ | -0.0079 | -0.0033 | $u_{land}$ | -0.0047 | $u_{water}$ | -0.4866 | -0.2214 | $u_{land}$ | -0.3406 | $u_{water}$ | -0.7292 | -0.3500 | $u_{land}$ | -0.5834 | $u_{water}$ |
| **Daito:** | | | | | | | | | | | | | | | |
| $U_{DA}$ ( * ) | 0.0 | 0.8 | $u_{env}$ | 0.2 | $u_{res}$ | 0.1481 | 0.1111 | $u_{env}$ | 0.0333 | $u_{res}$ | 0.3207 | 0.2245 | $u_{env}$ | 0.0786 | $u_{res}$ |
| $U_{env}$ | -0.2041 | -0.0714 | $u_{COD}$ | -0.1429 | $u_{SO_2}$ | -0.5926 | -0.2667 | $u_{COD}$ | -0.4445 | $u_{SO_2}$ | -0.8036 | -0.4500 | $u_{COD}$ | -0.6429 | $u_{SO_2}$ |
| $U_{res}$ | -0.079 | -0.0332 | $u_{land}$ | -0.0474 | $u_{water}$ | -0.4866 | -0.2214 | $u_{land}$ | -0.3406 | $u_{water}$ | -0.7292 | -0.3500 | $u_{land}$ | -0.5834 | $u_{water}$ |
| **Higashi-Osaka:** | | | | | | | | | | | | | | | |
| $U_{HG}$ | -0.2083 | -0.1666 | $u_{env}$ | -0.0500 | $u_{res}$ | -0.0635 | -0.0476 | $u_{env}$ | -0.0167 | $u_{res}$ | 0.3453 | 0.2314 | $u_{env}$ | 0.0925 | $u_{res}$ |
| $U_{env}$ | -0.2083 | -0.0500 | $u_{COD}$ | -0.1666 | $u_{SO_2}$ | -0.2222 | -0.0667 | $u_{COD}$ | -0.1667 | $u_{SO_2}$ | -0.2041 | -0.0714 | $u_{COD}$ | -0.1429 | $u_{SO_2}$ |
| $U_{res}$ | -0.3550 | -0.1615 | $u_{land}$ | -0.2308 | $u_{water}$ | -0.4082 | -0.1714 | $u_{land}$ | -0.2857 | $u_{water}$ | -0.4675 | -0.1800 | $u_{land}$ | -0.3506 | $u_{water}$ |
| **East Osaka:** | | | | | | | | | | | | | | | |
| $U_{EO}$ | $1/-0.1587[(1-0.0952U_{YAO})(1-0.0381\ U_{DA})(1-0.0333\ U_{HG})-1]$ | | | | | $1/-0.3067[(1-0.1840\ U_{YAO})(1-0.0828\ U_{DA})(1-0.0736\ U_{HG})-1]$ | | | | | $1/-0.4228[(1-0.2537\ U_{YAO})(1-0.1268\ U_{DA})(1-0.1142\ U_{HG})-1]$ | | | | |
| **Region:** | | | | | | | | | | | | | | | |
| $U_R$ | 0.6122 | 0.4285 | $u_{OS}$ | 0.1286 | $u_{EO}$ | 0.8283 | 0.5384 | $u_{OS}$ | 0.1884 | $u_{EO}$ | 1.1111 | 0.6667 | $u_{OS}$ | 0.2667 | $u_{EO}$ |

* Additive form: $u = a_1 u_1 + a_2 u_2$

**Table 11.11 Numerical evaluation of environmental management program: 1975**

| | Short term ( t=1 ) | Intermediate term (t=3) | Long term ( t=5 ) |
|---|---|---|---|
| Osaka | 0.0285 | 0.0110 | 0.0038 |
| environment | 0.7518 | 0.6452 | 0.6509 |
| COD | 0.85 | 0.21 | 0.68 |
| $SO_2$ | 0.94 | 0.86 | 0.93 |
| resources | 0.1190 | 0.0450 | 0.0160 |
| land | 0.05 | 0.02 | 0.24 |
| water | 0.17 | 0.16 | 0.02 |
| Yao | 0.0209 | 0.1076 | 0.1613 |
| environment | 0.0140 | 0.0473 | 0.3120 |
| COD | 0.09 | 0.09 | 0.08 |
| $SO_2$ | 0.02 | 0.00 | 0.39 |
| resources | 0.1309 | 0.5740 | 0.7680 |
| land | 0.72 | 0.46 | 0.08 |
| water | 0.22 | 0.82 | 0.96 |
| Daito | 0.1628 | 0.0393 | 0.0490 |
| environment | 0.0700 | 0.6076 | 0.7360 |
| COD | 0.06 | 0.52 | 0.56 |
| $SO_2$ | 0.10 | 0.81 | 0.92 |
| resources | 0.5340 | 0.1750 | 0.2000 |
| land | - | 0.03 | 0.03 |
| water | 0.89 | 0.25 | 0.25 |
| Higashi-Osaka | 0.1326 | 0.0221 | 0.1145 |
| environment | 0.0744 | 0.6377 | 0.1540 |
| COD | 0.31 | - | 0.80 |
| $SO_2$ | - | 0.85 | 0.22 |
| resources | 0.5526 | 0.0840 | 0.4275 |
| land | 0.08 | 0.05 | 0.05 |
| water | 0.85 | 0.12 | 0.57 |
| East Osaka ( Yao, Daito, Higashi-Osaka ) | 0.2782 | 0.0053 | 0.0309 |
| Region ( Osaka, East Osaka ) | 0.0058 | 0.0012 | 0.0074 |

The second layer is also decomposed into two levels. The infimal decision unit corresponds to a regional decomposition (coastal and inland) and the supremal decision unit (the Otsu River Basin Authority) corresponds to an overall systems coordination.

In the first layer, there are interface transactions of parameters via the input-output relationship between the main program unit and the simulation units. Main information channels have their counter-flow in each phase. The first layer corresponds to the second layer via feedback information channels. Interactive evaluation and calculation for finding the preferred policy program are iteratively executed through

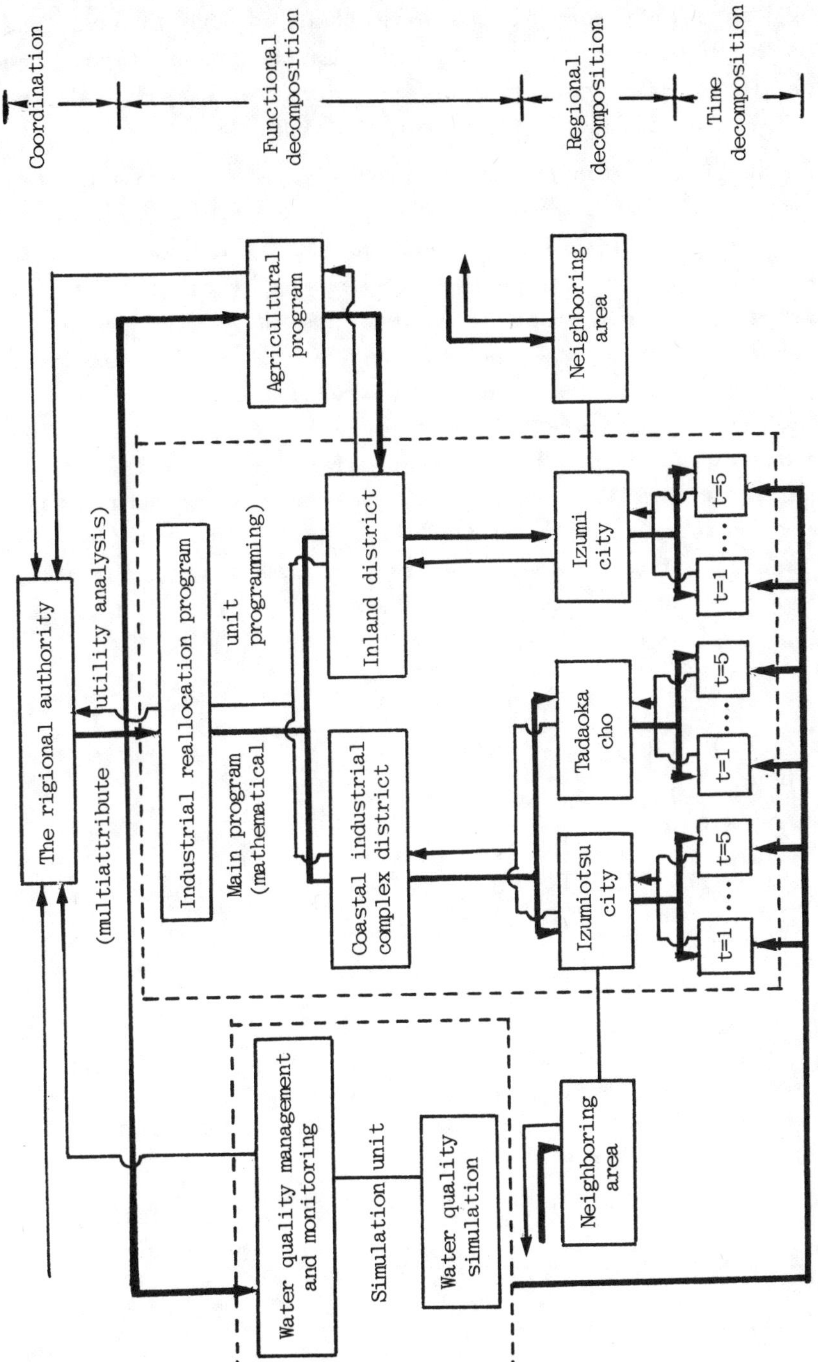


Figure 11.5 Systems decomposition and hierarchical modeling of the problem complex for the Otsu Riber basin.

learning and adaptation processes in the vertical transactions of information between the two layers. In the second-layer, the decision unit is concerned with worth assessments for alternative regional policies in terms of MUF.

The whole decision system has three major objectives: (1) to promote economic growth, (2) to control river water pollution, and (3) to preserve land quality. The land quality is taken up as a surrogate representing the quality for environmental factors other than water, such as air pollution and noise from factory and traffic congestion. The preservation of land quality is represented in the regulations of industrial land-use, by which spatial environmental quality will be conserved. Thus in the main program unit, mathematical programming is formulated for a land-use program connected with industrial reallocation under the water quality restrictions in each planning period in each subregion. The whole planning period is ten years. The local problem formulation for each subregion i is as follows:

$$\underset{K_j^i,\ L_j^i,\ D_j^i,}{\text{maximize}} \quad \sum_{j=1}^{n_i} H_j^i(t)$$

$$= \sum_{j=1}^{n_i} A_{jt_o}^i \, e^{\mu_j^i t} \, K_j^i(t)^{\alpha_j^i} \, L_j^i(t)^{\beta_j^i} \, D_j^i(t)^{1-\alpha_j^i-\beta_j^i} \qquad (11.34)$$

subject to

$$\sum_{j=1}^{n_i} (\kappa_j^i \,/\, \delta_{jt_o} e^{-\psi_j t}) \, D_j^i(t) \geq K^i(t), \qquad (11.35)$$

$$\sum_{j=1}^{n_i} (\omega_{jt_o} \, e^{-\rho t}/\kappa_j^i) \, K_j^i(t) \leq W^i(t), \qquad (11.36)$$

$$\sum_{j=1}^{n_i} L_j^i(t) \leq L^i(t), \qquad (11.37)$$

$$\sum_{j=1}^{n_i} D_j^i(t) \leq D^i(t), \tag{11.38}$$

$$(K/L)_j^{L^i} \leq K_j^i(t)/L_j^i(t) \leq (K/L)_j^{U^i}, \quad j = 1,\ldots,n_i, \tag{11.39}$$

$$K_{jt_o}^i e^{-\pi t} \leq K_j^i(t) \leq K_{jt_o}^i e^{\pi' t}, \quad j = 1,\ldots,n_i, \tag{11.40}$$

$$L_{jt_o}^i e^{-\pi t} \leq L_j^i\,(t) \leq L_{jt_o}^i e^{\pi' t}, \quad j = 1,\ldots,n_i, \tag{11.41}$$

where $i$ denotes a subregion, $i$ = Izumi-Otsu, Tadaoka, Izumi; $j$ is an industry, $j = 1,\ldots,n_i$, and $t$ is a planning period, $t = 1,\ldots,5$. Decision variables for each industry are capital value $K_j^i(t)$ (million yen/year), labor force $L_j^i(t)$ (persons), and industrial land area $D_j^i(t)$ ($100m^2$); $H_j^i(t)$ is industrial output (million yen/year), and $\kappa_j^i$ is the average value of the capital coefficient calculated from time-series data. The $\delta_{jt_o}$ is a land coefficient per industrial output $H_{jt_o}$, and $\omega_{jt_o}$ is a unit load of COD effluent discharge (ton/year) per industrial output. Subscript $t_o$ shows an initial value of the decision variable or parameter and is taken as $t_o = 1975$. Thus, $\delta_{jt_o} = D_{jt_o}/H_{jt_o}$ and $\omega_{jt_o} = W_{jt_o}/H_{jt_o}$. These values are calculated from aggregated data for the districts and thus are used in common for each subregion. $K^i(t)$ is the total capital value (million yen/year) and represents an economic growth policy. $W^i(t)$ is the total COD effluent discharge (ton/year) and represents a water pollution control policy. These policy aims, economic growth and water pollution control, take discretionary ranges and are varied in each planning period. $L^i(t)$ and $D^i(t)$ are the predicted upper-bounds of total labor and land supply for industry use. The $K^i(t)$, $W^i(t)$, $L^i(t)$, and $D^i(t)$ are target constraint constants imposed by the upper-level decision unit. The number of selected industries for each subregion is three to nine.

The objective function (11.34) is the sum of the Cobb-Douglas-type production function for each industry, in which the

Hicks-neutral technological progress is included as $A^i_{jt_o} e^{\mu^i_j t}$, where $\mu^i_j$ shows a growth rate due to unembodied technological progress. The Cobb-Douglas production function is homogeneous of degree one and shows that, if each production factor, $K^i_j$, $L^i_j$, $D^i_j$, is paid its marginal product, total output is distributed among these production factors in the proportions $\alpha^i_j$, $\beta^i_j$, and $(1 - \alpha^i_j - \beta^i_j)$, respectively.

In the constraint (11.35), the land variable $D^i_j(t)$ is related to the growth policy for total capital formation $K^i(t)$ via the capital coefficient $k^i_j$ and land coefficient $\delta_j(t) \triangleq \delta_{jt_o} e^{-\psi_j t}$. The $\delta_{jt_o} e^{-\psi_j t}$ is imposed as an indicative policy parameter sent down from the upper-level decision unit. The reduction rate $\psi_j$ is varied for each industry depending on alternative land-use policies, but is taken as being the same for each subregion during the whole planning period. In the constraint (11.36), the capital variable $K^i_j(t)$ is related to the water pollution control policy for total COD effluent discharge, $W^i(t)$, in each subregion i. The $\omega_{jt_o} e^{-\rho t}$ is used as a policy parameter, and the $\rho$-value is taken to be the same among industries and subregions, and also fixed during the whole planning period.

Constraint (11.37) shows that the labor requirements of local industries should not exceed the predicted local labor supply, and constraint (11.38) shows that the land availability for industrial use is restricted in each subregion. The constraint constants, $K^i(t)$, $W^i(t)$, $L^i(t)$, and $D^i(t)$, are all varied according to alternative policies.

Constraint (11.39) is a technical constraint. Constraints (11.40) and (11.41) are frictional constraints and are set for avoiding radical changes of the local industrial structure, which would cause some social problems due to the "frictional" unemployment of local capital and labor in the subregion. The $\pi$ and $\pi'$ are the policy parameters set for avoiding such social conflict.

The decision problem is to find the optimal reallocation program for capital, labor, and land that maximizes the local industrial output under the resource and environmental constraints. These constraints prescribe indicative levels of economic growth and water quality control under the given conditions on the labor supply and land availability for each subregion. For solving the nonlinear mathematical programming (11.34)-(11.41), the Generalized Reduced Gradient (GRG) Algorithm developed by Lasdon et al. (1974, 1976, 1977) has been effectively used.

Data was obtained with some necessary calculations from the Input-Output Table for Industrial Pollution Analysis in the Kinki area in 1973, by the Division of Trade and Industry, Osaka Prefecture; Industrial Statistics Survey Results Table in 1973, and 1975; by the Statistical Office of Osaka Prefecture; White Paper on Pollution in Osaka Prefecture. 1977 by the Pollution Prevention Program in Osaka Prefecture; and Census of Manufacture: Report on Industrial Land and Water, by the Japan Ministry of International Trade and Industry, 1975 (all in Japanese).

In the water quality simulation unit, an ecological model is used for describing the interrelationship among ecological constituents acting in self-purification mechanisms in the river. The water quality simulation model is presented as an extension of the Streeter-Phelps model and includes dissolved oxygen (DO) and biochemical oxygen demand (BOD) concentrations as affected by sunlight, water temperature, and photosynthetic activity of plants and algae (Beck, 1978a, 1978b). Experiments for alternative models having this property have been executed based on the continuously-stirred tank reactor (CSTR) idealization without transportation delay and measurement error by Beck and Young (1975, 1976). However, from their experiment on the River Cam, it has been shown that including parameters for the algae population in the water quality model does not largely improve the model-fitting of the observed water system. Thus their Type-II model were utilized for simulating self-purification mechanisms of river water quality and were extended for a one-year (day-by-day) data for the present study. In this model, water temperature $\theta$ is explicitly introduced via sunlight effects $h$ and DO saturation concentration $C$ to represent the influence of algae on DO-BOD balance.

The simulation model is as follows.

$$X_1 = -(k_1 + Q(\tau)/V)\ x_1(\tau) - k_2x_2(\tau) + (Q(\tau)/V)\ U_1(\tau) + k_1C(\tau) + k_4(h(\tau) - \bar{h}) + S(\tau), \tag{11.42}$$

$$X_2 = -(k_2 + k_3 + Q(\tau)/V)\ x_2(\tau) + (Q(\tau)/V)U_2(\tau) + k_5(h(\tau) - \bar{h}) + R, \tag{11.43}$$

where

$$h(\tau_k) = h(\tau_{k-1}) + \frac{1}{T}[\nu(\tau_k)\ \{\frac{\theta(\tau_k) - \bar{\theta}}{\bar{\theta}}\} - h(\tau_{k-1})], \tag{11.44}$$

$$(h(\tau_k) - \bar{h}) = 0 \text{ for } h(\tau_k) < \bar{h}, \tag{11.45}$$

$$h(\tau_0) = 0.0, \tag{11.46}$$

and

$$C(\tau) = 14.5412 - 0.3928\,\theta(\tau) - 0.0073(\theta(\tau))^2 - 0.000066(\theta(\tau))^3, \tag{11.47}$$

$$\tau_0 \leqslant \tau_k \leqslant \tau_{365}, \quad \tau_k - \tau_{k-1} = 1(\text{day}). \tag{11.48}$$

The values of some parameters, such as reaeration rate $k_1$ for DO, BOD decay rate $k_2$, and BOD sedimentation rate $k_3$, are assumed to be the same as those for the river Cam experiment because of the common properties of both rivers flowing in catchment areas through open fields. The flow rates of both the rivers are assumed to be approximately same. Coefficients for the sustained sunlight effects on DO and BOD equations, $k_4$ and $k_5$, are also taken to be the same as those for the river Cam with the assumption that meteorological conditions in the early summer season in central England resemble the average conditions in Japan. However, the parameter value S for decomposition of bottom mud deposit was revised to make the river Cam data applicable to the year-round data in Japan. The increase of BOD generated from the local surface runoff $R$ is also assumed to take a positive value, differing from the river Cam experiment, because rainfall effects during the long rainy season in Japan cannot be neglected. Other parameters, such as the threshold level for sunlight effect $\bar{h}$ and time constant $T$, are taken as the same as those for the river Cam. For the Otsu River experiment, empirical time-series data on water temperature $\theta(\tau)$ and sunlight hours $\nu(\tau)$ in Osaka Prefecture are used. Data on the volumetric flow rate $Q(\tau)$ and on mean volumetric hold up in the reach $V$ are also taken from empirical data for the Otsu River. Initial values, $x_1(\tau_0)$ and $x_2(\tau_0)$, are newly set for our experiment.

Data for the Otsu river experiment are obtained with calculations from the Year Book on Japanese River Quality 1975, by the Division of Rivers, Japan Ministry of Construction; Osaka Environmental Management Plan 1973, by Osaka Prefecture; and Reports of the Osaka Meteorological Observatory. Data for the water quality is collected in the vicinity of the final point of COD effluent discharge from Otsu river into Osaka Bay (White Paper on Pollution by Osaka Prefecture).

The dynamic loop of interactive processes of mathematical optimization and simulation is depicted in the hierarchical and interface configuration in Figure 11.6. The mathematical programming unit is combined with the simulation unit via the input-output relationship of parameters. The mathematical programming unit solves the industrial land-use problem (11.34)-(11.41) in each subregion by receiving information on the reduction rate $\rho$ of COD discharge along with the parameter $\psi_j$, $j = 1,\dots,n_i$, as input from the upper-level decision unit, and then sends information on the total industrial product in each period $t$, $\sum_{i=1}^{3} \sum_{j=1}^{n_i} H_j^{i*}(t)$, as output to the simulation unit. In the simulation unit, the control parameter EPSI is imposed, based on information on total pollution in the whole region $\sum_{i=1}^{3} \sum_{j=1}^{n_i} \omega_j(t) H_j^{i*}(t)$. The control parameter EPSI is assigned to the input variable $U_2(\tau)$ in the simulation model in the beginning of each period $t$ as follows:

$$\frac{\text{EPSI} \sum_{r=1}^{3} \sum_{j=1}^{n_i} \omega_j^i(t)\, H_j^{i*}(t)}{365\; Q(\tau)} = U_2(\tau). \tag{11.49}$$

The simulation unit starting with the input variables $U_1(\tau)$ and $U_2(\tau)$ which are sequentially revised in each period t provides, via (11.42)-(11.48), $X_1(\tau)$ and $X_2(\tau)$ as output. Then the predicted value of controlled pollution effluent discharge in total is calculated as

$$\sum_{k=1}^{365} X_2(\tau_k)\, Q(\tau_k) = \sum_{i=1}^{3} W^i(t). \tag{11.50}$$

The predicted value of COD, $\sum_{i=1}^{3} W^i(t)$, is allocated to each subregion i in proportion to the amount of local industrial

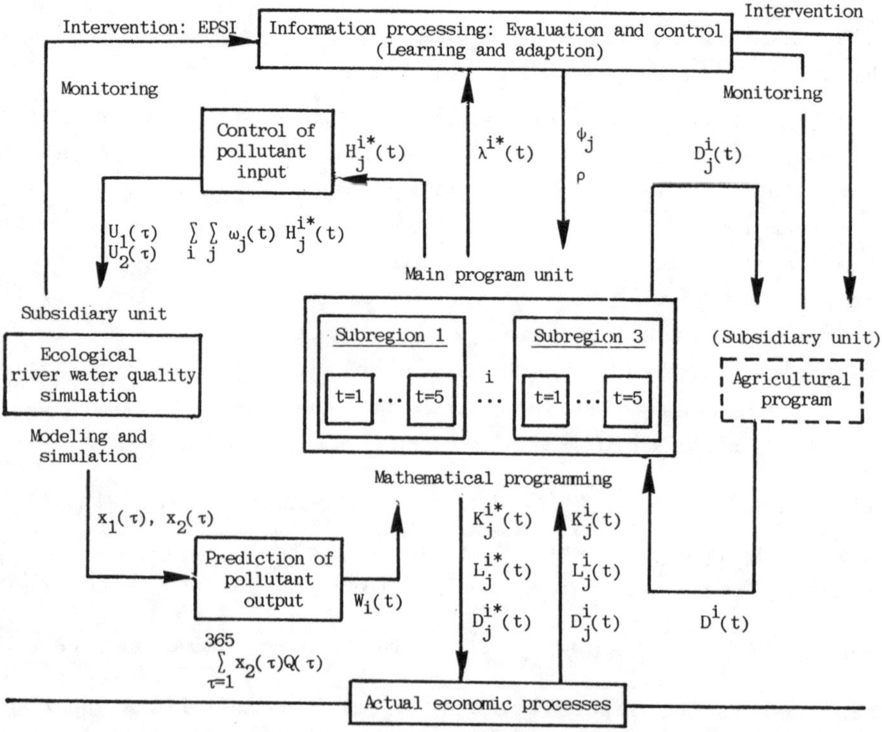


**Figure 11.6 An interactive loop of regional planning combined with water quality control**

shipments and assigned as the constraint constant $W^i(t)$. The input-output relationship between the main program unit and the simulation unit forms an interactive dynamic loop which shows a learning and adaptation process.

The iterative procedure via the dynamic loop is operated for alternative policy programs for land-use, which are formed and evaluated over the five planning periods. Parameters are depicted in Table 11.12. Total reduction rates of policy constraint constants are shown in Table 11.13.

Alternative I is a radical industrial reallocation plan between the coastal and inland areas. Total capital formation at the end of the planning period is reduced about 18% in the coastal industrial complex district, while it is increased about

**Table 11.12 Parameters for the industrial land-use reallocation problem**

(A)

| Parameter | Value | Percentage change from $t_0$ to $t=5$ |
|---|---|---|
| $\rho$ | 0.05754 | (-) 25% |
| $\pi$ | 0.071 | (-) 30% |
| $\pi'$ | 0.139 | (-) 100% |

(B)

| Alternative policy program | Parameter ($\phi_j$) | Percentage change of $\delta_{jt}$ from $t_0$ to $t=5$ | Industry code (j) |
|---|---|---|---|
| AI | 0.0220 | (-) 10% | No. 21, 22, 24, 34, 36 |
| | 0.08616 | (-) 35% | No. 18, 19, 20, 26, 30, 31, 33 |
| AII | 0.0220 | (-) 10% | No. 21, 22, 34, 36 |
| | 0.08616 | (-) 35% | No. 24, 30, 31 |
| | 0.1386 | (-) 50% | No. 18, 19, 20, 26, 33 |
| AIII | 0.0220 | (-) 10% | No. 21, 22, 34 36 |
| | 0.04463 | (-) 20% | No. 18, 19, 20, 24 26, 30, 31, 33 |

**Table 11.13**
**Percentage change of constraint constants for the alternatives (from $t_0$ to t=5)**

| | AI | | | AII | | | AIII | | |
|---|---|---|---|---|---|---|---|---|---|
| | Costal land | | inland | Costal land | | inland | Costal land | | inland |
| | IO | TA | IZ | IO | TA | IZ | IO | TA | IZ |
| $K^i(t)$ | -18.3% | -18.6% | +25.8% | +22.1% | +27.8% | +17.1% | +21.9% | +28.4% | +29.4% |
| $W^i(t)$ | -27.8 | -27.8 | -27.8 | -26.8 | -26.8 | -33.4 | -36.7 | -27.1 | -27.1 |
| $L^i(t)$ | -16.3 | -1.3 | +17.5 | +23.0 | +8.8 | -29.4 | -21.6 | +3.0 | +5.0 |
| $D^i(t)$ | -50.8 | -43.3 | -20.3 | -29.0 | -19.8 | -38.5 | -31.8 | +2.4 | +6.2 |
| Industrial output $\sum_i H_i^*(t)$ | +17.1 | +80.8 | +44.6 | +45.4 | +133.5 | +14.8 | +15.5 | +141.7 | +58.0 |

Note. IO = Izumi-Otsu, TA = Tadaoka, IZ = Izumi

26% in the inland district. Alternative II is an overall reduction policy for industrial land use. Although trends of capital growth in the period 1973-75 in the coastal as well as inland districts are maintained as a typical example, drastic reduction rates for the land coefficients are introduced. In both Alternatives I and II, industrial land areas are reduced about 20%-50% in each subregion. Alternative III is a moderate plan whereby an overall capital growth policy compatible with water quality management is sought. The growth rates for both districts are assured at about 22%-30%. In Izumi-Otsu, the industrial land area is reduced about 32%, but in other cities it is slightly increased.

The Kuhn-Tucker multipliers $\lambda_s^{i*}$ obtained from the mathematical optimization in the local level planning are linearly transformed to the quasi-utility functions $u_s^i(\lambda_s^i)$, where $s = 1,...,4$ denotes the policy constraint constants $K^i(t)$ $W^i(t)$, $L^i(t)$, and $D^i(t)$ in each subregion $i$. A numerical example for Alternative III is shown in Table 11.14.

The analytical results are interpreted as follows. Generally the opportunity costs of the constraint constant for the COD discharge measured in terms of the local objective function do not have high values. Thus the local satisfaction with the COD control show considerably high levels.

For Alternative I, the coastal and inland districts have

Table 11.14 Kuhn-Tucker multiplier ($\lambda_s^i$) and scaled worth assessment ($u_s^1$) for Alternative III

| | t=1 | | t=2 | | t=3 | | t=4 | | t=5 | |
|---|---|---|---|---|---|---|---|---|---|---|
| | $\lambda_s^1$ | $u_s^1$ | $\lambda_s^1$ | $u_s^1$ | $\lambda_s^1$ | $u_s^1$ | $\lambda_s^1$ | $u_s^1$ | $\lambda_s^1$ | $u_s^1$ |
| Izumi-Otsu | | | | | | | | | | |
| K(t) | 0.503 | 0.1033 | 0.4879 | 0.0003 | 0.337 | 0.0068 | 0.455 | 0.0089 | 0.288 | 0.0040 |
| W(t) | 3.837 | 0.9582 | 1461.44 | 0.9976 | 33.58 | 0.9592 | 37.90 | 0.9488 | 21.47 | 0.9763 |
| L(t) | 2.059 | 0.5023 | 2.065 | 0.0013 | 2.16 | 0.0590 | 2.65 | 0.0640 | 19.95 | 0.9065 |
| D(t) | 0.1915 | 0.0235 | 0.178 | $5.5 \times 10^{-5}$ | 0.8631 | 0.0219 | 0.1427 | 0.0011 | 2.511 | 0.1061 |
| Tadaoka | | | | | | | | | | |
| K(t) | 0.265 | 0.0016 | 0.291 | 0.0018 | 0.218 | $2.87 \times 10^{-4}$ | 0.1231 | 0.0003 | 0.04 | 0.0002 |
| W(t) | 37.80 | 0.9438 | 49.40 | 0.9889 | 61.27 | 0.9881 | 76.0 | 0.9715 | 93.30 | 0.9794 |
| L(t) | 2.33 | 0.0535 | 2.469 | 0.0456 | 3.0617 | 0.0463 | 3.83 | 0.0477 | 4.97 | 0.0520 |
| D(t) | 1.34 | 0.0286 | 1.343 | 0.0230 | 1.816 | 0.0261 | 2.40 | 0.0294 | 3.29 | 0.0343 |
| Izumi | | | | | | | | | | |
| K(t) | 0.769 | 0.0385 | 0.944 | 0.0191 | 0.7569 | 0.0157 | 0.888 | 0.0259 | 1.30 | 0.0134 |
| W(t) | 14.584 | 0.9724 | 33.79 | 0.9947 | 40.94 | 0.9761 | 21.893 | 0.9522 | 58.14 | 0.9684 |
| L(t) | 1.7836 | 0.1071 | 1.55 | 0.0371 | 1.811 | 0.0409 | 1.56 | 0.0556 | 2.125 | 0.0273 |
| D(t) | 0.307 | 0.0072 | 0.4179 | 0.0035 | 0.118 | 0.0004 | 0.36 | 0.0027 | 0.796 | 0.0050 |

different characteristics. In the coastal industrial complex district, the constraint constant for capital formation denotes the lowest values for the quasi-utility function, which shows the greatest difficulty for it in this subregion; while, in the inland district, the land constraint presents the most difficulty, which is shown by the low value of the quasi-utility function for it. The labor constraint shows low values of the quasi-utility function, which represents a large difficulty for it, in the industrial district, but shows relatively high values in the inland district.

For Alternative II, the land constraint shows the lowest values of the quasi-utility function for all subregions and represents the greatest difficulty, particularly in Tadaoka. For the capital constraint, Tadaoka also shows the lowest value among the subregions.

For Alternative III, the evaluation reveals that the situation falls between those for Alternatives I and II. The capital constraint shows the lowest value of the quasi-utility function in Tadaoka, while the land constraint shows the lowest value in Izumi. Izumi-Otsu is in a medium situation. In Alternative III, however, there is no subregion showing extreme difficulty for any constraint constant, except during a few periods.

Those results of numerical evaluation primarily correspond to the policy implications for the alternatives, but there are some local peculiarities that result from the parameter relationship specific to each subregion.

Assessment of preferences for the alternative policy programs are performed in the second layer where the MUFs are derived.

**Remarks.**

1. As pointed out in Chapter 10, the NLM method depends on the units of measurement taken for the original data because values of the Kuhn-Tucker multiplier are affected by them. The present case study may suggest that comparisons of the numerical values of the quasi-utility functions will provide more meaningful assessment for a particular constraint constant among alternative policy programs for each subregion and for each

subperiod. Thus, interregional and interperiod comparisons of the quasi-utility values for a particular policy constraint may often, if it is not always, be more recommendable.

2. In the assessment process of MUF-values, the component quasi-utility functions are primarily based on the Kuhn-Tucker multipliers which are generated with an extremal method as mathematical optimization. Thus, these values are not only deterministically obtained but also extremely sensitive to marginal variations of the parameters. For mitigating this characteristic of the generated values, the component utility values $u_s^i(\lambda_s^i)$ can be treated as if they are uncertain quantities, for which probability distributions can be assessed with some other information. As a result, the expected value of $u_s^i(\lambda_s^i)$ can be used in place of the original quasi-utility value. First, for constructing the cumulative distribution function $F_s^i(u_s^{iq})$, the quasi-utility value (u-value) $u_s^{iq}$ is assessed judgmentally as an uncertain quantity for a fractile q, $q = 1,\ldots,Q$, of the distribution $F_s^i$ which takes the values between 0 and 1:

$$F_s^i(u_s^{iq}) = p_s^i(u_s^i \leqslant u_s^{iq}) = \sum_{u_s^{it} \leqslant u_s^{iq}} f_s^i(u_s^{it}),$$

$$q = 1,\ldots,Q, \tag{11.51}$$

where $p_s^i$ is a probability, $0 \leqslant p_s^i \leqslant 1$, and $f_s^i$ is a density function. Then the cumulative distribution function $F_s^i(u_s^i)$ is converted to the density function $f_s^i(u_s^i)$. Uncertainty of the $u_s^i$- values can be examined with the standard deviation for the probability distribution function. Assessment of the probability distribution is based on the some ground rules. Finally, the expected values of the quasi-utility function are calculated in the following form:

$$\bar{u}_s^i \triangleq Eu_s^i \triangleq \sum_t f_s^i(u_s^{it})\, u_s^{it}(\lambda_s^{it}). \tag{11.52}$$

The evaluation of the expected utility values can be performed with the CDISPRI program of the MANECON collection or ICOPSS package. In the expected utility values obtained as a

**Table 11.15 Ranking of the alternatives (AI, AII, AIII) in subregions**

| t | Izumiotsu | | | Tadaoka | | | Izumi | | | Region | | |
|---|---|---|---|---|---|---|---|---|---|---|---|---|
| | AI | AII | AIII | AI | AII | AIII | AI | AII | AIII | AI | AII | AIII |
| 1 | 3 | 2 | 1 | 1 | 2 | 3 | 2 | 3 | 1 | 1 | 2 | 3 |
| 3 | 3 | 1 | 2 | 3* | 2* | 1 | 1 | 3 | 2 | 1* | 3 | 2* |
| 5 | 3 | 2 | 1 | 1 | 1 | 2 | 1* | 3 | 2* | 3 | 2 | 1 |

Note. *indicate that the ranking of the two alternatives indicated for a given region in a particular period is almost the same.

result of assessing the probability density functions for the $u_s^i(\lambda_s^i)$, dispersion of the original values of the quasi-utility functions is generally reduced.

The preferred policy is found by comparing the regional MUF-values for all the alternatives and finding the order of priority. Ranking of all the alternatives based on those MUF-values is depicted in Table 11.15. It can be found that Alternative III dominates the other alternatives by the termination of the planning periods. The ranking shows that the degree of satisfaction for Alternative III is the best among all the alternatives for all the subregions. Alternative I is the least preferable for Izumi-Otsu and Alternative II is the least preferable for Izumi.

For further results, see Seo and Sakawa (1980, 1981a).

# Chapter 12

# Interpretation of Duality in Game Theory

## 12.1 Introduction

In this chapter, we extend the consideration on socio-economic interpretation of duality in mathematical programming to multiple agents decision problems.

The game theory as an analytical tool for multiple agents decision making, which is based on the maximin (or minimax) principle, is closely related to mathematical programming. The equivalence of the matrix game problem and the programming problem has been pointed out since an early stage of development in game theory (Dantzig 1951c; Dorfman 1951; Gale 1960, etc.). Recently much interest is increasingly focused upon the usefulness of the game theoretic approach for administrative planning. From this point of view, studies on interrelations between the mathematical programming problems and the game problems become more attractive for multiple agents decision analysis, because problem formulations as mathematical programming provide efficient solution techniques for the game problems, and thus greatly enhance their practical usefulness.

This chapter intends to examine the socio-economic interpretations of solutions of games attained by various forms of mathematical programming problems. In recent works, the equivalence of mathematical programming and game theory have paid much attention on proving the necessary and sufficient conditions for existence of the optimal mixed strategies (in noncooperative games) and of a core having the Pareto optimal property in payoff vectors (in cooperative games). In these works, some implications of the equivalence are also discussed. The purpose of this chapter is to examine the interpretation of the dual optimal solutions obtained by the formulations of mathematical programming problems for game theory. This examination will contribute to check the acceptability of solutions of games obtained in alternative forms with different parameters and constants constructed for realistic administrative planning.

## 12.2 Noncooperative Games (Two-person Zero-sum)

In noncooperative games, the interpretation of duality in programming problems converted from matrix games has been considered to be rather trivial in its original form and has been known since Dantzig (1956, 1963).

In a noncooperative zero-sum two-person game, a payoff vector obtained by each player participating in a game is represented in a payoff matrix A for Player I.

$$A \triangleq [a_{ij}] \triangleq \begin{bmatrix} a_{11} & \cdots & a_{1j} & \cdots & a_{1n} \\ \vdots & & \vdots & & \vdots \\ a_{i1} & \cdots & a_{ij} & \cdots & a_{in} \\ \vdots & & \vdots & & \vdots \\ a_{m1} & \cdots & a_{mj} & \cdots & a_{mn} \end{bmatrix}. \tag{12.1}$$

The column $a_j \triangleq (a_{1j}, a_{2j}, \ldots, a_{mj})$ represents a payoff vector of Player I when Player II takes a strategy $j$. An element $a_{ij}$ is a payoff value of Player I when Player I takes a strategy $i$, given the strategy $j$ of Player II. The payoff values of Player II are shown to be the same as $[a_{ij}]$ with the negative sign. The game in which a payoff vector obtained from each strategy is represented in a payoff matrix (12.1) is called a matrix game.

Let $A \triangleq [a_{ij}]$ be a payoff matrix, Player I take his pure strategy $i = 1,\ldots,m$, $i \in S$, and Player II take his pure strategy $j = 1,\ldots,n$, $j \in T$. Let $x \triangleq (x_1,\ldots, x_m)$ and $y \triangleq (y_1,\ldots, y_n)$ be the sets of mixed strategies for Player I and Player II, respectively, which are the probability distributions on the sets of the pure strategies for Player I and Player II, and where $x_i \geqslant 0$, $\sum_{i=1}^{m} x_i = 1$, $y_i \geqslant 0$, $\sum_{j=1}^{n} y_j = 1$. Let $\Pi : (i, j) \to A$ be the payoff function, where the matrix $A$ denotes an amount that Player I pays Player II when the strategies $i$ and $j$ are taken by each respectively. The expected payoff of the game $\Gamma(S, T; \Pi)$ is defined as

$$A(x, y) \triangleq \sum_{i=1}^{m} \sum_{j=1}^{n} x_i a_{ij} y_j \tag{12.2}$$

or, in matrix form,

$$A(x, y) \triangleq x^T A y. \tag{12.3}$$

Consider the following dual program.

P

$$\begin{aligned} &\underset{x_i,\ v^I}{\text{Maximize}} \quad v^I \\ &\text{subject to} \quad \sum_{i=1}^{m} a_{ij} x_i \geqslant v^I, \quad j = 1,\ldots,n, \\ &\qquad \sum_{i=1}^{m} x_i = 1 \\ &\qquad x_i \geqslant 0, \quad i = 1,\ldots,m, \end{aligned} \tag{12.4}$$

or, in matrix form,

P

$$\begin{aligned} &\underset{x,\ v^I}{\text{Maximize}} \quad v^I \\ &\text{subject to} \quad x^T A \geqslant v^I \\ &\qquad \mathbf{1}x = 1 \\ &\qquad x \geqslant 0, \end{aligned} \tag{12.5}$$

and

D

$$\begin{aligned}&\underset{y_j,\, v^{II}}{\text{minimize}} \quad v^{II}\\ &\text{subject to} \quad \sum_{j=1}^{n} a_{ij}y_j \leqslant v^{II}, \quad i = 1,\ldots,m,\\ &\qquad\qquad \sum_{j=1}^{n} y_j = 1 \qquad\qquad (12.6)\\ &\qquad\qquad y_j \geqslant 0, \quad j = 1,\ldots,n,\end{aligned}$$

or, in matrix form,

D

$$\begin{aligned}&\underset{y,\, v^{II}}{\text{Minimize}} \quad v^{II}\\ &\text{subject to} \quad Ay \leqslant v^{II} \qquad\qquad (12.7)\\ &\qquad\qquad \mathbf{1}y = 1\\ &\qquad\qquad y \geqslant 0\end{aligned}$$

where $\mathbf{1} \triangleq (1,1,\ldots,1)^T$ is a row vector, $v^I \triangleq \{v^I\}$, and $v^{II} \triangleq \{v^{II}\}$. $v^I$ is the largest gain-floor for Player I, and $v^{II}$ is the lowest loss-ceiling for Player II. It is clear that the problem P represents the maximin strategy for Player I and the problem D represents the minimax strategy for Player II, because $v^I = \min_j \sum_{i=1}^{m} a_{ij}x_i$ and $v^{II} = \max_i \sum_{j=1}^{n} a_{ij}y_j$. The fundamental duality theorem of linear programming assures that, for both feasible and bounded problems,

$$\max \ v^I = \min \ v^{II}, \qquad (12.8)$$

from $v^I = \min_j \sum_{i=1}^{m} a_{ij}x_i \leqslant \sum_{i=1}^{m} a_{ij}x_i \sum_{j=1}^{n} y_j = \sum_{i=1}^{m} \sum_{j=1}^{n} a_{ij}x_iy_j = \sum_{i=1}^{m} x_i \sum_{j=1}^{n} a_{ij}y_j \leqslant \max_i \sum_{j=1}^{n} a_{ij}y_j = v^{II}$. Furthermore, von Neumann-Morgenstern's minimax theorem assures, in terms of the expected payoff, that

$$\max_{x} \min_{y|x} \sum_{i=1}^{m} \sum_{j=1}^{n} a_{ij} x_i y_j = \min_{y} \max_{x|y} \sum_{i=1}^{m} \sum_{j=1}^{n} a_{ij} x_i y_j . \qquad (12.9)$$

This result is regarded as a precise expression of the duality (12.8) for the problems P and D. Thus the dual program P and D is a statement of the minimax principle in the two-person zero-sum game, and optimal values of variables $x_i^*$ and $y_j^*$ as the solution show the mutual optimal strategies of both players.

Formulating the Lagrange function of P brings another interpretation of the dual optimal value $y_j^*$. Consider, with

$$v^I = \min_j \sum_{i=1}^{m} a_{ij} x_i \ , \ L = v^I - \sum_{j=1}^{n} y_j (v^I - \sum_{i=1}^{m} a_{ij} x_i) + \dots .$$

The dual variable $y_j$ represents a weight for the difference between the minimum expected gain from the mixed strategy of Player I for the strategy $j$, $j = 1,\dots,n$, of Player II and his every expected gain for every strategy $j$. This dual "price" for Player I represents a mixed strategy of Player II in an equilibrium and thus indicates an opportunity cost for the minimum expected gain of Player I.

In the constrained game, consider the following problem in matrix form (Owen 1968, 1982):

M

$$\begin{aligned} &\underset{y}{\text{minimize}} \ \underset{x}{\text{maximize}} \quad x^T A y \\ &\text{subject to} \quad x^T B \leqslant c^T \\ &\qquad\qquad\quad x \geqslant 0 \qquad\qquad\qquad (12.10) \\ &\qquad\qquad\quad y^T F \geqslant g^T \\ &\qquad\qquad\quad y \geqslant 0 \end{aligned}$$

where B and F are matrices of weights as constraint parameters on the mixed strategies $x$ and $y$, respectively. This problem is converted to the dual program:

P

$$\underset{y|x}{\text{minimize}} \quad (x^T A)y$$

$$\text{subject to} \quad y^T F \geqslant g^T \qquad (12.11)$$

$$y \geqslant 0,$$

D

$$\underset{z|x}{\text{maximize}} \quad z^T g$$

$$\text{subject to} \quad z^T F^T \leqslant x^T A \qquad (12.12)$$

$$z \geqslant 0.$$

The $z$ is interpreted as the valuation price by Player I for the constraint constant $g$ on the mixed strategy $y$ of Player II. Then the dual problem (12.12) shows that the total values of the constraint constants for the mixed strategy $y$ of Player II, which are evaluated by the price $z$ for Player I, should be maximized under the condition that the total evaluation of the constraint parameters on the mixed strategy $y$ of Player II should not exceed the expected payoff for Player I. When the constraints in the original problem (12.10) are included, the dual problem (12.12) is reformulated as

P*

$$\underset{z,x}{\text{maximize}} \quad z^T g$$

$$\text{subject to} \quad z^T F^T - x^T A \leqslant 0$$

$$x^T B \leqslant c^T \qquad (12.13)$$

$$z, x \geqslant 0.$$

Then the dual problem $D^*$ to $P^*$ (12.13) is constructed.

D*

$$\underset{y,s}{\text{minimize}} \quad s^T c$$

$$\text{subject to} \quad F^T y \geqslant g \tag{12.14}$$

$$Ay - Bs \leqslant 0$$

$$y, s, \geqslant 0.$$

The dual program, P* and D*, brings about a duality in the total evaluation with the prices z and s imposed by each player on the constraint constants g and c for the mixed strategies of the opponents, respectively. The $P^*$ shows that the price z is selected by Player I as the maximizer to keep total evaluation for the weights F on the mixed strategies of Player II less than or equal to the expected payoff for Player I. The $D^*$ shows that the price s is selected by Player II as the minimizer to keep the total evaluation for the weights B on the mixed strategies x of Player I larger than or equal to the expected payoff for Player II.

For another interpretation, formulate the Lagrange function of P*:

$$L \triangleq z^T g - y(z^T F^T - x^T A) - s(x^T B - c^T) \tag{12.15}$$

for $z, x \in X$, $X \triangleq \{z, x \mid z, x \geqslant 0\}$. Considering that the decision variables, z and x, and the dual variables (Kuhn-Tucker multipliers), y and s, are all functions of $c^T$ yields, at optimal,

$$\frac{\partial L}{\partial c^T} = \frac{\partial (z^T g)}{\partial c^T} = s, \quad \text{for} \quad s > 0. \tag{12.16}$$

It is known that, at the optimal, the dual variable s indicates inversely marginal values of constraint constants c for the mixed strategy of Player I measured in terms of a marginal change of the total evaluation of the constraint constant g on the mixed strategy of Player II. In this sense, the dual variable s represents a "price" vector imputed to the constraint constants c on the mixed strategy for Player I. Furthermore, at optimal, from the complementary slackness condition, the total evaluation with z* by Player I for the weights F on the mixed strategies of Player II is equal to the expected payoff of Player I when $y^* > 0$. Similarly, the total evaluation with $s^*$ by Player II for the weights B for Player I is equal to the expected payoff for Player II when $x^* > 0$. From the duality theorem, total evaluations of both players for constraint constants on the mixed strategy of the opponent coincide with each other, i.e., $z^Tg = s^Tc$.

## 12.3 N-Person Cooperative Games and Nucleolus

### 1. Balanced game

The concept of the balanced game is closely related to a market game embodied Pareto optimality. Many works have appeared in this field since Shapley (1967), and Shapley and Shubik (1969), in which main interest is concentrated in presenting the balanced game as the necessary and sufficient condition for a game to have a core. In their researches, a cooperative game with transferable utility is defined in terms of linear programming. A more recent work by Owen (1975) asserts that an imputation in a core is obtained from an equilibrium price vector that is generated as the dual solution vector. Samet and Zemel (1984) provided some conditions for coincidence of the core of an LP-game that is represented as linear programming and the set of the "dual payoff" vector that is defined with the dual optimal solutions. In this subsection, the interpretation of the dual "price" vector as an evaluation factor, with which the dual payoff vector is constructed, are examined.

Consider the following dual program (Scarf 1967, 1973):

P

$$\underset{x_p}{\text{minimize}} \quad \sum_{p\in N} x_p \tag{12.17}$$

$$\text{subject to} \quad \sum_{p\in S} x_p \geq v(S), \qquad S \subset N, \tag{12.18}$$

D

$$\underset{\gamma_S}{\text{maximize}} \quad \sum_{S \subset N} \gamma_S v(S) \tag{12.19}$$

$$\text{subject to} \quad \sum_{\substack{S \ni p \\ S \subset N}} \gamma_S = 1, \qquad p \in N \tag{12.20}$$

$$\gamma_S \geqslant 0, \qquad S \subset N, \tag{12.21}$$

where $x \triangleq (x_1, x_2, \ldots, x_n)$ is a payoff vector for a game $\Gamma(N, v)$, and $N$ is a set of $n$ players. $v(S)$ is a function from a subset $S$ (coalition) of $N$ to a real number satisfying $v(\phi) = 0$ and is called the characteristic function. An n-person cooperative game in characteristic function form is defined with the real-valued function $v(S)$ that is an amount of "utility" for the members of $S$ to obtain from the game. $\gamma_S$ is the dual variable. The constraints (12.20) and (12.21) in D define the balanced set. The dual problem D defines the cover of the game $\Gamma(N, v)$ when it is considered for $S \subset R$, $R \subseteq N$, $p \in R$.

An imputation is defined as a vector $x \triangleq (x_1, \ldots, x_n)$ satisfying

(i) $\sum_{p \in N} x_p = v(N)$ (collective rationality), and

(ii) $x_p \geqslant v(\{p\})$ for all $p \in N$ (individual rationality).

An imputation $x$ is said to dominate another imputation $y$ through the coalition $S$, when

(a) $x_p > y_p$ for all $p \in S$ (preference condition) and

(b) $\sum_{p \in S} x_p \leqslant v(S)$ (feasibility condition)

are satisfied. The core of a game $\Gamma(N, v)$ is defined as the set of all undominated imputation. When the superadditivity $v(S \cup T) \geqslant v(S) + v(T)$ for coalitions $S$ and $T$, $S \cap T = \phi$, holds, the payoff vector $x$ in a core satisfies (i) and

(iii) $\sum_{p \in S} x_p \geqslant v(S)$ for all $S \subset N$ (coalitional rationality).

The Bondareva-Shapley Theorem asserts that the game $\Gamma(N, v)$ has a nonempty core if and only if, when the game is balanced, i.e., for $\gamma_S$ satisfying (12.20) and (12.21),

$$\sum_{S \subset \beta} \gamma_S v(S) \leqslant v(N) \tag{12.22}$$

holds, where $\beta$ is the balanced set. It means that a game has a core if the problem P has a solution with which the objective function is equal to v(N). Because, by formulating the dual problem D, $\sum_{S \subset N} \gamma_S v(S) \leqslant \sum_{p \in N} x_p$ holds for feasible solutions, which leads to the condition (10.22) when the collective rationality (efficiency) (i) $\sum_{p \in N} x_p = v(N)$ is assured.

In addition that the dual variable $\gamma_S$ in D shows the weight for the characteristic value v(S) of a coalition S, the dual program, P and D, has further implications.

(1) Formulate the Lagrange function of P:

$$L = \sum_{p \in N} x_p + \sum_{S \subset N} \gamma_S (v(S) - \sum_{p \in S} x_p). \tag{12.23}$$

Let $x(N) \triangleq \sum_{p \in N} x_p$. Then considering $x_p = x_p(v(S))$ and $\gamma_S = \gamma_S(v(S))$, from the complementary slackness condition, yields

$$\frac{\partial L}{\partial v(S)} = \frac{\partial x(N)}{\partial v(S)} = \gamma_S \tag{12.24}$$

for $\gamma_S > 0$ at optimal. Put differently, the weight $\gamma_S$ indicates a trade-off between a marginal change of the characteristic value v(S) of a coalition S and a marginal change of the total payoff values allocated for all players. The $\gamma_S$ indicates inversely an imputed price of the characteristic value v(S) measured in terms of a marginal change of the total payoff value.

In the case of the core, the weight $\gamma_S$ indicates a trade-off value

$$\gamma_S = \frac{\partial v(N)}{\partial v(S)} . \tag{12.25}$$

In other words, $\gamma_S$ implies a trade-off between the characteristic values of the coalition S and the "grand coalition" N.

(2) At optimal, when $\gamma_S > 0$,

$$x(S) = v(S) \tag{12.26}$$

where $x(S) \triangleq \sum_{p \in S} x_p$. Namely, a value of the game for a coalition S is equal to the total allocation for all players in S. If there exists some deficiency, then the weight for the coalition S will vanish. It means that, when $\gamma_S > 0$, all players in the coalition S should have an equivalent value, in a total, to the value of the game v(S) for the coalition S in its allocation program.

(3) From the duality theorem, at optimal,

$$x(N) = \sum_{S \subset N} \gamma_S v(S) \tag{12.27}$$

holds. It means that the total allocation for all players is equal to the weighted sum of the value of the game for each coalition $S \subset N$. In the case of the core,

$$v(N) = \sum_{S \subset N} \gamma_S v(S) \tag{12.28}$$

holds.

It is known from (12.28) that, when $\gamma_S > 0$, the balanced collection of the coalition $\boldsymbol{\beta} = \{S\}$ satisfying (12.20) and (12.21) is simply formed as a reallocation of the total payoff value for the grand coalition to all (nondummy) players as the carrier participating in the game with positive weights for all the coalition $S \subset N$. These weights $\gamma_S$ construct the dual "price" vector.

## 2. Market game

Define a market which is composed of a finite set N of traders, a finite set M of commodities, an initial bundle $a_p \in E_+^M$ for each $p \in N$, and a continuous concave utility function $u_p\colon E_+^M \to R^1$, where $E_+^M$ denotes the nonnegative quadrant of the vector space $E^M$ with coordinates indexed by the components of M. A market generates a market game

$\Gamma(N, v)$ which is represented by

P

$$v(S) = \underset{x_p}{\text{maximize}} \sum_{p \in S} u_p(x_p) \tag{12.29}$$

$$\text{subject to} \quad \sum_{p \in S} x_p = \sum_{p \in S} a_p \tag{12.30}$$

for all $S \subseteq N$, where $x_p \in X_S$ is a commodity bundle in $E_+^M$. This market game can be converted, via the concept of direct market that has $u_p: I_+^M \to R^1$ in the place of $u_p: E_+^M \to R^1$ for the market game and using the characteristic function $v(S) = u(e^S)$ for the direct market , to a new game $\Gamma(N, \bar{v})$ that is the cover of $\Gamma(N, v)$;

C

$$\bar{v}(R) = \underset{\gamma_S}{\text{maximize}} \sum_{S \subseteq R} \gamma_S v(S), \quad R \subseteq N. \tag{12.31}$$

$$\text{subject to} \quad \sum_{\substack{S \subseteq R \\ S \ni p}} \gamma_S = 1, \quad p \in R, \tag{12.32}$$

$$\gamma_S \geqslant 0, \quad S \subseteq R, \tag{12.33}$$

where $I_+^M$ is the collection of unit vectors in $E_+^M$, and $e^S$ denotes an n-dimensional vector, whose element $e_p^S$ takes 1 or 0 according to whether $p \in S$ or $p \notin S$, respectively. It is assumed that, in the direct market, each trader starts with one unit of his personal commodity.

Shapley and Shubik (1969, 1975) proved that a game $\Gamma(N, v)$ has a core if and only if $\bar{v}(N) = v(N)$. When $R = N$, the cover C is equivalent to the dual problem D in the form of the balanced game. Thus the solution $\gamma_S$ to C has the same implication as in the dual problem. This shows an extension of the notion of the imputed price in the balanced game to the market game.

On the other hand, the market game has its own imputed

price. Putting $\sum_{p \in S} u_p(x_p) \triangleq u(S)$ and $\sum_{p \in S} a_p \triangleq a(S)$, from the Lagrange function

$$L_S \triangleq u(S) - \pi_S\left(\sum_{p \in S} a_p - \sum_{p \in S} x_p\right), \tag{12.34}$$

yields at optimal

$$\frac{\partial u(S)}{\partial a(S)} = \pi_S, \quad \pi_S > 0. \tag{12.35}$$

The Kuhn-Tucker multiplier $\pi_S$ is imputed to the difference between the total of initial bundles and the sum of the reallocated (traded) commodities, and as the imputed price represents a trade-off between a marginal change of the sum of initial holding and a marginal change of the total value of the individual utility functions obtained from the trading activity in the coalition $S$. Put it differently, the imputed price $\pi_S$ represents inversely a marginal evaluation of the total initial endowment for the coalition $S$ in terms of a marginal unit of the total utility value for the coalition $S$.

## 3. Nucleolus of an n-person game

The nucleolus as a solution concept for an n-person cooperative game in characteristic function form $\Gamma(N, v)$ is represented as a solution of a linear programming problem (Kohlberg 1971; Owen 1974).

Define the excess of a value of a game $v(S)$ for a coalition $S$ over a total payoff $x(S)$ for all players in the coalition $S$ to be

$$e(S, x) \triangleq v(S) - x(S), \quad S \subset N, \tag{12.36}$$

where $v(\phi) = 0$ and $x(S) \triangleq \sum_{p \in S} x_p$. $x_p$ is not necessarily an imputation. The excess is regarded as a measure of dissatisfaction of a coalition $S$ at $x \triangleq \{x_p\}$. The core is defined as a set of all payoff vectors that cannot be improved by any coalition, and is shown by

$$e(S, x) \leq 0 \tag{12.37}$$

along with $x(N) - v(N) = 0$.

The existence and uniqueness of the core are not necessarily assured in all cases. Thus, by relaxing the definition of the core (12.37), the concept that defines the quasi-core is constructed (Shapley and Shubik 1966; Schmeidler 1969; Maschler, Peleg and Shapley 1979).

Define the $\varepsilon$-core as a quasi-core concept relaxed with a parameter $\varepsilon$, using

$$e(S, x) \triangleq v(S) - x(S) \leq \varepsilon, \quad \text{for all } S \neq \phi, N, \tag{12.38}$$

along with $v(N) = x(N)$. It means that the payoff vector for all $p \in S$ cannot be improved by any coalition $S$, when a tax transfer or a subsidy of $\varepsilon$ is imposed to the payoff $x(S)$. Based on this concept, the smallest $\varepsilon$-core that maximizes the excess is defined as

$$\varepsilon_o(\Gamma) = \min_{x \in \chi} \max_{S \neq \phi, N} e(S, x) \tag{12.39}$$

where $\chi$ is a set of preimputation that satisfies the total rationality $x(N) = v(N)$. $\varepsilon_o(\Gamma)$ is called the least core and provides the nucleolus $\mathcal{N}(v)$ of the game $\Gamma(N, v)$ via the lexicographic ordering of the excess. The lexicographic ordering is defined as follows: Let $\Theta(x) \triangleq (\Theta_1(x), \Theta_2(x), \ldots, \Theta_{2^n}(x))$ be a $2^n$-dimensional vector whose elements are the numbers $\Theta_k = e(S_k, x)$, $K = 1, \ldots, 2^n$, $S \subset N$, arranged in a nonincreasing order. The lexicographic order is given by the relation $\Theta(x) \leq_L \Theta(y)$, which holds when $\Theta_i(x) = \Theta_i(y)$ for all $i < j$ and $\Theta_j(x) < \Theta_j(y)$ for $j$. It means that, if equality exists between the maximal values of the excess $\Theta_i(x)$ and $\Theta_i(y)$, $i = 1,2,\ldots,$ that are arranged in a nonincreasing order, then the next greatest values of the excess $\Theta_j(x)$ and $\Theta_j(y)$ are compared with each other, and so on. The comparison is continued sequentially until the inequality is found. Then, the nucleolus of a game is defined as the set of payoff vectors such that

$$\mathcal{N}(x) \triangleq \{x \in \chi \mid \Theta(x) <_L \Theta(y) \quad \text{for all} \quad y \in \chi\}. \tag{12.40}$$

Naturally, the payoff vector $x$ is more acceptable than $y$. Thus the nucleolus is defined as the payoff vector that minimizes the maximum excess. The theorems that the nucleolus $\mathcal{N}(v) \triangleq \mathcal{N}(x)$ belongs to every nonempty $\varepsilon$-core and the nucleolus is a continuous function of the characteristic function can be derived directly from the definition of the nucleolus, as suggested by Schmeidler (1969).

The nucleolus as the solution concept for the quasi-core is obtained by solving at most $n-1$ linear programming problems (Kopelowitz 1967; Littlechild 1974; Owen 1974).

In a similar discussion, the concept of $\varepsilon$-core (12.38) is augmented with a parameter $\mu$ as

$$e_\mu(S, x) \triangleq v(S) - x(S) \leqslant \mu\varepsilon , \tag{12.41}$$

along with $v(N) = x(N)$. The augmented nucleolus $\mathcal{N}(\mu)$ is defined on the augmented $\varepsilon$-core, and is obtained as a solution to a linear program. Consider the 0- normalization of a value $v$ of game $\Gamma(N, v)$, that is defined with $v(\{p\}) = 0$ for all $p \in N$. The augmented nucleolus $\mathcal{N}(\mu)$ is obtained by solving the following linear program.

P

$$\underset{x_p,\ \varepsilon}{\text{minimize}} \quad \varepsilon$$

$$\text{subject to} \quad x_p \geqslant 0 \qquad \text{for} \quad p \in N$$

$$v(S) - (x(S) + \mu\varepsilon) \leqslant 0 \quad \text{for all} \quad S \subset N$$

$$v(N) - x(N) = 0 \tag{12.42}$$

In matrix form,

P

$$\underset{\hat{x}}{\text{minimize}} \quad e^T\hat{x}$$

$$\text{subject to}\quad \begin{matrix} n \\ \sum_{r=1}^{n-1} {}_nC_r \\ 1 \end{matrix} \overset{\begin{matrix} n & 1 \end{matrix}}{\begin{bmatrix} I & 0 \\ E & \boldsymbol{\mu} \\ \mathbf{1}^T & 0 \end{bmatrix}} \overset{1}{\begin{pmatrix} x \\ \varepsilon \end{pmatrix}}\begin{matrix} n \\ 1 \end{matrix} \geqslant \overset{1}{\begin{pmatrix} \mathbf{0} \\ \mathbf{v}(S) \\ v(N) \end{pmatrix}} \begin{matrix} n \\ \sum_{r=1}^{n-1} {}_nC_r, \\ 1 \end{matrix} \qquad (12.43)$$

where $e^T$ is an $n+1$ dimensional row vector whose n elements are all 0 and the $n+1^{th}$ element is 1, and $\hat{x} \triangleq (x_1, \ldots, x_n, \varepsilon)$. $\mathbf{1}^T$ is an n-dimensional row vector whose elements are all 1. I is an $n \times n$ identity matrix and E is a $\sum_{r=1}^{n-1} {}_nC_r \times n$ matrix whose element is 1 when a payoff $x_p$ for $p \in S$, $S \subset N$, appears, and otherwise 0. $\boldsymbol{\mu} \triangleq \{\mu\}$ denotes a numerical vector. The dual problem to (12.43) is :

D

maximize $\quad v^T\hat{y}$

$$\begin{matrix} n \\ 1 \end{matrix} \overset{\begin{matrix} n & \sum_{r=1}^{n-1} {}_nC_r & 1 \end{matrix}}{\begin{bmatrix} I & E^T & \mathbf{1} \\ 0 & \mu^T & 0 \end{bmatrix}} \overset{1}{\begin{pmatrix} \mathbf{0} \\ \mathbf{y}(S) \\ y(N) \end{pmatrix}} \begin{matrix} n \\ \sum_{r=1}^{n-1} {}_nC_r \\ 1 \end{matrix} \leqslant \overset{1}{\begin{pmatrix} 0 \\ 1 \end{pmatrix}} \begin{matrix} n \\ 1 \end{matrix} \qquad (12.44)$$

where $v^T \triangleq (\mathbf{0}, v(S), v(N))^T$ and $\hat{y} \triangleq (\mathbf{0}, \mathbf{y}(S), y(N))$.

The interpretation of the primal problem (12.42) with the augmenting parameter $\mu$ is clear. When $\mu = 1$, the solution to P provides the nucleolus. When $\mu = s$, the weak nucleolus is obtained, in terms of the weak least core $\varepsilon_o(\Gamma, s)$ in (12.39), where s denotes the number of players in S (Shapley and Shubik 1966). When $\mu = v(S)$, the proportional nucleolus is obtained, in terms of the proportional least core $\varepsilon_o(\Gamma, v(S))$ in (12.39) (Young, Okada, and Hashimoto 1982). Sakawa, Tada, and Nishizaki (1983) proposed the concession nucleolus when $\mu = \sum_{p \in S} \Phi_p$, where $\Phi_p$ is the Shapley value. The Shapley value is defined as

$$\Phi_p(v) \triangleq \sum_{\substack{S \subset N \\ S \ni p}} \frac{(s-1)!(n-s)!}{n!} [v(S)-v(S-\{p\})]. \qquad (12.45)$$

The second term of the Shapley value represents the marginal amount of contribution of a player $p$ to the value of coalition $S$. The first term represents a total of the relative frequency for a player $p$ to appear in every coalition $S$. Thus the value $\sum_{p \in S} \Phi_p$ shows a total of the marginal contribution by each player to every coalition $S$ weighted by the relative frequency of appearance of each player. The concept of the concession nucleolus defined in terms of (12.41) shows that the excess, or the dissatisfaction, of a coalition $S$ should be weighted according to the sum of marginal contribution of each player in the coalition $S$. In this concept, some kind of external effects, or "opportunity cost", for participation of each player $p$ is taken into account for every coalition $S$.

Alternatively, when $\mu = v(N) - v(N - S)$, the contribution nucleolus, as we will call it here, is found for a coalition $S$. This represents that a contribution of a coalition $S$ to the grand coalition should be weighted for the excess.

In these different formulations, the dual variables $y_S$ and $y_N$ represent alternative evaluations for the coalition values $v(S)$ and $v(N)$.

In general form, the dual problem (12.44) is to maximize a sum of an evaluation for every coalition value under the conditions that a sum of a unit evaluation for each coalition $S$ with the 0-1 weight for appearance of each player should not exceed an evaluation for the grand coalition and, for the augmenting parameter, the total evaluation for the coalitions $S$ should be less than or equal to one.

This interpretation of the dual variables can be represented by forming the Lagrange function of the primal problem (12.42): for $x_p \geqslant 0$,

$$L \triangleq \varepsilon + \sum_{S \neq N} y_S(v(S) - (x(S) + \mu\varepsilon)) + y_N(v(N) - x(N)). \qquad (12.46)$$

Then, considering that $\varepsilon$, $x_p$, $y_S$ and $y_N$ are all functions of v(S) and v(N), from the Kuhn-Tucker conditions, yields

$$\frac{\partial \varepsilon}{\partial v(S)} = y_S \quad \text{for} \quad y_S > 0, \quad S \subset N, \tag{12.47}$$

$$\frac{\partial \varepsilon}{\partial v(N)} = y_N \tag{12.48}$$

at optimal. It is also known, from the first order optimality conditions, that $-\sum_{\substack{S \subset N \\ S \ni p}} y_S = y_N$ and $\sum_{S \subset N} y_S \mu = 1$. The dual variable $y_S$ represents a trade-off between the "tax" transfer variable $\varepsilon$ and the coalition value v(S) for every coalition S. This property also holds for the grand coalition. This is an expression of the result of the duality theorem:

$$\varepsilon = \sum_{S \subset N} v(S) y_S + v(N) y_N. \tag{12.49}$$

The dual prices $y_S$, $S \subset N$, for each coalition and $y_N$ are imputed inversely corresponding to the marginal changes of the coalition values v(S) and v(N), respectively, in terms of a marginal increment of the "tax" transfer $\varepsilon$. It means that the dual prices $y_S$ and $y_N$ indicate marginal evaluations of the coalition values measured commonly in the marginal terms of the "tax" transfer $\varepsilon$. Larger values of $y_S$ and $y_N$ show relative inefficiency of v(S) and v(N), because only smaller values of v(S) and v(N) is traded-off for a given $\varepsilon$-value, but it is not desirable for $\varepsilon$ in this case where the minimization of the $\varepsilon$-values is intended. Thus $y_S$ and $y_N$ indicate the opportunity benefit, or the imputed price, of the coalition values v(S) and v(N) in terms of the "tax" transfer $\varepsilon$. These values $y_S$ and $y_N$ can be used inversely as the measure of satisfaction with (or efficiency of) the coalition S and N, respectively. The augmenting parameter $\mu$ denotes a weighting factor that indicates a deviation from the balanced game. When $\mu = 1$, the nucleolus implies that the game is balanced.

## 4 Extension

When the core is nonempty, the concept of a coalition's propensity to disrupt for a game $\Gamma(N, v)$ is defined as follows:

$$d(S, x) \triangleq \frac{x(N-S) - v(N-S)}{x(S) - v(S)} = \frac{-e(N-S, x)}{-e(S, x)} > 0. \tag{12.50}$$

The disruption nucleolus, or relative nucleolus, is defined as a payoff that minimizes the maximum propensity to disrupt in the lexicographic ordering sense (Littlechild and Vaidya 1976). The mathematical programming for computing the disruption nucleolus is formulated as follows.

P

$$\underset{r,x}{\text{minimize}} \quad r \tag{12.51}$$

$$\text{subject to} \quad d(S, x) \leq r, \quad S \subset N \tag{12.52}$$

$$x(N) = v(N), \tag{12.53}$$

$$x_p \geq 0. \tag{12.54}$$

The constraint (12.52) shows that the relative ratio of the dissatisfaction of a coalition $S$ in $N$ to that of the complementary elements (players) $N - S$ should not exceed a threshold value $r$. Considering that the normal game is constant-sum, $v(S) + v(N-S) = v(N)$ for all $S \subset N$, yields the transformed problem. Since $x(N-S) = v(N) - x(S)$, (12.52) is rearranged in the following formulation.

P

$$\underset{r,x}{\text{minimize}} \quad r \tag{12.55}$$

$$\text{subject to} \quad (1+r)(x(S)-v(S)) \geq 0, \quad S \subset N \tag{12.56}$$

$$x(N) = v(N) \tag{12.57}$$

$$x_p \geq 0. \tag{12.58}$$

The Lagrange function for P is formulated as

$$L \triangleq r + \sum_{S\subset N} y_S[v(S) - (1+r)x(S) + rv(S)] + y_N(v(N) - x(N)), \tag{12.59}$$

where $y_S$ and $y_N$ are Lagrange multipliers associating with the constraints (12.56) and (12.57). Considering that the decision variables, $x_p$ and r, and the dual variables, $y_S$ and $y_N$, are all functions of v(S) and v(N), $S \subset N$, from the Kuhn-Tucker conditions, yields at optimal

$$\frac{\partial r}{\partial v(S)} = (1+r)y_S, \quad \text{for} \quad y_S > 0, \quad S \subset N, \tag{12.60}$$

$$\frac{\partial r}{\partial v(N)} = y_N. \tag{12.61}$$

The first order optimality conditions for P show that, for $y_S \geq 0$, $1 + r = - y_N \Big/ \sum_{\substack{S\subset N\\ S\ni p}} y_S$ and $-(v(S) - x(S)) \sum_{S\subset N} y_S = 1$. In other words, the constraint parameter $1 + r$ associated with (12.56) represents a relative ratio of the imputed price for the grand coalition N to the total of the imputed price for each coalition S. This parameter indicates a trade-off between both values. By examining this value, the threshold value r can be chosen discretionally as a desirable solution obtained from alternative formulations. The excess $v(S) - x(S)$ represented in the propensity of disruption indicates the weighting factor that shows a deviation from the balanced game at the optimal.

## 5. Concluding remarks

Development of solution algorithms for a game using mathematical programming will greatly contributes to applicability of game theory to practical cases. However, criteria for selecting the preferred solution from among alternative computational results that are obtained by using alternative parameters and solution concepts still remain to be developed. Comparative examination of the Kuhn-Tucker multipliers as the evaluation factor, will provide some measure for selecting the best compromised solution among the alternative solution concepts. Table 12.1 shows, in a summary, the comparative evaluation for the dual variables as alternative solution concepts for the augmented nucleolus. It is known that the augmenting parameter $\mu$ has no influence on the evaluation in terms of the dual variables. Thus, by examining comparably the trade-offs among the "tax" transfer variable and the coalition values, the preferred solution among alternative solution concepts can be obtained. The augmenting parameter $\mu$ indicates a weighting factor that shows a deviation from the

**Table 12.1 Evaluation for nucleolus**

| $y_S$ for $v(S)$ | $y_N$ for $v(N)$ | Equilibrium conditions |
|---|---|---|
| Nucleolus | | |
| $\frac{\partial \varepsilon}{\partial v(S)} = y_S$ | $\frac{\partial \varepsilon}{\partial v(N)} = y_N$ | $-\sum_{S \subset N, S \ni p} y_S = y_N$ |
| $y_S > 0$ | | $\sum_{S \subset N} y_S = 1,$ |
| | | $y_S \geq 0$ |
| Augmented nucleolus | | |
| $\frac{\partial \varepsilon}{\partial v(S)} = y_S$ | $\frac{\partial \varepsilon}{\partial v(N)} = y_N$ | $-\sum_{S \subset N, S \ni p} y_S = y_N$ |
| $y_S > 0$ | | $\sum_{S \subset N} y_S \mu = 1,$ |
| | | $y_S \geq 0$ |
| Disruption nucleolus | | |
| $\frac{\partial r}{\partial v(S)} = (1+r) y_S$ | $\frac{\partial r}{\partial v(N)} = y_N$ | $-(1+r) \sum_{S \subset N, S \ni p} y_S = y_N$ |
| $y_S > 0$ | | $-\sum_{S \subset N} y_S(v(S)-x(S)) = 1,$ |
| | | $y_S \geq 0$ |

Note. $\mu = 1$: nucleolus. $\mu = s$: weak nucleolus. $\mu = v(S)$: proportional nucleolus. $\mu = \sum_{i \in S} \Phi_i$: concession nucleolus. $\mu = v(N) - v(N - S)$: contribution nucleolus.

"balanced" state of a game in a characteristic function form. In the disruption nucleolus, $\mu = -(v(S) - x(S))$ and $(1 + r)$ indicate the augmenting factor for $y_S$. In terms of marginal changes of the threshold variable $r$, the most desirable value of trade-off between the threshold value $r$ and the coalition value can be chosen.

The results of the comparative evaluation of the Kuhn-Tucker multiplier, which are generated from alternative formulations of mathematical programming, can be used as the base or reference of the discretionary decisions in the judgmental process for DM as the mediator. In this sense, the multiple agents decision making in game theory is also composed of two phases: analytical and judgmental. By introducing the coordination function of DM in the judgmental phase, the multiple agents decision making represented in a game is structured in a hierarchical two-layer system. If it is necessary, the normalization process for the comparative evaluation can be introduced, where the quasi-utility concept that is used in the NLM method will also provide a device for commensurating the plural evaluations.

## 12.4 Example: Evaluation for Efficient Formation of Interregional Agreement

As a case study, effective formation of interregional agreements for environmental management is assessed in terms of augmented nucleolus. A hierarchical systems analysis in two levels is used: regional and interregional. At the regional level, a multidimensional risk function for each region is constructed, which independently reflects regional interests in conflict with each other. At the interregional level, formation of interregional concordances for compromising the regional interests is considered. A n-person cooperative game in the characteristic function form is used to examine the effectiveness of the alternative formation of interregional agreements for the regional conflict solving. Based on the multidimensional risk function, the characteristic function for the game is derived. The augmented nucleolus as a solution concept is used in its alternative function forms.

At the regional level, the multidimensional risk function (MRF) of an event A that is the cause of an interregional spillover of the pollution is defined on the risk profile p and represented in terms of m attributes as

$$R(p) = R(p_1,\ldots,p_m). \tag{12.62}$$

where $p_j \triangleq p(\mathbf{x}_j)$, $j = 1,\ldots,m$, shows a risk for $\mathbf{x}_j$ to occur and is assessed with the probability.

The MRF is evaluated for each region as a counterpart of the MUF with the corresponding procedures. For solving the interregional conflicts, interregional concords are constructed as the results of multilateral negotiations, which is treated as formation of coalitions and evaluate their efficiency in terms of an n-person cooperative game. Each region i is treated as a player who is a member of a coalition S. A characteristic function v(S) for a coalition S is defined on the total of decremental values of MRF due to formation of the coalition S:

$$v(S) = \sum_{i\in S} \frac{1}{s} R_{\{i\}}(p_{\{i\}}) - R_S(p_S) \tag{12.63}$$

where $S \subseteq N$, $N \triangleq \{1,\ldots n\}$. $R_{\{i\}}$ and $R_S$ are MRFs for a region i and a coalition S, respectively. $p_{\{i\}}$ and $p_S$ are the risk profiles of the event for them. The v(S) in (12.63) is a coalition value, which indicates a decrease of the degree of the interregional risk that occurs from the regional event.

Define a payoff vector as $z \triangleq \{z_1,\ldots z_n\}$, whose elements are decremental values of MRF for a player (region) i, $i = 1,\ldots,n$, due to construction of a coalition.

At the interregional level, in which the game theoretic approach is used, the obtained MRF-value for a region i is shown as

$$w_i^\dagger = R_{\{i\}} - z_i^\dagger, \quad i \in N, \tag{12.64}$$

where $w_i$, $\sum_{i\in N} w_i \triangleq R_N$, represents an interregional allocation of total risk generated from a regional event with interregional effects to each region i after the construction of an interregional concord among n regions. Alternative solutions $z^\dagger \triangleq (z_1^\dagger, \ldots, z_n^\dagger)$ of the augmented nucleolus provide alternative payoff values for each region.

Suppose that a region intends to promote an industrial development program A on the basin of the upper stream of a large, interregional river. This development program will have multiple adverse effects.

Suppose that five regions are affected from A. Suppose that, at the regional level, the evaluation of MRF $R_{\{i\}}(p_{\{i\}})$, $i = 1, \ldots, 5$, has already been done for each region i. These values are shown in Table 12.2. Then, at the interregional level, the characteristic function v(S) is defined as (12.63) where $S \subseteq N$, $N \triangleq \{1, \ldots, 5\}$, and evaluated as shown in Table 12.2. The payoff values generated from alternative concepts of the nucleolus are shown in Table 12.3. The obtained risk values (12.64) are also calculated there. As a result, the payoff

**Table 12.2 Estimated values of the characteristic function**

$$v(S) \triangleq 100 \left( \sum_{i \in S} \frac{1}{s} R_{\{i\}}(p_{\{i\}}) - R_S(p_S) \right) \qquad S \subseteq N$$

$$N \triangleq (1, 2, 3, 4, 5)$$

| | |
|---|---|
| v({1}) = 0, | $R_1$ = 0.75 |
| v({2}) = 0, | $R_2$ = 0.65 |
| v({3}) = 0, | $R_3$ = 0.80 |
| v({4}) = 0, | $R_4$ = 0.90 |
| v({5}) = 0, | $R_5$ = 0.60 |

| | |
|---|---|
| v(1, 2) = 70 - 60 = 10 | v(1,3,4) = 82 - 50 = 32 |
| v(1, 3) = 78 - 65 = 13 | v(1,3,5) = 72 - 53 = 19 |
| v(1, 4) = 83 - 68 = 15 | v(1,4,5) = 75 - 50 = 25 |
| v(1, 5) = 68 - 55 = 13 | v(2,3,4) = 78 - 48 = 30 |
| v(2, 3) = 73 - 59 = 14 | v(2,3,5) = 68 - 50 = 18 |
| v(2, 4) = 78 - 59 = 19 | v(2,4,5) = 72 - 48 = 24 |
| v(2, 5) = 63 - 55 = 8 | v(3,4,5) = 77 - 45 = 32 |
| v(3, 4) = 85 - 70 = 15 | v(1,2,3,4) = 78 - 38 = 40 |
| v(3, 5) = 70 - 58 = 12 | v(1,2,3,5) = 70 - 37 = 33 |
| v(4, 5) = 75 - 55 = 20 | v(1,2,4,5) = 73 - 35 = 38 |
| v(1, 2, 3) = 73 - 55 = 18 | v(1,3,4,5) = 76 - 34 = 42 |
| v(1, 2, 4) = 77 - 50 = 27 | v(2,3,4,5) = 74 - 33 = 41 |
| v(1, 2, 5) = 67 - 50 = 17 | v(1,2,3,4,5 ) = 74 - 20 = 54 |

**Table 12.3 Numerical results for nucleolus**

| Player: $i$ | 1 | 2 | 3 | 4 | 5 |
|---|---|---|---|---|---|
| Individual risk: $R_{\{i\}}$ | 0.75 | 0.65 | 0.80 | 0.90 | 0.60 |
| Payoff vector: $z_i$ (× 100) | | | | | |
| Nucleolus: $\mu = 1$ | 8.60 | 7.60 | 11.60 | 16.60 | 9.60 |
| Weak nucleolus: $\mu = s$ | 8.60 | 7.60 | 11.60 | 16.60 | 9.60 |
| Proportional nucleolus: $\mu = v(S)$ | 8.35 | 7.24 | 11.69 | 17.26 | 9.46 |
| Concession nucleolus: $\mu = \sum_{i \in s} \Phi_i$ | 8.44 | 7.38 | 11.64 | 17.07 | 9.46 |
| Contribution nucleolus: $\mu = v(N) - v(N-S)$ | 8.60 | 7.60 | 11.60 | 16.60 | 9.60 |
| Obtained risk value: $w_i$ (× 100) | | | | | |
| Nucleolus: $\mu = 1$ | 66.40 | 57.40 | 68.40 | 73.40 | 50.40 |
| Weak nucleolus: $\mu = s$ | 66.40 | 57.40 | 68.40 | 73.40 | 50.40 |
| Proportional nucleolus: $\mu = v(S)$ | 66.65 | 57.76 | 68.31 | 72.74 | 50.54 |
| Concession nucleolus: $\mu = \sum_{i \in s} \Phi_i$ | 66.56 | 57.62 | 68.36 | 72.93 | 50.54 |
| Contribution nucleolus: $\mu = v(N) - v(N-S)$ | 66.40 | 57.40 | 68.40 | 73.40 | 50.40 |

**Table 12.4 The dual vectors for coalitions and maximal ε-value**

| | Nucleolus | Weak nucleolus | Proportional nucleolus | Concession nucleolus | Contribution nucleolus |
|---|---|---|---|---|---|
| $y_S$ for $v(S)$: | | | | | |
| $v(1,2,3,4)$, $v(1,2,3,5)$, $v(1,2,4,5)$, $v(1,3,4,5)$, $v(2,3,4,5)$ | 0.20 | 0.05 | 0.00515 | 0.00463 | 0.0037 |
| $y_N$ for $v(N)$: | | | | | |
| $v(1,2,3,4,5)$ | −0.80 | −0.20 | −0.02062 | −0.01852 | −0.01481 |
| maximum ε-value | −4.4 | −1.1 | −0.1134 | −0.10185 | −0.08148 |

values show that the largest benefit will be brought to Player (Region) 4, the largest risk taker. However, among the alternative concepts, there are still conflicts of regional interests. For Regions 3 and 4, the proportional nucleolus is most beneficial but, for the other regions, the nucleolus, weak nucleolus and contribution nucleolus are most beneficial. As a reference for choosing the preferred policy for the agreement, the dual optimal vectors are generated and examined for the alternative nucleolus concepts. The results are shown in Table 12.4 which shows a descending preference order among them toward the right hand. The final decision can be made by the mediator on these evaluation results, but it can still be performed discretionally without any rigorous restraint in these results.

# CHAPTER 13

# PROPRIETY OF MULTIPLE CRITERIA DECISION MAKING FOR HUMAN AFFAIRS: SOCIAL IMPLEMENTATION AND PERSONAL BEHAVIOR

## 13.1 Introduction

Difficulty in social implementation of multiple criteria decision analysis (MCDA), particularly in social science fields, is a major trap to overcome in development of this method, and also is a major source of criticism against the effectiveness of MCDA. This chapter concerns conceptual reflection upon how the difficulty can be coped with.

The difficulty of MCDA is threefold. First, MCDA primarily presumes the function of the decision maker (DM) for the social decision making, which presumes as if a single person has made decisions. Even though DM in MCDA is defined as an assessor or analyst in a decision support system and thus is not meant to be an administrator or a policy maker, and also even though his decisions usually represent final results of the brain storming by team members, it will still be doubted if there is any legitimacy for such the presumption. Above all, many economists have traditionally denied the necessity of scrutinizing the function of DM and purge it from their field (e.g., Robbins 1932; Friedman 1953). This tide of thought is combined with their value-free or value-neutral attitudes for scientific thought. The importance of knowing how people can go about making decisions through the social decision maker as an impersonate "body" in any sense has been disregarded. However, this suspicion raises a problem theoretically similar to various discourses in classical works about the raison d'etre of political societies since the seventeenth century, because both discussions present the common problem of how individual decision making in a community can be agglomerated with a legitimacy into the social decision making of DM impersonated as the representative of the social or collective body.

Second, social implementation of MCDA presumes existence and function of reason in human behavior, for which there also seems to be great suspicion. Recently Simon (1983) presented a criticism about the limits of reason in human affairs, in particular against the von Neumann-Morgenstern type expected utility theory, or the Olympian model, because the theory presumes a comprehensiveness of human knowledge and consistencies of human reasoning that are difficult to fulfill in the actual decision processes. It has been discussed, in the previous chapters, that MCDM in fact does not depend on such an overall comprehensiveness and consistency, because in the judgmental phase of MCDM, only local value assessment is performed for any device even with some fuzziness. However, the grounds for reason in human affairs still remain to be discussed. Recently behavioral models are presented as an alternative to the rational or the Olympian model. The behavioral approach seems after all to clarify the foundations of reason in biological as well as human behaviors based on the development of genetic theory.

Third, social implementation of MCDA depends on cultural environments. Evolution of human reason is restricted in the institutional as well as natural environment, which evolves from different social and cultural domains. Thus, recent works of biologists juxtapose a cultural gene ("culturgen") with the biological gene (Lumsden and Wilson 1981), while an author in management science talks about the "habitual domain" of human behavior (Yu 1981, 1984, 1985). The dynamism of the evolution of MCDM cannot be elucidated without regard to its cultural environment.

In the following sections, the above points at issue are discussed. First, properties and functions of DM as the social decision maker are discussed in relation to its social propriety, its genetic origin and its legitimacy (13.2). Second, a micromechanism of human behavior for an individual decision maker is examined in a conceptual model. The personal basis of human reason in DM is scrutinized according to development processes of individual human needs, which are constructed in the hierarchical structure from lower to higher levels. This discussion will provide a behavioral basis of the legitimacy of DM (13.3). Finally, a macromechanism of human behavior is examined. The effects of the cultural domain on human decisions are discussed. Teleology in the social implementation of MCDA is also considered (13.4).

## 13.2 Properties and Functions of the Decision Maker

### 13.2.1 Agglomeration Process of Decision Making

This section deals with the propriety or legitimacy of functions of DM as the social decision maker in implementation of MCDA. The judgmental phase of MCDM presumes, as its essential part, the existence of a formal function as the social decision maker, even though multiplicity and fuzziness of decision making are taken into account to some extent (see Chapters 4 and 7). This presumption raises suspicions as to why the individual behavior with self-interested motivation can be transferred in the social behavior of the decision maker and how this mechanism can be explained in the evolution of human reason if we intend to avoid metaphysical and theological discussions. The problem is discussed in twofold: one is to examine how the personal behavior of many individual decision makers can be merged, transferred, and converted into the particular behavioral form of a (conceptual or formal) single personality and why it can be approved as social decision making by the individual decision makers (IDM); another is to examine how personal characteristics which are held by plural IDM can be kept in this personality. The former question is about the social legitimacy of agglomeration of individual behaviors (or individual rights) and the latter is the propriety of the projection of a personal behavior onto the social decision maker (SDM). These two aspects are interrelated, and the latter provides the basis for the former legitimacy. In this subsection, we will discuss, as the personal basis of the agglomeration, the propriety of the projection of a personal behavior onto the social decision making. The social legitimacy of the agglomeration will be discussed in the next subsection.

The proposition that the *decision maker should be personalized in itself, not as this or that particular person but as all mankind or human beings,* has been presented in classical works and has succeeded with special emphasis in early modern societies. This proposition is the origin of political thought about modern societies, but often criticized, due to its normative tone, as unrealistic and idealistic. However, the interpretation of this assertion can be made more descriptive and behavioral than is usually conceived. In particular, the validity of this assertion can be verified by some considerations on its behavioral basis.

As a microfoundation, it has been noted in classical works that the similitude of thought and passions of one person to those of others is the basis for reading (knowing) the thought and passions of all other persons. This similitude has been regarded as the basis for the creation of the civil society, as a "common-wealth" (Hobbes 1651). The validity of this proposition is not restricted within its original age, the seventeenth century, where civilized absolutism was governing. The maxim since Socrates, *read thy self*, is used for explaining the personal basis of the decision maker as the representative of a social or a political body. In the Assembly and Parliament systems as democratic political systems at the present time, as long as their intrinsic property as the "political common-wealth" or "common-wealth by institution" remains unchanged, the decision making revealed in legislations should have a personal basis that represents the reflection or projection of many individual decision making. In this sense, the personal basis is still kept in some form of a unified collectivity that is composed of individual decision makers.

To reconsider the above proposition, we call your attention to another aspect of the personal basis of a social body, assembly or association. In recent studies on motivation theory, an individual is regarded as an integrated, organized whole, or rather a *horon* in the new word, having varied desires, perceptions, emotions, and thinking (Maslow 1954; Argyris 1957; Koestler 1967). The individual as a *horon* is motivated by a unified body rather than just by a part of one person. In particular, in selecting aims and means to attain to them, an individual should act in a personal integration. Thus the integrated property of a societal behavior of associations does not invalidate the similitude of a personal behavior to the societal behavior representing many persons. The recognition of the integrated property of an individual personality will make the agglomeration process of IDM into SDM more understandable and persuasive.

It should be noted here that to assert the existence of the function of the decision maker (DM) in which the personality of IDM is merged and projected is not at all the same as to presume despotism. The distinction between despotism or tyranny and "civil power" (civilian authority) has been highly regarded by many authors although both of them demand the constituent's complaisance or accommodation to the power or decision once it is established (e.g., Locke 1690; Rousseau 1762). Despotical power can be exercised arbitrarily for one particular personal interest over the others and thus his own interests are separated from many other people. On the contrary, civilian power is based on the voluntary abandonment of private rights on decision making originally belonging to IDM and on their transfer to SDM for the constituents' own best (or better) interest. This definite distinction has been the basis of many kinds of modern political discourse and also is the basis of the legitimacy of DM in MCDM.

Here is another factor to be taken into account. Conflict among multiple goals can also be included in an integrated personality of an individual. Some level of conflict can motivate evolution of the human mind by evoking a counterpower to restore unification of the personality and by promoting robustness against deviation from its integrated property. However, too much conflict, compared with a certain degree of robustness in the human mind, may lead to destroying the personality physically, mentally, or morally. Thus management processes for conflict solving should be embedded in human behavior if it is desirable for the individual to hold a unified personality for better enjoyment of his life. This perception and conception in human behavior actually lead to the motivation of embedding the conflict solving process in it, consciously or unconsciously. This observation can be extended to any societal and organizational behavior (see Chapter 7, and Chapter 8.3.3). Recognition of the personal base of an association has been the basis of modern organization theory since Barnard (1938), in which the functions of leadership are carefully examined. In particular, an organization of the personality is conceptualized as *the Self*, and its psychological basis is regarded as the source of energy for the association as well as for the individual. In this context, the importance of conflict management is a highly regarded (Argyris 1957; March and Simon 1958). This recognition treats the organizational decision making in a social body as the projection of the individual decision making of its constituents. To embed the conflict solving processes in an organization is regarded as the basis of innovation and evolution of the organization.

Now, we shall discuss about the social legitimacy of DM in the transfer or agglomeration process of the private rights in decision making.

### 13.2.2 Legitimacy of the Decision Maker

The legitimacy or competency of the decision maker (SDM) to take over the private rights of IDM for decision making is primarily based on the confidence that the "public" right will be exercised on behalf of the IDMs' own interests. This source of power should be contemplated more deeply because social acceptance and effectiveness in implementation of MCDM rests with this consideration.

The problem of the legitimacy of DM is raised because, in any case, a decision is made as if it were done by a single person in the declaration and execution of the results of the decision. Thus, for instance, a business organization as a corporation is said to hold a legal personality. A nation also behaves as if it is a single decision maker (SDM), legally or illegally. The decision maker in MCDM has the same property. A decision, once it has been made in any form with any procedure, is regarded as if SDM had done it, and multiplicities of evaluation are merged in its declaration.

In the following, the legitimacy of DM in transferring of individual rights for decision making is examined. This transference occurs in the evaluation process in MCDM as the awakened or illuminated aspect performed by individuals (project team members).

**1. Comprehensiveness of understanding and consistency of evaluation.**

It is asserted that the decision maker (DM) as a personality should possess the capability for a comprehensive understanding of problems (objectives and constraints) and of possible alternatives, the consistency of evaluations, and complete capabilities of problem solving. This assertion is a major point that so far has been attacked because of the limits of reason in human affairs. The assertion is often treated as representing Platon's Heaven of Ideas, or the Country of the Omniscient God. This requirement is regarded not to have been met by decision making in the fields of experimental psychology, where exist a great incomprehensiveness in the range of human attentions and many inconsistencies in human choices. The problem solving capability is also limited due to an incompleteness of information. Factorization of complete actions, or a whole behavioral system, into separate components has been presented as a device for coping with the limits of human reason (Simon 1969, 1983). This device only requires with its local assessment a bounded rationality that is a substitute for the entire rationality in a global optimization, as in mathematical programming and the expected utility theory in their original forms. As seen in the previous chapters, in addition to primary dependence of MCDM on the locality of assessment, the decomposition device is another core of MCDM and is on the same line as Simon's factorization.

**2. Propensity for other persons**

The proposition that *an individual has a great concern or an inclination for all other persons* is one of the major inheritances in human thought. This propensity for other persons presents one fundamental principle by which human reason is guided and, due to this other-regarding property common to every person, DM can make decisions like the representative for all other persons.

This proposition is in contrast to Leibnizian monachism on

which modern scientific thought has been based and on which the neo-classical school of economics also depends. This Leibnizian way of thinking is known today as reductionism. It has been already noted in Chapter 10 that Adam Smith (1759), a representative of the classical school of economics, early in the eighteenth century stated that the pleasure of mutual sympathy and compassion is a major principle of human nature that sometimes has a function to guard and protect the civil society. This altruistic mind of human nature has been recognized as indicating one direction of human motivations led by human preferences, and is regarded as the base to overcome the impossibility of the social utility function (Harsanyi 1955). The alienability of private rights in decision processes and the amendment of preference of liberalistic individuals, discussed by Sen (1976), can also be approved on this recognition. Recently, an author suggested that an individual determines his own utility to society and seeks to maximize the group utility from his own perception of group-interest. Thus it is presumed that an individual has his own group-interest utility as well as his own self-interest utility (Margolis 1982). This work presents a weighting function which is defined on the spending to maximize both of the utilities, respectively, and in equilibrium corresponds to the value ratio, the ratio of marginal utility for pure group-interest to that for pure self-interest. The twofold property of the individual utility function, self-interest and group-interest, is examined in Chapter 7, where the value ratio used for assessing the weighting constants for the individual utility functions is constructed as a relative ratio of magnitude of the total value of the individual utility function to that of its social component. Comparison of absolute levels of the social components of the utility functions is regarded there as more important than that of their marginal values in the weighting process of individual utility functions. Although the same values of the marginal rates of substitution can correspond to the different levels of the group-interest utility functions for an attribute level, this almost does not make sense for "aggregation" of the individual group-interest utility functions.

Recent works on the utilitarian approach pay much attention

| | | Prisoner 2 | | | |
|---|---|---|---|---|---|
| | | Cooperate (Not confess) | | Defect (Confess) | |
| Prisoner 1 | Cooperate (Not confess) | 0.9 | 0.9 | 0 | 1.0 |
| | Defect (Confess) | 1.0 | 0 | 0.1 | 0.1 |

**Table 13.1 The payoff matrix (utility value) for the prisoner's dilemma**

to the "externality," or to the process in which private preference merges into public choice via game theoretic approaches (Harsanyi 1977; Moreh 1985; etc.). An interesting result from an experiment in game theory, called the Computer Prisoner's Dilemma Tournament, has also appeared (Axelrod 1980a, b, 1981, 1984). The Prisoner's Dilemma (Luce and Raiffa 1957) assumes that, as shown in the payoff matrix in Table 13.1, two prisoners have different values of utility for rewards (or punishment) from their alternative behavior, and concludes that their intentions to maximize their own interest lead to mutual defection and thus they obtain a worse result for both than if both had cooperated. In an attempt to get out from this dilemma, an iterated computer tournament has been executed. In result, it is shown that the TIT FOR TAT strategy has won and thriven with robustness against other exploitative strategies. The TIT FOR TAT strategy embodies mutual cooperation only in reciprocity: TIT FOR TAT cooperates on the first move, and then does whatever the other player did on the subsequent move. Although this strategy includes a punishment process for self-protection, the result reveals the positive role of "niceness" and "forgiveness" in human behavior for constructing better resolutions in group decision making under situations with conflicting interests. This experiment also shows that concentrating or clustering of the strategy, even if it has only a small proportion of interactions, is an important factor for TIT FOR TAT strategy to win the other strategies, to thrive, and to be robust against invasion by uncooperative strategies. These findings are presented for explaining how cooperation emerges in a world of egoists without a central authority. It is asserted that there is no need to assume the existence of rational players, or even conscious and deliberate choice by the players. The results are explained in a genetic way, and the resemblance of human behavior appearing in that experiment to the evolution of cooperation for survival in biological systems (Maynard Smith 1982, etc.) is particularly stressed. The findings of the Computer Prisoner's Dilemma Tournament provide the foundation for insight into the human reason which guides human behavior. The success of the players using TIT FOR TAT depends on the following conditions (Axelrod 1984):

(i) regards on the future (forward-looking rule),
(ii) possibility of seeing and interacting again with each other (intimacy rule),
(iii) provocability of retaliatory strategy of a player with reciprocity (provocation rule),
(iv) capability of discriminating the other players' strategy (discerning capacity rule),
(v) regards on adaptation with sensitivity to the other players rather than simply maximizing their own advantage (the "not too clever" rule), and
(vi) extinction of defeated players ("not ever exploited" rule).

It has been pointed out that these conditions (ii)-(iv) can be found even in biological behavior of animals with its genetic base. Perhaps conditions (i) and (v) also have some findings in biological systems along with the specialization of a species as a form of fitness and the dispersion and elaboration of niches where some species can find new living places. These findings also provide the behavioral source of reason in human beings which has developed with great enlightenment and cultivation of the human mind, via learning, thinking, and introspection processes of human behavior. In short, reason in human beings as a biological species has a behavioral foundation, although it has been evolved, educated, and enlightened from a simple genetic base. The condition (i) has been particularly enlightened in mankind, and is another basis of the legitimacy of DM. The condition (vi), however, is one part to be criticized in the Computer Tournament if the social behavior of humans is considered.

In the Computer Prisoner's Dilemma Tournament by Axelrod, ecological success of alternative decision rules is simulated for over 1000 generations. In this simulation, many strategies based on exploitative rules disappear because, as exploited rules die out, the exploiters' base of survival becomes eroded and the exploiters suffer a similar fate. Here is a major difference, however, between the simulation test for biological success and human behavior. First, human beings can not wait for so many generations, even for 100 generations, although they can assume themselves to be great forward-lookers into the future. Second, differing from the computer simulation, the players with defeated strategies cannot walk off their playing field: they must still struggle for their living, and thus they may have to ever exploited until their death. This is the natural state for mankind, and this situation presents the raison d'être of civil society to which some private rights on decision making are transferred. The existence of the function of the social decision maker as the mediator has been approved to supply this defect and imperfection in the natural state (Locke 1690). Third, altruistic or cooperative propensity is one aspect of human nature, which has evolved for keeping and preserving mankind as a species and on which the reason of human beings is based. There are some observations for this assertion. (a) If the egoism that seeks its own interest is governing, then unconditional defection will prevail in the world of the Prisoners' Dilemma, which leads to a worse result for every player. (b) It is better for human beings to compare their behavior with that of others in order to understand and improve their performances. This comparison needs the acquisition of information from other people. Cooperation with others makes it easy to obtain such information. Egoism calls forth isolation of an individual from his fellows because he never provides any benefit to other people. This situation is a cause of stiffness to external information and thus will lead the individual to worse situations due to the lack of good quality information from others. (c) Here is a more novel situation that will promote an altruistic attitude. Survival of some species has been assured to some extent by the partitions of niches and the variations in forms of fitness with different strategies under competitive situations (Simon 1984). The recent advancement of high technology in human society, however, is promoting the uniformity of information, which will pervade very widely and rapidly and will destroy small, varied societal and cultural niches in which some fellows in the minority are still living successfully under different societal and cultural conditions. This large-scale information system will behave as a modern Leviathan over all individuals and may become a major source of mental, psychological, and social conflict for some personalities, which may lead to a dissolution of human associations, morally and institutionally. The other-regarding propensity in human preference (decisions) with concern for the independency of the others is particularly important for the mutual interest of all individuals in a modern society.

In short, the construction of a social body, or an association, for assuring social decision making originates from promoting an altruistic attitude in mankind and is a particular characteristic that has evolved in human behavior, showing the wisdom of human beings. The grounds for the legitimacy of DM is embedded in the origin of human societies, and thus is on human propensity for other persons.

### 3. Propensity for future

Another legitimacy of DM is on the propensity for the future. This forward-looking propensity also has a behavioral basis in every individual.

First, in general, foresight of the future behavior of other individuals will contribute to better performance of an individual, and mutual interest in this situation forms the basis of human cooperation. Thus, Axelrod also suggested that the clearness of the strategy of one player with reciprocity to the others will promote mutual cooperation among players and leads to their better consequences.

Second, an individual's enjoyment of psychic income (including physical and monetary income) needs to be calculated for a long period of time. The long-term enjoyment of the psychic income is one characteristic of modern industrial societies, and one example of it in economics is shown by the round-about production principle of Böhm-Bawerk (1889). Fisher (1930) discussed the problem of time valuation to translate the future into the present. He stressed that valuations as a human process are always anticipations, and that the value of the good itself is the discounted value in which foresight enters and its future services are considered. Time preference (or human impatience for the future) is the fundamental cause which determines the rate of interest, and reveals a price in the trade-off or exchange between present goods and future goods.

Thus, dynamic utility, in which the discounting rate for the future is embodied, can be constructed, and the expected utility maximization principle can be replaced by the maximization principle of the present value of the expected utility. Let $u^s(t, x) \triangleq u_t^s(x)$ be a time-dependent valuation of the psychic income, or dynamic utility function, for a time $t$, $t = 0,\ldots,T$ at a time $s$, where $t$ is counted in the forward direction from $s$, and let $i_t^s$ be the interest rate which is also time-variant. Then, the present value $V^s$ of the utility flow $u_0^s, u_1^s,\ldots, u_T^s$, is

$$V^s \triangleq u_0^s + \frac{u_1^s}{1 + i_1^s} + \ldots + \frac{u_T^s}{(1 + i_1^s)(1 + i_2^s) \ldots (1 + i_T^s)}, \tag{13.1}$$

where $\alpha_1(s) \triangleq \dfrac{1}{1 + i_1^s}$, $\alpha_2(s) \triangleq \dfrac{1}{(1 + i_1^s)(1 + i_2^s)}$, etc., are the discount factor and $d_t^s$ in $\alpha_t(s) \triangleq (1 - d_t^s)$ is the discount rate. The maximization condition is, putting $dx = 1$,

$$dV^s = \partial u_0^s + \frac{\partial u_1^s}{1 + i_1^s} + \ldots + \frac{\partial u_T^s}{(1 + i_1^s)(1 + i_2^s) \ldots (1 + i_T^s)} = 0. \tag{13.2}$$

Consider the local conditions for each pair of terms. For example,

$$\partial u_0^s + \frac{\partial u_1^s}{1 + i_1^s} = 0, \qquad \frac{\partial u_1^s}{1 + i_1^s} + \frac{\partial u_2^s}{(1 + i_1^s)(1 + i_2^s)} = 0, \text{ etc.} \tag{13.3}$$

Then

$$-\frac{\partial u_1^s}{\partial u_0^s} = 1 + i_1^s, \quad -\frac{\partial u_2^s}{\partial u_1^s} = 1 + i_2^s,$$
$$-\frac{\partial u_3^s}{\partial u_1^s} = (1 + i_2^s)(1 + i_3^s), \text{ etc.} \tag{13.4}$$

The discount factor shows the time trade-off, or a marginal rate of substitution, for the time-dependent utilities for two adjoining periods. Thus the expected utility function can be redefined as follows.

$$Eu \triangleq \sum_{r=1}^{n} p_r V^s(x_r), \tag{13.5}$$

where $x_r$ is an event represented as a vector or a scalar, and $p_r$ shows its probability. It should be noted here that the present value of the dynamic utility function (13.1) is based on the local assessment at time $s$. It presumes implicitly the bounded rationality when the evaluation is extended to future. The concept of time preference has been used in describing the economic behavior for capital investments, for which it is discussed that social considerations will bring about lower social rates of discount than its private, or market rate (Marglin 1963a,b; Mishan 1967). An example is found in afforestation activity. Axelrod (1984) also suggested that the discount rate $d_t^s$ should be held not too high in order to promote the cooperative human behavior because mankind is interested in preservation of its species in the future, for which mutual cooperation is necessitated.

Third, the concern for the future is extended beyond the present generation and their direct offspring in kinship. In the forward-looking attitude, which is one of the eminent characteristics of human behavior that differs from biological behavior, human beings, besides the preservation of the species, highly regard the preservation and evolution of culture including societal and technological inventions, which have needed the accumulation of knowledge and experience obtained over many generations. This retrospective recognition is naturally extended to the future. The recognition for the necessity of cultural preservation and evolution for the future provides a better environment for human lives with nice feeling, and thus is positively connected with individual self-interest. This propensity for the future will be reinforced by the religious mind of individuals, which is one aspect of human nature, consciously or unconsciously.

These observations confirm the behavioral basis of the forward-looking attitude of human beings. The future consideration is one major source of the transference of the private rights to DM in an association. Self-interested motivation of an individual is usually more myopic and often dominates the group-interested mind of the individual, which evokes a more long-range perspective. The necessity to cope with this weakness of humanity has been discussed as the origin of government (e.g., Hume 1752) and is one major source of the legitimacy of DM.

## 4. Promotion of adaptability

One source of the legitimacy of DM is in its capability, in a short range or a long range, for promotion of the adaptability of mankind to changing environments and contingencies. In general, environments for human beings are mutable and changing. They are variable in themselves and as results of human actions. Some of these variations have adverse effects on human lives. Thus the promotion of the adaptation of human behavior to the changing environments is one of the major roles of DM who possesses the capability for evaluating, managing, and controlling these environments through influencing human behavior. The variations and fluctuations in individual traits are increasingly regarded as the basis of the robustness of biological systems to the changing environments. The occurrence of a mutation is regarded as a result of an adaptive change of a species, successful or unsuccessful. The social decision making in human society can promote the variations and fluctuations in individual traits by establishing effective education systems, which promote the differentiation of personal characteristics and specialities and thus will make the adaptation process easier in the niche partition and its elaboration. The function of DM as the coordinator is emphasized in particular in this adaptation process which requires a wider scope of recognition and long-ranging foresight in making decisions.

## 5. Provision of information

The above discussions lead to the recognition of another basis of the legitimacy of DM, the capability for providing individuals with information. In the ancient Japanese literature in the eighth century (*Kojiki*, The Memoirs of Old Histories, etc.), it is shown that to govern is to hear, or to know, from people and also to inform them of their situations. These words, "hear," "know," and "inform," in Japanese are used as synonyms for the word that means "govern." This etymological analysis presents the principal role of the provision of information in the origin of the function of DM. When DM defaults on this primal role, then the revolution will come, which means in the old Chinese letters that the Command of Heaven Has Been Renewed.

The preservation and evolution of human beings in the changing environments require a great deal of good quality information for their adaptive behavior without much delay. The advantage of the social decision maker is in collecting and providing the good quality information in various fields and is in making its mutual comparison and screening possible with promptness. The position of the social decision maker in forming advisory boards will raise the quality and reliability of information over individual capacities. Thus the major source and consequence of the function of the social decision maker is in the capability to possess and provide information, and also in the effectiveness in assembling, examining, and conveying information. The ground of existence of DM in an assembly, or an association, is in expectation to provide a great advantage for its constituents through the provision of information. This is one of the major sources of the legitimacy of DM.

There is some risk, however, in the existence of DM. The function of DM can be used for collection and manipulation of large-scale information, which may have adverse effects on the advantages of IDM and may lead to informational despotism in modern societies. For avoiding this risk, the propriety and usefulness of information which is collected and provided by DM should be rigorously checked from the individuals' points of view. The usefulness of DM for IDM in information processing and provision is one of the most fundamental bases of the legitimacy of DM.

## 13.3 Hierarchical Structure of Human Needs

In this section, the behavioral basis of reason in humans is considered in its evolutionary process. Reason in humans, on which MCDM is founded, can be seen not only in their normative propositions, but also in observation and description of the personal behavior of IDM. This section concerns the observable characteristics of human reason revealed in the personal behavior of an individual.

The personal behavior is based on human needs, which seem to be intuitively constructed but actually are formed with human experience and logic and evolve in a hierarchical configuration. Experience reflects an accumulation of human behavior in the course of time. Logic evokes human motivation. Even if it takes an "illogical" form such as intuition and emotion, they are also considered a sudden comprehension or understanding of how to behave at a point of time, and the mental activity for this understanding always occurs through a course of logic, correctly or incorrectly. For example, an assertion that "I like to drink water because I am thirsty" is one of the most primitive logics, and this logic motivates an action to drink water; it is also a result of his experience including a potential memory in a gene. Thus human needs are defined on both of experience and logic. It also means that an assertion representing a human need is always defined on a specific point of time. For that example, the assertion that represents a human need to drink water will be described as "I'd like to drink water because I am thirsty right now."

A morphological diagram for the above phases of human needs is depicted in Figure 13.1 in a hierarchical configuration.

The human needs are largely partitioned into physiological,

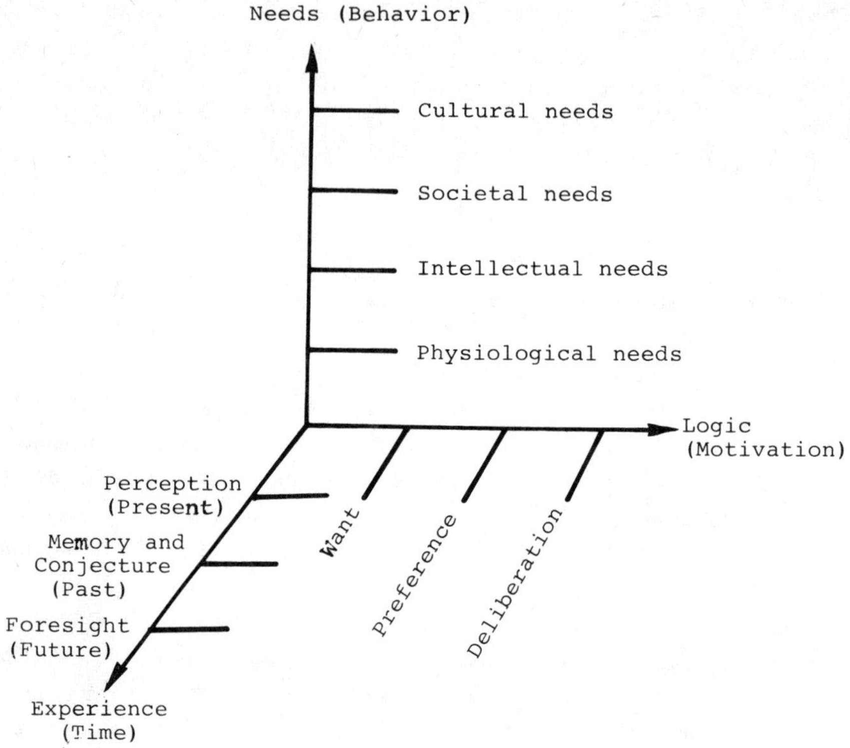


**Figure 13.1 The morphological diagram for a hierarchical structure of human behavior.**

intellectual, societal, and cultural needs. Each need has two dimensions, experience and logic. Experience reflects the cumulative memory of time-dependent human behavior and its extension to the future. It has the time dimensions: present, past, and future. The present experience is recognized simply as perception of objects. The past experiences are stored as memory and recalled for conjecture about present objects via comparison with the memory. The future experience is the foresight of objects which have not yet occurred. These experiences form the human needs in the different time phases. Logic stimulates human motivation in different levels by putting human thinking in order: the logic in want, the logic in preference, and the logic in deliberation. The logic in want is in the lowest level and sometimes appears to be "illogical." It arouses the human motivation for meeting primal necessities. The logic in preference is in the second level, and to order the preference requires more imaginative or conceivable activity of the human mind via comparison and evaluation of alternatives. The logic in deliberation is in the highest level for motivation, and shows the highly enlightened and elaborated results of the mental activities of humans. On these phases, logic and experience, the human needs are formed in a hierarchical structure. For example, a physiological need with a past experience and a logic in preference will intend to eat beef rather than oysters for dinner in the summer season. For another example, an intellectual need with a present experience and a logic in want will lead a person to go to an opera performance despite his having an important appointment with a client this evening, because this person has just got the scarce ticket that he was eager to obtain. It should be noted here that the morphological diagram in Figure 13.1 is open-ended. It may be supposed that the ends of the arrows in three dimensions will perhaps converge into a point in a very far distance. Or alternatively, the diagram may be supposed to be a quadrihedral cone having a vertex in an upward direction. The end point or the vertex seems to suggest a theological phase which is not the subject of the present work.

In the following, some properties of the human needs will be considered.

**1. Physiological needs.**

The physiological needs are the elementary needs of human beings and have an instinctive nature primary for individual survival. Preservation of an individual and the population of its species is the primal aim sought with these needs. It should be noted, however, that even for these primal needs, the phase with deliberation and foresight for their self-interest is embedded in human behavior for its more effective achievement.

**2. Intellectual needs.**

Human actions for meeting the physiological needs develop more elaborate ways of thinking and evolve the intellectual needs. The use of copper and iron for more effective hunting in the Neolithic age promoted the development of scientific knowledge in a primitive sense. The process of development of the intellectual needs is shown in Figure 13.2. (i) The

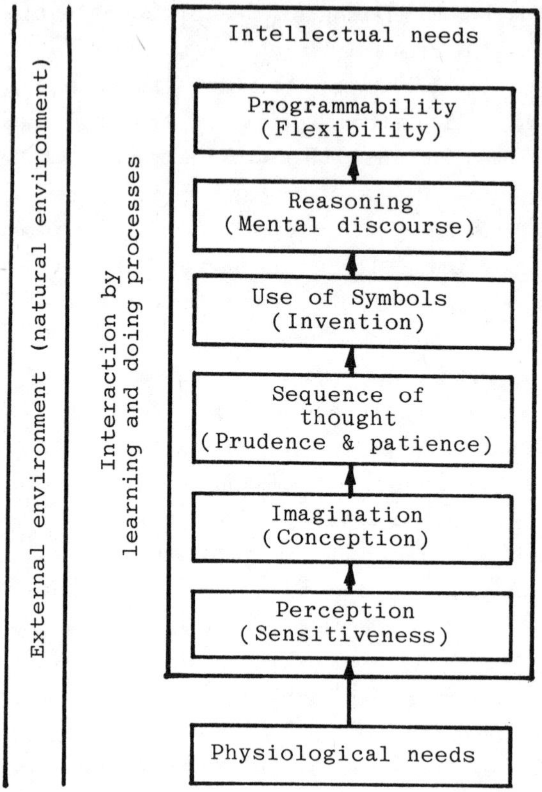


**Figure 13.2 Development of the intellectual needs.**

conversion of the physiological needs to intellectual needs is initiated and promoted by perception, the primal function of thinking. Sensitiveness, susceptivity, and curiosity in human nature have greatly enlightened the power of perception. (ii) Then imagination evolves the power of perception towards conception based on experiences. Some emotional inclination and passion particularly promote this psychological or mental activity. These two stages (i) and (ii) are still primitive, but provide the basis of intellectual development. Advanced stages show more elaborate processes of cognitive power in human nature. Namely (iii) a sequence of thought, unguided or guided, forms some findings for more effective performances in order. Prudence and patience promote this ability and present the virtue favorable for its acquisition. Note that these stages are common to some extent in any species, or living thing in biological worlds. (iv) The use of symbols, various kinds of languages, was the critical event for the evolution of effective preservation, processing, and conveyance of information. Human beings could evolve crucially in this stage, differing from other species. By using the symbolic media, the capacity of invention, for which an augmentation, concentration, and convergence of a sequence of thinking into ideas are required, is definitely evolved in this stage. (v) Reasoning is a more effective function for proper arrangement and its extensions of knowledge and information, and the core of intellectual activity. Mental discourses and dialogs promote this capacity. The development of the power of reasoning leads to the next stage: (vi) programmability. The programmability is the capacity to detect a problem, to structure it, and to prescribe a resolution for it, intentionally and discretionally. Increasing this capacity requires malleability of the human mind, which allows the variation and fluctuation of human thinking with toughness and thus makes it more effective to adapt to changing environments. Development of the problem-finding and problem-solving capabilities in human nature is promoted by the human needs for the programmability.

During these stages, the cognitive power of human beings was not at all completed at the beginning of their genesis, but it has greatly been enlightened in the process of its evolution. The development of the intellectual needs motivated in the evolution of the cognitive power, and the above stages (i)-(vi) correspond to its evolution process. A major product of this process is the recognition of the effectiveness of interpersonal comparisons among individual behaviors for finding better performances. For this purpose, the cognitive power of human beings led to the invention and use of language. The development of societal needs are a natural result of this process. The consciousness of the societal needs comes after the development of the programmability, because the societal needs are developed to a new dimension according to the necessity of interaction and cooperation which are evoked by the problem-finding and problem-solving capability in human behavior.

**3. Societal needs.**

The societal needs are the natural result of the development of the intellectual needs. The learning and doing processes, which the intellectual needs stimulate and by which they are stimulated, induce the sense of comparison with the different behaviors of other persons and then lead to recognition of the benefit of cooperation with other individuals. It has been emphasized that the cooperation and mutual assistance in civil society are not originally the effect of human wisdom, but have the behavioral basis known as "self-love." Transactions among individuals are more likely to prevail if some person can interest the self-love of other persons and show them that it is for their own advantage to cooperate with each other (Smith 1776, etc.). This intention of individuals stimulates the societal needs. The societal needs have the following components in a hierarchical structure (Figure 13.3).

(i) Needs for self-understanding.

As discussed before, the need for self-understanding of an individual is the basis of his interest for other individuals and also is stimulated by this interest. We cannot understand ourselves unless we understand others, and we cannot understand others unless we understand ourselves. In particular, the Self is built up through social contacts or mutual interactions with others. A person cannot make his "whole" personality by himself (cf. Argyris 1957).

(ii) Needs for others' interests.

The recognition of self-advantages from progress in other individuals evoke the needs for others' interest. To have a better neighbor is to get information with better quality, directly or indirectly. Thus the "enlightened self-interest" (Simon 1983) will accompany the needs for others' interests and, standing by itself, forms an altruistic attitude in human nature. The recognition of others' contributions to one's self-enrichment forms the basis of one's contribution to the others mutual and places cooperation on a sound base.

(iii) The belongingness needs.

The need for belongingness (Maslow 1954) evolves from the

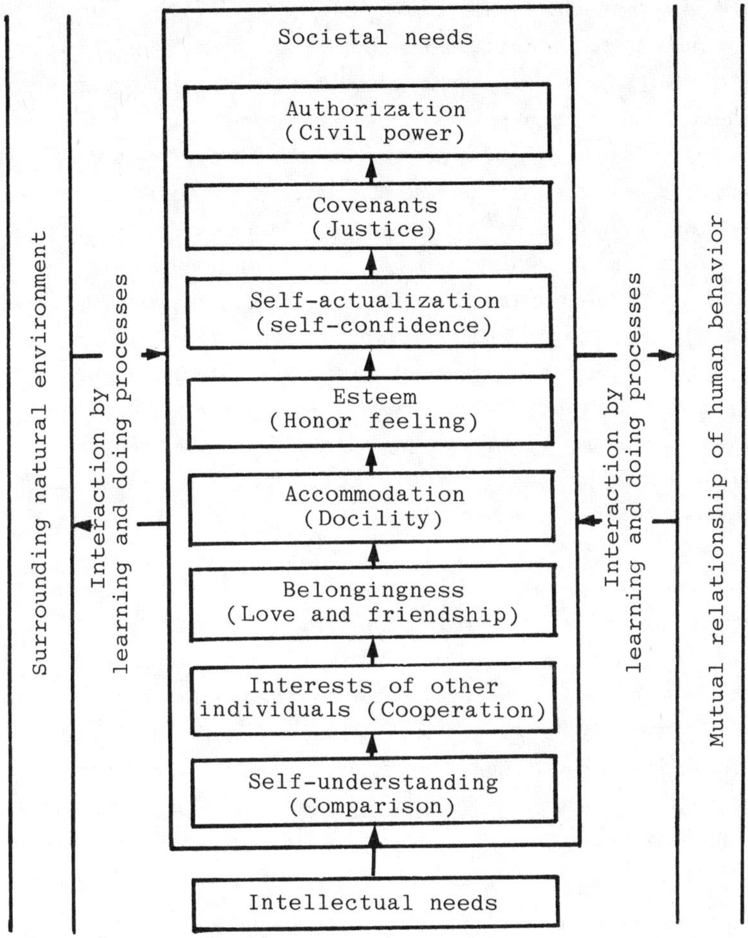


**Figure 13.3 The hierarchical structure of societal needs.**

need for others' interests and forms the psychological basis of love and friendship. A relatedness or kinship provides the genetic origin of this needs because the feeling of belongingness in a sexual or a blood relationship is stronger than in other relationships in its primitive cases, and thus promotes the fellow-feeling among individuals as found in many biological species. These belongingness needs, or fellow-feelings, greatly contribute to the societal progress in an association, because they can excite the imaginative capacity for protection and evolution of their fellows and promote the intellectual progress in a society.

(vi) Accommodation needs.

The need for adaptation to others has been discussed in classical works. The sense of fitness, or the perception of coincidence (correspondent affection), has been discussed as the basis of the sense of propriety (Smith 1759). Complaisance, or docility, in adaptation has been regarded as one of the Laws of Nature, and has been treated as necessary condition for evolution, because every person shall endeavor all he can to obtain what is necessary for his own preservation (Hobbes 1651) and knowledge for them often comes from others. The psychological or behavioral base of social obedience is threefold: the advantages for self-protection and group-protection, which correspond to the safety needs (Maslow 1954), and the advantage for the acquisition of knowledge and experience, which requires a lot of learning and doing processes (Simon 1983).

The evolution of the accommodation needs leads to the desire for contribution, which has positive and creative effects on the association. This desire may sometimes make an individual's behavior plunge into an inadequate or unacceptable range to the others. Although negative effects of the accommodation needs, when they fail, may not be harmful to the individual, an association can suffer from the failure of the desire for contribution.

(v) Esteem needs.

The accommodation needs which evoke the desire for contribution lead to desire for social acceptance or approval of the contribution. This desire forms the esteem needs. The needs for esteem (Maslow 1954), or the feeling of honor as a reward, are derived from the evolution of the accommodation needs and are the result of the desire for contribution. They are accompanied by the sense of shame or a guilt feeling when the contribution is regarded to be inadequate to the society. An individual who behaves in the expectation to contribute to others asks in result that the adequacy or propriety of his contributions be approved, estimated, and highly regarded by others. These needs for esteem will be extended, on the one hand, to the desire for praise and acclaim (Simon) if the performance is successful. If it is unsuccessful, these needs lead to the desire for forgiveness or pardon with the desire for revenge on the other side of the coin (Hobbes, Axelrod). The desire for gratitude has also been regarded as one of the Laws of Nature (Hobbes). It is the reciprocal attitude for contribution and corresponds to the self-interest of an individual by promoting the reciprocity of the gifts of grace and assistance.

Here is some discussion about the esteem needs, which may evoke envy in human nature. The envy has a negative effect on the evolution of human behavior, because the envy originates from an egoism only intending self-interest and thus is incompatible with enlightened personal wisdom which intends collective or social interests. An envious person can be clever in seeking self-interest from a myopic point of view, but cannot be wise in seeking a long-range self-interest which is closely combined with the social interest in its reciprocity. Although envious minds seek esteem for a short term, this cannot evolve the needs for self-actualization, because only a myopic comparison with particular other persons is the matter of interest in envy. As a natural result, the social approbation is not bestowed so much on it; and in turn, the need for self-actualization will not well develop from this source, because social approbation is particularly important for the envious mind; it leads to a contradiction.

In short, the esteem needs cannot be confused with the desire of envious minds because the latter have no momentum to evolve into the more social-oriented and self-cultivable needs, the need for self-actualization.

(vi) Needs for self-actualization.

The needs for self-actualization, which are particularly emphasized in motivation theory (e.g., Maslow), are the result of the evolution and divergence of the esteem needs. The needs for self-actualization have been developed in the process of the struggle of mankind with its natural surrounding for its survival. Interactive relationships between humans and nature have promoted the needs for self-actualization through learning and doing processes. Although these needs have been originally stimulated with the expectation of esteem and natural rewards, their achievement proceeds in itself to behavior without regard to the esteem and reward. Thus, although the needs for self-actualization as a major incentive to human behavior can be found even in animal behavior in its primal forms, it has evolved in its most elaborate forms in human activities and has provided the basis of culture. The intellectual capacity of human beings has greatly cultivated these needs and brought gratification for their physical and mental activities at a higher level, which often accompanies social praise. The toughness of these needs as developed in mankind, however, leads to the self-confidence and the self-respect of individuals as to their ability, and then brings the individuals to the situation where every man is the enemy to every man in the natural condition, a state of mutual invasion upon others' rights, as discussed by Hobbes, Locke, etc. The struggle for power is a result of this development in the human nature. On the contrary, in the animals' world, there is no state of such the severe struggle due to other motivations than simply seeking and preserving predator territories with food chains.

(vii) Covenant needs.

The needs to make covenants, or social contracts, have been developed to restrain the retaliatory situations in human societies and have been promoted by evolution of the needs for self-actualization which intend to pursue more and more the high-level performances. Formation of various kinds of contracts is one of the major accomplishments invented by humans.

Covenants, or social contracts, have a behavioral basis on the intention of human beings to cooperate with each other, and are its completed forms. The basis of voluntary assurance of the covenants is in the Golden Rule: *Don't do unto others what you would not have them do unto you* (The *Didache* AC 200, The *Tobit* IV 15, Confucius *The Lun Yu* Bk. VIII 15). In particular, Confucius regarded this proposition as a primal interpretation of the compassion that is considered to be the fundamental principle of human behavior. Although this assertion has a normative form as if it were an absolute proposition, it actually has a behavioral basis for preserving the self-interest in a reciprocity. The reciprocal preservation of the self-interest of individuals is the personal wisdom of human beings, which has matured through long-term experience. Legal contracts have been evolved from this behavioral basis with various forms. An assembly, a team or an association, for working in MCDM is one form of covenant, as are other scientific or practical associations.

(viii) Authority needs.

The need to establish authorities in an association developed originally from the necessity of the mediator to execute the covenants or contracts with justice or equity. Justice or equity manifests a consensus for keeping the promises and for guaranteeing its reciprocity. The power of the authorities is expected to exist in the personalization of collective wisdom and to be the projection of the formation and evolution of such a personality. It has the behavioral basis in this expectation.

A major problem here is to construct the common understanding between the authority of an assembly and the constituents as IDM, which are often in conflict with one another. A primal form of the resolution is the majority rule whereby the authority simply obeys the consensus formed by the majority. Insight into organizational behavior, however, reveals the independent functions of DM as a representative in associations, corporations, or business firms. The final decision is not necessarily made as a simple aggregation of the constituents' opinions whether the representative person is actually trusted by a law or agreement. The Japanese maxim, *three people make the wisdom of Monju (a buddha)*, shows an example of a convergence of group decision making through the interaction, which implies that a consensus is not usually obtained by a simple aggregation of opinions among independent and separate individuals. The final decision can be made more wisely with the enlightened reason constructed via human interactions. The presentation of the conclusion will take a form of an agreement by each individual.

The properties of contracts between individuals and the established authorities have been discussed in classical works. Our considerations for these problems in relation to MCDM are summarized for the following topics.

First, the authority of DM originates from the illuminated

societal needs in human nature. The recognition of its necessity is primarily based on the self-interested component as well as the altruistic component in the propensity of human beings, and therefore can be merged into a collective body. The propensities for cooperation with the authority are also embedded in the individuals' self-regarding propensity as well as the other-regarding propensity as long as the legitimacy of DM holds.

Second, the legitimacy of decision making depends on diversified cultural conditions, to some extent, by which the processes of decision making are constrained. Thus the discussion about the legitimacy cannot be completed until the cultural legitimacy of decision making is examined.

Third, the establishment of the authority and its illuminating role for individuals will promote the human needs for culture which are developed through their great advantages held for construction of educational and training processes. Thus the need for authority evolves into the higher level of human needs, the cultural needs, which are particularly based on the need for self-actualization in human nature and promoted by them. The contracts for that function stimulate largely this progress.

Fourth, the cultural needs forms the cultural domain of human behavior. The formation of different cultural conditions is a natural consequence of human behavior, which is primarily based on the differentiation in evolution of the self-actualization needs. MCDM concerns in particular the cultural domain as an environment for making decisions, because it provides an overall constraint for social decision making.

Fifth, the institutional conditions, in which DM and the constituents are living and making their decisions, are formed on the cultural domain. Without much attention to this fact, no decisions, organizational, social, economic, political and technical, can succeed in their implementation.

In the next section, the cultural domain in decision making is considered in relation to human behavior, and problems raised by the different cultural and institutional conditions are discussed.

## 13.4 Cultural Domain in Decision Making

### 13.4.1 A Primitive Model

The cultural domain in human behavior has historical characteristics and a primitive model for it is shown as a functional J defined on the societal and individual phases in personal behavior. A primitive model for the cultural domain $C(t)$ is formulated as

$$C(t) = J[f(c^t, S(t), H(t))], \tag{13.6}$$

where $S(t)$ denotes a societal phase, and $H(t)$ shows an individual phase at time $t$ for personal behavior. $c^t$ is a cultural stock in a society at time $t$, and evaluated with a discount factor:

$$c^t = c_0^t + \frac{c_1^t}{(1+r_1^t)} + \frac{c_2^t}{(1+r_1^t)(1+r_2^t)} + \dots,$$

$$+ \frac{c_\tau^t}{(1+r_1^t)(1+r_2^t)\dots(1+r_\tau^t)} + \dots \quad , \tag{13.7}$$

where the sequence of cultural products,..., $c_\tau^t$,.., and the discount factor form a backward flow toward the past. The interest rate $r_i^t$, $i = 1,\dots,\tau,\dots$, is evaluated at time $t$ for a cultural stock $c_i^t$ formed at a time $i$ and is supposed to be varied for each time $i$ and $t$. The individual phase for personal behavior is described with a functional,

$$H(t) = I[B^t(L(t), E(t))], \tag{13.8}$$

where $L(t)$ denotes a logic at time $t$, $E(t)$ is an experience, and $B^t$ is an individual behavior function at $t$. The past experiences $E(t)$, which are not only in a clear remembrance $E_R^t(\tau)$, but also in a fuzzy memory $\tilde{E}^t(\tau)$ and in subconsciousness $E_P^t(\tau)$. They are shown as

$$E(t) = F^t[W^t(E_p^t, \tilde{E}^t), E_R^t] \tag{13.9}$$

$$= F^t \left[ \sum_{\tau=0}^{\infty} \omega_\tau^t (E_P^t(\tau) + \tilde{E}^t(\tau)), \sum_{\tau=0}^{\infty} \nu_\tau^t E_R^t(\tau) \right]. \tag{13.10}$$

In (13.10), $\omega_\tau^t$ and $\nu_\tau^t$ are the discount factors. The "interest rate" for $\nu_\tau^t$ is time variant as the same in (13.7). However, the first term in the square bracket is written, putting $W_\tau^t \triangleq (E_p^t(\tau) + \tilde{E}^t(\tau))$, as

$$W^t \triangleq W_0^t + \frac{W_1^t}{1+\rho^t} + \frac{W_2^t}{(1+\rho^t)^2} + \ldots + \frac{W_\tau^t}{(1+\rho^t)^\tau} + \ldots , \tag{13.11}$$

where the "interest rate" $\rho^t$, $\rho < 1$, is time invariant for $\tau$, because $\rho$ generally depends on potential inclination and cannot clearly be discerned in consciousness for each point of time when the memory is formed.

The societal phase is described with two parts: one depends on the past societal behavior, and the other does not. The functional form is described as

$$S(t) = K [s(N(\tau), A(\tau); \beta)] \tag{13.12}$$

$$= K [\{\alpha_j^t \int_0^T s_j(N_j(\tau), A_j(\tau))d\tau; \beta_j(B)\}], \tag{13.13}$$

where $N_j(\tau)$ denotes the contract and $A_j(\tau)$ is the authority for an association $j$, $j = 1,\ldots,J$. $s_j$ is a societal behavior function representing a collective behavior as an operation of the collective body or an assembly. $\alpha_j^t$ is an adjustment parameter and represents a discount factor:

$$\alpha_j(t) = \frac{1}{1+\theta_j^t} \tag{13.14}$$

where $\theta_j^t$ denotes an "interest rate" at $t$ for an association $j$. $\beta_j(B)$ shows an innovation parameter which is determined depending on human behavior in the association. T is a fixed point of time in the past. The first term in the square brackets in (13.13) shows an accumulation of the previous operations of a society, which is composed of associations j, j = 1,...,J, with a weighting parameter $\alpha_j^t$ depending on the characteristic of the association. The second term shows an innovative characteristic of the association.

The cultural domain in human behavior is determined with the societal and individual phases of personal behavior at a given time t as shown in (13.6). The cultural domain represented by the primitive model includes different kinds of conflicts. Major conflicts exist (i) between the societal phase and the individual phase of the cultural domain, (ii) between the cumulative factor and the innovative factor in the societal phase, (iii) between the contract factor and the authority factor in the societal behavior, and (iv) between the logical (motivation) factor and the experience factor in the individual phase. These conflicts give impetus to some extent to evolve the cultural domain if they can be well managed. For cultivating this function of conflict embedded in the cultural domain, however, some insight for an interpretative understanding of the primitive model is necessary. In the next subsection, an interpretative investigation of the cultural domain is presented mainly in the context of its societal phase.

### 13.4.2 Interpretative Inquiry

#### 1. Formation of institutions

The differentiation of human needs in its evolution processes forms the cultural domain; it provides the origin of the formation of institutions in which associations are included. The differentiation of human needs brings individuals into mutual exchanges of information and fruits of work, which lead to the formation of contracts. The contracts, or covenants, are made in general as the mutual transfer of individuals' rights in exchange for the security of the individual's person in his life and in the means of having his life well-preserved so as not to be weary of it (Hobbes 1651). It is a voluntary act for good for oneself in modern societies. In return for this transference of individuals' rights, justice or equity is asked for the fulfillments of the mutual obligations in the covenant. The recognition that the covenant is a combination of the individuals' interests and that the origin of justice consists in keeping the confidence of the covenant early appeared in Plato (Bk. II) and has succeeded in the modern rationalism. For keeping the validity of the covenant, a collective power in an association is requested as a mediator. This is the origin of the authority in institutions. The constitution of civil power has the highest form in the conclusion of the social covenant or contract, which is also a result of the innovative personal behavior. In short, the origin of a collective power is in the contracts by which individuals intend to preserve their own interests. The collective power functions as a person in representation of the collective or agglomerated will of the individuals. The authority of the civil power is established in extensions of this aspect to more wide-ranging perspective. Thus its innovative functions are most regarded and scrutinized.

## 2. **Reasonability of institutions**

The reasonability of an institution originates in its functions to be expected, in particular in the appropriateness for keeping the contracts, for execution of authority, and for manipulating innovative behavior as shown in (13.12). Some discussions are extended for the following points.

(i) Function of authority as the mediator.

The function of DM as an authority for mediation, or coordination, depends on the purpose of the association.

First, the primal source of the DM's power of mediation is in the contract, or covenant, among every person, by which the right to represent the individual *person* is transferred to some extent to the representative in a society. In the function of DM as a mediator, a multitude of persons constitutes one social or legal personality as a collective body. Thus, the foundation of power of authority for the mediation is in its unity as a person. In this sense, the representative has the behavioral basis.

Second, the mediation function of DM is requested in particular in the "post-industrial" society, where even the consequences of individual economic behavior cannot fully be incorporated via market price systems. There is no mediation by the market adjustment mechanism for the differentiated "production" and "consumption" activities (see Chapter 9). It is known as the market failure due to the existence of the externality. In particular, aesthetic and psychic enjoyment of natural as well as artistic beauty, and altruistic attitudes for other persons are not properly valuated in market prices. Thus, nonmarket goods or "bads" should be evaluated, monetarily or nonmonetarily, only via the mediation of DM, on the confidence that this is the best way to protect all of the individuals' self-interest.

Third, the voluntary submission to DM as the representative in an association originates in the confidence in DM for the protections and enjoyments of individual lives. From this foundation, the sanctions of the decisions made by DM and the adaptations to them are regarded as the proper and sound personal behavior of the constituents under the "correct" operations in organizations.

Fourth, the propensity of an individual to adapt to the organizational decision making, however, will still produce some conflicts at certain stages. The basic incongruency between the needs of a mature and healthy person and the requirements of formal or informal organizations has attracted much attention in modern organization theory (Argyris 1957; March and Simon 1958, etc.). Decreasing the degree of the incongruence between individual needs and organizational requirements is a major problem for any kind of association. The embedment of proper functions for conflict-finding and conflict-solving in an association is an innovative device for the institutional as well as human protection and their evolution. As discussed before, conflicts to a certain extent provide a momentum or a source of constructive energy for organizational as well as human evolution by inducing conflict-solving intention, which will stimulate human behavior to climb up toward a higher level of the cultural needs.

The mediation for the conflict-resolution is one of recent major topics in systems research (e.g., Raiffa 1982), and it forms in particular a crucial role for DM in MCDM. A decision problem with a single objective for a multiple persons can be treated as a negotiation problem only at one level even though it often includes an arbitration process by DM. In contrast, MCDM cannot function without the explicit existence of DM as the mediator. The extension of game theory to MCDM also includes this aspect (Chapter 12).

(ii) Assurance of variation.

Modern Darwinian biological theory claims that one origin of biological evolution is in the generation of a variation or a mutation in the selective adaptation process of a species. This is the consequence of a conflict-finding and conflict-solving process by interaction between a living creature and its environment. In organization theory, Argyris (1957) proposed job enlargement, the increase of the number of tasks performed by workers, as well as job specialization, as one way to increase the gratification of the self-actualization. The recognition of the necessity to increase the degree of variety in the individual's work with some specialization proceeds to the consideration of job enrichment which corresponds to individuals' demands at higher levels (Herzberg 1966). These discussions stress that the variations in human activities have a vital importance for organizational activation and evolution, which will be promoted by decreasing the degree of incongruence between the organization and the individual persons. In firm theory, an evolutionary approach stresses the new Schumpeterian innovation process which requires variations in the innovation process for evolution of firms (Nelson and Winter 1982).

The innovation process, however, requires the variations of the way of thinking and includes some interruption of habitual conditions. This disruption will generate a counteraction by the law of inertia, which resists the generation of variations, washes it away from the mainstream of thinking, and as a result retards the evolution process. The majority rule may operate to resist the innovative process because a variation always appears as a minority in the beginning. Thus assurance for variants to appear is regarded as one of the reasonability of an institution to well-operate, to a proper extent.

(iii) Propriety of goals.

Finally, the propriety of goals in associations can also be checked on the behavioral base. The Law of Nature has been the theme of discourses since Plato and also appears in religious literature including the original Buddhist teachings. The Law of Nature in its simplest terms is reduced to concern for the individual and collective preservation of human beings. The Platonic rule, *the community of pain and pleasure* (*the Republic* Bk. V), or *the happiness of the city as a whole* (Bk. IV), has been often regarded as an unrealistic utopia, or the Heaven of Ideas, and the Golden Rule, mentioned before, has also seemed to have similar characteristics. Plato, however, discussed that the genesis of justice is in setting down a compact among people (Bk. II). Buddhist teachings (*The Suttanipāta*) also suggests that the grounds of the compassion, *don't kill*, is the recognition of the identity of the self, I and the other. Other literature (*The Saṃyutta-Nikāya: Sagātha-vagga*) suggests that *every person, I or the other, loves the self most, and therefore the person who loves the self must not harm the others*. The assertions in the second half of the Decalogue (Ten Commandments), in particular the prohibition of murder, theft, and false accusation, have a similar behavioral source for survival of the individuals in a collective body in harmony under the severe natural conditions. Thus, the most primal rules in the Law of Nature have common behavioral properties to other moral assertions along with more extended rules which appear in many of the Classics. Hobbes (1651) and Locke (1690) also treated the safety and security of persons in multitudes as the purpose for which the civil society was originally instituted. This original recognition, the preservation of the self and others in harmony or in peace, is the grounds of the propriety of goals in an association, and in more advanced forms, gratification and evolution of the human mind at higher levels, such as graceful and agreeable mind, are sought as the purpose of associations. An institution which is composed of various associations is expected thus to operate with the corresponding goals.

Preserving the reasonability in institutions induces the institutional evolution, which promotes in repercussions the differentiation of the cultural needs. In the next part, the effects of the cultural differentiation are discussed.

**3. Differentiation of culture.**

The differentiation of the cultural needs comes from the cumulative properties of the individual phase (13.8) and societal phase (13.12) in our primitive model. In this sense, culture is a historical product of human behavior. Different cultural conditions provide constraints for decision making and form its artificial environment. Without regard to these cultural differences, no decision making will succeed in its social implementation.

The cultural differences are considered in the following aspects.

(1) Differentiation of temperament.

Differentiation of temperament in the human population is mainly formed by the cumulative properties of the individual phase, which partially depends on living environments under various natural, geographical and meteorological conditions. The characteristics of the cognitive power of human beings such as quick-wittedness, sharpness, and sensitiveness, the behavioral patterns such as conservativeness, persistency, and curiosity, the personality such as mildness, meanness, and cleverness, and so on, prescribe the special dispositions of the human population, which are also different depending on societal conditions such as nations, regions, occupations, social status, and so on.

The differentiation of temperament forms the basis of the cultural differences. Some aspects in relation to MCDM are considered.

(i) Degree of ambiguousness.

The degree of ambiguousness or nonlogical factors in linguistic representations originates from the temperament of the human population and forms cultural differences. Linguistic characteristics, such as the utilization of the hieroglyphics or the phonetic alphabet, will have some effects on the logical structure in a language and thus give rise to differences in perceptions and thought. They are revealed in different degrees of dependence on a logical representation, or the logical clarity, in linguistic expressions, which come from different habits for human communication and recognition. These characteristics for ambiguousness that is inherent in human behavior will make large differences in particular for the fuzzy evaluation as discussed in Chapters 4 and 7.

(ii) Consideration for the future.

Considerations on the future also vary greatly under different cultural conditions. Some people have a long-range view for personal behavior, covering even the world after their death, but some other people seem to exclusively be interested in their daily lives at the present time. The differences in human attitudes for the future are represented in the difference of the discount rates for the future (Fisher 1930). The rate of time preference may gradually decrease, depending on the increase of income, if other situations remain unvaried. Knowledge extension and invention as well as geographical conditions also influence on the discount rate via the variation of the future-regarding attitude.

(iii) Intention for collectivity.

The intention for collectivity is also different, depending on the temperament of the human population. The individualistic way of thinking and behavior has long been a characteristic of Western European countries and the United States, although this temperament is now spreading to other countries. The intention for uniformity in personal behavior is a result of the mind of collectivity and thus varies in the human populations. The characteristics of ethnological compositions of the human population and the degrees of industrial development in regions have contributed to the differences in the attitude toward collectivity and uniformity. Agriculture, for example, has promoted the collective pattern of personal behavior more than does stockfarming, because efficiency of the working process in agriculture has required the collective labor in cooperation, while the labor of a shepherd boy has been isolated from other people in his working environment in the stock farming. The individualistic mind greatly develops in the high technology society because concentration on intellectual work usually requires an isolated condition for its successful achievement.

(2) Succession of institutions.

Although the differentiation of culture produces diversification of institutions where the human population lives and makes decisions, this variety succeeds in the behavioral processes of the constituents with some evolution. While the evolution process makes interruption and disconnection in the succession of culture, the law of inertia will operate in the behavioral process of the institution more than in that of individuals and resist the evolution processes to preserve cultural uniformity and continuity in the institution. An institution is a historical product and an alteration of the institution is not easy because its establishment is based on the cumulative, habitual behavior of the human population. Innovation in decision making has some effects by parametric changes on institutional behavior as shown in the primitive model (13.12). However, due to the property of the institution for preserving the majority of lives, the magnitude of the innovation parameter $\beta$ will not generally be very large. Even the revolution, an abrupt and radical alteration of an institution, has cultural characteristics resulting from the cumulative, habitual effects in the cultural differentiation, and thus the forces of the aftermath will easily turn the alteration processes back to the previous course with some modifications. This is the case of the dynamic process in evolutions of institutions.

(3) Conflicts of values.

Although the differentiation of culture produces a conservative tendency in the succession of institutions, conflicts in the value sense will be embedded in it. This embedment of conflicts is a necessary condition for the evolution of institutions. First, the conflicts in the value sense originate in variations in human behavior and result in the differentiation of culture. Each ramification or division of culture yields its own sense of values, and bears its variations and mutations which form the origin of evolution. In a cumulative process, these activities produce a great diversification of values and conflicts among them in more advanced stages, even though these new values will be resisted by the law of inertia and thus will not proceed very far. Second, the conflict-finding and the conflict-solving processes intend to compromise and reconcile the diversified sense of values. The successful operation of conflict management processes will sublate the conflict in a higher level and also enhance the cultural domain of human behavior at a higher level. Conflict resolution among multiple objectives is the ultimate goal of MCDM and will enhance human behavior in a new dimension.

## 13.5 Concluding Remarks

Now we shall make some concluding remarks.

1. In MCDM, the final results of the decision making are presented in the form of a proposition presented by one person in any form, chained or not, even though it is constructed through brain-storming processes by multiple participants. In this aspect, some people will be suspicious about human reason, and in particular, doubtful of the legitimacy of DM in MCDM. Thus contemplation about the role of DM and its legitimacy should be one of the major subjects of MCDM.

2. An inquiry of human nature provides the behavioral basis of DM for elucidating upon the above suspicion. An assembly or an association entrusts DM with handling final decisions via the transference of individual rights under the proper procedures through the covenants, explicitly or implicitly. It is shown that this agglomeration of the personal rights of IDM into DM has been founded on the behavioral basis.

3. An institution, which is composed of associations formed for various kinds of decision making, is based on behavioral characteristics of human nature and evolves itself independently. In result, it produces great effects on the human behavior of the constituents. Thus an institution provides an environment in which decisions are made. Cultural differentiations have large effects on the institution and thus on the social decision making.

4. The major factors that should be taken into account in the decision making are the hierarchical characteristics of human needs from lower to higher levels and their evolutionary properties. Having regards for variations are a necessary condition for institutional as well as human evolution and their robustness. Cultural differentiation originates in human variation, and thus the propensity for the fluctuation (malleability or the "soft" structure) in human nature

stimulates the cultural evolution. The same propensity in associations and institutions provides a necessary condition for assuring the generation of new variants and thus promotes their evolution to new stages.

5. The evolutionary processes via cultural differentiations produce value conflicts. The function of mediation by DM will be highly regarded in this aspect. The proposition that *the mediation function of DM originates in the agglomerative property of personal rights* is not contrary to human freedom or the Natural Right, because the formation of the agglomerative right in DM is a reflection of personal wisdom for the self-preservation of individuals, which is a result of the behavioral evolution of human beings, and thus the proposition should be decisively distinguished from the cleverness, which exclusively concern the particular interest of an individual, even though his decision has some social benefit. Plato (Bk. VIII) suggested that tyranny can arise out of a regime of democracy and the greatest slavery can come from the extreme of freedom. The insight of Plato seems to still be proper if the fellow-feeling is purged from the democratic society. First, this situation can be a result of manipulation of public opinions, and does not depend on the education level of the society. The distance between the speciality in an advanced knowledge and the uniformity in the average level of knowledge seems to remain almost the same, or rather to be enlarged over a long period (Figure 13.4). At least, no counterexample can be presented because, in the differentiation of culture, the specialization of the advanced knowledge is relatively broadened and deepened even in the progress of the average level of education. Second, fascination in human nature, which is regarded as unvaried, can easily lead to the manipulation of opinions, and may result in modern despotism. Nazism in the twentieth century, for example, appeared with an enthusiastic atmosphere in exercise of the majority rule which had been highly regarded in the Weimar Republic. Witch-hunts in the Middle Ages are another example. Thus the mediation of DM should be executed with deliberate consideration for the remainder of the human population along with the special regards on the individual thought that is not absorbed in the majority rule.

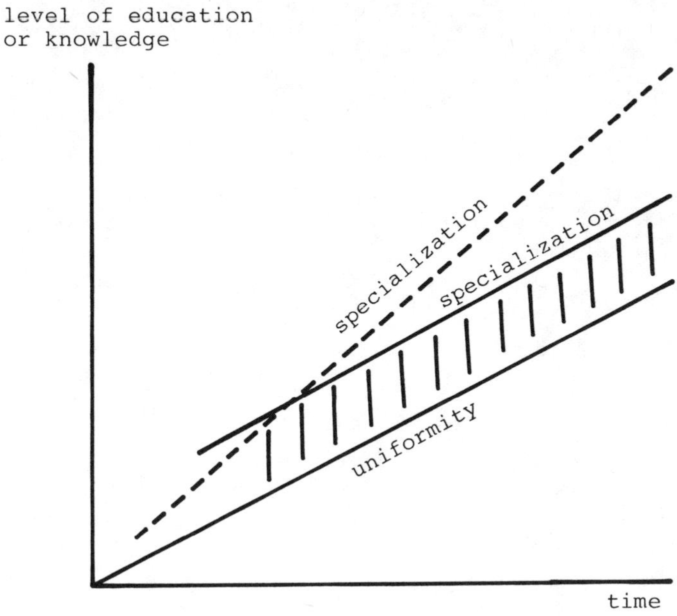


**Figure 13.4 Trend of human knowledge.**

6. It should be noted here that, although teleological considerations are the basis of the legitimacy of DM, preservation of individuals and their gratification, the promotion of more agreeable lives of individuals, are the behavioral source of the human teleology. MCDM which concerns the teleological considerations originates in this behavioral source, and the effectiveness of MCDM depends on their proper functions in the varied decision problems.

7. It should be stressed here that MCDM only concerns the decision support for selecting the preferred policy program from among decision alternatives. Thus the execution of MCDM should not be confused with the execution of actual decision making in administration. MCDM should hold the "political neutrality" in this sense. The assessment should be only "scientifically" reasonable in any sense, and thus should not "fluctuate" depending on the changes of "political atmosphere."

# REFERENCES


Allais, M., and Hagen, O. (1979). *Expected Utility Hypothesis and Allais Paradox*, D. Reidel Publishing Company, Dordrecht, Netherland.

Argyris, C. (1957). *Personality and Organization*, Harper & Row, New York.

Armacost, R. L., and Fiacco, A. V. (1975). Second-order parametric sensitivity analysis in NLP and estimates by penalty function methods Serial T-324, Institute for Management Science and Engineering, George Washington University, Washington, D. C.

Armacost, R. L., and Fiacco, A. V. (1976). NLP sensitivity analysis for RHS perturbations: a brief survey and second-order extensions, Serial T-334, Institute for Management Science and Engineering, George Washington University, Washington, D. C.

Armstrong, W. E. (1939). The determinateness of the utility function, *Economic Journal* 49, 453-467.

Armstrong, W. E. (1948). Uncertainty and the utility function, *Economic Journal* 58, 1-10.

Arrow, K. J. (1950a). An extension of the basic theorems of classical welfare economics, in *Proceedings of the Second Berkeley Symposium on Mathematical Statistics and Probability* (J. Neyman, ed.), 507-532.

Arrow, K. J. (1950b). A difficulty in the concept of social welfare, *Journal of Political Economy* 58, 328-346.

Arrow, K. J. (1951, 2nd ed. 1963). *Social Choice and Individual Values*, Wiley, New York.

Arrow, K. J. (1971). Theory of risk aversion, in *Essays in the Theory of Risk Bearing*, Chap.3, North-Holland, Amsterdam.

Arrow, K. J., and Debreu, G. (1954). Existence of an equilibrium for a competitive economy, *Econometrica* 22, 265-290.

Arrow, K. J., and Hurwicz, L. (1960). Decentralization and computation in resource allocation, in *Essays in Economics and Econometrics* (R. W. Pfouts, ed.), 34-104.

Ashby, W. R. (1952, 2nd ed. 1960). *Design for a Brain,* Chapman & Hall, London.

Ashby, W. R. (1956). *An Introduction to Cybernetics,* Chapman & Hall, London.

Axelrod, R. (1980a). Effective choice in the Prisoners Dilemma, *Journal of Conflict Resolution* 24, 3-25.

Axelrod, R. (1980b). More effective choice in the Prisoner's Dilemma, *Journal of Conflict Resolution* 24, 379-403.

Axelrod, R. (1981). The emergence of cooperation among egoists, *American Political Science Review* 75, 306-318.

Axelrod, R. (1984). *The Evolution of Cooperation,* Basic Books, New York.

Axelrod, R., and Haimilton, W. D. (1981). The evolution of cooperation, *Science* 211, 1390-1396.

Balinski, M. L., and Baumol, W. J. (1968). The dual in nonlinear programming and its economic interpretation, *Review of Economic Studies* 35, 237-256.

Baptistella, L. F. B., and Ollero, A. (1980). Fuzzy methodologies for interactive multicriteria optimization, *IEEE Transactions on Systems, Man and Cybernetics, SMC.* 10, 355-365.

Barnard, C. I. (1938). *The Functions of the Executive,* Harvard University Press, Massachusetts.

Barrager, S. M. (1975). Preferences for dynamic lotteries: assessment and sensitivity, Ph. D. dissertation, Department of Engineering-Economic Systems, Stanford University, California.

Bator, F. M. (1958). The anatomy of market failure, *Quarterly Journal of Economics* 72, 351-379.

Baumol, W. J., and Fabian, T. (1964). Decomposition, pricing for decentralization and external economies, *Management Science* 11, 1-32.

Bawa, V. S. (1975). Optimal rules for ordering uncertain prospects, *Journal of Financial Economics* 2, 95-121.

Bawa, V. S. (1982). Stochastic dominance: a research bibliography, *Management Science* 28(6), 698-712.

Beck, M. B. (1978a). Modelling of dissolved oxygen in a non-tidal stream, *Mathematical Models in Water Pollution Control* (A. James, ed.), Wiley, New York.

Beck, M. B. (1978b). A comparative case study of dynamic models for DO-BOD-algae interaction on a freshwater river, RR-78-19, IIASA, Laxenburg, Austria.

Beck, B., and Young, P. C. (1975). A Dynamic model for DO-BOD relationship in a non-tidal stream, *Water Research* 9, 769-776.

Beck, B., and Young, P. C. (1976). Systematic identification of DO-BOD model structure, *Journal of Environmental Engineering Division* 102, ASCE, 907-927.

Bell, D. E. (1982). Regret in decision making under uncertainty, *Operations Research* 30(5), 961-981.

Bell, D. E. (1983). Risk premiums for decision regret, *Management Science* 29(10), 1156-1166.

Bell, D. E., and Raiffa, H. (1982). Marginal value and intrinsic risk aversion, in *Risk: a seminar series* (H. Kunreuther ed.), IIASA Collective proceedings series CP-82-S2, 325-349.

Bellman, R. E., and Zadeh, L. A. (1970). Decision making in a fuzzy environment, *Management Science* 17(4), 141-164.

Bernoulli, D. (1738). Exposition of a new theory on the measurement of risk, *Econometrica* 22, 1954.

Blin, J. M. (1974). Fuzzy relations in group decision theory, *Journal of Cybernetics* 4(2), 17-22.

Blin, J. M., and Whinston, A. B. (1974). Fuzzy sets and social choice, *Journal of Cybernetics* 3(4), 28-36.

Bodily, S. E. (1981). Stability, equality, balance, and multivariate risk, in *Organizations: Multiple Agents with Multiple Criteria* (J. N. Morse ed.), Springer, Verlag, Berlin.

Bowman Jr., V. J. (1976). On the relationship of the Tchebycheff norm and the efficient frontier of multiple-criteria objectives, in *Multiple Criteria Decision Making* (H. Thiriez and S. Zionts, eds.), 76-86.

Chankong, V. (1977). Multiobjective decision-making analysis: the Interactive Surrogate Worth Trade-off method, Ph. D. dissertation, Case Western Reserve University, Cleveland, Ohio.

Chankong, V., and Haimes, Y. Y. (1978). The interactive surrogate worth trade-off (ISWT) method for multiobjective decision-making, in *Multiple Criteria Problem Solving* (S. Zionts, ed.), Springer-Verlag, Berlin.

Chankong, V., and Haimes, Y. Y. (1982). On characterization of noninferior solutions of a vector optimization problem, *Automatica* 18, 697-707.

Chankong, V., and Haimes, Y. Y. (1983a). *Multiobjective Decision Making: Theory and Methodology,* North-Holland, Amsterdam.

Chankong, V., and Haimes, Y. Y. (1983b). Optimization-based methods for multiobjective decision-making: An overview, *Large Scale Systems* 5(1), 1-33.

Charnes, A., and Cooper, W. W. (1961). *Management Models and Industrial Applications of Linear Programming,* Wiley, New York.

Charnes, A., and Cooper, W. W. (1977). Goal programming and multiple objective optimizations, *European Journal of Operational Research* 1(1), 39-54.

Chipman, J. S. (1960). The foundations of utility, *Econometrica* 28, 193-224.

Choo, E. U., and Atkins, D. R. (1983). Proper efficiency in nonconvex multicriteria programming, *Mathematics of Operations Research* 8(3), 467-470.

Cohon, J. L., and Marks, D. H. (1973). Multiobjective screening models and water resource investment, *Water Resources Research* 9, 826-836.

Coombs, C. H., Dawes, R. H., and Tversky, A. (1970). *Mathematical Psychology,* Prentice-Hall, New Jersey.

Dantzig, G. B. (1951). A proof of the equivalence of the programming problem and the game problem, in ed. by T.C. Koopmans, *Activity Analysis of Production and Allocation,* Wiley, New York.

Dantzig, G. B. (1956). Constructive proof of the min-max theorem, *Pacific Journal of Mathematics* 6(1), 25-33.

Dantzig, G. B. (1963). *Linear Programming and Extensions,* Princeton University Press, New Jersey.

Dantzig, G. B. (1982). Reminiscences about the origins of linear programming, *Operations Research Letters* 1-2, 43-48.

Dantzig, G. B., and Wolfe, P. (1960). Decomposition principle for linear programs, *Operations Research* 8, 101-110.

Dantzig, G. B., and Wolfe, P. (1961). The decomposition algorithm for linear programs, *Econometrica* 29, 767-778.

Davidson, D., and Suppes, P. (1956). A Finitistic axiomatization of subjective probability and utility, *Econometrica* 24, 264-275.

Davidson, D., and Marschak, J. (1959). Experimental test of a stochastic decision theory, in *Measurement: Definitions and Theories* (C. H. Churchman and D. Ratoosh, eds.), Wiley, New York, 233-269.

Debreu, G. (1954). Valuation equilibrium and Pareto optimum, in *Proceedings of the National Academy of Science* 40, 588-92.

Debreu, G. (1958). Stochastic choice and cardinal utility, *Econometrica* 26, 440-444.

Debreu, G. (1959a). Cardinal utility for even-chance mixtures of pairs of sure prospects, *Review of Economic Studies* 26, 174-177.

Debreu, G. (1959b). *Theory of Value,* Wiley, New York.

Debreu, G. (1960). Topological methods in cardinal utility theory, in *Mathematical Methods in the Social Science 1959* (K.J. Arrow, S. Karlin and P. Suppes, eds.), Stanford University Press, California.

Diamond, P. A. (1967). Cardinal welfare, individualistic ethics, and interpersonal comparison of utility: Comment, *Journal of Political Economiy* 75, 765-766.

Dorfman, R. (1951). Application of the simplex method to a game theory problem, in ed. by T. C. Koopmans, ibid.

Dorfman, R. (1972). Conceptual model of a regional water quality authority, in *Models for Managing Regional Water Quality* (R. Dorfman, H. D. Jacoby, and H. A. Thomas, eds.), Harvard University Press, Massachusetts.

Dorfman, R., and Jacoby, H. D. (1972). An Illustrative model of river basin, in *Models for Managing Regional Water Quality* (R. Dorfman, H. D. Jacoby, and H. A. Thomas, eds.), Harvard University Press, Massachusetts.

Dorfman, R., Samuelson, P. A., and Solow, R. M. (1958). *Linear Programming and Economic Analysis*, McGraw-Hill, New York.

Dubois, D., and Prade, H. (1978). Operations on fuzzy numbers, *International Journal of Systems Science* 9, 613-626.

Dubois, D., and Prade, H. (1980). *Fuzzy Sets and Systems: Theory and Applications*, Academic Press, New York.

Dyer, J. S. (1972). Interactive goal programming, *Management Science* 19, 62-70.

Dyer, J. S. (1973). An empirical investigation of a man-machine interactive approach to the solution of the multiple criteria problem, in *Multiple Criteria Decision Making* (J. L. Cochrane and M. Zeleny, eds.), University of South Carolina Press, South Carolina.

Dyer, J. S., and Sarin, R. K. (1978). Cardinal preference aggregation rule for the case of certainty, in *Multiple Criteria Problem Solving* (S. Zionts ed.), Springer-Verlag, Berlin, 68-86.

Dyer, J. S., and Sarin, R. K. (1979a). Measurable multiattribute value functions, *Operations Research* 27(4), 810-822.

Dyer, J. S., and Sarin, R. K. (1979b). Group preference aggregation rules based on strength of preference, *Management Science* 25(9), 822-832.

Dyer, J. S., and Sarin, R. K. (1982). Relative risk aversion, *Management Science* 28(8), 875-886.

Eckstein, O. (1958). *Water-Resource Development*, Harvard University Press, Massachusetts.

Edgeworth, F. Y. (1881). *Mathematical Psychics*, Kelley, New York, 1953.

Ellsberg, D. (1954). Classic and current notions of measurable utility, *Economic Journal* 64, 528-556.

Ellsberg, D. (1961). Risk, ambiguity and the Savage axioms, *Quarterly Journal of Economics* 75, 643-669.

Ellsberg, D. (1963). Risk, ambiguity and the Savage axiom: a reply, *Quarterly Journal of Economics* 77, 336-341.

Everett, H. (1963). Generalized Lagrange multiplier method for solving problems of optimum allocation of resources, *Operations Research* 11, 399-417.

Fiacco, A. V. (1976). Sensitivity analysis for nonlinear programming using penalty method, *Mathematical Programming* 10, 287-311.

Fiacco, A. V. (1983). *Introduction to Sensitivity and Stability Analysis in Nonlinear Programming*, Academic Press, New York.

Fiacco, A. V. and McCormick, G. P. (1968). *Nonlinear Programming: Sequential Unconstrained Minimization Techniques*, Wiley, New York.

Fishburn, P. C. (1964). *Decision and Value Theory*, Wiley, New York.

Fishburn, P. C. (1967a). Methods of estimating additive utilities, *Management Science* 13, 435-453.

Fishburn, P. C. (1967b). Preference-based definitions of subjective probability, *The Annals of Mathematical Statistics* 38, 1605-1617.

Fishburn, P. C. (1970). *Utility Theory for Decision Making*, Wiley, New York.

Fishburn, P. C. (1982). Nontransitive measurable utility, *Journal of Mathematical Psychology* 26, 31-67.

Fishburn, P. C., and Kochenberger, G. A. (1979). Two-piece von Neumann-Morgenstern utility functions, *Theory and Decision* 9, 161-171.

Fishburn, P. C., and Vickson, R. G. (1978). Theoretical foundations of stochastic dominance, in *Stochastic Dominance* (G. A. Whitmore and M. C. Findlay, eds.), Lexington, 39-113.

Fisher, I. (1930). *The Theory of Interest*, Kelley, New York, 1970.

Fleming, M. (1952). A cardinal concept of welfare, *Quarterly Journal of Economics*, 66, 366-384.

Friedman, M. (1953). *Essays in Positive Economics*, University of Chicago Press, Chicago.

Friedman, M. and Savage, L. J. (1948). The utility analysis of choices involving risk, *Journal of Political Economy* 56, 279-304.

Gale, D. (1960) *The Theory of Linear Economic Models*, McGraw-Hill, New York.

Geoffrion, A. M. (1968). Proper efficiency and the theory of vector maximization, *Journal of Mathematical Analysis and Applications* 22, 618-630.

Geoffrion, A. M. (1971). Duality in nonlinear programming: a simplified applications-oriented development, *SIAM Review* 13, 1-37.

Geoffrion, A. M., Dyer, J. S., and Feinberg, A. (1972). An interactive approach for multi-criterion optimization, with an application to the operation of an academic department, *Management Science* 19, 357-369.

Gossen, H. H. (1854, 3rd ed. 1927). *Entwicklung der Gesetze des Menschlichen Verkehrs und der Daraus Fliessenden Regeln fur Menschliches Handeln*, Prager, Berlin.

Grauer, M. (1983a). A dynamic interactive decision analysis and support system (DIDASS), user's guide, WP-83-60, IIASA, June.

Grauer, M. (1983b). Reference point optimization - the nonlinear case, in *Essays and Surveys on Multiple Criteria Decision Making* (P. Hansen ed.), Springer-Verlag, New York, 126-135.

Grauer, M., and Kaden, S. eds. (1984). A nonlinear dynamic interactive decision analysis and support system (DIDASS/N), WP-84-23, International Institute for Applied Systems Analysis A-2361 Laxenburg, Austria.

Griffith, R. E., and Stewart, R. A. (1961). A nonlinear programming technique for the optimization of continuous processing systems, *Management Science* 7, 379-392.

Hadar, J., and Russell, W. R. (1969). Rules for ordering uncertain prospects, *American Economic Review* 59, 25-34.

Hadar, J., and Russell, W. R. (1971). Stochastic dominance and diversification, *Journal of Economic Theory* 3, 288-305.

Haimes, Y. Y. (1973). Decomposition and multilevel approach in the modeling and management of water resources systems, in *Decomposition of Large-Scale Problems* (D. M. Himmelblau, ed.), North-Holland, Amsterdam.

Haimes, Y. Y. (1977) *Hierarchical Analysis of Water Resources Systems, Modeling and Optimization of Large Scale Systems,* McGraw-Hill, New York.

Haimes, Y. Y., and Chankong, V. (1979). Kuhn-Tucker multipliers as trade-offs in multiobjective decision-making analysis, *Automatica* 15, 50-72.

Haimes, Y. Y., Foley, J., and Yu, W. (1972). Computational results for water pollution taxation using multilevel approach, *Water Resources Bulletin* 8, 761-772.

Haimes, Y. Y., and Hall, W. A. (1974). Multiobjectives in water resource systems analysis: the surrogate worth trade-off method, *Water Resources Research* 10, 615-624.

Haimes, Y. Y., Hall, W. A., and Friedman, H. T. (1975). *Multiobjective Optimization in Water Resources Systems,* Elsevier, Amsterdam.

Haimes, Y. Y., Kaplan, M. A., and Husar, M. A. (1972). A multilevel approach to determining optimal taxation for the abatement of water pollution, *Water Resources Research* 8, 851-860.

Haimes, Y. Y., Lasdon, L. S., and Wismer, D. A. (1971). On a bicriterion formulation of the problems of integrated systems identification and systems optimization, *IEEE Transactions on Systems Man, and Cybernetics* SMC-1, 296-297.

Haimes, Y. Y., and Macko, D. (1973). Hierarchical structures in water resources systems management, *IEEE Transactions on Systems, Man and Cybernetics* SMC-3, 396-402.

Hall, W. A., and Haimes, Y. Y. (1976). The surrogate worth trade-off method with multiple decision makers, in *Multiple Criteria Decision Making, Kyoto* 1975 (M. Zeleny, ed.), Springer-Verlag, Berlin.

Handa, J. (1977). Risk, probabilities, and a new theory of cardinal utility, *Journal of Political Economy* 85, 97-122.

Hannan, E. L. (1981). Linear programming with multiple fuzzy goals, *Fuzzy Set and Systems* 6, 235-248.

Hanoch, G., and Levy, H. (1969). The efficiency analysis of choices involving risk, *Review of Economic Studies* 36, 335-346.

Harsanyi, J. C. (1955). Cardinal welfare, individualistic ethics, and interpersonal comparisons of utility, *Journal of Political Economy* 63, 309-321.

Harsanyi, J. C. (1977). *Rational Behavior and Bargaining Equilibrium in Games and Social Situations*, Cambridge University Press, London.

Herstein, I. N., and Milnor, J. (1953). An axiomatic approach to measurable utility, *Econometrica* 23, 291-297.

Herzberg, F. (1966). *Work and the Nature of Man*, Staples Press, London.

Hicks, J. R. (1939, 2nd ed. 1946). *Value and Capital*, Oxford University Press, London.

Hicks, J. R. (1962). Liquidity, *Economic Journal* 72, 787-802.

Hinloopen, E., Nijkamp, P., and Rietveld, P. (1983). Qualitative descrete multiple criteria choice models in regional planning, *Regional Science and Urban Economics*, 13(1), 78-102.

Hobbes, T. (1651). *Leviathan*, Dutton, New York, 1950.

Hottel, H. C., and Howard, J. B.(1971). *New Energy Technology*, MIT Press, Massachusetts.

Huang, C. C., Vertinsky, I., and Ziemba, W. T. (1978). On multiperiod stochastic dominance, *Journal of Financial and Quantitative Analysis* 13, 1-13.

Huang, C. C., Kira, D., and Vertinsky, I. (1978). Stochastic dominance rules for multiattribute utility functions, *Review of Economic Studies* 45, 611-615.

Hume, D. (1777). *Of the Origin of Government*, in *David Hume's Political Essays*, ed. by C. W. Hendel, Liberal Art Press, New York, 1953.

Ignizio, J. P. (1976). *Goal Programming and Extensions, Heath*: (Lexington Series), Lexington, Massachusetts.

Ignizio, J. P. (1982). *Linear Programming in Single and Multiple Objective Systems*, Prentice-Hall, Englewood Cliffs, New Jersey.

Ignizio, J. P. (1983). Generalized goal programming: An Overview, *Computer and Operations Research* 10(4), 277-289.

Ijiri, Y. (1965). *Management Goals and Accounting for Control*, North-Holland, Amsterdam.

Intriligator, M. D. (1971). *Mathematical Optimization and Economic Theory*, Prentice-Hall, New Jersey.

Isard, W. (1960). *Methods of Regional Analysis: An Introduction to Regional Science*, The MIT Press, Cambridge.

Kahneman, D., and Tversky, A. (1979). Prospect theory: an analysis of decision under risk, *Econometrica* 47, 263-291.

Karlin, S. (1959). *Mathematical Methods and Theory in Games, Programming and Economics*, I, and II, Addison-Sesley, Massachusetts.

Karmarkar, U. S. (1978). Subjectively weighted utility: a descriptive extension of the expected utility model, *Organizational Behavior and Human Performance* 21, 61-72.

Karmarkar, U. S. (1979). Subjectively weighted utility and the Allais paradox, *Organizational Behavior and Human Performances* 24, 67-72.

Keelin, T. W. (1976). A protocol and procedure for assessing multi-attribute preference function, Ph. D. dissertation, Department of Engineering-Economic Systems, Stanford University, California.

Keeney, R. L. (1974). Multiplicative utility functions, *Operations Research* 22, 22-34.

Keeney, R. L. (1976) A group preference axiomatization with cardinal utility, *Management Science* 23(2), 140-145.

Keeney, R. L. (1980a). Equity and public risk, *Operations Research*, 28(3), 527-534.

Keeney, R. L. (1980b). Utility functions for equity and public risk, *Management Science* 26(4), 345-353.

Keeney, R. L., and Kirkwood, C. (1975). Group decision making using cardinal social welfare functions, *Management Science* 22(4), 430-437.

Keeney, R. L., and Raiffa, H. (1976). *Decisions with Multiple Objectives, Preferences and Value Tradeoffs*, Wiley, New York.

Kirkwood, C. W. (1978). Social decision analysis using multiattribute utility theory, in *Multiple Criteria Problem Solving* (S. Zionts, ed.), Springer-verlag, Berlin, 335-344.

Kirkwood, C. W. (1979). Pareto optimality and equity in social decision analysis, *IEEE Transactions on Systems, Man and Cybernetics*, SMC-9(2), 89-91.

Koestler, A. (1967). *The Ghost in the Machine*, Hutchinson, London.

Kohlberg, E. (1971). On the nucleolus of a characteristic function game, *SIAM Journal of Applied Mathematics* 20(1), 62-66.

Koopmans, T. C. (1951). Analysis of production as an efficient combination of activities, in *Activity Analysis of Production and Allocation* (T. C. Koopmans, ed.), Wiley, New York.

Koopmans, T. C. (1957). Allocation of resources and the price system, in *Three Essays on the State of Economic Science*, McGraw-Hill, New York.

Kopelowitz, A. (1967). Computation of the kernels of simple games and the nucleolus of n-person games, R.M. 31, Dept. of Math., Hebrew University.

Kornbluth, J. S. M. (1973). A survey of goal programming, *OMEGA* 1, 193-205.

Krantz, D. H., Luce, R. D., Suppes, P., and Tversky, A. (1971). *Foundations of Measurement* 1, Academic Press, New York.

Kuhn, H. W., and Tucker, A. W. (1951). Nonlinear programming, *Proceedings of the Second Berkeley Symposium on Mathematical Statistics and Probability* (J. Neyman, ed.), University of California Press, California, 481-492.

Kunisawa, K. (1975). *Entropy Model*, Nikkagiren, Tokyo, (in Japanese).

Krutilla, J. V., and Eckstein, O. (1958). *Multiple Purpose River Development*, Johns Hopkins Press, Baltimore.

Lange, O. (1962). *Calosci i Rozwoj w Swietle Cybernetyki*, PWN, Warszawa. (The Wholes and the Development in the Light of Cybernetics).

Lange, O. (1965). *Wstep do Cybernetyki Ekonomiczej*, PWN, Warszawa. (Introduction to Economic Cybernetics).

Lasdon, L. S. (1968). Duality and decomposition in mathematical programming, *IEEE Transactions on Systems Science and Cybernetics* 4, 86-100.

Lasdon, L. S. (1970). *Optimization Theory for Large Systems*, Macmillan, London.

Lasdon, L. S., Fox, R. L., and Ratner, M. W. (1974). Nonlinear optimization using the generalized reduced gradient method, *Revue Francaise d' Automatique Informatique et Recherche Operationnelle* 3, 73-103.

Lasdon, L. S., Waren, A. D., Jain, A., and Ratner, M. (1976). Design and testing of a generalized reduced gradient code for nonlinear programming, Technical Report SOL 76-3, Systems Optimization Laboratory, Department of Operations Research, Stanford University, California.

Lasdon, L. S., Waren, A. D., and Ratner, M. W. (1980). *GRG2 user's guide*, Technical Memorandum, University of Texas.

Leberling, H. (1981). On finding compromise solutions in multicriteria problems using the fuzzy min-operator, *Fuzzy Set and Systems* 6(2), 105-118.

Lee, S. M. (1972). *Goal Programming for Decision Analysis*, Auerbach, Philadelphia.

Leontief, W. (1970). Environmental repercussions and the economic structure: an input-output approach, *Review of Economics and Statistics* 37, 262-271.

Levy, H. (1973). Stochastic dominance, efficiency criteria and efficient portfolios: the multi-period case, *American Economic Review* 63(5), 986-994.

Levy, H., and Paroush, J. (1974). Multi-period stochastic dominance, *Management Science* 21(4), 428-435.

Levy, H., and Sarnat, M. (1970). Alternative efficiency criteria: an empirical analysis, *Journal of Finance* 25(5), 1153-1158.

Lewandowski, A., and Grauer, M. (1982). The reference point optimization approach - methods of efficient implementation, Working paper, WP-82-26, International Institute for Applied Systems Analysis, Laxenburg, Austria.

Littlechild, S. C. (1974). A simple expression for the nucleolus in a special case, *International Journal of Game Theory* 3(1), 21-29.

Littlechild, S. C., and Vaidya, K. G. (1976). The propensity to disrupt and the disruption nucleolus of a characteristic function game, *International Journal of Game Theory* 5(2/3), 151-161.

Locke, J. (1690). *Two Tracts on Government*, ed. and tr. by Philip Abrams, The University Press, Cambridge, 1967.

Loomes, G., and Sugden, R. (1982). Regret theory: an alternative theory of rational choice under uncertainty, *Economic Journal* 92, 805-824.

Luce, R. D. (1956). Semiorders and a theory of utility discrimination, *Econometrica* 24, 178-191.

Luce, R. D., and Raiffa, H. (1957). *Games and Decisions,* Wiley, New York.

Luce, R. D., and Suppes, P. (1965). Preference, utility and subjective probability, in *Handbook of Mathematical Psychology* III (R. D. Luce, R. R. Bush and E. Galanter, eds.), Wiley, New York.

Luenberger, D. G. (1973). *Introduction to Linear and Nonlinear Programming,* Addison-Wesley, Massachusetts.

Lumsden, C. J., and Wilson, E. O. (1981). *Genes, Mind, and Culture,* Cambridge, Massachusetts.

Maass, A., Hufschmidt, M. M., Dorfman, R., Thomas, H. A., Marglin, S. A., and Fair, G. M. (1962). *Design of Water-Resource Systems,* Harvard University Press, Massachusetts.

March, J. G., and Simon, H. A. (1958). *Organizations*, Wiley, New York.

Marglin, S. A. (1962). Objectives of water-resource development: a general statement, in *Design of Water-Resource Systems* (A. Maass, M. M. Hufschmidt, R. Dorfman, H. A. Thomas, S. A. Marglin, and G. M. Fair, eds.), Harvard University Press, Massachusetts.

Marglin, S. A. (1963a). The social rate of discount and the optimal rate of investment, *Quarterly Journal of Economics* 77, 95-111.

Marglin, S. A. (1963b). The opportunity costs of public investment, *Quarterly Journal of Economics* 77, 274-289.

Margolis, H. (1982). *Selfishness, Altruism and Rationality,* Cambridge University Press, Cambridge.

Markowitz, H. M. (1959). *Portfolio Selection: Efficient Diversification of Investment*, Yale University Press, New Haven.

Marschak, J. (1950). Rational behavior, uncertain prospects, and measurable utility, *Econometrica* 18, 111-141.

Marschak, J. (1964). Scaling of utilities and probability, in *Game Theory and Related Approaches to Social Behavior* (M. Shubik, ed.), Wiley, New York.

Marschak, J., and Radner, R. (1972). *Economic Theory of Teams*, Yale University Press, New Haven.

Marx, K. (1867-1894). *Das Kapital*, Bd. I 1867, Bk.II 1885, Bd III 1894, Dietz, Berlin, 1962-64.

Maschler, M., Peleg, B., and Shapley, L. S. (1979). Geometric properties of the kernel, nucleolus, and related solution concepts, *Mathematics of Operations Research* 4(4), pp.303-338.

Maslow, A. H. (1954, 2nd ed. 1970). *Motivation and Personality*, Harper & Row, New York.

Maynard Smith, J. (1982). *Evolution and the Theory of Games*, Cambridge University Press, Cambridge, Massachusetts.

Mesarovic, M. D., Macko, D., and Takahara, Y. (1970). *Theory of Hierarchical, Multilevel, Systems*, Academic Press, New York.

Miller, W. L., and Byers, D. M. (1973). Development and display of multiple-objective project impacts, *Water Resources Research* 9, 11-20.

Mishan, E. J. (1967). A proposed normalisation procedure for public investment criteria, *Economic Journal* 77, 777-796.

Moreh, J. (1985). Conflict of interests, *Journal of Conflict Resolution* 29(1), 137-159.

Musselman, K., and Talavage, J. (1980). A trade-off cut approach to multiple objective optimization, *Operations Research* 28(6).

Nash, J. (1951). Non-Cooperative game, *Annals of Mathematics* 54(2), 286-295.

Nelson, R. R., and Winter, S. G. (1982). *An Evolutionary Theory of Economic Change*, Harvard University Press, Cambridge, Massachusetts.

Nijkamp, P. (1977). *Theory and Application of Environmental Economics*, North-Holland, Amsterdam.

Nijkamp, P. (1979). *Multidimensional Spatial Data and Decision Analysis*, Wiley, New York.

Nijkamp, P. (1980). *Environmental Policy Analysis: Operational Methods and Models*, Wiley, New York.

Nijkamp, P., and Spronk, J. eds. (1981). *Multiple Criteria Analysis: Operational Methods*, Gower, Hampshire.

Oppenheimer, K. R. (1978). A proxy approach to multiattribute decision making, *Management Science* 24, 675-689.

Orlovski, S. A. (1983a). Multiobjective programming problems with fuzzy parameters, IIASA Working Paper, International Institute for Applied Systems Analysis, Laxenburg, Austria.

Orlovski, S. A. (1983b). Problems of decision-making with fuzzy information, IIASA Working Paper WP-83-28, International Institute for Applied Systems Analysis, Laxenburg, Austria.

Owen, G. (1968, 2nd ed. 1982). *Game Theory*, Academic Press, New York.

Owen, G. (1974). A note on the nucleolus, *International Journal of Game Theory,* 3(2), 101-103.

Owen, G. (1975). On the core of linear production game, *Mathematical Programming,* 9, 358-370.

Pareto, V. (1906). *Manual di Economia Politica*, Trans. in French, *Le manual d'economie politique*, 1909, Trans. in English, by A. S. Schwier, *Manual of Political Economy*, Macmillan, 1971.

Parsons, T. (1951). *The Social System,* The Free Press, New York.

Payne, H. J., Polak, E., Collins, D. C., and Meisel, W. S. (1975). An algorithm for bicriteria optimization based on the sensitivity function, IEEE *Transactions on Automatic Control* AC-20, 546-548.

Phipps, C. G. (1952). Maxima and minima under restraint, *American Mathematics Monthly* 59, 230-235.

Pierre, D. A., and Lowe, M. J. (1975). *Mathematical Programming via Augmented Lagrangians*, Addison-Wesley, Massachusetts.

Platon. *Politica* (BC 375). *The Republic of Plato*, Trans. by A. Bloom, Basic Books, New York, 1968.

Pratt, J. W. (1964). Risk aversion in the small and in the large, *Econometrica* 32, 122-136.

Pratt, J. W., Raiffa, H., and Schlaifer, R. (1964). The foundations of decision under uncertainty: an elementary exposition, *Journal of American Statistical Association* 59, 353-375.

Quirk, J. P., and Saposnik, R. (1962). Admissibility and measurable utility functions, *Review of Economic Studies* 29, 140-146.

Quiggin, J. (1982). A theory of anticipated utility, *Journal of Economic Behavior and Organization* 3, 323-343.

Raiffa, H. (1968). *Decision Analysis*, Addison Wesley, Massachusetts.

Raiffa, H. (1982). *The Art and Science of Negotiation*, Harvard University Press, Massachusetts.

Raiffa, H. (1983). Mediation of Conflicts, *American Behavioral Scientist* 27(2), 195-210.

Ramsey, F. P. (1926). Truth and probability, in *The Foundations of Mathematics* (R. B. Braithwaite, ed.), Kegan Paul, Trench, Trubner & Co., 1931.

Ricardo, D. (1817, 3rd ed. 1821). *On the Principles of Political Economy and Taxation.*

Richard, S. F. (1975). Multivariate risk aversion, utility independence and separable utility functions, *Management Science* 22(1), 12-21.

Rietveld, P. (1980). *Multiple Objective Decision Methods and Regional Planning*, North-Holland, Amsterdam.

Robbins, L. (1932, 2nd ed. 1935). *An Essay on the nature and Significance of Economic Science*, Macmillan, London, 1969.

Robinson, S. M. (1974). Perturbed Kuhn-Tucker points and rates of convergence for a class of nonlinear-programming algorithms, *Mathematical Programming* 7, 1-16.

Rousseau, J. J. (1762). *Du Contract Social*, ed. by Ronald Grimsley, The Clarendon Press, Oxford, 1972.

Roy, B. (1977a). Partial preference analysis and decision-aid: the fuzzy outranking relation concept, in *Conflicting Objectives in Decisions* (D. E. Bell, R. L. Keeney, and H. Raiffa, eds.), Wiley, New York.

Roy, B. (1977b). A conceptual frame work for a prescriptive theory of "decision-aid", *TIMS Studies in the Management Science* 6, 179-210

Sakawa, M. (1979). Multiobjective analysis in water supply and management problems for a single river basin, *Water Supply and Management* 3, 55-64.

Sakawa, M. (1980). Interactive multiobjective decision making by the sequential proxy optimization technique: SPOT, WP-80-66, IIASA, Laxenburg, Austria.

Sakawa, M. (1981). An interactive computer program for multiobjective decision making by the sequential proxy optimization technique, *International Journal of Man-machine Studies* 14, 193-213.

Sakawa, M. (1982). Interactive multiobjective decision making by the sequential proxy optimization technique: SPOT, *European Journal of Operational Research* 9, 386-396.

Sakawa, M. (1983a). Interactive computer programs for fuzzy linear programming with multiple objectives, *International Journal of Man-Machine Studies* 18(5), 489-503.

Sakawa, M. (1983b). Interactive fuzzy decision making for multiobjective linear programming problems and its application, in *Proceedings of IFAC Symposium on Fuzzy Information, Knowledge Representation and Decision Analysis* (E. Sanchez, ed.), 19-21.

Sakawa, M. (1984a). Interactive fuzzy decision making for multiobjective nonlinear programming problems, in *Interactive Decision Analysis* (M. Grauer and A. P. Wierzbicki, eds), Springer Verlag, Berlin, 105-112.

Sakawa, M. (1984b). Interactive fuzzy goal programming for multiobjective nonlinear programming problems and its application to water quality management, *Control and Cybernetics* 13(3), 217-228)

Sakawa, M., Ito, K., Ainai, T., Takahashi, H., and Sawaragi, Y. (1980). A man-machine interactive approach to a nonlinear multiobjective optimal planning problem on water management of a river basin, *Proceedings of IFAC Symposium of Water and Related Land Resource Systems*, 1-10.

Sakawa, M., and Mori, N. (1983). Interactive multiobjective decision-making for nonconvex problems based on the weighted Tchebycheff norm, *Large Scale Systems* 5(1), 69-82.

Sakawa, M., and Mori, N. (1984). Interactive multiobjective decisionmaking for nonconvex problems based on the penalty scalarizing functions, *European Journal of Operational Research* 17(3), 320-330.

Sakawa, M., Sawaragi, Y., Narutaki, R., and Sawada, K. (1977). Multiobjective optimization in water resources problems of Kakogawa River basin, *Proceedings of IFAC Symposium on Environmental Systems Planning, Design, and Control*, 255-262.

Sakawa, M., Sawaragi, Y., and Sasakura, T. (1978). Multiobjective analysis in water resources problem for multiple river basins: a case study of the southern part of Hyogo prefecture, in *Proceedings of the International Conference on Cybernetics and Society*, 761-766

Sakawa, M., and Seo, F. (1980a). An interactive computer program for subjective systems and its application, WP-80-64, IIASA, Laxenburg, Austria.

Sakawa, M., and Seo, F. (1980b). Interactive multiobjective decision-making for large-scale systems and its application to environmental systems, *IEEE Transactions on Systems, Man and Cybernetics* SMC-10, 796-806.

Sakawa, M., and Seo, F. (1982a). Interactive multiobjective decision making in environmental systems using sequential proxy optimization techniques (SPOT), *Automatica* 18, 155-165.

Sakawa, M., and Seo, F. (1982b). Integrated methodology for computer-aided decision analysis, in *Progress in Cybernetics and Systems Research* (X. R. Trapple, F. de P. Hanika, and R. Tomlinson, eds.), Hemisphere Publishing Corporation, New York.

Sakawa, M., and Seo, F. (1983). Interactive multiobjective decision-making in environmental systems using the fuzzy sequential proxy optimization technique, *Large Scale Systems* 4(3), 233-243.

Sakawa, M., Tada, K., and Nishizaki, I. (1983). A new solution concept in a cooperative n-person game and its application, *Journal of Electronics and Communication Society* J.66-A(12) (in Japanese).

Sakawa, M., and Yano, H. (1984a). An interactive fuzzy satisficing method using penalty scalarizing problems, *Proceedings of International Computer Symposium*, Tamkang University, Taiwan, 1122-1129.

Sakawa, M., and Yano, H. (1984b). An interactive goal attainment method for multiobjective nonconvex problems, in *Cybernetics and Systems Research* 2 (R. Trapple, ed.), North-Holland, Amsterdam.

Sakawa, M., and Yano, H. (1985a). Interactive fuzzy decision-making for multiobjective nonlinear programming using reference membership intervals, International Journal of Man-Machine Studies, 23, 407-421.

Sakawa, M., and Yano, H. (1985). An interactive fuzzy satisficing method using augmented minimax problems and its application to environmental systems, *IEEE Transaction on Systems, Man and Cybernetics,* SMC-15, 720-729.

Sakawa, M., and Yano, H. (1986a). An interactive fuzzy decisionmaking method using constraint problems, *IEEE Transactions on Systems, Man and Cybernetics,* SMC-16, 179-182.

Sakawa, M., and Yano, H. (1986b). An interactive method for multiobjective nonlinear programming problems with fuzzy parameters, in *Cybernetics and Systems '86* (R. Trappl, ed.), D. Reidel Publishing Company, Dordrecht, 607-614.

Sakawa, M., and Yano, H. (1986c). An interactive fuzzy satisficing method for multiobjective nonlinear programming problems with fuzzy parameters, CP-86-15, IIASA, Laxenburg, Austria.

Sakawa, M., and Yumine, T. (1983). Interactive fuzzy decision-making for multiobjective linear fractional programming problems, *Large Scale Systems* 5(2), 105-114.

Sakawa, M., Yumine, T., and Yano, H. (1984). An interactive fuzzy satisficing method for multiobjective nonlinear programming problems, CP-84-18, IIASA, Laxenburg, Austria.

Samet, D., and Zemel, E. (1984). On the core and dual set of linear programming game, *Mathematics of Operations Research* 9(2), 309-316.

Samuelson, P. A. (1947). *Foundations of Economic Analysis*, Harvard University Press, Massachusetts.

Sannomiya, N., and Nishikawa, Y. (1978). A method of linear programming with relaxable constraints and its application to a rural regional planning, *Proceedings of 7th IFAC World Congress*, Helsinki, 1661-1668.

Sarin, R. K. (1982). Strength of preference and risky choice, *Operations Research* 30(5), 982-997.

Savage, L. J. (1954). *The Foundations of Statistics*, Wiley, New York.

Scarf, H. E. (1967). The core of an n person game, *Econometrica* 35(1), 50-69.

Scarf, H. E. (1973). *The Computation of Economic Equilibria,* Yale University Press, New Haven.

Schlaifer, R. (1969). *Analysis of Decision under Uncertainty,* McGraw-Hill, New York.

Schlaifer, R. (1971). *Computer Programs for Elementary Decision Analysis*, Division of Research, Graduate School of Business Administration, Harvard University, Massachusetts.

Schmeidler, D. (1969). The nucleolus of a characteristic function game, *SIAM Journal of Applied Mathematics* 17(6), PT.1163-1170.

Schubik, M. (1983). *Game Theory in the Social Sciences, Concepts and Solutions*, The MIT Press, Massachusetts.

Schubik, M. (1984). *A Game Theoretic Approach to Political Economy*, The MIT Press, Massachusetts.

Sen, A. (1976). Liberty, unanimity and rights, *Economica* 43, 217-245.

Seo, F. (1975). Economic evaluation and its policy implications for environmental control, *Proceedings of the International Congress on the Human Environment*, Kyoto, 813-824.

Seo, F. (1977). Environmental assessment with multiobjective optimization in the region, *Studies on Regional Science* 7, 95-111 (in Japanese).

Seo, F. (1978a). Evaluation and control of regional environmental systems in the Yodo river basin: socio-economic aspects, *Proceedings of IFAC Symposium on Environmental Systems Planning, Design and Control* (Y. Sawaragi and H. Akashi, eds.), Pergamon Press, Oxford, 601-608.

Seo, F. (1978b). Regional environmental assessment and industrial reallocation in the greater Osaka area, *Studies on Regional Science* 8, 137-158 (in Japanese).

Seo, F. (1980). An integrated approach for improving decision-making processes, *Behavioral Science* 25, 387-396.

Seo, F. (1981). Organizational aspects of multicriteria decision making, in *Organizations: Multiple Agents With Multiple Criteria* (J. N. Morse, ed.), Springer-Verlag, Berlin, 363-379.

Seo, F., and Sakawa, M. (1979a). An evaluation for environmental systems planning: an alternative utility approach, *Environment and Planning A* 11, 149-168.

Seo, F., and Sakawa, M. (1979b). A methodology for environmental systems management: dynamic application of the nested Lagrangian multiplier method, *IEEE Transactions on Systems, Man, and Cybernetics* SMC-9, 794-804.

Seo, F., and Sakawa, M. (1979c). Technology assessment and decision-aid utility analysis in fossil fuel-to-fuel conversion, *Proceedings of the IFAC Symposium on Criteria for Selecting Appropriate Technologies under Different Cultural, Technical and Social Conditions* (A. De Giorgio, and C. Roveda, eds.), Pergamon Press, Oxford, 205-213.

Seo, F., and Sakawa, M. (1980). Evaluations for industrial land-use program related to water quality management WP-80-49, IIASA, Laxenburg, Austria.

Seo, F., and Sakawa, M. (1981). A regional land-use program combined with water quality management and its evaluation, *Proceedings of the IFAC Symposium on Water and Related Land Resource Systems*, (Y. Haimes, ed.), Pergamon Press, Oxford, 403-411.

Seo, F., and Sakawa, M. (1984a). An experimental method for diversified evaluation and risk assessment with conflicting objectives, *IEEE Transactions on Systems, Man, and Cybernetics* 14(2).

Seo, F., and Sakawa, M. (1984b). Fuzzy assessment of multiattribute utility functions, in *Interactive Decision Analysis and Interpretative Computer Intelligence* (A. Wierzbicki and M. Grauer, eds.), Springer-Verlag, Berlin, 97-104.

Seo, F., and Sakawa, M. (1985). Fuzzy multiattribute utility analysis for collective choice, *IEEE Transactions on Systems, Man and Cybernetics* 15(1).

Seo, F., Sakawa, M., Yamane, K., and Fukuchi, T. (1986a). Interactive systems analysis for impact evaluation of the Hokuriku Shinkansen (Super-Express railroad), *Large-Scale Modeling and Interactive Decision Analysis* (G. Fandel, M. Grauer, A. Kurzhanski and A. P. Wierzbicki, eds.), Springer-Verlag, Berlin.

Seo, F., Sakawa, M., Yamane, K., and Fukuchi, T. (1986b). Multiobjective systems analysis for impact evaluation of the Hokuriku Shinkansen (Super-Express Railroad): the extended version, Discussion Paper No. 212, Kyoto Institute of Economic Research, Kyoto University.

Shapley, L. S. (1967). On balanced sets and cores, *Naval Research Logistic Quality* 14, 453-460.

Shapley, L. S., and Shubik, M. (1966). Quasi-cores in a monetary economy with nonconvex preferences, *Econometrica* 34(4), 805-827.

Shapley, L. S., and Shubik, M. (1969). On Market game, *Journal of Economic Theory* 1, 9-25.

Shapley, L. S., and Shubik, M. (1973). Game Theory in Economics-Chapter 6: Characteristic Function, Core and Stable Set, R-904/6-NSF, RAND Corporation.

Shapley, L. S., and Shubik, M. (1975). Competitive outcomes in the core of market games, *International Journal of Game Theory* 4(4), 229-237.

Shimizu, K., Kawanabe, H., and Aiyoshi, E. (1978). A theory for interactive preference optimization and its algorithm - generalized SWT method - Trans. Institute of Elec., Commun. Eng. Japan J61-a (11), 1075-1082 (in Japanese).

Sicherman, A. (1975). An interactive computer program for assessing and using multiattribute utility functions, Technical Paper, No. 111. Operations Research Center, MIT, Massachusetts.

Simon, H. A. (1945). *Administrative Behavior*, Macmillan, London.

Simon, H. A. (1969). *The Science of the Artificial*, MIT Press, Cambridge, Massachusetts.

Simon, H. A. (1978). Rationality as process and as product of thought, *American Economic Review* 68, 1-16.

Simon, H. A. (1979). Rational decision making in business organizations, *American Economic Review* 69, 493-512.

Simon, H. A. (1983). *Reason in Human Affairs*, Stanford University Press, California.

Smith, A. (1759, 6th ed. 1790). The Theory of Moral Sentiments, in the works of Adam Smith, Vol. 1, Aalen Otto Zeller, 1963.

Smith, A. (1776). *An Inquiry into the Nature and Causes of the Wealth of Nations*, the Modern Library, New York, 1937.

Steuer, R. E., and Choo, E. U. (1983). An interactive weighted Tchebycheff procedure for multiple objective programming, *Mathematical Programming* 26, 326-344.

Suppes, P., and Winet, M. (1955). An axiomatization of utility based on the notion of utility differences, *Management Science* 1, 259-270.

Tanino, T., and Sawaragi, Y. (1979). Duality theory in multiobjective programming, *Journal of Optimization Theory and Applications* 27, 509-529.

Thrall, R. M. (1954). Applications of multidimensional utility theory, in *Decision Processes* (R. M. Thrall, ed.), Wiley, New York.

von Bertalanffy, L. (1968). *General Systems Theory*, Braziller, New York.

von Bohm-Bawerk, E. (1889). *Positive Theorie des Kapitales*, Trans. by W. Smart, The Positive Theory of Capital, Books for Libraries Press, New York, 1971.

von Mises, L. (1957). *Theory and History, An Interpretation of Social and Economic Evaluation*, Arlington House, New York.

von Neumann, J., and Morgenstern, O. (1944, 2nd ed. 1947). *Theory of Games and Economic Behavior*, Wiley, New York.

Voogd, H. (1983). *Multicriteria Evaluation for Urban and Regional Planning*, Pion Limited, London.

Weber, M. (1921). *Wirtschaft und Gesellschaft, Grundriss der Verstehenden Soziologie:* English translation: Economy and Society, an Outline of Interpretive Sociology, Bedminster Press, 1968.

Whitmore, G. A. (1970). Third-degree Stochastic dominance, *American Economic Review* 60(3), 457-459.

Wiener, N. (1948, 2nd ed. 1961). *Cybernetics*, MIT Press, Massachusetts.

Wierzbicki, A. P. (1975). Penalty methods in solving optimization problems with vector performance criteria, *Proceedings of VI-th IFAC World Congress*, Cambridge, Massachusetts.

Wierzbicki, A. P. (1977). Basic properties of scalarizing functionals for multiobjective optimization, mathematical operations, *Forshung und Statistik, Ser. Optimization* 8(1), 55-60.

Wierzbicki, A. P. (1978). On the use of penalty functions in multiobjective optimization, *Proceedings of the International Symposium on Operations Research*, Mannheim.

Wierzbicki, A. P. (1979). The use of reference objectives in multiobjective optimization: theoretical implications and practical experience WP-79-66, IIASA, Laxenburg, Austria.

Wierzbicki, A. P. (1981). A mathematical basis for satisficing decision making, in *Organizations: Multiple Agents with Multiple Criteria* (J. N. Morse, ed.), 465-485.

Wieser, F. (1889). *Der Naturiche Wert*, Holder, Wien.

Wismer, D. A. (ed.) (1971). *Optimization Methods for Large-Scale Systems*, McGraw-Hill, New York.

Wolfe, P. (1961). A duality theorem for non-linear programming, *Quarterly of Applied Mathematics* 19, 239-244.

Yano, H., and Sakawa, M. (1985). Trade-off rates in the weighted Tchebycheff norm method, *Transactions on* S.I.C.E. 21(3), 248-255 (in Japanese).

Young, H. P., Okada, N., and Hashimoto, T. (1982). Cost allocation in water resources development, *Water Resources Research* 18(3), 463-475.

Yu, P. L. (1973). A class of solutions for group decision problems, *Management Science* 19, 936-946.

Yu, P. L. (1981). Behavior bases and habitual domains of human decision/behavior, *International Journal of Systems, Measurement, and Decisions* 1, 39-62.

Yu, P. L. (1984). Behavior mechanism in decision making, in *Decision Making with Multiple Objectives* (Y. Y. Haimes and V. Chankong, eds.), Springer-Verlag, Berlin.

Yu, P. L. (1985). *Multiple-Criteria Decision Making, Concepts, Techniques, and Extensions*, Plenum Press, New York.

Zadeh, L. A. (1963). Optimality and non-scalar valued performance criteria, *IEEE Transactions on Automatic Control* AC-8, 59-60.

Zadeh, L. A. (1965). Fuzzy sets, *Information and Control* 8, 338-353.

Zadeh, L. A. (1971). Similarity relations and fuzzy orderings, *Information Sciences* 3, 177-200.

Zeleny, M. (1973). Compromise programming, in *Multiple Criteria Decision Making* (J. L. Cochrane, and M. Zeleny, eds.), University of South Carolina Press, South Carolina.

Zeleny, M. (1976). The theory of displaced ideal, in *Multiple Criteria Decision Making, Kyoto*, 1975, ed. by Zeleny, Springer-Verlag, Berlin.

Zeleny, M. (1981). *Multiple Criteria Decision Making*, McGraw-Hill, New York.

Zimmermann, H. J. (1978). Fuzzy programming and linear programming with several objective functions, *Fuzzy Sets and Systems* 1(1), 45-55.

Zimmermann, H. J. (1983). Fuzzy mathematical programming, *Computer and Operations Research* 10(4), 291-298.

## Bibliography on Multiple Criteria Decision Making (Books)

Arrow, K. J., and Raynaud, H. (1986). *Social Choice and Multicriterion Decision-Making,* MIT Press, Cambridge.

Chankong, V., and Haimes, Y. Y. (1983). *Multiobjective Decision Making: Theory and Methodology,* North-Holland, Amsterdam.

Charnes, A., and Cooper, W. W. (1961). *Management Models and Industrial Applications of Linear Programming,* Vol. 1, Wiley, New York.

Cohon, J. L. (1978). *Multiobjective Programming and Planning,* Academic Press, New York.

Dubois, D. and Prade, H. (1980). *Fuzzy Sets and Systems, Theory and Applications,* Academic Press, New York.

Fishburn, P. C. (1964). *Decision and Value Theory,* Wiley, New York.

Fishburn, P. C. (1970). *Utility Theory for Decision Making,* Wiley, New York.

Fishburn, P. C. (1982). *The Foundations of Expected Utility,* D. Reidel Publishing Company, Dordrecht.

Fraser, N. M., and Hipel, K. W. (1984). *Conflict Analysis, Models and Resolutions,* North-Holland, Amsterdam.

Goicolchea, A., Hansen, D. R., and Duckstein, L. (1982). *Multiobjective Decision Analysis with Engineering and Business Applications,* Wiley, New-York.

Guddat, J., Vasquez, F. G., Tammer, K., and Wendler, K. (1985). *Multiobjective and Stochastic Optimization Based on Parametric Optimization,* Akademic-Verlag, Berlin.

Haimes, Y. Y. (1977). *Hierarchical Analyses of Water Resources Systems: Modeling and Optimization of Large-scale Systems,* McGraw-Hill, New York.

Haimes, Y. Y., Hall, W. A., and Freedman, H. T. (1975). *Multiobjective Optimization in Water Resources Systems: The Surrogate Worth Trade-off Method,* Elsevier, The Netherlands.

Harsanyi, J. C. (1977). *Rational Behavior and Bargaining Equilibrium in Games and Social Situations,* Cambridge University Press, Cambridge.

Hwang, C. L., and Masud, A. S. Md. (1979). *Multiple Objective Decision-Making --Methods and Applications,* Springer-Verlag, Berlin.

Hwang, C. L., and Yoon, K. (1981). *Multiple Attribute Decision Making -- Methods and Applications,* Springer-Verlag, Berlin.

Ignizio, J. P. (1976). *Goal Programming and Extensions,* Heath, Boston, Massachusetts.

Ignizio, J. P. (1982). *Linear Programming in Single and Multiple Objective Systems,* Prentice-Hall, Englewood Cliffs, New Jersey.

Ijiri, Y. (1965). *Management Goals and Accounting for Control,* North-Holland Publishing Co., Amsterdam.

Isard, W., and Smith, C. (1982). *Conflict Analysis and Practical Conflict Management Procedures,* Ballinger Publishing Company, Cambridge.

Keeney, R. L., and Raiffa, H. (1976). *Decisions with Multiple Objectives: Preferences and Value Tradeoffs,* Wiley, New York.

Kickert, W. J. M. (1978). *Fuzzy Theories on Decision-making,* Martinus, Nijhoff.

Lee, S. M. (1972). *Goal Programming for Decision Analysis,* Auerbach, Philadelphia.

Luce, R. D., and Raiffa, H. (1957). *Games and Decisions,* Wiley, New York.

Nijkamp, P. (1977). *Theory and Application of Environmental Economics,* North-Holland, Amsterdam.

Nijkamp, P. (1979). *Multidimensional spatial Data and Decision Analysis,* Wiley, New York.

Nijkamp, P. (1980). *Environmental Policy Analysis, Operational Methods and Models,* Wiley, New York.

Ordeshook, P. C. (1986). *Game Theory and Political Theory,* Cambridge University Press, Cambridge.

Owen, G. (1982). *Game Theory,* Second Edition. Academic Press, New York.

Raiffa, H. (1968). *Decision Analysis,* Addison-Wesley, Reading, Massachusetts.

Raiffa, H. (1982). *The art and Science of Negotiation,* Harvard University Press, Massachusetts.

Rietveld, P. (1980). *Multiple Objective Decision Methods and Regional Planning,* North Holland, New York.

Roy, B. (1985). *Methodologie Multicritere d'aide a la decision,* Economica, Paris.

Saaty, T. L. (1980). *The Analytic Hierarchy Process, Planning, Priority Setting, Resourse Allocation,* McGraw-Hill, New York.

Sawaragi, Y., Nakayama, H., and Tanino, T. (1985). *Theory of Multiobjective Optimizations,* Academic Press, New York.

Shubik, M. (1983). *Game Theory in the Social Sciences, Concepts and Solutions*. MIT Press, Cambridge.

Shubik, M. (1984). *A Game Theoretic Approach to Political Economy*, MIT Press, Cambridge.

Spronk, J. (1981). *Interactive Multiple Goal Programming: Applications to Financial Planning*, Martinus Nijhoff Publishing, Boston.

Stancu-Minasian, I. M. (1984). *Stochastic Programming with multiple objective Functions* (translated from Rumanian by V. Giurgiutiu), D. Reidel Publishing Company, Dordrecht.

Steuer, R. E. (1986). *Multiple Criteria Optimization: Theory, Computation, and Application*, Wiley, New York.

Szidarovsky, F., Gershou, M. E., and Duckstein, L. (1986). *Techniques for Multiobjective Decision Making in Systems Management*, Elsevier, Amsterdam.

White, D. J. (1982). *Optimality and Efficiency*, John Wiley & Sons, Inc. New York.

Yu, P. L. (1985). *Multiple-Criteria Decision Making: Concepts, Techniques, and Extensions*, Plenum Press, New York.

Zimmermann, H. J. (1985). *Fuzzy Set Theory-and Its Application*, Kluwer-Nijhoff Publishing, Dordrecht.

Zimmerman, H. J. (1987). *Fuzzy Set, Decision Making and Expert Systems*, Kluwer-Nijhoff Publishing, Dordrecht.

Zeleny, M. (1974). *Linear Multiobjective Programming*, Springer-Verlag, New York.

Zeleny, M. (1982). *Multiple Criteria Decision Making*, McGraw-Hill, New York.

**(Collective Papers)**

Bell, D. E., Keeney, R. L., and Raiffa, H. (eds.) (1977). *Conflicting Objectives in Decisions*, IIASA International Series on Applied Systems Analysis, Wiley, New York.

Carlsson, C., and Kochetkov, Y. (eds.) (1983). *Theory and Practice of Multiple Criteria Decision Making*, North-Holland, Amsterdam.

Cochrane, J. L., and Zeleny, M. (eds.) (1973). *Multiple Criteria Decision Making*, University of South Carolina Press, Columbia.

Fandel, G., and Gal, T. (eds.) (1980). *Multiple Criteria Decision Making: Theory and Applications*, Springer-Verlag, Berlin.

Fandel, G., Grauer, M., Kurzhanski, A., and Wierzbicki, A. P. (eds.) (1986). *Large-Scale Modeling and Interactive Decision Analysis, Proceedings, Eisenach, GDR, 1985*, Springer-Verlag, Berlin.

Fandel, G., and Spronk, J. (eds.) (1985). *Multiple Criteria Decision Methods and Applications*, Springer-Verlag, Berlin.

Grauer, M., Lewandowski, A., and Wierzbicki, A. P. (eds.) (1982). *Multiobjective and Stochastic Optimization,* Proceedings of an IIASA Task Force Meeting, November 30-December 4, 1981, IIASA Collaborative Proceedings series, CP--82-S12, International Institute for Applied Systems Analysis, Laxenburg, Austria.

Grauer, M., Thompson, M., and Wierzbicki, A. P. (eds.) (1985). *Plural Rationality and Interactive Decision Processes,* Proceedings, Springer-Verlag, Berlin.

Grauer, M., and Wierzbicki, A. P. (eds.) (1984). *Interactive Decision Analysis,* Proceedings, Laxenburg, Austria, 1983, Springer-Verlag, Berlin.

Haimes, Y. Y., and Chankong, V. (eds.) (1985). *Decision Making with Multiple Objectives, Proceedings, 1984,* Springr-Verlag, Berlin.

Hansen, P. (ed.) (1983). *Essays and Surveys on Multiple Criteria Decision Making, Proceedings, 1982,* Springer-Verlag, Berlin.

Isard, W., and Nagao, Y. (eds.) (1983). *International and Regional Conflict, Analytic Approaches,* Ballinger Publishing Company, Cambridge.

Koopmans, T. C. (ed.) (1951). *Activity Analysis of Production and Allocation,* Cowles Commission for Research in Economics, Monograph no.13, Wiley, New York.

Leitmann, G. (ed.) (1972). *Multicriteria Decision Making and Differential Games,* Plenum Press, New York.

Leitmann, G., and Marzollo, A. (eds.) (1975). *Multicriteria Decision Making,* Springer-Verlag, New York.

McGuire, C. B., and Radner, R. (eds.) (1986). *Decision and Organization,* University of Minnesota Press, Minneapolis.

Morse, J. N. (ed.) (1981). *Organizations: Multiple Agents with Multiple Criteria,* Proceedings, Newark, 1980, Springer-Verlag, Berlin.

Nijkamp, P., and Spronk, J. (eds.) (1981). *Multiple Criteria Analysis: Operational Methods,* Gower, Hampshire.

Sawaragi, Y., Inoue, K., and Nakayama, H. (eds.) (1987). *Toward Interactive and Intelligent Decision Support Systems, vol 1&2, Proceedings, Kyoto, Japan, 1986,* Springer-Verlag, Berlin.

Serafini, P. (ed.) (1985). *Mathematics of Multi-objective Optimization,* Springer-Verlag, Wien.

Starr, M. K., and Zeleny, M. (eds.) (1977). *Multiple Criteria Decision Making,* North Holland, Yew York.

Thiriez, H., and Zionts, S. (eds.) (1976). *Multiple criteria Decision Making: Jouy-en-Josas, France,* Springer-Verlag, Berlin.

Yager, R. R., Ovchinnikov, S., Tong, R. M., and Nguyen, H. T. (eds.) (1987). *Fuzzy Set and Applications, Selected Papers by Zadeh,* Wiley, New York.

Zeleny, M. (ed.) (1976). *Multiple Criteria Decision Making: Kyoto 1975,* Springer-Verlag, Berlin.

Zimmermann, H. J., Gaines, B. R., and Zadeh, L. A. (eds.) (1984). *Fuzzy Sets and Decision Analysis*, North Holland, New York.

Zionts, S. (ed.) (1978). *Multiple Criteria Problem Solving*, Springer-Verlag, Berlin.

# INDEX

**J**



**K**



**L**



**M**

## N

Q



R



S

**T**



**U**